Cisco ASA: All-in-One Firewall, IPS, and VPN Adaptive Security Appliance

Jazib Frahim, CCIE No. 5459
Omar Santos

Cisco Press

800 East 96th Street
Indianapolis, Indiana 46240 USA

Cisco ASA: All-in-One Firewall, IPS, and VPN Adaptive Security Appliance

Jazib Frahim, Omar Santos

Copyright © 2006 Cisco Systems, Inc.

Published by:
Cisco Press
800 East 96th Street
Indianapolis, IN 46240 USA

Printed in the United States of America 1 2 3 4 5 6 7 8 9 0

First Printing October 2005

Library of Congress Cataloging-in-Publication Number: 2004108505

ISBN: 1-58705-209-1

Trademark Acknowledgments

All terms mentioned in this book that are known to be trademarks or service marks have been appropriately capitalized. Cisco Press or Cisco Systems, Inc., cannot attest to the accuracy of this information. Use of a term in this book should not be regarded as affecting the validity of any trademark or service mark.

Warning and Disclaimer

This book is designed to provide information about **Cisco ASA.** Every effort has been made to make this book as complete and as accurate as possible, but no warranty or fitness is implied.

The information is provided on an "as is" basis. The authors, Cisco Press, and Cisco Systems, Inc., shall have neither liability nor responsibility to any person or entity with respect to any loss or damages arising from the information contained in this book or from the use of the discs or programs that may accompany it.

The opinions expressed in this book belong to the author and are not necessarily those of Cisco Systems, Inc.

Corporate and Government Sales

Cisco Press offers excellent discounts on this book when ordered in quantity for bulk purchases or special sales.

For more information please contact: **U.S. Corporate and Government Sales**   1-800-382-3419
corpsales@pearsontechgroup.com

For sales outside the U.S. please contact: **International Sales**   international@pearsoned.com

Feedback Information

At Cisco Press, our goal is to create in-depth technical books of the highest quality and value. Each book is crafted with care and precision, undergoing rigorous development that involves the unique expertise of members from the professional technical community.

Readers' feedback is a natural continuation of this process. If you have any comments regarding how we could improve the quality of this book, or otherwise alter it to better suit your needs, you can contact us through e-mail at feedback@ciscopress.com. Please make sure to include the book title and ISBN in your message.

We greatly appreciate your assistance.

Publisher	John Wait
Editor-in-Chief	John Kane
Executive/Acquisitions Editor	Brett Bartow
Cisco Representative	Anthony Wolfenden
Cisco Press Program Manager	Jeff Bradley
Production Manager	Patrick Kanouse
Development Editor	Sheri Cain
Project Editor	Marc Fowler
Copy Editor	Bill McManus
Technical Editors	David White, Jr., Andrew Yourtchenko, and Wen Zhang
Team Coordinator	Tammi Barnett
Cover Designer	Louisa Adair
Composition	Interactive Composition Corporation
Indexer	Tim Wright

CISCO SYSTEMS

Corporate Headquarters
Cisco Systems, Inc.
170 West Tasman Drive
San Jose, CA 95134-1706
USA
www.cisco.com
Tel: 408 526-4000
    800 553-NETS (6387)
Fax: 408 526-4100

European Headquarters
Cisco Systems International BV
Haarlerbergpark
Haarlerbergweg 13-19
1101 CH Amsterdam
The Netherlands
www-europe.cisco.com
Tel: 31 0 20 357 1000
Fax: 31 0 20 357 1100

Americas Headquarters
Cisco Systems, Inc.
170 West Tasman Drive
San Jose, CA 95134-1706
USA
www.cisco.com
Tel: 408 526-7660
Fax: 408 527-0883

Asia Pacific Headquarters
Cisco Systems, Inc.
Capital Tower
168 Robinson Road
#22-01 to #29-01
Singapore 068912
www.cisco.com
Tel: +65 6317 7777
Fax: +65 6317 7799

Cisco Systems has more than 200 offices in the following countries and regions. Addresses, phone numbers, and fax numbers are listed on the
Cisco.com Web site at www.cisco.com/go/offices.

Argentina • Australia • Austria • Belgium • Brazil • Bulgaria • Canada • Chile • China PRC • Colombia • Costa Rica • Croatia • Czech Republic
Denmark • Dubai, UAE • Finland • France • Germany • Greece • Hong Kong SAR • Hungary • India • Indonesia • Ireland • Israel • Italy
Japan • Korea • Luxembourg • Malaysia • Mexico • The Netherlands • New Zealand • Norway • Peru • Philippines • Poland • Portugal
Puerto Rico • Romania • Russia • Saudi Arabia • Scotland • Singapore • Slovakia • Slovenia • South Africa • Spain • Sweden
Switzerland • Taiwan • Thailand • Turkey • Ukraine • United Kingdom • United States • Venezuela • Vietnam • Zimbabwe

About the Authors

Jazib Frahim, CCIE No. 5459, has been with Cisco Systems for more than 6 years. Having a bachelor's degree in computer engineering from Illinois Institute of Technology, he started out as a TAC engineer in the LAN Switching team. He then moved to the TAC Security team, where he acted as a technical leader for the security products. He led a team of 20 engineers as a team leader in resolving complicated security and VPN technologies. He is currently working as a Senior Network Security Engineer in the Worldwide Security Services Practice of Cisco's Advanced Services for Network Security. He is responsible for guiding customers in the design and implementation of their networks with a focus in network security. He holds two CCIEs, one in Routing and Switching and the other in Security. He has written numerous Cisco online technical documents and has been an active member on Cisco's online forum, NetPro. He has presented at Networkers on multiple occasions and has taught many onsite and online courses to Cisco customers, partners, and employees. He is also pursuing masters of business administration (MBA) from North Carolina State University.

Omar Santos is a Senior Network Security Engineer in the Worldwide Security Services Practice of Cisco's Advanced Services for Network Security. He has more than 12 years of experience in secure data communications. Omar has designed, implemented, and supported numerous secure networks for Fortune 500 companies and the U.S. government, including the United States Marine Corps (USMC) and Department of Defense (DoD). He is also the author of many Cisco online technical documents and configuration guidelines. Prior to his current role, he was a technical leader of Cisco's Technical Assistance Center (TAC), where he taught, led, and mentored many engineers within the organization. He is an active member of the InfraGard organization. InfraGard is a cooperative undertaking between the Federal Bureau of Investigation and an association of businesses, academic institutions, state and local law enforcement agencies, and other participants that is dedicated to increasing the security of the critical infrastructures of the United States of America. Omar has also delivered numerous technical presentations to Cisco customers, partners, and other organizations.

About the Technical Reviewers

David White, Jr., CCIE No. 12021, has more than 9 years of networking experience with a focus in network security. He is currently a Technical Leader in the Cisco TAC, where he has been for over 5 years. In his role at Cisco, he is involved in new product design and implementation and is an active participant in producing Cisco documentation, both online and in print. David holds a CCIE in Security, and is also NSA IAM certified. Prior to joining Cisco, David worked for the U.S. government, where he helped secure its worldwide communications network. He was born and raised in St. Petersburg, Florida and received his bachelor's degree in computer engineering from the Georgia Institute of Technology.

Andrew Yourtchenko, CCIE No. 5423, is a Customer Support Engineer working in the security area in the Cisco Technical Assistance Centre in Brussels, which he joined in 2000. Born in St. Petersburg, Russia, his first experience with computers was in 1989, which sparked his interest in computers and motivated him to start self-study in computer science while still in school. He graduated St. Petersburg State Technical University in 1997. Andrew's networking experience started around 1992, when he commenced work for a systems integration company in St. Petersburg. In parallel with the job—which varied from fiber cable installations to custom Perl programming—he obtained Novell CNE certification for NetWare 4.1. He became a CCIE in Routing and Switching in 1999 and in Security in 2002.

Wen Zhang, CCIE No. 4302, is a senior engineer in the Cisco TAC Escalation Team, with a focus in network security and VPN technologies. In this role, he is responsible for handling difficult and complex escalation issues, working on critical software defects, and participating in the new product design and implementation process. He earned his B.S. and M.S. degrees in electrical engineering from Clemson University.

Dedications

I would like to dedicate this book to my parents, Frahim and Perveen, who support and encourage me on all of my endeavors. I would also like to dedicate it to my siblings, including my brother Shazib and my sisters Erum and Sana, my sister-in-law Asiya, and my cute nephew Shayan for their patience and understanding during the development of this book.
—Jazib Frahim

I would like to dedicate this book to my lovely wife Jeannette, who has always stood by me and supported me throughout the development of this book. I also dedicate this book to my two beautiful children, Hannah and Derek.
—Omar Santos

Acknowledgments

We would like to thank the technical editors (David White, Andrew Yourtchenko, and Wen Zhang) for their time and technical expertise. They verified our work and corrected us in all the major and minor mistakes that were hard to find.

Special thanks go to Jay Biersbach and James Cline for reviewing the manuscript and making this a better-looking book.

We would like to thank the Cisco Press team, especially Brett Bartow, Sheri Cain, Dayna Isley, Michelle Grandin and Marc Fowler for their patience, guidance, and consideration. Their efforts are greatly appreciated.

Many thanks to our managers, William Beach and Joe Dallatore, for their continuous support. They highly encouraged us throughout this project.

Kudos to the Cisco ASA product development team for delivering such a great product. Their support is also greatly appreciated during the development of this book.

This Book Is Safari Enabled

The Safari® Enabled icon on the cover of your favorite technology book means the book is available through Safari Bookshelf. When you buy this book, you get free access to the online edition for 45 days.

Safari Bookshelf is an electronic reference library that lets you easily search thousands of technical books, find code samples, download chapters, and access technical information whenever and wherever you need it.

To gain 45-day Safari Enabled access to this book:

- Go to http://www.ciscopress.com/safarienabled
- Enter the ISBN of this book (shown on the back cover, above the bar code)
- Log in or Sign up (site membership is required to register your book)
- Enter the coupon code BBCZ-BRWD-A1AZ-VKD7-3BXN

If you have difficulty registering on Safari Bookshelf or accessing the online edition, please e-mail customer-service@safaribooksonline.com.

Contents at a Glance

Table of Contents

Foreword

Network security is at a critical juncture where no single technology can solve the problem in silos. Hundreds of millions of dollars are being spent in reactively solving the virus, worms, malware problem and the rapid propagation of these vile threats. Recognizing this, Cisco has modeled the Self-Defending Network (SDN) similar to the way our bodies protect us and deal with diseases.

The SDN has several protective and integrated layers—VPNs, firewalls, intrusion prevention, and anomaly mitigation. When combined with advanced virtualization, deeper packet intelligence, and behavioral linkages with end systems, the SDN is able to proactively prevent dangerous elements from causing havoc on networks. But akin to the human body, no network can completely stop all bad things from entering. People need to eat, drink, and breathe, and networks need to process and deliver information from a wide variety of external sources. With this in mind, Cisco is constructing SDN to work at or near capacity even when invaded by detrimental entities, just as the human body can keep on functioning even when it has an infection.

This book offers deep insight into one of Cisco's flagship and recently introduced products, the Adaptive Security Appliance, ASA 5500. ASA exemplifies the importance of integration, collaboration, and adaptation to different threat patterns in security. It is one of the industry's first all-in-one network security platforms, focused on uncompromised performance and security.

The authors of this book, Jazib Frahim and Omar Santos, have intimate knowledge of security as well as internetworking. Together they have about two decades of network security expertise and have been strong advocates of thoughtful security practices and designs for Cisco. I have found this book really highlights the practical aspects needed for building real-world security. It offers the insider's guidance needed to plan, implement, configure, and troubleshoot the Cisco ASA in customer environments and demonstrates the potential and power of SDNs. I hope you enjoy the insights of this book as much as I and come to appreciate the ground-breaking security pioneered by Cisco over the past few years.

Jayshree Ullal
Senior Vice President, Security Technology Group
October 2005

Icons Used in This Book

 Cisco ASA

 NAT

 PIX Right

 PIX Left

 CiscoCA

 Bridge

 Web Browser

 Web Server

 End User Male

 End User Male, Video

 Cisco IP Phone

 Hub

 Communication Server

 PC

 PC with Software

 Sun Workstation

 Macintosh

 Branch Office

 Headquarters

 Terminal

 File Server

 Web Server

 Cisco Works Workstation

 House, Regular

 Printer

 Laptop

 Unity Server

 Gateway

 Router

 Catalyst Switch

 Multilayer Switch

 Route/Switch Processor

 Network Cloud

 Line: Ethernet

Line: Serial

Line: Switched Serial

Command Syntax Conventions

The conventions used to present command syntax in this book are the same conventions used in the *Cisco IOS Command Reference,* which describes these conventions as follows:

- **Boldface** indicates commands and keywords that are entered literally as shown.
- *Italics* indicate arguments for which you supply actual values.
- Vertical bars (I) separate alternative, mutually exclusive elements.
- Square brackets, [ ], indicate optional elements.
- Braces, { }, indicate a required choice.
- Braces within brackets, [{ }], indicate a required choice within an optional element.

Introduction

Network security has always been a challenge for many organizations that cannot deploy separate devices to provide firewall, intrusion prevention, and virtual private network (VPN) services. Cisco ASA is a high-performance, multifunction security appliance that offers firewall, IPS, network anti-virus, and VPN services. Cisco ASA delivers these features through improved network integration, resiliency, and scalability.

This book is an insider's guide to planning, implementing, configuring, and troubleshooting Cisco ASA. It delivers expert guidance from senior Cisco network security consulting engineers. It demonstrates how adaptive identification and mitigation services on Cisco ASA provide a sophisticated network security solution to small, medium, and large organizations. This book brings together expert guidance for virtually every challenge you will face—from building basic network security policies to advanced VPN and IPS implementations.

Who Should Read This Book

This book serves as a guide for any network professional who manages network security or installs and configures firewalls, VPN devices, or intrusion detection/prevention systems. It encompasses topics from an introductory level to advanced topics on security and VPNs. The requirements of the reader include a basic knowledge of TCP/IP and networking.

How This Book Is Organized

This book has five parts, which provide a Cisco ASA product overview and then focus on firewalls, intrusion prevention, VPNs, and Adaptive Security Device Manager (ASDM). Each part comprises many sample configurations, accompanied by in-depth analyses of design scenarios. Your learning is further enhanced by a discussion of a set of debugs included in each technology. Ground-breaking features, such as WebVPN and virtual and Layer 2 firewalls, are discussed extensively.

- Part I, "Product Overview," includes the following chapters:
  - **Chapter 1, "Introduction to Network Security"**—This chapter provides an overview of different technologies that are supported by Cisco ASA and widely used by today's network security professionals.
  - **Chapter 2, "Product History"**—Historically, Cisco PIX security appliances, the Cisco IOS Advanced Security Feature Set, and the security services modules for Cisco Catalyst 6500 Series Switches have provided integrated security solutions to small and large organizations. As described in this chapter, Cisco ASA incorporates features from each of these products, integrating comprehensive firewall, intrusion detection and prevention, and VPN technologies in a cost-effective, single-box format.
  - **Chapter 3, "Hardware Overview"**—This chapter provides a hardware overview of Cisco ASA, including detailed technical specifications and installation guidelines. It also covers an overview of the Adaptive Inspection and Prevention Security Services Module (AIP-SSM).

- Part II, "Firewall Solution," includes the following chapters:

  — **Chapter 4, "Initial Setup and System Maintenance"**—A comprehensive list of initial setup tasks and system maintenance procedures is included in this chapter. These tasks and procedures are intended to be used by network professionals who will be installing, configuring, and managing Cisco ASA.

  — **Chapter 5, "Network Access Control"**—Cisco ASA can protect one or more networks from intruders. Connections between these networks can be carefully controlled by advanced firewall capabilities, enabling you to ensure that all traffic from and to the protected networks passes only through the firewall based on the organization's security policy. This chapter shows you how to implement your organization's security policy using the features that Cisco ASA provides.

  — **Chapter 6, "IP Routing"**—This chapter covers the different routing capabilities of Cisco ASA.

  — **Chapter 7, "Authentication, Authorization, and Accounting (AAA)"**—Cisco ASA supports a wide range of AAA features. This chapter provides guidelines on how to configure AAA services by defining a list of authentication methods applied to various implementations.

  — **Chapter 8, "Application Inspection"**—Cisco ASA stateful application inspection helps to secure the use of applications and services in your network. This chapter describes how to use and configure application inspection.

  — **Chapter 9, "Security Contexts"**—Cisco ASA virtual firewall feature introduces the concept of operating multiple instances of firewalls (contexts) within the same hardware platform. This chapter shows how to configure and troubleshoot each of these security contexts.

  — **Chapter 10, "Transparent Firewalls"**—This chapter introduces the transparent (Layer 2) firewall model within Cisco ASA. It explains how users can configure Cisco ASA in transparent single mode and multiple mode while accommodating their security needs.

  — **Chapter 11, "Failover and Redundancy"**—This chapter discusses the different redundancy and failover mechanisms that Cisco ASA provides. It includes not only the overview and configuration, but also detailed troubleshooting procedures.

  — **Chapter 12, "Quality of Service"**—QoS is a network feature that lets you give priority to certain types of traffic. This chapter covers how to configure and troubleshoot QoS in Cisco ASA.

- Part III, "Intrusion Prevention System (IPS) Solution," includes the following chapters:

  — **Chapter 13, "Intrusion Prevention System Integration"**—Intrusion detection and prevention systems provide a level of protection beyond the firewall by securing the network against internal and external attacks and threats. This chapter describes the integration of Intrusion Prevention System (IPS) features within Cisco ASA.

- **Chapter 14, "Configuring and Troubleshooting Cisco IPS Software via the CLI"** — This chapter provides expert guidance on how to configure the AIP-SSM IPS software via its command-line interface (CLI). Troubleshooting scenarios are also included to enhance learning.

- Part IV, "Virtual Private Network (VPN) Solution," includes the following chapters:

  - **Chapter 15, "Site-to-Site IPSec VPNs"** — Cisco ASA supports IPSec VPN features that allows you to connect networks in different geographic locations. This chapter provides configuration and troubleshooting guidelines to successfully deploy site-to-site IPSec VPNs.

  - **Chapter 16, "Remote Access VPNs"** — This chapter discusses many different remote-access VPN solutions that are supported on Cisco ASA. A large number of sample configurations and troubleshooting scenarios are provided.

  - **Chapter 17, "Public Key Infrastructure (PKI)"** — This chapter starts by introducing PKI concepts. It then covers the configuration and troubleshooting of PKI in Cisco ASA.

- Part V, "Adaptive Security Device Manager," includes the following chapters:

  - **Chapter 18, "Introduction to ASDM"** — This chapter introduces Cisco ASA GUI—the Adaptive Security Device Manager (ASDM).

  - **Chapter 19, "Firewall Management Using ASDM"** — This chapter guides you on how to configure and manage firewall features using ASDM.

  - **Chapter 20, "IPS Management Using ASDM"** — This chapter shows you how to configure and manage IPS features using ASDM.

  - **Chapter 21, "VPN Management Using ASDM"** — The configuration and management of remote-access and site-to-site VPNs using ASDM are covered in this chapter.

  - **Chapter 22, "Case Studies"** — In this chapter, you gain greater insight into how the implementation of Cisco ASA advanced features can benefit your organization. Several sample configurations and deployment scenarios are covered in detail.

Product Overview

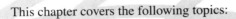

This chapter covers the following topics:

- Firewall technologies
- Intrusion detection technologies
- Network-based attacks
- Virtual private network (VPN) technologies

CHAPTER 1

Introduction to Network Security

The cost of reported computer and network security breaches at enterprises, schools, and government organizations has risen dramatically during the last couple of years. Hints and detailed instructions for creating exploits to break into networks and computer systems are becoming more easily available on the Internet, consequently requiring network security professionals to carefully analyze what techniques they deploy to mitigate these risks.

Security threats vary from distributed denial-of-service (DDoS) attacks to viruses, worms, Trojan horses, and theft of information. These threats can easily destroy or corrupt vital data, requiring difficult and expensive remediation tasks to restore business continuity.

This chapter introduces the essentials of network security technologies and provides the necessary foundation for technologies involved in the Cisco Adaptive Security Appliances security features and solutions.

Firewall Technologies

A detailed understanding of how firewalls and their related technologies work is extremely important for all network security professionals. This knowledge will help them to configure and manage the security of their networks accurately and effectively. The word *firewall* commonly describes systems or devices that are placed between a trusted and an untrusted network.

Several network firewall solutions offer user and application policy enforcement that provide multivector attack protection for different types of security threats. They often provide logging capabilities that allow the security administrators to identify, investigate, validate, and mitigate such threats.

Additionally, several software applications can run on a system to protect only that host. These types of applications are known as *personal firewalls*. This section includes an overview of network and personal firewalls and their related technologies.

Network Firewalls

It is important to recognize the value of perimeter security in today's networking world. Network-based firewalls provide key features used for perimeter security. The primary task of a network firewall is to deny or permit traffic that attempts to enter the network based on explicit preconfigured policies and rules. The processes that are used to allow or block traffic may include the following:

- Simple packet-filtering techniques
- Multifaceted application proxies
- Stateful inspection systems

Packet-Filtering Techniques

The purpose of packet filters is simply to control access to specific network segments by defining which traffic can pass through them. They usually inspect incoming traffic at the transport layer of the Open System Interconnection (OSI) model. For example, packet filters can analyze TCP or UDP packets and judge them against a set of predetermined rules called access control lists (ACLs). They inspect the following elements within a packet:

- Source address
- Destination address
- Source port
- Destination port
- Protocol

NOTE   Packet filters do not commonly inspect additional Layer 3 and Layer 4 fields such as sequence numbers, TCP control flags, and TCP acknowledgement (ACK) field.

Various packet-filtering firewalls can also inspect packet header information to find out if the packet is from a new or an existing connection. Simple packet-filtering firewalls have several limitations and weaknesses:

- Their ACLs or rules can be relatively large and difficult to manage.
- They can be deceived into permitting unauthorized access of spoofed packets. Attackers can orchestrate a packet with an IP address that is authorized by the ACL.
- Numerous applications can build multiple connections on randomly negotiated ports. This makes it difficult to determine which ports will be selected and used until after the connection is completed. Examples of this type of application are several multimedia applications, including RealAudio, QuickTime, and other streaming audio and video applications. Packet filters do not understand the underlying upper-layer protocols used by this type of application, and providing support for this type

of application is difficult because the ACLs need to be manually configured in packet-filtering firewalls.

Application Proxies

Application proxies, or proxy servers, are devices that operate as intermediary agents on behalf of clients that are on a private or protected network. Clients on the protected network send connection requests to the application proxy in order to transfer data to the unprotected network or the Internet. Consequently, the application proxy sends the request on behalf of the internal client. The majority of proxy firewalls work at the application layer of the OSI model. Few proxy firewalls have the ability to cache information to accelerate their transactions. This is a great tool for networks that have numerous servers that experience considerably high usage. A disadvantage of application proxies is their inability to scale. This makes them difficult to deploy in large environments.

Network Address Translation

Several Layer 3 devices can provide Network Address Translation (NAT) services. The application proxy translates the internal host's IP addresses to a publicly routable address. NAT is often used by firewalls; however, other devices such as wireless access points provide support for NAT. By using NAT, the firewall exposes its own network address or public address range of an unprotected network. This enables a network professional to use any IP address space as the internal network. A best practice is to use the address spaces that are reserved for private use (see RFC 1918, "Address Allocation for Private Internets"). Table 1-1 lists the private address ranges specified in RFC 1918.

Table 1-1   *RFC 1918 Private Address Ranges*

Network Address Range	Network/Mask
10.0.0.0–10.255.255.255	10.0.0.0/8
172.16.0.0–172.31.255.255	172.16.0.0/12
192.168.0.0–192.168.255.255	192.168.0.0/16

It is important to think about the different private address spaces when you plan your network (for example, number of hosts and subnets that can be configured). Careful planning and preparation will lead to substantial time savings if changes are encountered down the road.

Port Address Translation

Normally, application proxies perform a technique called Port Address Translation (PAT). This feature allows many devices on the internal protected network to share one IP address by inspecting the Layer 4 information on the packet. This address is usually the firewall's public address. Figure 1-1 shows how PAT works.

Figure 1-1 *PAT Example*

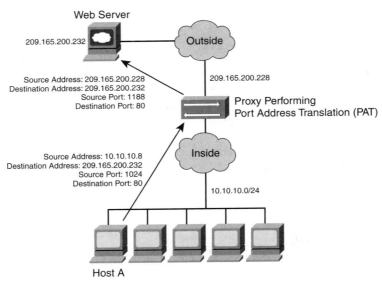

As illustrated in Figure 1-1, several hosts on a protected network labeled "inside" are configured with an address from the network 10.10.10.0 with a 24-bit subnet mask. The application proxy is performing PAT for the internal hosts and translating the 10.10.10.x addresses into its own address (209.165.200.228). In this example, Host A sends a TCP port 80 packet to the web server located in the "outside" unprotected network. The application proxy translates the request from the original 10.10.10.8 IP address of Host A to its own address. It does this by randomly selecting a different Layer 4 source port when forwarding the request to the web server.

Static Translation

A different methodology is used when hosts in the unprotected network need to contact specific hosts behind the NAT device. This is done by creating a static mapping of the public IP address and the address of the internal protected device. For example, static NAT can be configured when a web server has a private IP address but needs to be contacted by hosts located in the unprotected network or the Internet. Figure 1-2 demonstrates how static translation works.

In Figure 1-2, the web server address (10.10.10.230) is statically translated to an address in the outside network (209.165.200.240, in this case). This allows the outside host to initiate a connection to the web server by directing the traffic to 209.165.200.240. The device performing NAT then translates and sends the request to the web server on the inside network.

Figure 1-2   *Example of Static Translation*

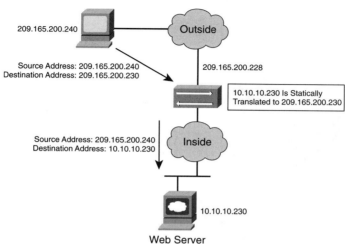

Address translation is not limited to firewalls. Nowadays, devices from simple small office, home office (SOHO) routers to very sophisticated stateful inspection firewalls are able to perform different types of NAT techniques.

Stateful Inspection Firewalls

Stateful inspection firewalls provide enhanced benefits when compared to the simple packet-filtering firewalls. They track every connection passing through their interfaces by assuring that they are valid connections. They examine not only the packet header contents, but also the application layer information within the payload. This is done to find out more about the transaction than just the source and destination addresses and ports. A stateful firewall monitors the state of the connection and maintains a database with this information. This database is usually called the state table. The state of the connection details whether such connection has been established, closed, reset, or is being negotiated. These mechanisms offer protection for different types of network attacks.

Numerous firewalls have the capability to configure a network (or zone) where you can place devices to allow outside or Internet hosts to access them. These areas or network segments are usually called demilitarized zones (DMZs). These zones provide security to the systems that reside within them, but with a different security level than your network within your inside network. Sophisticated firewall solutions can be configured with several DMZs. Figure 1-3 exemplifies this technique.

The example in Figure 1-3 shows how a firewall (a Cisco ASA 5500 appliance, in this case) can be deployed and configured to protect several DMZ networks. DMZs minimize the exposure of devices and clients on your external network by allowing only recognized and managed services on those hosts to be accessible by hosts on the Internet.

Figure 1-3   *Firewall DMZ Configurations*

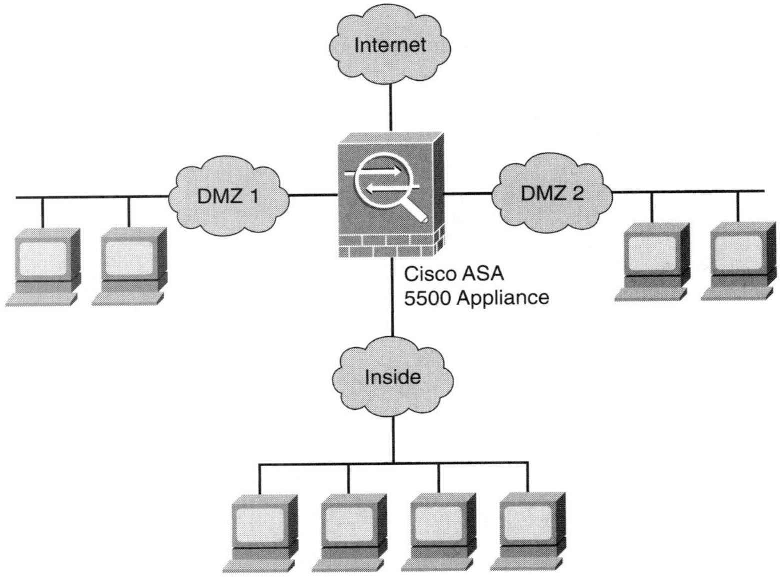

Personal Firewalls

Personal firewalls use similar methods as network-based firewalls. They provide filtering techniques and stateful inspection of connections directed to the specific host. Conversely, they abridge the operation of the application to meet the needs of a less technically inclined consumer. Personal firewall applications can restrict access to services and applications installed within a single host. This is commonly deployed to telecommuters and remote mobile users. Several personal firewalls generally protect the host from inbound connections and attacks; however, they allow all outbound connections.

There are many differences between personal firewalls and network-based firewalls. One of the major differences is the deployment model and the security services each of them provides.

Intrusion Detection and Prevention Technologies

In the security world, intrusion detection systems (IDSs) are devices that detect attempts from an attacker to gain unauthorized access to a network or a host to create performance degradation or to steal information. They also detect DDoS attacks, worms, and virus outbreaks. The number and complexity of security threats have skyrocketed over recent years. Achieving efficient network intrusion security is vital to maintaining a high level of protection. Cautious protection ensures business continuity and minimizes the effects of costly interruption of services. Like firewalls, there are two different types of intrusion detection systems:

- Network-based intrusion detection systems (NIDS)
- Host-based intrusion detection systems (HIDS)

Network-Based Intrusion Detection and Prevention Systems

Network-based intrusion detection and prevention systems are designed to precisely identify, categorize, and protect against known and unknown threats targeting a network. These threats include worms, DoS attacks, and any other detected vulnerabilities. Several detection methodologies are widely deployed. These techniques or methodologies embrace the following:

- Pattern matching and stateful pattern-matching recognition
- Protocol analysis
- Heuristic-based analysis
- Anomaly-based analysis

Pattern Matching and Stateful Pattern-Matching Recognition

Pattern matching is a methodology in which the intrusion detection device searches for a fixed sequence of bytes within the packets traversing the network. Generally, the pattern is aligned with a packet that is related to a respective service or, in particular, associated with a source and destination port. This approach reduces the amount of inspection made on every packet. However, it is limited to services and protocols that are associated with well-defined ports. Protocols that do not use any Layer 4 port information will not be categorized.

This tactic uses the concept of signatures. A *signature* is a set of conditions that point out some type of intrusion occurrence. For example, if a specific TCP packet has a destination port of 1234 and its payload contains the string "ff11ff22," an alert will be triggered to detect such string.

Alternatively, the signature could include an explicit starting point and endpoint for inspection within the specific packet.

The benefits of the plain pattern-matching technique include the following:

- Direct correlation of an exploit
- Trigger alerts on the pattern specified
- Can be applied across different services and protocols

One of the main disadvantages is that pattern matching can lead to a considerably high rate of false positives. *False positives* are alerts that do not represent a genuine malicious activity. In contrast, any alterations to the attack can lead to overlooked events of real attacks, which are normally referred as *false negatives*.

To address some of these limitations, a more refined method was created. This methodology is called *stateful pattern-matching recognition*. This process dictates that systems performing this type of signature analysis must consider the chronological order of packets in a TCP stream. In particular, they should judge and maintain a stateful inspection of such packets and flows.

The advantages of stateful pattern-matching recognition include the following:

- It has the capability to directly correlate a specific exploit within the pattern.
- Supports all non-encrypted IP protocols.

Systems that perform stateful pattern matching keep track of the arrival order of packets in a TCP stream and handle matching patterns across packet boundaries.

However, stateful pattern-matching recognition shares some of the same restrictions of the simple pattern-matching methodology, which was discussed previously, including an uncertain rate of false positives and a possibility of some false negatives.

Protocol Analysis

Protocol analysis (or protocol decode-base signatures) is often referred to as the extension to stateful pattern recognition. A NIDS accomplishes protocol analysis by decoding all protocol or client-server conversations. The NIDS identifies the elements of the protocol and analyzes them while looking for an infringement. Some intrusion detection systems look at explicit protocol fields within the inspected packets. Others require more sophisticated techniques, such as examination of the length of a field within the protocol or the number of arguments. For example, in SMTP, the device may look at specific commands and fields such as HELO, MAIL, RCPT, DATA, RSET, NOOP, and QUIT. This technique diminishes the possibility of encountering false positives if the protocol being analyzed is properly defined and enforced. On the other hand, the system can alert numerous false positives if the protocol definition is ambiguous or tolerates flexibility in its implementation.

Heuristic-Based Analysis

A different approach to network intrusion detection is to perform heuristic-based analysis. Heuristic scanning uses algorithmic logic from statistical analysis of the traffic passing through the network. Its tasks are CPU and resource intensive. This is an important consideration while planning your deployment. Heuristic-based algorithms may require fine tuning to adapt to network traffic and minimize the possibility of false positives. For example, a system signature can generate an alarm if a range of ports is scanned on a particular host or network. The signature can also be orchestrated to restrict itself from specific types of packet (for example, TCP SYN packets). Heuristic-based signatures call for more tuning and modification to better respond to their distinctive network environment.

Anomaly-Based Analysis

A different practice keeps track of network traffic that diverges from "normal" behavioral patterns. This practice is called *anomaly-based analysis.* The limitation is that what is considered to be normal must be defined. Systems and applications whose behavior can be easily considered as normal could be classified as heuristic-based systems.

However, sometimes it is challenging to classify a specific behavior as normal or abnormal based on different factors. These factors include negotiated protocols and ports, specific application changes, and changes in the architecture of the network.

A variation of this type of analysis is *profile-based detection.* This allows systems to orchestrate their alarms on alterations in the way that other systems or end users interrelate on the network.

Another kind of anomaly-based detection is *protocol-based detection.* This scheme is related to, but not to be confused with, the protocol-decode method. The protocol-based detection technique depends on well-defined protocols, because it detects as an anomaly any unpredicted value or configuration within a field in the respective protocol.

Devices doing protocol decoding can look at information within the packets that will look similar to a possible buffer-overflow pattern.

NOTE   A buffer overflow occurs when a program attempts to store more data in a temporary storage area within memory (buffer) than what it was designed to hold. In view of the fact that buffers are fashioned to contain a specific amount of information, the "extra" data or information can overflow to adjoining buffers. Attackers can generate extra data containing malicious code designed to galvanize specific actions. The attacker might send instructions to the targeted system that could damage or change data.

Host-Based Intrusion Detection Systems

Host-based intrusion detection systems are employed to safeguard critical computer systems containing crucial data. Whereas network-based intrusion detection systems examine activity within a network, a host-based IDS resides on a server or client machine while sharing CPU and other resources with other existing applications.

Cisco Systems offers both network- and host-based intrusion detection systems:

- Cisco Adaptive Security Appliances provide a network-based intrusion detection solution.
- Cisco Security Agent (CSA) provides a complete host-based intrusion detection solution.

The deployment of a host-based IDS can provide protection against both viruses and worms. The system supervises routines on the host by using a database of system policies and prevents malicious activity on the host by concentrating on the behavior of those activities. Host-based intrusion detection systems, such as CSA, use static and user-configured security policies to determine whether a specific behavior is allowed. In addition to personal firewall services, CSA offer spyware, adware, worm protection, and operating-system integrity assurance.

Network-Based Attacks

During recent years, the number of different types of network attacks has been on the rise. This section covers some of the major types of network attacks and their purpose, in relation to their perpetrators and victims. Several common types of attacks are discussed, such as the following:

- DoS attacks
- DDoS attacks
- Session hijacking (such as man-in-the-middle attacks)

It is extremely important to understand that everyone has the potential to be exploited by a network attack. Consequently, a full understanding of these threats is imperative.

DoS Attacks

DoS attacks are exercised to disrupt service to a single system or an entire network. An attacker uses this type of attack to overburden and overutilize system or network resources. DoS attacks can cause network devices to drop packets. They can also force applications to stop functioning properly. With a DoS attack, an attacker's goal is to prevent the system or network users from using its services.

NOTE   DoS attacks can also be used to degrade the performance of IDS and IPS devices. They are often used to add other attacks, like penetration attempts and reconnaissance.

Most frequently, DoS attacks try to damage network connectivity, while trying to open counterfeited TCP or UDP connections. The target device tries to handle the additional connections to the best of its extent, thus consuming all of its available resources. Three common types of DoS attacks are designed to disrupt network connectivity:

- TCP SYN flood attacks
- land.c attacks
- Smurf attacks

TCP SYN Flood Attacks

TCP SYN flood attacks are designed to take advantage of the methodology used in establishing a new TCP connection, referred as a TCP three-way handshake. Figure 1-4 illustrates how the TCP connections are established.

Figure 1-4   *TCP Connection Establishment*

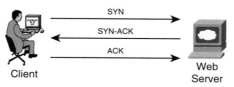

In the example presented in Figure 1-4, the client tries to establish a TCP connection to the web server. First, it sends out a SYN (synchronize) packet to the server to synchronize the sequence numbers. It stipulates its initial sequence number (ISN). To initialize a connection, the client and server must synchronize each other's sequence numbers. The Acknowledgment (ACK) field is set to 0 because this is the first packet of the three-way handshake and there are no acknowledgements thus far. In the second packet, the server sends an acknowledgment and its own SYN (SYN-ACK) back to the client. The server acknowledges the request from the client, but also sends its own request for synchronization. The server increments the client's sequence number by one and, in addition, uses it as the acknowledgment number. To conclude the connection, the client sends an acknowledgment (ACK) packet to the web server. The client uses the same methodology the server used by providing an acknowledgment number.

In TCP SYN flood attacks, the attacker generates spoofed packets to appear as valid new connection requests. These packets are received by the server, but the connection never completes. On the other hand, the server tries to reply without successfully completing the connections. After several of these packets are sent to the server, the server may quit responding to new connections until its resources are available to process the additional requests or when the attack stops attacking. Figure 1-5 shows how SYN flood attacks work. The attacker sends numerous spoofed SYN packets to the web server.

NOTE   Spoofing is the technique where the attacker sends IP packets with someone else's source address to hide their identity. Sometimes attackers use authorized external or internal IP addresses that are trusted by firewalls and other devices, in order to obtain access to internal resources.

NOTE   The server keeps all spoofed connections open until they time out. This causes substantial performance degradation.

Figure 1-5 *SYN Flood Attack*

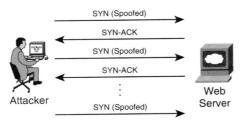

land.c Attacks

Another primitive example of a DoS attack is the land.c attack. In this type of attack, an attacker sends numerous SYN packets with the same source and destination IP addresses and the identical source and destination ports to its victim. The purpose of this attack is to make the victim send the reply packet to itself. Because the attacker repeatedly sends these packets, the victim can run out of resources by replying to itself. Technically, the attacker uses the server's own resources against itself.

Smurf Attacks

Attackers can also consume bandwidth by directing unnecessary traffic to the victim's network. A classic example of this type of attack is the smurf attack. There are two major components in a smurf attack:

- The use of bogus Internet Control Message Protocol (ICMP) echo request packets
- The routing of packets to IP broadcast addresses

Normally, ICMP handles errors and barters control messages. For example, the popular tool called ping uses ICMP. It is used to verify that a specific system on the network is responding. It does this by sending an ICMP echo request packet to such a system. Consequently, it expects the system to return an ICMP echo reply packet.

In smurf attacks, ICMP echo request packets are sent to IP broadcast addresses of remote subnets to degrade network performance. Figure 1-6 illustrates the essentials of smurf attacks. In smurf attacks, usually there is an attacker, an intermediary, and a victim (in this case, a web server). If the network is 192.168.1.0 with a 24-bit subnet mask of 255.255.255.0, the broadcast address will be 192.168.1.255. If the ICMP traffic is sent to the broadcast address, all the systems or nodes on the network will receive the ICMP echo request packets and, consequently, send ICMP echo reply packets in return. Additionally, the intermediary can also become the victim, because it receives an ICMP echo request packet sent to the IP broadcast address of its network. Attackers make this technique successful by using spoofed packets. By doing this, the victim responds with ICMP echo reply packets that consume available bandwidth.

Figure 1-6   *Smurf Attack Example*

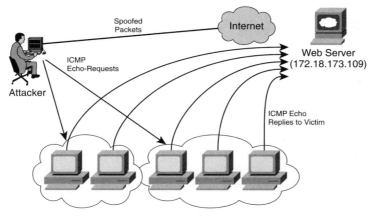

DDoS Attacks

DoS attacks may be orchestrated collectively to structure a more sophisticated technique called distributed DoS (DDoS) attacks. DDoS attacks coordinate the use of several systems in different locations to attack a specific victim, making them very difficult to trace. In DDoS attacks, the attackers compromise numerous systems on the Internet by installing malicious code to launch coordinated attacks on victim sites. These compromised systems are often referred as bots (short for robots). These attacks characteristically deteriorate bandwidth and other network resources. Figure 1-7 explains how an attacker compromises numerous systems (agents) on the Internet and then launches a chained attack from them to a target system/network (victim).

Figure 1-7   *DDoS Attacks*

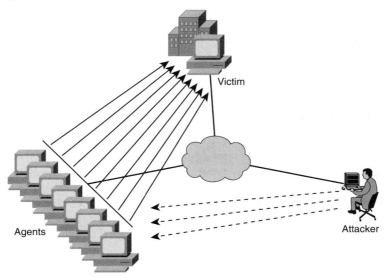

In general, attackers control the agents to generate these packets with spoofed source addresses.

Session Hijacking

Session hijacking occurs when an attacker intercepts a connection or session between two systems. The most common type of session hijacking attack uses TCP-based connections and source-routed packets. In other words, the hacker sits in on a given location on the network to take part in a session between two systems, routing all the TCP packets to pass through its system. Figure 1-8 shows a basic session hijacking example, which is known as a man-in-the-middle attack. An attacker sits in between the hosts and, by using a sniffer, intercepts and routes packets from Host A to Host B without them knowing that the information has been compromised by the attacker.

Figure 1-8 *Session Hijacking Example*

If an attacker is not able to use source routing, they can also use a method called blind hijacking. By using this technique, the attacker guesses the replies of the two hosts. The only disadvantage to the attacker is that they may send a command and never see its response. However, the attacker can impersonate the receiver of both devices.

NOTE   Source routing is a technique by which the sender can specify the route that a packet should take through the network.

Virtual Private Networks

Since the advent of the Internet, network administrators have looked for ways to leverage the low-cost, widespread medium to transport data while still providing data integrity and confidentiality to protect the information within the data packets, all while maintaining transparency to the end user. This is where the idea of virtual private networks (VPNs) originated, and the Internet Engineering Task Force (IETF) was engaged to craft the standard protocols and procedures to be used by all vendors to achieve these goals.

Point-to-Point Tunneling Protocol (PPTP), Layer 2 Forwarding (L2F) Protocol, Layer 2 Tunneling Protocol (L2TP), Generic Routing Encapsulation (GRE) protocol, Multiprotocol Label Switching (MPLS) VPN, and Internet Protocol Security (IPSec) are just a few examples of VPN protocols that were defined in their respective RFCs.

IPSec became an obvious choice for the majority of the vendors because of its robust features. It was designed to provide data integrity to ensure that packets have not been modified during transmission, packet authentication to make sure that packets are coming from a valid source, and data encryption to assure confidentiality of the content.

VPN protocols can be categorized into two distinct groups:

- Site-to-site protocols
- Remote-access protocols

Site-to-site protocols allow a corporation to establish VPN connections between two or more offices so that they can send traffic back and forth using a shared medium such as the Internet. This eliminates the need to have dedicated leased lines to connect the remote offices to the corporate network. GRE, IPSec, and MPLS VPN are some commonly used site-to-site VPN protocols.

On the other hand, the remote-access protocols benefit an organization by allowing mobile users to work from remote locations such as home, hotels, and Internet cafes as if they were directly connected to their corporate network. Corporations do not need to maintain a huge pool of modems and access servers to accommodate remote users. Additionally, they save money by not having to pay for the toll-free numbers and long-distance phone charges. Some commonly used remote-access VPN protocols are PPTP, L2TP, L2F, and IPSec.

As you can see, IPSec can be used as either a site-to-site or remote-access protocol. Furthermore, IPSec can be used in conjunction with other VPN protocols, like GRE and L2TP, to provide enhanced security.

Understanding IPSec

Figure 1-9 shows a simple IPSec VPN topology that the fictional SecureMe Company is looking to deploy. SecureMe wants to ensure that the two locations (Chicago and London) can communicate over the Internet without worrying too much about crackers looking at the data content. In this network diagram, Host A, behind the Chicago router, sends a packet to Host B, behind the London router. When the Chicago router receives the clear-text packet, it encrypts the datagram based on the negotiated security policies and then forwards the encrypted datagram to the other end of the VPN tunnel. The London router receives and decrypts the datagram and eventually forwards it to the destination Host B. Because the cracker does not have the security policies (or keys) to decrypt the packet, he cannot look at the content inside.

Figure 1-9 *Example of an IPSec VPN Tunnel*

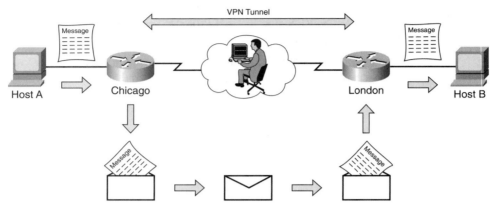

IPSec VPN devices go through a series of packet exchanges to negotiate security parameters, as discussed in the next section.

Internet Key Exchange

Internet Key Exchange (IKE) uses the framework provided by the Internet Security Association and Key Management Protocol (ISAKMP) and parts of two other key management protocols, namely Oakley and Secure Key Exchange Mechanism (SKEME). The purpose of IKE, as defined in RFC 2409, "The Internet Key Exchange," is to negotiate different security associations (SAs) by using the available key management protocols.

ISAKMP defines two phases when negotiating an IPSec tunnel. It uses Phase 1 to create a secure and authentic communication channel between the peers. By using this bidirectional channel, also known as the ISAKMP SA, the VPN peers can agree on how the further negotiation should be handled by sending protected messages to one another. Because this is a bidirectional channel, either side can initiate Phase 2 negotiations.

IKE Phase 1

The IPSec implementers have the option to use either main mode or aggressive mode to establish Phase 1 SA. The Cisco Systems implementation of IPSec typically employs main mode for site-to-site tunnels and aggressive mode for remote-access VPN tunnels. This is the default behavior when preshared keys are used as the authentication method.

Main mode goes through six packet exchanges in three round trips to negotiate the ISAKMP SA, while aggressive mode completes the SA negotiation in three packet exchanges. One of the biggest advantages of using main mode is its capability to provide identity protection if preshared key (the most commonly used authentication method) is used. Aggressive mode also provides identity protection if public key encryption is used as the authentication method.

Many different ISAKMP attributes are negotiated in Phase 1. Table 1-2 lists these attributes.

Table 1-2   *ISAKMP Attributes*

Attribute	Possible Values
Encryption	DES, 3DES, AES 128, AES 192, AES 256
Hashing	MD5 or SHA
Authentication method	Preshared keys, RSA signature, or DSA signature
DH group	1, 2, 5 or 7

Figure 1-10 shows the sequence of events that takes place on a VPN device, such as a Cisco ASA, if a preshared key is employed using main mode in Phase 1.

Figure 1-10   *Main Mode Packet Exchanges*

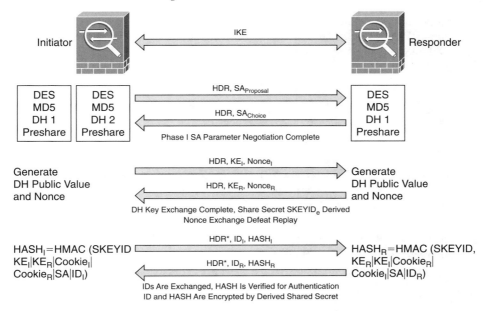

In the first and second packets, the ISAKMP peers complete their Phase 1 proposal negotiations. In the first packet, the initiator generates a proposal that it considers appropriate to send to the other side. An IPSec vendor may choose to send multiple proposals in this packet. The responder evaluates the received proposal and, if there is a match to one of its configured proposals, sends the accepted proposal back to the initiator in the second packet.

In the third and fourth packets, the initiator and the responder exchange their nonces (randomly generated values) and Diffie-Hellman public values to come up with SKEYID states.

In the fifth and sixth packets, the ISAKMP peers exchange their identity information. They protect this by encrypting the packets using the keying material derived from SKEYID. Thus, in the fifth packet, the initiator sends its identity information to the responder for peer verification. Once the responder validates the peer, it sends out its identity information so that the initiator can also validate the responder. After both peers authenticate each other, the Phase 1 SA is successfully negotiated.

NOTE   Using Preshared key is a widely deployed authentication method for small and medium-sized VPN deployments. RSA signatures, commonly referred to as certificates, provide a scalable and secure environment in which to authenticate VPN peers.

IKE Phase 2

As previously mentioned, after the ISAKMP SA is established, either VPN device can initiate Phase 2 IPSec tunnel negotiation using quick mode. The IPSec SAs are protected by the ISAKMP SA. This means that all payloads are encrypted except for the ISAKMP header.

A single IPSec SA negotiation always creates two security associations—one inbound and one outbound. Each SA is assigned a unique security parameter index (SPI) value—one by the initiator and the other by the responder.

TIP   The security protocols (AH or ESP) are Layer 3 protocols and do not have Layer 4 port information. If an IPSec peer is behind a PAT device, the ESP or AH packets are typically dropped. To work around this, many vendors, including Cisco Systems, use a feature called IPSec pass-thru. The PAT device that is IPSec pass-thru capable builds the Layer 4 translation table by looking at the SPI values on the packets.

Many industry vendors, including Cisco Systems, implement another new feature called NAT Traversal (NAT-T). With NAT-T, the VPN peers dynamically discover whether an address translation device exists between them. If they detect a NAT/PAT device, they encapsulate the data packets using UDP port 4500.

Another interesting point is that if the VPN router needs to connect multiple networks over the tunnel, it will need to negotiate twice as many IPSec SAs. Remember, each IPSec SA is unidirectional. So, if three local subnets need to go over the VPN tunnel to talk to the remote network, then six IPSec SAs will be negotiated. IPSec can use quick mode to negotiate these multiple Phase 2 SAs using the single pre-established ISAKMP SA. The number of IPSec SAs can, however, be reduced if source and/or destination networks are summarized.

Many different IPSec attributes are negotiated in quick mode, as shown in Table 1-3.

Table 1-3   *IPSec Attributes*

Attribute	Possible Values
Encryption	None, DES, 3DES, AES128, AES192, AES256
Hashing	MD5, SHA or null
Identity information	Network, Protocol, Port number
Lifetime	120 – 2,147,483,647 seconds 10 – 2, 147, 483, 647 kilobytes
Mode	Tunnel or transport
PFS group	None, 1, 2, or 5

In addition to generating the keying material, quick mode also negotiates identity information. The Phase 2 identity information specifies what network, protocol, and/or port number to encrypt. Hence, the identities can vary anywhere from an entire network to a single host address, allowing a specific protocol and port.

Quick mode goes through three packet exchanges to successfully negotiate the IPSec SA, as shown in Figure 1-11.

Figure 1-11   *Quick Mode Packet Exchanges*

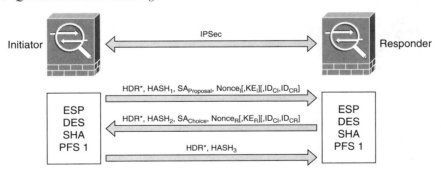

In the first quick mode packet, the initiator sends the identity information, IPSec SA proposal, Nonce payload, and the optional Key Exchange (KE) payload in case Perfect Forward Secrecy (PFS) is used. The responder evaluates the received proposal against its configured proposal. If it finds a match, it sends the accepted proposal back to the initiator along with its identity information, nonce payload, and the optional KE payload. The initiator evaluates the responder's proposal and then sends the third packet. The last packet acts as a confirmation that the IPSec SAs have been successfully negotiated and that the VPN devices can start the data encryption process.

IPSec uses two different IP protocols to encapsulate the data over the VPN tunnel. These protocols are discussed in the next section.

IPSec Protocols

IPSec uses Authentication Header (AH) and Encapsulation Security Payload (ESP) to provide data security. These protocols add an IPSec header that provides the necessary information for the VPN peer to decrypt the received packet.

Authentication Header

AH uses IP protocol 51 as defined in RFC 2402, "IP Authentication Header." It provides data integrity by encapsulating traffic to make sure that the packet has not been altered during transmission. It also provides source origination authentication to ensure that packets were originated by the right peer.

As an option, the VPN devices can use AH's antireplay service. The use of this service is determined by the receiver; hence, the sender has no knowledge whether or not the feature is in use. As a result, the sender is required to use the Sequence Number field in the AH header, as shown in Figure 1-12.

Figure 1-12 *AH Packet Header*

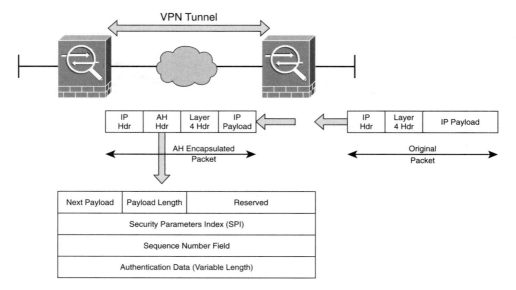

NOTE	The Cisco ASA does not support AH encapsulation.

One of the shortcomings of using AH is its lack of data confidentially (encryption). Thus, data packets are sent in clear text over the VPN tunnel when AH is used.

NOTE	AH uses a hash function on the entire packet, including the IP header. When the packet passes through a NAT device, the IP header is modified. Consequently, the output of the hash function is different when the packet is received by the other end of the VPN tunnel.

Encapsulation Security Payload

ESP, as defined in RFC 2406, "IP Encapsulating Security Payload (ESP)," uses IP protocol 50 to encapsulate the data packet. ESP provides:

- **Data confidentiality**—Encrypts the packet
- **Data integrity**—Ensures that the packet is not altered during transmission
- **Source origination authentication**—Ensures that the packet was originated by the correct peer
- **Antireplay service**—Avoids replay attacks and provides limited traffic flow confidentiality

The VPN device adds an ESP header and trailer to the original packet. The ESP header contains an SPI value and a Sequence Number field. The trailer, on the other hand, contains a Padding field, a Pad Length field, Next Protocol field, and an Integrity Check Value (ICV) field. The Padding field is used to ensure that the Authentication Data is aligned on a 4-byte boundary. It is also used to hide the actual length of the payload. The Pad Length field specifies the number of bytes used as padding. The Next Header field indicates what Layer 4 protocol is being carried in the encrypted packet. The optional ICV field is also present if authentication is used.

Figure 1-13 breaks down the ESP header and trailer when transport mode is used. IPSec modes are discussed in the next section.

NOTE	If AH and ESP are both used in an IPSec transform set, the AH header gets used as the outermost encapsulation.

Figure 1-13 *ESP Packet Header and Trailer*

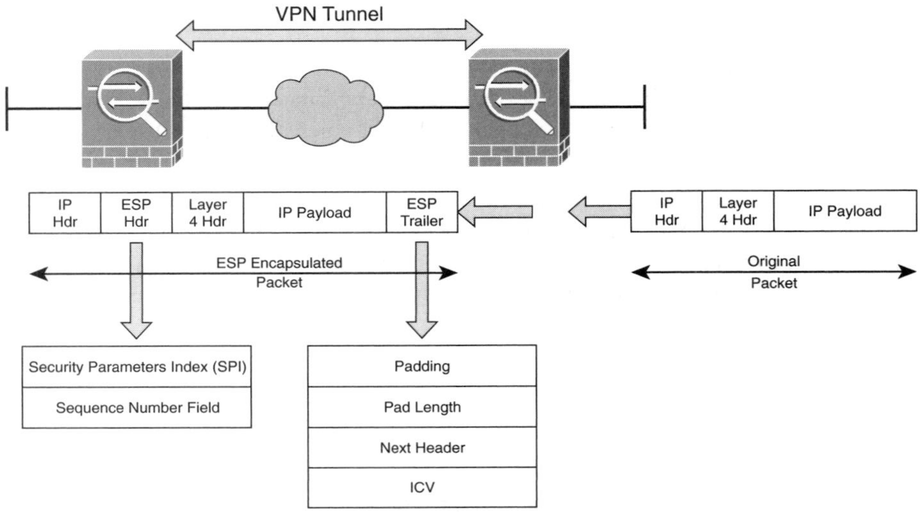

Table 1-4 lists the major differences between AH and ESP.

Table 1-4 *Contrasting AH and ESP*

Authentication Header	Encapsulation Security Payload
Uses IP protocol 51 for data encapsulation	Uses IP protocol 50 for data encapsulation
Cannot have a NAT device between the VPN peers	Supports NAT device between the peers
Does not provide payload encryption (confidentiality)	Provides payload encryption (confidentiality)
Authenticates the entire packet including the outermost IP header	Does not authenticate the outermost IP header
Adds an AH header on the packet	Adds an ESP header and a trailer on the packet

IPSec Modes

IPSec can use two modes with either AH or ESP:

- **Transport mode**—Primarily protects the upper-layer protocols (for example, UDP and TCP)

- **Tunnel mode**—Protects the entire IP packet

This section covers both modes in further detail.

Transport Mode

Transport mode is used to encrypt and/or to authenticate the data packets that are either sourced by or destined to the IPSec termination points. Most of the Cisco VPN products can act as host devices that terminate the clear-text as well as the IPSec connections. L2TP over IPSec and GRE over IPSec tunnel generally use transport mode where the IP packets are also sourced by the VPN device. Transport mode can also be used for management purposes of the VPN devices, because both clear-text and IPSec packets are originated from or destined to them.

When AH is used in transport mode, a new AH header is added between the IP header and the IP payload. The entire IP packet is then authenticated by the AH process, including the newly added AH header, as shown in part A of Figure 1-14.

ESP can also be deployed in transport mode where the original IP payload is encrypted. The authentication mechanism authenticates the ESP header and trailer in addition to the IP payload. The original IP address is kept intact even after encryption. Part B of Figure 1-14 shows an ESP packet in transport mode.

Figure 1-14 *AH and ESP Headers in Transport Mode*

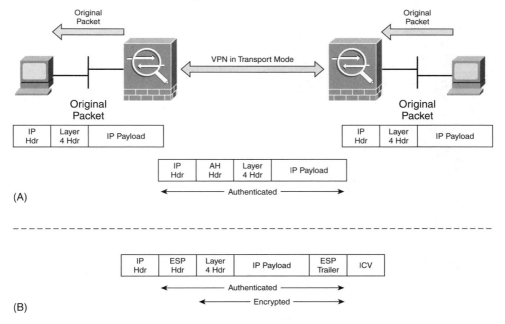

Tunnel Mode

Tunnel mode is used to encrypt and/or authenticate the IP packets when they are originated by the hosts connected behind the VPN device. In the Cisco VPN devices, tunnel mode is the default mode for IPSec.

When AH is used in tunnel mode, two additional headers get added to the original IP packet:

- An AH header (as shown in the preceding section)
- A new IP header

In AH, the entire IP packet is authenticated, including the new headers; thus, if any bit is changed during transmission, the entire packet is discarded by the receiving VPN device. Figure 1-15, part A, shows an AH packet in tunnel mode.

ESP in tunnel mode encrypts the original IP packet and adds an ESP header and trailer and a new IP header, as shown in part B of Figure 1-15. The ESP authentication process is applied to the original IP header and the ESP header. Thus, if there is a NAT device between the IPSec peers, the IPSec tunnel will successfully work.

Figure 1-15 *AH and ESP Headers in Tunnel Mode*

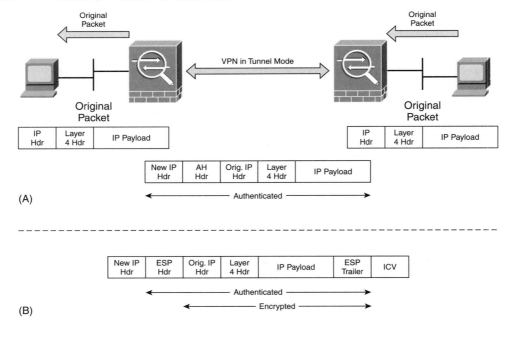

Summary

Network security is a science that needs to be carefully put into practice. There are different techniques to prevent attackers and crackers from accessing networks and computer systems. This chapter provides an overview of the different technologies, principles, and protocols related to the integrated features of Cisco ASA.

This chapter covers the following topics:

- ASA product history
- Cisco firewall products
- Cisco IDS products
- Cisco VPN products
- Cisco ASA all-in-one solution

CHAPTER 2

Product History

Cisco Systems has integrated security solutions and products to enable organizations to protect their voice and data assets. Cisco offers a range of security products, including the following:

- Firewalls
- Network intrusion detection and protection devices
- VPN devices

This chapter covers the Cisco ASA product history and describes how this product puts all of these offerings into a single-box solution.

Cisco Firewall Products

Traditionally, Cisco has provided robust network security through the use of firewalls, which create a strong defense for fast-changing network deployments. The Cisco firewall family includes the following devices and solutions:

- Cisco PIX Firewalls
- Cisco Firewall Services Module (FWSM) for Cisco Catalyst 6500 Series Switches and Cisco 7600 Series Routers
- Cisco IOS Firewall

Cisco PIX Firewalls

Cisco PIX Firewalls have always played a vital role in the Cisco security strategy. The different Cisco firewall models provide security solutions for small and large enterprises. The current Cisco PIX Firewall models are as follows:

- Cisco PIX 501 Firewalls
- Cisco PIX 506 and 506E Firewalls
- Cisco PIX 515 and 515E Firewalls
- Cisco PIX 525 Firewalls
- Cisco PIX 535 Firewalls

Cisco PIX 501, 506 and 506E offer a firewall solution for small office, home office (SOHO) environments. Cisco PIX 515, 515E, 525, and 535 are widely deployed in medium and large enterprises.

Cisco FWSM

The Cisco FWSM is a high-speed firewall module for Cisco Catalyst 6500 Series Switches and Cisco 7600 Series Routers. It currently provides one of the fastest firewall data rates in the industry (a total of 5-Gbps throughput, 100,000 cycles per second [CPS], and 1 million concurrent connections). Additionally, you can install up to four FWSMs in a single chassis. This will scale to up to 20 Gbps per chassis.

The Cisco FWSM is designed for large enterprises and service providers. It includes virtualization services at Layer 2 and Layer 3, as well as resource management capabilities. The virtualization capability allows you to split a single Cisco FWSM into multiple logical security contexts (virtual firewalls). The concept of a Layer 2 firewall, also known as a transparent firewall, allows you to deploy the FWSM in stealth mode, in which it is not seen as an extra Layer 3 hop.

Cisco IOS Firewall

The Cisco IOS Firewall feature set is available for a wide range of Cisco IOS software-based routers. Numerous organizations deploy Cisco routers with the IOS Firewall feature set for security and policy enforcement of their intranet and extranets. Additionally, it is widely deployed to secure Internet connections on remote and branch offices.

Cisco IDS Products

As mentioned in Chapter 1, "Introduction to Network Security," intrusion detection systems (IDSs) alert security administrators when they detect unauthorized or malicious activity. It also covers how the new intrusion prevention systems provide a more sophisticated way of protecting your network. There are two types of IDS and intrusion prevention systems (IPS):

- host based IDS/IPS
- network based IDS/IPS

Cisco offers the Cisco Security Agent (CSA) for host-based intrusion prevention software (HIPS) and the Cisco 4200 Series Sensors for network-based IDS/IPS, along with modules for Catalyst switches and IOS routers. The Cisco 4200 Series includes the following models:

- Cisco IDS 4215 Sensor
- Cisco IDS 4235 Sensor

- Cisco IDS 4240 Sensor
- Cisco IDS 4250 Sensor
- Cisco IDS 4250 XL Sensor
- Cisco IDS 4255 Sensor

The IDS Services Module-2 (IDSM-2) for Cisco Catalyst 6500 offers a solution for large enterprises. It is designed to protect switched environments in the Cisco Catalyst chassis. Cisco also offers an IDS network module (CIDS-NM) for IOS routers. Similarly, Cisco ASA offers an integrated Intrusion Prevention System (IPS) solution with Cisco ASA 5510, 5520, and 5540 IPS Security Services Modules (ASA-SSM-AIP-10 and ASA-SSM-AIP-20). The Cisco ASA AIP-SSM modules accelerate security application execution by offloading IDS/IPS processing from the main chassis and offer numerous enhanced IPS and Anti-X features. Anti-x is the Cisco codename for features that deliver a new generation of highly accurate and intelligent in-line prevention services. These features include network anti-virus, anti-spyware, and worm mitigation capabilities for improved threat defense.

Cisco VPN Products

Cisco ASA includes features from the different Cisco VPN product families. Cisco products such as the PIX Firewall, IOS routers, and VPN 3000 Series Concentrators offer VPN capabilities to small, medium, and large organizations. Cisco ASA integrates and enhances several IPSec and SSL VPN features from the Cisco VPN 3000 Series Concentrators and PIX Firewalls, respectively. The VPN 3000 Series Concentrator family includes the following models:

- Cisco VPN 3005 Concentrator
- Cisco VPN 3015 Concentrator
- Cisco VPN 3020 Concentrator
- Cisco VPN 3030 Concentrator
- Cisco VPN 3060 Concentrator
- Cisco VPN 3080 Concentrator

Cisco also offers an IPSec VPN Services Module for the Cisco Catalyst 6500 Series Switch and the Cisco 7600 Series Internet routers. They are designed to provide IPSec VPN services to large enterprises and service providers.

Cisco ASA All-in-One Solution

Cisco ASA integrates all the firewall, IDS, and VPN capabilities of the previously mentioned products. This provides an all-in-one solution for your network. Incorporating all of these solutions into Cisco ASA secures the network without the need for extra overlay equipment or network alterations. This is something that many Cisco customers and network professionals have requested in a security product.

Firewall Services

All firewall capabilities from the Cisco PIX Firewall and the Cisco FWSM are included in Cisco ASA. All the features available on Cisco PIX 7.x software are available in Cisco ASA. For example, the Cisco ASA virtualization capabilities allow you to configure multiple firewalls on a single appliance. You can configure, implement, and manage these firewalls as if they were separate devices. In addition, you can screen and manage resources separately for specific applications.

NOTE   Chapter 9, "Security Contexts," covers virtualization in detail.

Cisco ASA enhances security for numerous Voice over IP (VoIP) and multimedia standards. It performs in-depth inspection for Layers 4–7 on several applications and protocols.

NOTE   Chapter 8, "Application Inspection," covers application inspection in detail.

Cisco ASA also provides high-availability and failover mechanisms to assure business continuity. It also offers advanced authentication, authorization, and accounting (AAA) services.

NOTE   Chapter 11, "Failover and Redundancy," shows you how to configure and troubleshoot the Cisco ASA redundancy mechanisms. Chapter 7, "Authentication, Authorization, and Accounting (AAA)," covers the details on configuring and troubleshooting AAA services.

IPS Services

Cisco ASA remains vigilant for attacks and notifies network administrators about them in real time. The strong integration with Cisco IPS version 5.x enables Cisco ASA to automatically shun (block) devices that it recognizes as being malicious. Additionally, Cisco ASA supports virtual packet reassembly. This enables the Cisco ASA to search for attacks that are hidden over a series of fragmented packets.

The AIP-SSM modules running Cisco IPS 5.x also have the ability to run in inline mode. When running in inline mode, all packets are forwarded to the AIP-SSM to be inspected. All packets that do not conform to security policies can be dropped before reaching the protected network, making this a true intrusion prevention system.

NOTE   Chapters 13, "Intrusion Prevention System Integration," provides details on the integration of IPS services in Cisco ASA, and Chapter 14, "Configuring and Troubleshooting Cisco IPS Software via the CLI," covers configuration and troubleshooting of IPS services in Cisco ASA.

VPN Services

Cisco ASA offers site-to-site and remote-access VPN solutions. The supported connectivity mechanisms include IPSec, and Cisco WebVPN clientless SSL-based VPN connectivity.

One of the biggest advantages of Cisco ASA is the unprecedented cost savings and performance offered through its ability to terminate site-to-site and remote-access VPN connections.

Summary

This chapter introduced and offered a history of Cisco ASA. This all-in-one appliance integrates and enhances the firewall, IPS, and VPN solutions of several Cisco security products, such as the PIX Firewalls, Cisco IPS sensors, and VPN 3000 Series Concentrators. This enables Cisco ASA to secure the network without the need for any extra equipment or network alterations.

This chapter covers the following topics:

- Cisco ASA 5510 hardware overview
- Cisco ASA 5520 hardware overview
- Cisco ASA 5540 hardware overview
- Cisco ASA AIP-SSM module overview

CHAPTER 3

Hardware Overview

The Cisco ASA 5500 Series Adaptive Security Appliance provides an advanced Adaptive Identification and Mitigation (AIM) architecture and is a key component of the Cisco Self-Defending Network. Three Cisco ASA 5500 Series models are available:

- Cisco ASA 5510
- Cisco ASA 5520
- Cisco ASA 5540

This chapter provides an overview of the Cisco ASA 5500 Series Adaptive Security Appliance hardware, including performance and technical specifications. It also provides an overview of the Adaptive Inspection and Prevention Security Services Module (AIP-SSM), which is required for IPS features.

Cisco ASA 5510 Model

The Cisco ASA 5510 model is designed to deliver advanced security services for small and medium-sized businesses and enterprise branch offices. This model provides advanced firewall and VPN capabilities and has optional Anti-X (Adaptive Threat Defense) and IPS services that use the Cisco AIP-SSM-10 module.

Figure 3-1 shows a front view of the Cisco ASA 5510 model.

Figure 3-1　*Cisco ASA 5510 Front View*

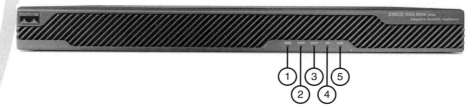

The front panel has the following five LEDs:

1 **Power**—Solid green indicates that the appliance is powered on.

2 **Status**—Flashing green indicates that the system is booting and power-up tests are running. Solid green indicates that the system tests passed and the system is operational. Amber solid indicates that the system tests failed.

   3   **Active**—Flashing green indicates network activity.

   4   **VPN**—Solid green indicates that one or more VPN tunnels are active.

   5   **Flash**—Solid green indicates that the Flash memory card is being accessed.

The three ASA models, 5510, 5520, and 5540, offer a one-rack unit (1RU) design. They also have an expansion slot for security-services modules. Figure 3-2 shows a back view of the Cisco ASA 5510 model.

Figure 3-2   *Cisco ASA 5510 Back View*

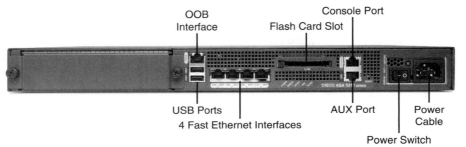

The Power, Status, Active, VPN, and Flash LEDs are also present on the back of the Cisco ASA 5510. The Cisco ASA 5510 includes five integrated 10/100 Fast Ethernet network interfaces. Three of these five Fast Ethernet ports are enabled by default (0 to 2). The fifth interface is reserved for out-of-band (OOB) management. The Security Plus license allows you to enable the fourth Fast Ethernet port, and the restriction on the OOB port is also removed. Therefore, you can use all five Fast Ethernet interfaces for the through traffic and apply security services.

NOTE   The OOB Ethernet port restriction is removed with the Security Plus license; however, it is highly recommended that you solely use this port for OOB management.

Each Fast Ethernet port has an activity LED and a link LED:

●   The activity LED shows that data is passing on the network to which the port is attached.

●   The link LED shows that the correct cable is in use and the port is operational.

The Cisco ASA 5510 Security Plus license enables Cisco ASA 5510 to provide VLAN support on switched networks (up to 10 VLANs). The Security Plus upgrade license also provides a greater number of concurrent virtual private network (VPN) connections for remote users and site-to-site connections.

NOTE   Similar to the Cisco PIX firewalls, Cisco ASA requires a unique license key to enable certain features. This license key is a 40-digit hexadecimal number represented in 5 tuples (set of fixed-length data types). The security appliance allows an administrator to enter the license key by using the activation-key command.

The output of the **show version** command includes information about the license installed on the Cisco ASA. The following is an example of the output:

```
Cisco Adaptive Security Appliance Software Version 7.0(1)
Device Manager Version 5.0(1)
Compiled on Thu 31-Mar-05 14:37 by builders
System image file is "disk0:/ASA701.bin"
Config file at boot was "startup-config"
ASA-5510-A up 4 days 5 hours
Hardware:   ASA5510, 256 MB RAM, CPU Pentium 4 Celeron 1600 MHz
Internal ATA Compact Flash, 64MB
BIOS Flash AT49LW080: @ 0xffe00000, 1024KB
Encryption hardware device : Cisco ASA-55x0 on-board accelerator (revision
0x0)
                               Boot microcode    : CNlite-MC-Boot-Cisco-1.2
                               SSL/IKE microcode: CNlite-MC-IPSEC-Admin-3.03
                               IPSec microcode   : CNlite-MC-IPSECm-MAIN-2.03
 0: Ext: Ethernet0/0       : media index  0: irq 9
 1: Ext: Ethernet0/1       : media index  1: irq 9
 2: Ext: Ethernet0/2       : media index  2: irq 9
 3: Ext: Not licensed      : media index  3: irq 9
 4: Ext: Management0/0     : media index  4: irq 11
 5: Int: Not licensed      : media index  0: irq 11
 6: Int: Not licensed      : media index  5: irq 5
Licensed features for this platform:
Maximum Physical Interfaces : 4
Maximum VLANs              : 0
Inside Hosts              : Unlimited
Failover                 : Disabled
VPN-DES                  : Enabled
VPN-3DES-AES             : Enabled
Security Contexts         : 0
GTP/GPRS                 : Disabled
VPN Peers                : 50
This platform has a Base license.
Serial Number: JMX0921L03L
Running Activation Key: 0x0610c842 0x1c8a31b4 0xb8c32858 0x8e987cc8
0xc222eabf
Configuration register is 0x1
Configuration last modified by enable_15 at 07:22:28.233 UTC Wed Jun 15 2005
```

The highlighted lines show the license (features) enabled on the Cisco ASA version.

The RJ-45 console port allows you to physically connect to the appliance to access its command-line interface (CLI) for initial configuration. The AUX (auxiliary) port allows you to connect an external modem for OOB management. The Flash card slot allows you to use an external Flash card to save system images and configuration files.

Two USB ports in the back of all Cisco ASA models are designed for future features. The Reset button is a multifunction switch. It provides the following functionality:

- If pressed longer than 1 second and less than 5 seconds, the system initiates a hardware reset. The saved configuration will be loaded at boot time.
- If pressed longer than 5 seconds, the system clears the configuration and loads the default configuration.

Table 3-1 lists the capabilities of the Cisco ASA 5510 appliance, as well as performance and connection limit numbers.

Table 3-1   *Cisco ASA 5510 Model Capabilities*

Description	Without Security Plus License	With Security Plus License
Firewall throughput	Up to 300 Mbps	Up to 300 Mbps
3DES/AES IPSec VPN throughput	Up to 170 Mbps	Up to 170 Mbps
Connections	32,000	64,000
IPSec VPN peers	50	150
WebVPN peers	50	150
Interfaces	Three Fast Ethernet ports for security services and one OOB management port	Five Fast Ethernet ports for security services (including the OOB management port)
Virtual interfaces (VLANs)	0	10
High availability	—	Active/Standby

NOTE   Performance numbers vary depending on the packet size and other applications running on the appliance.

NOTE   For more information about licensing, go to http://www.cisco.com/go/asa.

NOTE   The Cisco ASA 5510 model does not support virtualization (security contexts).

For a complete list of all product part numbers, see the Cisco ASA 5500 Series platform data sheet at http://www.cisco.com/go/asa.

Cisco ASA 5520 Model

Cisco ASA 5520 provides security services for medium-sized enterprises. The Cisco ASA 5520 and 5540 models are similar to the Cisco ASA 5510 model. They are all 1RUs, and the chassis external layouts are similar with the exception of the interfaces. The Cisco ASA 5520 and ASA 5540 models have four Gigabit Ethernet (10/100/1000) copper-based RJ-45 ports instead of the four Fast Ethernet ports in the Cisco ASA 5510 model. They also include a Fast Ethernet port for OOB management. Virtualization (security contexts) is supported in the Cisco ASA 5520 and 5540 models.

Figure 3-3 illustrates the front view of the Cisco ASA 5520 model.

Figure 3-3   *Cisco ASA 5520 Front View*

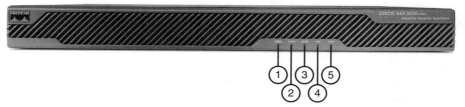

The front panel has the following five LEDs:

1 **Power**—Solid green indicates that the appliance is powered on.

2 **Status**—Flashing green indicates that the system is booting and power-up tests are running. Solid green indicates that the system tests passed and the system is operational. Amber solid indicates that the system tests failed.

3 **Active**—Flashing green indicates network activity.

4 **VPN**—Solid green indicates that one or more VPN tunnels are active.

5 **Flash**—Solid green indicates that the Flash memory card is being accessed.

Figure 3-4 illustrates the back view of the Cisco ASA 5520 model.

Figure 3-4   *Cisco ASA 5520 Back View*

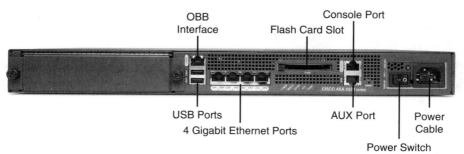

The back view of ASA 5520 is identical to that of ASA 5510, except that the Cisco ASA 5520 has four Gigabit Ethernet (10/100/1000) ports whereas the Cisco ASA 5510 has four Fast Ethernet ports.

With the installation of a VPN Plus upgrade license, Cisco ASA 5520 can terminate up to 750 IPSec or WebVPN tunnels.

Table 3-2 lists the capabilities of the Cisco ASA 5520 appliance and its performance and connection limit numbers.

Table 3-2 *Cisco ASA 5520 Model Capabilities*

Description	Without VPN Plus License	With VPN Plus License
Firewall throughput	Up to 450 Mbps	Up to 450 Mbps
3DES/AES IPSec VPN throughput	Up to 225 Mbps	Up to 225 Mbps
Connections	130,000	130,000
IPSec VPN peers	300	750
WebVPN peers	300	750
Interfaces	Four Gigabit Ethernet ports for security services and one Fast Ethernet port for OOB management	Four Gigabit Ethernet ports for security services and one Fast Ethernet port for OOB management
Virtual interfaces (VLANs)	25	25
High availability	Active/Active and Active/Standby	Active/Active and Active/Standby
VPN scalability	VPN clustering and load balancing	VPN clustering and load balancing
Threat mitigation throughput (IPS, firewall, and Anti-X)	Up to 225 Mbps with AIP-SSM-10 Up to 375 Mbps with AIP-SSM-20	Up to 225 Mbps with AIP-SSM-10 Up to 375 Mbps with AIP-SSM-20
Security contexts	Up to 10	Up to 10

NOTE   Performance numbers vary depending on the packet size and other applications running on the appliance.

NOTE   For more information about licensing, go to http://www.cisco.com/go/asa.

Cisco ASA 5540 Model

The Cisco ASA 5540 appliances provide security services to medium to large enterprises. The Cisco ASA 5540 model supports a higher number of security contexts (50) to provide more flexibility and compartmentalized control of security policies. It also provides support for up to 10 appliances in a VPN cluster, supporting a maximum of 50,000 IPSec VPN peers per cluster (25,000 for WebVPN).

Cisco ASA 5540 is also a 1RU device. The external front and back layouts of Cisco ASA 5540 appliance are identical to those of the Cisco ASA 5510 and 5520 appliances. Figure 3-5 illustrates the front view of Cisco ASA 5540.

Figure 3-5   *Cisco ASA 5540 Front View*

Figure 3-6 illustrates the back view of Cisco ASA 5540.

Figure 3-6   *Cisco ASA 5540 Back View*

Table 3-3 lists the capabilities of the Cisco ASA 5540 appliance and its performance and connection limit numbers.

Table 3-3   *Cisco ASA 5540 Model Capabilities*

Description	Without VPN Plus License	With VPN Plus License	With VPN Premium License
Firewall throughput	Up to 650 Mbps	Up to 650 Mbps	Up to 650 Mbps
3DES/AES IPSec VPN throughput	Up to 325 Mbps	Up to 325 Mbps	Up to 325 Mbps
Connections	280,000	280,000	280,000
IPSec VPN peers	500	2000	5000
WebVPN peers	500	1250	2500
Interfaces	Four Gigabit Ethernet ports for security services and one Fast Ethernet port for OOB management	Four Gigabit Ethernet ports for security services and one Fast Ethernet port for OOB management	Four Gigabit Ethernet ports for security services and one Fast Ethernet port for OOB management
Virtual interfaces (VLANs)	100	100	100

continues

Table 3-3 *Cisco ASA 5540 Model Capabilities (Continued)*

Description	Without VPN Plus License	With VPN Plus License	With VPN Premium License
High availability	Active/Active and Active/Standby	Active/Active and Active/Standby	Active/Active and Active/Standby
VPN scalability	VPN clustering and load balancing	VPN clustering and load balancing	VPN clustering and load balancing
Threat mitigation throughput (IPS, firewall, and Anti-X)	Up to 450 Mbps with AIP-SSM-20	Up to 450 Mbps with AIP-SSM-20	Up to 450 Mbps with AIP-SSM-20
Security contexts	Up to 50	Up to 50	Up to 50

AIP-SSM Modules

The following are the two Adaptive Inspection and Prevention Security Services Module (AIP-SSM) models, which provide support for IPS services delivered by Cisco IPS version 5.*x* software and later:

- **AIP-SSM-10**—Supported only on the Cisco ASA 5510 and 5520 appliances
- **AIP-SSM-20**—Supported only on the Cisco ASA 5520 and 5540 appliances

Table 3-4 lists the specifications of the AIP-SSM-10 and AIP-SSM-20 modules.

Table 3-4 *AIP-SSM Modules*

Description	AIP-SSM-10	AIP-SSM-20
Concurrent threat mitigation throughput (firewall + Anti-X services)	Up to 100 Mbps with Cisco ASA 5510 Up to 225 Mbps with Cisco ASA 5520	Up to 375 Mbps with Cisco ASA 5520 Up to 450 Mbps with Cisco ASA 5540
Processor	2.0 GHz	2.4 GHz
RAM	1 GB	2 GB
System flash	256 MB	256 MB
Cache	256 MB	512 MB

NOTE   For a complete list of environmental operating ranges, see the Cisco ASA site at http:// www.cisco.com/go/asa.

Summary

This chapter provided a hardware overview of all Cisco ASA 5500 Series appliances and the AIP-SSM modules. It provided information about the broad range of firewall, VPN, application inspection, IPS, and Anti-X services they offer to small, medium, and large enterprises. In-depth technical information for each feature and capability is provided in subsequent chapters.

Firewall Solution

This chapter covers the following topics:

- Accessing the Cisco ASA appliances
- Managing licenses
- Initial setup
- IP version 6
- Setting up the system clock
- Configuration management
- Remote system management
- System maintenance
- System monitoring

CHAPTER 4

Initial Setup and System Maintenance

Cisco Adaptive Security Appliance (ASA) can be set up in a number of ways to adapt any network topology. However, proper planning is essential for successful implementations of the security features that Cisco ASA offers. This chapter guides you through the initial configuration of the security appliance and shows ways to monitor the health and status of the system.

Accessing the Cisco ASA Appliances

Cisco ASA provides two types of user interface:

- Command-line interface (CLI)
- Graphical user interface (GUI)

The CLI provides nongraphical access to the Cisco ASA. The CLI can be accessed from a console, Telnet, or Secure Shell (SSH) session. Telnet and SSH are discussed later in the chapter, in the "Remote System Management" Section. The security appliance can also use Adaptive Security Device Manager (ASDM), a GUI-based application to configure the different security and networking features. ASDM is discussed in later chapters within Part V, "Adaptive Security Device Manager."

Establishing a Console Connection

A new security appliance, by default, has no IP addresses assigned to its interfaces. To access the CLI, you need to have a successful connection to the console port of the security appliance. The console port is a serial asynchronous port with the settings listed in Table 4-1.

Table 4-1 *Console Port Settings*

Parameters	Value
Baud rate	9600
Data bits	8
Parity	None
Stop bits	1
Flow control	Hardware

The console port on the security appliance can be connected to a serial port on a PC using a flat rolled console cable, with a DB9 serial adapter on one end and a RJ-45 port on the other. The DB9 side of the cable goes to the serial port of a PC, while the RJ-45 end of the cable goes to the console port of the security appliance, as illustrated in Figure 4-1.

Figure 4-1 *Console Port Connectivity from a Computer*

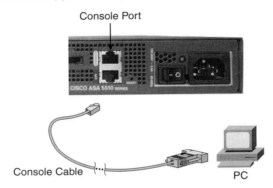

After connecting the console cable to the security appliance and the computer, launch terminal-emulation software, such as HyperTerminal or TeraTerm, to send and receive output. You can launch HyperTerminal by navigating to **Start > Programs > Accessories > Communications > HyperTerminal** on a Windows-based PC. The initial configuration window of HyperTerminal is shown in Figure 4-2. In the Connection Description dialog box, you can enter a connection name to identify this session as a unique connection. A connection name of **Console Connection to the Cisco ASA** is specified in Figure 4-2. You can choose an icon to associate with the connection entry. After filling out the connection name and selecting an icon, click **OK** to proceed to the Connect To window.

Figure 4-2 *Initial Configuration of HyperTerminal*

Specify the connection type in the Connect To window. Because the console port uses an asynchronous serial connection, the HyperTerminal setting must use a COM port. As illustrated in Figure 4-3, **COM3** is being set up for the serial connection to the security appliance. After you are done, click **OK** to proceed to the last configuration window.

Figure 4-3   *Setting HyperTerminal Connection Type*

The next window is used to configure port properties, such as the baud rate and flow control. Figure 4-4 shows HyperTerminal set up with the values listed in Table 4-1. After configuring the port settings, click **OK** to complete the configuration setup.

Figure 4-4   *Setting HyperTerminal Port Specification*

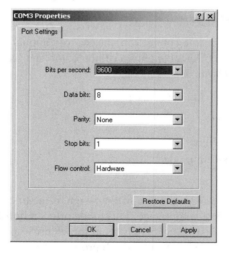

The HyperTerminal application is ready to transmit and receive data from the security appliance. If you press Enter a few times, you should see a ciscoasa> prompt in the HyperTerminal window, as shown in Figure 4-5.

Figure 4-5   *Initial Command Prompt in HyperTerminal*

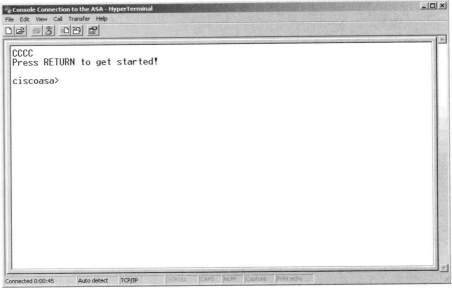

The next section describes how to use the CLI after establishing a successful console connection.

Command-Line Interface

After a successful console connection, the security appliance is ready to accept your commands. The Cisco ASA contains a similar command set structure as a Cisco IOS router and offers the following access modes:

- User mode, also known as user access mode
- Privileged mode
- Configuration mode
- Sub-configuration mode
- ROMMON mode

User mode, shown as the hostname with a **>** sign, is the first mode of access available when you log into the security appliance. This mode offers a limited set of commands that is useful in obtaining basic information about the security appliance. One of the important commands in this mode is **enable**, which prompts a user to specify a password to log into privileged mode.

Privileged mode, shown as the host name with a **#** sign, gives full access to a user after a successful logon. This mode also allows execution of all the commands that are available in user mode. The security appliance offers a rich set of monitoring and troubleshooting commands to check the health of different processes and features in the security appliance. One of the important commands in this mode is **configure terminal**, which places a user in configuration mode.

NOTE   The security appliance enables you to restrict what a user can do by implementing command authorization. This is covered in Chapter 7, "Authentication, Authorization, and Accounting (AAA)."

Configuration mode, displayed as the host name with a **(config)#** prompt, allows a user to enable or disable a feature, set up security and networking components, and tweak the default parameters. This mode not only allows the user to configure the security appliance, but also allows the use of all the commands that are available in the user and privileged modes. A user may enter into the sub-configuration mode of different features from this mode.

Sub-configuration mode, displayed as the hostname with a **(config-xxxx)#** prompt, lets a user configure specific networking or security features on the security appliance. The *xxxx* is replaced by the process/feature keyword that is being configured on the security appliance. For example, if a user is setting up specific parameters on an interface, the prompt changes to **(config-if)**. Sub-configuration mode allows the user to execute all the configuration mode commands as well as the user and privileged mode commands.

In Example 4-1, a user logs into privileged mode from user access mode by typing the **enable** command. The security appliance prompts a user to specify a password to gain privileged mode access. If the security appliance has the default configuration, it uses a null (no) password to grant access. After logging into privileged mode, the user types **configure terminal** to access configuration mode. The user enters into interface subconfiguration mode by typing the **interface GigabitEthernet0/0** command. To go back to the previous mode, the user can enter **exit** or **quit**, as shown in Example 4-1.

Example 4-1   *Accessing the Privileged and Configuration Modes*

```
ciscoasa> enable
Password: <cr>
ciscoasa# configure terminal
ciscoasa(config)# interface GigabitEthernet0/0
ciscoasa(config-if)# exit
ciscoasa(config)# exit
ciscoasa#
```

In the preceding example, the administrator of the security appliance typed **exit** twice to return to the privileged mode prompt. Optionally, you can type **end** to return to privileged mode from any configuration mode.

TIP Like a Cisco IOS router, the security appliance also allows you to press the Tab key to complete a partial command. For example, to enter a **show** command, type **sho** and press the Tab key. The security appliance displays the complete **show** command on the screen.

The security appliance allows you to abbreviate commands and keywords to the number of characters that identify a distinct abbreviation. For example, you can abbreviate the **enable** command as **en**.

All the supported options and arguments of a command are displayed when you type **?** after the command. For example, you can type **show ?** to see all the options that are supported under the **show** command.

The security appliance also provides a brief description and command syntax when you type **help** followed by the command. For example, when you type **help reload**, the security appliance shows the command syntax for **reload**, a description, and the supported arguments.

The security appliance uses *ROMMON mode (Read-Only-Memory Monitor mode)* when it does not find a bootable image or when an administrator forces it to enter into that mode. In ROMMON mode, you can use a TFTP server to load a system image into the security appliance. ROMMON mode is also used to recover the system password, discussed later in this chapter under "Image Recovery Using ROMMON."

Managing Licenses

As mentioned in Chapter 3, "Hardware Overview," the security appliance controls security and networking features through the use of a license key. The information of the currently installed license key can be obtained by issuing the **show version** command. This command also displays other system information, such as:

- The current version and the location of the system image
- The ASDM version, if installed
- The security appliance uptime
- The security appliance hardware model number, including the memory and flash information
- The physical interface and the associated IRQs (Interrupt Requests)
- The current features that are active on the security appliance
- The license information
- The serial number of the security appliance
- Configuration register setting
- Information on last configuration modification

Example 4-2 shows the output of **show version**, which has a VPN Plus-based license key installed.

Example 4-2   *Output of* **show version**

```
Chicago> show version

Cisco ASA Software Version 7.0(1)
Device Manager Version 5.0(1)

Compiled on Thu 31-Mar-05 14:37 by builders
System image file is "disk0:/ASA701.bin"
Config file at boot was "startup-config"

Chicago up 8 hours 32 mins

Hardware:   ASA5540, 1024 MB RAM, CPU Pentium 4 2000 MHz
Internal ATA Compact Flash, 63MB
BIOS Flash M50FW016 @ 0xffe00000, 2048KB

Encryption hardware device : Cisco ASA-55x0 on-board accelerator (revision 0x0)
                             Boot microcode    : ?CNlite-MC-Boot-Cisco-1.2
                             SSL/IKE microcode: ?CNlite-MC-IPSEC-Admin-3.03
                             IPSec microcode   : ?CNlite-MC-IPSECm-MAIN-2.03
 0: Ext: GigabitEthernet0/0  : media index  0: irq 9
 1: Ext: GigabitEthernet0/1  : media index  1: irq 9
 2: Ext: GigabitEthernet0/2  : media index  2: irq 9
 3: Ext: GigabitEthernet0/3  : media index  3: irq 9
 4: Ext: Management0/0       : media index  0: irq 11
 5: Int: Not licensed        : media index  4: irq 11
 6: Int: Not licensed        : media index  1: irq 5

License Features for this Platform:
Maximum Physical Interfaces : Unlimited
Maximum VLANs               : 100
Inside Hosts                : Unlimited
Failover                    : Active/Active
VPN-DES                     : Enabled
VPN-3DES-AES                : Enabled
Security Contexts           : 20
GTP/GPRS                    : Enabled
VPN Peers                   : 2000

This machine has a Plus license.

Serial Number: JABXXXXXXXX
Running Activation Key: 0xXXXXXXXX 0xXXXXXXXX 0xXXXXXXXX 0xXXXXXXXX 0xXXXXXXXX
Configuration register is 0x1
Configuration last modified by enable_15 at 22:11:22.123 UTC Fri Aug 1 2005
```

In Example 4-2, the security appliance is running a system image of 7.0(1) with the ASDM image of 5.0(1). The hardware model is ASA5540 running the Plus license. The serial number and the license activation key are masked to protect the identity of this system. The configuration register is set to 0x1, which instructs the security appliance to load the image from flash. The configuration register is discussed later in this chapter, in the section "Configuring the Password Recovery Process."

You can change the installed license key by using the **activation-key** command followed by the five-tuple key, as shown in Example 4-3. Once the new activation key is entered, the security appliance shows the features set activated by the new license key. In this example, a VPN premium license key is installed.

Example 4-3 *Changing the Activation Key*

```
Chicago# activation-key 0x11223344 0x55667788 0x9900aabb 0xccddeeff 0x01234567

Licensed features for this platform:
Maximum Physical Interfaces : Unlimited
Maximum VLANs               : 100
Inside Hosts                : Unlimited
Failover                    : Active/Active
VPN-DES                     : Enabled
VPN-3DES-AES                : Enabled
Security Contexts           : 50
GTP/GPRS                    : Disabled
VPN Peers                   : 5000
This machine has a VPN Premium license.

Both running and flash activation keys were updated with the requested key.
```

Initial Setup

When the security appliance is booted with no configuration, it offers a setup menu that enables you to configure the initial parameters such as the device name and the IP address. You can choose to go through the initial setup menu for quick configuration.

In Example 4-4, a security appliance is prompting the user to specify whether they wish to go through the interactive menu to preconfigure the device. If a user types **yes** or selects the default option, the security appliance walks them through the configuration of ten parameters. The security appliance shows the default values in brackets ([]) before prompting the user to accept or change them. To accept the default input, press Enter. After going through the initial setup menu, the security appliance displays the summary of the new configuration before prompting the user to accept or reject them.

Example 4-4 *Initial Setup Menu*

```
Pre-configure Firewall now through interactive prompts [yes]? yes
Firewall Mode [Routed]:
Enable password [<use current password>]: cisco123
Allow password recovery [yes]?
Clock (UTC):
  Year [2003]: 2005
  Month [Aug]:
  Day [16]: 5
```

Example 4-4   *Initial Setup Menu (Continued)*

```
      Time [02:02:48]: 23:30:00
Inside IP address: 192.168.10.1
Inside network mask: 255.255.255.0
Host name: Chicago
Domain name: securemeinc.com
IP address of host running Device Manager: 192.168.10.100

The following configuration will be used:
Enable password: cisco123
Allow password recovery: yes
Clock (UTC): 23:30:00 Aug 5 2005
Firewall Mode: Routed
Inside IP address: 192.168.10.1
Inside network mask: 255.255.255.0
Host name: Chicago
Domain name: securemeinc.com
IP address of host running Device Manager: 192.168.10.100

Use this configuration and write to flash? yes
INFO: Security level for "inside" set to 100 by default.
Cryptochecksum: 1d3c3c10 b029b36d 9c95faaa 3b8dca37
1252 bytes copied in 3.330 secs (417 bytes/sec)
Chicago>
```

Table 4-2 lists all the parameters that can be configured in the initial setup menu. It also provides a brief description of each parameter along with the default and configured values.

Table 4-2   *Initial Setup Parameters and Their Values*

Parameter	Description	Default Value	Configured Value
Enable password	Specifies the enable password	None	cisco123
Firewall mode	Sets up the security appliance as a Layer 2 or 3 firewall	Routed	Routed
Inside IP address	Specifies the IP address on the inside interface	None	192.168.10.1
Inside subnet mask	Specifies the subnet mask on the inside interface	None	255.255.255.0
Host name	Sets the host name on the device	ciscoasa	Chicago
Domain name	Sets the domain name on the device	None	securemeinc.com
IP address of host running Device Manager	Specifies the IP address of the host machine responsible for managing the Cisco ASA	None	192.168.10.100

continues

Table 4-2 *Initial Setup Parameters and Their Values (Continued)*

Parameter	Description	Default Value	Configured Value
Clock	Sets up the current time on the Cisco ASA	varies	4:18 PM August 5th 2005
Save configuration	Prompts the user if configuration needs to be saved	Yes	Yes
Allow password recovery	Prompts the user if password recovery is allowed	Yes	Yes

If a user bypasses the initial setup, the same parameters and features can be set up by using the CLI commands discussed throughout this chapter. The next section discusses how to configure a device name from the CLI.

TIP   The initial setup process can be rerun by using the **setup** command in configuration mode.

Setting Up the Device Name

The default device name, also known as the host name, of a security appliance is ciscoasa. It is highly recommended that you set a unique device name to identify the security appliance on the network. In Example 4-5, the host name of the security appliance is changed to **Chicago** by using the **hostname** command. Because it is a configuration change, the administrator needs to go to configuration mode before the **hostname** command can be used. As soon as the host name is altered, the CLI prompt is changed to reflect this modification.

Example 4-5 *Setting Up the Host Name*

```
ciscoasa# configure terminal
ciscoasa(config)# hostname Chicago
Chicago(config)#
```

Networking devices usually belong to a network domain. A domain name can be specified on the security appliance, which appends the unqualified host names with the configured domain name. For example, if the security appliance tries to reach a host, secweb, by its host name and the configured domain name is securemeinc.com, then the fully qualified domain name (FQDN) will be secweb.securemeinc.com. The domain name is specified by using the **domain-name** command followed by the actual name of your organization's domain. As shown in Example 4-6, a domain name of **securemeinc.com** is set up in configuration mode.

Example 4-6 *Setting Up the Domain Name*

```
Chicago# configure terminal
Chicago(config)# domain-name securemeinc.com
```

NOTE The domain name is necessary if RSA (Rivest, Shamir, and Adleman) keys need to be generated. These keys are used for Public Key Infrastructure (PKI) implementation and for secure access such as SSH and Secure Sockets Layer (SSL).

Configuring an Interface

Cisco ASA 5510 comes with four Fast Ethernet interfaces (Ethernet0/0–Ethernet0/3) and a management interface (Managament0/0), while Cisco ASA 5520 and Cisco ASA 5540 have four Gigabit Ethernet interfaces (GigabitEthernet0/0–GigabitEthernet0/3) and a management interface (Management0/0). The Fast Ethernet and Gigabit Ethernet interfaces are used to route traffic from one interface to another based on the configured policies, while the management interface is designed to establish out-of-band connections. By default, all of these interfaces are shut down, meaning no traffic can pass through them. You can enable these interfaces by issuing the **no shutdown** command under the interface sub-configuration mode. As shown in Example 4-7, the administrator is enabling the **GigabitEthernet0/0** interface.

Example 4-7 *Enabling an Interface*

```
Chicago# configure terminal
Chicago(config)# interface GigabitEthernet0/0
Chicago(config-if)# no shutdown
```

Cisco ASA protects the internal network from external threats. Each interface is assigned a name to designate its role on the network. The most secure network is typically labeled as the inside network, whereas the least secure network is tagged as the outside network. For semitrusted networks, you can define them as demilitarized zones (DMZs).

If you go through the initial setup and configure an IP address and a subnet mask, the security appliance designates the GigabitEthernet0/1 interface as the inside interface on the Cisco ASA 5520 and 5540, while it designates Ethernet0/1 as the inside interface on the Cisco ASA 5510. You can also use the **nameif** command followed by the name to be assigned to the interface. You must use the interface name to set up the configuration features that are linked to an interface. In Example 4-8, the administrator has designated the GigabitEthernet0/0 interface as outside and GigabitEthernet0/1 as inside.

Example 4-8 *Assigning Names to Interfaces*

```
Chicago# configure terminal
Chicago(config)# interface GigabitEthernet0/0
Chicago(config-if)# nameif outside
Chicago(config-if)# exit
Chicago(config)# interface GigabitEthernet0/1
Chicago(config-if)# nameif inside
```

The security appliance also uses the concept of assigning security levels to the interfaces. The higher the security level, the more secure an interface is. Consequently, the security level is used to reflect the level of trust of this interface with respect to the level of trust of another interface on the Cisco ASA. The security level can be between 0 and 100. Therefore, the most secure network is placed behind the interface with a security level of 100. The security level is assigned by using the **security-level** command, as shown in Example 4-9. The inside interface has been configured with a security level of 100, and the outside interface with a security level of 0.

NOTE   The Cisco ASA allows you to assign the same security level to more than one interface. If communication is required for the hosts on the same security level interfaces, use the global configuration **same-security-traffic permit inter-interface** command.

Example 4-9   *Assigning Security Levels*

```
Chicago# configure terminal
Chicago(config)# interface GigabitEthernet0/0
Chicago(config-if)# nameif outside
Chicago(config-if)# security-level 0
Chicago(config-if)# exit
Chicago(config)# interface GigabitEthernet0/1
Chicago(config-if)# nameif inside
Chicago(config-if)# security-level 100
```

NOTE   When an interface is configured with a **nameif** command, the security appliance automatically assigns a preconfigured security level. If an interface is set up with an inside name, the security appliance assigns a security level of 100. For all the other interface names, the security appliance sets the security level to 0.

Additionally, if an interface is not assigned a security level, it does not respond back on the network layer.

The most important parameter under the interface configuration is the assignment of an IP address. This is required if an interface is to be used to pass traffic in the Layer 3 firewall, also known as routed mode. An address can be either statically or dynamically assigned. To assign an IP address to an interface, use the **ip address** command followed by an IP address and subnet mask. The complete syntax of the **ip address** command is shown here:

```
ip address ip_address [mask] [standby ip_address]
ip address dhcp setroute
```

The *ip_address* next to the **ip address** command is the static address to be configured to this interface and *mask* is the subnet mask for the respective IP address. If there is no mask specified, the security appliance assigns a default mask of a class for the configured IP address. The **standby** *ip_address* is also optional and it is used only if this interface participates in failover, discussed in Chapter 11, "Failover and Redundancy."

If a security appliance is deployed in transparent mode, discussed in Chapter 10, "Transparent Firewalls," the IP address is configured in global configuration mode.

The security appliance also supports interface address assignment through a Dynamic Host Configuration Protocol (DHCP) server. This is a preferred method if an ISP dynamically allocates an IP address to the outside interface. The **dhcp** keyword indicates that a DHCP server will assign an IP address, while the **setroute** keyword informs the security appliance to use the DHCP server's specified default gateway as the default route.

NOTE   Chapter 6, "IP Routing," discusses how to configure default route to get connectivity to the networks that are not in the routing table.

In Example 4-10, a DHCP server is responsible for assigning an IP address on the outside interface, while a static IP address of 192.168.10.1 with a mask of 255.255.255.0 is set up on the inside interface.

Example 4-10 *Assigning Interface IP Addresses*

```
Chicago# configure terminal
Chicago(config)# interface GigabitEthernet0/0
Chicago(config-if)# nameif outside
Chicago(config-if)# security-level 0
Chicago(config-if)# ip address dhcp setroute
Chicago(config-if)# exit
Chicago(config)# interface GigabitEthernet0/1
Chicago(config-if)# nameif inside
Chicago(config-if)# security-level 100
Chicago(config-if)# ip address 192.168.10.1 255.255.255.0
```

Optionally, you can configure **speed** and **duplex** on an interface. Both parameters are set to **auto** by default and can be changed to avoid link negotiations. The command syntax to change the speed and duplex is as follows:

```
speed {auto | 10 | 100 | 1000}
duplex {auto | full | half}
```

The **speed** option is used to hard-code the interface connection speed to 10, 100, or 1000 Mbps. This option does not allow an interface to auto-negotiate link speed on the interface. The **duplex** option disables auto-negotiation of duplex parameters and limits an interface to act either in full or half-duplex mode. As demonstrated in Example 4-11, the outside interface is set up with a connection speed of 1000 Mbps using full-duplex mode.

Example 4-11 *Configuring Speed and Duplex on an Interface*

```
Chicago# configure terminal
Chicago(config)# interface GigabitEthernet0/0
Chicago(config-if)# nameif outside
Chicago(config-if)# security-level 0
Chicago(config-if)# ip address dhcp setroute
Chicago(config-if)# speed 1000
Chicago(config-if)# duplex full
```

NOTE   The management interface, discussed in the section titled "Configuring a Management Interface," is a FastEthernet interface, which only allows either 10 or 100 Mbps as the interface speed.

The Ethernet-based interfaces on the Cisco ASA 5500 series use the auto-MDI/MDIX (media-dependent interface/media-dependent interface crossover) feature, which does not require a crossover cable when connecting two similar type interfaces. They perform an internal crossover when a straight network cable connects two similar interfaces. This feature only works when both the **speed** and **duplex** parameters are set for auto-negotiations.

CAUTION   If the speed and duplex settings do not match the speed and duplex settings on the other end of the Ethernet connection, you will see packet loss, which will result in performance degradation.

The security appliance shows the output of interface-related parameters and counters information when the **show interface** command is used. As illustrated in Example 4-12, **GigabitEthernet0/0** is set up as the outside interface and has an IP address of **209.165.200.225**, while **GigabitEthernet0/1** is set up as the inside interface with an IP address of **192.168.10.1**.

Example 4-12 *Output of* **show interface**

```
Chicago# show interface
Interface GigabitEthernet0/0 "outside", is up, line protocol is up
  Hardware is i82546GB rev03, BW 1000 Mbps
        Auto-Duplex(Full-duplex), Auto-Speed(100 Mbps)
        MAC address 0013.c480.90ee, MTU 1500
        IP address 209.165.200.225, subnet mask 255.255.255.224
        79855 packets input, 6345439 bytes, 0 no buffer
        Received 79692 broadcasts, 0 runts, 0 giants
        0 input errors, 0 CRC, 0 frame, 0 overrun, 0 ignored, 0 abort
        75 packets output, 7806 bytes, 0 underruns
        0 output errors, 0 collisions
```

Example 4-12 *Output of* **show interface** *(Continued)*

```
        0 late collisions, 0 deferred
        input queue (curr/max blocks): hardware (0/5) software (0/0)
        output queue (curr/max blocks): hardware (0/1) software (0/0)
        Received 79220 VLAN untagged packets, 4869649 bytes
        Transmitted 75 VLAN untagged packets, 6420 bytes
        Dropped 14202 VLAN untagged packets
Interface GigabitEthernet0/1 "inside", is up, line protocol is up
   Hardware is i82546GB rev03, BW 1000 Mbps
        Auto-Duplex(Full-duplex), Auto-Speed(100 Mbps)
        MAC address 0013.c480.90ef, MTU 1500
        IP address 192.168.10.1, subnet mask 255.255.255.0
        79693 packets input, 6331839 bytes, 0 no buffer
        Received 79693 broadcasts, 0 runts, 0 giants
        0 input errors, 0 CRC, 0 frame, 0 overrun, 0 ignored, 0 abort
        1 packets output, 64 bytes, 0 underruns
        0 output errors, 0 collisions
        0 late collisions, 0 deferred
        input queue (curr/max blocks): hardware (0/6) software (0/0)
        output queue (curr/max blocks): hardware (0/1) software (0/0)
        Received 79059 VLAN untagged packets, 4859061 bytes
        Transmitted 1 VLAN untagged packets, 28 bytes
        Dropped 14114 VLAN untagged packets
```

Configuring a Subinterface

Cisco ASA has a limited number of Ethernet-based interfaces and it currently does not allow adding more physical interfaces. However, you can divide a physical interface into multiple logical interfaces to increase the total number of interfaces. This is achieved by tagging each subinterface with a unique virtual LAN (VLAN) ID, which keeps the network traffic separate from other VLANs using the same physical interface. The security appliance uses the IEEE-specified 802.1Q trunking to connect the physical interface to an 802.1Q-enabled device.

The number of VLANs (subinterfaces) can range from 0 to 100 depending on the security appliance model and the license key used, as shown in Table 4-3.

Table 4-3 *Supported Subinterfaces on the Security Appliances*

Appliance Model	License Feature	Number of VLANs
ASA5510	Base License	0
ASA5510	Security Plus	10
ASA5520	Base Plus	25
ASA5520	VPN Plus	25
ASA5540	Base Plus	100
ASA5540	VPN Plus	100
ASA5540	VPN Premium	100

To create subinterfaces on an appliance, you can use the **interface** command followed by the interface name and the subinterface number, as shown in the following syntax:

```
interface physical_interface.subinterface
```

Here, *physical_interface* is the actual physical interface and *subinterface* is an integer between 1 and 4,294,967,295. Example 4-13 demonstrates how to create a subinterface 300 on GigabitEthernet0/0.

Example 4-13 *Creating a Subinterface*

```
Chicago# configure terminal
Chicago(config)# interface GigabitEthernet0/0.300
```

Once you have created a subinterface, the next step is to associate the interface with a unique VLAN identity. Assign a VLAN ID by using the **vlan** subinterface configuration command followed by the actual VLAN ID, which ranges between 1 and 4096. In Example 4-14, the administrator has linked **GigabitEthernet0/0.300** to **vlan 300**. Although the subinterface number and the VLAN ID do not have to match, it is a good practice to use the same number for ease of management.

Example 4-14 *Associating a VLAN ID to a Subinterface*

```
Chicago# configure terminal
Chicago(config)# interface GigabitEthernet0/0.300
Chicago(config-if)# vlan 300
```

CAUTION   If the main physical interface is shut down, all the associated subinterfaces are disabled as well.

The subinterface is configured identically to a physical interface, using the **nameif**, **security-level**, and **ip address** commands. It does not, however, allow the use of speed and duplex commands, discussed in the previous section. Example 4-15 shows a subinterface GigabitEthernet0/0.300 configuration that is set up as a DMZ interface with the security level 30 and an IP address of 192.168.20.1/24 in VLAN 300.

Example 4-15 *Configuring Subinterface Parameters*

```
Chicago# configure terminal
Chicago(config)# interface GigabitEthernet0/0.300
Chicago(config-if)# vlan 300
Chicago(config-if)# nameif DMZ
Chicago(config-if)# security-level 30
Chicago(config-if)# ip address 192.168.20.1 255.255.255.0
```

NOTE   Even after creating the subinterfaces, a security appliance can still pass untagged traffic over the physical interface if the **nameif**, **security-level**, and **ip address** commands are configured.

Configuring a Management Interface

Cisco ASA 5500 appliances have a built-in Management0/0 port, which is designed to pass management-related traffic only. The management interface blocks all the traffic that is trying to pass through it and only permits traffic destined to the security appliance. This ensures that the management traffic is separate from the data traffic on an appliance. You can change this default behavior, however, to allow through traffic similar to the Gigabit Ethernet interfaces. Additionally, any Gigabit Ethernet or Fast Ethernet interface can act as a dedicated management interface when it is configured with the **management-only** command. As shown in Example 4-16, the Management0/0 interface is set up to allow through traffic, while **GigabitEthernet0/2** is set up as the **management-only** interface.

NOTE   The base license on the Cisco ASA 5510 does not allow you to enable through traffic on the management interface.

Example 4-16 *Configuring a Management-Only Interface*

```
Chicago# configure terminal
Chicago(config)# interface GigabitEthernet0/2
Chicago(config-if)# management-only
Chicago(config-if)# exit
Chicago(config)# interface Management0/0
Chicago(config-if)# no management-only
```

Some general characteristics about a management interface include the following:

- Routing protocols such as RIP and OSPF are supported on a management interface.
- A subinterface can also act as a management interface if configured with the **management-only** command.
- Multiple management interfaces are supported on an appliance.
- Traffic through the security appliance is dropped on a management interface and a syslog message is generated to log this event.
- VPN tunnels for remote management are allowed on a management interface.

DHCP Services

Cisco ASA can act as a DHCP server to hand out IP addresses to the end machines that are running the DHCP client services. The supported DHCP server options can be enabled by using the **dhcpd** command, as shown in Example 4-17.

Example 4-17 *Supported DHCP Server Options*

```
Chicago# configure terminal
Chicago(config)# dhcpd ?
configure mode commands/options:
  address       Configure the IP pool address range after this keyword
  auto_config   Enable auto configuration from client
  dns           Configure the IP addresses of the DNS servers after this keyword
  domain        Configure DNS domain name after this keyword
  enable        Enable the DHCP server
  lease         Configure the DHCPD lease length after this keyword
  option        Configure options to pass to DHCP clients after this keyword
  ping_timeout  Configure ping timeout value after this keyword
  wins          Configure the IP addresses of the NETBIOS servers after this
                keyword
```

To configure the DHCP server on the security appliance, use the following steps:

Step 1 Enable the DHCP server.

The first step in setting up the DHCP server is to enable it on an interface. Use the **dhcpd enable** command followed by the name of an interface. The security appliance runs the DHCP services on the configured interface. As shown in the following example, the administrator is enabling the DHCP services on the inside interface.

```
Chicago(config)# dhcpd enable inside
```

Step 2 Define a DHCP pool of addresses.

The next step in setting up the DHCP server is to define a pool of addresses that can be assigned to a DHCP client. Use the **dhcpd address** command and configure a range of IP addresses. The pool of addresses is then bound to an interface. As shown in the following example, the administrator is setting up a pool of addresses that starts at 192.168.10.100 and ends at 192.168.10.200. This pool of addresses is bound to the inside interface.

```
Chicago(config)# dhcpd address 192.168.10.100-192.168.10.200 inside
```

Step 3 Set up WINS, DNS, and domain-name options.

The DHCP server sends the WINS, DNS, and domain name when an address is offered to a DHCP client. The client computers do not need to be manually set up for these addresses. Use the **dhcpd dns**, **dhcpd wins**, and **dhcpd domain** commands to assign the DNS, WINS, and domain names to the DHCP clients. In the following example, the security appliance assigns 192.168.10.50 and 192.168.10.51 as the primary and secondary DNS addresses, 192.168.10.51 and 192.168.10.50 as the primary and secondary WINS addresses, and securemeinc.com as the domain name:

```
Chicago(config)# dhcpd dns 192.168.10.50 192.168.10.51
```

```
Chicago(config)# dhcpd wins 192.168.10.51 192.168.10.50
Chicago(config)# dhcpd domain securemeinc.com
```

Step 4   Specify the DHCP timeout parameters.

Before the security appliance allocates an IP address to a DHCP client, it sends two ICMP request packets to the address it is about to assign. It waits for 50 milliseconds to receive an ICMP response. If a response is received, the security appliance assumes that the address is being used and thus does not assign it. This default ping timeout value can be changed by using the **dhcpd ping_timeout** command. If a response is not received, the security appliance allocates the IP address until the DHCP lease expires. Once the lease expires, the DHCP client is expected to return the assigned IP address. The default lease time setting of 3600 seconds can be changed by using the **dhcpd lease**. In the following example, the administrator has set up a ping timeout value of 20 milliseconds and a DHCP lease time of 86,400 seconds (1 day).

```
Chicago(config)# dhcpd lease 86400
Chicago(config)# dhcpd ping_timeout 20
```

Step 5   Set up additional DHCP options (optional).

The security appliance allows you to assign DHCP option codes ranging from 0 to 255. These DHCP option codes are defined in RFC 2132 and can be set up on the security appliance by using the **dhcp option** command. In the following example, the DHCP option code **66** (TFTP server) is assigned to the DHCP clients with a TFTP server address of **192.168.10.10**. This DHCP option code is typically used by the Cisco IP Phones to retrieve their configuration from the TFTP server.

```
Chicago(config)# dhcpd option 66 ip 192.168.10.10
```

Step 6   Set up DHCP auto-configuration (optional).

In many network implementations, the security appliance acts as a DHCP client on one interface and a DHCP server on another interface. This is usually the case when the security appliance gets an IP address from the ISP's DHCP server on its outside interface. At the same time, it acts as a DHCP server to assign addresses to the DHCP clients connected on the inside networks. In this network scenario, the security appliance can pass the DNS, WINS, and domain-name information to the DHCP clients after it receives them from the DHCP server on its interface that acts as a DHCP client. This is achieved if the **dhcpd auto_config** command is set up with the interface name that acts as a DHCP client. In the following example, the security appliance is set up to pass DNS, WINS, and domain-name information, obtained on the outside interface, to the DHCP clients:

```
Chicago(config)# dhcpd auto_config outside
```

IP Version 6

IP version 6 (IPv6) is a new IP protocol developed to fix the shortcomings of the current IPv4 implementations. When IPv4 was standardized in 1981, the current challenges were not anticipated. The challenges include:

- Exponential growth of Internet usage
- Scalability of large routing tables on the Internet backbone routers
- Supportability of real-time data delivery

IPv6 not only fixes these problems but also provides improvements to IPv4 in areas such as IP security and network auto-configuration.

With the increased use of IP-enabled wireless phones and PDAs, the IPv4 address space is running out. Although network techniques such as Network Address Translation (NAT) and short-term DHCP leases have helped to conserve these addresses, more and more home users are demanding always-on Internet connections.

To accommodate the growing global demand for IP addresses, the new IPv6 implementation quadruples the number of bits used in an IPv4 address-from 32 bits to 128 bits. It provides 2^{128} routable IP addresses, enough to assign over a thousand IP addresses per person on this planet.

IPv6 Header

IPv6 specifications, defined in RFC 2460, describe an IPv6 header, as shown in Figure 4-6. Table 4-4 lists and describes the fields in an IPv6 header.

Figure 4-6   *IPv6 Header*

Table 4-4   *IPv6 Header Fields*

Field	Description
Version	A 4-bit Internet Protocol version number = 6
Traffic Class	An 8-bit field that enables the source to specify a desired delivery priority of its packets relative to other packets
Flow Label	A 24-bit field that may be set to request special handling of the packets by the IPv6-based router
Payload Length	A 16-bit integer that specifies the length of the data payload
Next Header	An 8-bit field that identifies the type of header following the IPv6 header
Hop Limit	An 8-bit integer that is decremented by 1 whenever the packet passes through a network node
Source Address	A 128-bit address to identify the source of the packet
Destination Address	A 128-bit address to identify the destination of the packet

In case of IPv4, an IP address is represented in four octets, separated by dots (.). To accommodate a 128-bit IPv6 address, it is divided into 8 blocks of 16 bits each, separated by colons (:). Consequently, this representation is referred to as *colon-hexadecimal notation.*

The following are a few examples of IPv6 addresses:

```
FEDC:BA98:0001:3210:FEDC:BA98:0001:3210
1080:0000:0000:0000:0008:0800:200C:417A
0000:0000:0000:0000:0000:0000:0000:0001
```

In an IPv6 address, it is not required to write the leading zeros in the individual block, similar to an IPv4 address. Thus the preceding addresses can be rewritten as follows:

```
FEDC:BA98:1:3210:FEDC:BA98:1:3210
1080:0:0:0:8:800:200C:417A
0:0:0:0:0:0:0:1
```

As you can see from the preceding addresses, an IPv6 address may have long strings of zero bits. For the ease of representation, an IPv6 address with long sequences of zeros can be compressed and replaced with ::. This notation, also known as *double colon,* can compress contiguous blocks of zeros. However, the :: notation can only appear once in an address, to avoid confusion on how many zeros should go to which instance of ::. The preceding addresses, with zero compression, can be written as follows:

```
FEDC:BA98:1:3210:FEDC:BA98:1:3210
1080::8:800:200C:417A
::1
```

Configuring IPv6

The security appliance supports a limited set of IPv6 features, which includes IP address assignment, packet filtering, and basic routing using static routes. This section discusses IP address assignment, whereas packet filtering and basic routing using static routes are discussed in subsequent chapters.

IP Address Assignment

The security appliance supports simultaneous IPv4 and IPv6 addresses on an interface. An IPv6 address can be configured on an interface by using the **ipv6 address** command. The syntax for the **ipv6 address** command is as follows:

```
ipv6 address {autoconfig | ipv6-prefix/prefix-length [eui-64] | ipv6-address link-
   local}
```

Table 4-5 lists the arguments of the **ipv6 address** command.

Table 4-5   *The **ipv6 address** Command Arguments*

Syntax	Syntax Description
autoconfig	Configures the assignment of IPv6 addresses using Router Advertisement messages. These messages are used to announce the network prefix.
ipv6-prefix	Specifies the IPv6 network address.
prefix-length	Specifies the high-order contiguous bits in the IPv6 prefix to determine the network part of the IPv6 address.
eui-64	Uses the EUI-64 format interface ID as the host part of the IPv6 address.
ipv6-address	Overrides the auto-generated IPv6 link-local address.
link-local	Identifies that the IPv6 address is a link-local address.

The security appliance supports four types of interface address assignments:

- Global address
- Site-local address
- Link-local address
- Auto-configuration address

NOTE   For detailed information about these types, consult RFC 3513.

Global Address

A global IPv6 address, similar to an IPv4 public routable address, is used for Internet connectivity. It uses a prefix of 2000::/3 and requires a 64-bit interface identifier in the extended universal identifier 64 (EUI-64) format.

Each physical interface has an embedded 48-bit MAC address that specifies a unique link-layer address. The EUI-64 format interface ID is derived from the interface MAC address by using the following rules:

1 Insert FFFE between the upper and the lower 24 bits. For example, if the interface's MAC address is 000F.F775.4B57, the modified address will be 000F.F7FF.FE75.4B57.

2 Change the 7th bit in the leftmost byte to 1. For example, if the 64-bit address is 000F.F7FF.FE75.4B57 (derived in the previous step), after the 7th bit is changed, the new address becomes 020F.F7FF.FE75.4B57. This new address is in the EUI-64 format.

Example 4-18 shows how to set up a global IPv6 address of 2001:1ae2:123f with a mask of /48 followed by the EUI-64 format identifier.

Example 4-18 *Assigning a Global IPv6 Address*

```
Chicago(config-if)# ipv6 address 2001:1ae2:123f::/48 eui-64
```

NOTE   You can set up multiple IPv6 addresses on an interface.

Site-Local Address

A site-local IPv6 address, similar to an IPv4 private address, is used for the hosts on the trusted networks that do not require Internet connectivity. It uses a prefix range of FEC0::/10 and uses the EUI-64 format interface ID for a complete IPv6 address. Example 4-19 shows how to set up a global IPv6 address of fec0:1ae2:123f with a mask of /48 and using EUI-64 format identifier.

Example 4-19 *Assigning a Site-Local IPv6 Address*

```
Chicago(config-if)# ipv6 address fec0:1ae2:123f::/48 eui-64
```

Link-Local Address

A link-local IPv6 address allows IPv6-enabled hosts to communicate with each other using the neighbor discovery protocol without the need to configure a global or site-local address. The neighbor discovery protocol provides a messaging channel on which the neighbor IPv6 devices can interact. It uses a prefix of FE80::/10 and the EUI-64 format interface ID as the complete link-local address. The link-local address is auto-assigned to an interface when IPv6 is enabled. To manually assign a different link-local address, use the **ipv6 address** command with the **link-local** keyword, as shown in Example 4-20, where an IPv6 address of **fe80::20f:f7ff:fe75:4b58** is being assigned.

Example 4-20 *Assigning a Static Link-Local IPv6 Address*

```
Chicago(config-if)# ipv6 address fe80::20f:f7ff:fe75:4b58 link-local
```

Auto-Configuration Address

The auto-configuration method assigns a link-local address on the interface when the **ipv6 address autoconfig** command is set up, as shown in Example 4-21. The security appliance listens for the Router Advertisement messages to determine the prefix, and generates an IPv6 address by using the EUI-64 format interface ID.

Example 4-21 *Assigning an Auto-Configuration Address*

```
Chicago(config-if)# ipv6 address autoconfig
```

NOTE   The current implementation of IPv6 on the security appliances does not support anycast addresses.

Setting Up the System Clock

One of the most important tasks when setting the security appliance is to verify that the clock settings are accurate. The security appliances can timestamp the syslog messages using the system clock before sending them to the configured types if **logging timestamp** is enabled, as discussed in the "Enabling Logging" section. The system clock is also checked when the VPN tunnels, using PKI, are being negotiated to verify the validity of the certificate presented by the VPN peer. The security appliance supports two methods to adjust the system clock:

- Manual clock adjustment using **clock set**
- Automatic clock adjustment using the Network Time Protocol

Manual Clock Adjustment Using clock set

Similar to a Cisco IOS router, the security appliance allows the use of the **clock set** command to adjust the system clock. After setting the clock, the security appliance updates the system memory powered by a battery on the motherboard. Consequently, if the security appliance is rebooted, the time setting does not need to be reconfigured. The complete command syntax is as follows:

```
clock set hh:mm:ss {month day | day month} year
```

Table 4-6 describes the syntax.

Table 4-6   *The **clock set** Command Syntax*

Syntax	Syntax Description
hh:mm:ss	Specifies the time in hour, minutes, and seconds using the 24-hour time format
month	Specifies the time in month, such as January or February

Table 4-6   *The* **clock set** *Command Syntax (Continued)*

Syntax	Syntax Description
day	Sets the day of the month, an integer from 1 to 31
year	Sets the time in hour as a four-digit number ranging between 1993 and 2035

In Example 4-22, the clock on the security appliance is updated to use the current time of 23:30 and the current date is August 5, 2005.

Example 4-22 *Setting the System Clock*

```
Chicago# clock set 23:30:00 august 5 2005
```

To check the current time on the security appliance, use the **show clock** command, as shown in Example 4-23.

Example 4-23 *Output of* **show clock**

```
Chicago# show clock
23:30:05.142 UTC Fri Aug 5 2005
```

Automatic Clock Adjustment Using the Network Time Protocol

Cisco ASA provides support for the Network Time Protocol (NTP) to synchronize the system clock with an NTP server. The device administrator does not need to update the system clock manually because the security appliance overrides the manual clock setting when it synchronizes the time with the NTP server. Setting up an NTP server is important when an organization uses certificates (PKI) to authenticate users and devices on the network.

NTP is set up by using the **ntp** commands, as shown in the following command syntaxes:

```
ntp server ip_address [key key_id] [source interface_name] [prefer]
ntp authenticate
ntp authentication-key key_id md5 md5_key
ntp trusted-key key_id
```

Table 4-7 lists and describes the options in the **ntp** command.

Table 4-7   *The* **ntp** *Command Arguments*

Syntax	Syntax Description
server	Keyword to specify the IP address of the NTP server
ip_address	Specifies the actual IP address of the NTP server
key	Optional keyword to specify the authentication key
key_id	Specifies the authentication key number, between 1 and 4,294,967,295
source	Optional keyword to specify the source of the NTP packets

continues

Table 4-7   *The **ntp** Command Arguments (Continued)*

Syntax	Syntax Description
interface_name	Specifies the name of the interface to source the packets destined to the NTP server
prefer	If multiple NTP servers are specified, the security appliance chooses the NTP server with this keyword.
authenticate	Keyword to enable NTP authentication
authentication-key	Keyword to specify the authentication key to authenticate to an NTP server
md5	Keyword to enable MD5 authentication
md5_key	Specifies the actual key, up to 35 characters, used for MD5 authentication
trusted-key	Keyword to specify an authentication key for all the configured NTP servers

Example 4-24 shows how to configure two NTP servers located on the inside interface. The server at 192.168.10.200 is a preferred server, while the server at 192.168.10.201 is the secondary NTP server. Both servers use an authentication key of 919919. They require an MD5 authentication key of cisco123 to successfully authenticate the security appliance.

Example 4-24 *Configuration of NTP Server*

```
Chicago(config)# ntp authentication-key 919919 md5 cisco123
Chicago(config)# ntp authenticate
Chicago(config)# ntp server 192.168.10.200 key 123456 source inside prefer
Chicago(config)# ntp server 192.168.10.201 key 123456 source inside
```

To verify whether the system clock is synchronized with the NTP server, use the **show ntp status** command, as shown in Example 4-25.

Example 4-25 *Output of **show ntp status***

```
Chicago(config)# show ntp status
Clock is synchronized, stratum 9, reference is 192.168.10.200
nominal freq is 99.9984 Hz, actual freq is 99.9984 Hz, precision is 2**6
reference time is c69e0e0b.1dfbb8db (23:35:51.117 UTC Fri Aug 5 2005)
clock offset is -11.9016 msec, root delay is 7.02 msec
root dispersion is 15902.56 msec, peer dispersion is 15890.63 msec
```

Time Zones and Daylight Savings Time

Cisco ASA supports displaying the system time in the correct time zone. It maintains the system clock in Universal Time, Coordinated (UTC) but shows it in the configured time zone. Use the **clock timezone** command followed by the name of the time zone to set the time zone on the security appliance, as shown in Example 4-26. The configured time zone is Eastern Standard Time (EST), which is 5 hours behind UTC time.

Example 4-26 *Setting Time Zone*

```
Chicago(config)# clock timezone EST -5
```

The security appliance can automatically display the system clock in daylight savings time (DST) if it is configured to do so using the **clock summer-time** command. The security appliance enables you to set the DST in two formats:

- Using specific date and time settings
- Using recurring date and time settings

The command syntax for both formats is as follows:

```
clock summer-time zone date {day month | month day} year hh:mm {day month | month day}
    year hh:mm [offset]

clock summer-time zone recurring [week weekday month hh:mm week weekday month hh:mm]
    [offset]
```

By using the **clock summer-time date** option, you can specify to start and end DST on a specific day and time. For example, you can specify to always start DST at 2 a.m., April 1 and end at 2 a.m., October 31 of every year, as illustrated in Example 4-27. The *offset* indicates the number of minutes to add or remove from DST. The default is 60 minutes.

Example 4-27 *Setting DST Using the Date Format*

```
Chicago(config)# clock summer-time EST date Apr 1 2005 2:00 Oct 31 2035 2:00 60
```

Alternatively, you can use the **clock summer-time recurring** option to specify the day and time based on the day of the week. For example, you can set a policy to always start DST at 5 a.m. on the first Sunday of April and end it at 5 a.m. on the last Sunday of October, as shown in Example 4-28. If no day and time settings are specified, the security appliance uses a policy based on the U.S. DST rules (start DST at 2 a.m. on the first Sunday of April and end at 2 a.m. on the last Sunday of October).

Example 4-28 *Setting DST Using the Recurring Format*

```
Chicago(config)# clock summer-time EST recurring 1 Sun Apr 5:00 last Sun Oct 5:00
```

Configuration Management

The security appliance keeps two copies of the configuration in the system:

- The active, or running, configuration
- The saved, or startup, configuration

These configurations are discussed in the next two subsections. Removing configurations from the security appliance is also discussed.

Running Configuration

The running configuration is the actual configuration that the security appliance loads in its memory. When the security appliance boots up, it copies the saved configuration in its memory and then uses it to function as configured. Use the **show running-config** command to display the current configuration that the security appliance is using. This is the most important command to verify that the security appliance is configured properly. The running configuration is not stored in nonvolatile RAM (NVRAM) until the security appliance is instructed to store it there.

Example 4-29 shows the current configuration on an appliance. As you can see, the configuration file can be fairly large and complex depending on the number of features configured on the security appliance. The configuration file displays the current version of the system image, and then the rest of the configuration parameters.

Example 4-29 *Output of* **show running-config**

```
Chicago# show running-config
: Saved
:
ASA Version 7.0(1)
names
!
interface GigabitEthernet0/0
 nameif outside
 security-level 0
 ip address 209.165.200.225 255.255.255.224
!
interface GigabitEthernet0/1
 nameif inside
 security-level 100
 ip address 192.168.10.1 255.255.255.0
!
interface GigabitEthernet0/2
 shutdown
 no nameif
 no security-level
no ip address
!
interface GigabitEthernet0/3
 shutdown
 no nameif
 no security-level
 no ip address
!
interface Management0/0
 shutdown
 no nameif
 no security-level
 no ip address
!
enable password 8Ry2YjIyt7RRXU24 encrypted
passwd 2KFQnbNIdI.2KYOU encrypted
```

Example 4-29 *Output of* **show running-config** *(Continued)*

```
hostname Chicago
domain-name securemeinc.com
ftp mode passive
pager lines 24
mtu outside 1500
mtu inside 1500
no failover
monitor-interface outside
monitor-interface inside
asdm image disk0:/asdm501.bin
no asdm history enable
arp timeout 14400
route outside 0.0.0.0 0.0.0.0 209.165.200.226 1
timeout xlate 3:00:00
timeout conn 1:00:00 half-closed 0:10:00 udp 0:02:00 icmp 0:00:02 sunrpc 0:10:00
 h323 0:05:00 h225 1:00:00 mgcp 0:05:00 mgcp-pat 0:05:00 sip 0:30:00 sip_media 0
:02:00
timeout uauth 0:05:00 absolute
telnet timeout 5
ssh timeout 5
console timeout 0
!
class-map inspection_default
 match default-inspection-traffic
!
!
policy-map global_policy
 class inspection_default
  inspect dns maximum-length 512
  inspect ftp
  inspect h323 h225
  inspect h323 ras
  inspect netbios
  inspect rsh
  inspect rtsp
  inspect skinny
  inspect esmtp
  inspect sqlnet
  inspect sunrpc
  inspect tftp
  inspect sip
  inspect xdmcp
!
 service-policy global_policy global
Cryptochecksum:533c1e606d18c43ea3c6d1cfb7f00d52
: end
```

Cisco ASA allows you to display the specific part of the configuration by using **show running-config** followed by the name of the command you are interested in checking, as shown in Example 4-30. The **show running-config ?** command shows all possible keywords you can use, while the **show running-config interface gigabitEthernet0/0** command shows the running configuration of the GigabitEthernet0/0 interface.

Example 4-30 *Partial Output of* **show running-config**

```
Chicago# show running-config ?
  aaa                      Show aaa configuration information
  aaa-server               Show aaa-server configuration information
  access-group             Show access group(s)
  access-list              Show configured access control elements
  alias                    Show configured overlapping addresses with dual NAT
  all                      Current operating configuration including defaults
  arp                      Show configured arp entries, arp timeout
  asdm                     Show ASDM configuration
! Output omitted for brevity
Chicago# show running-config interface gigabitEthernet0/0
!
interface GigabitEthernet0/0
 nameif outside
 security-level 0
 ip address 209.165.200.225 255.255.255.224
```

NOTE   The **show running-config command** does not display the default configuration of the security appliance. Use **show running-config all** to display the entire running configuration.

The Cisco ASA operating system allows you to enhance the search capabilities when a **show** command is executed, by using **| grep** at the end of the command. Alternatively, **| include** displays the output when the exact phrase matches a **show** command. In Example 4-31, the administrator is only interested in looking at the IP addresses set up on the security appliance and their respective subnet masks in the running configuration.

Example 4-31 *Selective Output of* **show running-config**

```
Chicago# show running-config | include ip address
 ip address 209.165.200.225 255.255.255.224
 ip address 192.168.10.1 255.255.255.0
 no ip address
 no ip address
 no ip address
```

The security appliance can also display the selective output of a **show** command when the **| begin** option is used. In this case, the security appliance displays the output beginning from a specific keyword. As shown in Example 4-32, the administrator is interested in looking at the running configuration beginning from the physical interfaces. This is done by using the **show running-config | begin interface** command.

Example 4-32 *Output of* **show running-config** *Beginning from the Interface Configuration*

```
Chicago# show running-config | begin interface
interface GigabitEthernet0/0
 nameif outside
 security-level 0
 ip address 209.165.200.225 255.255.255.224
!
interface GigabitEthernet0/1
 nameif inside
 security-level 100
 ip address 192.168.10.1 255.255.255.0
!
interface GigabitEthernet0/2
 shutdown
 no nameif
 no security-level
 no ip address
! Output omitted for brevity
```

Startup Configuration

The security appliance uses the saved configuration during the bootup process as the running configuration. This saved configuration is known as the startup configuration. The startup configuration can be viewed by using the **show startup-config** command, as shown in Example 4-33.

TIP   You can also use **show configuration** to display the startup configuration.

Example 4-33 *Output of* **show startup-config**

```
Chicago# show startup-config
: Saved
: Written by enable_15 at 23:35:53.100 UTC Sat Aug 5 2005
:
ASA Version 7.0(1)
names
!
interface GigabitEthernet0/0
 nameif outside
 security-level 0
 ip address 209.165.200.225 255.255.255.224
!
interface GigabitEthernet0/1
 nameif inside
 security-level 100
 ip address 192.168.10.1 255.255.255.0
!
```

continues

Example 4-33 *Output of* **show startup-config** *(Continued)*

```
interface GigabitEthernet0/2
 shutdown
 no nameif
 no security-level
 no ip address
! Output omitted for brevity
```

The output of **show running-config** and **show startup-config** may or may not be identical depending on whether the two configurations were synced. Use the **copy running-config startup-config** command to copy the active configuration into NVRAM, as shown in Example 4-34.

TIP   You can also use **write memory** command to copy the running configuration as the startup configuration.

Example 4-34 *Output of* **copy running-config startup-config**

```
Chicago# copy running-config startup-config
Source filename [running-config]?
Cryptochecksum: 28b8d710 e2eaeda0 bc98a262 2bf3247a
3205 bytes copied in 3.230 secs (1068 bytes/sec)
```

Removing the Device Configuration

A configured command can be removed from the configuration by using the **no** form of the command. This will undo the command that was previously entered into the configuration. In Example 4-35, the security appliance is set up for ISAKMP processing on the outside interface. It is being disabled with the **no isakmp enable outside** command.

Example 4-35 *Disabling ISAKMP Processing on the Outside Interface*

```
Chicago(config)# isakmp enable outside
Chicago(config)# no isakmp enable outside
```

The security appliance can also remove the current configuration for a specific feature if the **clear configure** command is used. If the security appliance is set up with an ISAKMP policy 10 for Phase 1 negotiations, the **clear configure isakmp** command will remove all the **isakmp** commands from the running configuration. This is demonstrated in Example 4-36.

NOTE   The use of **no** in a command removes a single line, while **clear configure** removes the parts of the configuration for a feature.

Example 4-36 *Clearing All ISAKMP Commands from the Running Configuration*

```
Chicago(config)# show running-config | include isakmp
isakmp enable outside
isakmp policy 10 authentication pre-share
isakmp policy 10 encryption 3des
isakmp policy 10 hash md5
isakmp policy 10 group 2
isakmp policy 10 lifetime 86400
Chicago(config)# clear configure isakmp
Chicago(config)# show running-config | include isakmp
```

The preceding example not only cleared the ISAKMP policy but also removed the **isakmp enable outside** command from the running configuration. Use the **clear configure isakmp policy** command to only remove the ISAKMP policy from the active configuration, as shown in Example 4-37.

Example 4-37 *Clearing ISAKMP Policy Commands from the Running Configuration*

```
Chicago(config)# show running-config | include isakmp
isakmp enable outside
isakmp policy 10 authentication pre-share
isakmp policy 10 encryption 3des
isakmp policy 10 hash md5
isakmp policy 10 group 2
isakmp policy 10 lifetime 86400
Chicago(config)# clear configure isakmp policy
Chicago(config)# show running-config | include isakmp
isakmp enable outside
```

Unlike the Cisco IOS routers, the Cisco ASA can clear the running configuration without going through the reboot process. This is helpful in a scenario where the security appliance needs to be in the default configuration. Use the **clear configure all** command to clear the running configuration, as shown in Example 4-38.

Example 4-38 *Clearing the Running Configuration*

```
Chicago(config)# clear configure all
ciscoasa(config)#
```

CAUTION   The use of this command will reset your connection if you are connected to the security appliance using a remote-management protocol. This is discussed in the in the next section.

The security appliance can also erase the startup configuration from NVRAM if the **write erase** command is issued from privileged mode, as shown in Example 4-39.

Example 4-39 *Clearing the Startup Configuration*

```
Chicago# write erase
Chicago#
```

Remote System Management

You do not have to be physically connected to the console port of the security appliance to be able to access the CLI. The security appliance supports two remote-management protocols:

- Telnet
- Secure Shell (SSH)

Telnet

Cisco ASA comes with a Telnet server that allows users to manage it remotely. The default behavior of the security appliance is to deny Telnet access from all clients unless they are explicitly permitted.

NOTE   The communication between a client and the security appliance is not encrypted; therefore, it is highly recommended to use SSH instead of Telnet for remote management.

You may choose to enable Telnet on all interfaces. However, the security appliance does not allow clear-text Telnet communication on the outside interface unless the session is protected by an IPSec tunnel. The security appliance requires a user to establish an IPSec tunnel to the outside interface to encrypt the traffic destined to the security appliance. Once the tunnel is successfully negotiated, the user can start a Telnet session to the outside interface.

When a Telnet client tries to connect, the security appliance verifies the following two conditions:

- The client's address space falls in the configured address space.
- The interface that is receiving the request is allowed to accept requests from the client's address space.

If either one of the conditions is not valid, the security appliance simply drops the request and generates a syslog message for this incident.

An external authentication server, such as CiscoSecure Access Control Server (ACS), can be used to leverage the authentication process for the Telnet sessions. Consult Chapter 7, "Authentication, Authorization, and Accounting (AAA)," for more information.

You can configure the security appliance to accept Telnet sessions on an interface by using the **telnet** command. The complete command syntax follows:

```
telnet {{IP_address mask} | ipv6_address/prefix} interface} | {timeout number}}
```

Table 4-8 lists and defines the arguments used in the **telnet** command.

Table 4-8   *The* **telnet** *Command Definition*

Syntax	Syntax Description
ip_address	Specifies a host or a network address that is allowed to connect.
mask	Associates a network mask to an IP address.
interface	Specifies which interface the Telnet clients should be coming in from.
ipv6_address/prefix	Specifies a host or a network IPv6 address that is allowed to connect.
timeout	Keyword that specifies the idle timeout for a Telnet session.
number	Specifies the actual number of minutes used by the **timeout** keyword. The security appliance disconnects a Telnet session if the idle timeout is reached. The allowed range is between 1 and 1440 minutes, with a default value of 5 minutes.

In Figure 4-7, the inside network, 192.168.10.0/24, is allowed to establish Telnet sessions to the security appliance's inside interface, while only two hosts from the DMZ network, 192.168.20.10 and 192.168.20.20, are permitted for the Telnet access.

Figure 4-7   *Telnet Services for the Inside and DMZ Networks*

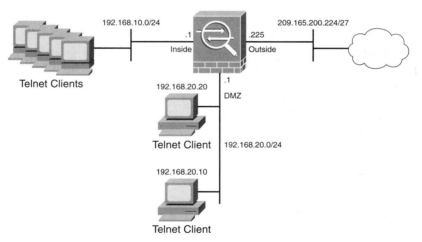

Example 4-40 shows the relevant configuration for this setup. For the inside network, all hosts are allowed to connect, so the mask is set to 255.255.255.0. For hosts on the DMZ network, the subnet mask is configured as 255.255.255.255. If the Telnet connection is idle, the security appliance is set up to time it out after 20 minutes.

If a user is allowed to connect, the security appliance goes through the user authentication phase and prompts them for login credentials. The default password to gain user access mode is **cisco**. This password can be changed by using the **passwd** command followed by

Example 4-40 *Configuration of Telnet Access on the Inside and DMZ Interfaces*

```
Chicago# configure terminal
Chicago(config)# telnet 192.168.10.0 255.255.255.0 inside
Chicago(config)# telnet 192.168.20.10 255.255.255.255 dmz
Chicago(config)# telnet 192.168.20.20 255.255.255.255 dmz
Chicago(config)# telnet timeout 20
```

the new password. As demonstrated in Example 4-41, the user access mode password is being changed to **cisco123**.

Example 4-41 *Changing the User Access Mode Password*

```
Chicago# configure terminal
Chicago(config)# passwd cisco123
```

NOTE   It is highly recommended that you change the default password of the security appliance to avoid unauthorized access.

If the authentication is successful, the security appliance grants user access mode CLI to the authenticated user.

The **who** command can be used to monitor active Telnet sessions. This displays the Telnet connection ID along with the client's IP address. You can use the connection ID to clear out a session if you believe that it should not be established. This is done by using the **kill** command followed by the connection ID. In Example 4-42, the security appliance has assigned a connection ID of 0 to a Telnet client 192.168.10.10 and a connection ID of 1 to a client 192.168.10.20. The connection ID 0 is cleared to terminate the client's session.

Example 4-42 *Monitoring and Clearing Active Telnet Sessions*

```
Chicago# configure terminal
Chicago# who
        0: 192.168.10.10
        1: 192.168.10.20
Chicago# kill 0
Chicago# who
        1: 192.168.10.20
```

Secure Shell

SSH is the recommended way to connect to the security appliance for remote management, because the data packets are encrypted using industry-standard algorithms such as 3DES and AES. The SSH implementation on the security appliance supports both versions 1 and 2.

Before the SSH client and the Cisco ASA SSH server encrypt data, they go through an exchange of the RSA security keys. These keys are used to ensure that an unauthorized user cannot look at the packet content. When a client tries to connect, the security appliance presents its public keys to the client. After receiving the keys, the client generates a random key and encrypts it using the public key sent by the security appliance. These encrypted client keys are sent to the security appliance, which decodes them using its own private keys. This completes the key exchange phase, and the security appliance starts the user authentication phase. Cisco ASA supports a number of security algorithms, listed in Table 4-9.

Table 4-9   *Security Algorithms Supported by Cisco ASA*

Attributes	Supported Algorithm
Data encryption	3DES and AES
Packet integrity	MD5 and SHA
Authentication method	RSA public keys
Key exchange	Diffie-Hellman group 1

To configure SSH on the security appliance, use the following steps:

Step 1   Generate the RSA keys.

The SSH daemon on the security appliance uses the RSA keys to encrypt the sessions. The public and private key pair is generated using the **crypto key generate rsa** command, as shown in the following output. For detailed information about generating the RSA keys, consult Chapter 17, "Public Key Infrastructure (PKI)."

```
Chicago(config)# crypto key generate rsa
INFO: The name for the keys will be: <Default-RSA-Key>
Keypair generation process begin. Please wait...
```

You can change the default modulus size, 1024 bits, to 512, 768, or 2048 bits. Once the keys have been generated, you can view the public keys by using the **show crypto key mypubkey rsa** command:

```
Chicago(config)# show crypto key mypubkey rsa
Key pair was generated at: 22:41:07 UTC Aug 21 2005
Key name: <Default-RSA-Key>
 Usage: General Purpose Key
 Modulus Size (bits): 1024
 Key Data:
  30819f30 0d06092a 864886f7 0d010101 05000381 8d003081 89028181
    00b85a0c
  7af04bc1 028c072e 4be49fad 29e7c8e2 9b1341cc e6ace229 2556b310
    66a12627
  05166501 30ca3360 e32307d7 31d2f839 7a36005e 0656cc36 4fa23aa5
    7d9a3f09
```

```
fd5b35b2 cdf1b393 8e4ba10f 0752f2ec c29915cf f058945a 4ac11cd6
d46c72d7
a45766e1 851d1093 e1cd4a93 f222631f 6c51a55f e9ef229a 4481f719
55020301 0001
```

Step 2 Enable SSH on an interface.

You can configure the security appliance to accept SSH sessions on an interface by using the **ssh** command. The complete command syntax follows:

```
ssh {ip_address mask | ipv6_address/prefix} interface
```

The arguments used by the **ssh** command are similar to the arguments used by the **telnet** command listed earlier in Table 4-7.

Configure the security appliance to accept an SSH session from the inside network, 192.168.10.0, and from an outside host, 209.165.201.1:

```
Chicago(config)# ssh 192.168.10.0 255.255.255.0 inside
Chicago(config)# ssh 209.165.201.1 255.255.255.255 outside
```

Note   Because SSH sessions are encrypted, the security appliance does not require an IPSec tunnel for users connecting on an outside interface.

After a client negotiates the security parameters, the security appliance prompts the user for authentication credentials. If the authentication is successful, the user is put into user access mode.

Note   If AAA settings are not used, the default username is **pix** and the password is the user access mode password.

Step 3 Restrict the SSH version.

The security appliance can restrict a user to use either SSH version 1 (SSHv1) or SSH version 2 (SSHv2) when a connection is made. By default, the security appliance accepts both versions. SSHv2 is the recommended version due to its strong authentication and encryption capabilities. However, the security appliance does not provide support for the following SSHv2 features:

— X11 forwarding

— Port forwarding

— Secure File Transfer Protocol (SFTP) support

— Kerberos and AFS ticket passing

— Data compression

To set a specific SSH version, use the **ssh version** command followed by the actual version of the shell. Configure the security appliance to use SSHv2 only:

```
Chicago(config)# ssh version 2
```

Note	The security appliance must have the 3DES-AES feature set in the license to support SSHv2 sessions.

Step 4 Modify the idle timeout (optional).

Similar to the Telnet **timeout** command, you can fine-tune the idle timeout value between 1 and 60 minutes. If the organizational security policy does not allow long idle connections, the idle timeout value can be changed to a lower value, such as 3 minutes, from its default value of 5 minutes, as follows:

```
Chicago(config)# ssh timeout 3
```

Step 5 Enable secure copy (SCP).

The SCP file transfer protocol is used to move files to the network device by using SSH keys. It functions similarly to FTP but with the added advantage of data encryption. The security appliance can act as an SCP server to allow SSHv2 clients to copy files in the flash. SCP can be enabled by using the **ssh scopy enable** command as follows:

```
Chicago(config)# ssh scopy enable
```

Note	The SSH client must be SCP capable to be able to transfer files.

Step 6 Monitor the SSH sessions.

You can monitor the SSH session connected to the security appliance by using the **show ssh sessions** command in privileged mode:

```
Chicago# show ssh sessions
SID Client IP      Version Mode Encryption Hmac  State          Username
0   192.168.10.10 2.0      IN   aes256-cbc sha1  SessionStarted user1
                            OUT  aes256-cbc sha1  SessionStarted user1
```

```
1    209.165.201.1 1.99    IN    aes256-cbc sha1 SessionStarted user2
                           OUT   aes256-cbc sha1 SessionStarted user2
2    192.168.10.20 1.5     -     3DES       -    SessionStarted user3
```

The output of this command displays useful information, including the following:

— In the first column, SID, the security appliance shows the session ID, similar to Telnet's session ID.

— The second column, Client IP, displays the IP address of the client establishing the SSH session.

— The third column, Version, identifies the SSH version that the client is using, described in Table 4-10.

— The fourth column, Mode, specifies the direction of the session, whether inbound or outbound. SSHv1 uses a single session for both inbound and outbound communication.

— The fifth column, Encryption, shows the type of encryption used by the SSH client. SSHv2 supports both 3DES- and AES-based encryption, whereas SSHv1 only supports DES and 3DES encryption.

— The sixth column, Hmac, shows the hashing algorithm used by the SSH client. SSHv2 supports both SHA and MD5 for session authentication.

— The seventh column, State, displays the state of the session when the SSH client is connecting to the security appliance. If a session is successful, the state will always be SessionStarted.

— The last column, Username, shows the username the SSH client is using for this session.

In the output, three users are connected to the security appliance. User1 is using an SSHv2 client and is connecting to the security appliance from 192.168.10.10. User2's SSH client is capable of running both version 1 and version 2. However, the established session is version 2 from 209.165.201.1. User3 is using an SSHv1 client to connect to the security appliance from 192.168.10.20.

Table 4-10 *Supported SSH Versions*

SSH Version	Description
1.5	SSH client can only use SSH version 1
1.99	SSH client can only use SSH version 2 with SSH version 1 compatibility enabled
2.0	SSH client can only use SSH version 2

Step 7   Disconnect an SSH session.

You can manually disconnect an active SSH session by using the **ssh disconnect** command followed by the session ID number. In the following example, the administrator is disconnecting an active session 2:

```
Chicago# ssh disconnect 2
```

System Maintenance

This section explains how to manage and install a different system image file on the Cisco ASA and ways to recover a device with no operating system. This section also talks about how to recover authentication passwords if they are lost.

Software Installation

Cisco ASA supports two methods for upgrading a system image file to flash:

- Image upgrade via the Cisco ASA CLI
- Image upgrade via the ASDM

You learn about the image upgrade process for the ASDM in Chapter 18, "Introduction to ADSM." The image upgrade process for the Cisco ASA CLI is discussed next. In case the security appliance does not have an image, this section also discusses steps to upload the image from ROMMON.

Image Upgrade via the Cisco ASA CLI

The security appliance supports a number of file server types, including TFTP and FTP, to download a system image into flash (disk0). The image upgrade process uses the **copy** command followed by the name of the file transfer type. The **copy** command copies the specified files from the source location or URL to the destination location (flash). The command syntax for the **copy** command is as follows:

```
copy [/noconfirm] {url:[path]} {local:[path]}
```

The security appliance uses HTTP, HTTPS, FTP, and TFTP protocols as the source location of the image file. The *url* keyword specifies the file transfer protocol and the exact location of the system image file. The full syntax of the *url* keyword is as follows:

```
ftp://[user[:password]@]server[:port]/[path/]filename[;type=xx]
http://[user[:password]@]server[:port]/[path/]filename
https://[user[:password]@]server[:port]/[path/]filename
tftp://[user[:password]@]server[:port]/[path/]filename[;int=interface_name]
```

Table 4-11 lists and defines the arguments used in the **url** keyword.

Table 4-11 *The **url** Keyword Arguments*

Syntax	Description
ftp	Keyword to specify that the protocol used for file transfer is FTP.
http	Keyword to specify that the protocol used for file transfer is HTTP.
https	Keyword to specify that the protocol used for file transfer is HTTPS.
tftp	Keyword to specify that the protocol used for file transfer is TFTP.
user	Specifies a username if the file transfer protocol uses authentication. HTTP, HTTPS, and FTP protocols usually prompt for user credentials.
password	Specifies a password for the username authentication.
server	Specifies the IP address or the host name of the file transfer server.
port	Specifies the port number that the security appliance can use to connect to the file transfer server. No need exists to specify a port if the file transfer protocol uses the default ports.
path	Specifies the complete path of the file, if the image file does not reside on the default directory.
filename	Specifies the filename that the security appliance needs to get from the server.
type=*xx*	The **type** option is explicitly used for the FTP protocol. The following types are supported: • **ap**—ASCII passive • **an**—ASCII normal • **ip**—Binary passive • **in**—Binary normal The default transfer type is **ip**.
int=*interface name*	Forces the security appliance to route the TFTP packets out to a different interface.

The destination location of the system image is the local file system. The security appliance has an internal storage disk, referred to as disk0: or flash. Additionally, an external storage device, referred to as disk1:, can be used to save system images.

The **noconfirm** option is used to notify the security appliance to accept the parameters without prompting the user for confirmation. This is useful if system images are uploaded using the customized scripts.

Example 4-43 illustrates how to configure the security appliance to download an image file, called **ASA702.bin**, from a TFTP server located at **192.168.10.250**. The security appliance initiates the download process and stores the image file as **ASA702.bin**.

Example 4-43 *Copying a System Image from a TFTP Server to the Local Flash*

```
Chicago# copy tftp: flash:
Address or name of remote host []? 192.168.10.250
Source filename []? ASA702.bin
Destination filename [ASA702.bin]? ASA702.bin

Accessing tftp://192.168.10.250/ASA702.bin...!!!!!!!!!!!!!!!!!!!!!!!!!!!!!!!!!!!
! Output omitted for brevity
Writing file disk0:ASA702.bin...
!!!!!!!!!!!!!!!!!!!!!!!!!!!!!!!!!!!!!!!!!!!!!!!!!!!!!!!!!!!!!!!!!!!!!!!!!!!!!!!!!!!
! Output omitted for brevity
5124096 bytes copied in 151.370 secs (33934 bytes/sec)
```

You can verify that the downloaded image file was successfully saved in flash by typing the **dir flash** command, as demonstrated in Example 4-44.

Example 4-44 *Output of the* **dir flash** *Command*

```
Chicago# dir flash:
Directory of disk0:/

8       -rw-  5124096      05:37:16 Aug 6 2005  ASA702.bin
10      -rw-  5919340      04:29:18 Aug 5 2005  asdm-501.bin
```

The security appliance allows multiple system image files to reside in flash. If rebooted, the security appliance loads the first available system image. This default behavior can be modified by using the **boot system** command to ensure that the newly uploaded image file is used for bootup. This is shown in Example 4-45, where the security appliance is set up to boot from **ASA702.bin**.

Example 4-45 *Setting the Boot Parameter*

```
Chicago(config)# boot system disk0:/ASA702.bin
Chicago(config# exit
```

After configuring the Cisco ASA to boot a specific image upon bootup, the running configuration needs to be saved to NVRAM, as shown in Example 4-46.

Example 4-46 *Copy Running-Config to NVRAM*

```
Chicago# copy running-config startip-config
```

To reboot the security appliance, you can use the **reload** command, as shown in Example 4-47. The security appliance shuts down all the processes, and reloads itself. Based on the boot system parameters, it loads the ASA702.bin image.

Example 4-47 *Reloading the Security Appliance*

```
Chicago# reload
Proceed with reload? [confirm] <cr>
***
*** --- START GRACEFUL SHUTDOWN ---
```

continues

Example 4-47 *Reloading the Security Appliance (Continued)*

```
Shutting down isakmp
Shutting down File system
! Output omitted for brevity

Loading disk0:/ASA702.bin... Booting...
#############################################################################
! Output omitted for brevity
Cryptochecksum(unchanged): 13b1d99f 59fffda6 58618094 bd58950d
Type help or '?' for a list of available commands.
Chicago>
```

NOTE   Before you reload the security appliance, schedule a maintenance window to avoid disrupting the production traffic.

The last step in verifying that the security appliance is running the desired version of code is to issue the **show version** command, as shown in Example 4-48.

Example 4-48 *Output of* **show version**

```
Chicago# show version | include Version
Cisco ASA Software Version 7.0(2)
Device Manager Version 5.0(1)
```

Image Recovery Using ROMMON

The security appliance provides a way to recover the system image in case the image file is lost or gets corrupted and the security appliance ends up in ROMMON mode. If the security appliance is actively running an image file, you can upload a new image in flash by using the guidelines described previously in the "Image Upgrade via the Cisco ASA CLI" section. However, if an image file is not present and the security appliance is reloaded, ROMMON mode can be invoked to upload an image using the TFTP protocol.

Before an image can be uploaded, verify that the TFTP server hosts the file in the root directory and that network connectivity exists between the security appliance and the TFTP server. Assign an IP address to the security appliance by using the **address** command, and configure a TFTP server using the **server** command. The configured IP address can be mapped to an interface by using the **interface** command followed by the physical interface name. The name of the system image file can be set using the **file** command. Example 4-49 assigns an IP address of **192.168.10.1** to the **GigabitEthernet0/0** interface. The TFTP server is **192.168.10.250** and the name of the system image file is **ASA702.bin.**

Example 4-49 *Setting Up TFTP Parameters*

```
rommon #0> ADDRESS 192.168.10.1
rommon #1> SERVER 192.168.10.250
rommon #2> interface GigabitEthernet0/0
GigabitEthernet0/0
MAC Address: 000f.f775.4b54
rommon #3> file ASA702.bin
```

| NOTE | If the security appliance and the TFTP server reside on different IP subnets, then you must define a default gateway on the security appliance by using the **gateway** command: |

```
rommon #2> GATEWAY 192.168.10.100
```

To verify whether all the attributes are properly configured, use the **set** command, as shown in Example 4-50. Start the TFTP process by issuing the **tftpdnld** command.

Example 4-50 *Verifying the TFTP Parameters*

```
rommon #4> set
ROMMON Variable Settings:
  ADDRESS=192.168.10.1
  SERVER=192.168.10.250
  PORT=GigabitEthernet0/0
  VLAN=untagged
  IMAGE=ASA702.bin
  CONFIG=

rommon #5> tftpdnld
tftp ASA702.bin@192.168.10.250
!!!!!!!!!!!!!!!!!!!!!!!!!!!!!!!!!!!!!!!!!!!!!!!!!!!!!!!!!!!!!!!!!!!!!!!!!!!!!!!!!!!!
```

| NOTE | The security appliance downloads the system image file in memory and boots up the device. However, the downloaded system image is not stored in flash. Follow the guidelines described previously in the section "Image Upgrade via the Cisco ASA CLI" to upload the image in the system flash. |

Password Recovery Process

The password recovery process on a security appliance is used when the system password is either locked out, due to configured authentication parameters, or lost. This process for Cisco ASA is similar to the password recovery process for an IOS router, which uses ROMMON mode to recover. You should schedule a maintenance window in which to recover the system passwords, because this process will require you to reboot the security appliance. Use the following steps for password recovery:

Step 1   Establish a console connection.

This process requires you to have physical access to the security appliance, for security reasons. This is to ensure that remote or unauthorized users cannot reset passwords. Consequently, a console connection to the security appliance is required. Consult the section "Establishing a Console Connection" earlier in the chapter.

Step 2   Reload the security appliance.

The password recovery process starts by turning the security appliance off and then turning it back on.

Step 3   Break into ROMMON.

When the security appliance starts to reboot, the startup messages are displayed on the console. You can press the **Esc** (Escape) key after "Use BREAK or ESC to interrupt boot" is shown. This will take you into ROMMON mode, as follows:

```
Evaluating BIOS Options ...
Launch BIOS Extension to setup ROMMON
Cisco Systems ROMMON Version (1.0(3)0) #0: Sat  6 14:51:06 EST 2005
Platform ASA5540
Management0/0
Ethernet auto negotiation timed out.
Interface-4 Link Not Established (check cable).
Default Interface number-4 Not Up
Use BREAK or ESC to interrupt boot.
Use SPACE to begin boot immediately.
Boot interrupted.
Use ? for help.
rommon #0>
```

Step 4   Set the ROMMON configuration register.

ROMMON mode includes the **confreg** command, which sets the configuration register responsible for changing the security appliance boot behavior. It can be used to specify how an appliance should boot (ROMMON, NetBoot, and Flash boot) or if it should ignore the default configuration during bootup. When the **confreg** command is entered, the security appliance displays the current configuration register value and prompts the user for several options. Record the current configuration register value and press **y** to enter interactive mode:

```
rommon #0> confreg
Current Configuration Register: 0x00000011
Configuration Summary:
  boot TFTP image, boot default image from Flash on netboot failure
Do you wish to change this configuration? y/n [n]: y
```

The security appliance prompts the user for new values to be assigned to the configuration register. Select all the default values until the system prompts the user to disable system configuration. Enter **y** as shown in the following configuration:

```
rommon #0> confreg
Current Configuration Register: 0x00000011
```

```
Configuration Summary:
  boot TFTP image, boot default image from Flash on netboot failure

Do you wish to change this configuration? y/n [n]: y
enable boot to ROMMON prompt? y/n [n]:
enable TFTP netboot? y/n [n]:
enable Flash boot? y/n [n]:
select specific Flash image index? y/n [n]:
disable system configuration? y/n [n]: y
go to ROMMON prompt if netboot fails? y/n [n]:
enable passing NVRAM file specs in auto-boot mode? y/n [n]:
disable display of BREAK or ESC key prompt during auto-boot? y/n [n]:

Current Configuration Register: 0x00000040
Configuration Summary:
  boot ROMMON
  ignore system configuration

Update Config Register (0x40) in NVRAM...
```

Step 5 Boot up the security appliance.

After setting up the configuration register to ignore the configuration file, you can boot the security appliance by using the **boot** command:

```
rommon #1> boot
Launching BootLoader...
Boot configuration file contains 1 entry.
Searching / for images to boot.
Loading /sa702.bin... Booting...
```

Step 6 Access privileged mode.

The security appliance loads the default configuration, which does not use an enable password to access privileged mode. Once the security appliance shows the default ciscoasa prompt, you can type the **enable** command to gain privileged mode access:

```
ciscoasa>
ciscoasa> enable
Password:<cr>
ciscoasa#
```

Step 7 Load the saved configuration.

Once you have privileged mode access to the security appliance CLI, the next step is to load the saved configuration from NVRAM. This is done by using the **copy** command, which copies the startup-config file to the running-config as follows:

```
ciscoasa# copy startup-config running-config
Destination filename [running-config]?<cr>
Cryptochecksum(unchanged): 3a3748e9 43700f38 7712cc11 2c6de52b
1104 bytes copied in 0.60 secs
Chicago#
```

Step 8   Reset the passwords.

After loading the saved configuration, you can change the login, enable, and user passwords. The login password is used to get user mode access, while the enable password is used to gain privileged mode access. In the following example, login and enable passwords are changed to cisco123:

```
Chicago# config terminal
Chicago(config)# passwd cisco123
Chicago(config)# enable password cisco123
```

If the security appliance is using local user authentication, the user passwords can also be changed, as shown here for user cisco:

```
Chicago# config terminal
Chicago(config)# username cisco password cisco123
```

Step 9   Restore the original configuration register value.

To ensure that the security appliance does not ignore the saved configuration in the next reboot, you must change the configuration register value to reflect this. Restore the original configuration register value of 0x11 by using the **config-register** configuration mode command:

```
Chicago(config)# config-register 0x11
```

Step 10 Save the current configuration into NVRAM

The last step in this process is to make sure that the newly specified passwords are stored in the saved NVRAM configuration. This is done by using the **copy** command to copy the running-config file in NVRAM as the startup-config, as follows:

```
Chicago(config)# copy running-config startup-config
Source filename [running-config]?
Cryptochecksum: 6167413a 17ad1a46 b961fb7b 5b68dd2b

1104 bytes copied in 3.270 secs (368 bytes/sec)
```

NOTE   The **write memory** command also copies the running-config file into NVRAM as startup-config.

Disabling the Password Recovery Process

Cisco ASA can disable the password recovery process discussed in the previous section to enhance device security. This ensures that even if an unauthorized user gets access to the console port, they should not be able to compromise the device or configuration settings. Use the **no service password-recovery** command to disable password recovery from configuration mode, as shown in Example 4-51. The security appliance displays a warning message saying that the only way to do password recovery is by erasing all files in flash and then downloading a new image and a configuration file from an external server such as TFTP. With this option, access to ROMMON mode is disabled to protect the system from unauthorized users.

Example 4-51 *Disabling the Password Recovery Process*

```
Chicago(config)# no service password-recovery
WARNING: Executing "no service password-recovery" has disabled the password recovery
mechanism and disabled access to ROMMON.  The only means of recovering from lost or
forgotten passwords will be for ROMMON to erase all file systems including
configuration files and images. You should make a backup of your configuration and
have a mechanism to restore images from the ROMMON command line.
```

The password recovery process can also be disabled by going through the initial setup as demonstrated in Example 4-52. The security appliance prompts the user to reconfirm if they really want to disable the password recovery process after displaying a warning that specifies the consequences of this option.

Example 4-52 *Disabling Password Recovery Using Initial Setup*

```
Pre-configure Firewall now through interactive prompts [yes]?
! Output omitted for brevity
Allow password recovery [yes]? no
WARNING: entering 'no' will disable password recovery and disable access
  to ROMMON CLI. The only means of recovering from lost or forgotten passwords
  will be for ROMMON to erase all file systems including configuration files
and images.
If entering 'no' you should make a backup of your configuration and have a
  mechanism to restore images from the ROMMON command line...
Allow password recovery [yes]?no
Clock (UTC):
! Output omitted for brevity
```

If you have forgotten the security appliance password and the password recovery process is disabled, the only way to recover out of this state is to erase all system files (including the software image and the configuration file). Make sure that the configuration and system image files are stored in an external server with IP connectivity to the security appliance. Use the following procedure to recover system passwords when password recovery is disabled:

Step 1   Establish a console connection.

This process requires you to have physical access to the security appliance, for security reasons. This is to ensure that remote or unauthorized users cannot reset passwords. Consequently, a console connection to the security appliance is required. Consult the section "Establishing a Console Connection" earlier in the chapter.

Step 2 Reload the security appliance.

The password recovery process starts by turning off the security appliance and then turning it back on.

Step 3 Break into ROMMON.

When the security appliance starts to reboot, the startup messages are displayed on the console. You can press the **Esc** (Escape) key after "Use BREAK or ESC to interrupt boot" is shown. This will display a warning message saying that all files will be erased from flash if access to ROMMON is made. The following example illustrates this process:

```
Evaluating BIOS Options ...
Launch BIOS Extension to setup ROMMON
Cisco Systems ROMMON Version (1.0(3)0) #0: Mon Aug  9 14:51:06 MDT 2004
  Platform ASA5540-K8
Management0/0
Ethernet auto negotiation timed out.

WARNING:  Password recovery and ROMMON command line access has been
disabled by your security policy.  Choosing YES below will cause ALL
configurations, passwords, images, and files systems to be erased.
ROMMON command line access will be re-enabled, and a new image must be
downloaded via ROMMON.

Erase all file systems? y/n [n]:
```

Step 4 Erase system files from flash.

Before the security appliance allows a user to get access to ROMMON mode, it prompts them to erase all file systems. Press **y** to start the process of erasing all system files. Once all files have been erased, the security appliance enables the password recovery process and grants access to ROMMON mode.

```
Erase all file systems? y/n [n]: yes
Permanently erase Disk0: and Disk1:? y/n [n]: y
Erasing Disk0:
............................................................
! Output omitted for brevity

Disk1: is not present.
Enabling password recovery...
rommon #0>
```

Step 5   Upload a system image.

Once access to ROMMON mode is available, you can go through the image upgrade process discussed earlier in this chapter. The following example shows a system image, asa702.bin, being uploaded from a TFTP server, 192.168.10.250:

```
rommon #0> ADDRESS=192.168.10.1
rommon #1> SERVER=192.168.10.250
rommon #3> interface GigabitEthernet0/0
GigabitEthernet0/0
MAC Address: 000f.f775.4b54
rommon #4> file asa702.bin
rommon #5> tftpdnld
tftp asa702.bin@192.168.10.250
!!!!!!!!!!!!!!!!!!!!!!!!!!!!!!!!!!!!!!!!!!!!!!!!!!!!!!!!!!!!!!!!!!!!!!!!!!!!!!
!!!!!!!!!!!
```

Note   The security appliance downloads the system image file in memory and boots up the device. However, the downloaded system image is not stored in flash.

Step 6   Upload a configuration file.

The security appliance loads a default configuration file without an interface configured. To upload a configuration file, the interface closest to the external file server must be set up to upload the saved file. In the following example, GigabitEthernet 0/1 is set up to upload a configuration file called Chicago.conf from a TFTP server located at 192.168.10.250 toward the inside interface:

```
ciscoasa> enable
Password:<cr>
ciscoasa# configure terminal
ciscoasa(config)# interface GigabitEthernet0/1
ciscoasa(config-if)# ip address 192.168.10.1 255.255.255.0
ciscoasa(config-if)# nameif inside
INFO: Security level for "inside" set to 100 by default.
ciscoasa(config-if)# no shutdown
ciscoasa(config)# exit
ciscoasa# copy tftp: running-config
Address or name of remote host []? 192.168.10.250
Source filename []? Chicago.conf
Destination filename [running-config]?
Accessing tftp://192.168.10.250/Chicago.conf...!
!
```

```
Cryptochecksum(unchanged): 1c9855a1 2cca93c7 a9691450 9bab6e92
1246 bytes copied in 0.90 secs
Chicago#
```

Step 7   Reset the passwords.

After uploading the saved configuration, you can change the login, enable, and user passwords. The login password is used to get user mode access, while enable password is used to gain privileged mode access. In the following example, login and enable passwords are changed to cisco123:

```
Chicago# config terminal
Chicago(config)# passwd cisco123
Chicago(config)# enable password cisco123
```

If the security appliance is using local user authentication, the user passwords can also be changed, as follows:

```
Chicago# config terminal
Chicago(config)# username cisco password cisco123
```

Step 8   Save the current configuration into NVRAM.

The next step in this process is to make sure that the newly specified passwords are stored in the saved NVRAM configuration. This is done by using the **copy** command to copy the running-config file in NVRAM as the startup-config:

```
Chicago(config)# copy running-config startup-config
Source filename [running-config]?
Cryptochecksum: 6167413a 17ad1a46 b961fb7b 5b68dd2b
```

Step 9   Save the current configuration into NVRAM.

The last step is to load the image from the TFTP server to the local flash. Follow the guidelines discussed under the "Image Upgrade via the Cisco ASA CLI" section earlier in this chapter.

System Monitoring

The security appliance can generate system and debug messages when an event occurs. These messages can be logged to the local buffer or to an external server, depending on an organization's security policies. This section discusses how to enable event logging and Simple Network Management Protocol (SNMP) polling, which can be used to check the status of the security appliance. This section also discusses how to monitor the health of the security appliance by monitoring the CPU and memory utilization.

System Logging

System logging is a process by which the Cisco ASA generates an event for any significant occurrence that affects the system, such as network problems, error conditions, and threshold breaches. These messages can either be stored locally on the system buffer or be transferred to external servers. You can use these logs for event correlations to detect network anomalies or you can use them for monitoring and troubleshooting purposes.

The security appliance assigns a message ID to each event it generates. These message IDs range from 101001 to 720073 and contain a brief description of the event. The security appliance also associates each message ID to a severity level ranging from 0 to 7. The lower the severity level number is, the more critical the message is. Table 4-12 lists the severity levels, along with the associated keyword and a brief description.

Table 4-12   *Severity Levels and Their Description*

Severity Level	Level Keyword	Level Description
0	emergencies	Event used to indicate that the system is unusable
1	alerts	Message used to specify that an immediate action is needed, such as when a power failure on the standby failover appliance has occurred
2	critical	Message used to identify a critical condition, such as spoofed attacks
3	errors	Event used for error messages such as memory allocation failures
4	warnings	Event used to inform about the warning messages, such as exceeding certain thresholds
5	notifications	Message used to identify a normal but significant condition, such as when a user logs in
6	informational	Event used to classify informational messages, such as the creation of IKE security associations
7	debugging	Event used to indicate the low-level debug messages, like the acknowledgement of VPN hello requests

Each severity level not only displays the events for that level but also shows the messages from the lower severity levels. For example, if logging is enabled for debugging (level 7), the security appliance also logs levels 0 through 6.

NOTE

For a complete list of all the severity messages, please consult the *System Log Messages Guide* located at Cisco.com.

The next subsection discusses how to enable logging on the security appliance to log relevant events.

Enabling Logging

To enable logging of system events, use the **logging enable** command, as shown in Example 4-53. This global command sends logs to all the terminals and devices set up to receive the syslog messages.

Example 4-53 *Enabling System Logging*

```
Chicago(config)# logging enable
```

Once the logging is enabled, ensure that the messages are timestamped before they are sent. Use the **logging timestamp** command to enable the timestamp in the syslog messages, as shown in Example 4-54.

Example 4-54 *Enabling Syslog Timestamps*

```
Chicago(config)# logging timestamp
```

The security appliance's robust operating system allows specific events and severities to be logged to specific hosts. For example, the VPN-related log messages can be stored in the local buffer, while all other events can be sent to an external syslog server. This is done by defining a logging list to specify the interesting event messages. The following are the command syntaxes of **logging list**:

```
logging list event_list level sev_level [class event_class]
logging list event_list message start_id[-end_id]
```

NOTE   The default severity level for a logging list is 3 (errors).

---

event_list is a list name that specifies the level of messages the security appliance should be logging. Use the **level** keyword followed by a logging level to identify messages by the specified severity level, which also covers the higher severity level messages. You can optionally classify the messages within the logging level by using the **class** keyword and an event class name. The security appliance comes with predefined event classes to log specific processes. These classes include:

- **auth**—Identifies user authentication messages
- **bridge**—Classifies transparent firewall events
- **ca**—Logs PKI certificate authority messages

- **config**—Logs the command interface-specific events
- **email**—Logs WebVPN e-mail proxy messages
- **ha**—Logs failover events
- **ids**—Classifies the intrusion detection system events
- **ip**—Identifies IP stack messages
- **np**—Logs network processor events
- **ospf**—Classifies OSPF routing events
- **rip**—Logs RIP routing messages
- **rm**—Identifies resource manager events
- **session**—Identifies user session-specific messages
- **snmp**—Classifies SNMP-specific events
- **sys**—Logs system-specific events
- **vpdn**—Is not currently used
- **vpn**—Classifies the IKE- and IPSec-related messages
- **vpnc**—Identifies the VPN client-specific events
- **vpnfo**—Logs VPN failover messages
- **vpnlb**—Logs VPN load-balancing events
- **webvpn**—Logs WebVPN related messages

In Example 4-55, a logging list called **IPSec_Crit** is set up to group all the IPSec messages. The selected severity level is **critical**, which also includes level 0 and level 1 events.

Example 4-55 *Setting Up a Logging List*

```
Chicago# configure terminal
Chicago(config)# logging list IPSec_Crit level critical class vpn
```

Logging Types

Cisco ASA supports the following types of logging capabilities:

- Console logging
- Terminal logging
- Buffered logging
- E-mail logging
- ASDM logging
- External syslog server logging

The followings sections describe each logging type in detail.

Console Logging

Console logging enables the security appliance to send syslog messages to the console serial port. This method is useful for viewing specific live events during troubleshooting. Use the **logging console** command to set up console logging. The complete command syntax for **logging console** is as follows:

```
logging console event_list|sev_level
```

In Example 4-56, event logs that are identified in an event list called **IPSec_Cric** are being viewed on the console port.

Example 4-56 *Enabling Console Logging*

```
Chicago# configure terminal
Chicago(config)# logging list IPSec_Cric level critical class vpn
Chicago(config)# logging console IPSec_Cric
```

CAUTION   Enable console logging with caution; the serial port is only 9600 bits per second, and the syslog messages can easily overwhelm the port.

If the port is already overwhelmed, access the security appliance from an alternate method, such as SSH or Telnet, and lower the severity.

Terminal Logging

Terminal logging sends syslog messages to a remote terminal monitor such as a Telnet or a SSH session. It is useful for viewing live events during troubleshooting. Use the **logging monitor** command to set up terminal monitoring, which uses the same arguments as the **logging console** command. In Example 4-57, event logs that are identified in an event list called IPSec_Cric and all the messages with the severity level set to 0 (emergencies) and 1 (alerts) are being viewed.

Example 4-57 *Setting Up Terminal Logging*

```
Chicago# configure terminal
Chicago(config)# logging list IPSec_Cric level critical class vpn
Chicago(config)# logging monitor IPSec_Cric
Chicago(config)# logging monitor alerts
```

Buffered Logging

The security appliance allocates 4096 bytes of memory to store log messages in the buffer. This is the preferred method to troubleshoot an issue because it does not overwhelm the console or terminal ports. Buffered logging can be enabled by using the **logging buffered** command, as shown in Example 4-58. All severity levels up to level 3 (errors) are being sent to the buffer. To ensure that the security appliance does not run out of the allocated memory, the buffer size is increased to 16,384 bytes by using the **logging buffer-size** command.

Example 4-58 *Setting Up Buffered Logging*

```
Chicago# configure terminal
Chicago(config)# logging buffered errors
Chicago(config)# logging buffer-size 16384
```

The allocated memory is a circular buffer; consequently, the security appliance will not run out of memory.

View the buffered logs by using the **show logging** command, as demonstrated in Example 4-59. This shows all different types of logging supported on the security appliance and indicates whether they are enabled or disabled. Additionally, it provides the number of messages logged on each of the configured logging types with the logging severity. Each syslog message starts with %ASA, to indicate that a Cisco security appliance generated the message, followed by the logging level, the unique message ID, and then a brief string to describe the log message.

Example 4-59 *Output of* **show logging**

```
Chicago# show logging
Syslog logging: enabled
    Facility: 20
    Timestamp logging: disabled
    Standby logging: disabled
    Deny Conn when Queue Full: disabled
    Ambiguous interface parameters: 98
    Console logging: disabled
    Monitor logging: list IPSec_Cric, 293 messages logged
    Buffer logging: level errors, 174 messages logged
    Trap logging: disabled
    History logging: disabled
    Device ID: disabled
    Mail logging: disabled
    ASDM logging: disabled
%ASA-3-109013: User must authenticate before using this service
%ASA-3-109020: Downloaded ACL has config error; ACE
%ASA-3-113001: Unable to open AAA session. Session limit 3
! Output omitted for brevity
```

The buffered log messages can be saved to the local flash or to an FTP server for future analysis. The security appliance supports three methods to save buffered logs:

- Manual flash logging
- Automatic flash logging
- Automatic FTP logging

Using the manual flash logging method, you can save the log messages located in the buffer space to the local flash (disk0: or disk1:). The security appliance creates a file in the /syslog directory of flash using the default name of LOG-*YYYY-MM-DD-HHMMSS*.TXT, where *YYYY* stands for year, the first *MM* for month, *DD* for days, *HH* for hours, the second *MM* for minutes, and *SS* for seconds. In Example 4-60, the buffered logs are saved in flash using the **logging savelog** command and the default filename. Check the flash directory to make sure that the file is successfully saved, by using the **dir /recursive** command.

Example 4-60 *Manual Saving of Logs in Flash*

```
Chicago# logging savelog
Chicago# dir /recursive
Directory of disk0:/*
9       -rw-  5124096      05:37:16 Aug 6 2005  ASA702.bin
Directory of disk0:/syslog
5461    -rw-  16384        06:25:26 Aug 6 2005  LOG-2005-08-06-062527.TXT
```

NOTE   The Cisco ASA uses the local clock settings to add the timestamp. Consult the section "System Clock" earlier in this chapter.

The security appliance can auto-save the buffered log messages to the local flash using the **logging flash-bufferwrap** command, as shown in Example 4-61. The security appliance uses the same format of the filename discussed in the previous example. Each file size depends on the buffer size, discussed in the "Buffered Logging" section. To ensure that there is room left in flash for other administrative tasks, use the **logging flash-minimum-free** command and specify the minimum space in kilobytes (4 MB in this case) that the security appliance should maintain. You can, optionally, specify the maximum space the security appliance can use to store the buffered logs in flash. This is accomplished by using the **logging flash-maximum-allocation** command. Example 4-61 shows that the security appliance is allocating 2 MB of space to save logs in flash.

Example 4-61 *Automatic Saving of Logs in Flash*

```
Chicago# configure terminal
Chicago(config)# logging flash-bufferwrap
Chicago(config)# logging flash-maximum-allocation 2000
Chicago(config)# logging flash-minimum-free 4000
```

The security appliance can transfer the buffer logs to an FTP server to conserve disk space. This is done by using the **logging ftp-bufferwrap** command. An FTP server is specified to store the log files. In Example 4-62, an appliance is set up to send log files to an FTP server, located at 192.168.10.150. The username to log into the FTP server is cisco with a password of cisco123. The logs will be stored in the root directory (.) for that user.

Example 4-62 *Automatic Saving of Logs in the FTP Server*

```
Chicago# configure terminal
Chicago(config)# logging ftp-bufferwrap
Chicago(config)# logging ftp-server 192.168.10.150 . cisco cisco123
```

E-Mail Logging

The security appliance supports sending log messages directly to individual e-mail addresses. This feature is extremely useful when you are interested in getting immediate notification when the security appliance generates a specific log message. Use the **logging mail** command followed by the name of the event list or the logging level to set up e-mail logging. When an interesting event is produced, the security appliance contacts the specified e-mail server and sends out an e-mail message to the e-mail recipient from a preconfigured e-mail account. The **smtp-server** command is used to configure an e-mail server, while the **recipient-address** command specifies an e-mail address to which to send messages. The **logging from-address** command uses a preconfigured e-mail address to generate the log messages.

In Example 4-63, a logging list called FO_Cable is set up with a message ID of 101002 to classify the failover cable issues. This logging list is linked to send e-mail messages from Chicago@securemeinc.com to e-mail address admin@securemeinc.com using 209.165.201.10 as the primary e-mail server and 209.165.201.11 as the secondary e-mail server.

Example 4-63 *Configuration of E-Mail Logging*

```
Chicago(config)# logging list FO_Cable message 101002
Chicago(config)# logging mail FO_Cable
Chicago(config)# logging from-address Chicago@securemeinc.com
Chicago(config)# logging recipient-address admin@securemeinc.com level errors
Chicago(config)# smtp-server 209.165.201.10 209.165.201.11
```

ASDM Logging

Cisco Adaptive Security Device Manager (ASDM) is a GUI that you can use to configure and monitor the security appliance. Use the **logging asdm** command to send log messages to a connected ASDM host. You can specify the number of messages that can exist in the ASDM buffer. You do this by using the **logging asdm-buffer-size** command followed by the actual number of messages, as shown in Example 4-64. The security appliance is set up to send messages with the logging level set to notifications or lower, while the ASDM buffer size is set to hold 512 messages.

Example 4-64 *Setting Up ASDM Logging*

```
Chicago# configure terminal
Chicago(config)# logging asdm notifications
Chicago(config)# logging asdm-buffer-size 512
```

NOTE	ASDM is discussed in Chapter 18 in greater detail.

Syslog Server Logging

Cisco ASA supports sending the event logs to an external syslog server. Messages can be stored for use in anomaly detection or event correlation. The security appliance allows the use of both TCP and UDP protocols to communicate with a syslog server. To configure a syslog server, use the **logging host** command followed by the IP address of the server. For UDP-based syslogs, the security appliance allows logging of messages in the Cisco EMBLEM format. Many Cisco devices, including the Cisco IOS routers and CiscoWorks management server, use this format of syslogging. In Example 4-65, two syslog servers are defined to send the log messages. The first server collects the logs using UDP and in the Cisco EMBLEM format, while the other server uses TCP port 1300 to accept the syslog messages. The security appliance will send all logging level 7 and below messages to these servers. This is done by using the **logging trap debugging** command.

Example 4-65 *Setting Up Syslog Servers*

```
Chicago# configure terminal
Chicago(config)# logging host inside 192.168.10.160 format emblem
Chicago(config)# logging host outside 192.168.10.170 TCP/1300
Chicago(config)# logging trap debugging
```

For TCP-based syslog servers, the security appliance drops the new connections if the session to the syslog server cannot be established. This default behavior can be changed by using the **logging permit-hostdown** command, as demonstrated in Example 4-66.

Example 4-66 *Allowing Syslog Messages when a TCP-Based Syslog Server Is Down*

```
Chicago# configure terminal
Chicago(config)# logging permit-hostdown
```

Additional Syslog Parameters

The security appliance does not send debug logs, such as debug crypto, to a syslog server unless the **logging debug-trace** command is turned on, as shown in Example 4-67.

Example 4-67 *Allowing Syslog Messages when a TCP-Based Syslog Server Is Down*

```
Chicago# configure terminal
Chicago(config)# logging debug-trace
```

The security appliance sends all log messages to the logging devices, internal and external. However, if you are not interested in logging a particular message, you can suppress it by using the **no logging message** command followed by the message ID number, as shown in Example 4-68, where message ID 101001 is disabled.

Example 4-68 *Disabling a Message ID*

```
Chicago# configure terminal
Chicago(config)# no logging message 101001
```

Simple Network Management Protocol

SNMP is an application layer protocol that was developed to monitor the health of network devices. It has become a de facto standard because of its simple protocol design. A successful SNMP implementation requires a management station, also known as the *manager,* and at least one agent, such as the Cisco ASA. The network management station, such as CiscoWorks, monitors the agents by collecting the device and network information and presenting it in a GUI. The agents, on the other hand, respond to the manager's request for information. If an important event occurs, the agents can also initiate a connection to the manager to send the message.

The SNMP implementation uses the following five message types, known as protocol data units (PDUs), for the communication between the management station and the agent:

- GET
- GET-NEXT
- GET-RESPONSE
- SET
- TRAP

The GET and GET-NEXT messages are initiated by the network manager to request specific information by using the Management Information Base (MIB). The agent replies with a GET-RESPONSE, which provides the requested information, if available. In a case where the requested information is not available, the agent sends an error with a reason why the request cannot be processed.

The SET message type is used by the network manager to change or add values in the configuration rather than retrieve the information. The agent replies with a GET-RESPONSE message to indicate whether the change was successful. The TRAP messages are agent-initiated to inform the network manager about an event, such as a link failure, so that an immediate action can be taken. Figure 4-8 illustrates the PDU communication between a security appliance, as an agent, and a CiscoWorks server, as a management server.

NOTE   The security appliance does not allow SET PDUs, for device-security reasons. Consequently, the configuration of the security appliance cannot be modified using SNMP.

Figure 4-8 *SNMP Communication Between the Cisco ASA and CiscoWorks*

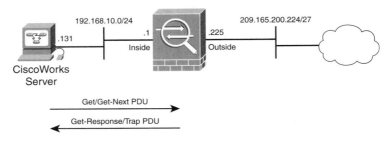

Configuring SNMP

The security appliance must be configured before a network management server can initiate a connection. The SNMP configuration is discussed in the following steps:

Step 1   Configure a global community string.

A community string acts as a password when the management server tries to connect to the security appliance to get information. It is used to validate the communication messages between the devices. You can set a global community string by using the **snmp-server community** command. The administrator has specified **ChicagoSNMP** as the snmp-community string in the following example:

```
Chicago(config)# snmp-server community ChicagoSNMP
```

Step 2   Define an SNMP server.

You can use the **snmp-server host** command to define an SNMP management server. The command syntax is as follows:

```
snmp-server host interface_name ip_addr [community commstr]
```

interface_name is the name of the interface where the SNMP server resides, *ip_addr* is the actual IP address of the server, and **community** *commstr* specifies a host-based community string. The SNMP server resides on the inside interface at **192.168.10.131** in the following example. The community string for this SNMP server is **s3cur3m3**.

```
Chicago(config)# snmp-server host inside 192.168.10.131 community
    s3cur3m3
```

Step 3   Specify the SNMP version.

The security appliance supports SNMP versions 1 and 2c. Version 2 overcomes the deficiencies and problems associated with version 1. It uses the administrative framework of version 1 but enhances protocol operations by increasing security capabilities. The following shows an appliance using SNMP version **2c** for an SNMP server located at **209.165.202.131**:

```
Chicago(config)# snmp-server host inside 192.168.10.131 version 2c
```

Step 4 Configure SNMP traps.

The security appliance does not send SNMP traps by default; however, it can be configured to send all supported traps, or a superset of all traps. This is done by using the **enable traps** option in the **snmp-server** command. The security appliance supports the following event trap types:

— **Standard event traps**—Traps such as interface link up/link down, authentication, and device cold start.

— **IPSec event traps**—These include IPSec tunnel start and stop traps.

— **Remote-access traps**—The security appliance generates a trap when remote-access sessions reach the session threshold limit.

— **Entity traps**—These traps are sent when changes are made to the device, such as configuration modification or insertion/removal of hardware modules into or from the chassis.

— **Syslog traps**—The security appliance sends syslog messages as SNMP traps to the management station.

In the following example, the security appliance is set up to send IPSec start and stop traps as well as the supported entity traps. The **remote-access session-threshold-exceeded** trap is also turned on.

```
Chicago(config)# snmp-server enable traps ipsec start stop
Chicago(config)# snmp-server enable traps entity config-change
    fru-insert fru-remove
Chicago(config)# snmp-server enable traps remote-access session-
    threshold-exceeded
```

To set up traps for the syslog messages, you must determine what severity of syslog messages need to be forwarded to the management server. This is done by using the **logging history** command followed by the syslog severity or a list name. The security appliance sends traps if the syslog severity is set to debugging or lower, as follows:

```
Chicago(config)# logging history debugging
Chicago(config)# snmp-server enable syslog
```

All supported traps can be sent using the **snmp-server enable traps all** command.

Step 5   Modify UDP ports.

The security appliance uses UDP port 162 when it needs to send SNMP traps to the management server. If the SNMP server listens on a different port, you can change the UDP port on the security appliance by using the **udp-port** keyword in the **snmp-server host** command, where the default port is changed to 172 for an SNMP server residing at 192.168.10.131, as follows:

```
Chicago(config)# snmp-server host inside 192.168.10.131 udp-port 172
```

The Cisco ASA can be configured to listen on a nondefault port for SNMP polls. In the following example, the security appliance is being configured to listen on UDP port 171 from its default UDP port, 161:

```
Chicago(config)# snmp-server listen-port 171
```

Step 6   Restrict traps and polls.

The security appliance allows an SNMP server to poll information from the security appliance. It also sends event traps when unusual incidents occur. You can optionally restrict the security appliance to allow either SNMP polls only or traps only. The following demonstrates how to set up an appliance to only allow SNMP polling from **192.168.10.131**:

```
Chicago(config)# snmp-server host inside 192.168.10.131 poll
```

Step 7   Set device information.

You can specify the location of the security appliance so that the SNMP server knows where the device is physically located. The security appliance enables you to set up contact information for an individual who is responsible for it. The following shows how to configure a security appliance for an SNMP **location** of **Chicago** with the contact name of **Jack Franklin** at extension **x5-1212**:

```
Chicago(config)# snmp-server location Chicago
Chicago(config)# snmp-server contact Jack Franklin at x5-1212
```

SNMP Monitoring

The **show snmp-server statistics** command is useful for checking the statistics of the SNMP engine. It displays not only the total SNMP packets received and transmitted but also any bad or illegal packets handled by the security appliance. Example 4-69 displays the output of this command, where the security appliance received 12 GET requests and replied to all of them as GET-RESPONSE.

Example 4-69 *Output of* **show snmp-server statistics**

```
Chicago# show snmp-server statistics
12 SNMP packets input
    0 Bad SNMP version errors
    0 Unknown community name
    0 Illegal operation for community name supplied
    0 Encoding errors
    36 Number of requested variables
    0 Number of altered variables
    12 Get-request PDUs
    0 Get-next PDUs
    0 Get-bulk PDUs
    0 Set-request PDUs (Not supported)
12 SNMP packets output
    0 Too big errors (Maximum packet size 1500)
    0 No such name errors
    0 Bad values errors
    0 General errors
    12 Get-response PDUs
    0 SNMP trap PDUs
```

CPU and Memory Monitoring

The **show cpu usage** command indicates current CPU utilization. It displays an approximation of load every 5, 60, and 300 seconds. Example 4-70 shows that the 5-second utilization is 2 percent, while the 1-minute and 5-minute utilizations are 1 percent.

Example 4-70 *Output of* **show cpu usage**

```
Chicago(config)# show cpu usage
CPU utilization for 5 seconds = 2%; 1 minute: 1%; 5 minutes: 1%
```

The security appliance can display memory usage through the **show memory** command. It shows a summary of the available and allocated memory in bytes and as a percentage. In Example 4-71, the free memory on the security appliance is 969,397,424 bytes (~921 MB), while the allocated or used memory is 104,344,400 bytes (~103 MB). The total memory on the security appliance is 1024 MB.

Example 4-71 *Output of* **show memory**

```
Chicago# show memory
Free memory:       969397424 bytes (90%)
Used memory:       104344400 bytes (10%)
-------------      ---------------
Total memory:      1073741824 bytes (100%)
```

NOTE   Using the **show memory detail command** with **show memory binsize** allows you to check the number of bytes allocated to a given size memory chunk. These commands should be used under a TAC engineer's supervision if advanced memory troubleshooting needs to be done.

The security appliance can display the system buffer utilization if the **show block** command is executed. When the security appliance boots up, the operating system carves out memory to create the maximum number of blocks for different block sizes. The maximum number of blocks does not change, except for the 256 and 1550 size blocks. For these blocks, the security appliance can dynamically create more blocks if necessary. The security appliance allocates a block from the pool when it needs to use it, and returns it when it is done using it.

There are nine different sizes of buffer blocks, and each buffer type is responsible for handling specific packets. Table 4-13 shows the buffer block sizes and provides a brief description on where they are used.

Table 4-13   *Buffer Sizes*

Buffer Block Size	Description
4	Used to duplicate existing blocks in applications such as DNS, ISAKMP, URL filtering, uauth, TFTP, H323, and TCP modules.
80	Used by the TCP intercept feature to generate an ACK packet. It is also used by the failover for hello messages.
256	Used by the stateful failover, syslog, and some TCP modules.
1550	Used to buffer Ethernet packets when they are processed by the security appliance.
2560	Used to buffer IKE messages.
4096	Used by the QoS metrics engine.
8192	Used by the QoS metrics engine.
16384	Used only for the 64-bit, 66-MHz Livengood Gigabit Ethernet cards (i82543).
65536	Used by the QoS metrics engine.

When you run the **show block** command, the security appliance displays the following counters:

- **MAX**—Indicates the maximum number of blocks available for a specific block size
- **LOW**—Indicates that the security appliance had that many lowest numbers of blocks available at one point since the last reboot or the last time the counters were cleared by the **clear block** command
- **CNT**—Displays the currently available blocks for each block size

In Example 4-72, the security appliance has allocated 300 blocks for 4-byte block size, and it is currently using one block. The LOW counter is set to 299 because the security appliance had allocated only one block of it since the last reboot.

Example 4-72 *Output of* **show block**

```
Chicago# show block
  SIZE     MAX     LOW     CNT
     4     300     299     299
    80    1200    1199    1200
   256    1100    1098    1100
  1550   13316   11777   11785
  2560    1990    1990    1990
  4096      80      80      80
  8192     160     160     160
 16384     250     250     250
 65536      16      16      16
```

Summary

This chapter introduced the different CLI modes and discussed the initial configuration of the Cisco ASA. It presented a brief overview of the networking technologies, such as IPv6, DHCP, NTP, and SNMP, and provided examples of how to set them up. Telnet and SSH were discussed as the remote-management protocols. This chapter also assisted in system maintenance features such as image upgrade, image, and password recovery methods. The last section discussed the security appliance monitoring capabilities, such as system logging, SNMP, and a set of **show** commands to check the status and health of the device.

This chapter covers the following topics:

- Packet filtering
- Advanced ACL features
- Content and URL filtering
- Deployment scenarios using access control lists
- Monitoring network access control
- Address translation
- DNS doctoring
- Monitoring address translations

CHAPTER 5

Network Access Control

Cisco Adaptive Security Appliances (ASA) can help protect one or more networks from intruders and attackers. Connections between these networks can be controlled and monitored by using the robust features that Cisco ASA offers. You can ensure that all traffic from the protected networks to the unprotected networks (and vice versa) passes through the firewall based on the organization's security policies. This chapter focuses on the features available for packet filtering and their implementations.

Packet Filtering

Cisco ASA can protect the inside network, the demilitarized zones (DMZs) and the outside network by inspecting all traffic that passes through it. You can specify policies and rules that identify what traffic should be permitted in or out of an interface. The security appliance uses access control lists (ACLs) to drop unwanted or unknown traffic when it attempts to enter the trusted networks. An ACL is a list of security rules or policies grouped together that allows or denies packets after looking at the packet headers and other attributes. Each permit or deny statement in the ACL is called an access control entry (ACE). These ACEs can classify packets by inspecting up to Layer 4 headers for a number of parameters, including the following:

- Layer 2 protocol information such as EtherTypes
- Layer 3 protocol information such as ICMP, TCP, or UDP
- Source and destination IP addresses
- Source and destination TCP or UDP ports

Once an ACL has been properly configured, you can apply it to an interface to filter traffic. The security appliance can filter packets in both the inbound and outbound direction on an interface. When an inbound ACL is applied to an interface, the security appliance inspects packets against the ACEs after receiving or before transmitting them. If a packet is allowed in, the security appliance continues to process it by sending it through the other configured engines. If a packet is denied by the ACL, the security appliance discards the packet and generates a syslog message indicating that such an event has occurred. In Figure 5-1, the security appliance administrator has applied to the outside interface an inbound ACL that permits only HTTP traffic destined for 209.165.202.131. All other traffic will be dropped at the interface by the security appliance.

Figure 5-1 *Inbound Packet Filtering*

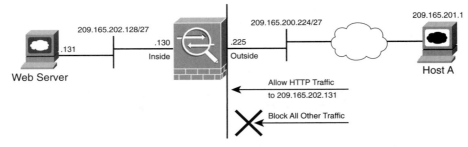

If an outbound ACL is applied on an interface, the security appliance processes the packets by sending them through the different processes (NAT, QoS, and VPN) and then applies the configured ACEs before transmitting the packets out on the wire. The security appliance transmits the packets only if they are allowed to go out. If the packets are denied by even one of the ACEs, the security appliance discards the packets and generates a syslog message indicating that such an event has occurred. In Figure 5-2, the security appliance administrator has applied to the inside interface an outbound ACL that permits only HTTP traffic destined for 209.165.202.131. All other traffic gets dropped at the interface by the security appliance.

Figure 5-2 *Outbound Packet Filtering*

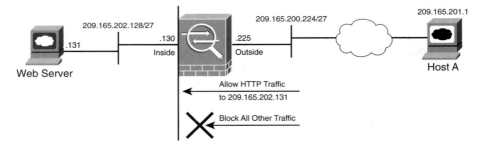

Types of ACLs

The security appliance supports five different types of ACLs to provide a flexible and scaleable solution to filter unauthorized packets into the network:

- Standard ACLs
- Extended ACLs
- IPv6 ACLs
- EtherType ACLs
- WebVPN ACLs

The following sections describe each type in turn.

Standard ACLs

Standard ACLs are used to identify packets based on the destination IP addresses. These ACLs can be used in scenarios such as split tunneling for the remote-access VPN tunnels (discussed in Chapter 16, "Remote Access VPNs") and route redistribution using the route maps. These ACLs, however, cannot be applied on an interface to filter packets. A standard ACL can be used only if the security appliance is running in routed mode. In routed mode, the Cisco ASA routes packets from one subnet to another subnet by acting as an extra layer 3 hop in the network.

Extended ACLs

Extended ACLs, the most commonly deployed ACLs, can classify packets based on the following attributes:

- Source and destination IP addresses
- Layer 3 protocols
- Source and/or destination TCP and UDP ports
- Destination ICMP type for ICMP packets

An extended ACL can be used for interface packet filtering, QoS packet classification, packet identification for NAT and VPN encryption, and a number of other features listed shortly in the "Comparing ACL Features" section. These ACLs can be set up on the security appliance in the routed and the transparent mode.

IPv6 ACLs

An IPv6 ACL functions similarly to an extended ACL. However, it only identifies IPv6 traffic passing through a security appliance in routed mode.

EtherType ACLs

EtherType ACLs can be used to filter IP- and non-IP-based traffic by checking the Ethernet type code field in the Layer 2 header. IP-based traffic uses an Ethernet type code value of 0x800, whereas Novell IPX uses 0x8137 or 0x8138 depending on the Netware version.

An EtherType ACL can be configured only if the security appliance is running in transparent mode, covered in Chapter 10, "Transparent Firewalls."

NOTE   The security appliance does not allow IPv6 traffic to pass through it, even if it is allowed to pass through an IPv6 EtherType ACL.

WebVPN ACLs

A WebVPN ACL allows security appliance administrators to restrict traffic coming through the WebVPN tunnels (discussed in Chapter 16). In the case where there is a WebVPN ACL defined but there is no match for a packet, the default behavior is to drop the packet. On the other hand, if there is no ACL defined, the security appliance allows traffic to pass through it.

Comparing ACL Features

Table 5-1 compares the ACLs. It also specifies whether they can be used in conjunction with supported features on the security appliance.

Table 5-1 *ASA Features and Support of ACL Types*

Feature	Standard	Extended	IPv6	EtherType	WebVPN
Layer 2 packet filtering	No	Yes	No	Yes	No
Layer 3 packet filtering	No	Yes	Yes	No	Yes
Capture	No	Yes	Yes	Yes	No
AAA	No	Yes	Yes	No	No
Time range	No	Yes	Yes	No	Yes
Object grouping	No	Yes	Yes	No	No
NAT 0	No	Yes	No	No	No
PIM	Yes	No	No	No	No
Packet inspection	No	Yes	No	No	No
IPS inspection	No	Yes	No	No	No
VPN encryption	No	Yes	No	No	Yes[1]
Remarks	Yes	Yes	Yes	Yes	Yes
Line numbers	No	Yes	Yes	No	No
Logging	No	Yes	Yes	No	Yes
QoS	No	Yes	No	No	No
Policy NAT	No	Yes	No	No	No
OSPF route-map	Yes	Yes	No	No	No

[1] Only WebVPN encrypted traffic.

Configuring Packet Filtering

The packet filtering on the security appliance requires three configuration steps:

Step 1 Set up an ACL.

Step 2 Apply an ACL to an interface.

Step 3 Set up an IPv6 ACL (optional).

Step 1: Set Up an ACL

The ACL identifies traffic that needs to be allowed or dropped when it tries to go through the security appliance. An ACE can be as simple as permitting all IP traffic from one network to another, to as complicated as permitting traffic originating from a unique source IP address on a particular port destined for a specific port on the destination address. An ACE is defined by using the **access-list** command. For interface filtering, you can define an extended ACL, an IPv6 ACL, or an EtherType ACL, as mentioned in the previous section. The command syntax to define an extended ACE is as follows:

```
access-list id [extended][line line-num] {deny | permit}{protocol | object-group
    protocol_obj_grp_id {source_addr source_mask} | object-group network_obj_grp_id |
    host src_host_addr [operator port [port] | object-group service_obj_grp_id]
    {destination_addr destination_mask} | object-group network_obj_grp_id | host
    dst_host_addr [operator port [port] | object-group service_obj_grp_id]} [log
    [[disable | default] | level] [interval secs] [time_range name]] [inactive]

access-list id [line line-num] remark text
access-list alert-interval secs
access-list deny-flow-max flow_num
```

NOTE The interface ACL does not block packets destined for the security appliance's IP addresses.

Table 5-2 lists and defines the arguments used in an ACE.

Table 5-2 *ACE Definition*

Syntax	Description
access-list	Keyword used to create an ACL.
id	Name or number of an ACL.
extended	Optional argument, used to specify an extended IP ACL.
line *line-num*	Optional argument, used to specify the line number at which to insert an ACE.
deny	Discards the packet if it matches the configured conditions.
permit	Allows the packet if it matches the configured conditions.
protocol	Name or number of an IP protocol.
object-group[1]	Grouping of different objects in a list.
protocol_obj_grp_id[1]	An object name containing the list of protocols to be filtered.

continues

Table 5-2   *ACE Definition (Continued)*

Syntax	Description
source_addr	Network or host address from which the packet is being sent.
source_mask	Network mask applied to *source_addr*. If an *src_host_addr* is used, this argument is optional.
network_obj_grp_id [1]	An object name containing the list of networks to be filtered.
host	A keyword used to specify a single IP address for traffic filtering.
src_host_addr	Specifies the source IP address to be filtered.
operator	An optional keyword used to compare the source or destination ports. Possible operands include **lt** for less than, **gt** for greater than, **eq** for equal, **neq** for not equal, and **range** for an inclusive range.
port	Name or number of TCP or UDP port to be filtered.
service_obj_grp_id [1]	An object name containing the list of services to be filtered.
destination_addr	Network or host address to which the packet is sent.
destination_mask	Network mask applied to *destination_addr*. If a *dst_host_addr* is used, this argument is optional.
dst_host_addr	Specifies the destination IP address to be filtered.
log	Generates a syslog message 106100 if a packet matches the ACE.
level	Specifies the logging level, 0 through 7, where: 0 = emergencies 1 = alerts 2 = critical 3 = errors 4 = warnings 5 = notifications 6 = informational (default) 7 = debugging
disable	Does not send syslog message if packets hit the configured ACE.
default	Uses the default behavior which generates a syslog 106023 message whenever packet matches a deny in the ACE.
interval	A keyword to specify the time interval to generate the subsequent new syslog messages.
secs	The actual time interval in seconds. The default time interval is 300 seconds.
time range[1]	A keyword to specify the time-range name.
name	A predefined time-range name.

Table 5-2   *ACE Definition (Continued)*

Syntax	Description
inactive	Keyword to disable an ACE.
remark	Keyword to specify remarks on an ACL.
text	Actual text, up to 100 characters, to be added as remarks.
alert-interval	Keyword to specify the number of seconds to generate a 106101 syslog message when the maximum number of deny flows is reached.
deny-flow-max	Keyword to limit the maximum number of concurrent deny flows allowed.
flow_num	Actual number of deny flows that can be created. This can be between 1 and 4096 (the default).

[1] These options are discussed in the "Object Grouping" section.

NOTE   The security appliance restricts the logging option to be implemented for interface filtering only. The logging option will be ignored if an ACL is used with another feature.

In Figure 5-3, SecureMe, the fictional company used in examples throughout this book, hosts a web server and an e-mail server at its location in Chicago. Both servers allow traffic to be destined for 209.165.202.131 on port 80 (HTTP) and 209.165.202.132 on port 25 (SMTP). However, the security appliance allows only two client hosts—209.165.201.1 and 209.165.201.2—to initiate the traffic. All other traffic passing through the security appliance will be dropped.

Figure 5-3   *Inbound Traffic Filtering*

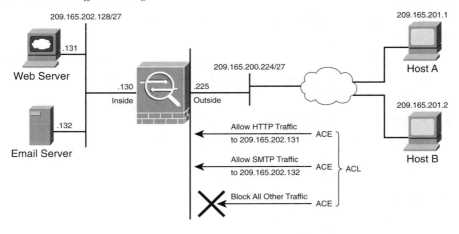

Example 5-1 shows the related configuration. An extended ACL called **inbound_traffic_
on_outside** is set up with four ACEs. The first two ACEs allow HTTP traffic destined for
209.165.202.131 from the two client machines, while the last two ACEs allow SMTP
access to 209.165.202.132 from both machines. Adding remarks to an ACL is
recommended, because it helps other to recognize its function. The system administrator
has added **This is the interface ACL to block inbound traffic** as the remark on this ACL.

Example 5-1   *Configuration of an Extended ACL*

```
Chicago# configure terminal
Chicago(config)# access-list inbound_traffic_on_outside remark This is the
   interface ACL to block inbound traffic
Chicago(config)# access-list inbound_traffic_on_outside extended permit tcp host
   209.165.201.1 host 209.165.202.131 eq www
Chicago(config)# access-list inbound_traffic_on_outside extended permit tcp host
   209.165.201.2 host 209.165.202.131 eq www
Chicago(config)# access-list inbound_traffic_on_outside extended permit tcp host
   209.165.201.1 host 209.165.202.132 eq smtp
Chicago(config)# access-list inbound_traffic_on_outside extended permit tcp host
   209.165.201.2 host 209.165.202.132 eq smtp
```

NOTE   The security appliance drops a packet if it does not find an ACE to explicitly permit the
packet. There is an implicit deny at the end of all ACLs.

The security appliance software allows you to stop processing an ACE temporarily without
removing the entry from the configuration. This is helpful if you are troubleshooting a
connection issue through the security appliance and want to disable the entry. You do so by
adding the **inactive** keyword at the end of the ACE.

Step 2: Apply an ACL to an Interface

After configuring an ACL to identify traffic allowed or denied by the security appliance, the
next step is to apply the ACL to an interface in either the inbound or the outbound direction.
You can apply the ACL by using the **access-group** command followed by the name of the
ACL, as shown in the following syntax:

```
access-group access-list {in | out} interface interface_name [per-user-override]
```

Table 5-3 lists and defines the arguments used in the **access-group** command.

Table 5-3   **access-group** *Command Definition*

Syntax	Description
access-group	Keyword used to apply an ACL to an interface.
access-list	The name of the actual ACL to be applied to an interface.
in	The ACL will be applied in the inbound direction.
out	The ACL will be applied in the outbound direction.
interface	Keyword to specify the interface to which to apply the ACL.

Table 5-3   **access-group** *Command Definition (Continued)*

Syntax	Description
interface_name	The name of the interface to which to apply an ACL.
per-user-override	Option that allows the downloadable ACLs to override the entries on the interface ACL. Downloadable ACLs are discussed later in this chapter.

Chapter 4 "Initial Setup and System Maintenance" discussed the concept of assigning security levels to an interface. In traffic filtering, the security appliance does not block the return TCP or UDP traffic on the lower security interface if the traffic is originated from a host on the higher security interface. For other protocols, such as GRE or ESP, you need to permit the return traffic in the ACL applied on that interface. For the ICMP, you can either allow the return traffic in the ACL or enable ICMP inspection (discussed in Chapter 8, "ASA Application Inspection").

In Example 5-2, an ACL called **inbound_traffic_on_outside** is applied to the outside interface in the inbound direction.

Example 5-2   *Applying an ACL on the Outside Interface*

```
Chicago# configure terminal
Chicago(config)# access-group inbound_traffic_on_outside in interface outside
```

NOTE   You can only apply one extended ACL in one direction. However, an inbound and an outbound extended ACL can be applied simultaneously on an interface.

You can, however, apply an extended and an IPv6 ACL in the same direction if the security appliance is set up to be in routed mode. In transparent mode, you can apply an extended and an EtherType ACL in the same direction.

Step 3: Set Up an IPv6 ACL (Optional)

As discussed previously in the "Types of ACLs" section, the security appliance supports filtering IPv6 traffic that is passing through interfaces. An IPv6 ACL is defined by using the **ipv6 access-list** command followed by the name of the ACL. Like an extended ACL, the IPv6 ACL uses similar command options, as shown in the following syntax:

```
ipv6 access-list id [line line-num] {deny | permit} {protocol | object-group
    protocol_obj_grp_id} {source-ipv6-prefix/prefix-length | any | host source-ipv6-
    address | object-group network_obj_grp_id} [operator {port [port] | object-group
    service_obj_grp_id}] {destination-ipv6-prefix/prefix-length | any | host
    destination-ipv6-address | object-group network_obj_grp_id} [{operator port [port] |
    object-group service_obj_grp_id}] [log [[level] [interval secs] | disable |
    default]]
```

```
ipv6 access-list id [line line-num] {deny | permit} icmp6 {source-ipv6-prefix/prefix-
  length | any | host source-ipv6-address | object-group network_obj_grp_id}
  {destination-ipv6-prefix/prefix-length | any | host destination-ipv6-address |
  object-group network_obj_grp_id} [icmp_type | object-group icmp_type_obj_grp_id]
  [log [[level] [interval secs] | disable | default]]
ipv6 access-list id [line line-num] remark text
```

Table 5-4 defines the unique arguments of an IPv6 ACE that are different from the ones listed in Table 5-2.

Table 5-4   *IPv6 ACE Definition*

Syntax	Description
ipv6	Keyword used to create an IPv6 ACL.
source-ipv6-prefix	Network or host IPv6 address from which the packet is being sent.
prefix-length	Network mask applied to an IPv6 address. It specifies how many higher-order bits compromise an IPv6 network address.
source-ipv6-address	Specifies the source IPv6 address to be filtered.
destination-ipv6-prefix	Network or host IPv6 address to which the packet is sent.
destination-ipv6-address	Specifies the destination IPv6 address to be filtered.
icmp6	Specifies that the protocol used is ICMPv6.

In Example 5-3, an ACL called **inbound-ipv6-traffic-on-outside** consists of two ACEs. The first ACE denies traffic from an IPv6 source fedc:ba98:1:3210:fedc:ba98:1:3210 if it is destined for a mail server (TCP port 25) located at 1080::8:800:200c:417a. The second ACE permits all mail traffic from the fedc:ba98:1:3210::/64 network if it is destined for 1080::8:800:200c:417a. The ACL is applied to the outside interface in the inbound direction.

Example 5-3   *Configuring and Applying an IPv6 ACL on the Outside Interface*

```
Chicago# configure terminal
Chicago(config)# ipv6 access-list inbound-ipv6-traffic-on-outside permit tcp host
  fedc:ba98:1:3210:fedc:ba98:1:3210 host 1080::8:800:200c:417a eq smtp
Chicago(config)# ipv6 access-list inbound-ipv6-traffic-on-outside permit tcp
  fedc:ba98:1:3210::/64 host 1080::8:800:200c:417a eq smtp
Chicago(config)# access-group inbound-ipv6-traffic-on-outside in interface
  outside
```

Advanced ACL Features

Cisco ASA provides many advanced packet-filtering features to suit any network environments. These features include:

- Object grouping

- Standard ACLs
- Time-based ACLs
- Downloadable ACLs
- ICMP Filtering

Object Grouping

Object grouping is a way to group similar items together to reduce the number of ACEs. Without object grouping, the configuration on the security appliance may contain thousands of lines of ACEs, which can become hard to manage. The security appliance follows the multiplication factor rule when ACEs are defined. For example, if three outside hosts need to access two internal servers running HTTP and SMTP services, the security appliance will have 12 host-based ACEs, calculated as follows:

Number of ACEs = (2 internal servers) ∗ (3 outside hosts) ∗ (2 services) = 12

By using object grouping, the number of ACEs can be reduced to just a single entry. Object grouping can cluster network objects such as internal servers into one group and outside hosts into another. The security appliance can also conglomerate both TCP services into a service object group. All of these groups can be linked to each other in one ACE.

NOTE	Although the number of viewable ACEs is reduced when object groups are used, the actual number of ACEs is not. Use the **show access-list** command to display the expended ACEs in the ACL. The security appliance supports nesting an object group into another one. This hierarchical grouping can further reduce the number of configured ACEs in Cisco ASA.

The following sections discuss how to configure object groups in a security appliance.

Object Types

The security appliance supports four different types of objects which can group similar items or services:

- Protocol
- Network
- Service
- ICMP type

You can configure object groups by using the **object-group** command followed by the object type. The complete command syntax is

```
object-group {{protocol | network | icmp-type} grp_id | service grp_id {tcp | udp |
    tcp-udp}}
```

Table 5-5 lists and defines the arguments used in the **object-group** command.

Table 5-5   **object-group** *Command Description*

Syntax	Description
object-group	Keyword used to define an object group.
protocol	Keyword to specify Layer 3 IP protocols such as TCP, UDP, ICMP, GRE, and IGMP.
network	Keyword to specify the host, subnet, or network addresses.
icmp-type	Keyword to specify ICMP types such as echo, echo-reply, and traceroute.
grp_id	Tag that identifies the object type. This tag can be linked to an ACE or to another object group.
service	Keyword to specify the Layer 4 services for TCP and UDP protocols.
tcp	Keyword to group TCP services such as HTTP, FTP, Telnet, and SMTP.
udp	Keyword to group UDP services such as DNS, TFTP, and ISAKMP.
tcp-udp	Keyword to group services that can use both TCP and UDP protocols such as DNS and Kerberos.

The different types of object groups are discussed in the following sections.

Protocol

A protocol-based object group specifies a list of IP protocols such as TCP, UDP, and ICMP, just to name a few. To set up a protocol-based object group, use the **object-group protocol** command followed by the name of the object group, as shown in Example 5-4. An object group called **TCP_UDP** is set up to group the TCP and UDP protocols by using the **protocol-object** command. The security appliance allows you to add a description under an object group. In this example, the description **Grouping of TCP and UDP protocols** identifies this group.

Example 5-4   *Configuration of Protocol-Based Object Group*

```
Chicago(config)# object-group protocol TCP_UDP
Chicago(config-protocol)# description Grouping of TCP and UDP protocols
Chicago(config-protocol)# protocol-object tcp
Chicago(config-protocol)# protocol-object udp
```

As mentioned earlier, an object group can be nested into another object group. This is done by using the **group-object** command. In Example 5-5, another protocol-based object group called **IP_Protocols** is set up to include GRE as the IP protocol. This object group also contains the **TCP_UDP** object group, defined in the preceding example. The description **nested object group to include GRE, TCP and UDP** is added to this group.

Example 5-5 *Nesting of Protocol-Based Object Groups*

```
Chicago(config)# object-group protocol IP_Protocols
Chicago(config-protocol)# description nested object group to include GRE, TCP and UDP
Chicago(config-protocol)# protocol-object gre
Chicago(config-protocol)# group-object TCP_UDP
```

CAUTION   When the protocol-based object group is used, all the protocols are expanded into different ACLs. Because of this, it is easy to permit unintended traffic if object groups are applied too liberally.

Network

A network-based object group specifies a list of IP host, subnet, or network addresses. Defining a network-based object group is very similar to defining a protocol-based object group. You use the **object-group network** command followed by the name of the object group, as shown in Example 5-6. An object group called **Local_Net** is set up to group together a subnet 209.165.202.128 255.255.255.224 and a host 192.168.10.100 by using the **network-object** command. The description **grouping of 192.168.10.100 and 209.165.202.128/27** is also added to this group.

Example 5-6 *Configuration of Network-Based Object Group*

```
Chicago(config)# object-group network Local_Net
Chicago(config-network)# description grouping of 192.168.10.100 and
  209.165.202.128/27
Chicago(config-network)# network-object host 192.168.10.100
Chicago(config-network)# network-object 209.165.202.128 255.255.255.224
```

Service

A service-based object group is used to cluster the TCP and/or UDP services together. By using the service-based object group, you can group either TCP, UDP, or TCP and UDP ports into a set by using the **object-group service** command followed by the name of the object group. If the object group is used to cluster only the TCP ports, then you need to specify the **tcp** keyword following the object name. For UDP-only services, use the **udp** keyword. If you are grouping services that are both TCP and UDP, such as DNS or Kerberos, you should use **tcp-udp** as the keyword. The services can be specified by using the **port-object** command in two ways:

- By using the **eq** (equal) option followed by the name of the service or the TCP/UDP port number
- By using the **range** option to group consecutive Layer 4 ports

In Example 5-7, an object group called **TCP_Ports** is set up to group the TCP-based services. The SMTP, Web, and HTTPS services are individually configured while FTP and FTP data are clustered using the **range** option. A description of **object group for SMTP, WWW, HTTPS and FTP services** is added to this group.

Example 5-7 *Configuration of Service-Based Object Group*

```
Chicago(config)# object-group service TCP_Ports tcp
Chicago(config-service)# description object group for SMTP, WWW, HTTPS and FTP
  services
Chicago(config-service)# port-object eq smtp
Chicago(config-service)# port-object eq www
Chicago(config-service)# port-object range ftp-data ftp
Chicago(config-service)# port-object eq https
```

ICMP-Type

The ICMP protocol uses unique types to send control messages, as documented in RFC 792. Using the ICMP-type object group, you can group the necessary types required to meet an organization's security needs. The configuration of an ICMP-type object group uses the **object-group icmp-type** command followed by the name of the object group, as shown in Example 5-8. An object group called **echo** is set up to group echo and echo-reply, two ICMP types used when a user issues the **ping** command. In the object group sub-configuration mode, the ICMP types can be configured by using the **icmp-object** command. The administrator has entered a description of **object group to allow ICMP echo and echo-reply** in this object group.

Example 5-8 *Configuration of ICMP-Type Object Group*

```
Chicago(config)# object-group icmp-type echo
Chicago(config-icmp)# description object group to allow ICMP echo and echo-reply
Chicago(config-icmp)# icmp-object echo
Chicago(config-icmp)# icmp-object echo-reply
```

Object Grouping and ACLs

Once object groups have been set up, you can map them in an ACL. In Figure 5-4, the inside network has two servers, both running HTTP and SMTP services. If two hosts on the outside network try to access those servers, then eight ACEs should be configured to allow the hosts to communicate with each other. By using object group parameters in the ACE, you can reduce the viewable number of ACEs to one.

The following is the command syntax to define an ACE using **object-group**:

```
access-list id [extended][line line-num] {deny | permit} object-group
  protocol_obj_grp_id  object-group network_obj_grp_id object-group
  service_obj_grp_id] object-group network_obj_grp_id object-group
  service_obj_grp_id] [log [[disable | default] | level] [interval secs]
  [time-range time_range_ID]] [inactive]
```

Figure 5-4   *Inbound Packet Filtering Using Object Groups*

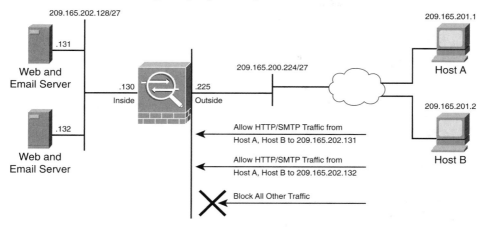

Table 5-6 lists and defines the arguments used in an ACE when object groups are specified. Some of these arguments are discussed in Table 5-2.

Table 5-6   *ACE Definition Using* **object-group**

Syntax	Description
access-list	Keyword used to create an ACL.
id	Name or number of an ACL.
extended	Optional argument, used to specify an extended IP ACL.
line *line-num*	Optional argument, used to specify the line number at which to insert an ACE.
deny	Discards the packet if it matches the configured conditions.
permit	Allows the packet if it matches the configured conditions.
object-group	Grouping of different objects in a list.
protocol_obj_grp_id	An object name containing the list of protocols to be filtered.
network_obj_grp_id	An object name containing the list of networks to be filtered.
service_obj_grp_id	An object name containing the list of services to be filtered.
log	Generates a syslog message 106100 if a packet matches the ACE
disable	Does not send syslog message if packets hit the configured ACE
default	Uses the default behavior, which generates a syslog 106023 message whenever packet matches a deny in the ACE.

continues

Table 5-6   *ACE Definition Using* **object-group** *(Continued)*

Syntax	Description
level	Specifies the logging level, 0 through 7, where: 0 = emergencies 1 = alerts 2 = critical 3 = errors 4 = warnings 5 = notifications 6 = informational (default) 7 = debugging
interval	A keyword to specify the time interval at which to generate the subsequent new syslog messages.
secs	The actual time interval in seconds. The default time interval is 300 seconds.
time-range*	A keyword to specify the time-range name.
*time_range_ID***	The predefined time-range name.
inactive	Keyword to disable an ACE

Example 5-9 shows the corresponding ACE using the object groups. A protocol-based object group called **TCP** is set up with the TCP protocol. The two network object groups configured are **internal_servers** and **internet_hosts**. The **internal_server** object group specifies the IP addresses of the servers that are on the inside network while **internet_hosts** is configured with the IP addresses of the hosts that are allowed to access the internal servers. A service based object group called **HTTP_SMTP** is set up to group the HTTP and SMTP services. An ACL, named **outside_in**, is used to link all the configured object groups together.

Example 5-9   *Configuration of an ACE Using Object Groups*

```
Chicago(config)# object-group protocol TCP
Chicago(config-protocol)# protocol-object tcp
Chicago(config-protocol)# object-group network internal_servers
Chicago(config-network)# network-object host 209.165.202.131
Chicago(config-network)# network-object host 209.165.202.132
Chicago(config-network)# object-group network internet_hosts
Chicago(config-network)# network-object host 209.165.201.1
Chicago(config-network)# network-object host 209.165.201.2
Chicago(config-network)# object-group service HTTP_SMTP tcp
Chicago(config-service)# port-object eq smtp
Chicago(config-service)# port-object eq www
Chicago(config-service)# exit
Chicago(config)# access-list outside_in extended permit object-group TCP
  object-group internet_hosts object-group internal_servers object-group
  HTTP_SMTP
```

The security appliance allows you to set up an ACE using any mix of object group and non–object group parameters. You can choose to use TCP as the protocol and an object group for source and destination IP addresses and subnet masks. This is shown in the first deployment scenario "Using ACLs to Filter Inbound and Outbound Traffic" under the outside_in ACL.

After configuring the ACL, you can bind it to an interface for traffic filtering, as shown in Example 5-10. The ACL **outside_in** is applied to the outside interface in the inbound direction.

Example 5-10 *Applying an ACL on the Outside Interface*

```
Chicago# configure terminal
Chicago(config)# access-group outside_in in interface outside
```

Standard ACLs

As mentioned earlier in this chapter, standard ACLs are used when the source network in the traffic is not important. These ACLs are used by processes, such as OSPF route-maps and VPN tunnels, to identify traffic based on the destination IP addresses.

Standard ACLs are defined by using the **access-list** command and the **standard** keyword after the ACL name. The command syntax to define a standard ACE is

```
access-list id standard {deny | permit} {any | host ip_address | ip_address
   subnet_mask}
```

In Example 5-11, the security appliance identifies traffic destined for host 192.168.10.100 and network 192.168.20.0/24 and ignores all other traffic.

Example 5-11 *Configuration of a Standard ACL*

```
Chicago(config)# access-list dest_net standard permit host 192.168.10.100
Chicago(config)# access-list dest_net standard permit 192.168.20.0 255.255.255.0
Chicago(config)# access-list dest_net standard deny any
```

In Example 5-12, a route map called **ospf** is set up to use the standard ACL configured in the previous example. Route maps will be discussed in Chapter 6, "IP Routing."

Example 5-12 *Route Map Using a Standard ACL*

```
Chicago(config)# route-map ospf permit 10
Chicago(config-route-map)# match ip address dest_net
```

Time-Based ACLs

The security appliance can apply the ACLs based on the time interval to allow or deny network access. These rules, commonly referred as *time-based ACLs,* can prevent users from accessing the network services when the packets arrive outside of the preconfigured time intervals. The ASA relies on the system's clock when time-based ACLs are evaluated.

Consequently, it is important to ensure that the system clock is accurate, and thus the use of Network Time Protocol (NTP) is highly recommended.

NOTE   The time-based restrictions can be used with the extended, IPv6, and WebType ACLs.

The time-based ACLs can be set up by using the **time-range** command followed by the name of the range. In Example 5-13, a time range called **business_hours** is set up.

Example 5-13 *Time-Range Configuration*

```
Chicago(config)# time-range business_hours
Chicago(config-time-range)#
```

In the time-range configuration mode, you can specify two different types of time restrictions:

- Absolute
- Periodic

Absolute

Using the absolute function, you can specify the values based on a start and/or an end time. This function is useful in cases where a company hires consultants for a period of time and wants to restrict access when they leave. In this case, you can set an absolute time and specify the start and the end time. Once the time period expires, the consultants will not be able to pass traffic through the security appliance.

The start and end times are optional. If there is no start time provided, the security appliance assumes that the ACL needs to be applied right away. If there is no end time configured, the security appliance applies the ACL indefinitely. Additionally, only one instance of the **absolute** parameter is allowed to be set up in a given time range.

The following is the command syntax to configure an absolute time range:

```
absolute [start time date] [end time date]
```

start *time date* specifies when to begin applying an ACE, and **end** *time date* directs the security appliance when to stop applying it. In Example 5-14, the administrator has created a time-range policy called **business_hours** for a new consultant whose start time/date is 8 a.m. on June 1, 2005 and end time/date is 5 p.m. on December 30, 2005.

Example 5-14 *Absolute Time-Range Configuration*

```
Chicago(config)# time-range business_hours
Chicago(config-time-range)# absolute start 08:00 01 June 2005 end 17:00 30
  December 2005
```

NOTE	The start and end times use the same format as the **clock set** command when configuring time and date values in the absolute function.

Periodic

Using the periodic function, you can specify the values based on the recurring events. The security appliance provides many easy-to-configure parameters to suit an environment. Time-based ACLs using this option is useful when a company wants to allow user access during the normal business hours on the weekdays and wishes to deny access over the weekends. Cisco ASA allows you to configure multiple instances of the periodic parameter. If both absolute and periodic parameters are configured in a time range, the absolute time parameters are evaluated first before evaluating the periodic time value. The following shows the command syntax to configure a periodic time range:

```
periodic <days-of-the-week> <hh:mm> to <days-of-the-week> <hh:mm>
```

The *days-of-the-week* values can be **Monday**, **Tuesday**, **Wednesday**, **Thursday**, **Friday**, **Saturday**, and **Sunday**. If you need to configure periodic days-of-the-week from Monday through Friday, you can use a shortcut of **weekdays** instead. For periodic Saturday and Sunday, you can use **weekend** as a shortcut. The security appliance can further the restrictions on the users by setting the optional 24-hour format *hh:mm* time specifications. In Example 5-15, the administrator has created a time-range policy called **business_hours** for the regular employees who work from 8 a.m. to 5 p.m. on weekdays and from 8 a.m. to 12 p.m. on Saturdays.

Example 5-15 *Periodic Time-Range Configuration*

```
Chicago(config)# time-range business_hours
Chicago(config-time-range)# periodic weekdays 8:00 to 17:00
Chicago(config-time-range)# periodic Saturday 8:00 to 12:00
```

Once a time-range entry has been set up, the next step is to map it to the ACL by using the **time-range** keyword, as illustrated in Example 5-16, in which the administrator allows outside users access to an internal web server, 209.165.202.131, during business hours (8 a.m. to 5 p.m. Monday through Friday and 8 a.m. to 12 p.m. Saturday). If the outside users try to access the servers outside of this time window, the security appliance will drop the packets and generate a syslog message logging this event. The ACL name is **inside_server** and the time-range name is **business_hours**. The ACL is applied to the outside interface in the inbound direction.

Example 5-16 *Configuration of a Time-Based ACL*

```
Chicago(config)# access-list inside_server extended permit tcp any host
   209.165.202.131 eq 80 time-range business_hours
Chicago(config)# access-group inside_server in interface outside
```

Downloadable ACLs

The security appliance can dynamically download the ACLs from an external authentication server such as Cisco Secure ACS (CS-ACS) using RADIUS. This feature is discussed in Chapter 7, "Authentication, Authorization, and Accounting (AAA)." When a user needs to access a service on the outside, the following sequence of events occurs, as illustrated in Figure 5-5:

1 User opens up a browser application and tries to navigate to a web server located at 209.165.201.1. The packets are sent to Cisco ASA for routing.

2 The ASA is set up for user authentication and thus prompts the user for authentication credentials.

3 The user provides username and password.

4 The security appliance forwards the username and password to an authentication server.

5 If authentication is successful, the server returns the ACLs to the security appliance.

6 Cisco ASA applies the downloadable ACLs to the user.

Figure 5-5   *Downloadable ACLs*

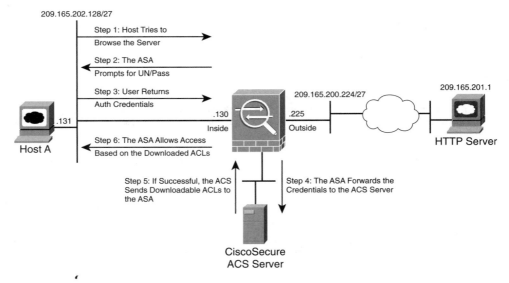

ICMP Filtering

The security appliance does not block ICMP traffic destined for its own interface when ACLs are deployed. Depending on an organization's security policy, an ICMP policy can be defined on the security appliance to block the ICMP traffic that terminates at a security appliance's interface. Use the **icmp** command to create an ICMP policy for an interface. In Example 5-17, an ICMP policy is enabled on the outside interface to block ICMP echo packets that are used to discover if network devices are alive. The second **icmp** statement permits all other ICMP that is destined for the security appliance's IP address.

Example 5-17 *Creating an ICMP Policy*

```
Chicago(config)# icmp deny any echo outside
Chicago(config)# icmp permit any outside
```

The ICMP commands are processed in sequential order, with an implicit deny at the end of the list. If an ICMP packet is not matched against a specific entry in the ICMP list, the packet is dropped. If there is no ICMP list defined, all ICMP packets are allowed to be terminated on the security appliance.

Content and URL Filtering

Traditionally, the firewalls block data packets by inspecting the Layer 3 and/or Layer 4 information in the packets. Cisco ASA can enhance this functionality by inspecting the content information in many Layer 7 protocols such as HTTP, HTTPS, and FTP. Based on the security policy of an organization, the security appliance can either pass or drop the packets if they contain content not allowed in the network. Cisco ASA supports two types of application layer filtering:

- Content filtering
- URL filtering

Both are discussed in turn in the following sections.

Content Filtering

Enabling Java or ActiveX in the production environment can cause naive users to download malicious executables that can cause loss of files and corruption in the user environment. A security network professional can disable Java and ActiveX processing in the browser, but this is not a very scalable solution. The other option is to use a network device such as Cisco ASA to remove the malicious content from the packets. Using the local content-filtering feature, the security appliance can inspect the HTTP header and filter out ActiveX and Java applets when the packets try to traverse through from nontrusted hosts.

Cisco ASA can differentiate between friendly applets and untrusted applets. If a trusted website sends Java or ActiveX applets, the security appliance can forward them to the host requesting the connection. If the applets are sent from untrusted web servers, the security appliance can modify the content and remove the applets from the packets. This way, the end user is not making decisions regarding which applet to accept or refuse. They can download any applets without being extra cautious.

ActiveX Filtering

As mentioned in the preceding section, ActiveX can cause potential problems on the network devices if malicious ActiveX code is downloaded on the machines. The ActiveX code is inserted into the web page by using the <OBJECT ID> and </OBJECT> HTML tags. The security appliance searches for these tags for traffic that originated on a preconfigured port. If the security appliance finds these tags, it replaces them with the comment tags <!-- and -->. When the browser receives the HTTP packets with <!-- and -->, it ignores the actual content by assuming that the content is the author's comments.

NOTE	The security appliance cannot comment out the HTML tags if they are split across multiple network packets.

Java Filtering

For Java-based content filtering, the security appliance looks for <applet and </applet> tags in the HTML data packets. Without Java filtering, the client browser tries to execute the code specified in <applet which begins with a 4-byte header, ca fe ba be. Therefore, to block Java applets, the security appliance searches for the <applet and </applet> tags and replaces them with the comment tags, <!-- and -->. Additionally, it blocks the applets if it sees the ca fe ba be string embedded in the packet.

Configuring Content Filtering

Local content filtering on the security appliance is set up by using the **filter** command followed by the content name to be removed. The following shows the complete command syntax:

```
filter activex | java port[-port] local_ip local_mask foreign_ip foreign_mask
```

Table 5-7 lists and describes the arguments used in the **filter** commands.

Table 5-7   *Syntax Description for* **filter java** *and* **filter activex** *Commands*

Syntax	Description
filter	Keyword used to enable content filtering.
activex	Keyword to enable ActiveX filtering.
java	Keyword to enable Java filtering.
port[-port]	TCP port number(s) for the security appliance to inspect HTTP packets. This can be either a single port or a range of ports. Typically, it is TCP port 80.
local_ip	Host IP or subnet address of the inside hosts where the connection originated.
local_mask	Subnet mask of the local host IP or subnet address.
foreign_ip	Host IP or subnet address of the outside servers to which the connection is made.
foreign_mask	Subnet mask of the outside host IP or subnet address.

In Figure 5-6, the security administrator of an appliance in Chicago has set up a content-filtering policy to remove ActiveX objects from the HTTP packets (TCP port 80). The policy will be enforced if packets originate from the inside subnet 209.165.202.128/27 and destined for the external subnet 209.165.201.0/27. If traffic originates from or is destined for a different host, the security appliance will not filter ActiveX content.

Figure 5-6   *ActiveX-Based Content Filtering*

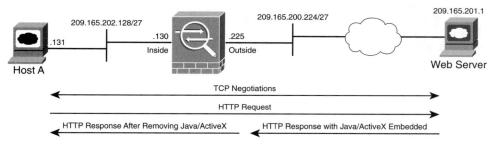

The relevant configuration is shown in Example 5-18.

Example 5-18 *ActiveX Content Filtering*

```
Chicago(config)# filter activex 80 209.165.202.128 255.255.255.224 209.165.201.0
   255.255.255.224
```

In Example 5-19, the security appliance is set up to filter Java applets from the TCP packets received on TCP port 8080. The Java applets will be removed if packets originate from the inside subnet 209.165.202.128/27 and are destined for external subnet 209.165.201.0/27.

Example 5-19 *Java Content Filtering*

```
Chicago(config)# filter java 8080 209.165.202.128 255.255.255.224 209.165.201.0
   255.255.255.224
```

URL Filtering

Traditionally, corporations monitor and control user Internet access by filtering questionable content. This prevents users from accessing sites that are deemed inappropriate based on the organization's security policies. Additionally, employees do not waste network resources by sending traffic to the blocked Internet sites, which results in lower bandwidth usage and increased employee productivity. Cisco ASA can delegate packet-filtering responsibilities to an external server, such as N2H2 or Websense. The URL-filtering process follows this sequence of events, shown in Figure 5-7:

1 A web client (Host A) opens a browser application for Server 1.

2 The security appliance forwards to the filtering server the URLs that the inside hosts try to reach. At the same time, the security appliance also forwards the original request to the external content server (Server 1).

3 The filtering server analyses the URLs and sends a permit or deny message back to the security appliance.

4 The web server sends a reply destined for Host A.

5 If the filtering server allows the connection, the security appliance forwards the response packet from the content server to the client. If the filtering server denies the connection, the security appliance drops the response packet from the content server and sends a message indicating a failed connection.

Figure 5-7 *URL Filtering*

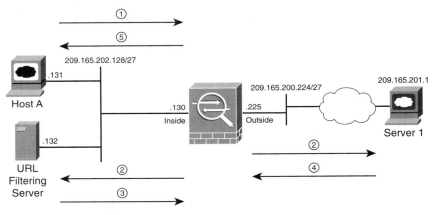

NOTE The inside users may experience longer access times if the response from the filtering server is slow or delayed.

Cisco ASA supports two external filtering servers:

- **Websense**—An external server that can filter HTTP, HTTPS, and FTP requests from the client machines based on many attributes, including destination host name, destination IP address, and username. The Websense Enterprise server can organize a list of Internet URLs into different categories and subcategorizes, including MP3, gambling, shopping, and adult content, for the ease of management. For more information about Websense and its features, visit http://www.websense.com.

- **N2H2**—Another external server that allows the security appliance to filter HTTP requests from the web clients when they try to access the web servers on the less-trusted network. With a huge database containing URLs organized into different categories, the N2H2 server ensures that users do not access restricted websites. For more information about N2H2, visit http://www.n2h2.com.

NOTE	N2H2 has been acquired by Secure Computing Corp. The product name has been renamed to Sentian.

Configuring URL Filtering

You can configure URL filtering as follows:

Step 1   Define a filtering server.

Step 2   Configure HTTP, HTTPS, and FTP filtering.

Step 3   Buffer server responses (optional).

Step 4   Enable long URL support (optional).

Step 5   Cache server responses (optional).

These steps are described in more detail in the sections that follow.

Step 1: Defining a Filtering Server

An external filtering server is defined by using the **url-server** command. The complete command syntax to specify a Websense server is

```
url-server [<(if_name)>] [vendor websense] host <local_ip> [timeout <seconds>]
    [protocol TCP|UDP] [connections num_conns] [version 1|4]
```

To define an N2H2 server, the command syntax is

```
url-server [<(if_name)>] vendor n2h2 host <local_ip> [port <number>] [timeout
    <seconds>] [protocol TCP|UDP] [connections num_conns]]
```

Table 5-8 lists and describes the arguments used in the **url-server** command.

Table 5-8   **url-server** *Command Syntax and Description*

Syntax	Description
url-server	Keyword used to enable URL filtering.
if_name	Specifies the interface toward the URL filtering server.
vendor	Keyword used to identify the vendors.
websense	Keyword to specify Websense as the URL-filtering server.
host	Keyword used to specify a host address for the filtering server.
local_ip	Specifies the IP address of the filtering server.
timeout	Keyword to specify the maximum idle timeout before the security appliance switches over to the next URL-filtering server.
seconds	The actual idle timeout in seconds. The default is 5 seconds.

continues

Table 5-8 url-server *Command Syntax and Description (Continued)*

Syntax	Description
protocol	Keyword to specify the protocol to be used for communication. The default is TCP.
TCP	Keyword to specify the TCP protocol to be used.
UDP	Keyword to specify the UDP protocol to be used.
version	Keyword to specify the version of protocol to be used when Websense server is set up as the filtering server.
1	Specifies version 1 for TCP protocol communication. This is the default.
4	Specifies version 4 for TCP or UDP protocol communication.
N2H2	Keyword to specify N2H2 as the URL-filtering server.
port	Keyword to specify the port number for the security appliance to communicate with the N2H2 server.
number	The actual port number. The default is port 4005.
connections	Keyword to limit the maximum number of connections permitted to a URL-filtering server.
num_cons	Specifies the maximum number of connections permitted.

The **url-server** command does not verify whether a Websense or N2H2 server is reachable from the security appliance. You can specify up to 16 filtering servers for redundancy. If the security appliance is not able to reach the first server in the list, it tries the second server from the list, and so on. Additionally, Cisco ASA does not allow setting up both N2H2 and Websense servers at the same time. You must delete the Websense server before you can use an N2H2 server, and vice versa.

In Example 5-20, the administrator has defined a Websense server located on the inside interface. The IP address of the server is 209.165.202.132 using TCP protocol version 4 with the timeout value of 30 seconds.

Example 5-20 *URL Filtering Using Websense*

```
Chicago(config)# url-server (inside) vendor websense host 209.165.202.132 timeout
  30 protocol TCP version 4
```

NOTE   The security appliance does not allow multiple N2H2 URL servers to use different port numbers.

Step 2: Configuring HTTP, HTTPS, and FTP Filtering

After identifying the URL server, the security appliance can forward the HTTP, HTTPS, and FTP requests to the appropriate filtering servers. In the current implementation, Cisco ASA supports HTTP, HTTPS, and FTP packet filtering on the Websense server and HTTP filtering on the N2H2 server. If the filtering server allows the connection, the security appliance forwards the response from the web and/or FTP server to the client host. If the filtering server denies the connection, the security appliance server drops the response and takes one of the following actions:

- Redirects the HTTP or HTTPS connection to a blocked page. The URL of the blocked page is returned by the filtering server.

- Returns "code 550: Directory not found" error message to the FTP client.

The command syntax to enable HTTP filtering is

```
filter url port[-port] local_IP local_mask foreign_IP foreign_mask [allow] [proxy-
    block] [longurl-truncate] [longurl-deny] [cgi-truncate]
```

The command syntax to enable HTTPS filtering is

```
filter https port[-port] local_IP local_mask foreign_IP foreign_mask [allow]
```

The command syntax to enable FTP filtering is

```
filter ftp port[-port] local_IP local_mask foreign_IP foreign_mask [allow]
    [interact-block]
```

Table 5-9 lists and describes the arguments used in the **filter** command for URL filtering.

Table 5-9   **filter** *Command Syntax and Description*

Syntax	Description
filter	Keyword used to enable content filtering.
url	Keyword to enable HTTP filtering.
port[-port]	TCP port number(s) for URL filtering. The security appliance inspects packets on this port(s). This can be either a single port or a range of ports.
local_ip	IP/subnet address of the inside hosts where the connection originated.
local_mask	Subnet mask of the local IP/subnet address.
foreign_ip	IP/subnet address of the outside servers to which the connection is made.
foreign_mask	Subnet mask of the outside IP/subnet address.
allow	Allows the response from the content server if the filtering server is not available.
proxy-block	Denies requests going to the proxy server.
longurl-truncate	Truncates URLs that are longer than the maximum allowed length before sending the request to the filtering server.
longurl-deny	Denies outbound connection if the URLs are longer than the maximum allowed length.
cgi-truncate	Truncates long CGI URLs before sending the request to the filtering server, to save memory resources and improve firewall performance.
https	Keyword to enable HTTPS filtering.
ftp	Keyword to enable FTP filtering.
interact-block	Denies interactive FTP sessions that do not provide the entire directory path.

In case a URL-filtering server is not available, the security appliance drops the response from the content (web or FTP) server. You can change this default behavior by specifying the **allow** keyword at the end of the **filter** command.

In Example 5-21, the Cisco ASA in Chicago is set up to filter HTTP, HTTPS, and FTP packets if the connections originate from 209.165.202.128/27 and are destined for any outside network (represented as 0.0.0.0 0.0.0.0). If the URL server is not available, the inside hosts are allowed to connect to the content servers. For the HTTP packets, the security appliance truncates CGI scripts and the long URLs. For the FTP connections, the security appliance restricts users to change directories without specifying the complete directory path.

Example 5-21 *Filtering of HTTP, HTTPS, and FTP Packet Content*

```
Chicago(config)# filter url 80 209.165.202.128 255.255.255.224 0.0.0.0 0.0.0.0 allow
  longurl-truncate cgi-truncate
Chicago(config)# filter https 443 209.165.202.128 255.255.255.224 0.0.0.0 0.0.0.0
  allow
Chicago(config)# filter ftp 21 209.165.202.128 255.255.255.224 0.0.0.0 0.0.0.0 allow
  interact-block
```

Step 3: Buffering Server Responses (Optional)

Using the URL-filtering feature, the security appliance sends the client request to the outside content server and simultaneously makes a URL lookup request to the filtering server. If the content server's reply arrives prior to the URL-filtering server's response, the security appliance drops the packet. This default behavior can be changed by buffering the response packets from the content server until a reply is received from the filtering server. The command to enable packet buffering is **url-block block** followed by the number of blocks to be buffered. In Example 5-22, the security appliance is set up to buffer up to 128 blocks in the HTTP response.

Example 5-22 *Buffering of Server Responses*

```
Chicago(config)# url-block block 128
```

Step 4: Enabling Long URL Support (Optional)

The security appliance identifies a URL greater than 1159 bytes as a long URL. You can change this behavior if a Websense server is deployed for filtering purposes by using the **url-block url-size** command followed by the size of the maximum long URL in kilobytes. In Example 5-23, the security appliance is set up to change the HTTP long URL size from 2 KB to 4 KB.

Example 5-23 *Configuration to Enable Long URL Support*

```
Chicago(config)# url-block url-size 4
```

When the security appliance receives a URL longer than 1024 bytes, it breaks the URL into multiple IP packets and copies the TCP payload, the content of the URL, into the buffer memory chunk. Each memory chunk is 1024 bytes, and the security appliance allocates another memory chunk for a URL longer than 1024 bytes for optimized memory management. Example 5-24 shows how to increase the allocated memory available for long URL support and packet buffering to 100 KB.

Example 5-24 *Configuration to Increase the Memory for Long URL Support*

```
Chicago(config)# url-block url-mempool 100
```

Step 5: Caching Server Responses (Optional)

The security appliance can cache the responses from the filtering servers for a certain period of time based on the destination and/or the source IP addresses. This way, when a user tries to access the same URL again, the security appliance does not forward the request to the filtering server but consults its local cache before allowing or denying the packets. Use the **url-cache** command to enable caching of server responses followed by the addressing policy. For destination address–based caching, use **dst** as the keyword in the **url-cache** command. If you prefer caching URL responses based on the source and destination addresses of a connection, use **src_dst** with the **url-cache** command. In Example 5-25, the security appliance allocates 128 KB of memory for destination-based URL caching.

Example 5-25 *URL Caching*

```
Chicago(config)# url-cache dst 128
```

Deployment Scenarios Using ACLs

Traffic filtering is the core functionality of any network or personal firewall. However, Cisco ASA integrates this core functionality with the novel features to provide a scalable packet identification and filtering mechanism that can be used in almost any environment. Although ACLs can be deployed in many different ways, this section covers the following two design scenarios for ease of understanding:

- Using ACLs to filter inbound and outbound traffic
- Enabling content filtering using Websense

NOTE   These design scenarios are discussed here to reinforce learning and thus they should be used for reference only.

Using ACLs to Filter Inbound and Outbound Traffic

SecureMe hosts three web servers, two e-mail servers, and a DNS server at its Chicago office. All of these servers are located on the DMZ network 209.165.201.0/27, as shown in Figure 5-8. SecureMe also provides connectivity to the Internet for its inside trusted users.

However, the inside hosts are allowed to access only Web Server1 and DNS server on the DMZ network.

Figure 5-8 *SecureMe ASA in Chicago Using ACLs*

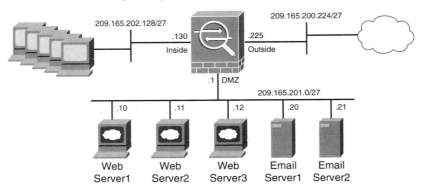

Table 5-10 lists all the servers and their corresponding IP addresses.

Table 5-10 *Server Address Assignments*

Server	IP Address
Web Server1	209.165.201.10
Web Server2	209.165.201.11
Web Server3	209.165.201.12
Email Server1	209.165.201.20
Email Server2	209.165.201.21
DNS	209.165.201.30

To achieve these requirements, the administrator has configured an inbound ACL, called outside_in, with two object groups. The first network object group, DMZ_Web_Servers, groups all the HTTP servers. The second network group, DMZ_Email_Servers, groups both e-mail servers. Both network groups are bound to the ACL to allow the HTTP and SMTP traffic only. All other traffic gets denied and logged by the security appliance. This ACL is applied on the outside interface in the inbound direction.

To limit the inside traffic to the DMZ network, the administrator has configured another ACL, called DMZ_out, to allow the trusted hosts on the inside network to access Web Server1 and DNS. The ACL is applied on the DMZ interface in the outbound direction. Example 5-26 shows the relevant configuration of the ASA in Chicago.

Example 5-26 *ASA's Full Configuration Using Inbound and Outbound ACLs*

```
Chicago# show running
ASA Version 7.0(1)
! GigabitEthernet0/0 interface set as outside
interface GigabitEthernet0/0
 nameif outside
 security-level 0
 ip address 209.165.200.225 255.255.255.224
! GigabitEthernet0/1 interface set as inside
interface GigabitEthernet0/1
 nameif inside
 security-level 100
 ip address 209.165.202.129 255.255.255.224
! GigabitEthernet0/2 interface set as DMZ
interface GigabitEthernet0/2
 nameif DMZ
 security-level 50
ip address 209.165.201.1 255.255.255.224
! Hostname of the security appliance
hostname Chicago
! Network Object-group to group the web-servers
object-group network DMZ_Web_Servers
 network-object host 209.165.201.10
 network-object host 209.165.201.11
 network-object host 209.165.201.12
! Network Object-group to group the Email-servers
object-group network DMZ_Email_Servers
 network-object host 209.165.201.20
 network-object host 209.165.201.21
! Access-list to filter inbound traffic on the outside interface
access-list outside_in remark ACL to block inbound traffic on the outside interface
access-list outside_in extended permit tcp any object-group DMZ_Web_Servers eq www
access-list outside_in extended permit tcp any object-group DMZ_Email_Servers eq
smtp
access-list outside_in extended deny ip any any log
! Access-list to filter outbound traffic on the DMZ interface
access-list DMZ_out remark ACL to block outbound traffic on the DMZ interface
access-list DMZ_out extended permit tcp 209.165.202.128 255.255.255.224 host
209.165.201.10 eq www
access-list DMZ_out extended permit udp 209.165.202.128 255.255.255.224 host
209.165.201.30 eq domain
! Access-list bound to the outside interface in the inbound direction
access-group outside_in in interface outside
! Access-list bound to the DMZ interface in the outbound direction
access-group DMZ_out out interface DMZ
! Default route is pointed to the outside interface
route outside 0.0.0.0 0.0.0.0 209.165.200.226 1
```

Enabling Content Filtering Using Websense

SecureMe wants to enable content filtering for its users to ensure that they do not access certain sites such as pornographic and gaming sites. The administrator has set up a Websense server to filter out the URLs if the packets are destined for these Internet sites using the HTTP, HTTPS, or FTP protocols. The administrator does not want to overload the filtering server by sending the duplicate request for the same source and destination addresses. SecureMe's policy allows users to go through the security appliance if the filtering server is unavailable. Additionally, if the reply from the content server arrives before the response is received from the filtering server, SecureMe wants the security appliance to buffer the reply rather than drop it.

To meet the company's goals, the administrator has specified a Websense server as a URL-filtering device in the network that is located on the DMZ interface at 209.165.201.50, as illustrated in Figure 5-9. To avoid overloading the filtering server, the maximum simultaneous limit is set to 15, while the server's responses are cached by allocating 100 KB of memory space. The security appliance is set up to buffer replies from the filtering server by using the **url-block block** command to store up to 128 packets.

Figure 5-9 *SecureMe Network Using Content Filtering*

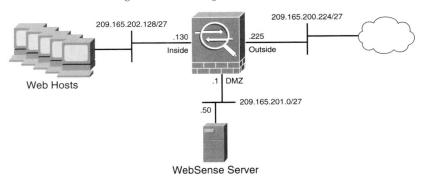

Example 5-27 shows the complete configuration for Cisco ASA used in this deployment.

Example 5-27 *ASA's Full Configuration Using a URL-Filtering Server*

```
Chicago# show run
ASA Version 7.0(1)
! GigabitEthernet0/0 interface set as outside
interface GigabitEthernet0/0
 nameif outside
 security-level 0
 ip address 209.165.200.225 255.255.255.224
! GigabitEthernet0/1 interface set as inside
interface GigabitEthernet0/1
 nameif inside
 security-level 100
 ip address 209.165.202.130 255.255.255.224
! GigabitEthernet0/2 interface set as DMZ
interface GigabitEthernet0/2
 nameif dmz
 security-level 50
 ip address 209.165.201.1 255.255.255.224
! Hostname of the security appliance
hostname Chicago
```

Example 5-27 *ASA's Full Configuration Using a URL-Filtering Server (Continued)*

```
! Access-list to filter inbound traffic on the outside interface
access-list outside_in remark ACL to block inbound traffic on the outside interface
access-list outside_in extended deny ip any any log
! Access-list to filter inbound traffic on the inside interface
access-list inside_in remark ACL to block inbound traffic on the inside interface
access-list inside_in extended permit tcp 209.165.202.128 255.255.255.224 any eq www
! Access-list bound to the outside interface in the inbound direction
access-group outside_in in interface outside
! Access-list bound to the inside interface in the inbound direction
access-group inside_in in interface inside
! Default route is pointed to the outside interface
route outside 0.0.0.0 0.0.0.0 209.165.200.226 1
url-server (dmz) vendor websense host 209.165.201.50 timeout 30 protocol TCP version
4 connections 15
url-cache src_dst 100
filter url http 209.165.202.128 255.255.255.128 0.0.0.0 0.0.0.0 allow
filter https 443 209.165.202.128 255.255.255. 128 0.0.0.0 0.0.0.0 allow
filter ftp 21 209.165.202.128  255.255.255. 128 0.0.0.0 0.0.0.0 allow
!
url-block block 100
```

Monitoring Network Access Control

The **show** commands provided by Cisco ASA are extremely useful in checking the health
and status of the hardware and in isolating network-related issues. The necessary **show**
commands to manage network access control are discussed in the following two sections.

Monitoring ACLs

Cisco ASA provides the **show access-list** command to determine if the packets are passing
through the configured ACLs. When a packet is matched against an ACE, the security
appliance increments the **hitcnt** (hit count) counter by one. This is useful when you want
to know if traffic is hitting a configured ACE. It is also useful to check if packets are allowed
or denied if there is a new virus outbreak in the network that might be sending traffic from
spoofed addresses. Example 5-28 shows the configuration of an ACL called outside_in. If
object groups are used and the **show access-list outside_in** command is executed, Cisco
ASA displays all the ACEs that are otherwise grouped into protocols, networks, and
services. As evident from this example, the security appliance processed 1009 packets that
were denied and logged by the ACE.

Example 5-28 *Output of* **show access-list outside_in**

```
Chicago(config)# show running-config access-list outside_in
access-list outside_in remark ACL to block inbound traffic on the outside interface
access-list outside_in extended permit tcp any object-group DMZ_Web_Servers eq www
access-list outside_in extended permit tcp any object-group DMZ_Email_Servers eq smtp
```

continues

Example 5-28 *Output of* **show access-list outside_in** *(Continued)*

```
access-list outside_in extended deny ip any any log
Chicago(config)#exit
Chicago(config)# show access-list outside_in
access-list outside_in; 6 elements
access-list outside_in line 1 remark ACL to block inbound traffic on the outside
interface
access-list outside_in line 2 extended permit tcp any object-group DMZ_Web_Servers
eq www
access-list outside_in line 2 extended permit tcp any host 209.165.201.10 eq www
(hitcnt=9)
access-list outside_in line 2 extended permit tcp any host 209.165.201.11 eq www
(hitcnt=100)
access-list outside_in line 2 extended permit tcp any host 209.165.201.12 eq www
(hitcnt=24)
access-list outside_in line 3 extended permit tcp any object-group DMZ_Email_Servers
eq smtp
access-list outside_in line 3 extended permit tcp any host 209.165.201.20 eq smtp
(hitcnt=3)
access-list outside_in line 3 extended permit tcp any host 209.165.201.21 eq smtp
(hitcnt=199)
access-list outside_in line 4 extended deny ip any any log informational interval
300 (hitcnt=1009)
```

To reset the hit-count counters, you can issue the **clear access-list** *<ACL_name>* **counters** command, as shown in Example 5-29, in which the counters for the outside_in ACL are being cleared.

Example 5-29 *Resetting Hit-Count Counters with* **clear access-list counters**

```
Chicago(config)# clear access-list outside_in counters
```

If a UDP, TCP, or, optionally an ICMP packet is allowed to pass through the security appliance, a connection entry is created, which can be shown by using the **show conn** command, as displayed in Example 5-30. The first column of the connection entry displays the protocol used followed by "out" to indicate IP address of the outside host and then "in" to display the inside hosts' IP addresses. It also shows the source and destination Layer 4 ports. The security appliance shows the idle timer per connection in hours, minutes, and seconds. The most important information to look at is the flags counter, which has the information about the current state of the connection. Table 5-11 lists and describes all the flags. The TCP entry has flags set to "UIO" to indicate that the connection is up and is passing traffic in both inbound and outbound directions.

Example 5-30 *Output of* **show conn**

```
Chicago# show conn
3 in use, 17 most used
UDP out 209.165.201.10:53 in 209.165.202.130:53376 idle 0:00:01 flags -
TCP out 209.165.201.10:23 in 209.165.202.130:11080 idle 0:00:02 bytes 108 flags UIO
ICMP out 209.165.201.10:0 in 209.165.202.130:15467 idle 0:00:00 bytes 72
```

Table 5-11 *Description of Flags in the* **show conn** *Command Output*

Flag	Description	Flag	Description
a	Awaiting outside ACK to SYN	A	Awaiting inside ACK to SYN
B	Initial SYN from outside	C	Computer Telephony Interface Quick Buffer Encoding (CTIQBE) media connection
d	Dump	D	DNS
E	Outside back connection	f	Inside FIN
F	Outside FIN	g	Media Gateway Control Protocol (MGCP) connection
G	Connection is part of a group	h	H.225 packet
H	H.323 packet	i	Incomplete TCP or UDP connection
I	Inbound data	k	Skinny Client Control Protocol (SCCP) media connection
m	SIP media connection	M	SMTP data
O	Outbound data	P	Inside back connection
q	SQL*NET data	R	Outside acknowledged FIN for TCP connection or UDP RPC
r	Inside acknowledged FIN	S	Awaiting inside SYN
s	Awaiting outside SYN	T	SIP connection
t	SIP transient connection	U	Up

Cisco ASA can act as a sniffer to gather information about the packets passing through the interfaces. This is important if you want to confirm that traffic from a particular host or network is reaching the interfaces. You can use an ACL to identify the type of traffic and bind it to an interface by using the **capture** command.

In Example 5-31, an ACL, called **inside-capture**, is set up to identify packets sourced from 209.165.202.130 and destined for 209.165.200.230. The security appliance is using this ACL to capture the identified traffic on the inside interface using a capture list named **cap-inside**.

To view the captured packets, use the **show capture** command followed by the name of the capture list. The security appliance captured 15 packets that matched the ACL on the inside interface. The highlighted entry shows that it is a TCP SYN (shown as S after the destination port) packet sourced from 209.165.202.130 with a source port of 11084 and it is destined for 209.165.200.230 on destination port 23. The TCP window size is 4128 while the Maximum Segment Size (MSS) is set to 536 bytes.

Example 5-31 *Packet Capturing*

```
Chicago(config)# access-list inside-capture permit ip host 209.165.202.130 host
  209.165.200.230
Chicago(config)# capture cap-inside access-list inside-capture interface inside
Chicago(config)# show capture cap-inside
15 packets captured
1: 02:12:47.142189 209.165.202.130.11084 > 209.165.200.230.23: S
433720059:433720059(0) win 4128 <mss 536>
   2: 02:12:47.163489 209.165.202.130.11084 > 209.165.200.230.23: . ack 1033049551
win 4128
!Output omitted for brevity
15 packets shown
```

NOTE   When the capture command is enabled, the security appliance allocates memory right away. The default memory allocation is 512 KB. The security appliance can overwrite content from the beginning in this buffer space when it is full. The capture command has minimal CPU impact and therefore it is one of the most important troubleshooting tools available in Cisco ASA.

TIP   The output of the capture command can be exported into pcap format, which can be imported into a sniffing tool such as Ethereal or TCPDUMP for further analysis.

Monitoring Content Filtering

If the security appliance is set up to filter traffic by inspecting the URLs, you can view the packet-filtering statistics to ensure that nonallowed traffic is denied. Use the **show url-server statistics** command to check how many packets have been allowed and dropped based on the responses from the URL server (such as Websense). In Example 5-32, the security appliance has denied 9000 URL (HTTP) attempts due to restricted or blocked content, whereas it has allowed 161,302 requests. The status of the Websense server is up which indicates that there is a bidirectional communication channel between the server and the security appliance.

Example 5-32 *Output of* **show url-server statistics**

```
Chicago# show url-server statistics
URL Server Statistics:
----------------------
Vendor                        websense
URLs total/allowed/denied     170302/161302/9000
HTTPSs total/allowed/denied   1765/876/889
FTPs total/allowed/denied     10/8/2

URL Server Status:
------------------
209.165.201.50           UP
```

Example 5-32 *Output of* **show url-server statistics** *(Continued)*

```
URL Packets Sent and Received Stats:
-----------------------------------
Message             Sent    Received
STATUS_REQUEST      496908  482321
LOOKUP_REQUEST      170694  170603
LOG_REQUEST         0       NA
-----------------------------------
```

If URL caching is enabled, as in the case of the deployment scenario, you can collect statistics such as allocated memory for this purpose. In Example 5-33, the security appliance shows that the total maximum number of cached URLs is 171, the total number of active URLs in the cache is 100, the total lookups it performed is 456, and the number of packets that matched the cached URLs is 306.

Example 5-33 *Output of* **show url-cache statistics**

```
Chicago# show url-cache statistics

URL Filter Cache Stats
----------------------
    Size :      100KB
 Entries :      171
  In Use :      100
 Lookups :      456
    Hits :      306
```

Understanding Address Translation

Cisco ASA, being a security device, can mask the network address on the trusted side from the untrusted networks. This technique, commonly referred to as *address translation,* allows an organization to hide the internal addressing scheme from the outside by displaying a different IP address space. Address translation is useful in the following network deployments:

- You use a private addressing scheme internally, and want to assign global routable addresses to those hosts.

- You change to a service provider that requires you to change the addressing scheme. Rather than redesign the entire IP infrastructure, you implement translation on the border appliance.

- You do not want to advertise the internal addressing scheme to the outside hosts, for security reasons.

- You have multiple internal networks that require Internet connectivity through the security appliance, but only one (or few) global address is available for translation.

- You have overlapping networks in your organization and you want to provide connectivity between the two without modifying the existing addressing scheme.

Cisco ASA supports the following two types of address translation:

- Network Address Translation
- Port Address Translation

The following sections discuss the two address translation types, packet flow sequence, address translation configuration steps, ways to bypass address translation, and address translation order of operation.

Network Address Translation

Network Address Translation (NAT) defines a one-to-one address mapping when a packet passes through the security appliance and matches criteria for translation. The security appliance either assigns a static IP address (static NAT) or allocates an address from a pool of addresses (dynamic NAT).

Cisco ASA can translate an internal address to a global address when packets are destined for the public network. With this method, also known as *inside NAT,* the security appliance converts the global address of the return traffic to the original internal address. Inside NAT is used when traffic originates from a higher security interface, such as the inside interface, and is destined for a lower-security interface, such as the outside interface. In Figure 5-10, a host on the internal network, 192.168.10.10, sends traffic to a host on the outside network, 209.165.201.1. The Cisco ASA converts the source IP address to 209.165.200.226 while keeping the destination IP address intact. When the web server responds to the global IP address, 209.165.200.226, the security appliance reverts the global IP address to an internal real IP address of 192.168.10.10.

Figure 5-10 *Inside Network Address Translation*

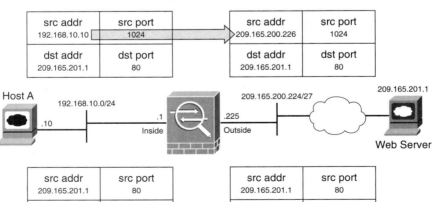

Optionally, the hosts on the lower security interface can be translated when traffic is destined for a host on the higher security interface. This method, known as *outside NAT*, is useful when you want the hosts on the outside network to appear as one of the internal IP addresses. In Figure 5-11, a host on the outside network, 209.165.201.1, sends traffic to a host on the inside network, 192.168.10.10, by using its global IP address as the destination address. Cisco ASA converts the source IP address to 192.168.10.100 while changing the destination IP address to 192.168.10.10.

Figure 5-11 *Outside Network Address Translation*

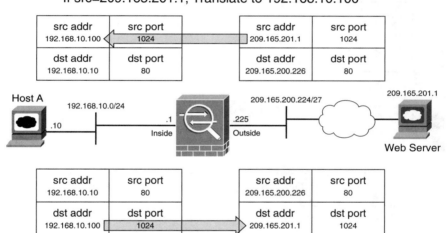

NOTE   If the packets are denied by the interface ACLs, the security appliance does not build the corresponding address translation table entry.

Port Address Translation

Port Address Translation (PAT) defines a many-to-one address mapping when a packet passes through the security appliance and matches criteria for translation. The security appliance creates the translation table by looking at the Layer 4 information in the header to distinguish between the inside hosts using the same global IP address.

Figure 5-12 illustrates an appliance set up for PAT for the inside network of 192.168.10.0/24. However, there is only one global address available for translation. If two inside hosts, 192.168.10.10 and 192.168.10.20, require connectivity to an outside host, 209.165.201.1, the security appliance will build the translation table by evaluating the Layer 4 header information. In this case, because both inside hosts have the same source port number, the security appliance assigns a different source port number to keep both entries unique from each other. This way, when the response from the web server returns to the security appliance, the security appliance knows which inside host to forward the packets to.

Figure 5-12 *Port Address Translation*

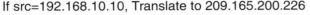

If src=192.168.10.10, Translate to 209.165.200.226

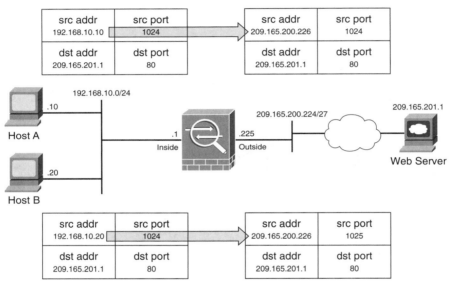

If src=192.168.10.20, Translate to 209.165.200.226

Packet Flow Sequence

When a packet passes through an appliance configured for address translation, the following sequence of events occurs:

1 The packet arrives at the ingress interface from the end host.

2 The security appliance checks the packet against the inbound ACL.

3 If the packet is allowed in, the security appliance consults the routing table to determine the outbound physical interface.

4 If address translation is enabled and the packet matches the translation criteria, the security appliance creates a translation for the host.

5 The security appliance creates a stateful connection entry for the TCP and UDP packets. The security appliance can, optionally, create a stateful connection entry for the ICMP traffic if ICMP inspection is turned on.

6 The packet is routed to the egress interface and is checked against the outbound ACL.

7 If allowed, the packet is transmitted.

Configuring Address Translation

Cisco ASA supports the following five types of address translation, each of which is configured uniquely:

- Static NAT
- Dynamic NAT
- Static PAT
- Dynamic PAT
- Policy NAT/PAT

Static NAT

Static NAT defines a fixed translation of an inside host or subnet address to a global routable address or subnet. The security appliance uses the one-to-one methodology by assigning one global IP address to an inside IP address. Thus, if 100 hosts residing on the inside network require address translation, the security appliance should be configured for 100 global IP addresses. Additionally, the inside hosts are assigned the same IP address whenever the security appliance translates the packets going through it. This is a recommended solution in scenarios in which an organization provides services, such as e-mail, web, DNS, and FTP, for outside users. Using static NAT, the servers use the same global IP address for all the inbound and outbound connections.

A static address translation can be defined by using the **static** command. The complete command syntax of **static** follows:

```
static (real_ifc,mapped_ifc) {mapped_ip} {real_ip [netmask mask]} [dns]
  [norandomseq] [[tcp] [max_conns [emb_lim]] [udp udp_max_conns]
```

Table 5-12 lists and defines the arguments used in the **static** command.

Table 5-12   *Syntax Description of* **static**

Syntax	Description
static	Keyword used to define a static address translation.
real_ifc	Interface name to which the actual (or real) hosts are connected. It is the higher security interface if inside NAT is used or the lower security interface if outside NAT is implemented.
mapped_ifc	Interface name that owns the *mapped_ip* of a host. It is the lower security interface if inside NAT is used or the higher security interface if outside NAT is implemented.

continues

Table 5-12 *Syntax Description of* **static** *(Continued)*

Syntax	Description
mapped_ip	Translated IP address(es).
real_ip	Original or nontranslated IP address(es).
netmask_mask	Subnet mask of the real IP subnet address. For host-based NAT, it is 255.255.255.255.
dns	Enables DNS doctoring, which is covered later in the "DNS Doctoring" section.
norandomseq	Disables randomization of TCP sequence number.
tcp	Keyword to enable TCP embryonic and connection limit.
max_conns	Maximum number of simultaneous TCP connections originated from the real host address.
emb_lim	Maximum number of simultaneous TCP embryonic connections that have not completed the three-way TCP negotiations. Exceeding this limit triggers the TCP interception feature, discussed later in this section.
udp	Keyword to enable UDP connection limit.
udp_max_conns	Maximum number of simultaneous UDP connections originated from or destined for the real host address.

The **static** command not only masquerades the original IP address, it also provides protection against TCP connection hijacking for hosts with weak SYN implementation. When a packet enters the higher security interface and is destined for a lower security interface during the TCP three-way handshake, the security appliance randomizes the original sequence numbers used by the hosts. This process is illustrated in Figure 5-13. When the host 192.168.10.10 sends a TCP SYN HTTP packet to host 209.165.201.1 with an Initial Sequence Number (ISN) of 0x12345678, the Cisco ASA changes the source IP address to 209.165.200.226 and also modifies the ISN to a randomly generated value of 0xa1b2e3c4.

In some deployment scenarios, such as BGP peering with MD5 authentication, it is recommended to turn off the randomization of TCP packets. When two routers establish BGP peering with each other, the TCP header and data payload are 128-bit hashed using the BGP password. When the sequence number is changed, the peering router fails to authenticate the packets because of mismatched hash. For more information about BGP MD5 authentication, consult RFC 2385.

Cisco ASA also provides protection against certain types of denial of service (DoS) attacks. By using the embryonic and maximum connection limit, the security appliance can restrict the establishment of new connections to the inside servers. An embryonic connection is a half-opened connection from the client to the server during the TCP three-way handshake. When the number of embryonic connections hits the maximum allowed limit, Cisco ASA starts intercepting the SYN packets from the client to the servers. When the client sends a

TCP SYN packet destined for the server, the security appliance responds with an ACK on behalf of the server. If the client acknowledges the receipt of the previous packet, the security appliance marks the connection as valid and starts a connection to the server on behalf of the client. It combines both connections transparently without any user interception. This process of intercepting the TCP packets is known as TCP interception and is illustrated in Figure 5-14.

Figure 5-13 *Randomization of ISN*

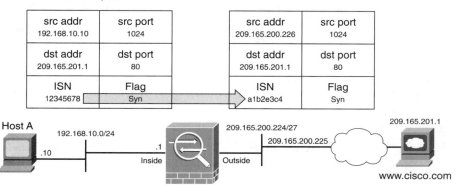

Figure 5-14 *TCP Interception*

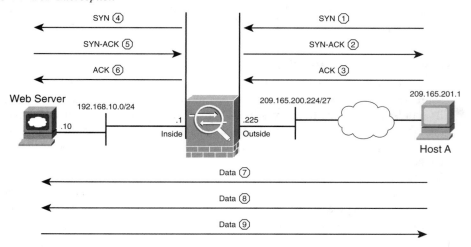

NOTE   The TCP intercept feature is available only for inbound NAT.

The security appliance can also protect network resources from an unexpected increase in the number of connections by setting maximum limits. This is applicable for both TCP- and

UDP-based connections. In Example 5-34, a static entry is created to translate an inside host, 192.168.10.10, to 209.165.200.226. The security appliance is also translating the 192.168.10.0/29 subnet to 209.165.200.232/29. Any host that falls in this range of IP addresses will be assigned an IP address from the 209.165.200.232/29 subnet. The maximum TCP and UDP simultaneous connection limits are set to 1000, while the embryonic connections are restricted to 100 before initiating the TCP intercept mode.

Example 5-34 *Inside NAT*

```
Chicago(config)# static (inside,outside) 209.165.200.226 192.168.10.10 netmask
   255.255.255.255 tcp 1000 100 udp 1000
Chicago(config)# static (inside,outside) 209.165.200.232 192.168.10.0 netmask
   255.255.255.248 tcp 1000 100 udp 1000
```

Example 5-35 illustrates how to set up an outside NAT static entry. An outside host, 209.165.201.1, is translated to an inside address, 192.168.10.100, before the packets enter the inside network.

Example 5-35 *Outside NAT*

```
Chicago(config)# static (outside,inside) 192.168.10.100 209.165.201.1 netmask
   255.255.255.255
```

NOTE   The security appliance does not support outside NAT if the Cisco CallManager server reside on the inside network and the IP phones connect from the outside network.

Dynamic Network Address Translation

Dynamic NAT assigns a random IP address from a preconfigured pool of global IP addresses. The security appliance uses a one-to-one methodology by allocating one global IP address to an inside IP address. Hence, if 100 hosts reside on the inside network, then the pool of addresses should be big enough to accommodate those hosts. This is a recommended solution in scenarios in which an organization uses protocols that don't contain Layer 4 information, such as Generic Routing Encapsulation (GRE), Reliable Datagram Protocol (RDP), and Data Delivery Protocol (DDP). Once the security appliance has built a dynamic NAT for an inside host, any machine can connect to the assigned IP address, assuming that the security appliance allows the inbound connection, as discussed in the "Monitoring Network Access Control" section earlier in this chapter.

A dynamic NAT is defined by using the **nat** and **global** commands. The following shows the complete command syntax of **nat**:

```
nat (real_ifc) nat_id local_ip [mask [dns] [outside] [[tcp] tcp_max_conns
   [emb_limit] [norandomseq]]] [udp udp_max_conns]
```

The NAT statement identifies the host or subnet that needs to be translated to a global IP address. Most of the arguments defined in the **nat** statement are the same as those outlined in Table 5-12. The *nat_id* is a positive number between 1 and 65,535 that groups hosts and subnets together so that an address can be allocated from the respective global pool.

NOTE   Nat_id with a value of 0 (zero) has a special meaning, because it is used to bypass address translation. This option is discussed later in the chapter, in the "Bypassing Address Translation" section.

The **outside** keyword is used if you want to define an outside dynamic NAT policy to allocate addresses when packets traverse from a lower security interface to a higher security interface.

After defining a NAT entry, the next step is to bind it to a global statement by using the same *nat_id*. A global statement specifies a range of translated addresses that can be assigned to the hosts. The command syntax of the **global** command is

```
global (mapped_ifc) nat_id {global_ip [-global_ip] [netmask global_mask]}
```

In Example 5-36, an administrator wishes to dynamically assign global addresses from a pool of IP addresses ranging from 209.165.200.230 to 209.165.200.237 for an inside subnet of 192.168.10.96 with a subnet mask of 255.255.255.248. Because these entries are dynamically created, the security appliance assigns these addresses in round-robin fashion by assigning 209.165.200.230 from the pool first. A NAT statement identifies the inside subnet 192.168.10.96/29 as *nat_id* 1. This *nat_id* is then mapped to a global statement that translates the inside hosts on the outside interface as 209.165.200.230-237.

Example 5-36 *Configuration of Dynamic NAT*

```
Chicago(config)# nat (inside) 1 192.168.10.96 255.255.255.248
Chicago(config)# global (outside) 1 209.165.200.230-209.165.200.237
```

NOTE   When address translation is turned on, the security appliance does proxy ARP for the configured translated addresses. Proxy ARP is a process in which the security appliance answers ARP requests on behalf of other addresses.

Static Port Address Translation

Static PAT, also known as *port redirection,* is useful when the security appliance needs to statically map multiple inside servers to one global IP address. Port redirection is applied on traffic when it passes through the security appliance from a lower security interface to a higher security interface. The outside hosts connect to the global IP address on a specific TCP or UDP port, which the security appliance redirects to the internal server, as shown in

Figure 5-15. The security appliance redirects traffic destined for 209.165.200.225 on TCP port 80 to 192.168.10.10. Similarly, any traffic destined for 209.165.200.225 on TCP port 25 is redirected to 192.168.10.20.

Figure 5-15 *Port Redirection*

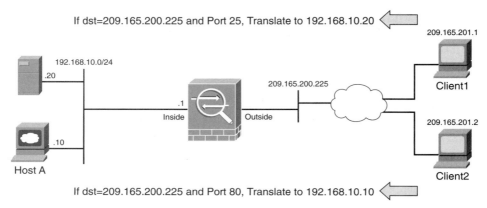

Port redirection is set up by using the **static** command (similar to static NAT) followed by the name of the Layer 4 protocol, as shown in the following command syntax:

```
static (real_ifc,mapped_ifc) {tcp | udp} {mapped_ip | interface} mapped_port {real_ip
real_port [netmask mask]} [dns] [norandomseq] [[tcp] [max_conns [emb_lim]] [udp
udp_max_conns]
```

The **static** command for port redirection uses most of the same arguments listed in Table 5-12. The **tcp** and **udp** keywords, after the real and mapped interface names, specify which protocol to consider for address translation. The security appliance allows the use of either a dedicated IP address or the global interface's IP address for port redirection.

When port redirection is set up to use the public interface's IP address, the security appliance uses the same address for:

- Address translation for the traffic traversing through the security appliance.
- Traffic destined for the security appliance.

Example 5-37 shows how to configure static PAT for an internal web server located at 192.168.10.10 and an e-mail server hosted at 192.168.10.20. The web and e-mail clients on the public network will connect to the server using the public IP address of the security appliance using the default web (TCP port 80) and SMTP (TCP port 25) ports.

Example 5-37 *Configuration of Static PAT*

```
Chicago(config)# static (inside,outside) tcp interface www 192.168.10.10 www netmask
  255.255.255.255
Chicago(config)# static (inside,outside) tcp interface smtp 192.168.10.20 smtp
  netmask 255.255.255.255
```

NOTE   If an inside host is configured for static PAT, then any packet sent from the host will also use the translated address. The security appliance creates a NAT and global entries for that host.

Dynamic Port Address Translation

Using dynamic PAT, the security appliance builds the address translation table by looking at the Layer 3 and Layer 4 header information. It is the most commonly deployed scenario because multiple inside machines can get outside connectivity using one global IP address. In dynamic PAT, the security appliance uses the source and destination IP addresses, the source and destination ports, and the IP protocol information (TCP or UDP) to translate an inside host.

Similar to setting up a static NAT entry, dynamic PAT also uses **nat** and **global** commands to configure address translation. You can choose to use either a dedicated global IP address or the public interface's IP address in this type. The complete command syntax for both commands follows:

```
nat (real_ifc) nat_id local_ip [mask [dns] [outside] [[tcp] tcp_max_conns
    [emb_limit] [norandomseq]]] [udp udp_max_conns]
global (mapped_ifc) nat_id global_ip | interface
```

Figure 5-16 illustrates a security appliance set up to translate the inside network, 192.168.10.0/24, by using the IP address on the outside interface, 209.165.200.225. The relevant configuration is shown in Example 5-38.

Figure 5-16 *Dynamic PAT*

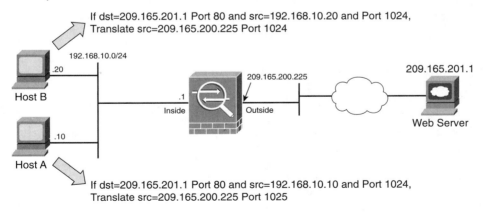

Example 5-38 *Configuration of Dynamic PAT*

```
Chicago(config)# nat (inside) 1 192.168.10.0 255.255.255.0
Chicago(config)# global (outside) 1 interface
INFO: outside interface address added to PAT pool
```

NOTE	If both dynamic NAT and dynamic PAT are set up using the same nat_id, then the security appliance tries to allocate addresses from the pool of addresses first. When all the addresses have been allocated, the security appliance starts using dynamic PAT.

The security appliance supports up to 65,535 PAT translations using a single address. The PAT addresses time out every 30 seconds of inactivity to accommodate as many hosts as possible.

Policy NAT/PAT

Policy NAT/PAT translates the IP address of the packets passing through the security appliance only if those packets match the configured criterion or policy. The policy is defined by using ACLs. The ACL matches traffic against the source and the destination IP addresses. As illustrated in Figure 5-17, an administrator has defined a policy to translate the source IP address to 209.165.200.226 if the packets originate 192.168.10.10 and are destined for 209.165.201.1. Similarly, if the packets are sourced from 192.168.10.10 and destined for 209.165.201.2, the security appliance will change the source IP address to 209.165.200.227.

Figure 5-17 *Policy-Based Network Address Translation*

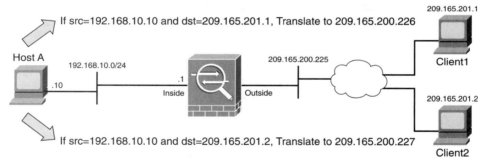

Policy NAT/PAT can be set up for static and dynamic address translations. An ACL identifies what traffic triggers the NAT or PAT engine for address translation. For static policy NAT/PAT, the security appliance uses the **static** command, as shown in the following syntax:

```
static (real_ifc,mapped_ifc) {tcp | udp} {mapped_ip | interface} mapped_port
   {real_ip real_port [netmask mask]} | {access-list access_list_name} [dns]
   [norandomseq] [[tcp] [max_conns [emb_lim]] [udp udp_max_conns]
```

For dynamic policy NAT/PAT, the security appliance uses both **nat** and **global** statements. The complete command syntax for these commands follows:

```
nat (real_ifc) nat_id access-list access_list_name [dns] [outside] [[tcp]
   tcp_max_conns [emb_limit] [norandomseq]]] [udp udp_max_conns]

global (mapped_ifc) nat_id {global_ip [-global_ip] [netmask global_mask]} |
   interface
```

Example 5-39 shows the configuration of the network scenario depicted in Figure 5-17. The administrator creates two ACLs to identify the traffic coming from 192.168.10.10 and

destined for 209.165.201.1 and 209.165.201.2. The ACLs are linked to the two **nat**
statements that are bound to the two **global** commands.

Example 5-39 *Configuration of Policy PAT*

```
Chicago(config)# access-list policy_PAT1 permit ip host 192.168.10.10 host
   209.165.201.1
Chicago(config)# access-list policy_PAT2 permit ip host 192.168.10.10 host
   209.165.201.2
Chicago(config)# nat (inside) 1 access-list policy_PAT1
Chicago(config)# nat (inside) 2 access-list policy_PAT2
Chicago(config)# global (outside) 1 209.165.200.226
Chicago(config)# global (outside) 2 209.165.200.227
```

The security appliance can be very granular in translating source IP addresses even when
static NAT needs to be defined. As shown in Example 5-40, an administrator allows the real
source IP address (192.168.10.190) to be changed to 209.165.200.227 only if traffic is
destined for 209.165.201.10. The same static entry will also change the destination address
from 209.165.200.227 to 192.168.10.190 if traffic is sourced from host 209.165.201.10.

Example 5-40 *Configuration of Static Policy NAT*

```
Chicago(config)# access-list static_NAT extended permit ip host 192.168.10.190 host
   209.165.201.10
Chicago(config)# static (inside,outside) 209.165.200.227   access-list static_NAT
```

NOTE   If host-based static policy NAT entries are defined, the access list should contain only host-
based source addresses to maintain the one-to-one mapping.

Bypassing Address Translation

Cisco ASA does not require an address translation policy to be created when the inside
machines need to access the hosts on the outside network. This is a necessity of many firewalls,
including the Cisco PIX Firewall running a pre-7.0 OS image. The security appliance translates
the addresses if the packets match a NAT/PAT policy. If the packets do not match a policy, they
are sent out without being translated. However, if an organizational security policy mandates
that a translation policy should be defined before hosts can send traffic through Cisco ASA, you
can enable the **nat-control** command. If implemented, any traffic trying to pass through the
security appliance without address translation will be dropped.

Cisco ASA allows the traffic to pass through it without being translated even if the **nat-
control** command is enabled. This way, if the security appliance is translating all traffic
flowing through it and you do not want some hosts or networks to be translated, you can
use the following methods to bypass address translation:

- Identity NAT
- NAT exemption

Identity NAT

Identity NAT bypasses address translation if traffic is initiated by a host or subnet address classified as the source. Consequently, an outside host cannot initiate traffic unless there is an entry in the translation table. Identity NAT is enabled by using the **nat 0** command followed by the host or subnet address to be bypassed for address translation, as shown in Example 5-41. The security appliance will not translate the outbound connections from the inside host, 192.168.10.200.

Example 5-41 *NAT Bypass Using Identity NAT*

```
Chicago(config)# nat (inside) 0 192.168.10.200 255.255.255.255
    nat 0 192.168.10.200 will be identity translated for outbound
```

NAT Exemption

NAT exemption disables address translation for the traffic identified by the hosts in an ACL. NAT exemption allows both inside and outside hosts to initiate traffic without being translated into a different address. In Figure 5-18, a security appliance is translating the inside network to its outside interface using dynamic PAT. However, the administrator does not want to change the addresses when the two e-mail servers send packets to each other. To accomplish this, NAT exemption is deployed, which uses an ACL called Email_Servers to identify the two servers. The ACL is then linked to the **nat 0** statement bound to the inside interface, as shown in Example 5-42.

Figure 5-18 *NAT Exemption*

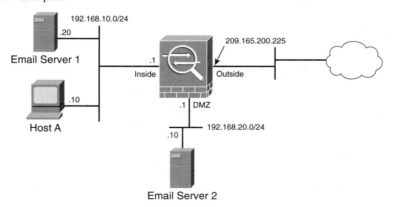

Example 5-42 *NAT Bypass Using NAT Exemption*

```
Chicago(config)# access-list Email_Servers permit ip host 192.168.10.20 host
    192.168.20.10
Chicago(config)# nat (inside) 0 access-list Email_Servers
Chicago(config)# nat (inside) 1 192.168.10.0 255.255.255.0
Chicago(config)# global (outside) 1 interface
```

The main difference between identity NAT and NAT exemption is that with identity NAT, the traffic must be sourced from the address specified with the **nat 0** statement, whereas with NAT exemption, traffic can be initiated by the hosts on either side of the security appliance. NAT exemption is a preferred method to bypass traffic when it is flowing over a VPN tunnel. This will be discussed in Chapter 15, "Site-to-Site IPSec VPNs," and Chapter 16, "Remote Access VPNs."

NOTE   In NAT exemption, the ACL cannot contain TCP/UDP port numbers.

NAT Order of Operation

In many network scenarios, it is necessary to configure different types of address translation on a single security appliance. To adapt to those scenarios, the security appliance needs to prioritize certain NAT rules over others to make sure that it knows what to do if there is a conflict. You also need to understand this order, shown next, to ensure that rules are properly set up:

1 **NAT exemption**—When multiple NAT types/rules are set up, the security appliance tries to match traffic against the ACL in the NAT exemption rules. If there are overlapping entries in the ACL, the security appliance analyzes the ACEs until a match is found.

2 **Static NAT**—If there is no match found in the NAT exemption rules, the security appliance analyzes the static NAT entries in sequential order to determine a match.

3 **Static PAT**—If the security appliance does not find a match in NAT exemption or static NAT entries, it goes through the static PAT entries until it locates a match.

4 **Policy NAT/PAT**—The security appliance evaluates the policy NAT entries if it is still not able to find a match on the packet flow.

5 **Identity NAT**—The security appliance tries to find a match using the identity NAT statement, if one is set up to do so.

6 **Dynamic NAT**—If the security appliance fails to find a match using the first five rules, it checks to see if the packets need to be translated using dynamic NAT.

7 **Dynamic PAT**—The packets are checked against the dynamic PAT rules as the last resort, if all the previously mentioned rules fail.

If the security appliance does not find an exact match using all the rules and policies and if nat-control is enabled, it drops the packet and generates a syslog message indicating such an event has occurred.

Integrating ACLs and NAT

Cisco ASA integrates two core features, ACLs and NAT, to provide enhanced network security. In Figure 5-19, both features are implemented on a security appliance.

Figure 5-19 *ACL and NAT*

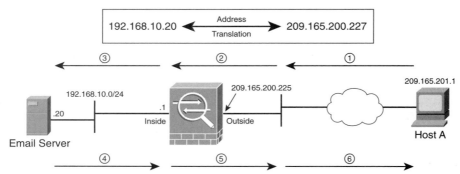

A host on the public network (209.165.201.1) sends a packet to an inside e-mail server. The security appliance handles the packet in the following sequence:

1 The packet arrives at the outside interface of the security appliance with a source address of 209.165.201.1 and a destination address of 209.165.200.227. Cisco ASA checks the inbound ACL to make sure that it is allowed in.

2 If the packet is permitted to pass through, the security appliance sends the packet to the NAT engine to determine if the addresses need to be translated. The destination address is changed to 192.168.10.20.

3 The security appliance forwards the packet to the outbound ACL to determine if it is allowed to leave the security appliance.

4 The e-mail server replies to Host A using a source IP address of 192.168.10.20.

5 The packet is forwarded to the NAT engine, which changes the source IP address to 209.165.200.227.

6 The security appliance sends the packet to Host A.

As depicted in Example 5-43, the e-mail server is being translated from 192.168.10.20 to 209.165.200.227 using static NAT. An ACL, named **inbound_traffic_on_outside,** allows any outside host to establish an SMTP connection to the e-mail server using the public IP address. The ACL is then applied to the outside interface to filter the inbound packets.

Example 5-43 *Configuration of NAT and Interface ACLs*

```
Chicago(config)# static (inside,outside) 209.165.200.227 192.168.10.20 netmask
  255.255.255.255
Chicago(config)# access-list inbound_traffic_on_outside extended permit tcp any
  host 209.165.200.227 eq smtp
Chicago(config)# access-group inbound_traffic_on_outside in interface outside
```

NOTE   Address translation is not supported in transparent mode. The **nat** and **static** commands are solely used to set embryonic and connection limits.

DNS Doctoring

In many network deployments, the DNS servers and DNS clients are located on different subnets which are connected through the security appliance, setup for address translation. This is illustrated in Figure 5-20. The web server (www.securemeinc.com) and the web clients are toward the inside network, whereas the DNS server is on the outside network. The real IP address of the server is 192.168.10.20 and the translated public address is 209.265.200.227.

Figure 5-20 *DNS and NAT Without DNS Doctoring*

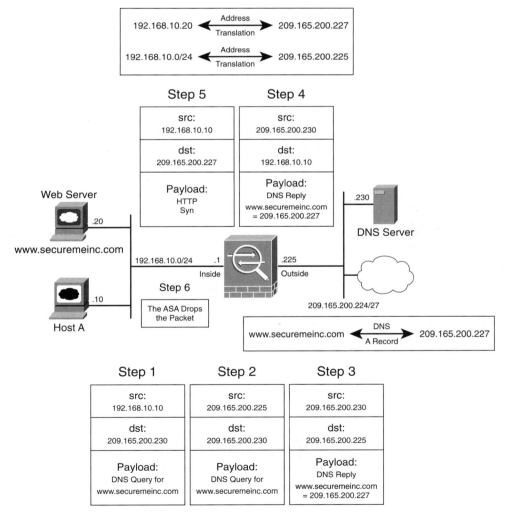

The problem arises when a web client (Host A) tries to access the web server using its host name. In this scenario, the following sequence of events occurs:

1 Host A sends a request to the DNS server, inquiring about the IP address of the web server.

2 The source IP address is translated to 209.165.200.225 using dynamic PAT.

3 The DNS server replies with the translated IP address of the web server (209.165.200.227) as a type A DNS record.

4 The security appliance translates the destination IP address to 192.168.10.10 (Host A's IP address).

5 The client, not knowing that the web server is on the same subnet, tries to connect to the public IP address.

6 The security appliance drops the packets, because it does not allow packet redirection on the same interface.

The DNS doctoring feature of Cisco ASA inspects the data payload of the DNS replies and changes the type A DNS record (IP address sent by the DNS server) to an address specified in the NAT configuration. In Figure 5-21, the security appliance modifies the IP address in the payload from 209.165.200.227 to 192.168.10.20 (Step 4) before forwarding the DNS reply to the client. The client uses this address to connect to the web server.

The DNS doctoring feature can be enabled by adding the **dns** keyword to the **static** and/or **nat** commands that are translating the real IP address of the server. In Example 5-44, a static NAT entry is set up to translate a real IP address from 192.168.10.20 to a global IP address, 209.165.200.227. The **dns** keyword is specified to enable DNS doctoring for this server.

Example 5-44 *Configuration of DNS Doctoring*

```
Chicago(config)# static (inside,outside) 209.165.200.227 192.168.10.20 netmask
   255.255.255.255 dns
```

NOTE   The security appliance also supports DNS doctoring using the **alias** command. However, the recommended method is to use DNS doctoring with **static** and **nat** commands, because the **alias** command will be deprecated in the future.

DNS doctoring can also be set up for the outside NAT connections. This is useful in deployments where the DNS server and the content (such as web or e-mail) server reside on the outside network and the clients are located on the inside network, as shown in Figure 5-22.

Figure 5-21 *DNS and NAT with DNS Doctoring*

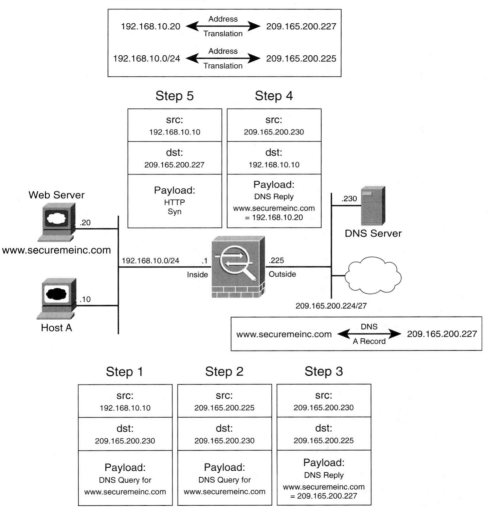

The following sequence of events takes place when a host on the inside network connects to a web server on the outside network:

1 Host A sends a DNS query to the server to resolve www.securemeinc.com.

2 The security appliance translates the source IP address to 209.165.200.225 before forwarding the packet to the DNS server.

3 The DNS server replies with the IP address of the web server, 209.165.201.20, in the data payload.

Figure 5-22 *DNS Doctoring for Outside NAT*

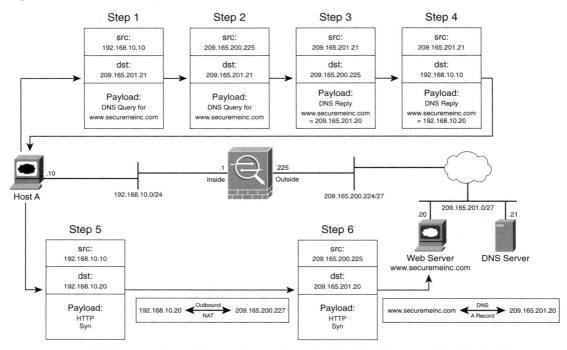

4   The security appliance changes the embedded IP address to 192.168.10.20 before it forwards the reply to Host A.

5   The client sends a TCP SYN packet to connect to the web server using as the destination IP address 192.168.10.20.

6   As the packet passes through, the security appliance changes the destination IP address to 209.165.201.20. The packet gets routed to the Internet before it reaches the web server.

Example 5-45 shows the respective configuration of the security appliance to enable DNS doctoring for outside NAT.

Example 5-45 *Configuration of DNS Doctoring for Outside NAT*

```
Chicago(config)# static (outside,inside) 192.168.10.20 209.165.201.20 netmask
   255.255.255.255 dns
```

Monitoring Address Translations

Cisco ASA provides a rich set of **show** commands to monitor and troubleshoot issues related to address translation. The most important monitoring command is **show xlate**, which displays the real (local) address and the mapped (global) IP address assigned to a host. In Example 5-46, the security appliance is translating an inside host located at

192.168.10.10 to 209.165.200.225 using PAT. Cisco ASA masks the source port number from 11085 (local) to 1024 (global) before forwarding the packet to the egress interface. The security appliance also shows the maximum number of simultaneous translations (10) it has performed since the last reboot and the current active translations (1).

Example 5-46 *Output of* **show xlate**

```
Chicago(config)# show xlate
1 in use, 10 most used
PAT Global 209.165.200.225(1024) Local 192.168.10.10(11085)
```

TIP   You can add the **debug** option at the end of **show xlate** to display the interfaces that the translations are bound to.

The **show local-host** command can display the connection and translation statistics using a single command, as shown in Example 5-47. It displays the network states of each host on the local network. The TCP and UDP flow counts exhibit the session going through the security appliance from that particular host.

Example 5-47 *Output of* **show local-host**

```
Chicago# show local-host
Interface inside: 1 active, 1 maximum active, 0 denied
local host: <192.168.10.10>,
    TCP flow count/limit = 1/unlimited
    TCP embryonic count to (from) host = 0 (0)
    TCP intercept watermark = unlimited
    UDP flow count/limit = 0/unlimited

  Xlate:
    PAT Global 209.165.200.225(1024) Local 192.168.10.10(11085)

  Conn:
    TCP out 209.165.200.240:23 in 192.168.10.10:11085 idle 0:00:13 bytes 87 flags UIO
```

NOTE   The **show local-host all** command can be used to see both the connections made to and from the security appliance and the connections made through the security appliance.

Summary

This chapter explained the features available to protect the critical network resources by using two important features: network access control and network address translation. Other features such as content filtering and DNS doctoring were discussed to exhibit the robustness of Cisco ASA. This chapter also discussed a number of **show** commands to monitor and troubleshoot these features.

This chapter covers the following topics:

- Configuring static routes
- Configuring and troubleshooting RIP
- Configuring and troubleshooting OSPF
- Configuring and troubleshooting IP multicast routing

CHAPTER 6

IP Routing

A routing decision is the process where a network device identifies which interface and gateway should be used to forward packets for a specific destination. This decision can be made by using dynamic routing protocols or static entries configured on such devices. This chapter covers the different routing capabilities of Cisco ASA. Cisco ASA supports static route entries, Routing Information Protocol (RIP), and Open Shortest Path First (OSPF). This chapter also covers IP multicast routing capabilities.

Configuring Static Routes

Deployment and configuration of static routes is appropriate when the Cisco ASAs cannot dynamically build a route to a specific destination. The device to which the Cisco ASA is forwarding the packets might not support any dynamic routing protocols or the deployment is basic and uncomplicated. Dynamic routing protocols, such as RIP and OSPF, must be considered if the network is fairly large and complex. Static routes are easy to configure. However, they do not scale well in large environments.

It is strongly recommended that you have a complete understanding of your network topology before configuring routing in your Cisco ASA. A best practice is to have a network topology diagram on hand that you can refer to when configuring your Cisco ASA.

Static routes are configured using the **route** command, as shown in the following syntax:

```
route interface network mask gateway metric [tunneled]
```

Table 6-1 details the options available within the **route** command.

Table 6-1   **route** *Command Options*

Option	Description
interface	The specific interface name for which the route will apply. It must match the interface name configured by the **nameif** command under the specific interface configuration section.
network	The address of the remote network or host. If configuring a default route, use 0.0.0.0 or just 0.
mask	The subnet mask of the remote network. If configuring a default route, use 0.0.0.0 or just 0 as the subnet mask.

continues

Table 6-1 **route** *Command Options (Continued)*

Option	Description
gateway	The gateway to which the ASA will forward the packets.
metric	The number of hops between the ASA and the destination network or host.
tunneled	This option is used to configure a tunnel default gateway. This option can be used only with default gateways.

Figure 6-1 shows a simple static route topology that includes a Cisco ASA with two interfaces configured (outside and inside).

Figure 6-1 *Basic IP Routing Configuration Using Static Routes*

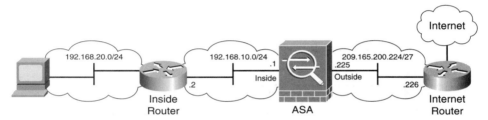

In the example shown in Figure 6-1, a static default route is configured for the Cisco ASA to be able to forward packets to the Internet through the Internet router. The **route** statement will look like this:

```
route outside 0.0.0.0 0.0.0.0 209.165.200.226 1
```

NOTE You can configure up to three default routes for traffic load-balancing. They should all point to the same interface.

A separate static route needs to be configured for the Cisco ASA to be able to reach the private network 192.168.20.0/24. This route entry must be configured as follows:

```
route inside 192.168.20.0 255.255.255.0 192.168.10.2 1
```

The **show route** command can be used to view the Cisco ASA's routing table and verify the configuration. Here is an example of the output of the **show route** command after configuring the previously mentioned static route statements:

```
Chicago# show route
S    0.0.0.0 0.0.0.0 [1/0] via 209.165.200.226, outside
C    192.168.10.0 255.255.255.0 is directly connected, inside
S    192.168.20.0 255.255.255.0 [1/0] via 192.168.10.2, inside
C    209.165.200.224 255.255.255.224 is directly connected, outside
```

The letter S by each route statement indicates that it is a statically configured route entry. The letter C indicates that it is a directly connected route. The first number in the brackets is the administrative distance of the information source; the second number is the metric for the route. Administrative distance is the feature used by routing devices to select the best path when there are two or more different routes to the same destination from two different routing protocols.

TIP   The **show** route command is useful when troubleshooting any routing problems. It provides not only the gateway's IP address for each route entry, but also the interface that is connected to that gateway.

The **show route** command can be used with an interface name to display only the routes going out of the specified interface.

Figure 6-2 shows another simple static route topology with the addition of a demilitarized zone (DMZ).

Figure 6-2   *IP Routing Configuration Using Static Routes to a Network on a DMZ Interface*

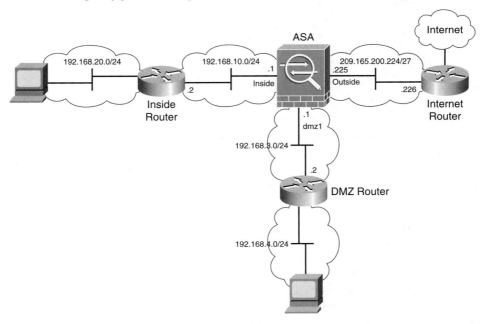

To forward IP packets to the 192.168.4.0/24 network, a static route must be configured as follows (assuming that the DMZ interface is labeled dmz1):

```
route dmz1 192.168.4.0 255.255.255.0 192.168.3.2 1
```

Earlier, the **tunneled** keyword on a default gateway was mentioned. This option configures a tunnel default gateway. When configured, the Cisco ASA forwards all tunnel (decrypted) traffic to the specified device. This is similar to the tunnel default gateway option on the Cisco VPN 3000 Series Concentrators. Chapter 15, "Site-to-Site IPSec VPNs," covers the use of the tunnel default gateway feature.

NOTE   Dynamic routing protocols are not supported when the security Cisco ASA is running in multimode. Cisco ASA has the ability to create multiple security contexts (virtual firewalls), as covered in Chapter 9, "Security Contexts."

A Cisco ASA configured with dynamic routing protocols can advertise configured static routes to its neighbors or peers. This process is called redistribution of static routes. This methodology is discussed later in this chapter under the "Configuring the Cisco ASA as an ASBR" section.

RIP

RIP is a fairly old Interior Gateway Protocol (IGP), but it is still deployed in many networks. It is typically used in small and homogeneous networks. RIP is a distance-vector routing protocol, and it is defined in RFC 1058, "Routing Information Protocol." Its second version is defined in RFC 2453, "RIP Version 2."

RIP uses broadcast or multicast packets—depending on the version—to communicate with its neighbors and exchange routing information. It uses the hop-count methodology to calculate its metric. *Hop count* is the number of routing devices that the packets forwarded by a router or a Cisco ASA (in this case) will traverse. RIP has a limit of 15 hops. A route to a network that is directly connected to the Cisco ASA has a metric of 0. However, a route with a metric reaching or exceeding 16 is considered unreachable.

Two versions of the RIP routing protocol are available (Cisco ASA supports both versions):

- **RIP version 1 (RIPv1)**—Does not support classless interdomain routing (CIDR) and variable-length subnet masks (VLSMs). VLSMs enable routing protocols to define different subnet masks for the same major network. For example, 10.0.0.0 is a Class A network. Its mask is 255.0.0.0. VLSM provides the ability to divide this network into smaller segments (i.e., 10.1.1.0/24, 10.1.2.0/24, etc.) Because RIPv1 does not support VLSM, no subnet mask information is present in its routing updates. RIP uses different techniques, such as holddowns, count-to-infinity, split horizon, and poison reverse, to prevent loops.

- **RIP version 2 (RIPv2)**—Supports CIDR and VLSMs. RIPv2 also converges faster than its predecessor. It also supports peer or neighbor authentication (plain-text or MD5 authentication), which provides additional security.

Configuring RIP

The configuration of the Cisco ASA is simple, but somewhat limited. Figure 6-3 illustrates the first example topology.

Figure 6-3 *Basic RIP Configuration*

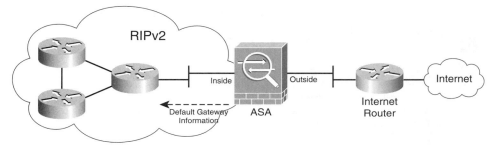

In the example shown in Figure 6-3, the Cisco ASA is connected to a router running RIPv2. This router is learning routes from two other routers. Subsequently, routes to all these networks are being advertised by the router connected to the Cisco ASA. The Cisco ASA is also injecting a default route to the inside router. Example 6-1 shows the necessary commands to configure RIPv2 on the Cisco ASA and to advertise a default route to the internal router.

Example 6-1 *Basic RIP Configuration*

```
Chicago# configure terminal
Chicago(config)# rip inside passive version 2
Chicago(config)# rip inside default version 2
Chicago(config)# exit
```

The **rip** command enables RIP on the Cisco ASA. The interface on which RIP will be enabled is also specified. The desired result is to learn the internal routes and advertise default route information. To do this, the **default** keyword is used. The **version** keyword specifies what RIP version is used. With the **passive** keyword, the Cisco ASA interface listens for RIP routing packets and uses that information to update its routing table, but it does not advertise any routing updates through the specified interface.

NOTE   Use the **clear configure rip** command to remove all the RIP related commands from the Cisco ASA.

The example shown in Figure 6-4 demonstrates how RIPv2 and RIPv1 are configured on two separate interfaces (inside and outside, in this example).

Figure 6-4 *Configuring RIPv1 and RIPv2 on Two Different Interfaces*

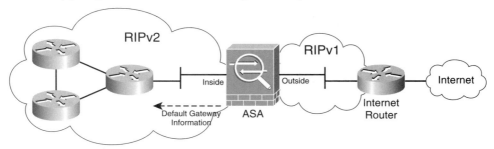

In the example shown in Figure 6-4, the inside interface is configured for RIPv2, as previously explained. Additionally, the Cisco ASA is learning RIPv1 routes on its outside interface from the Internet router. The commands needed for this configuration are shown in Example 6-2.

Example 6-2 *Configuring RIPv1 and RIPv2 on Two Different Interfaces*

```
Chicago# configure terminal
Chicago(config)# rip inside passive version 2
Chicago(config)# rip inside default version 2
Chicago(config)# rip outside passive version 1
Chicago(config)# exit
```

RIPv1 does not support authentication. Cisco ASA supports two modes of RIPv2 authentication: plain-text authentication and Message Digest 5 (MD5) authentication.

TIP   A best practice is to use MD5 instead of plain-text authentication, because MD5 authentication provides a higher level of security.

RIP authentication using MD5 is added in Figure 6-5. Example 6-3 shows the necessary commands to make this possible.

Figure 6-5 *RIPv2 MD5 Authentication*

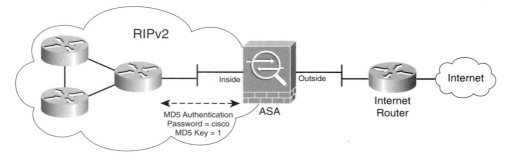

Example 6-3 *Configuring RIPv2 MD5 Authentication*

```
Chicago# configure terminal
Chicago(config)# rip inside default version 2 authentication md5 cisco 1
Chicago(config)# exit
```

The word cisco is the MD5 password in this example. The number 1 is the RIPv2 authentication key identification value. This key ID can be configured with a number from 0 to 255, but it must match the one in use on the peer router.

Verifying the Configuration

As mentioned earlier in this chapter, the **show route** command displays the routing table. With this command, you can also verify that the correct routes are being learned by the Cisco ASA via RIP. Example 6-4 shows the output of the Cisco ASA routing table while learning several routes via RIP from its peers.

Example 6-4 *Output of the Routing Table Showing Routes Learned via RIP*

```
Chicago# show route
R    0.0.0.0 0.0.0.0 [1/0] via 209.165.200.226, outside
C    192.168.10.0 255.255.255.0 is directly connected, inside
R    192.168.20.0 255.255.255.0 [1/0] via 192.168.10.2, inside
R    192.168.13.0 255.255.255.0 [2/0] via 192.168.10.2, inside
C    209.165.200.224 255.255.255.224 is directly connected, outside
```

Notice the letter R or C by each route entry. The letter R indicates that the route is learned via RIP; C indicates that it is directly connected.

Troubleshooting RIP

This section includes several commands and techniques that you can use while troubleshooting different issues that may arise throughout your deployment of RIP. A number of scenarios are provided to exemplify these troubleshooting techniques.

Scenario 1: RIP Version Mismatch

Using the topology illustrated in Figure 6-5, the internal router was intentionally configured with the incorrect RIP version. The Cisco ASA was configured with RIPv2 on the inside interface (as previously shown) and the internal router was configured with RIPv1. The output of the **show route** command does not display any routes learned via RIP. Example 6-5 shows the output of this command.

Example 6-5 *Output of* **show route** *Command Missing RIP Routes*

```
Chicago# show route
C    192.168.10.0 255.255.255.0 is directly connected, inside
C    209.165.200.224 255.255.255.224 is directly connected, outside
```

The command **debug rip** is used as a troubleshooting tool for this problem, as demonstrated in Example 6-6.

Example 6-6 *Output of* **debug rip** *Showing Incorrect RIP Version During Negotiation*

```
Chicago# debug rip
debug rip  enabled at level 1
Chicago# RIP: interface inside sending v2 update to 224.0.0.9
RIP: received packet from interface inside [pif=2] (192.168.10.2:520)
RIP: interface inside received v1 update from 192.168.10.2
```

In the highlighted line, the router sends the incorrect RIP version. The solution to this problem is to configure RIP version 2 on the internal router.

Scenario 2: RIP Authentication Mismatch

The topology shown in Figure 6-5 is also used in this example. The internal router and the Cisco ASA were configured to perform RIP authentication using MD5. The MD5 password was configured incorrectly in the Cisco ASA. The router is configured with an MD5 password of cisco and the Cisco ASA was configured with cisco123. Example 6-7 shows the output of **debug ip rip** on the router, which shows that there is a problem with MD5 authentication.

Example 6-7 *Output of* **debug ip rip** *on the Router While the Incorrect MD5 Password Was Configured*

```
Router# debug ip rip
2d09h: RIP: received packet with MD5 authentication
2d09h: RIP: ignored v2 packet from 192.168.10.1 (invalid authentication)
```

This message also appears if the incorrect authentication method or mode is selected.

Scenario 3: Multicast or Broadcast Packets Blocked

RIPv1 uses broadcast packets and RIPv2 uses multicast packets, as previously discussed. If broadcast or multicast packets (respectively) are blocked, the Cisco ASA will never be able to successfully establish a RIP neighbor relationship with its peers. The **debug rip** command is also useful to troubleshoot this problem. Example 6-8 shows the output of **debug rip** while RIPv2 multicast packets were being blocked.

Example 6-8 *Output of* **debug rip** *While Multicast Packets Are Being Dropped or Blocked*

```
Chicago# debug rip
debug rip  enabled at level 1
RIP: interface inside sending v2 update to 224.0.0.9
RIP: interface inside sending v2 update to 224.0.0.9
RIP: interface inside sending v2 update to 224.0.0.9
RIP: interface inside sending v2 update to 224.0.0.9
```

As you can see from this example, the Cisco ASA is sending the RIPv2 packets to the address 224.0.0.9 without receiving anything back from its peers. You will also see this behavior when RIP is not enabled on any routing device on that segment.

TIP	You can also ping the multicast address of 224.0.0.9 to verify that packets are not blocked.

Scenario 4: Correct Configuration and Behavior

It is impossible to troubleshoot a problem if you are not familiar with the behavior of the device(s) to determine whether or not they are configured correctly. Example 6-9 includes the output of **debug rip** when all devices are configured correctly. Again, the Cisco ASA is configured to support RIPv1 on its outside interface; support RIPv2 on its inside interface; broadcast a default route to the inside router; and use MD5 authentication for RIPv2 learned routes.

Example 6-9 *Output of* **debug rip**—*Correct Configuration*

```
Chicago# debug rip
Chicago# RIP: received packet from interface inside [pif=2] (192.168.10.2:520)
RIP: interface inside received v2 update from 192.168.10.2
RIP: update contains 2 routes
RIP: interface inside sending v2 update to 224.0.0.9
```

The highlighted line shows that a RIPv2 update was received on the Cisco ASA and it contained two routes from the router 192.168.10.2. Example 6-10 shows the complete routing table, showing the routes learned via both peers.

Example 6-10 *Routing Table—Correct Configuration*

```
Chicago# show route
R     0.0.0.0 0.0.0.0 [1/0] via 209.165.200.226, outside
C     192.168.10.0 255.255.255.0 is directly connected, inside
R     192.168.20.0 255.255.255.0 [1/0] via 192.168.10.2, inside
R     192.168.13.0 255.255.255.0 [2/0] via 192.168.10.2, inside
C     209.165.200.224 255.255.255.224 is directly connected, outside
```

OSPF

The OSPF routing protocol was drafted by the IGP Working Group of the Internet Engineering Task Force (IETF). It was developed because RIP was not able to scale for large, heterogeneous networks. The OSPF specification is defined in RFC 2338, "OSPF Version 2." It is based on the Shortest Path First (SPF) algorithm (usually referred to as the Dijkstra algorithm, per its author's name).

OSPF is a link-state routing protocol. It sends information about attached interfaces, metrics used, and other variables to its peers or neighbors. This information is called link-state advertisements (LSAs). They are sent to all the peers within a specific hierarchical area.

OSPF operates in hierarchies of separate autonomous systems. These autonomous systems can be divided into groups of contiguous networks called areas. Routers that are part of more than one area are referred to as Area Border Routers (ABRs). Figure 6-6 illustrates an example of this concept.

Figure 6-6   *Areas in OSPF*

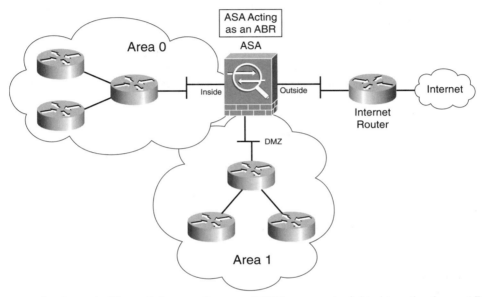

As shown in Figure 6-6, more than one OSPF area can be joined together by an ABR. On the other hand, an OSPF backbone, OSPF area 0, must be present to propagate routing information to all other areas. The Cisco ASA can be configured to act as an ABR. It will provide not only connectivity, but also security while performing type 3 LSA filtering. Type 3 LSAs refer to summary links and are sent by ABRs to advertise destinations outside the area. The OSPF ABR type 3 LSA filtering feature gives the user improved control of route distribution between OSPF areas. This feature also provides the capability of hiding the private networks by using Network Address Translation (NAT) without advertising them.

Figure 6-7 provides an example of how the Cisco ASA can be configured as an ABR and provide LSA type 3 filtering.

Figure 6-7   *Cisco ASA OSPF LSA Type 3 Filtering*

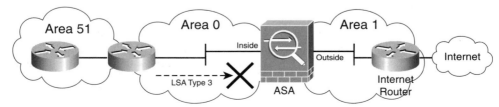

NOTE   If the Cisco ASA is configured as an Autonomous System Boundary Router (ASBR) in a private network, it will propagate Type 5 LSAs to the entire autonomous system, including public areas. Type 5 LSAs define external routes to the autonomous system. This is not a recommended security practice because this will cause all private networks to be externally advertised.

NOTE   The **ospf database-filter all out** command can be used to filter out all outgoing LSAs to an OSPF interface during synchronization and flooding.

The following section provides different sample configurations explaining all the OSPF features supported by Cisco ASA.

Configuring OSPF

Cisco ASA supports several OSPF features and capabilities. The following summarizes the Cisco ASA OSPF support:

- Intra-area, interarea, and external (Type 1 and Type 2) routes
- Support to act as a designated router (DR)
- Support to act as a backup designated router (BDR)
- Support to act as an ABR
- Support to act as an ASBR, with route redistribution between OSPF processes including OSPF, static, and connected routes
- Virtual links
- OSPF authentication (both clear-text and MD5 authentication)
- Stub areas and not-so-stubby areas (NSSAs)
- ABR type 3 LSA filtering
- OSPF **neighbor** command and dynamic routing over VPN
- Load balancing between a maximum of three peers on a single interface, using equal-cost multipath (ECMP) routes

The following sections provide configuration examples for most of these features.

Enabling OSPF

The topology illustrated in Figure 6-8 is used in this example. It includes a Cisco ASA connected to a router named R1 on its inside interface. This router is also connected to two other routers (R2 and R3).

Figure 6-8 *Basic OSPF Configuration*

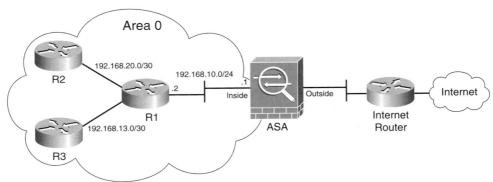

In this first example, the Cisco ASA, R1, R2, and R3 are all configured in area 0.

To initially configure OSPF, perform these tasks:

Step 1 Create an OSPF routing process.

To enable OSPF on the Cisco ASA, creating an OSPF routing process:

```
Chicago# configure terminal
Chicago(config)# router ospf 1
```

The number 1 is used as an identification parameter for the OSPF routing process. This number does not have to match the peer's OSPF process because it has only local significance. It can be configured with a value from 1 to 65,535. A unique value must be allocated for each OSPF routing process within the Cisco ASA.

Step 2 Define the interface(s) on which OSPF will run.

The **network** command specifies the interfaces that will run OSPF. Further-more, it specifies the area to be associated with that interface. You can use the network address or the address of the interface where you want to enable OSPF. Use the **network** command while enabling OSPF on the inside interface of the Cisco ASA:

```
Chicago# configure terminal
Chicago(config)# router ospf 1
Chicago(config-router)# network 192.168.10.0 255.255.255.0 area 0
Chicago(config-router)# exit
Chicago(config)# exit
```

In this example, the **network** command is added to the configuration. It is followed by the network address and a 24-bit mask. It also shows that this interface has been added to area 0. The OSPF peer must also be configured for area 0.

Note	Unlike the Cisco I OS routers, the Cisco ASA **network** command does not use an inverse mask.

The routing table is as follows:

```
Chicago# show route
C    192.168.10.0 255.255.255.0 is directly connected, inside
C    209.165.200.224 255.255.255.224 is directly connected, outside
O    192.168.20.0 255.255.255.0 [110/11] via 192.168.10.2, 0:00:55,
     inside
O    192.168.13.0 255.255.255.0 [110/11] via 192.168.10.2, 0:00:55,
     inside
```

NOTE   The output of **show route** has two routes learned via OSPF on the inside interface of Cisco ASA. The first number in the brackets is the administrative distance of the information source. The second number is the metric for the route.

Virtual Links

All areas must talk to area 0 (the backbone area). There is the probability that this will not always be possible. However, in OSPF, a mechanism provides a solution for this problem. Virtual links can be configured to connect an area through a nonbackbone area. They can also be used to connect two parts of a segmented backbone through nonbackbone areas. To configure a virtual link on the Cisco ASA, use the following command syntax:

```
area area_id virtual-link router_id [authentication [message-digest | null]]
   [hello-interval seconds] [retransmit-interval seconds] [transmit-delay seconds]
   [dead-interval seconds] [authentication-key password] [message-digest-key
   id md5 password]
```

Figure 6-9 illustrates a network topology where a Cisco ASA is configured with a virtual link to a router located on a DMZ interface.

At first, the virtual link is down because the Cisco ASA does not know how to reach the router labeled DMZ-R2. All the LSAs in area 1 need to be flooded, and the shortest path first (SPF) algorithm must run within area 1 in order for the Cisco ASA to successfully reach DMZ-R2 through area 1. In this example, area 1 is the transit area. After the Cisco ASA can reach DMZ-R2, they try to form an adjacency across the virtual link. Once the Cisco ASA and the DMZ-R2 router become adjacent on the virtual link, DMZ-R2 becomes an ABR because it now has a link in area 0. Consequently, a summary LSA for the networks in area 0 and area 1 is created. Example 6-11 shows the Cisco ASA OSPF virtual link configuration.

Figure 6-9 *Virtual Link Example*

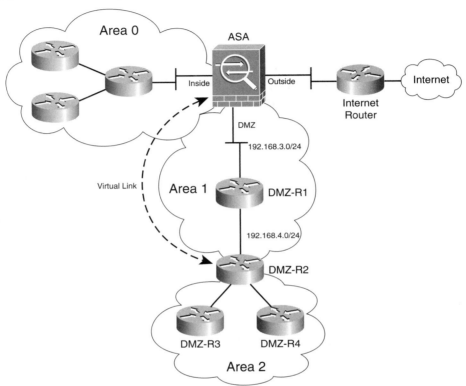

Example 6-11 *Virtual Link Configuration Example*

```
interface GigabitEthernet0/0
nameif outside
 security-level 0
 ip address 209.165.200.225 255.255.255.248
!
interface GigabitEthernet0/1
nameif inside
 security-level 100
 ip address 192.168.10.1 255.255.255.0
!
interface GigabitEthernet0/2
nameif DMZ
 security-level 50
 ip address 192.168.4.1 255.255.255.0
!
router ospf 1
 network 192.168.4.1 255.255.255.255 area 1
 network 192.168.10.0 255.255.255.0 area 0
 area 1 virtual-link 192.168.3.1
 log-adj-changes
```

In Example 6-11, the Cisco ASA is configured with a DMZ interface with the IP address of 192.168.4.1. DMZ-R2's IP address is 192.168.3.1. The output of the **show ospf virtual-links** is included in Example 6-12.

Example 6-12 *Output of* **show ospf virtual-links** *After Virtual Link Was Created*

```
Chicago# show ospf virtual-links
Virtual Link DMZ to router 192.168.3.1 is up
  Run as demand circuit
  DoNotAge LSA allowed.
  Transit area 1, via interface DMZ, Cost of using 10
  Transmit Delay is 1 sec, State UP,
  Timer intervals configured, Hello 10, Dead 40, Wait 40, Retransmit
```

Configuring OSPF Authentication

Cisco ASA supports both plain-text and MD5 OSPF authentication. MD5 authentication is recommended, because it is more secure than plain-text authentication. When configuring authentication, an entire area must be configured with the same type of authentication. For example, if area 1 is configured for authentication, all devices running OSPF must run the same type of authentication. Figure 6-10 includes an example of a Cisco ASA performing MD5 authentication on its inside interface. All routers and the Cisco ASA reside in area 0, and they must use the same authentication type and shared secret (password) to learn routes from each other.

Figure 6-10 *OSPF MD5 Authentication Example*

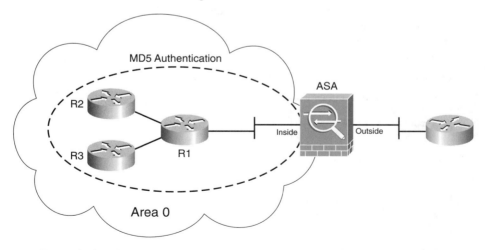

Example 6-13 includes the Cisco ASA configuration. The shared secret in use is cisco123. The Cisco ASA will only accept routes from the router labeled R1 if authentication is successful.

Example 6-13 *OSPF MD5 Authentication Configuration Example*

```
interface GigabitEthernet0/0
nameif outside
 security-level 0
 ip address 209.165.200.225 255.255.255.248
!
interface GigabitEthernet0/1
nameif inside
 security-level 100
 ip address 192.168.10.1 255.255.255.0
 ospf message-digest-key 1 md5 cisco123
 ospf authentication message-digest
!
interface GigabitEthernet0/2
nameif DMZ
 security-level 50
 ip address 192.168.4.1 255.255.255.0
 ospf message-digest-key 1 md5 cisco123
 ospf authentication message-digest
!
router ospf 1
 network 192.168.4.1 255.255.255.255 area 1
 network 192.168.10.0 255.255.255.0 area 0
 area 0 authentication message-digest
 area 1 authentication message-digest
 log-adj-changes
!
```

The Cisco ASA also provides plain-text authentication that can be configured under the Ethernet interfaces. Although plain-text authentication is less secure than MD5 authentication, it is sometimes used when communicating with Layer 3 devices that do not support MD5 authentication. Example 6-14 shows how to configure plain-text authentication.

Example 6-14 *OSPF Plain-Text Authentication Configuration Example*

```
interface GigabitEthernet0/0
nameif outside
 security-level 0
 ip address 209.165.200.225 255.255.255.248
!
interface GigabitEthernet0/1
nameif inside
 security-level 100
 ip address 192.168.10.1 255.255.255.0
 ospf authentication-key cisco123
 ospf authentication
!
interface GigabitEthernet0/2
nameif DMZ
 security-level 50
 ip address 192.168.4.1 255.255.255.0
 ospf authentication-key cisco123
 ospf authentication
```

Example 6-14 *OSPF Plain-Text Authentication Configuration Example (Continued)*

```
!
router ospf 1
  network 192.168.4.0 255.255.255.0 area 1
  network 192.168.10.0 255.255.255.0 area 0
  area 0 authentication
  area 1 authentication
  log-adj-changes
```

OSPF virtual links can also be authenticated using MD5 or plain-text authentication. Example 6-15 demonstrates how to enable MD5 authentication in the virtual link configuration previously discussed. The MD5 key ID value is 1 and the shared secret or password is cisco123.

Example 6-15 *Virtual Link MD5 Authentication Configuration Example*

```
router ospf 1
  network 192.168.4.1 255.255.255.255 area 1
  network 192.168.10.0 255.255.255.0 area 0
  area 1 virtual-link 192.168.3.1 authentication message-digest
  area 1 virtual-link 192.168.3.1 message-digest-key 1 md5 cisco123
  router-id 192.168.4.1
  log-adj-changes
```

NOTE   The authentication type in both areas should match.

Configuring the Cisco ASA as an ASBR

The Cisco ASA can be configured to act as an ASBR. It can perform route redistribution between different OSPF processes, static routes, or directly connected subnets. To configure redistribution, use the **redistribute** subcommand under the respective OSPF process by using the following command syntax:

```
redistribute static|connected [metric metric-value] [metric-type metric-type]
   [route-map name] [tag tag-value] [subnets]
redistribute ospf pid [metric metric-value] [metric-type metric-type] [route-map
   name] [tag tag-value ] [subnets] [match {internal | external [1|2] | nssa-external
   [1|2]}]
```

Table 6-2 lists all the options of the **redistribute** subcommand.

Table 6-2   **redistribute** *Subcommand Options*

Option	Description
connected	Redistributes directly connected subnets into OSPF
ospf	Redistributes routes from a different OSPF process
static	Redistributes static routes

continues

Table 6-2   **redistribute** *Subcommand Options (Continued)*

Option	Description
subnets	specifies that subnet information should be redistributed into OSPF
pid	Process ID of the OSPF process from which routes will be redistributed
metric-value	Metric used for the redistributed route
name	Identifier of a configured route map
metric-type	Used to select type 1 or type 2 external routes
tag-value	32-bit decimal value attached to each external route
external	Used to redistribute OSPF external routes
internal	Used to redistribute OSPF internal routes
nssa-external	Used to redistribute OSPF NSSA external routes

Example 6-16 shows how to redistribute all the static routes into OSPF.

Example 6-16 *Static Route Redistribution Example*

```
Chicago(config)# route inside 192.168.4.0 255.255.255.0 192.168.10.2 1
Chicago(config)# router ospf 1
Chicago(config-router)# network 192.168.10.0 255.255.255.0 area 0
Chicago(config-router)# redistribute static metric 10 subnets
```

A static routes is configured in Example 6-16. These are then redistributed into OSPF as shown in the highlighted line. The static routes are redistributed with a metric value of 10.

TIP   Use the **subnets** attribute to allow the Cisco ASA to consider any configured subnets. This is commonly used when redistributing other routing protocols into OSPF. Only classful routes are redistributed if you do not specify the **subnets** attribute.

Stub Areas and NSSAs

An ASBR advertises external routes throughout the OSPF autonomous system. However, in some situations, there is no need to advertise external routes into an area to reduce the size of the OSPF database. A *stub area* is an area that does not allow the advertisements of external routes. In stub areas, a default summary route is injected along with information about networks that belong to other areas within the same OSPF network. Use the **stub** option with the **area** OSPF subcommand to configure this feature in the Cisco ASA. The following is the command syntax:

```
area area-id stub [no-summary]
```

TIP	Use the **no-summary** attribute if you do not want to send summary LSAs into the stub area.

If an area is configured as a stub, all the routers within the area must also be configured as stub routers. Otherwise, the neighbor relationship will not be established.

The OSPF NSSA feature is defined in RFC 3101, "The OSPF Not-So-Stubby Area (NSSA) Option." Redistribution of routes into an NSSA area generates a special type of LSA known as LSA type 7. This type only exists in NSSA areas. Use the **nssa** option with the **area** OSPF subcommand to configure this feature in the Cisco ASA. The following is the command syntax:

```
area area-id nssa [no-redistribution][default-information-originate [metric metric]
    [metric-type 1|2]][no-summary]
```

Example 6-17 demonstrates how to configure the Cisco ASA as an NSSA router and generate a default route.

Example 6-17 *NSSA Configuration Example*

```
router ospf 1
  network 192.168.4.1 255.255.255.255 area 1
  area 1 nssa default-information-originate
```

The highlighted line in Example 6-17 specifies area 1 as an NSSA and enables the Cisco ASA to inject a default route.

ABR Type 3 LSA Filtering

To filter type 3 LSAs in the Cisco ASA, use the **prefix-list** command. Once configured, the Cisco ASA can control which prefixes are sent from one area to another. The syntax of the **prefix-list** command is as follows:

```
prefix-list list-name [seq seq-value] {deny | permit prefix/length} [ge min-value]
    [le max-value]
```

Table 6-3 lists all the options of the **prefix-list** command.

Table 6-3   **prefix-list** *Command Options*

Option	Description
list-name	Name of the prefix list
seq	The sequence number for the prefix list entry
seq-value	The sequence number value
deny	Denies access for a matching condition
permit	Permits access for a matching condition
prefix/length	The network number and length (in bits) of the network mask

continues

Table 6-3 **prefix-list** *Command Options (Continued)*

Option	Description
ge	Applies the *ge (greater or equal) value* to the range specified
min-value	Specifies the lesser value of a range (the "from" portion of the range description); range is 0 to 32
le	Applies the *le (less or equal) value* to the range specified
max-value	Specifies the greater value of a range (the "to" portion of the range description); range is 0 to 32

TIP You can enter a description (up to 225 characters) for each prefix list by using the **prefix-list** *list-name* **description** command.

Example 6-18 demonstrates how to configure a prefix list to filter type 3 LSAs.

Example 6-18 *Type 3 LSA Filtering Configuration Example*

```
prefix-list myfilter1 seq 5 deny 192.168.3.3/32
prefix-list myfilter2 seq 5 deny 192.168.1.1/32
prefix-list myfilter2 seq 10 permit 192.168.2.2/32
prefix-list myfilter2 seq 15 permit 192.168.1.0/24
router ospf 1
  network 192.168.10.0 255.255.255.0 area 1
  network 192.168.3.0 255.255.255.0 area 0
  area 1 filter-list prefix myfilter2 in
  area 1 filter-list prefix myfilter1 out
```

In Example 6-18, two prefix lists are configured. One is applied inbound and one outbound under the OSPF process. Each prefix list entry is identified with a sequence number. Notice that for the prefix list myfilter2, three sequence numbers are used to identify each entry (5, 10, and 15). When multiple entries of a prefix list match a given prefix, the entry with the lowest sequence number is matched first. In this case, the entry with sequence number 5 will be matched before the other two.

The Cisco ASA begins the search at the top of the prefix list. Once a match or deny occurs, the Cisco ASA does not need to go through the rest of the prefix list.

TIP For efficiency, you may want to put the most common matches or denials near the top of the list, using the *seq-value* argument in the **prefix-list** command.

In Example 6-18, 192.168.3.3/32 will not be advertised, and any routes received for 192.168.1.1/32 will be dropped. On the other hand, 192.168.2.2/32 and the rest of the 192.168.1.0/24 network will be permitted.

OSPF **neighbor** Command and Dynamic Routing over VPN

OSPF Hello messages are sent over multicast by default. However, IPSec does not support multicast over a VPN tunnel. Consequently, OSPF adjacency using multicast cannot be established over IPSec VPN tunnels. Cisco ASA provides a solution to this problem by supporting the configuration of statically defined neighbors with the **neighbor** command. With the **neighbor** command, the Cisco ASA communicates with its peers using the unicast packets. This allows the OSPF messages to be successfully encrypted and sent over the VPN tunnel. This is similar to the **neighbor** command in Cisco IOS routers.

NOTE	Chapter 15 covers site-to-site IPSec VPNs.

The OSPF neighbors can be defined only on nonbroadcast media. Because the underlying physical media is Ethernet (broadcast), the media type must be changed to nonbroadcast under the interface configuration. This would override the default physical broadcast media type. Example 6-19 demonstrates how to use the **neighbor** command for an IPSec peer located at 209.165.200.225.

Example 6-19 *OSPF* **neighbor** *Command Example*

```
Chicago(config)# router ospf 1
Chicago(config-router)# neighbor 209.165.200.225  interface outside
INFO: Neighbor command will take effect only after OSPF is enabled
and network-type is configured on the interface
```

Notice the warning message in Example 6-19. The command will not take effect until the network type is changed to nonbroadcast under the interface. Use the **ospf network point-to-point non-broadcast** interface command to accomplish this. Example 6-20 demonstrates this command.

Example 6-20 *Changing the Default Physical Media Type to Nonbroadcast*

```
Chicago(config-router)# interface GigabitEthernet0/0
Chicago(config-if)# ospf network point-to-point non-broadcast
```

Additionally, OSPF expects neighbors to belong to the same subnet. The subnet requirement is overlooked for point-to-point links. Because the IPSec site-to-site VPN tunnels are considered a point-to-point connection, the previous command provides the solution to this problem. Only one neighbor can be configured on a point-to-point link.

NOTE	Once an interface is declared to be a point-to-point nonbroadcast link, it cannot form adjacencies unless neighbors are configured explicitly.
	If OSPF is configured to run over a site-to-site IPSec tunnel, then that same interface cannot form an OSPF neighbor with the directly connected router.

On IPSec site-to-site and remote-access VPN configurations, you can optionally use reverse route injection (RRI). RRI is a feature on the Cisco ASA that provides a solution for topologies that require encrypted traffic to be diverted to the Cisco ASA and all other traffic to be sent to a separate router. In other words, RRI eliminates the need to manually define static routes on internal routers or hosts to be able to send traffic to remote site-to-site connections or remote-access VPN connections. RRI is not required if the Cisco ASA is used as the default gateway and all traffic passes through it to get into and out of the network.

NOTE	RRI is covered in detail in Chapter 15, "Site-to-Site IPSec VPN," and Chapter 16, "Remote Access VPNs."

There are several advantages to running OSPF over an IPSec VPN tunnel instead of using RRI. One of the major advantages is that when RRI is used, the routes to the remote networks or hosts are always advertised to the internal network, regardless of whether or not the VPN tunnel is operational. When using OSPF over an IPSec site-to-site tunnel, the routes to the remote networks or hosts are advertised only if the VPN tunnel is operational.

Troubleshooting OSPF

This section includes many mechanisms and techniques that are used to troubleshoot OSPF problems, such as several **show** and **debug** commands.

Useful Troubleshooting Commands

A commonly used command is **show ospf** [*process-id*]. It displays general information about OSPF routing-process IDs. The *process-ID* option displays information for a specific OSPF routing process. Example 6-21 shows the output of this command.

Example 6-21 *Output of the* **show ospf** *[process-id] Command*

```
Chicago# show ospf 1
 Routing Process "ospf 1" with ID 192.168.10.1 and Domain ID 0.0.0.1
 Supports only single TOS(TOS0) routes
 Does not support opaque LSA
 SPF schedule delay 5 secs, Hold time between two SPFs 10 secs
 Minimum LSA interval 5 secs. Minimum LSA arrival 1 secs
 Number of external LSA 0. Checksum Sum 0x       0
 Number of opaque AS LSA 0. Checksum Sum 0x       0
 Number of DCbitless external and opaque AS LSA 0
 Number of DoNotAge external and opaque AS LSA 0
 Number of areas in this router is 1. 1 normal 0 stub 0 nssa
 External flood list length 0
    Area BACKBONE(0)
        Number of interfaces in this area is 1
```

Example 6-21 *Output of the* **show ospf** *[process-id] Command (Continued)*

```
         Area has no authentication
         SPF algorithm executed 5 times
         Area ranges are
         Number of LSA 3. Checksum Sum 0x 1da9c
         Number of opaque link LSA 0. Checksum Sum 0x      0
         Number of DCbitless LSA 0
         Number of indication LSA 0
         Number of DoNotAge LSA 0
         Flood list length 0
```

As demonstrated in Example 6-21, the **show ospf** command gives you details about the OSPF configuration, LSA information, OSPF router ID, and number of areas configured in the Cisco ASA.

To display OSPF-related interface information, use the **show ospf interface** command. Example 6-22 includes the output of this command for the inside interface.

Example 6-22 *Output of the* **show ospf interface** *Command*

```
Chicago# show ospf interface inside
inside is up, line protocol is up
  Internet Address 192.168.10.1 mask 255.255.255.0, Area 0
  Process ID 1, Router ID 192.168.10.1, Network Type BROADCAST, Cost: 10
  Transmit Delay is 1 sec, State BDR, Priority 1
  Designated Router (ID) 192.168.10.2, Interface address 192.168.10.2
  Backup Designated router (ID) 192.168.10.1, Interface address 192.168.10.1
  Timer intervals configured, Hello 10, Dead 40, Wait 40, Retransmit 5
    Hello due in 0:00:00
  Index 1/1, flood queue length 0
  Next 0x0(0)/0x0(0)
  Last flood scan length is 1, maximum is 1
  Last flood scan time is 0 msec, maximum is 0 msec
  Neighbor Count is 1, Adjacent neighbor count is 1
    Adjacent with neighbor 192.168.10.2  (Designated Router)
  Suppress hello for 0 neighbor(s)
```

The output of the **show ospf interface** command shows not only information about the OSPF communication on that specific interface, but also other information, such as the network type, cost, designated router information, etc.

To display OSPF neighbor information, use the **show ospf neighbor** command. The following is the command syntax:

```
 show ospf neighbor [interface-name] [neighbor-id] [detail]
```

To show neighbor information on a per-interface basis, use the *interface-name* argument. Use the *neighbor-id* option to display information about a specific neighbor, and use the **detail** option to display detailed neighbor information. The *interface-name* and *neighbor-id* options are mutually exclusive. Example 6-23 shows the output of the **show ospf neighbor** command.

Example 6-23 *Output of the* **show ospf neighbor** *Command*

```
Chicago# show ospf neighbor
Neighbor ID     Pri   State        Dead Time   Address        Interface
192.168.10.2     1    FULL/DR       0:00:34     192.168.10.2    inside
```

When OSPF adjacency is formed, the Cisco ASA goes through several state changes before it becomes fully adjacent with its neighbor. The information that these states represent is crucial when troubleshooting OSPF problems in the Cisco ASA. These states are as follows:

- **Down**—The first OSPF neighbor state. It means that no Hello packets have been received from this neighbor, but Hello packets can still be sent to the neighbor in this state.

- **Attempt**—Only valid for manually configured neighbors in a non-broadcast multi-access (NBMA) environment. In Attempt state, the Cisco ASA sends unicast Hello packets every poll interval to the neighbor, if it has not received any Hello packets within the dead interval.

- **Init**—Specifies that the Cisco ASA has received a Hello packet from its neighbor, but the receiving router's ID was not included in the Hello packet. When the Cisco ASA or any router running OSPF receives a Hello packet from a neighbor, it should send its router ID in the Hello packet as an acknowledgment that it received a valid Hello packet.

- **2Way**—Designates that bidirectional communication has been established between the Cisco ASA and its neighbor.

- **Exstart**—The Cisco ASA is exchanging information to select who will be the DR and BDR (master-slave relationship) and chooses the initial sequence number for adjacency formation. The device with the higher router ID becomes the master and starts the exchange and, as such, is the only device that can increment the sequence number.

- **Exchange**—Indicates the exchange of database descriptor (DBD) packets. Database descriptors contain LSA headers only and describe the contents of the entire link-state database.

- **Loading**—The Cisco ASA is doing the actual exchange of link-state information with its neighbor.

- **Full**—The Cisco ASA and its neighbor are fully adjacent with each other. All the router and network LSAs are exchanged and the routing databases are fully synchronized.

Example 6-24 shows the output of the **show ospf neighbor** command with the **detail** option. The neighbor in this example is a router with IP address 192.168.10.2. In this example, you can see that the OSPF state is Full and that there were six state changes. Additionally, you can see that the neighbor has been up for 26 minutes and 21 seconds.

Example 6-24 *Output of the* **show ospf neighbor detail** *Command*

```
Chicago# show ospf neighbor inside 192.168.10.2 detail
Neighbor 192.168.10.2, interface address 192.168.10.2
    In the area 0 via interface inside
    Neighbor priority is 1, State is FULL, 6 state changes
    DR is 192.168.10.2 BDR is 192.168.10.1
    Options is 0x2
    Dead timer due in 0:00:31
    Neighbor is up for 00:26:21
    Index 1/1, retransmission queue length 0, number of retransmission 1
    First 0x0(0)/0x0(0) Next 0x0(0)/0x0(0)
    Last retransmission scan length is 1, maximum is 1
    Last retransmission scan time is 0 msec, maximum is 0 msec
```

Use the **show ospf database** command to display information related to the Cisco ASA OSPF database. The command displays information about the different OSPF LSAs. It displays detailed information about the neighbor router and the state of the neighbor relationship. Example 6-25 shows the output of the **show ospf database** command.

Example 6-25 *Output of the* **show ospf database** *Command*

```
Chicago# show ospf database
        OSPF Router with ID (192.168.10.1) (Process ID 1)
                Router Link States (Area 0)
Link ID         ADV Router      Age        Seq#      Checksum Link count
192.168.10.1     192.168.10.1    1943        0x80000005 0x99dd 1
192.168.10.2     192.168.10.2    20          0x80000003 0xa1d2 1
                Net Link States (Area 0)
Link ID         ADV Router      Age        Seq#      Checksum
192.168.10.2     192.168.10.2    1944        0x80000001 0xa2e6
                Type-5 AS External Link States
Link ID         ADV Router      Age        Seq#      Checksum Tag
192.168.20.0     192.168.10.2    19          0x80000001 0xfa25 0
192.168.13.0     192.168.10.2    19          0x80000001 0x8293 0
192.168.10.0     192.168.10.2    19          0x80000001 0xa72c 0
```

As demonstrated in Example 6-25, several external routes are learned from router 192.168.10.2. The 192.168.10.2 neighbor is advertising two routes for networks 192.168.20.0/24 and 192.168.13.0/24. Example 6-26 shows the output of the **show route** command for this example.

Example 6-26 *Output of the* **show route** *Command*

```
Chicago# show route
S     0.0.0.0 0.0.0.0 [1/0] via 209.165.200.226, outside
C     209.165.200.224 255.255.255.224 is directly connected, outside
C     192.168.10.0 255.255.255.0 is directly connected, inside
O E2 192.168.20.0 255.255.255.0 [110/10] via 192.168.10.2, 0:00:04, inside
O E2 192.168.13.0 255.255.255.0 [110/10] via 192.168.10.2, 0:00:04, inside
```

| TIP | Make sure that the exact subnet mask is configured on the interfaces that are running OSPF between the Cisco ASA and its neighbor. A subnet mismatch creates a discrepancy in the OSPF database that prevents routes from being installed in the routing tables. Furthermore, the maximum transmission unit (MTU) size must also match between peers. |

Table 6-4 lists some of the common reasons why OSPF neighbors have problems forming an adjacency and suggests the **show** commands that you can use to troubleshoot the problem.

Table 6-4   *OSPF Common Problems and Useful* **show** *Commands*

Problem	Command
OSPF is not enabled on an interface where it is needed.	**show ospf interface**
OSPF Hello or dead timer interval values are mismatched.	**show ospf interface**
OSPF network-type mismatch on the adjoining interfaces.	**show ospf interface**
OSPF area type is stub on one neighbor, but the adjoining neighbor in the same area is not configured for stub.	**show ospf interface**
OSPF neighbors have duplicate router IDs.	**show ospf**
OSPF Hellos are not processed due to a lack of resources, such as high CPU utilization or not enough memory.	**show memory** **show cpu usage**
Neighbor information is incorrect.	**show ospf neighbor**
An underlying layer problem is preventing OSPF Hellos from being received.	**show ospf neighbor** **show ospf interface** **show interface**

The **debug ospf** command is extremely useful for troubleshooting OSPF problems. However, only turn on debugs commands if any of the **show** commands discussed cannot help you solve the problem. Table 6-5 lists all the options of the **debug ospf** command.

Table 6-5   **debug ospf** *Options*

Option	Description
adj	Outputs information about the adjacency process transactions
database-timer	Outputs database timer information
events	Outputs OSPF transaction event information
flood	Includes OSPF flooding information
lsa-generation	Outputs OSPF LSA generation information

Table 6-5   **debug ospf** *Options (Continued)*

Option	Description
packet	Outputs detailed OSPF packet information
retransmission	Provides information about retransmissions during OSPF transactions
spf external	Outputs SPF information external to local area
spf internal	Outputs SPF information within a given area
spf intra	Outputs SPF intra-area information

TIP   If the **debug ospf** command is entered without any options, all options are enabled by default. This may not be appropriate for busy OSPF networks.

Example 6-27 shows the output of the **debug ospf events** command during a new adjacency. The first highlighted line shows that a two-way communication has been started to the router 192.168.10.2 on the inside interface and the state is 2WAY. The second highlighted line shows that NBR negotiation has been completed and the Cisco ASA is classified as the slave. The third and fourth highlighted lines indicate that the exchange has been completed and that the state is now FULL.

Example 6-27 *Output of the* **debug ospf events** *Command*

```
OSPF: Rcv DBD from 192.168.10.2 on inside seq 0x167f opt 0x2 flag 0x7 len 32  mtu
  1500 state INIT
OSPF: 2 Way Communication to 192.168.10.2 on inside, state 2WAY
OSPF: Neighbor change Event on interface inside
OSPF: DR/BDR election on inside
OSPF: Elect BDR 192.168.10.2
OSPF: Elect DR 192.168.10.1
        DR: 192.168.10.1 (Id)    BDR: 192.168.10.2 (Id)
OSPF: Send DBD to 192.168.10.2 on inside seq 0x7c1 opt 0x2 flag 0x7 len 32
OSPF: NBR Negotiation Done. We are the SLAVE
OSPF: Send DBD to 192.168.10.2 on inside seq 0x167f opt 0x2 flag 0x2 len 132
OSPF: Rcv DBD from 192.168.10.2 on inside seq 0x1680 opt 0x2 flag 0x3 len 152  mtu
  1500 state EXCHANGE
OSPF: Send DBD to 192.168.10.2 on inside seq 0x1680 opt 0x2 flag 0x0 len 32
OSPF: Rcv hello from 192.168.10.2 area 0 from inside 192.168.10.2
OSPF: Neighbor change Event on interface inside
OSPF: DR/BDR election on inside
OSPF: Elect BDR 192.168.10.2
OSPF: Elect DR 192.168.10.1
        DR: 192.168.10.1 (Id)    BDR: 192.168.10.2 (Id)
OSPF: End of hello processing
OSPF: Rcv DBD from 192.168.10.2 on inside seq 0x1681 opt 0x2 flag 0x1 len 32  mtu
  1500 state EXCHANGE
OSPF: Exchange Done with 192.168.10.2 on inside
OSPF: Synchronized with 192.168.10.2 on inside, state FULL
```

continues

Example 6-27 *Output of the* **debug ospf events** *Command (Continued)*

```
OSPF: Send DBD to 192.168.10.2 on inside seq 0x1681 opt 0x2 flag 0x0 len 32
OSPF: service_maxage: Trying to delete MAXAGE LSA
OSPF: Rcv hello from 192.168.10.2 area 0 from inside 192.168.10.2
OSPF: End of hello processing
```

Mismatched Areas

Example 6-28 shows the output of the **debug ospf events** command during an OSPF transaction where the Cisco ASA was configured with area 0 and the adjacent router was configured with area 1. Consequently, the mismatch area message is displayed in the debug output.

Example 6-28 *Mismatched OSPF Areas*

```
OSPF: Rcv pkt from 192.168.10.2, inside, area 0.0.0.0
      mismatch area 0.0.0.1 in the header
```

OSPF Authentication Mismatch

Here is an example in which the Cisco ASA was configured to perform OSPF authentication. OSPF authentication was not enabled on the neighbor router. Example 6-29 shows the output of the **debug ospf event** command.

Example 6-29 *Mismatched OSPF Authentication Parameters*

```
Chicago# debug ospf event
OSPF: Rcv pkt from 192.168.10.2, inside : Mismatch Authentication type. Input packet
specified type 0, we use type 1
Chicago#
```

Troubleshooting Virtual Link Problems

To display parameters and the current state of OSPF virtual links configured in the Cisco ASA, use the **show ospf virtual-links** command. Example 6-30 shows the output of the **show ospf virtual-links** command while the state of the virtual link to router 192.168.10.2 is down.

Example 6-30 *Output of the* **show ospf virtual-links** *Command During a Configuration Mismatch in the Neighbor Router*

```
Chicago# show ospf virtual-links
Virtual Link dmz to router 192.168.3.1 is down
  Run as demand circuit
  DoNotAge LSA allowed.
  Transit area 1, via interface dmz, Cost of using 10
  Transmit Delay is 1 sec, State DOWN,
  Timer intervals configured, Hello 10, Dead 40, Wait 40, Retransmit 5
```

The problem is a configuration error on the Cisco ASA's neighbor router. The administrator notices, by looking at the running configuration with the **show running-config** command, that the router does not have the Cisco ASA router ID in its configuration.

IP Multicast

IP multicast provides the capability to transmit information to multiple devices in the network by efficiently utilizing bandwidth. Several video and audio applications use IP multicast as their method of communication. Many other applications, such as database replication software and emergency alert systems, also operate using IP multicast.

Traditionally, a multicast device communicates with a group of receivers by using an associated Layer 3 Class D address. The lowest bit of the first byte of the Ethernet multicast destination addresses must be a 1, which allows the device to differentiate between multicast and unicast packets.

Multicast has a mechanism that tells the network about what hosts are members of a specific group. This technique prevents unnecessary flooding. The Internet Group Multicast Protocol (IGMP) is the protocol used to prevent unnecessary flooding. IGMP is defined in RFC 2236.

IGMP

To join a specific multicast group, a host sends an IGMP report or join message to the routing device. The routing device sends query messages to discover which devices are still associated to a specific group. The host sends a response to the router query if it wants to continue to be a member of the specific group. If the router does not receive a response, it prunes the group list. This minimizes unnecessary transmissions.

The Cisco ASA can be configured as an IGMP proxy. It can forward IGMP messages from the downstream hosts. Additionally, it can send multicast transmissions from upstream routers. It can also be configured to statically join a multicast group.

IP Multicast Routing

In IP multicast routing, the network must be able to assemble packet distribution trees that identify a unique forwarding path between the source and each subnet containing members of the multicast group. One of the key objectives in the creation of distribution trees is to allow at least one copy of each packet to be forwarded to each branch of the tree. Several IP multicast protocols exist, but the most commonly used is Protocol Independent Multicast (PIM).

There are two different flavors of PIM routing protocols:

- **Dense mode (PIM-DM)**—Routers running DM routing protocols are required to forward multicast traffic to each group by assembling distribution trees. This is done by flooding the entire network. Subsequently, they prune all the paths that do not have any receivers.

- **Sparse mode (PIM-SM)** — The SM protocols require that few routers in the network will be drawn in each multicast group. SM IP multicast routing protocols start with an empty distribution tree and add only devices that specifically request to join the distribution.

Cisco ASA supports PIM-SM as the multicast routing protocol. It can use unicast routing information base (RIB) or multicast-capable RIB (MURIB) to route multicast packets. PIM-SM assembles unidirectional joint trees rooted at a rendezvous point (RP) per multicast group. Additionally, it can create shortest-path trees (SPTs) per each source.

Configuring Multicast Routing

This section includes the necessary steps to configure multicast routing using the CLI. You can also configure multicast routing using the Cisco Adaptive Security Device Manager (ASDM), which is covered in Chapter 19, "Firewall Management Using ASDM."

Enabling Multicast Routing

The first step to configure IP multicast routing on the Cisco ASA is to enable it by invoking the **multicast-routing** command in global configuration mode. Example 6-31 shows how to enable multicast routing on the Cisco ASA.

Example 6-31 *Enabling Multicast Routing*

```
Chicago(config)# configure terminal
Chicago(config)# multicast-routing
Chicago(config)# exit
```

To disable IP multicast routing, use the **no multicast-routing** command.

NOTE   The **multicast-routing** command enables IGMP on all interfaces by default. To disable IGMP on a specific interface, use the **no igmp** subinterface command.

The **multicast-routing** command enables PIM on all interfaces by default. If configured globally, use the **no pim** interface command to disable PIM on a specific interface.

Statically Assigning an IGMP Group

You can configure the Cisco ASA to statically join a specific multicast group. This can be accomplished by using the **igmp static-group** command in interface configuration mode. Example 6-32 shows how to statically assign an IGMP group in the Cisco ASA.

Example 6-32 *Statically Assigning an IGMP Group*

```
interface GigabitEthernet0/1
  igmp static-group 239.0.10.1
```

In Example 6-32, the statically configured group in interface GigabitEthernet0/1 is 239.0.10.1.

Limiting IGMP States

The IGMP State Limit feature provides protection against DoS attacks when attackers use IGMP packets. You can use the **igmp limit** command in interface configuration mode to limit the number of hosts allowed to join the multicast group on a per-interface basis. Example 6-33 shows how to configure this feature.

Example 6-33 *Limiting IGMP States*

```
Chicago(config)# interface GigabitEthernet0/1
Chicago(config-if)# igmp limit 100
```

In Example 6-33, the limit is set to 100 states. The maximum number of IGMP states allowed on an interface is 500. The default is 0 (unlimited).

IGMP Query Timeout

In the Cisco ASA, you can configure the timeout period before the security Cisco ASA takes over as the multicast query router for the configured interface. To do this, use the **igmp query-timeout** command in interface configuration mode. The range is from 60 to 300 seconds. The default is 255 seconds. Example 6-34 shows how to configure this feature with the query timeout value of 100 seconds.

Example 6-34 *IGMP Query Timeout*

```
Chicago(config)# interface GigabitEthernet0/1
Chicago(config-if)# igmp query-timeout 100
```

Defining the IGMP Version

Cisco ASA supports IGMP versions 1 and 2. IGMP version 2 is the default. To specify the version you want, use the **igmp version** interface subcommand. Example 6-35 demonstrates how to specify IGMP version 1 on the GigabitEthernet0/1 interface.

Example 6-35 *Defining the IGMP Version*

```
Chicago(config)# interface GigabitEthernet0/1
Chicago(config-if)# igmp version 1
```

Configuring Rendezvous Points

Rendezvous points (RPs) are used as a temporary way to connect a multicast receiver to an existing shared multicast tree. The **pim rp-address** command configures the address of a PIM RP for a particular group. Example 6-36 demonstrates how to configure a PIM RP for a particular group.

Example 6-36 *Configuring a PIM RP*

```
Chicago# configure terminal
Chicago(config)# pim rp-address 192.168.10.2 bidir
```

In Example 6-36 a PIM RP with IP address 192.168.10.2 is configured. The **bidir** keyword indicates that the specified multicast groups operate in bidirectional mode. If the command is configured without this option, the specified groups operate in PIM sparse mode.

NOTE	You can, optionally, configure an ACL defining the groups that should map to the given RP. If no ACL is specified, the RP is used for all available groups.

Configuring Threshold for SPT Switchover

The **pim spt-threshold** command can be used to specify when a PIM leaf router should join the shortest-path source tree for a specific multicast group. The following is the command syntax:

```
pim spt-threshold infinity [group-list acl]
```

The **infinity** keyword forces the PIM router to always use the shared tree instead of switching to the shortest-path source tree. This command can be associated with a group list by using the **group-list** *acl* optional tag. This dictates which groups the threshold applies to, as specified by a previously configured ACL. If no ACL is configured, the threshold applies to all groups. To restore the default value, use the **no** form of this command.

Filtering RP Register Messages

The **pim accept-register** command can configure a candidate RP to filter PIM register messages. The following is the syntax of this command:

```
pim accept-register {list acl>| route-map map-name>}
```

This command can use a preconfigured ACL or a route map to define what will be filtered.

PIM Designated Router Priority

PIM elects a designated router (DR), which is similar to the mechanism in OSPF. You can use the **pim dr-priority** command in interface configuration mode to set the priority for which a router is elected as the DR. The following is the command syntax:

```
pim dr-priority value
```

The priority value can range from 1 to 4,294,967,295, and the default is 1. The highest value is the priority in the DR election process.

PIM Hello Message Interval

The Cisco ASA sends PIM hello messages to the neighbor routers. To configure the frequency of PIM hello messages, use the **pim hello-interval** command in interface configuration mode. The following is the command syntax:

```
pim hello-interval seconds
```

The number of seconds that the router waits before sending a hello message can vary from 1 to 3600 seconds. The default is 30 seconds.

Example 6-37 demonstrates all the PIM subcommand options.

Example 6-37 *Customizing PIM Values at the Interface Level*

```
interface GigabitEthernet0/1
  nameif inside
  security-level 100
  ip address 192.168.10.1 255.255.255.0
  pim hello-interval 100
  pim dr-priority 5
  pim join-prune-interval 120
```

In Example 6-37, the PIM hello interval is set to 100 seconds, the DR priority to 5, and the PIM join and prune interval to 120 seconds on interface GigabitEthernet0/1.

Configuring a Static Multicast Route

You can configure a static multicast route entry using the **mroute** command. The following is the command syntax:

mroute *src mask* [*in-interface-name*] [**dense** *out-interface-name*] [**distance**]

Table 6-6 lists and explains all the available options for the **mroute** command.

Table 6-6   **mroute** *Command Options*

Option	Description
src	IP address of the multicast source.
mask	Subnet mask of the multicast source.
in-interface-name	Incoming interface name for the multicast route.
out-interface-name	Outgoing interface name for the multicast route..
[**distance**] (optional)	Defines whether a unicast route or a static multicast route should be used for the Reverse Path Forwarding (RPF) lookup. The lower the distance, the higher the preference. A static multicast route takes precedence if it has the same distance as the unicast route. The default distance is 0.

Troubleshooting IP Multicast Routing

This section includes detailed information on several commands and mechanisms that are useful while troubleshooting IP multicast routing problems in the Cisco ASA.

One of the most common interoperability issues between the Cisco ASA and older Cisco IOS router versions is that the register messages were generated differently. The Cisco ASA and newer versions of Cisco IOS generate PIM RFC—compliant registers. To generate registers that are compatible with older versions of Cisco IOS, use the **pim old-register-checksum** command.

show Commands

The following **show** commands help you to monitor and view the current multicast (PIM or IGMP) configuration information:

- **show pim df**—Shows bidirectional PIM designated forwarder (DF) information
- **show pim group-map**—Displays PIM group-to-protocol mapping information
- **show pim interface**—Displays PIM interface information
- **show pim join-prune statistic**—Shows PIM join/prune information
- **show pim neighbor**—Displays PIM neighbor information
- **show pim range-list**—Shows PIM range-list information
- **show pim topology**—Displays the PIM topology table information
- **show pim traffic**—Displays PIM traffic counters
- **show pim tunnel**—Lists information about the PIM tunnel interfaces
- **show igmp groups**—Displays group membership information
- **show igmp interface**—Provides interface IGMP information
- **show igmp traffic**—Displays traffic counters
- **show mroute**—Displays the contents of the multicast routing table:

  ```
  show mroute source-address group-address [summary] [count] [pruned]
  ```

  To display the active multicast streams, use the **show mroute** [*group*] **active** [*kbps*] syntax of this command. The active multicast streams whose data rate is greater or equal to the specified value in *kbps* will be displayed. The default kbps is 4.

- **show mroute summary**—Displays a summary of the multicast routing table:

  ```
  Chicago# show mroute summary
  Multicast Routing Table
  Flags: D - Dense, S - Sparse, B - Bidir Group, s - SSM Group,
         C - Connected, L - Local, I - Received Source Specific Host Report,
         P - Pruned, R - RP-bit set, F - Register flag, T - SPT-bit set,
         J - Join SPT
  T
  (*, 224.55.55.55), 23:25:49/never, RP 192.168.10.2, OIF count: 0, flags: BP
  ```

debug Commands

The following commands are crucial for debugging IP multicast routing problems:

- **debug pim**—Enables debugging for PIM events
- **debug pim neighbor**—Enables debugging of PIM neighbor events
- **debug pim group** *group*—Enables PIM protocol activity debugging for only the matching group

- **debug pim interface** *interface*—Enables debugging of PIM protocol activity for only the specified interface.
- **debug pim df-election**—Enables debugging of PIM DF election exchange messages.
- **debug mrib route** [*group*]—Enables debugging of MRIB routing activity
- **debug mrib client**—Enables debugging of MRIB client management activity
- **debug mrib io**—Enables debugging of MRIB I/O events
- **debug mrib table**—Enables debugging of MRIB table management activity

Take into consideration the amount of traffic that is passing through the Cisco ASA and other activity before enabling some of the previously mentioned **debug** commands.

Deployment Scenarios

SecureMe is deploying a new Cisco ASA 5520 at a remote branch office in San Diego, California. The security administrator wants the Cisco ASA to learn all internal routes via OSPF. All routing updates should be authenticated using MD5. Additionally the security administrator wants to enable IP multicast routing and configure a static PIM RP.

Deploying OSPF

Figure 6-11 illustrates San Diego's network topology. There is a router (R1) in the inside of the Cisco ASA that has a connection to three other routers (R2, R3, and R4).

Figure 6-11 *San Diego's Network Topology*

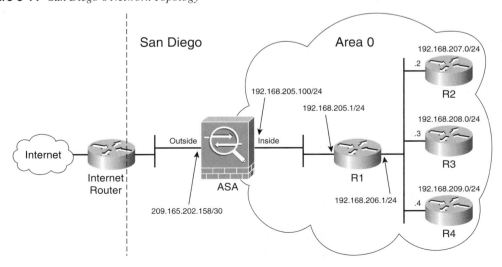

The goal is for the Cisco ASA to learn all authenticated routes from R1 via OSPF and to advertise a default route to the internal network. The following steps are completed to achieve this goal.

Step 1 An OSPF process (1) is enabled on the Cisco ASA:

```
SanDiego# configure terminal
SanDiego(config)# router ospf 1
```

Step 2 The internal network is added to the OSPF process to enable OSPF on the inside interface:

```
SanDiego(config-router)# network 192.168.205.0 255.255.255.0 area 0
```

Step 3 The command **default-information originate always** is entered for the Cisco ASA to send the inside interface's address as the default gateway to the internal devices:

```
SanDiego(config-router)# default-information originate always
```

Step 4 OSPF authentication using MD5 is configured on the Cisco ASA under the OSPF process and inside interface:

```
SanDiego(config-router)# area 0 authentication message-digest
SanDiego(config-router)# exit
SanDiego(config)# interface GigabitEthernet0/1
SanDiego(config-if)# ospf message-digest-key 1 md5 cisco
SanDiego(config-if)# ospf authentication message-digest
```

The MD5 key ID is 1 and the password is cisco.

Step 5 The **show ospf** command is issued to verify that OSPF is enabled:

```
SanDiego# show ospf
 Routing Process "ospf 1" with ID 192.168.205.100 and Domain ID 0.0.0.1
 Supports only single TOS(TOS0) routes
 Does not support opaque LSA
 It is an autonomous system boundary router
 Redistributing External Routes from,
 SPF schedule delay 5 secs, Hold time between two SPFs 10 secs
 Minimum LSA interval 5 secs. Minimum LSA arrival 1 secs
 Number of external LSA 1. Checksum Sum 0x  e4ab
 Number of opaque AS LSA 0. Checksum Sum 0x     0
 Number of DCbitless external and opaque AS LSA 0
 Number of DoNotAge external and opaque AS LSA 0
 Number of areas in this router is 1. 1 normal 0 stub 0 nssa
 External flood list length 0
    Area BACKBONE(0)
        Number of interfaces in this area is 1
        Area has message digest authentication
        SPF algorithm executed 12 times
        Area ranges are
        Number of LSA 4. Checksum Sum 0x 2430a
```

```
                 Number of opaque link LSA 0. Checksum Sum 0x     0
                 Number of DCbitless LSA 0
                 Number of indication LSA 0
                 Number of DoNotAge LSA 0
                 Flood list length 0
```

Step 6   The **show route** command is issued to verify the routing table:

```
SanDiego# show route
O     192.168.209.0 255.255.255.0 [110/21] via 192.168.205.1, 0:14:55, inside
O     192.168.208.0 255.255.255.0 [110/21] via 192.168.205.1, 0:14:55, inside
C     209.165.202.156 255.255.255.252 is directly connected, outside
C     192.168.205.0 255.255.255.0 is directly connected, inside
O     192.168.206.0 255.255.255.0 [110/11] via 192.168.205.1, 0:14:55, inside
O     192.168.207.0 255.255.255.0 [110/21] via 192.168.205.1, 0:14:55, inside
S*    0.0.0.0 0.0.0.0 [1/0] via 209.165.202.157, outside
```

Deploying IP Multicast

The security administrator needs to enable PIM and configure R1 as a PIM RP in the Cisco ASA. The following steps are followed to achieve this goal.

Step 1   The security administrator enables multicast routing on the Cisco ASA:

```
SanDiego# configure terminal
SanDiego(config)# multicast-routing
```

Step 2   R1's address is configured as a PIM RP in the Cisco ASA:

```
SanDiego(config)# pim rp-address 192.168.205.1
```

Step 3   To verify the PIM neighbor relationship, the administrator issues the **show pim neighbor** command, where the neighbor addresses and the uptime are shown:

```
SanDiego(config)# show pim neighbor
Neighbor Address  Interface         Uptime     Expires DR pri Bidir
209.165.202.157   outside           00:08:23   00:01:43 N/A
192.168.205.1     inside            00:09:58   00:01:37 N/A
```

Summary

This chapter covered the different routing protocols supported by Cisco ASA. Configuration examples included information on how to add a static route to configure dynamic routing protocols such as OSPF and RIP. Detailed sample configurations were provided, as well as tips on how to troubleshoot common problems when deploying these dynamic routing protocols.

Cisco ASA also supports IP multicast routing protocols. IGMP versions 1 and 2 are supported, as well as PIM-SM. PIM-SM allows Cisco ASA to have direct participation in the creation of a multicast tree. This technique enhances the multicast support for IGMP forwarding and provides an alternate to multicast transparent mode operations. At the end of the chapter, deployment scenarios were added to enhance the level of learning.

This chapter covers the following topics:

- AAA protocols and services supported by Cisco ASA
- Defining an authentication server
- Authenticating administrative sessions
- Configuring authorization
- Configuring downloadable ACLs
- Configuring accounting
- Troubleshooting AAA

Authentication, Authorization, and Accounting (AAA)

This chapter provides a detailed explanation of the configuration and troubleshooting of authentication, authorization, and accounting (AAA) network security services that Cisco ASA supports. AAA offers different solutions that provide access control to network devices. The following services are included within its modular architectural framework:

- **Authentication**—The process of validating users based on their identity and predetermined credentials, such as passwords and other mechanisms like digital certificates.

- **Authorization**—The method by which a network device assembles a set of attributes that regulates what tasks the user is authorized to perform. These attributes are measured against a user database. The results are returned to the network device to determine the user's qualifications and restrictions. This database can be located locally on Cisco ASA or it can be hosted on a RADIUS or TACACS+ server.

- **Accounting**—The process of gathering and sending user information to a AAA server used to track login times (when the user logged in and logged off) and the services that users access. This information can be used for billing, auditing, and reporting purposes.

AAA Protocols and Services Supported by Cisco ASA

Cisco ASA can be configured to maintain a local user database or to use an external server for authentication. The following are the AAA authentication underlying protocols and servers that are supported as external database repositories:

- RADIUS
- TACACS+
- RSA SecurID (SDI)
- Windows NT
- Kerberos
- Lightweight Directory Access Protocol (LDAP)

Table 7-1 shows the different methods and the functionality that each protocol supports.

Table 7-1 *AAA Support Matrix*

Method	Authentication	Authorization	Accounting
Internal server	Yes	Yes	No
RADIUS	Yes	Yes	Yes
TACACS+	Yes	Yes	Yes
SDI	Yes	No	No
Windows NT	Yes	No	No
Kerberos	Yes	No	No
LDAP	No	Yes	No

NOTE   Using an external authentication server in medium and large deployments is recommended, for better scalability and easier management.

Cisco ASA supports the authentication methods listed in Table 7-1 with the following services:

- Virtual private network (VPN) user authentication
- Administrative session authentication
- Firewall session authentication (cut-through proxy)

Table 7-2 includes the support for the authentication methods in correlation to the specific services.

Table 7-2 *Authentication Support Services*

Service	Local	RADIUS	TACACS+	SDI	Windows NT	Kerberos
VPN users	Yes	Yes	Yes	Yes	Yes	Yes
Administration	Yes	Yes	Yes	No	No	No
Firewall sessions	Yes	Yes	Yes	No	No	No

NOTE   Cisco ASA VPN user authentication support is similar to the support provided on the Cisco VPN 3000 Series Concentrator.

As previously mentioned, the authorization mechanism assembles a set of attributes that describes what the user is allowed to do within the network or service. Cisco ASA supports local and external authorization depending on the service used. Table 7-3 shows the authorization support matrix.

Table 7-3   *Authorization Support*

Service	Local	RADIUS	TACACS+	SDI	NT	Kerberos	LDAP
VPN users	Yes	Yes	No	No	No	No	Yes
Administration	Yes	No	Yes	No	No	No	No
Firewall sessions	No	No	Yes	No	No	No	No

NOTE   Local authorization for administrative sessions can be used only for command authorization.

NOTE   Cisco ASA does not support RADIUS command authorization for administrative sessions because of limitations in the RADIUS protocol.

Accounting is supported by RADIUS and TACACS+ servers only. Table 7-4 shows the Cisco ASA accounting support matrix.

Table 7-4   *Accounting Support*

Service	Local	RADIUS	TACACS+	SDI	NT	Kerberos	LDAP
VPN users	No	Yes	Yes	No	No	No	No
Administration	No	Yes	Yes	No	No	No	No
Firewall sessions	No	Yes	Yes	No	No	No	No

The following subsections introduce each of the authentication protocols and servers that Cisco ASA supports.

RADIUS

RADIUS is a widely implemented authentication standard protocol that is defined in RFC 2865, "Remote Authentication Dial-In User Service (RADIUS)." RADIUS operates in a client/server model. A RADIUS client is usually referred to as a network access server (NAS). A NAS is responsible for passing user information to the RADIUS server. Cisco ASA acts as a NAS and authenticates users based on the RADIUS server's response.

NOTE   Cisco ASA supports several RADIUS servers, such as the following:

- CiscoSecure ACS for NT

- CiscoSecure ACS for UNIX

- Cisco Access Registrar

- Livingston

- Merit

- Funk Steel Belted

- Microsoft Internet Authentication Server

These are some of the most commonly deployed RADIUS server vendors. Support and testing with other servers is a continuous effort between vendors.

The RADIUS server receives user authentication requests and subsequently returns configuration information required for the client (in this case, the Cisco ASA) to support the specific service to the user. The RADIUS server does this by sending Internet Engineering Task Force (IETF) or vendor-specific attributes. (RADIUS authentication attributes are defined in RFC 2865.) Figure 7-1 shows how this process works.

Figure 7-1   *Basic RADIUS Authentication Process*

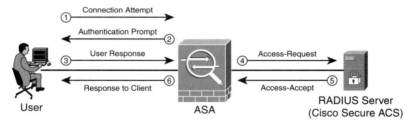

In this example, a Cisco ASA acts as a NAS and the RADIUS server is a Cisco Secure Access Control Server (ACS). The following sequence of events is shown in Figure 7-1:

1   A user attempts to connect to the Cisco ASA (i.e., administration, VPN, or cut-through proxy).

2   The Cisco ASA prompts the user, requesting his username and password.

3   User sends his or her credentials to the Cisco ASA.

4   The Cisco ASA sends the authentication request (Access-Request) to the RADIUS server.

5   The RADIUS server sends an Access-Accept message (if the user is successfully authenticated) or an Access-Reject (if the user is not successfully authenticated).

6   The Cisco ASA responds to the user and allows access to the specific service.

NOTE	The RADIUS server can also send IETF or vendor-specific attributes to the Cisco ASA depending on the implementation and services used. These attributes can contain information such as an IP address to assign the client and authorization information. RADIUS servers combine authentication and authorization phases into a single request and response communication cycle.

The Cisco ASA authenticates itself to the RADIUS server by using a preconfigured shared secret. For security reasons, this shared secret is never sent over the network.

NOTE	Passwords are sent as encrypted messages from the Cisco ASA to the RADIUS server. This is useful to protect this critical information from an intruder. The Cisco ASA hashes the password using the shared secret that is defined on the Cisco ASA and the RADIUS server.

The RADIUS servers can also proxy authentication requests to other RADIUS servers or other types of authentication servers. Figure 7-2 illustrates this methodology.

Figure 7-2   *RADIUS Server Acting as Proxy to Other Authentication Server*

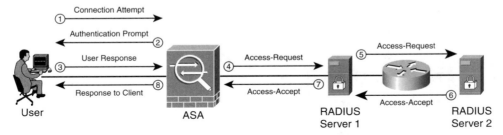

In Figure 7-2, RADIUS Server 1 acts as a proxy to RADIUS Server 2. It sends the authentication request from the Cisco ASA to RADIUS Server 2 and proxies the response back to the ASA.

TACACS+

TACACS+ is a AAA security protocol that provides centralized validation of users who are attempting to gain access to NASs. The TACACS+ protocol offers support for separate and modular AAA facilities. The TACACS+ protocol's primary goal is to supply complete AAA support for managing multiple network devices.

TACACS+ uses port 49 for communication and allows vendors to use either User Datagram Protocol (UDP) or TCP encoding. Cisco ASA uses the TCP version for its TACACS+ implementation.

The TACACS+ authentication concept is similar to RADIUS. The NAS sends an authentication request to the TACACS+ server (daemon). The server ultimately sends any of the following messages back to the NAS:

- **ACCEPT**—User has been successfully authenticated and the requested service will be allowed. If authorization is required, the authorization process will begin at this point.

- **REJECT**—User authentication was denied. The user may be prompted to retry authentication depending on the TACACS+ server and NAS.

- **ERROR**—A certain error took place during authentication. This can be experienced because of network connectivity problems or a configuration error.

- **CONTINUE**—User is prompted to provide further authentication information.

After the authentication process is complete, if authorization is required, the TACACS+ server proceeds with the authorization phase. The user must first successfully be authenticated before proceeding to TACACS+ authorization.

RSA SecurID

RSA SecurID (SDI) is a solution provided by RSA Security. The RSA ACE/Server is the administrative component of the SDI solution. It provides the usage of one-time passwords (OTPs). Cisco ASA supports SDI authentication natively only for VPN user authentication. However, if it is using an authentication server, such as CiscoSecure ACS for Windows NT, the server can use external authentication to an SDI server and proxy the authentication request for all other services supported by Cisco ASA. Cisco ASA and SDI use UDP port 5500 for communication.

The SDI solution uses small devices called tokens that provide users with an OTP that changes every 60 seconds. These OTPs are generated when a user enters a pin number and are synchronized with the server to provide the authentication service. The SDI server can be configured to require the user to enter a new pin when trying to authenticate. This process is called *new pin mode,* which Cisco ASA supports. Figure 7-3 demonstrates how this solution works when a user attempts to connect to the Cisco ASA using the Cisco VPN Client software.

Figure 7-3 *SDI Authentication Using New Pin Mode*

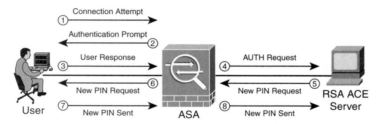

The purpose of new pin mode is to allow the user to change its PIN for authentication. The following sequence of events occurs when using SDI authentication with the new pin mode feature, as shown in Figure 7-3:

1   The user attempts to establish a VPN connection with the Cisco VPN client and negotiates IKE Phase 1. (Complete information about IKE and IPSec negotiations is provided in Chapter 1, "Introduction to Network Security.")

2   The Cisco ASA prompts the user for authentication via X-Auth (extended authentication)

3   The user provides its username and passcode. (X-Auth is also covered in Chapter 16, "Remote Access VPN.")

4   The Cisco ASA forwards the authentication request to the SDI server.

5   If new pin mode is enabled, the SDI server authenticates the user and requests a new PIN to be used during the next authentication session for that user.

6   The Cisco ASA prompts the user for a new PIN.

7   User enters new PIN.

8   The Cisco ASA sends the new PIN information to the SDI server.

NOTE   You can find more information about the RSA SecurID server at http://www.rsasecurity.com.

Microsoft Windows NT

Cisco ASA supports Windows NT native authentication only for VPN remote-access connections. It communicates with the Windows NT server using TCP port 139. Similarly to SDI, you can use a RADIUS/TACACS+ server, such as CiscoSecure ACS, to proxy authentication to Windows NT for other services supported by Cisco ASA.

Active Directory and Kerberos

Cisco ASA can authenticate VPN users via an external Windows Active Directory, which uses Kerberos for authentication. It can also communicate with a Unix/Linux-based Kerberos server. Support for this authentication method is available for VPN clients only. Cisco ASA communicates with the Active Directory and/or a Kerberos server using UDP port 88. Configuration and troubleshooting of remote access VPN tunnels are covered in Chapter 16.

Lightweight Directory Access Protocol

Cisco ASA supports LDAP authorization for remote-access VPN connections only. The LDAP protocol is defined in RFC 3377, "Lightweight Directory Access Protocol (v3)," and

RFC 3771, "The Lightweight Directory Access Protocol (LDAP) Intermediate Response Message." LDAP provides authorization services when given access to a user database within a Directory Information Tree (DIT). This tree contains entities called entries, which consist of one or more attribute values called distinguished names (DNs). The DN values must be unique within the DIT.

Cisco ASA communicates with an LDAP server over TCP port 389.

NOTE   LDAP only provides authorization services. Consequently, a separate protocol is required for authentication services.

Defining an Authentication Server

Before configuring an authentication server on Cisco ASA, you must specify AAA server groups with the **aaa-server** command. The syntax of the **aaa-server** command to specify a new AAA server group and the respective protocol is as follows:

aaa-server *server-tag* **protocol** *server-protocol*

server-tag is the server group name that is referenced by the other AAA command, and *server-protocol* is the name of the supported AAA protocol. Example 7-1 shows the different authentication protocols that can be defined within a AAA server group.

Example 7-1 *AAA Server Group Authentication Protocols*

```
Chicago(config)# aaa-server mygroup protocol ?
  kerberos   Protocol Kerberos
  ldap       Protocol LDAP
  nt         Protocol NT
  radius     Protocol RADIUS
  sdi        Protocol SDI
  tacacs+    Protocol TACACS+
```

In Example 7-1, the AAA server group tag is named mygroup. After defining the AAA server group with the respective authentication protocol, you are shown the (config-aaa-server) prompt, which has several subcommands and options that are shown in Example 7-2.

Example 7-2 *AAA Server Group Configuration Options*

```
Chicago(config)# aaa-server mygroup protocol radius
Chicago(config-aaa-server)# ?
aaa-server group configuration commands:
  accounting-mode      Enter this keyword to specify accounting mode
  max-failed-attempts  Specify the maximum number of failures that will be allowed
  for any server in the group before that server is deactivated
  no                   Remove an item from aaa-server group configuration
  reactivation-mode    Specify the method by which failed servers are reactivated
```

In Example 7-2, the AAA server group mygroup was configured for RADIUS authentication. You can specify the accounting mode using the **accounting-mode** subcommand with one of these options:

- **simultaneous**—Indicates that accounting messages are sent to all servers in the group
- **single**—Indicates that accounting messages are sent to a single server

NOTE	Accounting mode options are available only if you are configuring a AAA server group for RADIUS or TACACS+.

The **max-failed-attempts** subcommand specifies the maximum allowed number of communication failures for any server in the AAA server group before that server is disabled or deactivated. The maximum number of failures can be configured in a range from 1 to 5.

Cisco ASA supports two different AAA server reactivation policies or modes:

- **Timed mode**—The failed or deactivated servers are reactivated after 30 seconds of downtime. Example 7-3 includes the subcommand to enable server reactivation in timed mode.
- **Depletion mode**—The failed or deactivated servers remain inactive until all other servers within the configured group are inactive. Example 7-4 shows the Cisco ASA configured with a server group called mygroup, a maximum allowed number of communication failures set to 4, and server reactivation in depletion mode.

Example 7-3 *AAA Server Reactivation in Timed Mode*

```
Chicago(config-aaa-server)# reactivation-mode timed
```

Example 7-4 *AAA Server Reactivation in Depletion Mode*

```
Chicago# configure terminal
Chicago(config)# aaa-server mygroup protocol radius
Chicago(config-aaa-server)# max-failed-attempts 4
Chicago(config-aaa-server)# reactivation-mode depletion deadtime 5
Chicago(config-aaa-server)# exit
Chicago(config)# exit
```

The **deadtime** keyword stipulates the amount of time that will elapse between the disabling of the last server in the group and the subsequent re-enabling of all servers. The **deadtime** value in this example is set to 5 minutes.

To specify the AAA servers that will belong to specific groups, use the following command:

```
aaa-server server-tag host ip_address
```

Example 7-5 shows all the AAA server host configuration options.

Example 7-5 *AAA Server Host Available Configuration Options*

```
Chicago(config-aaa-server)# ?
aaa-server host configuration commands:
  accounting-port    Specify the port number to be used for accounting
  authentication-port Specify the port number to be used for authentication
  key                Specify the secret used to authenticate the NAS to the AAA
                     server
  no                 Remove an item from aaa-server host configuration
  radius-common-pw   Specify a common password for all RADIUS authorization
                     transactions
  retry-interval     Specify the amount of time between retry attempts
  timeout            Specify the maximum time to wait for response from configured
                     server
```

Example 7-6 shows the Cisco ASA configured with two AAA servers under the server group called mygroup.

Example 7-6 *AAA Server Host Configuration*

```
Chicago# configure terminal
Chicago(config)# aaa-server mygroup host 172.18.124.11
Chicago(config-aaa-server)# retry-interval 3
Chicago(config-aaa-server)# timeout 30
Chicago(config-aaa-server)# key cisco123
Chicago(config-aaa-server)# exit
Chicago(config)# aaa-server mygroup host 172.18.124.12
Chicago(config-aaa-server)# retry-interval 3
Chicago(config-aaa-server)# timeout 30
Chicago(config-aaa-server)# key cisco123
Chicago(config-aaa-server)# exit
Chicago(config)# exit
```

To view statistics about all AAA servers defined for a specific protocol, use the following command:

```
show aaa-server protocol server-protocol
```

Example 7-7 includes the output of this command for the RADIUS protocol.

Example 7-7 *Output of the show aaa-server protocol Command*

```
Chicago# show aaa-server protocol radius
Server Group:    mygroup
Server Protocol: radius
Server Address:  172.18.124.11
Server port:     1645(authentication), 1646(accounting)
Server status:   ACTIVE, Last transaction at unknown
Number of pending requests        0
Average round trip time           0ms
Number of authentication requests 55
Number of authorization requests  13
Number of accounting requests     45
```

Example 7-7 *Output of the* **show aaa-server protocol** *Command (Continued)*

```
Number of retransmissions          0
Number of accepts                  54
Number of rejects                  1
Number of challenges               54
Number of malformed responses      0
Number of bad authenticators       0
Number of timeouts                 0
Number of unrecognized responses   0
Server Group:    mygroup
Server Protocol: radius
Server Address:  172.18.124.12
Server port:     1645(authentication), 1646(accounting)
Server status:   ACTIVE, Last transaction at unknown
Number of pending requests         0
Average round trip time            0ms
Number of authentication requests  0
Number of authorization requests   0
Number of accounting requests      0
Number of retransmissions          0
Number of accepts                  0
Number of rejects                  0
Number of challenges               0
Number of malformed responses      0
Number of bad authenticators       0
Number of timeouts                 0
Number of unrecognized responses   0
Chicago#
```

To show the configuration of a specific AAA server, use the following command:

```
show running-config aaa-server [server-group [(if_name) host ip_address]]
```

To show statistics about a specific AAA server, use the following command:

```
show aaa-server [server-tag [host hostname]]
```

Example 7-8 includes the output of this command for server 172.18.124.11.

Example 7-8 *Output of the* **show aaa-server** *Command for a Specific Host*

```
Chicago# show aaa-server mygroup host 172.18.124.11
Server Group:    mygroup
Server Protocol: radius
Server Address:  172.18.124.11
Server port:     1645(authentication), 1646(accounting)
Server status:   ACTIVE, Last transaction at unknown
Number of pending requests         0
Average round trip time            0ms
Number of authentication requests  55
Number of authorization requests   13
Number of accounting requests      45
Number of retransmissions          0
Number of accepts                  54
Number of rejects                  1
```

continues

Example 7-8 *Output of the* **show aaa-server** *Command for a Specific Host (Continued)*

```
Number of challenges                54
Number of malformed responses        0
Number of bad authenticators         0
Number of timeouts                   0
Number of unrecognized responses     0
```

To clear the AAA server statistics for a specific server, use this command:

```
clear aaa-server statistics [tag [host hostname]]
```

To clear the AAA server statistics for all servers providing services for a specific protocol, use this command:

```
clear aaa-server statistics protocol server-protocol
```

To clear a specific AAA server group, use this command:

```
clear configure aaa-server [server-tag]
```

Configuring Authentication of Administrative Sessions

Cisco ASA supports authentication of administrative sessions using a local user database, a RADIUS server, or a TACACS+ server. An administrator can connect to the Cisco ASA via

- Telnet
- Secure Shell (SSH)
- Serial console connection
- Cisco ASA Device Manager (ASDM)

If connecting via Telnet or SSH, the user can retry authentication three times in case of user error. After the third time, the authentication session and connection to the Cisco ASA are closed. Authentication sessions via the console prompt the user continuously until the correct username and password are entered.

Before you start the configuration, you must decide which user database you will use (local or external AAA server). If you are using an external AAA server, configure the AAA server group and host, as covered in the previous section. You can use the **aaa authentication** command to require authentication verification when accessing Cisco ASA for administration. This section teaches you how to configure authentication for each type of connection.

Authenticating Telnet Connections

You can enable Telnet access to the Cisco ASA to any internal interface or to the outside (if an IPSec connection is established). Telnet sessions are allowed to the outside interface only over an IPSec connection. Example 7-9 includes the commands necessary to configure Telnet access using a local username and password.

Example 7-9 *Authenticating Telnet Connections*

```
Chicago# configure terminal
Chicago(config)# username admin password cisco
Chicago(config)# aaa authentication telnet console LOCAL
Chicago(config)# telnet 192.168.10.0 255.255.255.0 inside
Chicago(config)# exit
```

In Example 7-9, a user called admin will be able to be successfully authenticated when connecting via Telnet to the inside interface only from network 192.168.10.0/24. The keyword LOCAL can be used specify that the local user database on the Cisco ASA is used. This keyword can also be used to enable fallback to the local database if the configured authentication server is unavailable.

NOTE administrative sessions:Telnet:authenticating;authentication:of Telnet administrative sessions;Telnet connections:authenticationDo not confuse the keyword **console** with the serial console on the Cisco ASA. This keyword is used to force the Cisco ASA to require AAA authentication for any client trying to connect to it via Telnet, serial console, HTTP, or SSH. Telnet is used in Example 7-9.

Authenticating SSH Connections

To enable SSH on Cisco ASA, you configure a host name and domain name before generating the RSA key pair used by SSH. Example 7-10 shows how to generate the RSA key pair and enable SSH version 2 connections from any systems on the inside interface.

Example 7-10 *Generating RSA Key Pair and Enabling SSH Version 2*

```
Chicago# configure terminal
Chicago(config)# hostname ASA
Chicago(config)# domain-name cisco.com
Chicago(config)# crypto key generate rsa modulus 2048
INFO: The name for the keys will be: ASA.cisco.com
Keypair generation process begin.
Chicago(config)# ssh 0.0.0.0 0.0.0.0 inside
Chicago(config)# ssh version 2
```

After the RSA key pair has been generated and SSH has been enabled, complete your AAA server group and host configuration. In this example, a CiscoSecure ACS server (configured for TACACS+) is used for authentication. Enable SSH authentication as shown in Example 7-11.

Example 7-11 *Configuring SSH Authentication to a TACACS+ Server*

```
Chicago# configure terminal
Chicago(config)# aaa-server mygroup protocol tacacs+
Chicago(config-aaa-server)# max-failed-attempts 2
Chicago(config-aaa-server)# reactivation-mode timed
Chicago(config-aaa-server)# exit
Chicago(config)# aaa-server mygroup host 172.18.173.109
Chicago(config-aaa-server)# key cisco123
Chicago(config-aaa-server)# exit
Chicago(config)# aaa authentication ssh console mygroup
Chicago(config)# exit
```

In Example 7-11, the AAA server group is labeled as mygroup. The TACACS+ server's IP address is 172.18.173.109 and is configured with a shared secret of cisco123.

Complete the following steps to add Cisco ASA as a NAS in the CiscoSecure ACS:

Step 1   Log into the CiscoSecure ACS administration console.

Step 2   Click the **Network Configuration** tab from the navigation bar.

Step 3   Under AAA Clients, click **Add Entry**.

Step 4   Enter the Cisco ASA information as shown in Figure 7-4.

Figure 7-4   *Adding Cisco ASA as a NAS in ACS*

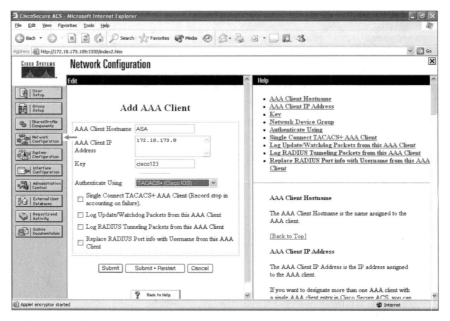

The AAA Client Hostname is the name given to the AAA client. The IP address of the interface that the Cisco ASA will source the TACACS+ packet (172.18.173.8) is entered under the **AAA Client IP Address** section. The Key is the shared secret that the Cisco ASA and CiscoSecure ACS use to encrypt their communication.

TIP	The shared key must be configured identically in both devices (key is case sensitive).

Authenticating Serial Console Connections

To configure authentication of serial console connections, use the **aaa authentication serial console** command. Be aware that you can get locked out of the Cisco ASA easily with any misconfiguration. Example 7-12 demonstrates how to configure serial console authentication using the AAA server group previously configured.

Example 7-12 *Configuring Serial Console Authentication*

```
Chicago(config)# aaa authentication serial console mygroup
```

TIP	Establishing two separate sessions to the Cisco ASA is always recommended when configuring AAA authentication. The purpose of this procedure is to avoid getting locked out of the CLI. Open one session using a Telnet or SSH connection and connect to the serial console of the Cisco ASA. One of the sessions can be disconnected once the configuration is verified and tested.
	If the administrator is locked out of the security appliance, follow the password recovery procedure discussed in Chapter 4, "Initial Setup and System Maintenance."

Authenticating Cisco ASDM Connections

The **aaa authentication http console** command can be configured to require authentication for Cisco ASDM users. Example 7-13 demonstrates how to configure ASDM authentication using the AAA server group previously configured.

Example 7-13 *Configuring HTTP Authentication for ASDM Users*

```
Chicago(config)# aaa authentication http console mygroup
```

If this command is not configured, Cisco ASDM users can gain access to the ASA by entering only the enable password, and no username, at the authentication prompt.

Authenticating Firewall Sessions (Cut-Through Proxy Feature)

Cisco ASA firewall session authentication is similar to the cut-through proxy feature on the CiscoSecure PIX Firewall. The firewall cut-through proxy requires the user to authenticate before passing any traffic through the Cisco ASA. A common deployment is to authenticate users before accessing a web server behind the Cisco ASA. Figure 7-5 illustrates how firewall session authentication works.

Figure 7-5 *Cut-Through Proxy Feature Example*

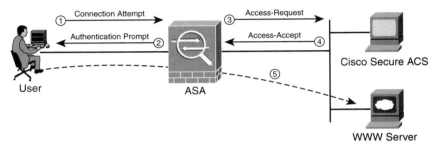

The following are the highlights of the steps in Figure 7-5:

1 The user on the outside of the Cisco ASA attempts to create an HTTP connection to the web server behind the ASA.

2 The Cisco ASA prompts the user for authentication.

3 The Cisco ASA receives the authentication information from the user and sends an AUTH Request to the CiscoSecure ACS server.

4 The server authenticates the user and sends an AUTH Accept message to the Cisco ASA.

5 The Cisco ASA allows the user to access the web server.

Cut-through proxy can be enabled with the **aaa authentication** command. The following is the command syntax:

```
aaa authentication include | exclude svc if_name l_ip l_mask [f_ip f_mask] server_tag
```

Table 7-5 lists all the **aaa authentication** command options.

Table 7-5 **aaa authentication** *Command Options*

Option	Description
include | exclude	Include or exclude the service, local, and foreign network, which needs to be authenticated, authorized, and accounted.
svc	Specifies the protocol and/or service used: *telnet* , *ftp* , *http* , *https* , *tcp/port* , and *tcp/0* .
if_name	The interface on the Cisco ASA that receives the connection request.
l_ip	The address of the local/internal host, which is the source or destination for connections requiring authentication.
l_mask	Network mask to apply to *l_ip* .
f_ip	The address of the foreign host, which is either the source or destination for connections requiring authentication.

Table 7-5 **aaa authentication** *Command Options (Continued)*

Option	Description
f_mask	Network mask to apply to *<f_ip>*.
server_tag	For authentication and accounting, use values defined by the **aaa-server** command.
	For cut-through and "to the box" authentication and command authorization, the server tag **LOCAL** can also be used.
	Only TACACS+ is supported for "through the box" authorization.

Using the **aaa authentication match** command is an alternate method of doing AAA authentication on Cisco ASA. It allows you to configure an access control list (ACL) to classify what traffic is authenticated. Using the **aaa authentication match** command replaces the use of the **include** and **exclude** options and it is now the preferred method to configure authentication through the Cisco ASA appliance. The following is the command syntax:

```
aaa authentication match acl interface server-tag
```

The *acl* keyword refers to the name or number of the ACL configured to define what traffic is authenticated. The *interface* keyword defines the interface that receives the connection request. The *server-tag* is the AAA server group defined by the **aaa-server** command.

Figure 7-6 illustrates an example of how the **aaa authentication match** command works. SecureMe Company has two users in the 209.165.200.224/27 network who need to access the web server in the 192.168.10.0/24 network. The Cisco ASA is configured to authenticate all users in the 209.165.200.224 network; however, User2 is allowed to connect to the web server without being authenticated.

Figure 7-6 *Firewall Session Authentication Exceptions*

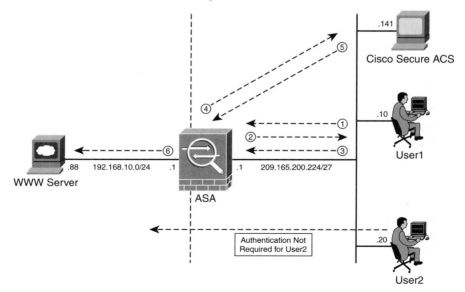

The following are the steps represented in Figure 7-6:

Step 1 User1 attempts to access the web server (192.168.10.88).

Step 2 The Cisco ASA prompts the user to authenticate.

Step 3 User1 replies with his credentials.

Step 4 The Cisco ASA sends the authentication request (Access-Request) to the CiscoSecure ACS RADIUS server (172.18.124.141).

Step 5 The CiscoSecure ACS server sends back its reply (Access-Accept) to the Cisco ASA.

Step 6 User1 is able to access the web server.

User2 is able to access the web server without being required to authenticate.

The commands to achieve this configuration are included in Example 7-14.

Example 7-14 *Configuring Firewall Session Authentication Exceptions*

```
!AAA server group called mygroup is configured for the 172.18.124.141 RADIUS server
aaa-server mygroup protocol radius
aaa-server mygroup host 172.18.124.141
 key cisco123!
!An ACL is configured to require authentication of all traffic except for User2
(172.18.124.20)
access-list 150 extended permit ip any any
access-list 150 extended deny ip host 172.18.124.20 any
!
!The aaa authentication match command is configured with the corresponding ACL.
aaa authentication match 150 inside mygroup
```

Cisco ASA is capable of excluding authentication for devices by using their MAC address. This feature is practical when bypassing authentication for devices such as printers and IP phones. You need to create a MAC address list, by using the **mac-list** command, to accomplish this task. Subsequently, you use the **aaa mac-exempt** command to bypass authentication for the specified MAC addresses on the list. Example 7-15 demonstrates how to configure the Cisco ASA to achieve this functionality.

Example 7-15 *Configuring Authentication Exceptions Using MAC Address Lists*

```
mac-list MACLIST permit 0003.470d.61aa ffff.ffff.ffff
mac-list MACLIST permit 0003.470d.61bb ffff.ffff.ffff
aaa mac-exempt match MAC
```

In Example 7-15, a MAC list named MACLIST is defined with two host MAC addresses and is associated with the **aaa mac-except** command.

NOTE Only one MAC list can be associated with **aaa mac-exempt**.

NOTE	Both authentication and authorization will be bypassed if this feature is turned on.

Authentication Timeouts

Authentication timeouts can be customized using the **timeout uauth** command. By using this command, you can specify how long the Cisco ASA should wait before requiring the user to reauthenticate after a period of inactivity or absolute duration. The following is the command syntax:

```
timeout uauth hh:mm:ss [absolute | inactivity]
```

The inactivity timer begins after a user connection becomes idle. The absolute timer runs continuously. If you use the inactivity and absolute timeouts at the same time, the absolute timeout duration should be longer than the inactivity timeout. If you set the timeouts the opposite way, the inactivity timeout will not work, because the absolute timeout always expires sooner.

NOTE	It is recommended to configure the **absolute timeout** command value for at least 2 minutes. Never configure the **timeout uauth** duration to 0, particularly when using passive FTP, because the authentication session will never time out.

Additionally, you can use the **clear uauth** command to delete all cached credentials and make all users reauthenticate when attempting to create a new connection through the Cisco ASA. You can append a username at the end of the command to make a specific user reauthenticate. For example, use **clear uauth joe** to force a user called "joe" to reauthenticate.

Customizing Authentication Prompts

Cisco ASA allows you to customize the authentication prompts by using the **auth-prompt** command. This customization is only available for Telnet, HTTP, or FTP authentication. The following is the usage and syntax of this command:

```
auth-prompt [prompt | accept |_reject] prompt text
```

Table 7-6 lists all the options of the **auth-prompt** command.

Table 7-6   **auth-prompt** *Command Options*

Option	Description
prompt text	The actual text that will be printed at challenge, accept, or reject time.
prompt	Specifies that text following this keyword is printed as the authentication prompt.
accept	The text following this keyword is printed at authentication acceptance time.
reject	The text following this keyword is printed at authentication rejection time.

NOTE	The **accept** and **reject** options apply only for Telnet connections.

Configuring Authorization

Cisco ASA supports authorization services over TACACS+ for firewall cut-through proxy sessions. It also supports authorization services over TACACS+ and its internal user database for administrative sessions. RADIUS-downloadable ACLs are also supported by Cisco ASA.

NOTE	Command access is authorized by privilege level only when authorization is done against the local database.

Additionally, authorization over RADIUS, LDAP, and internal user databases is available for VPN user connections. This is used for **mode-config** attributes for remote-access VPN clients. Information about **mode-config** and its attributes is provided in Chapter 16.

The **aaa authorization** command enables authorization for firewall cut-through proxy and administrative sessions. The following is the syntax for this command to enable authorization for firewall cut-through proxy sessions:

```
aaa authorization include | exclude svc if_name l_ip l_mask [f_ip f_mask] server_tag
```

Table 7-7 lists its options.

Table 7-7   **aaa authorization** *Command Options for Firewall Cut-Through Proxy Sessions*

Option	Description
include	Use this option to include authorization services for a specific host or network.
exclude	Use this option to exclude authorization services for a specific host or network.
svc	Specifies the protocol and/or service used: *telnet, ftp, http, https, tcp/port,* and *tcp/0*.
if_name	Name of the interface on which authorized connections are originated.
l_ip	The address of the local host or network that requires authorization.
l_mask	The network mask of the local host or network that requires authorization.
f_ip	The address of the foreign host or network whose connections require authorization.
f_mask	The network mask of the foreign host or network whose connections require authorization.
server_tag	The name of the AAA server tag. For cut-through and command authorization, the server tag **LOCAL** can also be used. Only TACACS+ is supported for cut-through authorization.

You can also use the **aaa authorization match** command to define a firewall cut-through proxy session:

```
aaa authorization match access_list_name if_name server_tag
```

The *access_list_name* option specifies the ACL name used to categorize which traffic requires authorization. Example 7-16 demonstrates how to use this command.

Example 7-16 *Enabling Authorization Using an ACL to Define Interesting Traffic*

```
access-list 100 extended permit ip 10.10.10.0 255.255.255.0 192.168.1.0
  255.255.255.0
aaa-server mygroup protocol tacacs+
aaa-server mygroup host 10.10.10.100
 key cisco123
aaa authorization match 100 inside mygroup
```

In Example 7-16, access list 100 defines that all IP traffic sourced from the 10.10.10.0/24 network destined to 192.168.1.0/24 requires authorization. This ACL is associated to the **aaa authorization match** command.

Command Authorization

To configure command authorization on the Cisco ASA, the following command is used:

```
aaa authorization command {LOCAL | tacacs_server_tag [LOCAL]}
```

The server tag **LOCAL** defines local command authorization. It can also be used as a fallback method in case the TACACS+ server is unreachable.

TIP   Establishing two separate sessions to the Cisco ASA is always recommended when configuring AAA authorization. The purpose of this procedure is to avoid getting locked out of the CLI. Open one session using a Telnet or SSH connection and connect to the serial console of the Cisco ASA. One of the sessions can be disconnected once the configuration is verified and tested.

When using authorization, the following attributes are passed to the TACACS+ server in the attribute payload of the authorization request message:

- **cmd**—The command string to be authorized (used for authorization for administrative sessions only)

- **cmd-arg**—The command arguments to be sent (used for authorization for administrative sessions only)

- **service**—The type of service for which authorization is requested

The following attributes may be received from a TACACS+ server in an authorization response message:

- **idletime**—Idle timeout value for firewall cut-through proxy sessions
- **timeout**—Absolute timeout value for firewall cut-through proxy sessions
- **acl**—The identifier of an ACL to be applied to a specific user

Configuring Downloadable ACLs

Cisco ASA provides support for a per-user ACL authorization by downloading an ACL from a RADIUS or TACACS+ server. This feature allows you to push an ACL to the Cisco ASA from a CiscoSecure ACS server. The downloadable ACL will work in combination with the ACLs configured in the ASA. The user traffic needs to be permitted by both ACLs in order for it to flow through the ASA. However, the **per-user-override** option can be configured at the end of the **access-group** command to bypass this requirement. The following is an example of applying the **per-user-override** option on an **access-group** command applied to the inside interface:

```
access-group 100 in interface inside per-user-override
```

All downloadable ACLs are applied to the interface from which the user is authenticated.

Figure 7-7 illustrates an example of how downloadable ACLs work.

Figure 7-7   *Downloadable ACL Example*

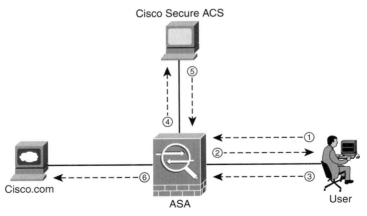

The following are the steps listed in Figure 7-7:

1   A user initiates a web connection to Cisco.com.

2   The Cisco ASA is configured to perform authentication (cut-through proxy) and prompts the user for authentication credentials.

3 The user replies with his credentials.

4 The Cisco ASA sends the RADIUS authentication request (Access-Accept) to the CiscoSecure ACS server.

5 The CiscoSecure ACS server authenticates the user and sends a RADIUS response (Access-Accept) including an ACL name associated with the user.

6 The Cisco ASA verifies whether it has an ACL named the same as the one downloaded from the CiscoSecure ACS server. There is no need to download a new ACL if there is an ACL identified with the same name.

You can configure downloadable ACLs in CiscoSecure ACS in a few different ways:

- Configure a Shared Profile Component (SPC), including both the ACL name and the actual ACL. This allows you to apply the ACL to any number of users within CiscoSecure ACS.

- Configure each ACL entry within a specific user profile.

- Configure the ACLs to be applied to a specific group.

These options are supported with Cisco ASA to better fit your security policies.

Configuring Accounting

To configure accounting on the Cisco ASA, use the **aaa accounting** command:

```
aaa accounting match access_list_name if_name server_tag
```

Example 7-17 demonstrates how to configure accounting on the Cisco ASA.

Example 7-17 *Enabling Accounting Using an ACL to Define Interesting Traffic*

```
Chicago(config)# access-list 100 permit ip 10.1.1.0 255.255.255.0 172.18.124.0
255.255.255.0
Chicago(config)# aaa accounting match 100 inside mygroup
```

In Example 7-17, an ACL is configured to enable accounting for all connections initiated from 10.1.1.0/24 to 172.18.124.0/24. The ACL is then applied to the **aaa accounting match** command. A previously defined AAA server group named mygroup is used with this command.

NOTE   You can also use the **aaa accounting include | exclude** command options, as demonstrated for the **aaa authentication** command. The **aaa accounting match** command makes the **include** and **exclude** options obsolete.

RADIUS Accounting

Table 7-8 lists all the RADIUS accounting messages supported by Cisco ASA.

Table 7-8 *RADIUS Accounting Messages Supported by Cisco ASA*

Attribute	Applicable Messages
acct-authentic	on, off, start, stop
acct-delay-time	on, off, start, stop
acct-status-type	on, off, start, stop
acct-session-id	start, stop
nas-ip-address	on, off, start, stop
nas-port	on, off, start, stop
user-name	on, off, start, stop
class	start, stop
service type	start, stop
framed-protocol	start, stop
framed-ip-address	start, stop
tunnel-client-endpoint	start, stop
acct-session-time	stop
acct-input-packets	stop
acct-output-packets	stop
acct-input-octets	stop
acct-output-octets	stop
acct-terminate-cause	stop
login-ip-host	on, off, start, stop
login-port	on, off, start, stop
Cisco AV pair (used to send source addr/port and dest addr/port)	on, off, start, stop
isakmp-initiator-ip	on, off, start, stop
isakmp-phase1-id	on, off, start, stop
isakmp-group-id	on, off, start, stop
acct-input-gigawords	stop
acct-output-gigawords	stop

The accounting-on message marks the start of accounting services. Subsequently, to mark the end of accounting services, use the accounting-off message. The start and stop accounting records are used to label when a user started a connection to a specific service. These sessions are labeled with their own accounting session IDs.

TACACS+ Accounting

Table 7-9 lists all the TACACS+ accounting messages that Cisco ASA supports.

Table 7-9   *TACACS+ Accounting Messages Supported by Cisco ASA*

Attribute	Applicable Messages
username (fixed field)	start, stop
port (NAS) (fixed field)	start, stop
remote_address (fixed field)	start, stop
task_id	start, stop
foreign_IP	start, stop
local_IP	start, stop
cmd	start, stop
elapsed_time	stop
bytes_in	stop
bytes_out	stop

Cisco ASA also allows you to configure command accounting depending on the user's privilege level. Use the following command to enable this feature:

```
aaa accounting command {privilege level} tacacs_server_tag
```

Example 7-18 demonstrates how to configure command accounting on the Cisco ASA depending on the user's privilege level.

Example 7-18 *Enabling Command Accounting*

```
Chicago(config)# aaa accounting command privilege 15 mygroup
```

In Example 7-18, the **accounting** command is enabled for users that execute a privilege level 15 command.

Deployment Scenarios

This section demonstrates how SecureMe Company deploys TACACS+ authentication, authorization, and accounting for administrative sessions connecting to its ASA. It also shows how cut-through proxy authentication is configured for all clients at a remote branch.

Deploying Authentication, Command Authorization, and Accounting for Administrative Sessions

The security administrator for SecureMe configures the Chicago ASA to perform authentication, command authorization, and accounting for all administrative sessions using TACACS+. Figure 7-8 illustrates the Chicago network topology. A TACACS+ server (172.18.124.101) and a management workstation (172.18.124.159) are configured in the management subnet (172.18.124.0/24). The Cisco ASA management interface is 172.18.124.205.

Figure 7-8 *Chicago Network Topology*

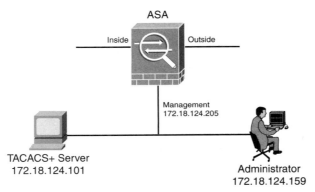

The goal is to configure two users. The first user, User1, has the ability to configure anything on the Cisco ASA. The second user, User2, is only allowed to add routes to the Cisco ASA. Accounting is configured for audit and monitoring purposes. Example 7-19 shows the Chicago ASA configuration.

Example 7-19 *AAA: Chicago ASA Configuration*

```
!outside interface configuration
interface GigabitEthernet0/0
 nameif outside
 security-level 0
 ip address 209.165.200.225 255.255.255.0
 !
!inside interface configuration
interface GigabitEthernet0/1
 nameif inside
 security-level 100
 ip address 192.168.10.1 255.255.255.0
 !
 !
!management interface configuration
interface Management0/0
 nameif management
 security-level 50
```

Example 7-19 *AAA: Chicago ASA Configuration (Continued)*

```
ip address 172.18.124.205 255.255.255.0
 management-only
!
!AAA server group configuration. A server group called mytacacs is configured. The
!172.18.124.101 TACACS+ server is added.
aaa-server mytacacs protocol tacacs+
aaa-server mytacacs (management) host 172.18.124.101
 key cisco123
!TACACS authentication for telnet, ssh, secure-http-client, and serial console
aaa authentication telnet console mytacacs
aaa authentication serial mytacacs
aaa authentication ssh mytacacs
aaa authentication secure-http-client mytacacs
!TACACS authorization is configured
aaa authorization command mytacacs
!TACACS accounting is enabled
aaa accounting command mytacacs
```

Figure 7-9 illustrates how the Cisco ASA is added as a AAA client in the TACACS+ server (CiscoSecure ACS).

Figure 7-9   *AAA Client Configuration in ACS*

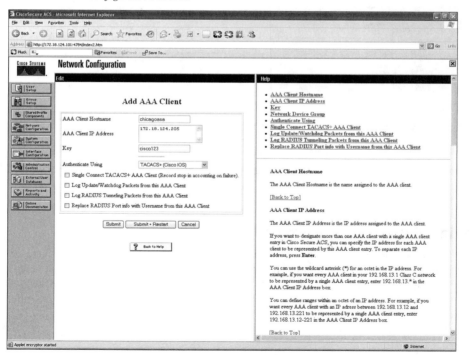

User1 belongs to Group 1 in the ACS server. User2 belongs to Group 2. Group level authorization is configured in the ACS server. Privilege level 15 is configured in Group 1 to allow User1 to freely modify the configuration of the Cisco ASA. Figure 7-10 illustrates how the CiscoSecure ACS group is configured.

Figure 7-10 *Privilege Level 15 Group Configuration in ACS*

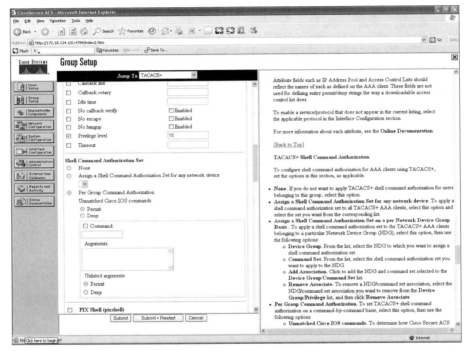

Group 2 is configured for privilege level 8, allowing User2 only to configure route statements on the ASA. Figure 7-11 illustrates how the CiscoSecure ACS is configured.

Deploying Cut-Through Proxy Authentication

A Cisco ASA at a branch office in Las Vegas, Nevada is configured to perform cut-through proxy. The ASA is configured to require authentication for network access to any protocol or services. Users can authenticate directly with HTTP(S), Telnet, or FTP only. However, they must first authenticate with one of these services before the Cisco ASA allows other traffic to pass through the appliance.

Figure 7-11 *Command Authorization*

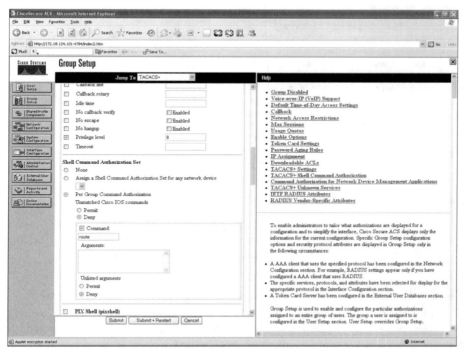

Figure 7-12 illustrates how an internal user (client1) attempts a connection to a server (209.165.201.2) on the outside, but first the ASA will prompt for authentication.

Figure 7-12 *Las Vegas Network Topology*

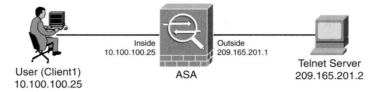

User (Client1)
10.100.100.25

Inside
10.100.100.25

ASA

Outside
209.165.201.1

Telnet Server
209.165.201.2

The Cisco ASA is configured to authenticate all internal users using its local database. Example 7-20 shows the Las Vegas ASA configuration.

Example 7-20 *AAA: Las Vegas ASA Configuration*

```
!outside interface configuration
interface GigabitEthernet0/0
 nameif outside
 security-level 0
 ip address 209.165.201.1 255.255.255.224
!
```

continues

Example 7-20 *AAA: Las Vegas ASA Configuration (Continued)*

```
!inside interface configuration
interface GigabitEthernet0/1
 nameif inside
 security-level 100
 ip address 10.100.100.1 255.255.255.0
 !
route outside 0.0.0.0 0.0.0.0 209.165.201.2 1
!user client1 is added to the local database
username client1 password W.a6bMRKDh/sWvbI encrypted
!access-list and aaa authentication match command are configured to require all
users in !the inside to be authenticated.
access-list 100 extended permit ip any any
aaa authentication match 100 inside LOCAL
```

Troubleshooting AAA

This section provides information about the AAA troubleshooting mechanisms available on Cisco ASA. Additionally, it includes several common problems and describes how to resolve them using the different commands available for troubleshooting.

Troubleshooting Administrative Connections to Cisco ASA

Administrative connections can be authenticated using RADIUS, TACACS+, or the Cisco ASA local user database. The following **debug** commands are available to troubleshoot AAA problems when you are trying to connect to the Cisco ASA for administration:

- **debug aaa**—Provides information about the authentication, authorization, or accounting messages generated and received by the Cisco ASA.

- **debug radius**—To troubleshoot RADIUS transactions, use this command, which has several options:

  - **all**—Enables all debug options

  - **decode**—Shows decoded RADIUS transaction messages

  - **session**—Provides information about all RADIUS sessions

  - **user**—Allows you to capture RADIUS transaction information for a specific user connection

- **debug tacacs**—To troubleshoot TACACS+ transactions, use this command with either of the following options:

  - **session**—Provides detailed information about all TACACS+ transactions

  - **user**—Allows you to capture TACACS+ transaction information for a specific user connection

If you enter **debug tacacs** without any options, the **debug** command is enabled with the **session** option by default. Example 7-21 includes the output of **debug tacacs** during a successful Telnet authentication.

Example 7-21 *Output of* **debug tacacs** *During a Successful Telnet Authentication*

```
Chicago# debug tacacs
 mk_pkt - type: 0x1, session_id: 4
 user: user1
 Tacacs packet sent
Sending TACACS Start message. Session id: 4, seq no:1
Received TACACS packet. Session id:4  seq no:2
tacp_procpkt_authen: GETPASS
Authen Message: Password:
mk_pkt - type: 0x1, session_id: 4
mkpkt_continue - response: ***
 Tacacs packet sent
Sending TACACS Continue message. Session id: 4, seq no:3
Received TACACS packet. Session id:4  seq no:4
tacp_procpkt_authen: PASS
TACACS Session finished. Session id: 4, seq no: 3
```

In Example 7-21, User1 connected to the Cisco ASA via Telnet. The Cisco ASA was configured to perform authentication via an external TACACS+ server. The first highlighted line shows that User1 attempted a connection to the Cisco ASA. The second highlighted line shows the ASA requesting the user's password. The user information is sent to the TACACS+ server and is finally authenticated. The third highlighted line shows that the authentication was successful.

Example 7-22 includes the output of **debug tacacs** during an authentication failure. In this example, the incorrect password was entered by the user and the TACACS+ server failed its authentication.

Example 7-22 *Output of* **debug tacacs** *During a Failed Authentication Because of Wrong Password*

```
Chicago# debug tacacs
 mk_pkt - type: 0x1, session_id: 5
 user: user1
 Tacacs packet sent
Sending TACACS Start message. Session id: 5, seq no:1
Received TACACS packet. Session id:5  seq no:2
tacp_procpkt_authen: GETPASS
Authen Message: Password:
mk_pkt - type: 0x1, session_id: 5
mkpkt_continue - response: ***
 Tacacs packet sent
Sending TACACS Continue message. Session id: 5, seq no:3
Received TACACS packet. Session id:5  seq no:4
tacp_procpkt_authen: FAIL
TACACS Session finished. Session id: 5, seq no: 3
```

The highlighted line in Example 7-22 shows the authentication FAIL message.

In Example 7-23, the TACACS+ server was offline or unreachable.

Example 7-23 *Output of* **debug tacacs** *While TACACS+ Server Is Unreachable*

```
Chicago# debug tacacs
mk_pkt - type: 0x1, session_id: 6
 user: user1
 Tacacs packet sent
Sending TACACS Start message. Session id: 6, seq no:1
Received TACACS packet. Session id:6  seq no:2
TACACS Request Timed out. Session id: 6, seq no:1
TACACS Session finished. Session id: 6, seq no: 1
mk_pkt - type: 0x1, session_id: 6
user: user1
 Tacacs packet sent
Sending TACACS Start message. Session id: 6, seq no:1
Received TACACS packet. Session id:6  seq no:2
TACACS Request Timed out. Session id: 6, seq no:1
TACACS Session finished. Session id: 6, seq no: 1
mk_pkt - type: 0x1, session_id: 6
 user: user1
 Tacacs packet sent
Sending TACACS Start message. Session id: 6, seq no:1
Received TACACS packet. Session id:6  seq no:2
TACACS Request Timed out. Session id: 6, seq no:1
TACACS Session finished. Session id: 6, seq no: 1
aaa server host machine not responding
```

The highlighted lines show how the Cisco ASA attempts to communicate with the TACACS+ server three times and finally finishes all authentication transactions.

The **show aaa-server** command is useful while troubleshooting and monitoring authentication transactions. Example 7-24 includes the output of the **show aaa-server** command for all TACACS+ transactions.

Example 7-24 *Monitoring and Troubleshooting TACACS+ Transactions with the* **show aaa-server** *Command*

```
Chicago# show aaa-server protocol tacacs+
Server Group:    mygroup
Server Protocol: tacacs+
Server Address:  172.18.173.109
Server port:     49
Server status:   ACTIVE, Last transaction at 21:05:43 UTC Sun Aug 8 2004
Number of pending requests         0
Average round trip time            43ms
Number of authentication requests  4
Number of authorization requests   0
Number of accounting requests      0
Number of retransmissions          0
Number of accepts                  3
Number of rejects                  1
Number of challenges               4
Number of malformed responses      0
Number of bad authenticators       0
Number of timeouts                 0
Number of unrecognized responses   0
```

In Example 7-24, the Cisco ASA processed a total of four authentication requests. Three of those requests were successfully authenticated and one was rejected by the TACACS+ server.

Troubleshooting Firewall Sessions (Cut-Through Proxy)

The techniques to troubleshoot cut-through proxy sessions on Cisco ASA are similar to the ones mentioned in the previous section. Additionally, the **show uauth** command can be used to display information about authenticated users and current transactions. Example 7-25 shows the output of this command.

Example 7-25 *Output of the* **show uauth** *Command*

```
Chicago# show uauth
                        Current     Most Seen
Authenticated Users        0           0
Authen In Progress         1           3
```

In Example 7-25, a total of three concurrent authentication requests were processed by the Cisco ASA. One is currently being processed.

Summary

Cisco ASA supports several AAA solutions for different services. It ensures the enforcement of assigned policies by allowing you to control who can log into the Cisco ASA or into the network. Additionally, it controls what each user is allowed to do. It can also record security audit information using accounting services. This chapter covered how Cisco ASA can use authentication services to control pass-through access by requiring valid user credentials. It also demonstrated how Cisco ASA is configured to authenticate administrative sessions from Telnet, SSH, serial console, and ASDM.

This chapter demonstrated how authorization can enforce per-user access control after authentication is done. It guided you to configure the Cisco ASA appliance to authorize management and administrative commands and network access.

The Cisco ASA accounting services track traffic that passes through the security appliance, enabling you to have a record of user activity. This chapter also demonstrated how you can enable accounting to track and audit user activity.

This chapter covers the following topics:

- Introduction to application inspection
- Enabling application inspection using the Modular Policy CLI
- Detailed information on the supported protocols and applications, such as HTTP, ESMTP, FTP, and H.323

CHAPTER 8

Application Inspection

This chapter describes how to use and configure application inspection on the Cisco ASA. The Cisco ASA mechanisms used for stateful application inspection enforce the secure use of applications and services in your network. The stateful inspection engine keeps information about each connection traversing through the security appliance's interfaces and makes sure they are valid. Stateful application inspection examines not only the packet header, but also the contents of the packet up through the application layer.

Several applications require special handling of data packets when they pass through the Layer 3 devices. These include applications and protocols that embed IP addressing information in the data payload of the packet or open secondary channels on dynamically assigned ports. The Cisco ASA application inspection mechanisms recognize the embedded addressing information, which allows Network Address Translation (NAT) to work and update any other fields or checksums.

Using application inspection, the Cisco ASA can identify the dynamic port assignments and allow data exchange on these ports during a specific connection. The application inspection capabilities are similar to the traditional fixup protocol functionality on the Cisco PIX firewalls. However, the Cisco ASA software dramatically enhances the capabilities of application inspection.

Table 8-1 lists all the applications and protocols supported by Cisco ASA. It also includes a list of the corresponding source and destination ports they use.

Table 8-1 *Supported Applications and Protocols*

Protocol Name	Protocol	Source Port	Destination Port
CTIQBE	TCP	Any	2748
DNS	UDP	Any	53
FTP	TCP	Any	21
GTP	UDP	2123, 3386	2123, 3386
H.323 H225	TCP	Any	1720
H.323 RAS	UDP	Any	1718–1719
HTTP	TCP	Any	80

continues

Table 8-1 *Supported Applications and Protocols (Continued)*

Protocol Name	Protocol	Source Port	Destination Port
ICMP	ICMP	—	—
ILS	TCP	Any	389
MGCP	UDP	2427, 2727	2427, 2727
NetBIOS	UDP	Any	137–138
SUNRPC	UDP	Any	111
RSH	TCP	Any	514
RTSP	TCP	Any	554
SIP	TCP, UDP	Any	5060
Skinny	TCP	Any	2000
SMTP/ESMTP	TCP	Any	25
SQLNet	TCP	Any	1521
TFTP	UDP	Any	69
XDMCP	UDP	Any	177

The following sections include thorough information on how to enable application inspection and details about these applications and protocols.

NOTE Certain protocol inspection requires a separate license. An example is GTP. More licensing information can be found at http://www.cisco.com/go/asa.

Enabling Application Inspection Using the Modular Policy Framework

Cisco ASA provides a Modular Policy Framework (MPF) to provide application security or to perform quality of service (QoS) functions. MPF provides a consistent and flexible way to configure the Cisco ASA application inspection and other features in a manner similar to the Cisco IOS Software Modular QoS CLI.

NOTE Chapter 12, "Quality of Service," covers the QoS functionality in detail.

As a general rule, the provisioning of inspection policies requires the following steps:

1 Configure traffic classes to identify interesting traffic.

2 Associate actions to each traffic class to create policies.

3 Activate the policies on an interface.

These policy provisioning steps can be completed using these three main commands of the MPF:

- **class-map**—Classifies the traffic that will be inspected. Various types of match criteria in a class map can be used to classify traffic. The primary criterion is the use of an access control list (ACL). Example 8-1 demonstrates this.

- **policy-map**—Configures security or QoS policies. A policy consists of a **class** command and its associated actions. Additionally, a policy map can contain multiple policies.

- **service-policy**—Activates a policy map globally (on all interfaces) or on a targeted interface.

Example 8-1 *Matching Specific Traffic Using an ACL*

```
Chicago(config)# access-list udptraffic permit udp any any
Chicago(config)# class-map UDPclass
Chicago(config-cmap)# match access-list udptraffic
Chicago(config-cmap)# exit
Chicago(config)# policy-map udppolicy
Chicago(config-pmap)# class UDPclass
Chicago(config-pmap-c)# inspect tftp
Chicago(config-pmap-c)# exit
Chicago(config-pmap)# exit
Chicago(config)# service-policy udppolicy global
```

In Example 8-1, an ACL named **udptraffic** is configured to identify all UDP traffic. This ACL is then applied to a class map named **UDPclass**.

A policy map named **udppolicy** is configured that has the class map **UDPclass** mapped to it. The policy map is set up to inspect all TFTP traffic from the UDP packets that are being classified in the class map. Finally, the service policy is applied globally.

The security appliance contains a default class map named **inspection_default** and a policy map named **asa_global_fw_policy**. Example 8-2 shows the default class map and policy map in the Cisco ASA.

Example 8-2 *Default Class and Policy Maps*

```
class-map inspection_default
 match default-inspection-traffic
!
!
policy-map global_policy
 class inspection_default
  inspect dns maximum-length 512
  inspect ftp
  inspect h323 h225
  inspect h323 ras
```

continues

Example 8-2   *Default Class and Policy Maps (Continued)*

```
  inspect netbios
  inspect rsh
  inspect rtsp
  inspect skinny
  inspect esmtp
  inspect sqlnet
  inspect sunrpc
  inspect tftp
  inspect sip
  inspect xdmcp
!
service-policy global_policy global
```

Selective Inspection

As previously mentioned, the **match** command allows you to specify what traffic the Cisco ASA inspection engine will process. It can be used in conjunction with an ACL to determine what traffic will be inspected. Example 8-3 shows all the supported options for traffic classification in a class map named **UDPclass**.

Example 8-3   *Supported Traffic Classification Options*

```
Chicago(config)# class-map UDPclass
Chicago(config-cmap)# match ?
mpf-class-map mode commands/options:
  access-list                 Match an Access List
  any                         Match any packet
  default-inspection-traffic  Match default inspection traffic:
                              ctiqbe----tcp--2748    dns-------udp--53
                              ftp-------tcp--21      gtp-------udp--2123,3386
                              h323-h225-tcp--1720    h323-ras--udp--1718-1719
                              http------tcp--80      icmp------icmp
                              ils-------tcp--389     mgcp------udp--2427,2727
                              netbios---udp--137-138 rpc-------udp--111
                              rsh-------tcp--514     rtsp------tcp--554
                              sip-------tcp--5060    sip-------udp--5060
                              skinny----tcp--2000    smtp------tcp--25
                              sqlnet----tcp--1521    tftp------udp--69
                              xdmcp-----udp--177
  dscp                        Match IP DSCP (DiffServ CodePoints)
  flow                        Flow based Policy
  port                        Match TCP/UDP port(s)
  precedence                  Match IP precedence
  rtp                         Match RTP port numbers
  tunnel-group                Match a Tunnel Group
```

Table 8-2 lists briefly describes all the options supported by the **match** command.

Table 8-2   match *Subcommand Options*

Option	Description
access-list	Specifies an ACL used to match or classify the traffic to be inspected.
any	Any IP traffic.
default-inspection-traffic	The default entry for inspection of the supported protocols. This match applies only to the **inspect** command. It cannot be associated with any action commands but **inspect**.
dscp	Matches based on IP DSCP (DiffServ CodePoints).
flow	Used for flow-based policy.
port	Used to match TCP and/or UDP ports.
precedence	Matches based on IP Precedence value represented by the TOS byte in the IP header. The precedence value can be in a range from 0 to 7.
rtp	Matches Real Time Protocol (RTP) port numbers.
tunnel-group	Matches VPN traffic of a specific tunnel group.

NOTE   Details on matching traffic based on DSCP, flow, precedence, and tunnel group are covered in Chapter 12.

To display statistics on the traffic being inspected on the Cisco ASA, use the **show service-policy** command. Example 8-4 shows the output of this command.

Example 8-4   *Output of* **show service-policy** *Command*

```
Chicago# show service-policy
Global policy:
  Service-policy: global_policy
    Class-map: inspection_default
      Inspect: dns maximum-length 512, packet 0, drop 0, reset-drop 0
      Inspect: ftp, packet 24, drop 0, reset-drop 0
      Inspect: h323 h225, packet 0, drop 0, reset-drop 0
      Inspect: h323 ras, packet 0, drop 0, reset-drop 0
      Inspect: netbios, packet 10, drop 0, reset-drop 0
      Inspect: rsh, packet 0, drop 0, reset-drop 0
      Inspect: rtsp, packet 0, drop 0, reset-drop 0
      Inspect: skinny, packet 0, drop 0, reset-drop 0
      Inspect: esmtp, packet 54, drop 0, reset-drop 0
      Inspect: sqlnet, packet 0, drop 0, reset-drop 0
      Inspect: sunrpc, packet 0, drop 0, reset-drop 0
      Inspect: tftp, packet 0, drop 0, reset-drop 0
      Inspect: sip, packet 0, drop 0, reset-drop 0
      Inspect: xdmcp, packet 0, drop 0, reset-drop 0
```

The following sections include information about each application inspection protocol supported on Cisco ASA.

Computer Telephony Interface Quick Buffer Encoding Inspection

Some Cisco Voice over IP (VoIP) applications use the Telephony Application Programming Interface (TAPI) and Java TAPI (JTAPI). TAPI-compatible applications can run on a wide variety of PC and telephony hardware and can support a variety of network services. The Cisco TAPI Service Provider (TSP) uses the Computer Telephony Interface Quick Buffer Encoding (CTIQBE) to communicate with Cisco CallManager on TCP port 2748. Figure 8-1 illustrates how CTIQBE works.

Figure 8-1 *Explanation of CTIQBE*

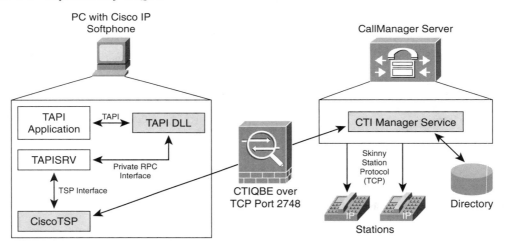

In Figure 8-1, a PC with Cisco IP SoftPhone communicates with a Cisco CallManager. CTIQBE inspection is not enabled by default. Use the **inspect ctiqbe** command to enable the Cisco ASA to inspect the TCP port 2748 CTIQBE packets, as shown in Example 8-5.

Example 8-5 *Enabling CTIQBE Inspection*

```
Chicago# configure terminal
Chicago(config)# policy-map asa_global_fw_policy
Chicago(config-pmap)# class inspection_default
Chicago(config-pmap-c)# inspect ctiqbe
```

In Example 8-5, CTIQBE inspection is enabled under the Cisco ASA global policy. Consequently, all traffic traversing the security appliance is inspected for CTIQBE, which successfully translates and transfers CTIQBE traffic to and from Cisco CallManager and IP SoftPhone.

NOTE	CTIQBE application inspection is not supported if the **alias** command is present in the configuration.

TIP	CTIQBE calls will fail if two Cisco IP SoftPhones are registered with different Cisco CallManagers connected to different interfaces of the Cisco ASA.

TIP	If the Cisco CallManager IP address is to be translated and you are also using PAT, TCP port 2748 must be statically mapped to the same port of the PAT (interface) address for Cisco IP SoftPhone registrations to succeed. The CTIQBE listening port (TCP 2748) is fixed and is not configurable on Cisco CallManager, Cisco IP SoftPhone, or Cisco TSP.

NOTE	Stateful failover of CTIQBE calls is not supported.

You can use the **show conn state ctiqbe detail** command to display the status of CTIQBE connections. The **C** flag represents the media connections allocated by the CTIQBE inspection engine. Example 8-6 includes the output of the **show conn state ctiqbe detail** command.

Example 8-6 *Output of the* **show conn state ctiqbe detail** *Command*

```
Chicago# show conn state ctiqbe detail
5 in use, 11 most used
Flags: A - awaiting inside ACK to SYN, a - awaiting outside ACK to SYN,
       B - initial SYN from outside, C - CTIQBE media, D - DNS, d - dump,
       E - outside back connection, F - outside FIN, f - inside FIN,
       G - group, g - MGCP, H - H.323, h - H.225.0, I - inbound data,
       i - incomplete, J - GTP, j - GTP data, k - Skinny media,
       M - SMTP data, m - SIP media, O - outbound data, P - inside back connection,
       q - SQL*Net data, R - outside acknowledged FIN,
       R - UDP RPC, r - inside acknowledged FIN, S - awaiting inside SYN,
       s - awaiting outside SYN, T - SIP, t - SIP transient, U - up
```

Domain Name System

Domain Name System (DNS) implementations require application inspection to allow the DNS queries not to rely on the generic UDP handling based on activity timeouts. As a security mechanism, the UDP connections associated with DNS queries and responses are torn down as soon as a reply to a DNS query has been received in the Cisco ASA. This is similar to the DNS Guard feature in Cisco PIX Firewall.

Cisco ASA DNS inspection provides the following benefits:

- Guarantees that the ID of the DNS reply matches the ID of the DNS query.

- Allows the translation of DNS packets using NAT.

- Reassembles the DNS packet to verify its length. The Cisco ASA allows DNS packets up to 65,535 bytes. When necessary, reassembly is done to verify that the packet length is less than the maximum length specified by the user. The packet is dropped if it is not compliant.

To enable DNS inspection, use the **inspect dns** command. You can also specify the maximum DNS packet length, as shown in Example 8-7.

Example 8-7 *Enabling DNS Inspection*

```
Chicago(config)# policy-map global_policy
Chicago(config-pmap)# class inspection_default
Chicago(config-pmap-c)# inspect dns maximum-length 1024
```

NOTE   The maximum DNS packet length can be configured in a range from 512 to 65,535 bytes. The default packet size is 512 bytes. It is recommended to use a maximum size of 1024 bytes, because several DNS applications use sizes larger than 512 bytes.

Extended Simple Mail Transfer Protocol

Cisco ASA Extended SMTP (ESMTP) inspection enhances the traditional SMTP inspection provided by Cisco PIX Firewall version 6.x or earlier. It provides protection against SMTP-based attacks by restricting the types of SMTP commands that can pass through the Cisco ASA. The following are the supported ESMTP commands:

- AUTH
- DATA
- EHLO
- ETRN
- HELO
- HELP
- MAIL
- NOOP
- QUIT
- RCPT
- RSET
- SAML
- SEND
- SOML
- VRFY

If an illegal command is found in an ESMTP or SMTP packet, it is modified and forwarded. This causes a negative server reply, forcing the client to issue a valid command. Figure 8-2 shows an example in which a user is trying to send TURN, which is an unsupported illegal command. The Cisco ASA modifies it and makes the receiver reply with an SMTP error return code of 500 (command not recognized) and tears down the connection.

NOTE   The Cisco ASA replaces the illegal command characters with X's, as illustrated in Figure 8-2.

Figure 8-2   *ESMTP Illegal Command Example*

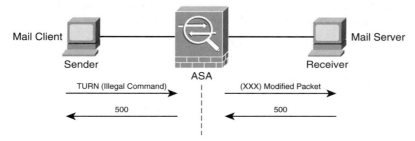

The Cisco ASA may perform deeper parameter inspection for packets containing legal commands. This type of inspection is required for SMTP and ESMTP extensions. The following SMTP and ESMTP extensions are inspected using deeper parameter inspection:

- Message Size Declaration (SIZE)
- Remote Queue Processing Declaration (ETRN)
- Binary MIME (BINARYMIME)
- Command Pipelining (PIPELINING)
- Authentication (AUTH)
- Delivery Status Notification (DSN)
- Enhanced Status Code (ENHANCEDSTATUSCODES)
- 8bit-MIMEtransport (8BITMIME)

To enable ESMTP inspection, use the **inspect esmtp** command. This command is enabled in the default class and policy maps on the Cisco ASA.

NOTE   If you enter the **inspect smtp** command, the Cisco ASA automatically converts the command to the **inspect esmtp** command.

The ESMTP AUTH command is used to indicate the authentication mechanism to the ESTMP server. If the server supports the requested authentication mechanism, it authenticates and identifies the user. The server sends a series of challenges that are answered by the client, depending on the authentication mechanism used. A server challenge (or ready response) is an ESMTP 334 reply with a Base64-encoded string. The client answer consists of a line containing a Base64-encoded string. The Cisco ASA inspects and keeps track of this exchange.

An important characteristic of ESMTP AUTH is that the client's reply is not associated with any SMTP command. The reply is sent with just a line containing a Base64-encoded string. The Cisco ASA has the ability to recognize the client's reply from other requests that contain ESMTP commands in the first 4 bytes and does not do command inspection for this reply. The Cisco ASA allows the keyword AUTH to be sent over the EHLO response when ESMTP inspection is enabled, allowing the client and server to use the authentication extension.

File Transfer Protocol

Cisco ASA FTP application inspection examines the FTP sessions to provide the following features:

- Enhanced security while creating dynamic secondary data connections for FTP transfers
- Enforcement of FTP command-response sequence
- Generation an audit trail for FTP sessions
- Translation of embedded IP address

Use the **inspect ftp** command to enable FTP inspection. The **strict** keyword (optional) allows the Cisco ASA to prevent client systems from sending embedded commands in FTP requests:

```
inspect ftp [strict] ftp-map-name
```

ftp-map-name is the name of an FTP map used to define FTP request commands to be denied. Example 8-8 demonstrates how to use the **inspect ftp strict** command in conjunction with an FTP map, called **myftpmap**, to deny several FTP commands.

Example 8-8 *Denying Specific FTP Commands*

```
ftp-map myftpmap
 deny-request-cmd cdup rnfr rnto stor stou
!
class-map inspection_default
 match default-inspection-traffic
!
policy-map asa_global_fw_policy
 class inspection_default
  inspect ftp strict myftpmap
```

CAUTION	The **strict** option may break FTP sessions from clients that do not comply with the RFC standards; however, it provides more security features.

When the **strict** option is enabled, the following anomalous activities in FTP commands and replies are denied:

- The total number of commas in the PORT and PASV reply commands is checked. If they are not 5, the PORT command is considered to be truncated and the connection is closed.

- The Cisco ASA inspects all FTP commands to see if they end with <CR><LF> characters, as specified by the RFC 959, "FTP Protocol". The connection is closed if these are not present.

- The PORT command is always expected to be sent from the FTP client. If the PORT command is sent from the server, the connection is dropped.

- The PASV reply command is always expected to be sent from the server. If the PASV command is sent from the client, the connection is dropped.

- The Cisco ASA checks the negotiated dynamic port value in the passive FTP mode. The port should not be in the range from 1 to 1024, because these are reserved for well-known protocols. The connection is closed if the negotiated port is within this range.

- The security appliance checks the number of characters included after the port numbers in the PORT and PASV reply commands. The maximum number of characters must be eight. The Cisco ASA closes the TCP connection if the number of character exceeds eight.

The FTP map **request-command deny** subcommand is used to deny specific FTP commands on the Cisco ASA. Table 8-3 lists all the **request-command deny** subcommand options that can be restricted under an FTP map.

Table 8-3   *List of FTP Commands Available for Restriction*

Option	Description
all	Denies all supported FTP commands
appe	Denies the ability to append to a file
cdup	Denies a user request to change to parent of current directory
help	Restricts the user to access the help information from the FTP server
retr	Denies the retrieval of a file from the FTP server
rnfr	User is not allowed to rename from a filename
rnto	User is not allowed to rename to a specific filename
site	User not allowed to specify server-specific command
stor	Denies the user permission to store a file
stou	Denies the user permission to store a file with a unique name

The SYST FTP command allows a system to ask for information about the server's operating system. The server accepts this request with code 215 and sends the requested information. The Cisco ASA replaces the FTP server response to the SYST command with an X for each character sent, to prevent FTP clients from seeing the FTP server system–type information. You can use the **no mask-syst-reply** subcommand in FTP map configuration mode to disable this default behavior, as shown in Example 8-9.

Example 8-9 **mask-syst-reply** *Subcommand*

```
ftp-map myftpmap
 no mask-syst-reply
```

General Packet Radio Service Tunneling Protocol

The General Packet Radio Service (GPRS) is a new carrier service for Global System for Mobile Communication (GSM) that enhances and simplifies wireless access to packet data networks. GPRS architecture uses a radio-packet technique to transfer user data packets in an efficient way between GSM mobile stations and external data networks. The GPRS Tunneling Protocol (GTP) allows multiprotocol packets to be tunneled through a GPRS backbone.

Figure 8-3 illustrates a basic representation of the GPRS architecture.

Figure 8-3 *GPRS Architecture Example*

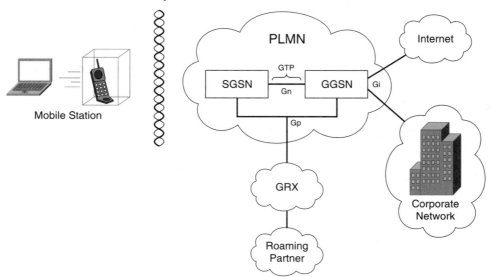

Figure 8-3 shows a mobile station (MS) logically connected to an SGSN. The SGSN provides data services to the MS. The SGSN is logically connected to a GGSN via GTP. If the GTP tunnel connection is over the same Public Land Mobile Network (PLMN), the interface connecting the tunnel is called the Gn interface. Connections between two different PLMNs are known as the Gp interfaces. The GGSN acts as a gateway to external networks such as the Internet or the corporate network via the Gi interface. In other words, the interface between a GGSN and an SGSN is called Gn, whereas the interface between the GGSN and an external data network is called Gi. GTP encapsulates data from the mobile station and controls the establishment, movement, and deletion of tunnels between SGSN and GGSN in roaming scenarios.

There are two versions of GTP:

- GTPv0
- GTPv1

GTPv0

In GTPv0, the GPRS mobile stations are connected to a SGSN without knowing GTP. A Packet Data Protocol (PDP) context is identified by the tunnel identifier (TID), which is a combination of the International Mobile Subscriber Identity (IMSI) and Network Service Access Point Identifier (NSAPI). The mobile stations can have up to 15 NSAPIs each. This allows the mobile stations to create multiple PDP contexts with different NSAPIs. These NSAPIs are based on application requirements for different QoS levels.

The common transport protocol for signaling messages for GTPv0 and v1 is UDP. GTPv0 can allow the use of TCP for the transport protocol data units (TPDUs). The Cisco ASA only supports UDP. The UDP destination port for requests is port 3386.

Figure 8-4 illustrates call flow and the signaling messages involved for GTPv0.

Figure 8-4   *GTPv0 Call Flow*

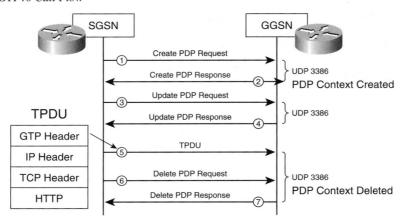

The following is the sequence of events in the call flow shown in Figure 8-4:

1 The SGSN sends a create PDP request to the GGSN.

2 The PDP context is created and the GGSN sends a PDP response back to the SGSN.

3 The SGSN sends an update PDP request message to the GGSN.

4 The GGSN replies back.

5 TPDUs are sent by the SGSN. (Figure 8-4 shows a sample of the TPDU as seen by the Cisco ASA inspection engine.)

6 The SGSN sends a request to delete the PDP context.

7 The PDP context is deleted and the GGSN sends its deletion response.

GTPv1

GTPv1 supports primary and secondary contexts for mobile stations. The primary context is identified with an IP address. Secondary contexts are created sharing the IP address and other parameters already associated with the primary context. The advantage of this technique is that the mobile station is able to initiate a connection to a context with different QoS requirements, while sharing the IP address obtained for the primary context.

GTPv1 uses UDP port 2123 for requests and UDP port 2152 for data transfer.

Figure 8-5 illustrates call flow and the signaling messages involved for GTPv1.

Figure 8-5 *GTPv1 Call Flow*

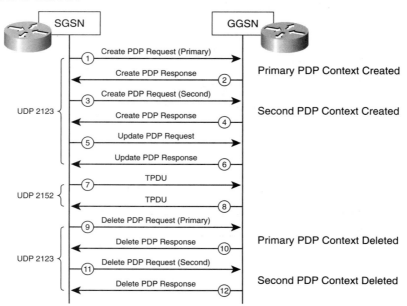

The following is the sequence of events in the call flow shown in Figure 8-5:

1   The SGSN sends a PDP context create request for the primary PDP context.

2   The primary context is created and the GGSN sends its response.

3   The SGSN sends a PDP context create request for the second PDP context.

4   The second context is created and the GGSN sends its response.

5   The SGSN sends a PDP update request to the GGSN.

6   The GGSN replies back with a PDP update response.

7   TPDU (data packets) are sent to the GGSN.

8   TPDU (data packets) are sent to the SGSN.

9   The SGSN sends a request to delete the primary PDP context.

10   The primary PDP context is deleted and the GGSN sends its response.

11   The SGSN sends a request to delete the second PDP context.

12   The second PDP context is deleted and the GGSN sends its response.

Figure 8-6 shows how the Cisco ASA can be positioned between GPRS networks.

Figure 8-6   *Cisco ASA in GPRS Network*

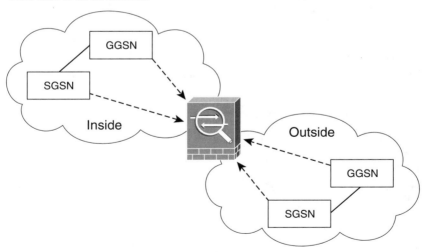

In Figure 8-6, the Cisco ASA is positioned between two GPRS PLMNs. This exemplifies how a mobile station may move from its home PLMN (HPLMN) to a visited PLMN (VPLMN) and communication will still be possible through the Cisco ASA. The Cisco ASA inspects all traffic between the respective SGSNs and GGSNs.

Configuring GTP Inspection

To enable GTP inspection, use the **inspect gtp** command. You can also associate a GTP map to create a more customizable configuration. This provides granular control of various GTP parameters and filtering options.

NOTE   GTP inspection is not supported with NAT or PAT. GTP inspection requires a special license from Cisco. For more information about licensing go to Cisco's website at www.cisco.com/go/nac

---

A GTP map can be created using the **gtp-map** command followed by the name of the map. Example 8-10 demonstrates how the Cisco ASA is configured with a GTP map, called **mygtpmap**, to enforce different restrictions.

Example 8-10 *GTP Inspection Example*

```
gtp-map mygtpmap
 tunnel-limit 1000
 request-queue 500
class-map inspection_default
 match default-inspection-traffic
policy-map asa_global_fw_policy
 class inspection_default
  inspect gtp mygtpmap
```

In Example 8-10, the Cisco ASA only allows a maximum of 1000 GTP tunnels and only allows a maximum of 500 requests to be queued. The GTP map is mapped to the default policy map under the default inspection class.

Table 8-4 lists all the subcommands available to configure under a GTP map.

Table 8-4   *GTP Map Subcommands*

Subcommand	Description
description	Used to enter a brief description of the GTP map.
drop	Used to drop messages based on three different keywords: • **apn**—The APN to be dropped after this keyword • **message**—The message ID to be dropped • **version**—Used to specify the version to be dropped
mcc	Used to specify a three-digit mobile country code. Values can be from 000 to 999. Country codes with one or two digits will be prepended with zeros.

Table 8-4   *GTP Map Subcommands (Continued)*

Subcommand	Description
message-length	Used to specify the minimum and maximum message length.
permit	Used to enable the Cisco ASA to allow packets with errors.
request-queue	Used to specify the maximum requests allowed on the queue.
timeout	Used to configure the idle timeout for the following: • GSN (GPRS Support Node) • PDP (Packet Data Protocol) contexts • Requests • Signaling connections • Tunnels
tunnel-limit	Used to configure the maximum tunnels allowed.

H.323

The H.323 standard stipulates the components, protocols, and procedures that provide multimedia communication services (audio, video, and data) over IP-based networks. Four kinds of H.323 components provide point-to-point and point-to-multipoint multimedia communication services:

- **Terminals**—Endpoints on the network that provide real-time two-way communications. For example, Cisco IP Phones.
- **Gateways**—Provide translation between circuit-switched networks and packet-based networks, enabling the endpoints to communicate.
- **Gatekeepers**—Responsible for call control and routing services to H.323 endpoints, system management, and some security policies.
- **Multipoint control units (MCUs)**—Maintain all the audio, video, data, and control streams between all the participants in the conference.

Figure 8-7 shows a basic network topology that illustrates the components of H.323.

H.323 Protocol Suite

Figure 8-8 illustrates the H.323 protocol suite:

- The G.7*xx* components are audio codecs.
- The H.26*x* components are video codecs. The standard is H.261.

Figure 8-7 *H.323 Components*

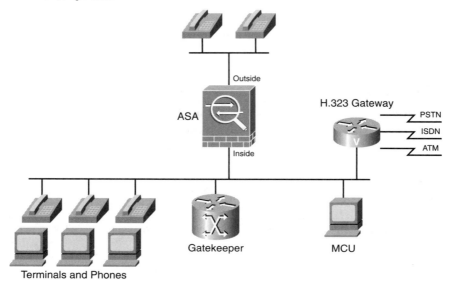

Audio and video components sit on top of the Real-Time Transport Protocol (RTP).

- The T.12x protocols are used in real-time exchange of data. One example is an online whiteboard application.

In Figure 8-8, the protocols are illustrated in relation to the respective OSI layers.

The H.323 suite of protocols may use up to two TCP connections and four to six UDP connections:

- RTP uses the Real-Time Transport Control Protocol (RTCP) to control and synchronize streaming audio and video. It allows the application to adapt the flow to specific network conditions.

- Terminals and gatekeepers use Registration, Admission, and Status (RAS) Protocol to exchange information about call registrations, admissions, and terminations. This protocol communicates over UDP.

Note	The FastConnect H.323 feature uses only one TCP connection, and RAS uses UDP requests and responses for registration, admissions, and status.

Figure 8-8   *H.323 Protocols*

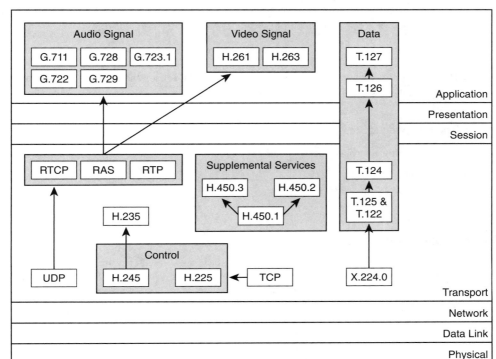

- H.225 is a protocol used to establish connections between two terminals. It runs over TCP.

- H.245 is a protocol used between two terminals to exchange control messages. These messages include flow control and channel management commands.

- Clients may request a Q.931 call setup over TCP port 1720 to H.323 servers. During the call setup process, the H.323 terminal provides the TCP port number for the client to use for an H.245 connection.

Note	The initial packet is transmitted over UDP if H.323 gatekeepers are used.

- The Cisco ASA can monitor the Q.931 TCP connection to determine the H.245 port number. It dynamically allocates the H.245 connection based on the inspection of the H.225 messages if FastConnect is not used.

- The terminals negotiate the port numbers to be used for subsequent UDP streams within each H.245 message. The Cisco ASA also monitors the H.245 messages to know about these ports and to create the necessary connections.

NOTE   RTP uses the negotiated port number; however, RTCP uses the next higher port number.

The following are the key TCP and UDP ports in H.323 inspection:

- **Gatekeeper discovery**—UDP port 1718
- **RAS**—UDP port 1719
- **Control port**—TCP port 1720

H.323 Version Compatibility

Cisco ASA is compatible with H.323 versions 1, 2, 3, and 4. Figure 8-9 and Figure 8-10 show a major difference between older versions of H.323 and H.323v3 and higher.

Figure 8-9   *Call Setup Pre-H.323v3*

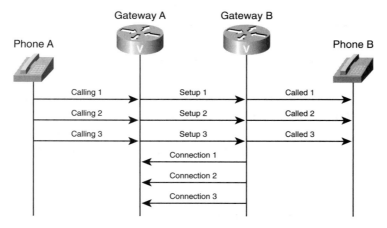

H.323v3 and higher supports multiple calls on one signaling connection. It accomplishes this by examining the call reference value (CRV) within the Q.931 message, as shown in Figure 8-10. This results in reduced call setup and clearing times.

Figure 8-10 *H.323v3 Call Setup Features*

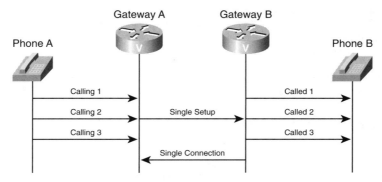

Enabling H.323 Inspection

To enable H.323 inspection for H.225, use the **inspect h323 h225** command. For RAS, use the **inspect h323 ras** command. Example 8-11 shows both commands.

Example 8-11 *H.323 Inspection Commands*

```
policy-map asa_global_fw_policy
  class inspection_default
    inspect h323 h225
    inspect h323 ras
```

The Cisco ASA can translate the necessary embedded IP addresses in the H.225 and H.245 packets. It also can translate H.323 connections. It uses an ASN.1 decoder to decode the H.323 Packet Encoding Rules (PER) encoded messages. The Cisco ASA also dynamically allocates the negotiated H.245, RTP, and RTCP sessions.

Additionally, the Cisco ASA analyses the TPDU Packet (TPKT) header to define the length of the H.323 messages. In H.323, Q.931 messages are exchanged over a TCP stream demarcated by TPKT encapsulations. It maintains a data structure for each connection also containing the TPKT length for the following H.323 messages.

NOTE   Cisco ASA also supports segmented TPKT messages.

Direct Call Signaling and Gatekeeper Routed Control Signaling

Two control-signaling methods are defined in the ITU-T H.323 recommendation:

- Direct Call Signaling (DCS)
- Gatekeeper Routed Control Signaling (GKRCS)

Cisco ASA supports both methods. The Cisco ASA inspects DSC and GKRCS to ensure that the negotiation messages and correct fields are transferred between the respective devices. GKRCS inspection is done when H.323 inspection is enabled in the Cisco ASA. No additional configuration is needed.

NOTE   The Cisco ASA must see the calling endpoint address within the initial H.225 setup information in order to allow the respective connection.

T.38

T.38 is the protocol used with Fax over IP (FoIP). This protocol is part of the ITU-T H.323 VoIP architecture. Cisco ASA supports inspection of this protocol. Because T.38 is a part of the H.323 protocol, inspection will be done if H.323 inspection is enabled on the Cisco ASA. No additional configuration is needed.

HTTP

The Cisco ASA HTTP inspection engine checks whether an HTTP transaction is compliant with RFC 2616 by checking the HTTP request message. The following are the predefined HTTP commands:

- OPTIONS
- GET
- HEAD
- POST
- PUT
- DELETE
- TRACE
- CONNECT

The Cisco ASA checks for these HTTP commands; if the message does not have any of these, the Cisco ASA verifies that it is an HTTP extension method/command (such as MOVE, COPY, EDIT). A syslog message is generated if both checks fail and the packet can be dropped. The Cisco ASA also has the ability to detect double-encoding attacks. This method, known as HTTP de-obfuscation, is one where an HTTP message is encoded by normalizing encoded characters to ASCII-equivalent characters (sometimes also referred to as ASCII normalization). In a double-encoding attack, the attacker sends an encoded HTTP URI request that has been through two rounds of encoding. Traditionally, firewalls and intrusion detection devices detect the first round of encoding and normalize it. The attack still evades the firewall or IDS. The Cisco ASA HTTP inspection engine is able to detect double encoding and prevent this from happening.

The Cisco ASA also provides a feature to filter HTTP messages based on keywords. This is useful when looking for specific applications running over HTTP, such as online instant messenger (IM) applications, music sharing applications, and so on.

Enabling HTTP Inspection

Use the **inspect http** command to enable HTTP inspection. You can also enable enhanced HTTP inspection by creating an HTTP map and associating it to the **inspect http** command. To create an HTTP map, use the **http-map** command, as shown in Example 8-12.

Example 8-12 *HTTP Inspection Using an HTTP Map*

```
http-map myhttpmap
 request-method rfc default action allow
 request-method ext move action reset
 request-method ext copy action reset
policy-map asa_global_fw_policy
 class inspection_default
 inspect http myhttpmap
```

In Example 8-12, an HTTP map named **myhttpmap** is configured. Request method inspection is enabled to allow all default RFC-compliant methods. The two extension methods, **move** and **copy**, are not allowed. If these two extensions are detected, the HTTP connection will be reset. The following HTTP extensions are supported by the Cisco ASA:

- **copy**
- **edit**
- **getattribute**
- **getattributenames**
- **getproperties**
- **index**
- **lock**
- **mkdir**
- **move**
- **revadd**
- **revlabel**
- **revlog**
- **revnum**
- **save**
- **setattribute**
- **startrev**

- **stoprev**
- **unedit**
- **unlock**

Several enhanced HTTP inspection options can be configured under the **http-map** subcommands. When you configure an HTTP map, you are placed into the **http-map** prompt. The following subcommands are available to configure the necessary rules for enhanced HTTP inspection:

- **strict-http**
- **content-length**
- **content-type-verification**
- **max-header-length**
- **max-uri-length**
- **port-misuse**
- **request-method**
- **transfer-encoding**

strict-http

The **strict-http** command changes the default action taken when noncompliant HTTP traffic is detected. The following is the subcommand syntax:

```
strict-http action {allow | reset | drop} [log]
```

Table 8-5 describes the **strict-http** command options.

Table 8-5   **strict-http** *Command Options*

Option	Description
allow	Allows the message to be transferred through the Cisco ASA.
reset	Causes Cisco ASA to send a TCP-RST (reset) message to client and/or server.
drop	Drops the packet and closes the connection.
log	Generates a syslog message.

The **strict-http** command is enabled by default. The default action is to log and send a TCP reset.

content-length

The **content-length** command limits the HTTP traffic allowed through the Cisco ASA based on the content length of the HTTP message body. The following is the command syntax:

```
content-length {min bytes max bytes} action {allow | reset | drop} [log]
```

Table 8-6 describes the **content-length** command options.

Table 8-6 **content-length** *Command Options*

Option	Description
min	Minimum content length allowed, in bytes. The range is from 0 to 65,535 bytes.
max	Maximum content length allowed, in bytes. The range is from 0 to 50,000,000 bytes.
bytes	The length, in bytes
allow	Allows the message to be transferred through the Cisco ASA.
reset	Causes Cisco ASA to send a TCP-RST (reset) message to client and/ or server.
drop	Drops the packet and closes the connection.
log	Generates a syslog message.

content-type-verification

When a web browser receives a document via HTTP, it must determine the document's encoding (sometimes referred to as charset). The browser must know this in order to display non-ASCII characters correctly. The **content-type-verification** command limits the content types in HTTP messages transferred through the Cisco ASA. The Cisco ASA verifies that the header content-type value is in the internal list of supported content types. Additionally, it checks that the header content type matches the actual content in the data or entity body portion of the message. Here are the currently supported HTTP content types:

- Text/HTML
- Application/ Microsoft Word
- Application/octet-stream
- Application/x-zip

The following is the **content-type-verification** command syntax:

```
content-type-verification [match-req-rsp] action {allow I reset I drop} [log]
```

The **match-req-rsp** keyword enables the Cisco ASA to verify that the **content-type** field in the HTTP response matches the accept field in the corresponding HTTP request message.

max-header-length

The **max-header-length** command limits the HTTP header length on traffic that passes through the Cisco ASA. Messages with a header length less than or equal to the configured value will be allowed; otherwise, the configured action will be taken. The following is the command syntax:

```
max-header-length {request bytes response bytes} action {allow | reset | drop} [log]
```

Table 8-7 describes the **max-header-length** command options.

Table 8-7   **max-header-length** *Command Options*

Option	Description
request	Used to specify the length of the request message header.
response	Used to specify the length of the response message header.
bytes	The length, in bytes. The range is 1 to 65,535.
allow	Allows the message to be transferred through the Cisco ASA.
reset	Causes Cisco ASA to send a TCP-RST (reset) message to client and/or server.
drop	Drops the packet and closes the connection.
log	Generates a syslog message.

max-uri-length

The **max-uri-length** command limits the length of the Universal Resource Identifier (URI) in a request message. The command syntax is as follows:

```
max-uri-length bytes action {allow | reset | drop} [log]
```

Table 8-8 describes the **max-uri-length** command options.

Table 8-8   **max-uri-length** *Command Options*

Option	Description
bytes	The length, in bytes. The range is 1 to 65,535.
allow	Allows the message to be transferred through the Cisco ASA.
reset	Causes Cisco ASA to send a TCP-RST (reset) message to client and/or server.
drop	Drops the packet and closes the connection.
log	Generates a syslog message.

port-misuse

The **port-misuse** command restricts applications, such as instant messengers, that use HTTP as a transport protocol. The following is the command syntax:

```
port-misuse {default | im | p2p | tunneling} action {allow | reset | drop} [log]
```

Table 8-9 describes the **port-misuse** command options.

Table 8-9   **port-misuse** *Command Options*

Option	Description
default	Allows inspection for all supported applications.
im	Enables IM application inspection (Yahoo Messenger).
p2p	Peer-to-peer application inspection. Applications include Kazaa and Gnutella.
tunneling	Enables tunneling application inspection. The following applications are inspected: • HTTPort/HTTHost • GNU Httptunnel • GotoMyPC • Firethru • Http-tunnel.com
allow	Allows the message to be transferred through the Cisco ASA.
reset	Causes Cisco ASA to send a TCP-RST (reset) message to client and/or server.
drop	Drops the packet and closes the connection.
log	Generates a syslog message.

NOTE   The **port-misuse** command is disabled by default.

request-method

The **request-method** command configures a specific action for each of the supported HTTP request methods. The following is the command syntax:

```
request-method  rfc rfc_method action {allow | reset | drop} [log]
request-method  ext ext_method action {allow | reset | drop} [log]
```

Table 8-10 describes the **request-method** command options.

Table 8-10   **request-method** *Command Options*

Option	Description
rfc	Used to specify methods defined in RFC 2616, "Hypertext Transfer Protocol".
ext	Used to specify extended methods.

continues

Table 8-10 **request-method** *Command Options (Continued)*

Option	Description
rfc_method	The RFC 2616 supported methods are as follows: • **connect** • **default** • **delete** • **get** • **head** • **options** • **post** • **put** • **trace**
ext_method	The extended methods are as follows: • **copy** • **default** • **edit** • **getattribute** • **getattribute** • **getproperties** • **index** • **lock** • **mkdir** • **move** • **revadd** • **revlabel** • **revlog** • **revnum** • **save** • **setattribute** • **startrev** • **stoprev** • **unedit** • **unlock**
allow	Allows the message to be transferred through the Cisco ASA.

Table 8-10   **request-method** *Command Options (Continued)*

Option	Description
reset	Causes Cisco ASA to send a TCP-RST (reset) message to client and/or server.
drop	Drops the packet and closes the connection.
log	Generates a syslog message.

NOTE   The **request-method** command is disabled by default.

transfer-encoding type

The **transfer-encoding type** command configures a specific action for each of the supported HTTP transfer-encoding types passing through the Cisco ASA. The following is the command syntax:

```
transfer-encoding type encoding_types action {allow | reset | drop} [log]
```

Table 8-11 describes the **transfer-encoding type** command options.

Table 8-11   **transfer-encoding type** *Command Options*

Option	Description
encoding_types	Used to specify the encoding type. The following encoding types are supported: • **default**—The default action. Enables all supported HTTP transfer-encoding types. • **chunked**—Message body is transferred in chunks. • **compress**—Unix file compression. • **deflate**—Supports ZLIB format, as specified in RFC 1950, and deflate compression, defined in RFC 1951. • **gzip**—GNU zip, as specified in RFC 1952. • **identity**—Used as default encoding (no transfer encoding is done).
action	Action taken when a violation occurs.
allow	Allows the message to be transferred through the Cisco ASA.
reset	Causes Cisco ASA to send a TCP-RST (reset) message to client and/or server.
drop	Drops the packet and closes the connection.
log	Generates a syslog message.

ICMP

Cisco ASA supports stateful inspection of Internet Control Message Protocol (ICMP) packets. To enable inspection of ICMP packets, use the **inspect icmp** command.

Additionally, Cisco ASA has the ability to translate ICMP error messages. It translates intermediate hops that send ICMP error messages based on the NAT configuration. Cisco ASA does this by overwriting the packet with the translated IP addresses.

NOTE   NAT for ICMP is disabled by default.

Cisco ASA also has the capability to inspect ICMP error messages. ICMP error messages always contain the full IP header, including options, of the IP packet that failed and the first 8 bytes of the IP data field. Cisco ASA makes sure that this information is present and that it is correct. To enable inspection of ICMP error messages, use the **inspect icmp error** command. If this command is disabled, Cisco ASA does not translate any ICMP error messages generated by intermediate devices.

ILS

Cisco ASA supports inspection for the Internet Locator Service (ILS) protocol. ILS is based on the Lightweight Directory Access Protocol (LDAP) specification. Numerous applications use ILS for directory services, including the following:

- Microsoft NetMeeting
- Microsoft SiteServer
- Microsoft Active Directory

To enable ILS inspection, use the **inspect ils** command. This command is disabled by default.

The Cisco ASA ILS inspection engine provides support for the following:

- Decoding of the LDAP REQUEST/RESPONSE PDUs using the BER decode functions
- Parsing the LDAP packet
- Extracting the IP addresses
- Translating IP addresses as necessary (PAT is not supported)
- Encoding the PDU with translated addresses using BER encode functions
- Copying the newly encoded PDU back to the TCP packet
- Performing incremental TCP checksum and sequence number adjustment

MGCP

The Media Gateway Control Protocol (MGCP) is the IETF standard for multimedia conferencing over IP. It offers a mechanism for controlling media gateways by providing conversion between the audio signals carried on telephone circuits and data packets carried over IP networks.

MGCP messages are ASCII based and are transmitted over UDP. This protocol is defined in RFC 3661. There are eight types of MGCP commands:

- CreateConnection
- ModifyConnection
- DeleteConnection
- NotificationRequest
- Notify
- AuditEndpoint
- AuditConnection
- RestartInProgress

Each command requires a mandatory reply. The first four commands are sent by the call agent to the gateway. The Notify command is sent by the gateway to the call agent. In some cases the gateway may also send a DeleteConnection command to tear down a connection to the call agent. The RestartInProgress command is used in the registration process of the MGCP gateway. The AuditEndpoint and the AuditConnection commands are sent by the call agent to the gateway.

The Cisco ASA performs the following tasks for MGCP inspection:

- Inspects all messages exchanged between the call agents and the media gateways
- Dynamically creates RTP and RTCP connections
- Supports and inspects retransmitted commands and responses
- Dynamically adapts to allow a command response to arrive from any of the call agents

A call agent is a device that provides call-processing functions, feature logic, and gateway control in an IP telephony system. An MGCP gateway handles the translation between audio signals and the IP packet network. In the MGCP configurations that Cisco IOS supports, the gateway can be a Cisco router, access server, or cable modem, and the call agent can be a server from Cisco (Cisco PGW or Cisco BTS Softswitches) or from a third-party vendor.

Figure 8-11 demonstrates how the Cisco ASA inspects messages exchanged between two media gateways residing in two different networks.

Figure 8-11 *MGCP Inspection*

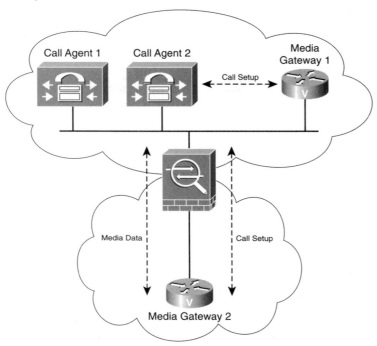

To enable MGCP inspection, use the **inspect mgcp** command. Create an MGCP map using the **mgcp-map** command to enable enhanced MGCP inspection. Example 8-13 demonstrates how to create an MGCP map for enhanced MGCP inspection.

Example 8-13 *Enhanced MGCP Inspection*

```
mgcp-map mymgcpmap
  call-agent 10.10.10.133 876
  command-queue 500
  gateway 192.168.11.23 876
policy-map asa_global_fw_policy
  class inspection_default
inspect mgcp mymgcpmap
```

In Example 8-13, an MGCP map named **mymgcpmap** is configured. The **call-agent** command specifies a group of call agents that can manage one or more gateways. A call agent with IP address **10.10.10.133** and the group ID **876** is configured.

NOTE   The group ID option can be any number between 0 and 2,147,483,647. Call agents with the same group ID belong to the same group. They may belong to more than one specific group.

The Cisco ASA can limit the maximum number of MGCP commands that will be queued waiting for a response to 500. The range of allowed values for the **command-queue limit** option is 1 to 2,147,483,647.

A gateway with IP address 192.168.11.23 in group 876 is also configured. This is used to specify which call agents are managing a particular gateway.

NetBIOS

NetBIOS was originally developed by IBM and Sytek as an API for client software to access LAN resources. NetBIOS has become the basis for many other networking applications. NetBIOS names are used to identify resources (e.g., workstations, servers, printers) on a network. Applications use these names to start and end sessions. NetBIOS names can consist of up to 16 alphanumeric characters. Clients advertise their name to the network. This is called the NetBIOS registration process and it is completed as follows:

1 The client broadcasts itself and its NetBIOS information when it boots up.

2 If there is another machine on the network that already has the broadcasted name, that NetBIOS client issues its own broadcast to advertise that the name is in use. Subsequently, the client that is trying to register stops all attempts to register that specific name.

3 The client finishes the registration process if there is no other machine with the same name on the network.

Cisco ASA supports NetBIOS by performing NAT of the packets for NetBIOS Name Server (NBNS) UDP port 137 and NetBIOS Datagram Service (NBDS) UDP port 138.

To enable NetBIOS inspection on the Cisco ASA, use the **ip inspect netbios** command.

PPTP

The Point-to-Point Tunneling Protocol (PPTP) is typically used for VPN solutions. (It is defined in RFC 2637.) Traditionally, the PPTP session negotiation is done over TCP port 1723 and the data traverses over the generic routing encapsulation (GRE) protocol (IP protocol 47). GRE does not have any Layer 4 port information. Consequently, it cannot be port address translated (PATed). PAT is performed for the modified version of GRE (RFC 2637) only when negotiated over the PPTP TCP control channel. PAT is not supported for the unmodified version of GRE (RFC 1701 and RFC 1702).

The Cisco ASA inspects PPTP protocol packets and dynamically creates the necessary translations to permit PPTP traffic.

NOTE   Cisco ASA supports only PPTP version 1.

Use the **inspect pptp** command to enable PPTP inspection on the Cisco ASA.

Sun RPC

The Sun Remote Procedure Call (RPC) is a protocol used by the Network File System (NFS) and Network Information Service (NIS). NIS clients attempt to communicate with their administratively configured NIS server through RPC Portmapper requests immediately after bootup. The RPC portmapper service converts RPC program numbers into TCP/UDP ports. The RPC server tells portmapper what port number it is listening to and what RPC program numbers it will use. The client first contacts portmap on the server machine to determine the port number to which RPC packets should be sent. The default RPC portmapper port is 111.

Cisco ASA Sun RPC inspection provides the following:

- Bidirectional inspection of Sun RPC packets
- Support of Sun RPC over TCP and UDP
- Support of Portmapper v2 and RPCBind v3 and v4
- Support of DUMP procedure used by the client to query the server for all the supported services
- NAT and PAT support

To enable Sun RPC inspection, use the **inspect rpc** command.

RSH

Remote Shell (RSH) is a management protocol used by numerous Unix systems. It uses TCP port 514. The client and server negotiate the TCP port number to be used by the client for the STDERR (standard error) output stream.

Cisco ASA supports NAT of the negotiated port number with RSH inspection. To enable this feature, use the **inspect rsh** command.

RTSP

The Real-Time Streaming Protocol (RTSP) is a multimedia streaming protocol that many vendors use. Cisco ASA supports inspection for this protocol in compliance with RFC 2326. The following are some of the applications that use RTSP:

- RealAudio
- Apple QuickTime
- RealPlayer
- Cisco IP/TV

Most RTSP applications use TCP port 554. On some rare occasions, UDP is used in the control channel.

The commonly used TCP control channel negotiates the data channels used to transmit audio and video. This is negotiated based on the transport mode specified on the client.

The following are the supported Real Data Transport (RDT) protocol transports:

- rtp/avp
- rtp/avp/udp
- x-real-rdt
- x-real-rdt/udp
- x-pn-tng/udp

Use the **inspect rtsp** command to enable RTSP inspection on the Cisco ASA.

SIP

The Session Initiation Protocol (SIP) is a signaling protocol used in multimedia conferencing applications, IP telephony, instant messaging, and some event-notification features on several applications. This protocol is defined in RFC 3261. SIP signaling is sent over UDP or TCP port 5060. The media streams are dynamically allocated. Figure 8-12 illustrates the basics of a SIP call flow between two SIP calling entities and gateways, respectively.

Figure 8-12 *SIP Call Flow*

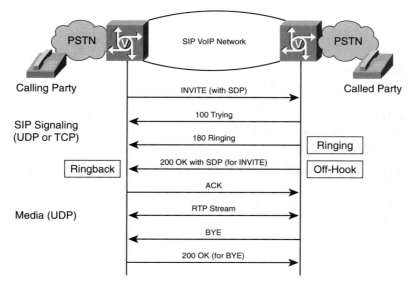

The Cisco ASA is able to inspect any NAT SIP transactions successfully. To enable SIP inspection, use the **inspect sip** command. You can see SIP connection statistics using the **show conn state sip** command. The **show service-policy** command provides you with SIP inspection statistics.

SIP is also used by IM applications. The details on SIP extensions for instant messaging are defined in RFC 3428. Instant messengers use MESSAGE/INFO requests and 202 Accept responses when users chat with each other. The MESSAGE/INFO requests are sent after registration and subscription transactions are completed. For example, two users may have their IM application connected at any time, but not talk to each other for a long period of time. The Cisco ASA SIP inspection engine maintains this information for a set period of time according to the configured SIP timeout value.

To configure the idle timeout after which a SIP control connection will be closed, use the **timeout sip** command. The default timeout value is 30 minutes. Use the **timeout sip_media** command to configure the idle timeout after which a SIP media connection will be closed. The default is 2 minutes.

Example 8-14 shows how the Cisco ASA is configured with a SIP timeout of 1 hour.

Example 8-14 *SIP Timeout Example*

```
Chicago(config)# timeout sip 1:00:00
Chicago(config)# timeout sip_media 0:30:00
```

NOTE   The SIP media timeout value must be configured at least 5 minutes longer than the subscription duration (**timeout sip**).

Skinny

Skinny is a protocol used in VoIP applications. (Skinny is another name for the Simple Client Control Protocol [SCCP].) Cisco IP Phones, Cisco CallManager, and Cisco CallManager Express use this protocol. Figure 8-13 demonstrates the registration and communication process between a Cisco IP Phone and all the respective components such as Cisco CallManager.

In Figure 8-13, the Cisco IP Phone is assigned to a specific VLAN. After that, it sends a request to the DHCP server to get an IP address, DNS server address, and TFTP server name or address. It also gets a default gateway address if you have set these options in the DHCP server.

Figure 8-13 *Cisco IP Phone Registration and Communication Flow*

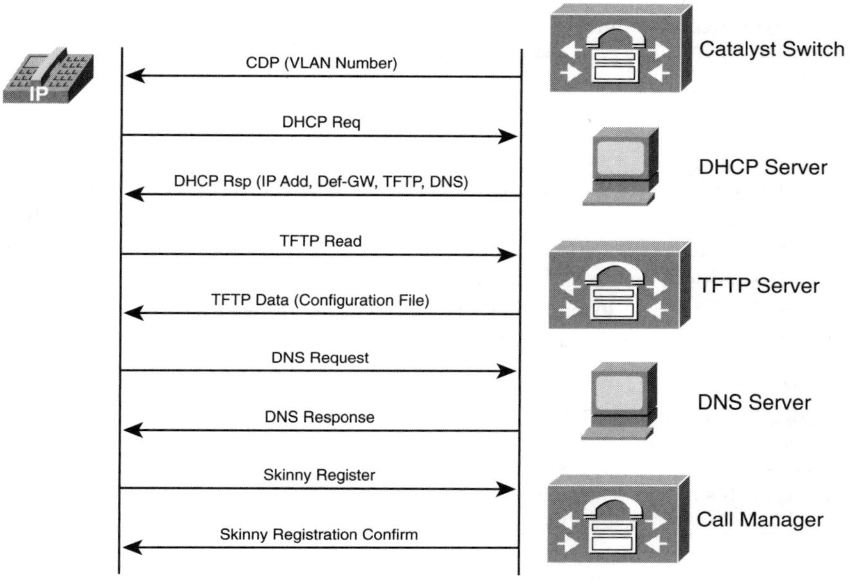

CDP (VLAN Number)	Catalyst Switch
DHCP Req	
DHCP Rsp (IP Add, Def-GW, TFTP, DNS)	DHCP Server
TFTP Read	
TFTP Data (Configuration File)	TFTP Server
DNS Request	
DNS Response	DNS Server
Skinny Register	
Skinny Registration Confirm	Call Manager

NOTE   If a TFTP server name is not included in the DHCP reply, the Cisco IP Phone uses the default server name.

The Cisco IP Phone obtains its configuration from the TFTP server. It resolves the Cisco CallManager name via DNS and starts the Skinny registration process.

The Cisco ASA inspects the Skinny transactions with the use of the **inspect skinny** command. This command is enabled by default.

NOTE   Cisco ASA does not support fragmented Skinny messages.

As previously discussed, Cisco IP Phones download their configuration information from a TFTP server. This information includes the name or IP address of the Cisco CallManager server to which they need to connect. You must use an ACL to open UDP port 69 when the Cisco IP Phones are on a lower security interface compared to the TFTP server. If the Cisco IP Phones are on a lower security interface compared to the Cisco CallManager, create a static NAT entry for the Cisco CallManager.

NOTE	Instructions on how to create ACLs and static NAT entries are covered in Chapter 5, "Network Access Control."

SNMP

The Simple Network Management Protocol (SNMP) manages and monitors networking devices. Cisco ASA SNMP inspection enables packet traffic monitoring between network devices. The Cisco ASA can be configured to deny traffic based on the SNMP packet version. Early versions of SNMP are less secure. Denying SNMPv1 traffic may be required by your security policy. This is done by configuring an SNMP map with the **snmp-map** command and then associating it to the **inspect snmp** command, as shown in Example 8-15.

Example 8-15 *SNMP Inspection*

```
snmp-map mysnmpmap
 deny version 1
policy-map asa_global_fw_policy
 class inspection_default
  inspect snmp mysnmpmap
```

In Example 8-15, the Cisco ASA is setup for an snmp map, called **mysnmpmap**, which denies any SNMPv1 packets. The following are the **deny version** subcommand options:

- **1** = SNMP version 1
- **2** = SNMP version 2 (party based)
- **2c** = SNMP version 2c (community based)
- **3** = SNMP version 3

SQL*Net

Cisco ASA provides support for Oracle SQL*Net protocol inspection. It supports both versions 1 and 2. Cisco ASA is able to perform NAT and look in the packets for all embedded ports to allow the necessary communication for SQL*Net. To enable SQL*Net inspection, use the **inspect sqlnet** command.

TFTP

The Trivial File Transfer Protocol (TFTP) allows systems to read and write files between them in a client/server relationship. One of the advantages of TFTP application inspection is that the Cisco ASA can prevent a host from opening invalid connections. Additionally, the Cisco ASA enforces the creation of a secondary channel initiated from the server. This restriction prevents the TFTP client from creating the secondary connection. Use the **inspect tftp** command to enable TFTP inspection on the Cisco ASA.

XDMCP

The X Display Manager Control Protocol (XDMCP) is a protocol that many Unix systems use to remotely execute and view applications.

TIP

Using XDMCP is inherently insecure; therefore, most of the Unix distributions shipped have XDMCP turned off by default. Use XDMCP only in a trusted network.

XDMCP uses UDP port 177 to negotiate X sessions using a TCP port. The X manager communicates with the X server over TCP port $6000 + n$ (n = negotiated port).

Cisco ASA supports the translation and inspection of XDMCP sessions with the **inspect xdmcp** command.

Deployment Scenarios

This section covers how SecureMe deploys a Cisco ASA in its London branch to perform application inspection for the following protocols:

* ESMTP
* HTTP
* FTP
* RTSP

Figure 8-14 illustrates the topology of SecureMe's London office.

Figure 8-14 *SecureMe London Office*

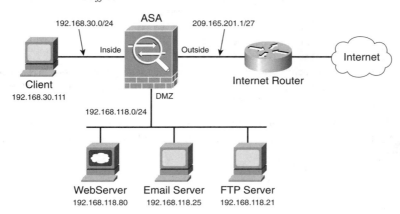

There are three interfaces configured in the London Cisco ASA (inside, outside, and DMZ). The DMZ has a web server, an e-mail server, and an FTP server. The outside is connected to the Internet via an ISP router. The goal is to configure application inspection for the previously mentioned protocols as outlined in the next sections.

ESMTP

The security administrator wants to inspect all ESMTP traffic from inside and outside hosts to the e-mail server (192.168.118.25) in the DMZ. The following steps are completed to achieve this goal:

Step 1   Configure an ACL to match all TCP port 25 (SMTP/ESMTP) traffic:

```
London(config)# access-list SMTPInspect extended permit tcp any
   192.168.118.25 eq smtp
```

Step 2   Configure a class map called **esmtpclass** to match this ACL:

```
London(config)# class-map esmtpclass
London(config-cmap)# match access-list SMTPInspect
```

Step 3   Configure two policy maps. Configure the policy map named **inside_inspection** for the traffic originating in the inside. Configure the policy map named **outside_inspection** for traffic coming from the outside. Apply the class map named **esmtpclass** to each policy map, along with the **inspect esmtp** command.

```
London(config)# policy-map inside_inspection
London(config-pmap)# class esmtpclass
London(config-pmap-c)# inspect esmtp
London(config-pmap-c)# exit
London(config-pmap)# exit
London(config)# policy-map outside_inspection
London(config-pmap)# class esmtpclass
London(config-pmap-c)# inspect esmtp
London(config-pmap-c)# exit
London(config-pmap)# exit
London(config)# service-policy outside_inspection interface outside
London(config)# service-policy inside_inspection interface inside
London(config)# exit
```

Each policy map is applied to the inside and outside interfaces, respectively. All TCP port 25 traffic that matches access list SMTPInspect will be inspected in the inside and outside interfaces.

HTTP

SecureMe's security policies dictate that the following HTTP extensions should not be allowed by any connections originating from the inside or outside hosts to the web server (192.168.118.80) in the DMZ:

- MOVE
- MKDIR
- COPY

You follow these steps to achieve this goal:

Step 1   Configure an HTTP map named **myhttpmap** to restrict the previously listed HTTP extensions:

```
London# configure terminal
London(config)# http-map myhttpmap
London(config-http-map)# request-method ext move action reset
London(config-http-map)# request-method ext mkdir action reset
London(config-http-map)# request-method ext copy action reset
London(config-http-map)# exit
London(config)#
```

Step 2   Configure a class map called **httpclass** to match all packets traversing the Cisco ASA:

```
London(config)# class-map httpclass
London(config-cmap)# match any
London(config-cmap)# exit
```

Step 3   Apply the class map **httpclass** to both of the previously configured policy maps. Also add the **inspect http** command, applying the HTTP map called **myhttpmap**.

```
London(config)# policy-map inside_inspection
London(config-pmap)# class httpclass
London(config-pmap-c)#  inspect http myhttpmap
London(config-pmap-c)# exit
London(config-pmap)# exit
London(config)# policy-map outside_inspection
London(config-pmap)# class httpclass
London(config-pmap-c)#  inspect http myhttpmap
London(config-pmap-c)# end
London#
```

Suppose that you receive several complaints from users a few days after you enter the commands in the Cisco ASA. The users are not able to successfully use several web-based applications to certain websites on the Internet. After further investigation, you notice that these applications use the HTTP extensions MOVE, COPY, and MKDIR for legitimate transactions. You proceed to modify the class map named **httpclass** to use an

ACL to only inspect traffic going to the web server (192.168.118.80) in the DMZ, as shown in Example 8-16.

Example 8-16 *Correcting the Class Map*

```
London(config)# access-list HTTPInspect permit tcp any host 192.168.118.80 eq 80
London(config)# access-list HTTPInspect permit tcp any host 192.168.118.80 eq 443
London(config)# class-map httpclass
London(config-cmap)# match access-list HTTPInspect
```

The access list **HTTPInspect** matches all HTTP (TCP port 80) and HTTPS (TCP port 443) traffic destined to 192.168.118.80.

FTP

Suppose that now you need to configure the Cisco ASA to inspect all FTP connections that originated from inside users to the FTP server (192.168.118.21) in the DMZ. The inside users must not be allowed to delete any files on the FTP server. Complete the following steps to achieve this goal.

Step 1   Configure an FTP map named **myftpmap** to deny any internal users when they are trying to delete any files in the FTP server:

```
London(config)# ftp-map myftpmap
London(config-ftp-map)# request-command deny dele
London(config-ftp-map)# exit
```

Step 2   Configure a class map called **ftpclass** to match all traffic:

```
London(config)# class-map ftpclass
London(config-cmap)# match port tcp 21
London(config-cmap)# exit
London(config)#
```

Step 3   Apply the class map to the policy map named **inside_inspection:**

```
London(config)# policy-map inside_inspection
London(config-pmap)# class ftpclass
London(config-pmap-c)# inspect ftp strict myftpmap
London(config-pmap-c)# exit
London(config-pmap)# exit
London(config)#
```

Example 8-17 shows how an internal user (user1) logs in to the FTP server and is denied while trying to delete a file.

Example 8-17 *FTP User Connection*

```
bash$ ftp 192.168.118.21
Connected to 192.168.118.21
220 (vsFTPd 2.0.3)
Username: user1
331 Please specify the password.
Password: *****
230 Login successful.
Remote system type is UNIX.
Using binary mode to transfer files.
ftp> ls
227 Entering Passive Mode (127,0,0,1,254,102)
150 Here comes the directory listing.
drwxr-xr-x    2 500       500          4096 Jul 07 19:20 Desktop
-rw-rw-r--    1 500       500          1216 Jul 08 01:03 order
-rw-rw-r--    1 500       500           944 Jul 08 01:58 test
226 Directory send OK.
ftp> dele test
550 Delete operation failed.
ftp>
```

The internal user (user1) attempts to delete a file called **test** and is denied by the Cisco ASA, as shown in the highlighted lines in Example 8-18.

Summary

This chapter described how to use and configure application inspection on Cisco ASA. It demonstrated how the application inspection features ensure the secure use of applications and services. Details on the protocols that require special application inspection were covered in detail.

This chapter covers the following topics:

- Architectural overview
- Configuration of security contexts
- Deployment scenarios
- Monitoring and troubleshooting

CHAPTER 9

Security Contexts

The virtual firewall methodology enables a physical firewall to be partitioned into multiple standalone firewalls. Each standalone firewall acts and behaves as an independent entity with its own configuration, interfaces, security policies, routing table, and administrators. In Cisco ASA, these virtual firewalls are known as *security contexts*.

The following are some example scenarios in which security contexts are useful in network deployments:

- You act as a service provider and you want to provide firewall services to customers. However, you do not want to purchase additional physical firewalls for each customer.

- You manage an educational institution and you want to segregate student networks from faculty networks for improved security using one physical security appliance.

- You administer a large enterprise with different departmental groups, and each department wants to implement its own security policies.

- You have overlapping networks in your organization and you want to provide firewall services to all of those networks without changing the addressing scheme.

- You currently manage many physical firewalls and you want to integrate security policies into one physical firewall.

In Figure 9-1, SecureMe, an enterprise headquartered in Chicago, has a Cisco ASA providing firewall services to two of its customers. To implement a cost-effective solution, SecureMe has configured two security contexts in the security appliance: CustA for Customer A and CustB for Customer B. Each customer can manage and administer its own security context without interfering with the other context. On the other hand, the security appliance administrator manages the system execution space, which is discussed in the next section.

In this figure, each horizontal dotted box represents a security context that has a Cisco ASA inspecting and protecting the packets going through it, while the vertical box represents the physical Cisco security appliance with multiple security contexts.

Figure 9-1 *Security Contexts in the ASA*

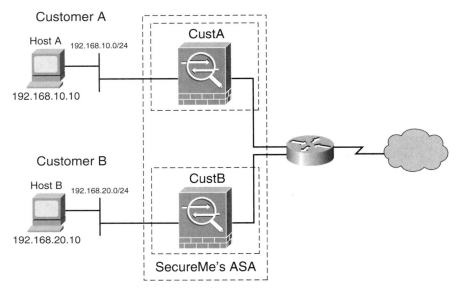

Architectural Overview

In multiple security context mode, the Cisco security appliance can be divided into three types:

- A system execution space
- An admin context
- One or more customer contexts

All contexts must be configured correctly for proper function. Similar to a real network, in which one misconfigured device can affect the operations of other network devices, misconfiguration of a security context can impact the overall operation of a security appliance.

System Execution Space

Unlike other contexts, the system execution space does not have any Layer 2 or Layer 3 interfaces or any network settings. Rather, it is mainly used to define the attributes of other security context attributes. Here are the three important attributes configured for each context in the system execution space:

- Context name.
- Location of context's startup configuration. The configuration of each context is also known as a configlet.
- Interface allocation.

Additionally, many optional features, such as interface and boot parameters, can be configured within the system execution space. Table 9-1 lists the important features that can be set up through the system execution space.

Table 9-1   *Options Available in System Execution Space*

Feature	Description
Interface	Sets up physical interfaces for speed and duplex. Interfaces can be enabled or disabled.
Banner	Specifies a login or session banner when connecting to the security appliance.
Boot	Specifies boot parameters to load proper image.
Activation key	Enables or disables security appliance features.
File management	Adds or deletes the security context configurations that are stored locally on the security appliance.
Firewall mode	Configures single- or multiple-mode firewall in the system execution space.
Failover	Sets the failover parameters to accommodate multiple physical security appliances.

The system execution space configuration resides in the nonvolatile random-access memory (NVRAM) area of the security appliance, while the configurations for security contexts are stored either in local Flash memory or on a network storage server using one of the following protocols:

- TFTP
- FTP
- HTTPS
- HTTP

The system execution space designates one of the security contexts as the admin context, which is responsible for providing network access when the system needs to contact resources. The admin context is discussed next.

Admin Context

The admin context provides connectivity to network resources, as mentioned earlier. The IP addresses on the allocated interfaces can be used for remote management purposes, such as SSH or Telnet. The security appliance also uses the IP addresses to retrieve configurations for other contexts if they are located on a network share. A system administrator with access to the admin context can switch into the other contexts to manage them. The security appliance uses the admin context to send the syslog messages that relate to the system.

The admin context must be created before defining other contexts. Additionally, it must reside on the local disk. A new admin context can be designated at any time by using the **admin-context** command, which is discussed in the "Configuration of Security Context" section, later in this chapter.

When a Cisco ASA is converted from single mode to multi-mode, the network-related configuration of the single-mode security appliance is saved as the admin context. The security appliance names this context as, admin.

NOTE   Changing the name of the admin context from admin is not recommended.

The admin context configuration is similar to a customer context. Aside from its relationship to the system execution space, it can be used as a regular context. However, using it as a regular context is not recommended, because of its significance.

Customer Context

Each customer context acts as a virtual firewall with its own configuration that contains almost all the options that are available in a standalone firewall. Table 9-2 lists the differences between a security appliance running in single mode and an appliance running in multiple mode.

Table 9-2   *Contrasting Single- and Multiple-Mode Firewalls*

Feature	Single Mode	Multiple Mode
Interface	All physical interfaces are available for use.	Only allocated interfaces are available in the contexts.
File management	Allows an administrator to copy system images and configurations.	Restricts a context administrator to manage the context configurations.
Firewall management	Allows a system administrator to fully manage the security appliance.	Allows a context administrator to manage the context.
Addressing scheme	Does not allow overlapping networks.	Allows overlapping networks between the contexts.
Routing protocols	Supports RIP and OSPF as the dynamic routing protocols.	Does not allow any dynamic routing protocols.
Licensing	There are no security contexts in single mode, hence no license is needed to turn on the security contexts.	Needs a license to activate more than two security contexts. The default license includes two customer security contexts and an admin context.
Resource allocation	The security appliance uses all the available resources.	The security appliance shares the system resources between the contexts.

Table 9-2   *Contrasting Single- and Multiple-Mode Firewalls (Continued)*

Feature	Single Mode	Multiple Mode
Failover	Does not allow Active/Active failover.	Allows Active/Active failover for redundancy and load-balancing.
Quality of service	Supports QoS.	Does not support QoS.
Multicast	Supports multicast using PIM-SM.	Does not support multicast.
VPN	Supports remote access and site-to-site VPN tunnels.	Does not support VPNs.

The number of customer contexts depends on the installed activation key. To find out how many customer contexts are allowed on a security appliance, look at the security context information in **show version**, as shown in Example 9-1. In this example, the ASA can have up to five customer contexts.

Example 9-1   *Verifying the Number of Security Contexts*

```
Chicago# show version | include Security Contexts
Security Contexts          : 5
```

NOTE   The number of available contexts does not include the admin context, because of its significance to the system execution space.

Packet Flow in Multiple Mode

When the packets traverse through the security appliance in multiple mode, they are classified and forwarded to the right context. The packets are then processed based on the configured security policies on a context. The packet classification and the forwarding mechanism are discussed in the following subsections.

Packet Classification

In multiple mode, the security appliance must classify the packets to find out which context should operate on them. The packet classification is done at the ingress interface point that tags the packets using the source IP address, source port, destination IP address, destination port, and the interface or VLAN. The packet is processed based on the security policies configured in that context. Cisco ASA uses the following fields or packet identifiers to classify them properly:

- **Source interface**—If all the contexts in the Cisco ASA use unique interfaces, the packet classification becomes easier because the security appliance classifies these packets based on the source interface. As illustrated in Figure 9-2, when the packet is sourced from 192.168.10.10, the classifier assigns the packet to context CustA because the packet originated from G0/0, which is a part of the CustA security context.

Figure 9-2 *Packet Classification Using Source Interface*

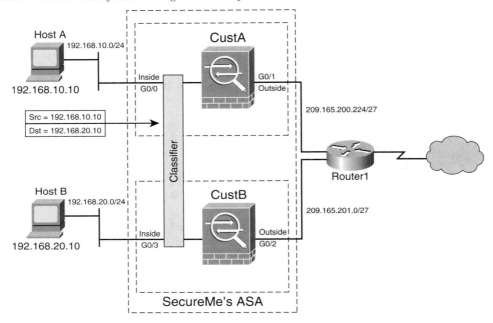

- **Destination IP address**—The security appliance allows you to share one or more interfaces between the security contexts. In this deployment model, the shared interface uses the same network space with unique IP addresses on the end hosts. If the security appliance is configured to use a shared ingress interface, then it uses the destination IP address to further clarify which of the security contexts using the shared interface should receive the packets. In this case, the security contexts within the Cisco ASA cannot use overlapping IP addresses, and therefore all destination IP addresses must be unique.

Packet Forwarding Between Contexts

In multiple mode, the two contexts communicate with each other as if two standalone appliances were communicating with one another. The security contexts can talk to each other in two ways:

- Without a shared interface
- With a shared interface

Depending on what mode you use, the packet flow is different, as discussed in the following subsections.

Forwarding Without a Shared Interface

As Figure 9-3 illustrates, SecureMe's ASA has four interfaces: two of them belong to the CustA context and the remaining two are allocated to CustB. The outside interface of both contexts is connected to Router1, which is responsible for routing packets from one context to another.

Figure 9-3   *Security Contexts Without a Shared Interface*

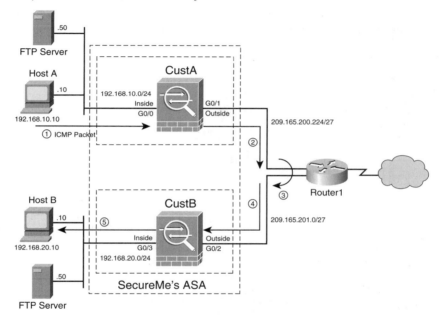

If NAT and packet filtering are set up on the security appliance, then the following sequence of events takes place when Host A sends an ICMP ping packet to Host B:

1 Host A sends an ICMP ping packet with a source address of 192.168.10.10 and a destination address of 192.168.20.10. The classifier tags the packet coming in on GigabitEthernet0/0 before sending it to the inside interface of CustA.

2 The packet is inspected by the inbound ACL and, if allowed, forwarded to the NAT engine for translation. The NAT engine translates the source address or leaves it unchanged as dictated by the configured policy. Before the security appliance forwards it to Router1, the packet is inspected by the outbound ACL to ensure that it is allowed to leave.

3 Router1 checks the destination IP address in the routing table and sends the packet to the G0/2 interface on the security appliance.

4 The appliance classifies the packet before sending it to the outside interface of the CustB context, where it is inspected by the inbound ACL. If it is allowed in, the packet passes through the NAT engine to determine if it needs to be translated.

5 The security context forwards the packet to Host B after verifying that the outbound ACL on the inside interface does not deny it.

Forwarding with a Shared Interface

Figure 9-4 illustrates another network topology, where SecureMe uses a shared outside LAN interface. To provide Internet connectivity, it has Router1 connected to the same shared interface. Using the shared interfaces, SecureMe can conserve the address space and the allocated interfaces. Additionally, shared contexts are useful when multiple security contexts need access to one public interface to get Internet connectivity.

Figure 9-4 *Security Contexts with a Shared Interface*

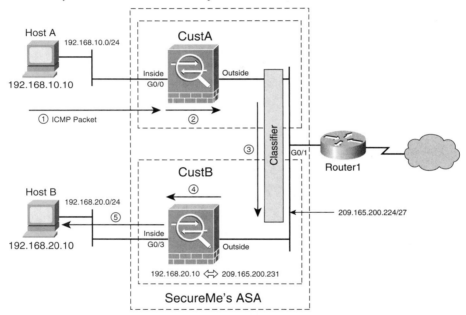

Using the previous example, when Host A sends an ICMP ping packet to Host B, the following steps are taken for successful communication:

1 Host A sends an ICMP ping packet with a source address of 192.168.10.10 and a destination address of 209.165.200.231, which can be translated by context CustB to 192.168.20.1. The classifier tags the packet coming in on GigabitEthernet0/0 before sending it to the inside interface of CustA.

2 The packet is inspected by the inbound ACL and, if allowed, forwarded to the NAT engine for translation. The NAT engine translates the source address or leaves it unchanged as dictated by the configured policy. The packet is then inspected by the outbound ACL to ensure that it is allowed to leave.

3 The packet passes through the context classifier, which looks at the destination IP address and forwards it to the outside interface of the CustB security context because 209.165.200.231 is owned by CustB.

Note	Because the security contexts reside on a physical security appliance, the packet never leaves the device when it moves from the outside interface of CustA to the outside interface of CustB.

4 The security context of CustB applies security policies after receiving the packet on the outside interface. The packet enters CustB's security context, where it is inspected by the inbound ACL. If it is allowed in, the NAT engine translates the destination address to 192.168.20.10.

Note	You will need to translate the destination IP addresses for the traffic traversing from a shared interface.

5 The security context forwards the packet to Host B after verifying that the outbound ACL on the inside interface does not deny it.

Note	Cisco ASA cannot classify packets if they are sourced from one shared interface and destined to another shared interface.

Configuration of Security Contexts

The configuration of a security context is broken down into seven steps:

1 Enable multiple security contexts globally.

2 Set up the system execution space.

3 Specify a configuration URL.

4 Allocate the interfaces.

5 Configure an admin context.

6 Configure a customer context.

7 Manage the security contexts (optional).

Refer to Figure 9-3 throughout this section to visualize how to configure a virtual firewall.

Step 1: Enabling Multiple Security Contexts Globally

The security context can be enabled by using the **mode multiple** command, as shown in Example 9-2. When this command is executed, the security appliance prompts the system administrator to verify mode conversion before proceeding further. This initiates the reboot process to complete mode conversion.

Example 9-2   *Enabling Security Context*

```
Chicago# configure terminal
Chicago(config)# mode ?
  multiple  Multiple mode; mode with security contexts
  single    Single mode; mode without security contexts
Chicago(config)# mode multiple
WARNING: This command will change the behavior of the device
WARNING: This command will initiate a Reboot
Proceed with change mode? [confirm]
Convert the system configuration? [confirm]
The old running configuration file will be written to disk0
The admin context configuration will be written to disk0
The new running configuration file was written to disk0
Security context mode: multiple
***
*** --- SHUTDOWN NOW ---
***
*** Message to all terminals:
***
***    change mode
Rebooting....
Booting system, please wait...
! Output omitted for brevity.
INFO: Context admin was created with URL disk0:/admin.cfg
INFO: Admin context will take some time to come up .... please wait.
Chicago>
```

When multiple-mode conversion is initiated, the security appliance prompts the administrator to convert the current running configuration into the system execution space and admin context. The appliance stores the system execution space in NVRAM and saves the admin context in the local Flash memory as admin.cfg. During conversion, it copies all the network-related information to the admin.cfg file, while all the device-related system information is stored in the NVRAM space.

NOTE   The security appliance saves the running configuration of the single-mode firewall as old_running.cfg in the Flash memory during the conversion process.

Once the appliance comes online, you can use **show mode** to verify whether it is running in multiple mode. Example 9-3 shows the output of **show mode**.

Example 9-3   *Verifying Virtual Firewall Mode*

```
Chicago# show mode
Security context mode: multiple
```

NOTE   If you do not have the license for multiple security contexts, the system key still lets you configure two customer contexts, in addition to one admin context. Refer to Chapter 4, "Initial Setup and System Maintenance," for more information about licensing.

To convert the device back to single mode, you have to copy the saved old_running.cfg as the startup configuration. After that, you need to switch the security appliance to single mode. Both of these steps are shown in Example 9-4.

Example 9-4   *Reverting to Single-Mode Firewall*

```
Chicago# copy disk0:/old_running.cfg startup-config
Source filename [old_running.cfg]?
Copy in progress...C
1465 bytes copied in 0.250 secs
Chicago# configure terminal
Chicago(config)# mode single
WARNING: This command will change the behavior of the device
WARNING: This command will initiate a Reboot
Proceed with change mode? [confirm]
Security context mode: single ***
*** --- SHUTDOWN NOW ---
***
*** Message to all terminals:
***
***     change mode
Rebooting....
```

Step 2: Setting Up the System Execution Space

As mentioned earlier, the system execution space is created as soon as multiple mode is enabled. To access the system execution space, you can do either of the following:

- Access the security appliance via the console or the auxiliary port.
- Log into the admin context using SSH or Telnet, and then switch to the system execution space. (The admin context is discussed earlier under the "Architectural Overview" section.

    If you are logged into the admin context, you need to use the **changeto system** command to get access to the system execution space. Example 9-5 demonstrates how to log into the system from the admin context.

    If you are in a security context, the host name contains a /. The text before the / is the host name of the security appliance, while the text after is the name of the security context. If the host name does not contain a /, you are in the system execution space.

NOTE   The system execution space can also be accessed through the GUI of ASA Device Manager (ASDM). Consult Chapter 19, "Firewall Management Using ASDM," for more information.

Example 9-5   *Switching to System Execution Space*

```
Chicago/admin# changeto system
Chicago#
```

The purpose of system execution space is to define the admin and customer contexts on the appliance. A context can be added by using the **context** command followed by the name of the context. Example 9-6 shows how to add CustA and CustB security contexts in the Chicago ASA. The security context name is case sensitive, so double-check it when adding the contexts. The appliance takes you into the context subconfiguration mode (config-ctx) to configure the necessary parameters.

Example 9-6   *Adding Customer Contexts in System Execution Space*

```
Chicago# configure terminal
Chicago(config)# context CustA
Creating context 'CustA'... Done. (2)
Chicago(config-ctx)# exit
Chicago(config)# context CustB
Creating context 'CustB'... Done. (3)
Chicago(config-ctx)# end
Chicago#
```

NOTE   The security appliance will not allow a system administrator to change to the newly created context until it is initialized, as discussed next in "Step 3: Specifying a Configuration URL."

The Cisco appliance allows you to add a description to the configured contexts. It is recommended that you add a description under each context for references purposes, as illustrated in Example 9-7.

Example 9-7   *Configuring a Description on the Security Context*

```
Chicago(config)# context CustA
Chicago(config-ctx)# description Customer A's Security Context
Chicago(config-ctx)# context CustB
Chicago(config-ctx)# description Customer B's Security Context
```

CAUTION   If you issue the **clear configure all** command from the system configuration, the Cisco ASA removes all security contexts from the device.

Step 3: Specifying a Configuration URL

The configuration URL specifies the location of the startup configuration for each context. The configured contexts (either admin or customer) are not active unless there is a configuration URL. The supported storage locations include the local disk and a network drive using the HTTP, HTTPS, FTP, or TFTP protocol. Once a configuration URL is specified, the Cisco ASA tries to retrieve the configuration from that location. If it does not find the configuration file, the Cisco security appliance creates a configuration file with the default settings.

An administrator can choose to specify different external servers as the configuration URL location for the security contexts. As shown in Figure 9-3, the Chicago ASA has an admin and two customer contexts. The system administrator prefers to use the following:

- A TFTP server, 192.168.10.50, to store the CustA configuration
- An FTP server, 192.168.20.50, to save the CustB configuration
- The local disk for the admin context configuration

By default, these configuration files are saved in the root directory of the network protocol used by the context. For example, if the root directory of an FTP server is C:\FTP\files, the configuration URL using the FTP protocol will save the configuration file at that location. The security appliance saves the configuration of these security contexts when either **write memory** or **copy running-config startup-config** is issued from within the security context. Example 9-8 shows the relevant configuration to define configuration URL.

Example 9-8   *Setting* **config-url** *for Security Contexts*

```
Chicago(config)# context admin
Chicago(config-ctx)# config-url disk0:/admin.cfg
Chicago(config-ctx)# context CustA
Chicago(config-ctx)# config-url tftp://192.168.10.50/CustA.cfg
Chicago(config-ctx)# context CustB
Chicago(config-ctx)# config-url ftp://cisco:cisco123@192.168.20.50/CustB.cfg
```

For the FTP protocol, you have to specify a username and a password to save and retrieve the configuration file. In the previous example, the CustB context is set up to use cisco as the username and cisco123 as the password.

NOTE   You cannot change the location of the configuration URL from within a context. You have to be in the system execution space to accomplish this.

When the configuration URL is changed, the appliance merges the running configuration of a context with the new configuration specified in the URL. This may add unnecessary commands and may cause system instability. If you do not want to merge the two configurations, you can follow these guidelines:

1   Log into the security context whose URL is to be changed, and clear the running configuration.

2   Log into the system execution space and enter into the context configuration mode.

3   Specify the new configuration URL that you want to use.

As soon as the new URL is entered, the appliance loads the new configuration immediately in the running configuration. Example 9-9 shows how the security appliance in Chicago can be configured to use a new configuration URL. The CustA context is currently using a

TFTP server to retrieve the startup configuration; however, the administrator wants to use an FTP server instead.

Example 9-9 *Changing the Configuration URL*

```
Chicago# change context CustA
Chicago/CustA# configure terminal
Chicago/CustA(config)# clear configure all
Chicago/CustA(config)# changeto system
Chicago(config)# context CustA
Chicago(config-ctx)# config-url ftp://cisco:cisco123@192.168.10.50/CustA.cfg
```

Step 4: Allocating the Interfaces

After defining the configuration URL, the next step is to allocate interfaces to each of the security contexts. You can assign either a physical interface or a subinterface to a security context. Do this by entering into the context subconfiguration mode and using the **allocate-interface** command:

```
allocate-interface physical_interface [map_name] [visible | invisible]
allocate-interface physical_interface.subinterface[-physical_interface.
  subinterface]
[map_name[-map_name]] [visible | invisible]
```

The **allocate-interface** command can hide the physical interface name from the security context if a mapped name is used. This provides additional security by displaying only the mapped name to the context administrator.

Table 9-3 lists and defines the arguments used in the **allocate-interface** command.

Table 9-3 **allocate-interface** *Command Definition*

Syntax	Description
physical_interface	Physical interface that is being allocated to a context, such as GigabitEthernet0/0.
subinterface	Subinterface that is being allocated to a context, such as GigabitEthernet0/0.1. A range of subinterfaces can also be specified.
map_name	By default, the allocated interface is displayed as the interface ID in the context. If you want to display the name for an interface instead of the interface ID, you can specify an alphanumeric mapped name. This is extremely useful when you do not want the context administrator to find out which physical interface is being used as the inside or the outside interface. You can also specify a range of mapped names for the corresponding range of subinterfaces.
invisible	If the **invisible** keyword is configured, the appliance does not display the interface ID in the configuration or the **show interface** command. This default option only shows the mapped name.
visible	If the **visible** keyword is configured, the appliance displays the interface ID in the configuration and the **show interface** command.

In Example 9-10, the ASA in Chicago is configured to allocate GigabitEthernet0/0 and GigabitEthernet0/1 to CustA and are mapped as A_inside and A_outside, respectively. The **invisible** option is used at the end to hide the physical interface name when the context administrator looks at the interface configuration or statistics. The appliance is also set up to allocate GigabitEthernet0/2 and GigabitEthernet0/3 to CustB. The context administrators will see these interfaces as B_inside and B_outside.

Example 9-10 *Allocating Interfaces to Security Contexts*

```
Chicago(config)# context CustA
Chicago(config-ctx)# allocate-interface GigabitEthernet0/0 A_inside invisible
Chicago(config-ctx)# allocate-interface GigabitEthernet0/1 A_outside invisible
Chicago(config-ctx)# exit
Chicago(config)# context CustB
Chicago(config-ctx)# allocate-interface GigabitEthernet0/2 B_inside invisible
Chicago(config-ctx)# allocate-interface GigabitEthernet0/3 B_outside invisible
```

NOTE   If the appliance is converted from a single- to multiple-mode firewall, it allocates all the non-shutdown interfaces to the admin context. It is highly recommended that you use the admin context only for management purposes. Reallocate the interfaces to the proper contexts if necessary.

Step 5: Configuring an Admin Context

Cisco ASA creates an admin context automatically, if you convert it from single to multiple mode and you answer "yes" to "Convert the system configuration?" The admin context is treated as any other customer context in the security appliance. To log into the admin context, use the **changeto context** command, as shown in Example 9-11, where an administrator logs into admin context called **admin**.

Example 9-11 *Logging into a Security Context*

```
Chicago# changeto context admin
Chicago/admin#
```

If you would rather designate a different context as the admin context, use the following command in the system execution space:

   admin-context *context_name*

where *context_name* is the name of the context you want to designate as the admin context. Before a context is declared to be an admin context, it must meet two requirements:

1   The context must be predefined and have a **config-url**.

2   The **config-url** must point to a file in the local disk.

Example 9-12 shows how to designate CustA as the admin context in a security appliance. Because CustA used a TFTP server to store the startup configuration, the administrator is modifying it to use the local disk0 before setting up the **admin-context** command.

Example 9-12 *Setting Up an Admin Context*

```
Chicago(config)# context CustA
Chicago(config-ctx)# config-url disk0:/CustA.cfg
Chicago(config-ctx)# exit
Chicago(config)# admin-context CustA
```

Not sure which context is set up as the admin context? Use one of the following three methods to find out:

- **show running-config | include admin-context**
- **show admin-context**
- **show context**, and look for the context name with an asterisk (*)

In Example 9-13, the highlighted entries indicate that CustA is currently set as the admin context.

Example 9-13 *Verifying the Admin Context*

```
Chicago# show running-config | include admin-context
admin-context CustA
Chicago# show admin-context
Admin: CustA disk0/:CustA.cfg
Chicago# show context
Context Name   Interfaces           URL
 admin         Management0/0         disk0:/admin.cfg
*CustA         GigabitEthernet0/0,   disk0:/CustA.cfg
               GigabitEthernet0/1
 CustB         GigabitEthernet0/2,   ftp://cisco:cisco123@192.168.20.50/CustB.cfg
               GigabitEthernet0/3
```

Step 6: Configuring a Customer Context

Any context that is not set up as the admin context is referred to as the customer context. As mentioned earlier in this chapter, a customer context is configured similarly to a standalone firewall, with a few exceptions that are listed in Table 9-1. When an administrator logs into a customer context, the command prompt displays the name of that context, as shown in Example 9-14.

Example 9-14 *Logging Into a Security Context*

```
Chicago# change to context CustA
Chicago/CustA#
```

After logging into the customer context, you can configure all the supported firewall-related options.

NOTE	The security appliance does not save the configuration of all security contexts if copy running-config startup-config is executed from the system execution space. If the security appliance needs to be reloaded, log into all the security contexts to save configuration.

Step 7: Managing the Security Contexts (Optional)

Cisco ASA provides many ways to manage and optimize system resources. For example, if a context name is mistyped or if it needs to be deleted, you can remove it by typing **no context** followed by the name of that context. In Example 9-15, the administrator of the Chicago ASA does not want to use CustB as a customer context anymore; instead, the administrator wants to remove it from system configuration. By deleting any unused security context, you do not waste security contexts, which are restricted by the system license. Additionally, the system does not have to allocate CPU and memory resources to maintain the unused contexts.

Example 9-15 *Removing a Security Context*

```
Chicago(config)# no context CustB
WARNING: Removing context 'CustB'
Proceed with removing the context? [confirm]
Removing context 'CustB' (4)... Done
```

In a situation where all contexts need to be removed, you can use the **clear configure context** command, as shown in Example 9-16.

Example 9-16 *Removing All Security Contexts*

```
Chicago(config)# clear configure context
```

CAUTION	The **clear configure context** command also removes the designated admin context. If you are remotely logged into the appliance over a telnet or a SSH session, you will lose connectivity to the security appliance.

Deployment Scenarios

The virtual firewall solution is useful in deployments where multiple firewalls are needed to protect traffic to and from the trusted networks. Although virtual firewalls can be deployed in many ways, for ease of understanding, we cover two design scenarios:

- Virtual firewall using two customer contexts
- Virtual firewall using a shared interface

NOTE	The design scenarios discussed in this section are used solely to reinforce learning. They should be used for reference purposes only.

Virtual Firewall Using Two Customer Contexts

SecureMe has an office in Brussels that provides firewall services to two small companies, Cubs and Bears. SecureMe's office is located in the same building as the offices of these companies. Cubs and Bears have specific requirements that SecureMe is obliged to meet. However, the appliance in Brussels has two active physical interfaces and, as a result, SecureMe wants to use subinterfaces to accommodate these customers. To conserve public addresses on the outside interfaces, the administrator uses a subnet mask of 255.255.255.248. Figure 9-5 shows SecureMe's new topology that will be set up in Brussels.

Figure 9-5 *SecureMe Brussels Multimode Topology*

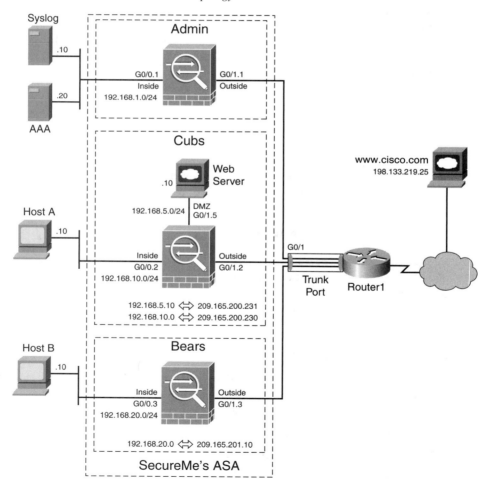

The security requirements for SecureMe, along with Cubs and Bears, are as follows:

SecureMe security requirements:

- For SSH and Telnet user authentication, use a AAA server.

- Log all the system-generated messages to a syslog server.

Cubs security requirements:

- All hosts on 192.168.10.0/24 should be able to access the Internet.

- The source IP address should be translated to 209.165.200.230 using PAT.

- Allow HTTP clients from the Internet to access Cub's web server (192.168.5.10) on the DMZ network. This address should appear as 209.165.200.231 for the Internet users.

- Deny and log all other inbound traffic on the outside interface.

Bears security requirements:

- Allow hosts on the 192.168.20.0/24 subnet to access www.cisco.com only. All other web traffic should be blocked.

- The source IP address should be translated to 209.165.201.10 using interface PAT.

- Block and log all inbound traffic on the outside interface.

Example 9-17 shows the relevant configuration to achieve the goals just listed.

Example 9-17 *ASA's Relevant Configuration with Multiple Security Contexts*

```
                        System Execution Space
Brussels# show run
ASA Version 7.0(1) <system>
! Main GigabitEthernet0/0 interface
interface GigabitEthernet0/0
! Sub-interface assigned to the admin context as the inside interface. A VLAN ID is
   !assigned to the interface
interface GigabitEthernet0/0.1
 vlan 5
! Sub-interface assigned to the Cubs context as the inside interface. A VLAN ID is
   !assigned to the interface
interface GigabitEthernet0/0.2
 vlan 10
! Sub-interface assigned to the Bears context as the inside interface. A VLAN ID is
   !assigned to the interface
interface GigabitEthernet0/0.3
 vlan 20
! Main GigabitEthernet0/1 interface
interface GigabitEthernet0/1

! Sub-interface assigned to the admin context as the outside interface. A VLAN ID
   is !assigned to the interface
interface GigabitEthernet0/1.1
 vlan 101
```

continues

Example 9-17 *ASA's Relevant Configuration with Multiple Security Contexts (Continued)*

```
! Sub-interface assigned to the Cubs context as the outside interface. A VLAN ID is
    !assigned to the interface
interface GigabitEthernet0/1.2
 vlan 110
! Sub-interface assigned to the Bears context as the outside interface. A VLAN ID
    is !assigned to the interface
interface GigabitEthernet0/1.3
 vlan 120
! Sub-interface assigned to the Cubs context as the DMZ interface. A VLAN ID is
    !assigned to the interface
interface GigabitEthernet0/1.5
 vlan 130
!
hostname Brussels
! context named "admin" is the designated Admin context
admin-context admin
! "admin" context definition along with the allocated interfaces.
context admin
  description admin Context for admin purposes
  allocate-interface GigabitEthernet0/0.1
  allocate-interface GigabitEthernet0/1.1
  config-url disk0:/admin.cfg
! "Cubs" context definition along with the allocated interfaces.
context Cubs
  description Cubs Customer Context
  allocate-interface GigabitEthernet0/0.2
  allocate-interface GigabitEthernet0/1.2
  allocate-interface GigabitEthernet0/1.5
  config-url disk0:/Cubs.cfg
! "Bears" context definition along with the allocated interfaces.
context Bears
  description Bears Customer Context
  allocate-interface GigabitEthernet0/0.3
  allocate-interface GigabitEthernet0/1.3
  config-url disk0:/Bears.cfg
```

Admin Context

```
Brussels/admin# show running
ASA Version 7.0(1) <context>
!inside interface of the admin context with security level set to 100
interface GigabitEthernet0/0.1
 nameif inside
 security-level 100
 ip address 192.168.1.1 255.255.255.0
!outside interface of the admin context with security level set to 0
interface GigabitEthernet0/1.1
 nameif outside
 security-level 0
 ip address 209.165.202.130 255.255.255.248
!
hostname admin
!configuration of a syslog server with logging level set to emergencies with
    timestamp
logging enable
```

Example 9-17 *ASA's Relevant Configuration with Multiple Security Contexts (Continued)*

```
logging timestamp
logging trap emergencies
logging host inside 192.168.1.10
!
route outside 0.0.0.0 0.0.0.0 209.165.202.129 1
!configuration of a AAA server using RADIUS for authentication
aaa-server uauth protocol radius
aaa-server uauth host 192.168.1.20
 key cisco123
!setting up telnet and SSH authentication
aaa authentication telnet console uauth
aaa authentication ssh console uauth
!Telnet to the admin context is allowed from the inside interface
telnet 192.168.1.0 255.255.255.0 inside
telnet timeout 5
!SSH to the admin context is allowed from the outside interface
ssh 0.0.0.0 0.0.0.0 outside
ssh timeout 5
```

                              Cubs Context

```
Brussels/Cubs# show running
ASA Version 7.0(1) <context>
!inside interface of the Cubs context with security level set to 100
interface GigabitEthernet0/0.2
 nameif inside
 security-level 100
 ip address 192.168.10.1 255.255.255.0
!outside interface of the Cubs context with security level set to 0
interface GigabitEthernet0/1.2
 nameif outside
 security-level 0
 ip address 209.165.200.225 255.255.255.248
!DMZ interface of the Cubs context with security level set to 50
interface GigabitEthernet0/1.5
 nameif dmz
 security-level 50
 ip address 192.168.5.1 255.255.255.0
!
hostname Cubs
!Access-list configuration to allow web traffic. The access-list is applied to the
  outside interface.
access-list outside-in extended permit tcp any host 209.165.200.231 eq www
access-list outside-in extended deny ip any any log
access-group outside-in in interface outside
!NAT configuration to allow inside hosts to get Internet connectivity
global (outside) 1 209.165.200.230
nat (inside) 1 192.168.10.0 255.255.255.0

!Static address translation for the Web-Server
static (dmz,outside) 209.165.200.231 192.168.5.10 netmask 255.255.255.255
!
route outside 0.0.0.0 0.0.0.0 209.165.200.226 1
```

continues

Example 9-17 *ASA's Relevant Configuration with Multiple Security Contexts (Continued)*

```
                              Bears Context
Brussels/Bears# show running
ASA Version 7.0(1) <context>
!inside interface of the Bears context with security level set to 100
interface GigabitEthernet0/0.3
 nameif inside
 security-level 100
 ip address 192.168.20.1 255.255.255.0
!outside interface of the Bears context with security level set to 0
interface GigabitEthernet0/1.3
 nameif outside
 security-level 0
 ip address 209.165.201.2 255.255.255.224
!
enable password 8Ry2YjIyt7RRXU24 encrypted
passwd 2KFQnbNIdI.2KYOU encrypted
hostname Bears
!Access-list configuration to permit web traffic initiated from the inside host and
    destined to 198.133.219.25. Deny all other traffic. The access-list is applied
    to the inside interface.
access-list inside-in extended permit tcp 192.168.20.0 255.255.255.0 host
198.133.219.25   eq 80
access-group inside-in in interface inside
!Access-list configuration to deny and log all inbound traffic. The access-list is
    applied to the outside interface
access-list outside-in extended deny ip any any log
access-group outside-in in interface outside
!NAT configuration to allow inside hosts to get Internet connectivity
global (outside) 1 interface
nat (inside) 1 192.168.20.0 255.255.255.0
!
route outside 0.0.0.0 0.0.0.0 209.165.201.1 1
```

Virtual Firewall Using a Shared Interface

An educational institute contacts SecureMe to provide firewall services for two of its departments—faculty and students—over a shared outside interface. The hosts in the student context are allowed to access a web server in the faculty context. Additionally, they are allowed to check their e-mail messages from 209.165.202.130. The faculty context, on the other hand, does not restrict anything going out to the Internet.

The SecureMe global policy restricts access of the security appliance to the valid and authorized users on the AAA servers. SecureMe does not have many public addresses available, so it is using interface PAT for address translation. Additionally, SecureMe does not want the administrators of the individual security contexts to be able to determine the interface assignment for their contexts. Figure 9-6 shows SecureMe's proposed topology for this institute.

Figure 9-6   *Security Contexts Using a Shared Interface*

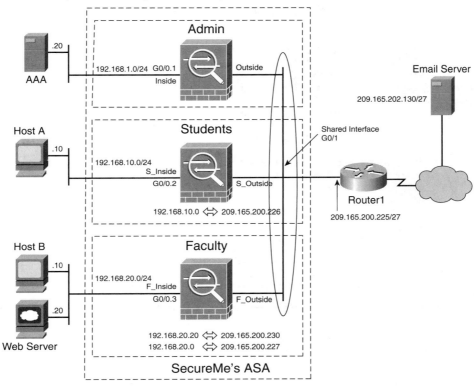

Example 9-18 shows the relevant configuration for the Cisco ASA used in this deployment.

Example 9-18 *ASA's Relevant Configuration Using a Shared Outside Interface*

```
                        System Execution Space
SecuremeInstitute# show run
ASA Version 7.0(1) <system>
! Main GigabitEthernet0/0 interface
interface GigabitEthernet0/0

! Sub-interface assigned to the admin context as the inside interface. A VLAN ID is
    !assigned to the interface
interface GigabitEthernet0/0.1
 vlan 5
! Sub-interface assigned to the Students context as the inside interface. A VLAN ID
 is !assigned to the interface
interface GigabitEthernet0/0.2
 vlan 10
! Sub-interface assigned to the Faculty context as the inside interface. A VLAN ID
    is !assigned to the interface
interface GigabitEthernet0/0.3
 vlan 20
```

continues

Example 9-18 *ASA's Relevant Configuration Using a Shared Outside Interface (Continued)*

```
! Main GigabitEthernet0/1 interface to be used as the shared interface
interface GigabitEthernet0/1
!
hostname SecuremeInstitute
! context named "admin" is the designated Admin context
admin-context admin
! "admin" context definition along with the allocated interfaces.
context admin
  description admin Context for admin purposes
  allocate-interface GigabitEthernet0/0.1 inside invisible
  allocate-interface GigabitEthernet0/1 outside invisible
  config-url disk0:/admin.cfg
! "Students" context definition along with the allocated interfaces.
context Students
  description Students Customer Context
  allocate-interface GigabitEthernet0/0.2 S_inside invisible
  allocate-interface GigabitEthernet0/1 S_outside invisible
  config-url disk0:/Students.cfg
! "Faculty" context definition along with the allocated interfaces.
context Faculty
  description Faculty Customer Context
  allocate-interface GigabitEthernet0/0.3 F_inside invisible
  allocate-interface GigabitEthernet0/1 F_outside invisible
  config-url disk0:/Faculty.cfg
```

Admin Context

```
SecuremeInstitute/admin# show running
ASA Version 7.0(1) <context>
!inside interface of the admin context with security level set to 100
interface inside
 nameif inside
 security-level 100
 ip address 192.168.1.1 255.255.255.0
!outside interface of the admin context with security level set to 0
interface outside
 nameif outside
 security-level 0
 ip address 209.165.200.225 255.255.255.224
!
hostname admin
!
route outside 0.0.0.0 0.0.0.0 209.165.200.230 1
!configuration of a AAA server using RADIUS for authentication
aaa-server uauth protocol radius
aaa-server uauth host 192.168.1.20
 key cisco123
aaa authentication telnet console uauth
aaa authentication ssh console uauth
!Telnet to the admin context is allowed from the inside interface
telnet 192.168.1.0 255.255.255.0 inside
telnet timeout 5
!SSH to the admin context is allowed from the outside interface
ssh 0.0.0.0 0.0.0.0 outside
ssh timeout 5
route outside 0.0.0.0 0.0.0.0 209.165.200.225 1
```

Example 9-18 *ASA's Relevant Configuration Using a Shared Outside Interface (Continued)*

Students Context

```
SecuremeInstitute/Students# show running
ASA Version 7.0(1) <context>
!inside interface of the Students context with security level set to 100
interface S_inside
 nameif inside
 security-level 100
 ip address 192.168.10.1 255.255.255.0
!outside interface of the Students context with security level set to 0
interface S_outside
 nameif outside
 security-level 0
 ip address 209.165.200.226 255.255.255.224
!Access-list configuration to allow email and web traffic. The access-list is
  applied to the inside interface.
access-list inside-in extended permit tcp 192.168.10.0 255.255.255.0 host
   209.165.202.130 eq smtp
access-list inside-in extended permit tcp 192.168.10.0 255.255.255.0 host
   209.165.200.230 eq www
access-group inside-in in interface S_inside
!
hostname Students
!NAT configuration to allow inside hosts to get Internet connectivity
global (S_outside) 1 interface
nat (S_inside) 1 192.168.10.0 255.255.255.0
!
route S_outside 0.0.0.0 0.0.0.0 209.165.200.225 1
```

Faculty Context

```
SecuremeInstitute/Faculty# show running
ASA Version 7.0(1) <context>
!inside interface of the Faculty context with security level set to 100
interface F_inside
 nameif inside
 security-level 100
 ip address 192.168.20.1 255.255.255.0
!outside interface of the Faculty context with security level set to 0
interface F_outside
 nameif outside
 security-level 0
 ip address 209.165.200.227 255.255.255.224
!
enable password 8Ry2YjIyt7RRXU24 encrypted
passwd 2KFQnbNIdI.2KYOU encrypted
hostname Faculty
!Access-list configuration to allow web traffic. The access-list is applied to the
   outside interface.
access-list outside-in extended permit tcp host 209.165.200.226 host 209.165.200.230
eq www
access-group outside-in in interface F_outside
!NAT configuration to allow inside hosts to get Internet connectivity
global (F_outside) 1 interface
```

continues

Example 9-18 *ASA's Relevant Configuration Using a Shared Outside Interface (Continued)*

```
nat (F_inside) 1 192.168.20.0 255.255.255.0
!Static address translation for the Web-Server
static (F_inside,F_outside) 209.165.200.230 192.168.20.20 netmask 255.255.255.255
!
route F_outside 0.0.0.0 0.0.0.0 209.165.200.225 1
```

Monitoring and Troubleshooting the Security Contexts

Cisco ASA provides **show** and **debug** commands that are useful to check the health of the appliance or to isolate a problem. The necessary **show** and **debug** commands that are used to manage multiple security contexts in the appliance are discussed here.

Monitoring

After the system is converted to multiple contexts, the first thing to verify is that the system is using the new mode by using the **show mode** command, as shown in Example 9-19.

Example 9-19 *Output of* **show mode**

```
Sydney# show mode
Security context mode: multiple
```

Once you verify that the system is running in multiple mode, configure the necessary contexts and assign the appropriate interfaces. A good way to check if the interfaces have been correctly assigned to the right context is to use the **show context** command. It lists all the configured contexts, the allocated interfaces, and the configuration URL. Example 9-20 shows the output of **show context** in the Chicago ASA, while logged into the system execution space.

Example 9-20 *Output of* **show context** *in the System Execution Space*

```
Chicago# show context
Context Name    Interfaces              URL
*admin          GigabitEthernet0/0.1    disk0:/admin.cfg
                GigabitEthernet0/1.1
 Cubs           GigabitEthernet0/0.2,   disk0:/Cubs.cfg
                GigabitEthernet0/1.2,
                GigabitEthernet0/1.5
 Bears          GigabitEthernet0/0.3    disk0:/Bears.cfg
                GigabitEthernet0/1.3
Total active Security Contexts: 3
```

The asterisk (*) next to admin indicates that this is an admin context. Another way to find out which context is designated as the admin context is to use the **show admin-context** command, as illustrated in Example 9-21.

Example 9-21 *Output of* **show admin-context** *in the System Execution Space*

```
Chicago# show admin-context
Admin: admin disk0:/admin.cfg
```

A context administrator can view the context settings from within his security context. In Example 9-22, the administrator of the Cubs context is verifying the allocated interfaces and the configuration URL.

Example 9-22 *Output of* **show context** *from a Security Context*

```
Chicago/Cubs# show context
Context Name       Interfaces                URL
  Cubs             GigabitEthernet0/0.2,     disk0:/Cubs.cfg
                   GigabitEthernet0/1.2,
                   GigabitEthernet0/1.5
```

Cisco ASA allows monitoring of CPU usage per security context. This is useful to determine which context is utilizing the most of the CPU cycles. Use the **show cpu usage context all** command to check the CPU utilization on each of the configured security contexts. In Example 9-23, the total system CPU utilization is 9.5 percent averaged over 5 seconds, 9.2 percent averaged over 1 minute, and 9.3 percent averaged over 5 minutes. The Cubs security context is using the most of the CPU cycles, averaging 5 percent over 5 seconds, 1 minute, and 5 minutes.

Example 9-23 *Output of* **show cpu usage context all** *from the System Execution Space*

```
Chicago# show cpu usage context all
5 sec  1 min  5 min  Context Name
9.5%   9.2%   9.3%   system
0.3%   0.0%   0.1%   admin
5.0%   5.0%   5.0%   Cubs
4.2%   4.2%   4.2%   Bears
```

Troubleshooting

For troubleshooting purposes, Cisco ASA includes a number of important debug and syslog messages to help you isolate the issue. This section discusses four troubleshooting scenarios related to security contexts:

- **Security contexts are not added**—When adding new contexts, the Cisco security appliance displays a message that the new security contexts creation failed, as shown in Example 9-24.

Example 9-24 *Security Context Creation Failure*

```
Chicago(config)# context  WhiteSox
Creating context 'WhiteSox'...
Cannot create context 'WhiteSox': limit of 3 contexts exceeded
ERROR: Creation for context 'WhiteSox' failed
```

The Cisco ASA appliance complains about exceeding the maximum number of security contexts allowed in this device. To verify the maximum number of allowed security contexts, use the **show version** command, as shown in Example 9-25.

Example 9-25 *Verifying the Maximum Number of Security Contexts*

```
Chicago# show version | include Security Contexts
Security Contexts              : 10
```

Depending on the security appliance model number, the administrator can add the maximum allowed security context number. Refer to Chapter 3, "Hardware Overview," for more information about the allowed number of security contexts in a Cisco ASA.

- **Security contexts are not saved on the local disk**—If the security context configuration files are stored locally on the disk, and the appliance is having trouble either retrieving or saving them, you can enable **debug disk** to gather information.

  In Example 9-26, **debug disk file**, **file-verbose**, and **filesystem** are enabled with a log level of 255. In this example, the administrator saves the running configuration into the Flash file system. The highlighted entries show that the appliance opens up the running configuration file from the disk and writes the new contents. If Flash is corrupt, the administrator will see failed attempts to read or write files. These messages are analyzed by the Cisco Technical Assistance (TAC) engineers.

Example 9-26 *Output of* **debug disk**

```
Chicago# debug disk file 255
Chicago# debug disk file-verbose 255
Chicago# debug disk filesystem 255
Chicago# write memory
Building IFS: Opening: file system:/running-config, flags 1, mode 0
IFS: Opened: file system:/running-config as fd 0
IFS: Fioctl: fd 0, fn 5, arg 370e7e0
configuration...
IFS: Read: fd 1, bytes 147456
IFS: Read: fd 1, bytes 146664
IFS: disk0:/.private/startup-config 100% chance ascii text
<snip>
1047 IFS: Close: fd 0
bytes copied in 4.40 secs (261 bytes/sec)IFS: Write: fd 0, bytes 1
```

- **Security contexts are not saved on the FTP server**—If the security appliance is having issues when saving and retrieving configuration files from an FTP server, use the **debug ftp client** command to isolate the issue. In Example 9-27, the appliance is being configured to use an FTP server. The debug shows that the user password is incorrect in the configuration URL.

Example 9-27 *Output of* **debug ftp client**

```
Chicago(config)# debug ftp client
Chicago# context CustB
Chicago(config-ctx)# config-url ftp://cisco:cisco123@172.18.124.27/CustB.cfg
IFS: Opening: file ftp://cisco:cisco123@192.168.20.50/CustB.cfg, flags 1, mode 0
IFS: Opened: file ftp://cisco:cisco123@192.168.20.50/CustB.cfg as fd 0
IFS: Fioctl: fd 0, fn 5, arg 279bc64
Loading CustB.cfg
FTP: 220 Please enter your user name.
FTP: ---> USER cisco
FTP: 331 User name okay, Need password.
FTP: ---> PASS *
FTP: 530 Password not accepted.
FTP: ---> QUIT
FTP: 221 Goodbye. Control connection closed.
IFS: Close: fd 0
```

- **User connectivity issues using shared security contexts**—As shown in Figure 9-6, when Host A in the Students context is not able to reach Host B in the Faculty context, the administrator can take the following steps to isolate the issue:

  Step 1   Ping the inside IP address of the S_inside interface from Host A. If successful, move to Step 2; otherwise, check to see if there is an inbound ACL applied to the inside interface. Also verify that physical connectivity exists between the host and the inside interface.

  Step 2   Ping the outside IP address of the F_outside interface from Host A. If successful, move to Step 3; otherwise, check the outbound ACL and NAT configuration on the Students context. Additionally, verify that the inbound ACL on the F_outside interface allows ICMP traffic from Host A.

  Step 3   Because this topology uses a shared interface, check the NAT configuration on the Faculty context. Ping from Host A to Host B and verify that the outbound ACL on F_inside does not block the ICMP packets.

  Step 4   If Host A is still not able to communicate with Host B in the other context, follow Step 1 through Step 3 and ping from Host B to Host A to verify connectivity and the contexts' configuration.

Summary

Security context is a robust feature available in Cisco ASA. It provides a cost-effective solution by having multiple firewalls integrated into one physical appliance. Each security context has its own interfaces, security policies, and routing tables. The packets traversed through the security contexts are classified based on the source interface or the destination IP address. This chapter discussed the configuration steps and provided deployment scenarios to help you to understand this concept better. For troubleshooting purposes, the chapter introduced the relevant **show** commands and walked you through how to isolate the issues related to security contexts.

This chapter covers the following topics:

- Architectural overview
- Configuration of transparent firewalls
- Deployment scenarios
- Monitoring and troubleshooting

CHAPTER 10

Transparent Firewalls

Traditionally, network firewalls have been deployed and used to filter traffic passing through them. These firewalls usually examine the upper-layer headers (Layer 3 or above) and, occasionally, the data payload in the packets. The packets are then either allowed or dropped based on the configured access control lists (ACLs). These firewalls, commonly referred to as routed firewalls, segregate protected networks from unprotected ones by acting as an extra hop in the network design. They route packets from one IP subnet to another subnet by using the Layer 3 routing table. In most cases, these firewalls are configured for address translation to protect the original IP addressing scheme used in the network.

Figure 10-1 illustrates a routed firewall protecting the inside network and translating the source address of Host A from 192.168.1.2 to 209.165.201.2 for the traffic destined to www.cisco.com.

Figure 10-1 *Routed Firewall*

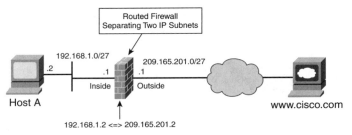

Routed firewalls do not provide a way to filter packets that traverse from one host to another in the same LAN segment. The Layer 3 firewalls require a new network segment to be created when they are inserted into a network, which requires quite a bit of planning, network downtime, and reconfiguration of network devices. To avoid these issues, stealth or transparent firewalls have been developed to provide LAN-based protection. An administrator can place a transparent firewall between the LAN and the next-hop layer 3 device (a router) without having to readdress the network devices.

By using transparent firewalls, administrators can optionally inspect Layer 2 traffic and filter disallowed traffic. Because all interfaces are in the same subnet, these firewalls, therefore, do not participate in address translation.

Figure 10-2 shows SecureMe's network running a transparent firewall. SecureMe wants to inspect all traffic before it hits the default gateway. When the host 192.168.1.2 sends traffic destined to www.cisco.com, the firewall makes sure that the packets are allowed before passing them to the default gateway, 192.168.1.1. The default gateway router is responsible for translating the 192.168.1.0/27 subnet to 209.165.201.0/27 to achieve the Internet connectivity.

Figure 10-2 *Transparent Firewall*

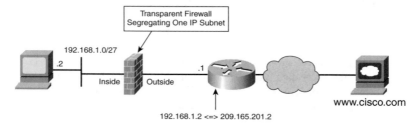

Table 10-1 summarizes major differences between routed and transparent mode firewalls.

Table 10-1 *Contrasting Routed and Transparent Firewalls*

Feature	Routed Firewall	Transparent Firewall
Interfaces	Supports up to five Fast-Ethernet or four Gigabit-Ethernet interfaces[1], which can be further subdivided.	Supports two interfaces.
Addressing	IP address assignment at the interface level.	IP address assignment at the global level, which is solely used for management purposes.
IPv6 addressing	IPv6 is supported.	IPv6 is not supported.
Routing protocols	Supports RIP and OSPF.	Does not participate in routing protocols but can still pass routing protocol traffic through it. You can define static routes for the traffic originated by the ASA.
Non-IP traffic	Does not allow passing non-IP traffic.	Allows IP and non-IP traffic to pass through it.
Network topology	Adds an extra hop on the network by setting up routed interfaces.	Does not add an extra hop; thus, no need to readdress one network.
NAT	Supports both static and dynamic address translation.	Does not support address translation.

Table 10-1   *Contrasting Routed and Transparent Firewalls (Continued)*

Feature	Routed Firewall	Transparent Firewall
Multicast	Supports multicast using sparse mode.	Does not participate in multicast. However, it allows passing the multicast traffic through it using the ACLs.
QoS	Supports QoS	Does not support QoS.
Inspection	Inspects Layer 3 and higher packet headers.	Inspects Layer 2 and higher packet headers.
VPN[2]	Supports remote access and site-to-site tunnels.	Only supports site-to-site VPN for management purposes.

1. Three Fast Ethernet interfaces are supported on the ASA5510 if a base license is used. ASA 5510 with a security plus license allows up to 5 Fast Ethernet interfaces. ASA 5520 and ASA 5540 support four Gigabit Ethernet interfaces and a Fast Ethernet interface.

2. Transparent firewalls and limitations related to VPN are discussed under the "Transparent Firewalls and VPNs" section.

Architectural Overview

As discussed in Chapter 9, "Security Contexts," Cisco ASA can be deployed in either single or multiple mode. A transparent firewall can coexist with these modes to provide a great deal of flexibility for network deployments. This section discusses these modes in detail.

Single-Mode Transparent Firewall

In a single-mode transparent firewall (SMTF), the ASA acts as a secured bridge that switches traffic from one interface to another. You do not configure IP addresses on either the inside or the outside interface. Rather, you must specify a global IP address that is primarily used for management purposes—Telnet and Secure Shell (SSH). The transparent firewall also uses the management IP address when it needs to source packets such as ARP requests.

This is the simplest form of configuration because it does not require configuration of security contexts, static or dynamic routes, or address translation. All that is needed is to set up the ACLs and inspection rules to determine what traffic is allowed. The next section talks about how a packet flows through an SMTF.

Packet Flow in an SMTF

Figure 10-3 shows SecureMe's office in Sydney, where the company has recently installed a Cisco ASA firewall in transparent mode. The network administrator in Sydney is curious to know how traffic traverses the ASA so that he can better implement network security. Therefore, he is monitoring the traffic sourced from Host A that is destined to www.cisco.com.

Figure 10-3 *Packet Flow in an SMTF*

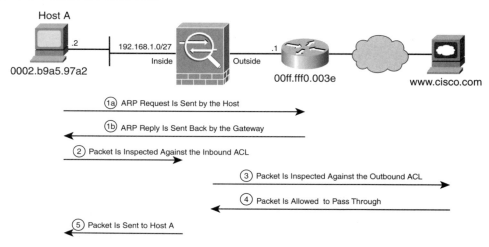

For a successful connection, the ASA follows these steps:

Step 1   **ARP resolution**—Because the Cisco website is located in a different
subnet from Host A's network, Host A needs to perform Address Resolution
Protocol (ARP) to determine its default gateway, 192.168.1.1. For the ARP
process through an ASA, there are four possible cases that we will discuss.

Case 1: Host A and ASA do not have gateway's MAC address

For ARP resolution, Host A sends out an ARP broadcast request, shown as
Step 1a. The ASA, after receiving this broadcast, performs two operations:

1   It populates the Layer 2 forwarding (L2F) table with the source MAC address
and the originating interface information.

2   It forwards the broadcast to all the interfaces except the originating interface.

Upon receipt of this ARP request, the default gateway replies with a
unicast ARP response packet, shown as Step 1b. The security appliance,
once again, does two things:

1   It forwards the response packet to Host A.

2   It inserts the MAC address of the default gateway router into its L2F table
along with the interface information on which the default gateway is located.

Case 2: Host A has gateway's MAC address but ASA does not

If, for some reason, the Cisco ASA does not learn the MAC address of
the default gateway (either it aged out or someone manually cleared it),
it goes through the process of learning the destination MAC address.

Hence, when Host A sends a packet to its default gateway, the Cisco ASA drops the packet and generates an ICMP request packet with TTL (time to live) set to 1. It sets the destination MAC address of the default gateway, which is learned from the packet sent by Host A. The security appliance sends the packet on all interfaces. If a response is received on an interface, the security appliance updates its L2F table accordingly.

Case 3: Host A does not have gateway's MAC address, but ASA does

When Host A needs to resolve a gateway's MAC address, it sends out an ARP broadcast. The Cisco ASA treats this case similarly to Case 1. If there is a discrepancy in what the Cisco ASA learns and in what is already in the L2F table, the ASA updates its table with the new information.

Case 4: Host A and ASA have MAC address resolution

If both devices know about the MAC address of the default gateway, they do not need to update either the ARP or the L2F table. As such, they do not participate in any address resolution process.

Note   For non-IP traffic, such as an Internetwork Packet Exchange (IPX) packet, there is no concept of ARP or ICMP to resolve destination MAC addresses. In this case, when the ASA receives a non-IP packet and it does not find an entry in its L2F table, it drops the packet and does not participate in resolution.

Step 2   **Inbound ACL checking**—Once Host A knows about the MAC address of its default gateway, it sends out a SYN packet to the web server to initiate a three-way TCP handshake. When the packet enters the inside interface of the security appliance, the packet is checked for uauth (user authentication) and an inbound ACL. If the packet is allowed in, a connection entry is created by verifying it against the inspection rules and TCP checks. It is then forwarded to the bridging engine, where the L2F table is used to determine the correct outbound interface (outside interface, in this case).

Step 3   **Outbound ACL checking**—After bridging the packet to the outside interface, the packet is then checked against the outbound interface ACL before transmitting it on the wire. If the packet is denied, it is dropped and a log entry is created in case the log keyword is specified in the ACL. The security appliance deletes the connection entry for this session if the packet is denied. If the packet is allowed, it is forwarded to the interface drivers for transmission.

Step 4 The web server replies with a SYN-ACK, the ASA allows the packet to pass because the connection had already been created.

Step 5 The packet is bridged to Host A after checking it against the outbound ACL on the inside interface. Finally, Host A and the web server complete the TCP three-way handshake and initiate data transmission.

As you can see from this packet flow, the security appliance applies security policies regardless of the firewall mode.

Multimode Transparent Firewall

In a multimode transparent firewall (MMTF), the ASA acts in a similar fashion to how it acts in single mode, with one major exception: packets are handled in different contexts. Because each context acts and behaves as an independent entity, you must configure an IP address in each context for administration and management purposes.

Packet Flow in an MMTF

Figure 10-4 illustrates SecureMe's topology for its Sydney office. SecureMe has recently acquired a small startup company (Site 2) in the same office building and is now responsible for providing the network services to the office. The new company currently uses an IP subnet of 192.168.2.0/27, and SecureMe wants to transparently add a firewall to inspect the Internet traffic destined to www.cisco.com.

Figure 10-4 *Packet Flow in an MMTF*

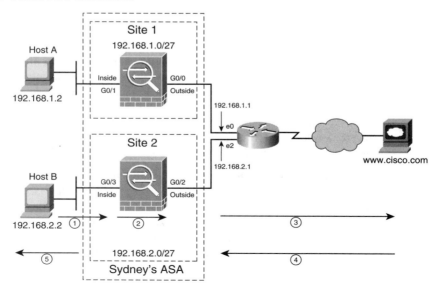

The following steps briefly talk about packet flow in an MMTF, as illustrated in Figure 10-4:

Step 1   **ARP resolution**—The process to resolve the default gateway's IP address is the same as discussed in the previous section. Host B sends a broadcast if it does not know the MAC address of its gateway. The ASA receives that packet on its GigabitEthernet0/3(G0/3) interface, which belongs to the "Site 2" context. The ASA forwards this request to its outside interface. Because the default gateway (192.168.2.1/27) is also on the same context, it sends a unicast reply to Host B. The ASA updates its L2F table once the reply packet traverses through it.

Step 2   **Inbound ACL checking**—Once the MAC address is known, Host B sends out the first packet to initiate the TCP three-way handshake. When the packet enters the inside interface of the security appliance, it is checked for uauth (user authentication) and an inbound ACL. If the packet is allowed in, a connection entry is created by verifying it against the inspection rules and TCP checks. These connection entries are segregated in each context and are used to forward the return packet to the correct destination.

Step 3   **Outbound ACL checking**—The packet is switched to the outside interface, where it is then checked against the outbound ACL. If the packet is allowed to leave the ASA, it is sent to the next hop router located in the same context. The packet is then routed out to the Cisco website.

Step 4   The web server sends a reply packet back to Host B.

Step 5   The ASA inspects this reply packet against the connection entry and, because an entry already exists, forwards the packet to Host B.

NOTE   You cannot use shared interfaces between the contexts in an MMTF.

Transparent Firewalls and VPNs

When the Cisco ASA runs in transparent mode, the following limitations and restrictions apply to configuring the IPSec tunnels on it:

- The ASA can terminate the IPSec tunnels for management purposes only. That means you cannot establish an IPSec tunnel to pass traffic through the Cisco ASA.

- An IPSec tunnel is allowed only if the ASA is running in single mode. Multimode transparent firewalls and IPSec VPNs are not supported.

- WebVPN and IPSec remote-access VPNs are not supported. You can configure only one site-to-site IPSec tunnel, which needs to be set up in answer mode to respond to a tunnel request.

- The ASA does not affect the IPSec tunnels going through it. You may still set up ACLs to block unnecessary IPSec traffic passing through the ASA.

- Because routing protocols are not supported in transparent mode, reverse route injection (RRI) is also not supported.

- The IPSec tunnel uses the management IP address to terminate the connection. The IPSec tunnel could be terminated on either interface—inside or outside.

- Load balancing, stateful failover, QoS, and NAT over the VPN tunnel are not supported in IPSec VPN implementations.

- NAT Traversal (NAT-T) and public key infrastructure (PKI) are fully supported in transparent mode for the management tunnel.

Configuration of Transparent Firewall

Implementing a transparent firewall increases design flexibility and network scalability. However, you need to consider some limitations before you implement a transparent firewall. This section discusses the configuration guidelines and configuration steps for a successful implementation of transparent firewalls in a network.

Configuration Guidelines

The following guidelines are useful if you are introducing a new ASA firewall into an environment where renumbering an existing network is not possible. They are also relevant if you are inspecting non-IP traffic through the firewall for improved security.

- Setting the Cisco ASA to either routed or transparent mode is a global feature. Thus, if you use multiple contexts and you set the ASA to transparent mode, all security contexts will use transparent mode to forward traffic between the interfaces.

- Switching from routed to transparent mode or vice versa clears the running configuration. Save active configurations prior to making this change.

- There is no support for dynamic routing protocols like RIP or OSPF in either SMTFs or MMTFs. All OSPF- and RIP-related commands are disabled.

- There is no support for NAT on the ASA if transparent mode is enabled. If address translation is required, it is recommended that you configure an Internet-facing router to provide address translation, as previously shown in Figure 10-2. Consequently, the "global" statement is disabled in the command-line interface (CLI).

- The static and nat commands are used to specify the embryonic and maximum connection limit. They can also be used to disable TCP sequence number randomization.

- Currently, only two interfaces—inside and outside—are used to pass traffic through the ASA transparent firewall running it either in SMTF or MMTF. These interfaces use different security levels.

- The ASA transparent firewall is implemented to inspect and filter out traffic traversing a subnet. This requires both inside and outside interfaces to be on the same subnet. The global IP address must belong to the same subnet as the directly connected interfaces.

- In an MMTF, interfaces cannot be shared between the contexts. Unique interfaces (either physical or logical) are required to segregate traffic between the security contexts.

- For traffic filtering, Layer 3 or EtherType ACLs can be used to allow IP or non-IP traffic to pass through the ASA.

- In transparent mode, the ASA does not support DHCP-relay and reverse-path forwarding features.

Configuration Steps

The following steps can be taken to configure Cisco ASA for transparent firewalls:

1 Enable transparent firewalls.

2 Set up interfaces.

3 Configure an IP address.

4 Configure interface ACLs.

5 Add static L2F table entries (optional).

6 Enable ARP inspection (optional).

7 Modify L2F table parameters (optional).

Step 1: Enabling Transparent Firewalls

The default routed mode can be changed to transparent mode by using the **firewall transparent** command, as shown in Example 10-1.

Example 10-1 *Enabling Transparent Firewall*

```
Sydney(config)# firewall transparent
Switched to transparent mode
```

After switching modes, the ASA clears the running configuration because most of the routed mode commands are not compatible in transparent mode. Example 10-2 illustrates how to revert to routed mode.

Example 10-2 *Enabling Routed Firewall*

```
Sydney(config)# no firewall transparent
Switched to router mode
```

Use the **show firewall** command to verify in which mode your firewall is running, as illustrated in Example 10-3.

Example 10-3 *Verifying Firewall Mode*

```
Sydney(config)# show firewall
Firewall mode: Transparent
```

Step 2: Setting Up Interfaces

After you turn on the transparent firewall on the security appliance, you can define the inside and outside interfaces. You do so by assigning a name and a security level on an interface. Example 10-4 shows how to define an inside interface with security level 100, and an outside interface with security level 0. By default, all interfaces are in the shutdown state, which can be enabled by using the **no shutdown** command.

Example 10-4 *Setting Up Interfaces*

```
Sydney(config)# interface GigabitEthernet0/0
Sydney(config-if)# no shutdown
Sydney(config-if)# nameif outside
INFO: Security level for "outside" set to 0 by default.
Sydney(config-if)# security-level 0
Sydney(config-if)# exit
Sydney(config)# interface GigabitEthernet0/1
Sydney(config-if)# no shutdown
Sydney(config-if)# nameif inside
INFO: Security level for "inside" set to 100 by default.
Sydney(config-if)# security-level 100
```

NOTE   Transparent firewall mode on the security appliance allows only two interfaces to pass through traffic. However, you can set up a dedicated management interface, which can be either a physical interface or a subinterface, as a third interface. This interface must be set up for the **management-only** command.

Step 3: Configuring an IP Address

Unlike routed mode, the ASA in transparent mode does not allow you to configure IP addresses on the interfaces. Rather, an IP address is assigned in global configuration mode.

This IP address is used exclusively for management purposes, such as SSH, Telnet, PDM, SNMP traps and polling, AAA, and ARP resolution. Here is the command syntax to configure an IP address:

```
ip address ip_address [mask] [standby sby_ip_addr]
```

ip_address is the configured IP address on the ASA, and *mask* is the network mask of the assigned IP address. Optionally, a standby IP address can be used for the appliance failover. This is covered in Chapter 11, "Failover and Redundancy."

Example 10-5 shows how to configure an IP address of 192.168.1.10 with a 27-bit mask on the ASA running in transparent mode.

Example 10-5 *Assigning an IP Address*

```
Sydney(config)# ip address 192.168.1.10 255.255.255.224
```

NOTE   In an MMTF, an IP address must be configured for each context. The command syntax remains the same as what was just discussed.

Step 4: Configuring Interface ACLs

As discussed in Chapter 5, "Network Access Control," extended ACLs can filter out IP packets by looking at various headers. EtherType-based ACLs can be used to filter IP- and non-IP-based traffic. Here is the command syntax for an EtherType ACL:

```
access-list id ethertype {deny | permit} {ether-value | bpdu | ipx | mpls-unicast |
    mpls-multicast | any}
```

ether-value is a 2-byte value specified in the Layer 2 datagram under the EtherType code field. For IP-based traffic, the EtherType code value is 0x800. Novell IPX uses 0x8137-8138 and 0xAAAA depending on the NetWare version.

NOTE   Cisco ASA only supports Ethernet II frames. The IEEE 802.3 frames do not contain an EtherType code field.

The security appliance does not restrict ARP packets to pass through it even if the ACL blocks ARP packets. On the other hand, the security appliance does not allow Cisco Discovery Protocol (CDP) packets to traverse through it, even if the ACL allows them. All other packets, such as DHCP, RIP, OSPF, BGP, BPDU, multicast, and MPLS packets, can be controlled by the ACL entries.

NOTE   Because the non-TCP and non-UDP packets do not create sessions, the security appliance must be configured for ACLs on both interfaces.

TIP	A list of commonly used EtherType codes is available on the following Cisco.com page: http://www.cisco.com/en/US/products/sw/iosswrel/ps1818/products_command_reference_chapter09186a00800803a6.html

Figure 10-5 shows an IPX packet captured using Ethereal, a sniffing tool. As you can see, the Ethernet type is 0x8137.

TIP	You can also use the **capture** command to sniff the IPX or non-IP packets traversing through the security appliance.

Figure 10-5 *Sniffer Trace Showing an IPX Packet*

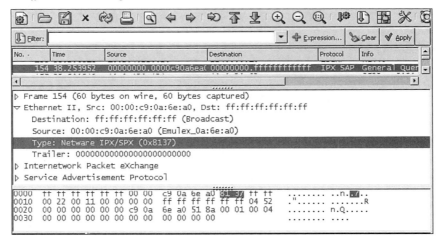

Example 10-6 shows how to restrict the LAN segment to allow IPX traffic to pass through, and how to block all other traffic.

Example 10-6 *Configuring an IPX-Based EtherType ACL*

```
Sydney(config)# access-list 100 ethertype permit ipx
Sydney(config)# access-list 100 ethertype deny any
```

NOTE	Cisco ASA does not forward bridge protocol data units (BPDUs) to prevent bridging loops. However, they can be allowed to pass through the security appliance if permitted in the ACL.

Step 5: Adding Static L2F Table Entries (Optional)

As mentioned earlier in this chapter, the L2F entries are learned dynamically when the IP packets traverse through the ASA. However, you can define a host-based static L2F entry to associate a host's MAC address to an interface. This disables the appliance to learn the MAC address and port binding dynamically for that particular host.

Example 10-7 shows how to add the static L2F entry for a router so that the ASA does not have to time out the entry and go through the learning process again.

Example 10-7 *Static L2F Entry*

```
Sydney(config)# mac-address-table static outside 00ff.fff0.003e
Added <00ff.fff0.003e> to the bridge table
```

TIP   If a static ARP entry is configured, the appliance also adds the corresponding static L2F table entry.

Step 6: Enabling ARP Inspection (Optional)

Cisco ASA, deployed in transparent mode, provides a way to prevent attacks related to ARP spoofing. This feature, called ARP inspection, is disabled by default. Once ARP inspection is enabled, the ASA examines all ARP packets (reply or gratuitous ARP) before forwarding them. ARP inspection can be configured to either flood the packet to other interfaces (by using the **flood** keyword) or drop the packet and generate a syslog (by using **no-flood**).

ARP inspection can be enabled per interface. When the Cisco ASA receives an ARP packet, it checks the static ARP table for a hit. Based on the hit or miss, it takes the following actions:

1 If there is a hit and it finds a matching entry, it forwards the packet to the correct interface.

2 If there is a hit but the entry does not match the interface, the appliance drops the packet and generates a syslog.

3 If there is a miss and the **flood** option is enabled, the ASA forwards the packet to all interfaces.

4 If there is a miss and **no-flood** is enabled, the appliance drops the packet and generates a syslog.

The command syntax to enable ARP inspection is

```
arp-inspection interface_name enable [flood | no-flood]
```

Example 10-8 illustrates how to turn on ARP inspection on the outside interface with **no-flood**. This will drop the packets if there is a miss on the static ARP table. With this option enabled, the security appliance needs to know the ARP entries of all the hosts that reside on that interface. This way, if an unknown host tries to connect through the security appliance, it will be denied access because there is no static ARP entry and the **no-flood** option is enabled.

Example 10-8 *Enabling ARP Inspection*

```
Sydney(config)# arp-inspection outside enable no-flood
```

NOTE   To set ARP inspection back to the default on all interfaces, use **clear configure arp-inspection**.

Step 7: Modifying L2F Table Parameters (Optional)

Cisco ASA is flexible in many ways to suit different security policies. For example, the default L2F table aging time can be changed from 5 minutes to a maximum of 12 hours. This way, dynamically learned entries for a specified host will not be aged out so frequently. Example 10-9 modifies the L2F aging time from 5 minutes to 60 minutes.

Example 10-9 *L2F Table Aging Time*

```
Sydney(config)# mac-address-table aging-time 60
```

If the security policy does not allow the ASA to learn the L2F table dynamically on an interface, the learning process can be disabled by using the **mac-learn disable** command. The complete command syntax is

```
mac-learn interface_name disable
```

Once you disable the learning process on an interface, you need to add static L2F entries for the hosts toward that interface. Example 10-10 shows how to turn off MAC address learning on the outside interface.

Example 10-10 *Disable L2F Learning on Outside Interface*

```
Sydney(config)# mac-learn outside disable
```

Deployment Scenarios

The robust transparent firewall solution can be deployed in different ways. This section covers two design scenarios for ease of understanding:

- SMTF deployment
- MMTF deployment using security contexts

NOTE   These design scenarios are discussed here to enforce learning and thus they should be used for reference only.

SMTF Deployment

SecureMe has a remote location in Brussels that uses IP as the Layer 3 protocol. SecureMe wants to deploy an ASA in transparent firewall mode so that it does not have to modify the existing network addresses. Figure 10-6 shows SecureMe's new topology in Brussels after setting up an ASA.

Figure 10-6 *SecureMe Brussels Network Topology*

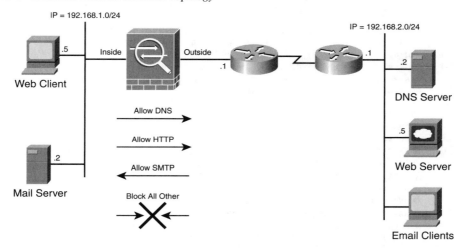

Additionally, SecureMe wants to achieve the following goals:

- Allow DNS traffic to query the DNS server
- Allow HTTP clients to talk to the remote web server
- Allow access to an email server for the remote client
- Protect the email server from TCP SYN attacks by setting the embryonic connections to 200 and maximum connections to 300
- Deny all other traffic

Example 10-11 shows the relevant configuration for the Cisco ASA in Brussels. SecureMe has set up an ACL that is applied to the inside interface to allow inbound DNS and HTTP traffic and filter out everything else. The security appliace is also configured with an ACL applied on the outside interface to allow SMTP traffic.

Example 10-11 *ASA Relevant Configuration to Allow IP Traffic*

```
Brussels# show running-config
! transparent firewall mode is enabled
firewall transparent
! outside interface
interface GigabitEthernet0/0
 nameif outside
 security-level 0
```

continues

Example 10-11 *ASA Relevant Configuration to Allow IP Traffic (Continued)*

```
! inside interface
interface GigabitEthernet0/1
 nameif inside
 security-level 100
!
hostname Brussels
! Access-list entry to allow DNS packets to pass through the ASA.
access-list inside_in extended permit udp 192.168.1.0 255.255.255.0 host 192.168.2.2
    eq 53
! Access-list entry to allow HTTP packets to pass through the ASA.
access-list inside_in extended permit tcp 192.168.1.0 255.255.255.0 host 192.168.2.5
    eq 80
! Access-list entry to deny and log all other packets.
access-list inside_in extended deny ip any any log
! Access-list entry to allow SMTP traffic.
access-list outside_in extended permit tcp 192.168.2.0 255.255.255.0 host
    192.168.1.2 eq 25
! Global IP address
ip address 192.168.1.10 255.255.255.0
! Static command is used to specify the maximum and embryonic connection limit
static (inside,outside) 192.168.1.2 192.168.1.2 netmask 255.255.255.255 tcp 300 200
! Access-list is applied to the inside interface of the ASA
access-group inside_in in interface inside
! Access-list is applied to the outside interface of the ASA
access-group outside_in in interface outside
! Default gateway. It is used by the ASA for the traffic originating from it
route outside 0.0.0.0 0.0.0.0 192.168.1.1 1
```

MMTF Deployment with Security Contexts

SecureMe plans to provide firewall services to two different organizations at its Brussels office. These organizations not only use different Layer 3 protocols but also have unique sets of requirements that SecureMe needs to account for. Figure 10-7 shows SecureMe's new topology in Brussels to provide these services.

Both customers—Cubs and Bears—have provided SecureMe with a list of requirements:

Cubs

- Allow all IPX traffic to pass
- Allow all BPDUs to pass
- Deny all other traffic
- Set L2F table timeout of 20 minutes

Figure 10-7 *SecureMe Brussels Multimode Topology*

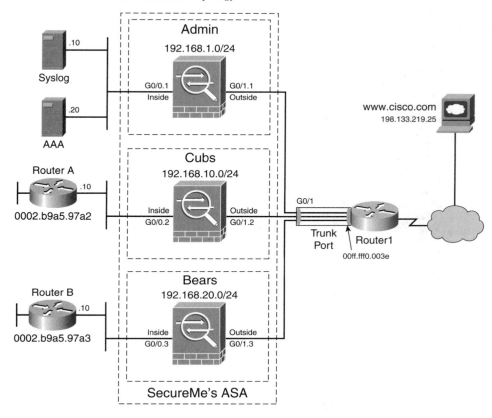

Bears

- Allow Enhanced Interior Gateway Routing Protocol (EIGRP) updates to pass
- Allow Virtual Router Redundancy Protocol (VRRP) updates to pass
- Deny and log all other inbound traffic on the outside interface
- Deny learning dynamic MAC address on the outside interface

Example 10-12 shows ASA's relevant configuration with three security contexts. The system execution space has been set up to allocate interfaces to customers' contexts. An admin context is configured to do the following:

- Use a AAA server for SSH and telnet user authentication
- Log all the system-generated messages to a syslog server

Additionally, there are two other contexts: Cubs and Bears. These security contexts are set up to meet the requirements of SecureMe's customers.

Example 10-12 *ASA's Relevant Configuration in Transparent Mode with Multiple Contexts*

```
                          System Execution Space
Brussels# show run
! transparent firewall mode is enabled in the system context
firewall transparent
! Main GigabitEthernet0/0 interface
interface GigabitEthernet0/0
! Sub-interface assigned to the admin context as the inside interface. A VLAN ID is
! assigned to the interface
interface GigabitEthernet0/0.1
 vlan 5
! Sub-interface assigned to the Cubs context as the inside interface. A VLAN ID is
! assigned to the interface
interface GigabitEthernet0/0.2
 vlan 10
! Sub-interface assigned to the Bears context as the inside interface. A VLAN ID is
! assigned to the interface
interface GigabitEthernet0/0.3
 vlan 20
! Main GigabitEthernet0/1 interface
interface GigabitEthernet0/1
! Sub-interface assigned to the admin context as the outside interface. A VLAN ID is
! assigned to the interface
interface GigabitEthernet0/1.1
 vlan 101
! Sub-interface assigned to the Cubs context as the outside interface. A VLAN ID is
! assigned to the interface
interface GigabitEthernet0/1.2
 vlan 110
! Sub-interface assigned to the Bears context as the outside interface. A VLAN ID is
! assigned to the interface
interface GigabitEthernet0/1.3
 vlan 120
hostname Brussels
! context named "admin" is the designated Admin context
admin-context admin
! "admin" context definition along with the allocated interfaces.
context admin
  description admin Context for admin purposes
  allocate-interface GigabitEthernet0/0.1
  allocate-interface GigabitEthernet0/1.1
  config-url disk0:/admin.cfg
! "Cubs" context definition along with the allocated interfaces.
context Cubs
  description Cubs Customer Context
  allocate-interface GigabitEthernet0/0.2
  allocate-interface GigabitEthernet0/1.2
  config-url disk0:/Cubs.cfg
```

Example 10-12 *ASA's Relevant Configuration in Transparent Mode with Multiple Contexts (Continued)*

```
! "Bears" context definition along with the allocated interfaces.
context Bears
  description Bears Customer Context
  allocate-interface GigabitEthernet0/0.3
  allocate-interface GigabitEthernet0/1.3
  config-url disk0:/Bears.cfg
```

Admin Context

```
Brussels/admin# show running
! transparent firewall mode is enabled in all contexts
firewall transparent
ASA Version 7.0(1) <context>
! inside interface of the admin context with security level set to 100
interface GigabitEthernet0/0.1
 nameif inside
 security-level 100
! outside interface of the admin context with security level set to 0
interface GigabitEthernet0/1.1
 nameif outside
 security-level 0
!
hostname admin
! Global IP address
ip address 192.168.1.10 255.255.255.0
! configuration of a syslog server with logging level set to emergencies with
timestamp
logging enable
logging timestamp
logging trap emergencies
logging host inside 192.168.1.100
!
route outside 0.0.0.0 0.0.0.0 192.168.1.1
! configuration of a AAA server using RADIUS for authentication
aaa-server uauth protocol radius
aaa-server uauth host 192.168.1.20
 key cisco123
!Telnet and SSH using RADIUS for authentication
aaa authentication telnet console uauth
aaa authentication ssh console uauth
! Telnet to the admin context is allowed from the inside interface
telnet 192.168.1.0 255.255.255.0 inside
telnet timeout 5
! SSH to the admin context is allowed from the outside interface
ssh 0.0.0.0 0.0.0.0 outside
ssh timeout 5
```

Security Context for Cubs

```
Brussels/Cubs# show running
! transparent firewall mode is enabled in all contexts
firewall transparent
ASA Version 7.0(1) <context>
```

continues

Example 10-12 *ASA's Relevant Configuration in Transparent Mode with Multiple Contexts (Continued)*

```
!inside interface of the Cubs context with security level set to 100
interface GigabitEthernet0/0.2
 nameif inside
 security-level 100
!outside interface of the Cubs context with security level set to 0
interface GigabitEthernet0/1.2
 nameif outside
 security-level 0
!
hostname Cubs
! Access-list entry to allow IPX and BPDU traffic
access-list layer2_acl ethertype permit ipx
access-list layer2_acl ethertype permit bpdu
access-list layer2_acl ethertype deny any
! Access-list is applied to the inside interface
access-group layer2_acl in interface inside
! Access-list is also applied to the outside interface
access-group layer2_acl in interface outside
! Management IP address
ip address 192.168.10.10 255.255.255.0
! Default route for management traffic
route outside 0.0.0.0 0.0.0.0 192.168.10.1 1
! L2F timeout is set to 20 minutes
mac-address-table aging-time 20
```

Security Context for Bears

```
Brussels/Bears# show running
! transparent firewall mode is enabled in all contexts
firewall transparent
ASA Version 7.0(1) <context>
!inside interface of the Bears context with security level set to 100
interface GigabitEthernet0/0.3
 nameif inside
 security-level 100
!outside interface of the Bears context with security level set to 0
interface GigabitEthernet0/1.3
 nameif outside
 security-level 0
!
enable password 8Ry2YjIyt7RRXU24 encrypted
passwd 2KFQnbNIdI.2KYOU encrypted
hostname Bears
! Access-list entry to allow all IP traffic on the inside interface
access-list inside_in extended permit ip any any
! Access-list entry to only allow EIGRP and VRRP traffic on the outside interface
access-list outside_in extended permit eigrp any any
access-list outside_in extended permit 112 any any
access-list outside_in extended deny ip any any log
!
! Global IP address
ip address 192.168.20.10 255.255.255.0
! Access-list is applied to the inside interface
```

Example 10-12 *ASA's Relevant Configuration in Transparent Mode with Multiple Contexts (Continued)*

```
access-group inside_in in interface inside
! Access-list is applied to the outside interface
access-group outside_in in interface outside
route outside 0.0.0.0 0.0.0.0 192.168.20.1 1
! learning MAC address on the outside interface is not allowed
mac-learn outside disable
! Static L2F entry of outside router as dynamic learning is not allowed
mac-address-table static outside 00ff.fff0.003e
```

Monitoring and Troubleshooting the Transparent Firewall

Cisco ASA provides **show** commands to ensure that the transparent firewall is working as expected. In the event of a problem, you can enable relevant debugs (which are discussed later in this section).

Monitoring

If transparent firewall mode is configured, first verify that the system is recognizing this mode. You achieve this by using the **show firewall** command, as shown in Example 10-13.

Example 10-13 *Output of* **show firewall**

```
Brussels# show firewall
Firewall mode: Transparent
```

Second, confirm that the system is running in the configured single or multiple mode, as shown in Example 10-14.

Example 10-14 *Output of* **show mode**

```
Brussels# show mode
Security context mode: multiple
```

Once you have verified that the system is switching packets in the correct mode, monitor the status of the L2F table, as demonstrated in Example 10-15. By using **show mac-address-table**, verify the entries in the bridge table if they look accurate, including static and dynamic entries. There are four dynamic L2F entries learned on the outside interface. There is also a static L2F entry pointing to the outside interface with no aging time.

Example 10-15 *Checking the L2F Table*

```
Brussels# show mac-address-table
interface          mac address     type    Age(min)
-----------------------------------------------------------------
outside            00d0.c0d2.8030  dynamic 1
outside            0040.8c5c.0e92  dynamic 4
outside            000b.cdf0.8e39  dynamic 4
outside            000e.8315.0bff  dynamic 2
outside            00ff.fff0.003e  static
```

show arp-inspection displays whether ARP inspection is enabled or disabled on all interfaces. Example 10-16 shows that ARP inspection is enabled on the outside interface with the no_flood option if a miss occurs on the static ARP table. ARP inspection is disabled on the inside interface.

Example 10-16 *Checking the Interfaces for ARP Inspection*

```
Brussels # show arp-inspection
interface          arp-inspection          miss
----------------------------------------------------------------
inside             disable                 -
outside            enable                  no_flood
```

If everything looks good yet traffic is still not flowing, verify the hit counts on the configured interface ACL. Example 10-17 shows 10 hit counts for IPX traffic.

Example 10-17 *Monitoring ACLs*

```
Brussels# show access-list
access-list inside ethertype permit ipx (hitcount=10)
access-list inside ethertype permit bpdu (hitcount=0)
access-list inside ethertype deny any (hitcount=0)
```

For TCP-, UDP-, and, optionally, ICMP-based traffic passing through the security appliance, you can use the **show conn** command and verify the connection status. As shown in Example 10-18, a connection is established from 192.168.1.10 to a Telnet server located at 192.168.1.1.

Example 10-18 *Output of* **show conn**

```
Brussels/admin# show conn
1 in use, 1 most used
TCP out 192.168.1.1:23 in 192.168.1.10:11018 idle 0:00:02 bytes 90 flags UIO
```

Troubleshooting

For troubleshooting purposes, Cisco ASA includes a number of important debug and syslog messages to help isolate the issue. This section discusses three troubleshooting scenarios related to the transparent firewalls:

- **Hosts are not able to communicate**—As shown in Figure 10-6, when the web client is not able to communicate with the web server located at 192.168.2.5, the administrator can take the following steps to isolate the issue:

Step 1   Ping the global IP address of the transparent firewall to ensure that the connectivity exists between the web client and the transparent firewall. If successful, move to Step 2; otherwise, check the cable and VLAN assignments if a switch is placed between the host and the transparent firewall. Additionally, check the L2F table on the appliance by using the **show mac-address-table** command to ensure that the host is being learned on the correct interface. If the MAC address is not learned, you can enable **debug mac-address-table**, which is used to view L2F table updates. The appliance uses this table to forward a packet out to an interface. This is shown in Example 10-19, where the security appliance adds a MAC address of 0003.a088.da86 in the table on the inside interface.

Example 10-19 *Debugging the L2F Table Entries*

```
Brussels# debug mac-address-table
add_l2fwd_entry: Going to add MAC 0003.a088.da86.
add_l2fwd_entry: Added MAC 0003.a088.da86 into bridge table thru inside.
add_l2fwd_entry: Sending LU to add MAC 0003.a088.da86.
set_l2: Found MAC entry 0003.a088.da86 on inside.
```

Step 2   Ping the IP address of the gateway router (192.168.1.1) from the web client. If successful, move to Step 3. If unsuccessful, check the inbound ACL and outbound ACL on the security appliance. If the ACLs look properly configured, enable **debug arp-inspection** to determine if the ARP requests are being forwarded and inspected through the transparent firewall. Example 10-20 shows the output of **debug arp-inspection**, where the appliance is forwarding the ARP requests from 192.168.1.5 destined to 192.168.1.1 located on the outside interface.

Example 10-20 *Output of* **debug arp-inspection**

```
Brussels# debug arp-inspection
arp_in_forward: Forwarding arp request from 192.168.1.5
to 192.168.1.1 smac 0003.a088.da86
learn_and_forward_arp_request: Forwarding arp request to outside
```

Step 3   Ping the remote gateway (192.168.2.1) from the web client. If it fails, check the inbound ACL and outbound ACL on the router for the ICMP traffic. If it works, make sure that the ACLs allow TCP and UDP connections necessary for browsing the website. Ports such as UDP 53 for DNS resolution and TCP 80 for web browsing should be opened.

● **Moved host is not able to communicate**—If a host is moved from an outside interface to the inside interface, or vice versa, and is not able to communicate after the move, check to ensure that a static L2F entry does not point to the old interface.

Additionally, **debug l2-indication** can be enabled to verify the processing of Layer 2 indications such as miss, learn, host move, and refresh of IP packets. Example 10-21 shows the output of **debug l2-indication** when a static entry is defined for a MAC address 00e0.b06a.412c toward the outside interface and the host is moved toward the inside interface. The Cisco ASA indicates a host move to the inside interface from the outside interface.

Example 10-21 *Output of* **debug l2-indication**

```
Brussels# debug l2-indication
debug l2-indication enabled at level 1
f1_tf_process_l2_hostmove:HOST MOVE: Host move indication cur_ifc outside, new_ifc
inside mac address: 00e0.b06a.412c
HOST MOVE: cur_vStackNum 0, new_vStackNum 1
HOST MOVE: Host move indication for static entry 00e0.b06a.412c
f1_tf_process_l2_hostmove:HOST MOVE: Host move indication cur_ifc outside, new_ifc
inside mac address: 00e0.b06a.412c
f1_tf_process_l2_hostmove:HOST MOVE: cur_vStackNum 0, new_vStackNum 1
f1_tf_process_l2_hostmove:HOST MOVE: Host move indication for static entry
00e0.b06a.412c
```

If the security appliance dynamically learns the MAC address of a host on a particular interface and the host is moved to another interface, the dynamic entries associated with an interface can be removed by using **clear mac-address-table** followed by the name of the interface. As shown in Example 10-22, the administrator wants to clear the L2F entries associated with the outside interface.

Example 10-22 *Clearing the L2F Table Associated with the Outside Interface*

```
Brussels# clear mac-address-table outside
```

Additionally, all dynamic entries in the entire table can be removed by issuing the **clear mac-address-table** command.

- **General syslogging**—The ASA includes four syslog messages to assist in preventing either MAC spoofing or ARP inspection issues. The ASA logs an L2F message when

  — A host is moved from one interface to another. This is known as host move.

  — The ASA detects MAC spoofing in the L2F table. MAC spoofing is similar to host move but the original MAC address was statically mapped to an interface.

  — The L2F table gets completely full.

  — The ARP packets are dropped because they fail the ARP inspection check.

Summary

The transparent firewall feature is designed for security professionals who do not want to change existing address schemes, but still require a firewall to inspect all packets leaving a subnet. Cisco ASA integrates features like security contexts with the transparent firewall and, therefore, presents a complete solution to fit any design scenario. This chapter covered the architectural overview of the transparent firewall and provided detailed configuration guides to suit any network deployments. This chapter also provided two deployment scenarios to enforce learning and to show the robustness of this feature. Extensive **show** and **debug** commands were discussed to assist a network administrator in troubleshooting complicated transparent firewall deployments.

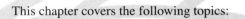

This chapter covers the following topics:

- Architectural overview
- Failover configuration
- Deployment scenarios
- Monitoring and troubleshooting

CHAPTER 11

Failover and Redundancy

With more organizations moving toward e-commerce, their dependence on both LANs and WANs have increased drastically. They cannot afford to lose connectivity with their core servers in the network infrastructure. This connectivity loss could cause multimillion-dollar revenue losses per minute. Consequently, organizations want to deploy and maintain reliable network devices to ensure nonstop availability and nearly 100 percent uptime. This is accomplished by implementing layers of redundant devices to prevent interruption should any network component fail.

Because Cisco Systems is fully committed to its customer base, it provides a resilient infrastructure. This is the reason why Cisco ASA provides many valuable failover features to suit your environment. In order for failover to work, you must have two Cisco ASA devices connected to each other using a network cable. Cisco ASA has to be identical in terms of hardware, software, and the software license. Thus, if one of Cisco ASA fails to perform its duties, the other Cisco ASA takes over and seamlessly starts passing traffic.

Architectural Overview

When two identical Cisco ASA are set up in failover, one of Cisco ASA (known as the *active Cisco ASA*) is responsible for creating the state and translation tables, transferring the data packets, and monitoring the other unit. The other security Cisco ASA (referred as the *standby Cisco ASA*) is responsible for monitoring the status of the active unit. The active and standby Cisco ASA are connected through a dedicated network link to send failover related messages to each other. This connection, known as a failover control link, is established over a dedicated failover LAN interface. When a failure occurs on the active Cisco ASA, the standby takes over the role and starts forwarding traffic. The standby Cisco ASA (now the active unit) also takes over the IP and MAC addresses that were used by the original active Cisco ASA. After the original active unit recovers from a failure, it can either assume the standby role or become the active Cisco ASA depending on its configuration.

The failover control link provides a medium over which the two security Cisco ASA can communicate with each other. Using this link, the Cisco ASA update one another about:

- The unit state (active or standby)
- Network link status

- Hello messages (which are sent on all interfaces)
- MAC address exchange
- Configuration synchronization

Figure 11-1 shows two Cisco ASA 5540 devices connected to each other through the Gigabit Ethernet interfaces to send the failover hello messages. For the failover link, they are using the GigabitEthernet0/2 interface, shown as the dashed line.

Figure 11-1 *Failover Connection Between Two ASAs*

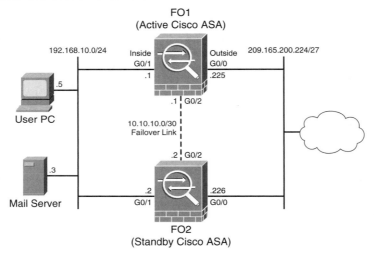

Conditions that Trigger Failover

For a failover to occur, any one of the following conditions has to be met:

- When an administrator manual switches over from active to standby. This happens when either **no failover active** is issued on the active unit or **failover active** is issued on the standby unit.

- When a standby Cisco ASA stops receiving keepalive packets on the failover command interface. In this condition, the standby unit waits for two consecutive polling periods before sending additional testing packets to the remaining interfaces. If it still does not receive a response from the active unit, it assumes that a failure has occurred and takes over the role as the active Cisco ASA.

- When the command interface link goes down. In this scenario, the security Cisco ASA sends additional testing packets to the remaining interfaces to determine if the peer's command interface is also down. If the command interface of the peer is not down and this unit is an active Cisco ASA, then it notifies the standby unit to become active using the other interfaces. If the peer's interface is also down, then the active Cisco ASA remains in the active state.

- When the link state of an interface goes down. In this condition, the Cisco ASA marks the interface as failed and initiates the failover process. Additionally, if the standby Cisco ASA does not receive keepalive packets for two consecutive polling periods on an interface, the Cisco ASA uses additional tests on the interface to determine the root cause of the problem. These tests are discussed in detail in the following section.

Failover Interface Tests

To ensure that an interface failure is properly detected before initiating a failover, the security Cisco ASA goes through four different interface tests. These tests are discussed in the order they are checked:

- **Link up/down test** — The security Cisco ASA determines the status of its network interface card (NIC) by doing the link up/down test, to determine if one of the ports on the security Cisco ASA is not plugged into an operational network. In this case, the security Cisco ASA marks the interface as failed, and initiates the failover process. Some examples of this failover include hardware port failure, unplugged cable of an interface, and a failure on the hub or switch that the interfaces are connected to. If the interface passes the link up/down test, the security Cisco ASA moves to the network activity test.

- **Network activity test** — In this test, the security Cisco ASA counts all received packets for up to 5 seconds. If the security Cisco ASA receives any packet during this time interval, it stops this test and marks the interface operational. If no traffic is received, the test is inconclusive regarding whether or not the interface is faulty, so the security Cisco ASA proceeds to the next test.

- **ARP test** — In the ARP test, the security Cisco ASA reads its ARP table for the last ten acquired entries. It sends an ARP request to those machines one at a time, and then counts packets for up to 5 seconds. If it receives traffic during this time window, it marks the interface as operational. If it does not receive a response from the host, it moves to the next host and sends an ARP request, and so on. At the end of the list, if the security Cisco ASA does not receive any traffic, it moves on to the ping test.

- **Broadcast ping test** — In this test, the security Cisco ASA sends out a broadcast ping request and then counts all received packets for up to 5 seconds. If it receives any packets during this time window, the security Cisco ASA declares this interface operational and stops the test. If the Cisco ASA does not receive any traffic, it marks the interface as failed and initiates failover.

NOTE   Although the network activity, ARP, and broadcast ping tests are time consuming, they do help avoid false failover on the security Cisco ASA. Even when the interface is going through these tests, the security Cisco ASA forwards traffic on the interfaces.

Stateful Failover

When a connection is established through the active Cisco ASA, the Cisco ASA updates its connection table. A connection entry includes the source and destination IP addresses, protocol used, current state of the connection, the interface it is tied to, and the number of bytes transferred. Depending on the failover configuration, the security Cisco ASA takes one of the following actions:

- **Stateless failover**—The security Cisco ASA maintains the connection table but does not replicate entries to the standby Cisco ASA.

- **Stateful failover**—The security Cisco ASA maintains the connection table and replicates it to the standby Cisco ASA.

In a stateless failover, the active Cisco ASA is not responsible for sending the state table updates to the standby Cisco ASA. When the standby unit becomes active (whether by detecting a failure or by manually switching over), it has to build all the connection entries from scratch. This causes all the stateful traffic, such as TCP-based connections, to get disrupted.

In a stateful failover, the active Cisco ASA sends an update to the standby unit whenever there is a change in the state table. In this mode, the active Cisco ASA sends stateful updates over a dedicated link to the standby unit. When the standby unit becomes active, it does not need to build any connection entries because all the entries already exist in its database.

NOTE   You can use the same physical interface for both failover control and stateful link updates.

Table 11-1 lists the entries and the types of traffic that are replicated to the standby Cisco ASA in the stateful failover.

Table 11-1   *Types of Traffic and Stateful Replication*

Type of Traffic	Stateful Replication
HTTP connection	Yes, if enabled
TCP connection	Yes
UDP connection	Yes
Xlate	Yes
Uauth cache	No
URL filtering cache	No
TCP intercept	No
SNMP firewall MIB	No
Routing table	No
IKE/IPSec SA	Yes

NOTE   The security Cisco ASA replicate IPSec states only if stateful failover is used in Active/Standby. IPSec VPN is not supported in multimode firewall, and Active/Active failover only works in multimode.

Hardware and Software Requirements

For failover to properly work, the following specifications must be identical:

- **Product or model number of the Cisco ASA**—For example, both Cisco ASA should be Cisco ASA 5520. You cannot use an ASA 5520 and an ASA 5540 in failover.

- **Amount of RAM**—You cannot use 512 MB of RAM in one Cisco ASA and 1024 MB in the other one.

- **Amount of Flash memory**—You cannot use 64 MB of Flash memory in one security Cisco ASA and 128MB of Flash memory in the other security Cisco ASA.

- **Number of interfaces**—The current hardware does not allow adding additional physical interfaces. If the number of interfaces on an Cisco ASA changes in the future, you cannot have mismatched interfaces on the two security Cisco ASA.

- **Activation key with the same features**—The activation key should have the same features, such as the failover mode, encryption level, and number of VPN peers.

NOTE   In the Cisco ASA, the software version does not have to be the same when running it in failover. This is called zero-downtime software upgrade, which is covered later in this chapter.

Before setting up security Cisco ASA for failover, verify that they have a valid activation key to run failover. After you verify the activation key, you can proceed with failover configuration.

Types of Failover

Cisco ASA supports two different types of failover:

- Active/Standby failover
- Active/Active failover

Active/Standby Failover

Active/Standby failover is identical to the failover scenario described in the previous section. In this failover type, when two security Cisco ASA are in failover, the active unit is responsible for passing the traffic. The standby's role is to monitor the status of the active Cisco ASA by sending periodic keepalive messages. The active Cisco ASA also sends keepalive messages to monitor the status of the standby Cisco ASA.

NOTE   You can have only two Cisco ASA set up in failover.

In Active/Standby failover, the Cisco ASA go through the following election process. They assume roles based on their designated status, whether primary or secondary.

1 When both Cisco ASA are up and running, one of them is designated as the active unit, while the other Cisco ASA assumes the standby role.

2 If both devices boot up simultaneously, the primary Cisco ASA takes over the active Cisco ASA role, and the secondary Cisco ASA goes into the standby state.

3 If one of the security Cisco ASA boots up and detects an active failover unit, it goes into the standby state regardless of its primary or secondary designation.

4 If one of the security Cisco ASA boots up and does not detect an active failover unit, it goes in the active state regardless of its primary or secondary designation.

5 If both Cisco ASA become active, the secondary changes its state to standby, while the primary remains active.

6 If both Cisco ASA become standby, the primary changes its state to active, while the secondary remains standby after they detect each other's state.

Active/Active Failover

Active/Active failover is a methodology in which both Cisco ASA, while monitoring the status of their peers, actively pass traffic. Cisco ASA in Active/Active failover mode can only be deployed in multimode. Figure 11-2 shows a network topology where two Cisco ASA are set up in stateful multimode Active/Active failover. They are set up for two customer contexts: Cubs and Bears. In this deployment, the Cubs security context is active on FO1 and standby on FO2. However, the Bears security context is active on FO2 and standby on FO1. If FO1 fails, the standby security context on FO2 for Cubs will become active and take over the IP and MAC addresses of FO1. As a result, both security contexts will be active on FO2.

The failover will be completely transparent to the end hosts because of the replication of state and connection tables. When the security Cisco ASA are deployed in this mode, the total throughput is doubled, because each Cisco ASA can allocate 100 percent of its system resources to inspect and route packets. However, if one of Cisco ASA fails, the total throughput is reduced by half, up to the capacity of one Cisco ASA. It is therefore recommended that you do not oversubscribe the failover pair.

A key point to remember is that the failover in the Cisco ASA is per failover redundancy group (discussed in the section, "Failover Configuration") as opposed to per-context failover. The Cisco ASA's failover is currently limited to only two failover groups.

Figure 11-2 *Cisco ASA in Active/Active Multiple Mode*

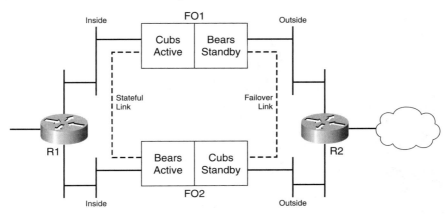

The biggest challenge in running Active/Active failover is that packets can leave from one active unit and can come back to the other active unit. Cisco ASA implements a feature known as asymmetric routing to work around this problem. This feature is discussed in the following section.

Asymmetric Routing

In their enterprise, many customers use multiple ISPs to get connectivity to the Internet or to the remote locations. Depending on their implementation, these enterprises can use these ISP to either load-balance the traffic or back each other up in the event of a failure.

Figure 11-3 depicts two Cisco ASA connected to two different ISPs and running in Active/Active failover with multiple contexts. Context Cubs is active on FO1 while context Bears is active on FO2. The problem arises when both ISPs are load-balancing the traffic out to the cloud and the security Cisco ASA are setup in Active/Active mode. If Host A, sitting behind context Cubs, sends out a TCP SYN packet to Host B, the packet can leave the active Cisco ASA (FO1). However, there is no guarantee that SYN-ACK, the reply from the server, will be routed back through the same unit. If the SYN-ACK packet lands on the other active Cisco ASA (FO2), FO2 will drop the packet because it is not active for the security context Cubs.

NOTE   The asymmetric routing feature is only supported in multimode. Asymmetric routing is not supported if Cisco ASA are using shared interfaces.

Figure 11-3 *Asymmetric Routing*

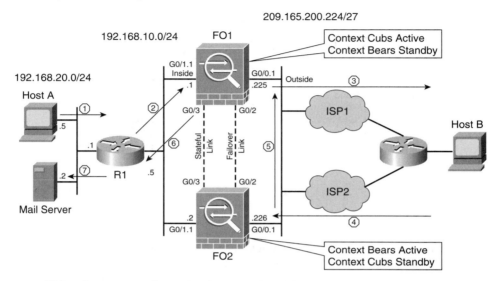

Using the asymmetric routing feature, FO1 will replicate the connection table entry for the SYN packet to FO2 over the stateful failover link. Thus, when the active context on FO2 (Bears) receives the SYN-ACK packet, it will forward the packet to FO1 because it belongs to context Cubs, which is active on FO1. Figure 11-3 depicts all the steps when Host A communicates with Host B.

1 Host A sends the SYN packet to its gateway router.

2 The gateway router consults its routing table and forwards the SYN packet to FO1, because it belongs to context Cubs.

3 FO1 looks at the routing table and forwards the SYN packet out to the Internet through ISP1.

4 Host B sends SYN-ACK, which gets routed to FO2 through ISP2.

5 When FO2 receives the packet on context Bears (as it is active) but it does not have an active connection. It checks the other interfaces that are in the same asymmetric routing group for the corresponding connection. In this case, it detects an active connection from FO1 for context Cubs. Therefore, it forwards the packet to FO1. It will continue to forward packets until the connection is terminated on FO1.

6 FO1 forwards the packet to its next-hop router (R1).

7 R1 forwards the packet to Host A, after checking the routing table.

NOTE   As a race condition, if the SYN-ACK packet arrives at FO2 before FO2 has the chance to process the state update message from FO1, then FO2 will drop the SYN-ACK packet. This problem can be remedied by using a high-bandwidth link as the stateful failover interface.

Failover Configuration

As mentioned in the previous section, the Cisco ASA supports two types of failover: Active/Standby and Active/Active. This section discusses how these failover types can be configured on the Cisco ASA.

Active/Standby Failover Configuration

The configuration of the Active/Standby failover feature in the Cisco ASA is broken down into seven steps:

Step 1   Select the failover link.

Step 2   Assign failover IP addresses.

Step 3   Set failover key (optional).

Step 4   Designate the primary Cisco ASA.

Step 5   Enable stateful failover (optional).

Step 6   Enable failover globally.

Step 7   Configure failover on the secondary Cisco ASA.

Figure 11-1 is used throughout this section to demonstrate how to configure failover functionality on the Cisco ASA.

NOTE   Before configuring the failover, verify that the secondary Cisco ASA is turned off. Also verify that the activation key on the security Cisco ASA supports failover and both Cisco ASA are using the same mode (single or multiple).

Step 1: Select the Failover Link

The first step is to decide which interface will be used to send failover control messages. The failover control link interface is defined by using the **failover lan interface** command followed by the interface name. Example 11-1 shows that Cisco ASA are using **GigabitEthernet0/2** as the failover control interface. In this example, the LAN interface is given a name of **FOCtrlIntf**. However, you can specify any name for this interface.

Example 11-1 *Assigning an Interface for LAN-based Failover*

```
Chicago(config)# failover lan interface FOCtrlIntf GigabitEthernet0/2
```

NOTE   If an interface already has the **nameif** statement configured, the security Cisco ASA displays an error stating that the interface is already in use. For example:

```
Chicago(config)# failover lan interface FOCtrlIntf GigabitEthernet0/2
Interface already in use
```

To fix this issue, issue the no nameif command under that interface.

After the **failover lan interface** command is configured, the Cisco ASA adds a description under the failover interface configuration. It also clears any configuration parameters on that interface, as shown in Example 11-2.

Example 11-2 *Description Under the Failover Interface Configuration*

```
Chicago# show running | begin interface GigabitEthernet0/2
interface GigabitEthernet0/2
 description LAN Failover Interface
```

Step 2: Assign Failover IP Addresses

After selecting what failover control interface the Cisco ASA is going to use, the next step is to configure the physical interfaces for the system and the standby IP addresses. The active Cisco ASA uses the system IP addresses, while the standby Cisco ASA uses the standby IP addresses. Example 11-3 shows that the Chicago Cisco ASA is using 209.165.200.225 and 192.168.10.1 as the system IP addresses and 209.165.200.226 and 192.168.10.2 as the failover IP addresses on the outside and inside interfaces, respectively.

Example 11-3 *Configuring Interface and Failover IP Addresses*

```
Chicago(config)# interface GigabitEthernet0/0
Chicago(config-if)# nameif outside
Chicago(config-if)# security-level 0
Chicago(config-if)# ip address 209.165.200.225 255.255.255.224 standby
  209.165.200.226
Chicago(config-if)# exit
Chicago(config)# interface GigabitEthernet0/1
Chicago(config-if)# nameif inside
Chicago(config-if)# security-level 100
Chicago(config-if)# ip address 192.168.10.1 255.255.255.0 standby 192.168.10.2
```

For two security Cisco ASA to communicate, the designated failover control interface should be configured with an IP address as well. Here is the complete command syntax to configure an IP address on the failover control interface:

```
failover interface ip interface_name ip_address mask standby ip_address
```

interface_name is the designated interface used for failover. The first IP address is the interface IP address used by the active Cisco ASA, and the second IP address is the IP address used by the standby Cisco ASA. The active unit uses its address to synchronize the running configuration with the standby. In Example 11-4, the active Cisco ASA is assigned a 10.10.10.1 IP address along with a standby IP address of 10.10.10.2.

Example 11-4 *Configuring LAN Interface for Failover IP Addresses*

```
Chicago# configure terminal
Chicago(config)# failover interface ip FOCtrlIntf 10.10.10.1 255.255.255.252
   standby 10.10.10.2
```

Step 3: Set Failover Key (Optional)

To secure the failover control messages sent between the Cisco ASA Cisco ASA, an administrator can optionally specify a shared secret key. The shared secret key encrypts and authenticates the failover messages if they are susceptible to unauthorized users. Example 11-5 illustrates how to configure a failover shared secret key of **cisco123**.

Example 11-5 *Configuring Shared Secret Key*

```
Chicago# configure terminal
Chicago(config)# failover key cisco123
```

The failover key uses DES or AES, depending on the installed license. It also uses MD5 as the hash to authenticate the message. Therefore, it is important that both Cisco ASA use the same cipher license key.

NOTE   If a failover key is not used, the active Cisco ASA sends all information in clear text, including the UDP/TCP states, the user credentials, and the VPN-related information.

Step 4: Designating the Primary Cisco ASA

The two security Cisco ASA send failover control messages through a network cable that has identical ends. Unlike a Cisco PIX firewall, in which the failover cable decides which firewall becomes primary, it is impossible to designate a Cisco ASA as primary based on the cable. To resolve the problem of which device should act as primary or secondary, you must designate the primary and secondary status through software configuration by using the **failover lan unit** command. In Example 11-6, FO1 is designated as the primary failover Cisco ASA.

Example 11-6 *Designating a Primary Cisco ASA*

```
Chicago# configure terminal
Chicago(config)# failover lan unit primary
```

Step 5: Enable Stateful Failover (Optional)

As discussed earlier, the stateful failover feature in the Cisco Cisco ASA replicates the state and translation tables from the active unit to the standby unit. In the event of a failure, the standby unit takes over the connections, and data flows do not get disrupted. The stateful failover requires a network interface to replicate the states. Cisco ASA can use either a dedicated or the failover control interface to replicate the updates. A stateful link interface is defined by using the **failover link** command followed by the name of the interface. In Example 11-7, the primary Cisco ASA is using **GigabitEthernet0/3** as the stateful interface. The interface IP address is **10.10.10.5** and the standby IP address is **10.10.10.6**. The administrator uses **statefullink** as the interface name.

Example 11-7 *Configuring Stateful Failover*

```
Chicago(config)# failover link statefullink GigabitEthernet0/3
Chicago(config)# failover interface ip statefullink 10.10.10.5 255.255.255.252
  standby 10.10.10.6
```

NOTE   Like the **failover lan interface** command, the Cisco ASA adds a description under the stateful link interface and clears any configuration on that interface.

For stateful failover, you can use the failover LAN interface if the stateful updates do not oversubscribe the interface bandwidth. Set up a different interface for stateful failover if you are concerned about possibly oversubscribing the failover control interface. If the security Cisco ASA uses the same interface for both control and stateful messages, you have to connect the security Cisco ASA through a switch. Crossover cable is not supported.

The stateful failover does not replicate HTTP-based connections. HTTP connections usually have a short lifetime and therefore are not replicated by default. Additionally, they add considerable load on the security Cisco ASA if the amount of HTTP traffic is large in comparison to other traffic.

If the HTTP connections need to be replicated to the standby Cisco ASA, use the **failover replication http** command, as illustrated in Example 11-8.

Example 11-8 *Configuring HTTP Replication*

```
Chicago(config)# failover replication http
```

Step 6: Enable Failover Globally

The last step in configuring failover on the primary Cisco ASA is to enable failover globally. Example 11-9 shows how to enable failover in the Chicago FO1 Cisco ASA.

Example 11-9 *Enabling Failover Globally*

```
Chicago(config)#failover
```

Step 7: Configure Failover on the Secondary Cisco ASA

In the Cisco failover feature, there is no need to manually configure the secondary Cisco ASA. Instead, you just need to configure some basic information about failover. After that, the primary/active Cisco ASA starts synchronizing its configuration. The bootstrap configuration includes the following five configuration parameters:

- Failover designation
- Failover link interface
- Failover interface IP address
- Failover shared key
- Failover enable

Example 11-10 shows the bootstrap configuration of the secondary Cisco ASA needed in LAN-based failover.

Example 11-10 *Bootstrap Configuration of the Secondary Cisco ASA*

```
failover lan unit secondary
failover lan interface FOCtrlIntf GigabitEthernet0/2
failover key cisco123
failover interface ip FOCtrlIntf 10.10.10.1 255.255.255.252 standby 10.10.10.2
failover
```

NOTE   Once failover is enabled on both Cisco ASA, their running configuration is identical except for the **failover lan unit** command.

Active/Active Failover Configuration

The configuration of the Active/Active failover feature in the Cisco ASA is broken down into 11 steps:

Step 1   Select the failover link.

Step 2   Assign failover interface IP addresses.

Step 3   Set failover key (optional).

Step 4   Designate the primary Cisco ASA.

Step 5   Enable stateful failover (optional).

Step 6   Set up failover groups.

Step 7   Assign failover-group membership.

Step 8   Assign interface IP addresses.

Step 9 Set up asymmetric routing (optional).

Step 10 Enable failover globally.

Step 11 Configure failover on the secondary Cisco ASA.

Figure 11-3 will be used throughout this section to demonstrate how to configure Active/ Active failover functionality on the Cisco ASA.

Step 1: Select the Failover Link

The first step is to configure a dedicated Ethernet interface to send the failover control messages. Example 11-11 illustrates how to configure **GigabitEthernet0/2** as the LAN failover interface in the Cisco ASA. In this example, the LAN interface is given a name of **FOCtrlIntf**.

Example 11-11 *Assigning an Interface for LAN-based Failover*

```
Chicago(config)# failover lan interface FOCtrlIntf GigabitEthernet0/2
```

Step 2: Assign Failover Interface IP Addresses

After selecting the failover control interface, the next step is to configure this interface with an IP address. In Example 11-12, the Chicago active Cisco ASA is assigned a 10.10.10.1 IP address along with a standby IP address of 10.10.10.2.

Example 11-12 *Configuring LAN Interface for Failover IP Addresses*

```
Chicago# configure terminal
Chicago(config)# failover interface ip FOCtrlIntf 10.10.10.1 255.255.255.252
    standby 10.10.10.2
```

Step 3: Set Failover Key

To protect the failover control messages sent between the Cisco ASA, you can optionally specify a shared secret key. Example 11-13 illustrates how to configure a failover shared secret key of cisco123.

Example 11-13 *Configuring Shared Secret Key*

```
Chicago# configure terminal
Chicago(config)# failover key cisco123
```

Step 4: Designate the Primary Cisco ASA

Because both ends of the network cables are identical, you can designate one Cisco ASA as primary and the other as secondary by using the **failover lan unit** command. In Example 11-14, FO1 is designated as the primary failover Cisco ASA.

Example 11-14 *Designating a Primary Cisco ASA*

```
Chicago# configure terminal
Chicago(config)# failover lan unit primary
```

Step 5: Enable Stateful Failover

To implement Active/Active failover, Cisco ASA use a stateful failover link to send continuous connection table updates. The asymmetric routing feature also heavily depends on the stateful failover link. In Example 11-15, the Chicago Cisco ASA is using **GigabitEthernet0/3** as the stateful interface with a system IP address of **10.10.10.5** and a standby IP address of **10.10.10.6**. The configured interface name is **statefullink**.

Example 11-15 *Configuring Stateful Failover*

```
Chicago(config)# failover link statefullink GigabitEthernet0/3
Chicago(config)# failover interface ip statefullink 10.10.10.5 255.255.255.252
   standby 10.10.10.6
```

Step 6: Set Up Failover Groups

In multimode Active/Active failover, an administrator can designate FO1 to be active for the Cubs security context while backing up the Bears security context. Similarly, FO2 can act as an active unit for Bears while backing up Cubs. This Active/Active failover is achieved by using the **failover group** command:

> **failover group** *group#*

Example 11-16 shows all the options that can be defined within a failover group. The Cisco ASA is configured to use failover with a group ID of 1. This group ID is later used to link the failover group to a context.

Example 11-16 *Failover Group Submenu Options*

```
Chicago(config)# failover group 1
Chicago(config-fover-group)# ?
  interface-policy  Set the policy for failover due to interface failures
  mac               Specify the virtual mac address for a physical interface
  no                Remove user failover redundancy group configuration
  polltime          Configure failover interface polling interval
  preempt           Allow preemption of lower priority active unit
  primary           Primary unit has higher priority
  replication       Configure the replication option
  secondary         Secondary unit has higher priority
```

NOTE   You can only configure a group ID of 1 or 2 in the current implementation. If you are using more than two contexts, then you must assign each context to one of the failover groups.

The **interface-policy**, **polltime**, and **mac** parameters are extensively discussed in the upcoming section "Optional Failover Commands."

The **preempt** option instructs the security Cisco ASA to immediately become the active unit for that group if it has a higher priority. This typically occurs when a security Cisco ASA goes through the reboot process. The priority is determined when the group is configured with the **primary** or the **secondary** options. **primary** means that this unit should be the active Cisco ASA for the group with a higher priority. **secondary**, on the other hand, assigns a lower priority and prefers the other unit to act as an active device in that group.

The **replication** option is useful if you want the active Cisco ASA to send updates about the HTTP state and connection entries to the standby Cisco ASA. Example 11-17 shows that the Chicago FO1 Cisco ASA is configured for two failover groups. Group 1 is set up to act as a primary failover device (the default option of a group) and to preempt the failover state in case it is rebooted. However, it will wait 10 seconds before initializing the preempt process. After 10 seconds, the failover Group 1 will become active once failover is up and running. Group 2, on the other hand, is set up to be in secondary mode. It will also try to preempt the state once it completes the boot sequence. Additionally, when it is acting as the active device, it will send updates regarding the HTTP connections to the other Cisco ASA.

Example 11-17 *Configuring Failover Groups*

```
Chicago(config)# failover group 1
Chicago(config-fover-group)# preempt 10
Chicago(config-fover-group)# failover group 2
Chicago(config-fover-group)# secondary
Chicago(config-fover-group)# preempt
Chicago(config-fover-group)# replication http
```

Step 7: Assign Failover Group Membership

After setting up the failover groups, you need to map these groups to the appropriate security contexts. In Figure 11-3, the administrator wants to designate FO1 as the active Cisco ASA for Cubs and standby for Bears, and wants to designate FO2 as the active Cisco ASA for Bears and standby for Cubs. Example 11-18 illustrates how the failover group to a context assignment is achieved by using the **join-failover-group** command. Context Cubs is a part of failover group 1, while context Bears is a member of failover group 2.

Example 11-18 *Failover Group Assignment*

```
Chicago(config)# context Cubs
Chicago(config-ctx)# allocate-interface GigabitEthernet0/0.1
Chicago(config-ctx)#  allocate-interface GigabitEthernet0/1.1
Chicago(config-ctx)#  config-url flash:/Cubs.cfg
Chicago(config-ctx)#  join-failover-group 1
Chicago(config-ctx)# context Bears
Chicago(config-ctx)# allocate-interface GigabitEthernet0/0.2
Chicago(config-ctx)# allocate-interface GigabitEthernet0/1.2
Chicago(config-ctx)# config-url flash:/Bears.cfg
Chicago(config-ctx)# join-failover-group 2
```

Step 8: Assign Interface IP Addresses

The interface system and standby IP addresses are configured in the security contexts. In Example 11-19, Cubs is configured to use **209.165.200.225** and **209.165.200.226** as the system and standby IP addresses, respectively, on the outside interface. It is also configured to use **192.168.10.1** and **192.168.10.2** as the system and standby IP address, respectively, on the inside interface.

Example 11-19 *Configuration of System and Standby IP Addresses*

```
Chicago(config)# change context Cubs
Chicago/Cubs(config)# interface GigabitEthernet0/0.1
Chicago/Cubs(config-if)# ip address 209.165.200.225 255.255.255.224 Standby
   209.165.200.226
Chicago/Cubs(config-if)# interface GigabitEthernet0/1.1
Chicago/Cubs(config-if)# ip address 192.168.10.1 255.255.255.0 standby 192.168.10.2
```

Step 9: Set Up Asymmetric Routing (Optional)

As discussed earlier, Cisco ASA enables you to set up asymmetric routing to ensure that return traffic can be forwarded to the active device in the Active/Active deployment. Use the **asr-group** interface command to enable asymmetric routing on the security Cisco ASA.

When the **asr-group** command is enabled on an interface and the incoming traffic reaches a context that is active on the other security Cisco ASA and does not have the associated flow, the security Cisco ASA:

- Reclassifies the incoming traffic to another interface of the same **asr-group** after determining the flow.

- Forwards the packet to the active unit for further processing.

In Example 11-20, the GigabitEthernet0/0.1 interface is configured for asymmetric routing. It belongs to **asr-group 1**.

Example 11-20 *Configuring Asymmetric Routing*

```
Chicago/Cubs(config)# interface GigabitEthernet0/0.1
Chicago/Cubs(config-if)# ip address 209.165.200.225 255.255.255.224 standby
   209.165.200.226
Chicago/Cubs(config-if)# asr-group 1
```

Step 10: Enable Failover Globally

The last step in configuring an Active/Active failover pair is to enable failover globally on the primary Cisco ASA. Example 11-21 shows how to enable failover on the Chicago Cisco ASA.

Example 11-21 *Enabling Failover Globally*

```
Chicago(config)# failover
```

Step 11: Configure Failover on the Secondary Cisco ASA

In the Cisco failover feature, there is no need to manually configure the secondary Cisco ASA. Instead, you just need to configure some basic information about the failover. After that, the primary Cisco ASA starts synchronizing its configuration to the secondary Cisco ASA. The bootstrap configuration includes the following five configuration parameters:

- Failover designation
- Failover link interface
- Failover interface IP address
- Failover shared key (optional)
- Failover enable

Optional Failover Commands

In addition to the failover commands discussed in the preceding section, you can optionally tweak many default parameters to optimize failover. These features include:

- Specifying failover MAC addresses
- Configuring interface policy
- Managing failover timers
- Monitoring failover interfaces

Specifying Failover MAC Addresses

In Active/Standby failover, the active device uses the primary unit's MAC addresses. In the event of a failover, the secondary Cisco ASA becomes active and takes over the primary unit's MAC addresses, while the active device (now standby) takes over the standby unit's MAC addresses. Once the standby Cisco ASA becomes active, it sends out a gratuitous ARP on the network. A *gratuitous ARP* is an ARP request that the Cisco ASA sends out on the Ethernet networks with the source and destination IP addresses of the active IP addresses. The destination MAC address is the Ethernet broadcast address, i.e., ffff.ffff.ffff. All devices on the Ethernet segment process this broadcast frame and update their ARP table with this information. Using gratuitous ARP, the Layer 2 devices, including bridges and switches, also update the Content Addressable Memory (CAM) table with the MAC address and the updated switch port information.

Using a virtual MAC address is recommended to avoid network disruptions. When a secondary Cisco ASA boots up before the primary Cisco ASA, it uses its physical MAC addresses as active Layer 2 addresses. However, when the primary Cisco ASA boots up, the secondary swaps the MAC addresses and uses the primary Cisco ASA's physical MAC addresses as active. With the virtual MAC address, Cisco ASA do not need to swap the MAC address.

In Example 11-22, the primary active Cisco ASA is being configured to use
0000.1111.2222 as the active MAC address and **0000.1111.2223** as the standby MAC
address on the **GigabitEthernet0/2** interface.

Example 11-22 *Configuration of System and Standby MAC Addresses for Active/Standby*

```
Chicago(config)# failover mac address GigabitEthernet0/2 0000.1111.2222
  0000.1111.2223
```

In Active/Active failover, the failover redundancy group uses a unique virtual MAC address
for each interface rather than using the physical MAC address of the interface. Cisco ASA
calculate this MAC address by using a simple formula, shown in Table 11-2. In this table, the
system will use a default MAC address of 00a0.c900.0101 for the GigabitEthernet0/0
interface if the failover group is 1 and the unit is acting as an active Cisco ASA.

Table 11-2   *Virtual MAC Addresses in Active/Active Failover*

Status	Formula	Example (GigabitEthernet0/0)
Active	00a0.c9{*physical interface #* }.{*failover group id*}01	00a0.c900.0101
Standby	00a0.c9{*physical interface #* }.{*failover group id*}02	00a0.c900.0102

The MAC address can be changed from its default by configuring the **mac address** command
under the failover group sub-configuration menu. In Example 11-23, the MAC address is
changed to **0000.1111.2222** for the active system and **0000.1111.2223** for the standby
system under **failover group 1**.

Example 11-23 *Configuration of System and Standby MAC Addresses for Active/Active*

```
Chicago(config)# failover group 1
Chicago(config-fover-group)# mac address GigabitEthernet0/2 0000.1111.2222
  0000.1111.2223
```

Configuring Interface Policy

The Cisco ASA monitors the status of all the interfaces. If one of the interfaces fails to
respond, failover occurs and the standby Cisco ASA takes over the connections. However,
if you prefer the system to fail over when two or more interfaces fail to respond, then you
can change this default behavior by using the **failover interface-policy** command for
Active/Standby failover, as shown in Example 11-24.

Example 11-24 **failover interface-policy** *Command in Active/Standby Failover*

```
Chicago(config)# failover interface-policy 2
```

In the Active/Active failover, the interface policy is applied under the failover group sub-
configuration menu, as shown in Example 11-25.

Example 11-25 failover interface-policy *Command in Active/Active Failover*

```
Chicago(config)# failover group 1
Chicago(config-fover-group)# interface-policy 2
```

Managing Failover Timers

The Cisco ASA, by default, send periodic keepalive packets to check the status of the peer failover unit. If the standby Cisco ASA does not receive acknowledgements for the keepalive packet it sends out, it initiates a failover only if it deems itself healthier than the current active. Cisco ASA support two types of failover keepalives:

- **Unit**—Sent every second to monitor the status of the failover control interface
- **Interface**—Sent every 15 seconds to monitor the health of the physical interfaces

Example 11-26 illustrates that the security Cisco ASA are configured to send keepalive packets every 500 milliseconds to monitor the status of the failover interface. They are also configured with a holdtime of 3 seconds. That means, the security Cisco ASA will send out up to six keepalive packets for 3 seconds every 500 milliseconds. If during that time they do not get an acknowledgment, the security Cisco ASA will go through the interface test, discussed earlier in the chapter. The results of the test dictate whether the secondary Cisco ASA needs to initiate a failover. This example also shows that the security Cisco ASA is configured for an interface polltime of 5 seconds.

Example 11-26 *Failover Polltime in Active/Standby Failover*

```
Chicago(config)# failover polltime unit msec 500 holdtime 3
Chicago(config)# failover polltime interface 5
```

In Example 11-27, the Active/Active failover is configured to use an interface polltime of 5 seconds.

Example 11-27 *Failover Polltime in Active/Active Failover*

```
Chicago(config)# failover group 1
Chicago(config-fover-group)# polltime interface 5
```

Monitoring Failover Interfaces

When an Cisco ASA is configured for failover, whether Active/Standby or Active/Active, it monitors the status of all the interfaces that have a **nameif** and an IP address configured. If you do not want the failover process to monitor a particular interface, you can use the **no monitor-interface** command for that interface. Example 11-28 illustrates how to disable failover monitoring on the inside interface.

Example 11-28 *Disabling Failover Interface Monitoring*

```
Chicago(config)# no monitor-interface inside
```

Zero-Downtime Software Upgrade

Certain firewalls are not compatible when they are deployed in failover and are running different software versions. The Cisco ASA allows you to run failover even if they are running different versions of images. This is useful when the security Cisco ASA need to be upgraded to a newer maintenance release without any service disruption. Follow these steps to complete the image-upgrade process without any network outage:

NOTE	Stateful failover is mandatory for zero-downtime software upgrade.

Step 1   Upload the new image to both security Cisco ASA.

You can use any of the supported transfer methods to upload the new maintenance image to both security Cisco ASA. In the following example, the administrator is loading the 7.0(2) system image from a TFTP server located at 172.18.108.26 to the system Flash:

```
Chicago(config)# copy tftp disk0:
Address or name of remote host []? 172.18.108.26
Source filename []? asa702-k8.bin
Destination filename [asa702-k8.bin]?
Accessing tftp://172.18.108.26/asa702-
k8.bin...!!!!!!!!!!!!!!!!!!!!!!!!!!!!!!!!!!!!!
<snip>
Writing file disk0:/asa702-k8.bin...
!!!!!!!!!!!!!!!!!!!!!!!!!!!!!!!!!!!!!!!!!!!!!!!!!!!!!!!!!!!!!!
<snip>
5124096 bytes copied in 58.630 secs (88346 bytes/sec)
Chicago(config)#
```

Once the image is uploaded, use the **show flash** command to verify if the image resides in the disk:

```
Chicago# show flash
-#- --length-- -----date/time------ path
 14 34778      Oct 04 2005 07:13:46 asa701.bin
 15 2516       Sep 06 2005 23:07:34 secureme.png
 16 5919340    Aug 18 2005 11:41:32 asdm501.bin
 17 5919976    Oct 04 2005 07:13:46 asa702-k8.bin
```

Note	The zero-downtime software upgrade process can be used to upgrade the maintenance image on the security Cisco ASA, such as going from 7.0(1) to 7.0(2). The failover is disabled if the security Cisco ASA run different major releases. That means you cannot run 7.0(1) on one security Cisco ASA and 7.1(1) on the other.

Step 2 Set boot parameters.

After an image is uploaded, log into the active Cisco ASA and set the system boot parameters to instruct the security Cisco ASA to load the newly uploaded image on the next reboot. Here, the administrator configures the active security Cisco ASA to load the asa702-k8.bin image on the next reboot:

```
Chicago(config)# boot system disk0:/asa702-k8.bin
```

Note   The commands entered on the active security Cisco ASA are synchronized with the standby unit.

Step 3 Reboot the standby Cisco ASA.

After the new image is uploaded, log into the standby security Cisco ASA and check failover status by using the **show failover** command. Verify that the security Cisco ASA is in the standby state. Here, the secondary security Cisco ASA is in standby mode:

```
Chicago# show failover
Failover On
Failover unit Secondary
Failover LAN Interface: FOCtrlIntf GigabitEthernet0/2 (up)
Unit Poll frequency 500 milliseconds, holdtime 3 seconds
Interface Poll frequency 3 seconds
Interface Policy 1
Monitored Interfaces 2 of 250 maximum
Last Failover at: 09:00:37 UTC Jul 13 2005
        This host: Secondary - Standby Ready
                Active time: 71475 (sec)
```

Use the **reload** command to reboot the standby security Cisco ASA:

```
Chicago# reload
Proceed with reload? [confirm]
***
*** --- START GRACEFUL SHUTDOWN ---
Shutting down isakmp
Shutting down File system
```

Step 4 Force failover.

After the standby Cisco ASA comes online, check the version of the system image. If it is running the newly uploaded image, then force the failover so that the standby security Cisco ASA becomes active and takes

over the connections. Issue the **failover active** command to switch
failover, as follows:

```
Chicago# show version
Cisco Adaptive Security Cisco ASA Software Version 7.0(2)
<snip>
Chicago# failover active
    Switching to Active
```

Step 5 Reboot the standby Cisco ASA.

Reboot the standby Cisco ASA (which was active before the forced
failover) so that it can also load the updated image. Use the **reload**
command on the standby Cisco ASA to initiate the reboot process.

Step 6 Force failover (optional).

Once the standby firewall comes online, you can optionally issue the
failover active command to switch the failover state.

NOTE   If the standby security Cisco ASA is set up with the **preempt** option, it will automatically
become active after coming online.

Deployment Scenarios

The failover feature is useful in deployments where redundancy is required to ensure near
100-percent uptime of the network devices. Although the failover feature can be deployed
in many ways, we will cover only two design scenarios for ease of understanding:

- Active/Standby failover in single mode
- Active/Active failover in multiple security contexts

NOTE   The design scenarios discussed in this section should be used solely to reinforce learning.
They should be used only for reference purposes.

Active/Standby Failover in Single Mode

In the first deployment scenario, SecureMe, Inc. is looking to implement failover at its
Chicago location. It has purchased two Cisco ASA 5540 Cisco ASA for this purpose. The
company requires implementation of the stateful failover feature to ensure that all the active
connections (excluding the HTTP connections) are replicated to the standby unit in case
there is a failure on the primary unit. Additionally, SecureMe requires the standby Cisco

ASA to become active if the primary Cisco ASA does not acknowledge the keepalive packets for 3 seconds. Figure 11-4 illustrates a proposed design for Active/Standby failover.

Figure 11-4 *Deployment Scenario Using Active/Standby Failover*

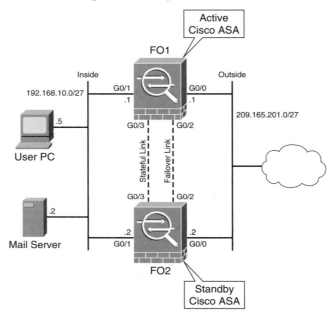

Example 11-29 shows relevant configuration of the primary Cisco ASA and the bootstrap configuration of the secondary Cisco ASA. The primary Cisco ASA, being the active unit, synchronizes the entire running configuration to the secondary Cisco ASA. The connection and translation tables are constantly replicated to the secondary Cisco ASA over a dedicated interface.

Example 11-29 *Cisco ASA Full Configuration Using Active/Standby Failover*

```
                    Configuration of Primary Cisco ASA
Chicago# show run
!outside interface with security level set to 0. The system IP address is
! 209.165.200.225 and the Standby IP address is 209.165.200.226
interface GigabitEthernet0/0
 nameif outside
 security-level 0
 ip address 209.165.200.225 255.255.255.224 standby 209.165.200.226
!inside interface with security level set to 100. The system IP address is
! 192.168.10.1 and the Standby IP address is 192.168.10.2
interface GigabitEthernet0/1
 nameif inside
 security-level 100
 ip address 192.168.10.1 255.255.255.0 standby 192.168.10.2
! Interface used as a failover control interface
interface GigabitEthernet0/2
 description LAN Failover Interface
```

Example 11-29 *Cisco ASA Full Configuration Using Active/Standby Failover (Continued)*

```
! Interface used as a Stateful link
interface GigabitEthernet0/3
 description STATE Failover Interface
<snip>
! Failover is enabled and the unit is acting as a Primary device
failover
failover lan unit primary
! Failover control interface is GigabitEthernet0/2
failover lan interface FOCtrlIntf GigabitEthernet0/2
! Cisco ASA will send periodic hellos every 500 milliseconds, and initiate a
! failover if hellos are not acknowledged for 3 seconds
failover polltime unit msec 500 holdtime 3
! Failover key to encrypt the control messages. This keys will be X'ed out
! in the configuration
failover key cisco123
! Stateful interface
failover link statefullink GigabitEthernet0/3
! IP address assignment on the failover control interface
failover interface ip FOCtrlIntf 10.10.10.1 255.255.255.252 standby 10.10.10.2
! IP address assignment on the stateful failover interface
failover interface ip statefullink 10.10.10.5 255.255.255.252 standby 10.10.10.6
! interfaces to be monitored for failover
monitor-interface outside
monitor-interface inside
! Address translation for the inside hosts to get Internet Access
global (outside) 1 interface
nat (inside) 1 192.168.10.0 255.255.255.0
<snip>
```

Configuration of Secondary Cisco ASA

```
! The unit is acting as a Secondary device
failover lan unit secondary
! Failover control interface is GigabitEthernet0/2
failover lan interface FOCtrlIntf GigabitEthernet0/2
! Failover key to encrypt the control messages. This keys will be X'ed out in the
  configuration
failover key cisco123
! IP address assignment on the failover control interface
failover interface ip FOCtrlIntf 10.10.10.1 255.255.255.252 standby 10.10.10.2
! Failover is enabled
failover
```

Active/Active Failover in Multiple Security Contexts

SecureMe's London office is currently using a Cisco ASA 5520 Cisco ASA as the security device. SecureUs, another firm in the same building, wants SecureMe to provide the firewall services for it as well. SecureMe's management is looking to implement an Active/Active failover solution where it can create two customer contexts—one for SecureMe and the other for SecureUs. It has purchased another Cisco ASA 5520 Cisco ASA to implement this solution. This requires one Cisco ASA to act as an active unit for SecureMe and the other Cisco ASA to act as an active unit for SecureUs while backing up each other in the event of a failure. Figure 11-5 illustrates a proposed design to meet these requirements.

Figure 11-5 *Deployment Scenario Using Active/Active Failover*

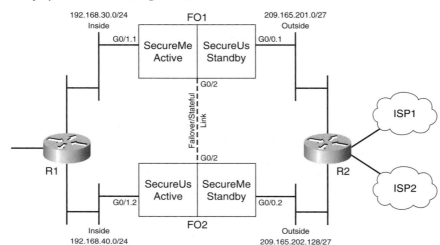

Example 11-30 shows relevant configuration of the primary Cisco ASA and the bootstrap configuration of the secondary Cisco ASA. The primary Cisco ASA synchronizes the entire running configuration to the secondary Cisco ASA. Once both Cisco ASA are active and passing traffic, the administrator also wants these devices to send connection and translation table updates to one another using the failover control interface. The administrator has implemented the asymmetric routing feature to avoid routing issues if packets arrive on the other active Cisco ASA.

Example 11-30 *Cisco ASA Configuration Using Active/Active Failover in Multiple Security Contexts*

```
                 Configuration of Primary Cisco ASA System Execution Space
! Main GigabitEthernet0/0 interface
interface GigabitEthernet0/0
! Sub-interface assigned to the SecureMe context as the
!  outside interface. A VLAN ID is assigned to the interface
interface GigabitEthernet0/0.1
 vlan 5
! Sub-interface assigned to the SecureUs context as the
! outside interface. A VLAN ID is assigned to the interface
interface GigabitEthernet0/0.2
 vlan 10
! Main GigabitEthernet0/1 interface
interface GigabitEthernet0/1
! Sub-interface assigned to the SecureMe context as the
! inside interface. A VLAN ID is assigned to the interface
interface GigabitEthernet0/1.1
 vlan 105
! Sub-interface assigned to the SecureUs context as the
! inside interface. A VLAN ID is assigned to the interface
interface GigabitEthernet0/1.2
 vlan 110
! Interface used as a Failover control and Stateful link
interface GigabitEthernet0/2
```

Example 11-30 *Cisco ASA Configuration Using Active/Active Failover in Multiple Security Contexts (Continued)*

```
  description LAN/STATE Failover Interface
<snip>
! Failover is enabled and the unit is acting as a Primary device
failover
failover lan unit primary
! Failover control interface is GigabitEthernet0/2
failover lan interface FOCtrlIntf GigabitEthernet0/2
! Failover key to encrypt the control messages
failover key cisco123
! IP address assignment on the failover control interface
failover interface ip FOCtrlIntf 10.10.10.1 255.255.255.252 standby 10.10.10.2
! Failover link interface is GigabitEthernet0/2
failover link FOCtrlIntf GigabitEthernet0/2
! Failover group configuration. Group 1 is primary and group 2 is secondary
failover group 1
  preempt 10
  polltime interface 10
! A virtual MAC address is defined for this group
  mac address Ethernet0 0000.1111.2222 0000.1111.2223
failover group 2
  secondary
  preempt
! A virtual MAC address is defined for this group
  mac address Ethernet0 0000.2222.3333 0000.2222.3334
! Context Assignment with the failover group ID
admin-context SecureMe
context SecureMe
  allocate-interface GigabitEthernet0/0.1 A_outside invisible
  allocate-interface GigabitEthernet0/1.1 A_inside invisible
  config-url disk0:/SecureMe.cfg
  join-failover-group 1
! Context Assignment with the failover group ID
context SecureUs
  allocate-interface GigabitEthernet0/0.2 B_outside invisible
  allocate-interface GigabitEthernet0/1.2 B_inside invisible
  config-url disk0:/SecureUs.cfg
  join-failover-group 2
```

Configuration of Primary Cisco ASA's SecureMe Context

```
!outside interface with security level set to 0. The system IP address is
!209.165.201.1 and the Standby IP address is 209.165.201.2. The asr-group ID is 1
interface A_outside
 nameif outside
 security-level 0
 ip address 209.165.201.1 255.255.255.224 standby 209.165.201.2
 asr-group 1
!inside interface with security level set to 0. The system IP address is
!192.168.30.1 and the Standby IP address is 192.168.30.2. The asr-group ID is 1
interface A_inside
 nameif inside
 security-level 100
 ip address 192.168.30.1 255.255.255.0 standby 192.168.30.2
<snip>
```

continues

Example 11-30 *Cisco ASA Configuration Using Active/Active Failover in Multiple Security Contexts (Continued)*

```
! interfaces to be monitored for failover
monitor-interface A_outside
monitor-interface A_inside
! Address translation Policies
global (A_outside) 1 209.165.201.3 netmask 255.255.255.224
nat (A_inside) 1 192.168.30.0 255.255.255.0
route A_outside 0.0.0.0 0.0.0.0 209.165.201.30
<snip>
```

Configuration of Primary Cisco ASA's SecureUs Context

```
!outside interface with security level set to 0. The system and standby IPs
!are 209.165.202.129 and 209.165.202.130 respectively. The asr-group ID is 1
interface B_outside
 nameif outside
 security-level 0
 ip address 209.165.202.129 255.255.255.224 standby 209.165.202.130
 asr-group 1
!inside interface with security level set to 0. The system and standby IPs are
!192.168.40.1 and 192.168.40.2 respectively.
interface B_inside
 nameif inside
 security-level 100
 ip address 192.168.40.1 255.255.255.0 standby 192.168.40.2
<snip>
! interfaces to be monitored for failover
monitor-interface B_inside
monitor-interface B_outside
! Address translation Policies
global (B_outside) 1 209.165.202.131 netmask 255.255.255.0
nat (B_inside) 1 192.168.40.0 255.255.255.0
route B_outside 0.0.0.0 0.0.0.0 209.165.202.158
<snip>
```

Monitoring and Troubleshooting Failovers

The Cisco ASA has a rich set of **show** and **debug** commands that are useful to monitor the status of the standby Cisco ASA. These commands are particularly important in isolating a problem if something behaves unexpectedly. The necessary **show** and **debug** commands that are used to manage Active/Standby and Active/Active failover in the Cisco ASA are discussed in this section. Deployment Scenario 1 is used for references in this section.

Monitoring

Once the primary Cisco ASA is configured for failover, the first thing to check is to verify that the Cisco ASA is recognizing failover as enabled. The status of an Cisco ASA's failover can be checked by using the **show failover** command, as shown in Example 11-31.

Example 11-31 *Output of* **show failover** *to Check if Failover Is Enabled*

```
Chicago(config)# show failover
Failover On
Failover unit Primary
Failover LAN Interface: FOCtrlIntf GigabitEthernet0/2 (up)
Unit Poll frequency 500 milliseconds, holdtime 3 seconds<snip>
```

After the secondary Cisco ASA is configured for bootstrap configuration, the primary Cisco ASA synchronizes the running configuration to the secondary Cisco ASA, as shown in Example 11-32.

Example 11-32 *Configuration Replication*

```
Beginning configuration replication: Sending to mate.
End Configuration Replication to mate
```

The secondary Cisco ASA loads the running configuration and becomes standby to monitor the status of the primary Cisco ASA. In Example 11-33, the secondary Cisco ASA is in standby with its current IP addresses set as the standby addresses.

Example 11-33 *Output of* **show ip**

```
Chicago# show ip
System IP Addresses:
Interface         Name          IP address       Subnet mask      Method
GigabitEthernet0/0 outside      209.165.200.225  255.255.255.224  CONFIG
GigabitEthernet0/1 inside       192.168.10.1     255.255.255.0    CONFIG
GigabitEthernet0/2 FOCtrlIntf   10.10.10.1       255.255.255.252  CONFIG
GigabitEthernet0/3 statefullink 10.10.10.5       255.255.255.252  CONFIG
Current IP Addresses:
Interface         Name          IP address       Subnet mask      Method
GigabitEthernet0/0 outside      209.165.200.226  255.255.255.224  CONFIG
GigabitEthernet0/1 inside       192.168.10.2     255.255.255.0    CONFIG
GigabitEthernet0/2 FOCtrlIntf   10.10.10.2       255.255.255.252  CONFIG
GigabitEthernet0/3 statefullink 10.10.10.6       255.255.255.252  CONFIG
```

The failover or standby IP addresses can also be checked by using the **show failover** command. If stateful failover is set up, **show failover** also displays the stateful failover statistics along with the number of updates it has received and transmitted. Example 11-34 shows the output of **show failover** with the system and standby IP addresses and information about stateful failover.

Example 11-34 *Output of* **show failover** *in Active/Standby Deployment*

```
Chicago# show failover
Failover On
Failover unit Secondary
Failover LAN Interface: FOCtrlIntf GigabitEthernet0/2 (up)
Unit Poll frequency 500 milliseconds, holdtime 3 seconds
Interface Poll frequency 3 seconds
```

continues

Example 11-34 *Output of* **show failover** *in Active/Standby Deployment (Continued)*

```
Interface Policy 1
Monitored Interfaces 2 of 250 maximum
Last Failover at: 16:50:50 UTC Jul 13 2005
        This host: Secondary - Standby Ready
                Active time: 4903 (sec)
                slot 0: ASA5520 hw/sw rev (1.0/7.0(1)5) status (Up Sys)
                slot 1: ASA-SSM-10 hw/sw rev (1.0/5.0(2)S152.0) status (Up)
                Interface outside (209.165.200.226): Normal
                Interface inside (192.168.10.2): Normal
        Other host: Primary - Active
                Active time: 26492 (sec)
                slot 0: ASA5520 hw/sw rev (1.0/7.0(1)5) status (Up Sys)
                slot 1: ASA-SSM-10 hw/sw rev (1.0/5.0(2)S152.0) status (Up)
                Interface outside (209.165.200.225): Normal
                Interface inside (192.168.10.1): Normal

Stateful Failover Logical Update Statistics
        Link : statefullink GigabitEthernet0/3 (up)
        Stateful Obj    xmit        xerr        rcv         rerr
        General         7509        0           23239       0
        sys cmd         4009        0           4009        0
        up time         0           0           0           0
        RPC services    0           0           0           0
        TCP conn        55001       0           43023       0
        UDP conn        3300        0           3205        0
        ARP tbl         3500        0           19230       0
        Xlate_Timeout   0           0           0           0
        VPN IKE upd     14          0           13          0
        VPN IPSEC upd   30          0           28          0
        VPN CTCP upd    0           0           0           0
        VPN SDI upd     0           0           0           0
        VPN DHCP upd    0           0           0           0
        Logical Update Queue Information
                        Cur     Max     Total
        Recv Q:         0       2       110826
        Xmit Q:         0       1       12417
```

NOTE   The xerr and rerr are transmit and receive errors that occur when Cisco ASA send stateful information to each other. Stateful failover is best effort and there will be times when errors increment because of congestion and other reasons.

In the Active/Active failover, the failover can be verified either from the system execution space or from the security context. The failover information from the security context displays the current status of the context along with the system and current IP addresses. Additionally, it also displays the stateful failover statistics, as shown in Example 11-35.

Example 11-35 *Output of* **show failover** *in Active/Active Deployment*

```
Chicago/SecureMe# show failover
Failover On
Last Failover at: 11:34:19 UTC Oct 1 2005
        This context: Active
                Active time: 155887 (sec)
                Interface outside (209.165.200.225): Normal
                Interface inside (192.168.10.1): Normal
        Peer context: Standby Ready
                Active time: 0 (sec)
                Interface outside (209.165.200.226): Normal
                Interface inside (192.168.10.2): Normal

Stateful Failover Logical Update Statistics
        Status: Configured.
        Stateful Obj    xmit        xerr        rcv        rerr
        RPC services    0           0           0          0
        TCP conn        40          0           0          0
        UDP conn        1984        0           18         0
<snip>
```

Troubleshooting

If the failover is properly set up, but the security Cisco ASA are not synchronizing the configuration, the first thing to verify is the status of security Cisco ASA. If the status of the other security Cisco ASA is failed, as shown in Example 11-36, the failover is not operational.

Example 11-36 *Failover Failure*

```
Chicago(config)# show failover | include Failed
        Other host: Secondary - Failed
```

To resolve this issue, check the following settings:

- The failover cable is physically connected between the security Cisco ASA. If they are connected via a Layer 2 switch, ensure that both failover control interfaces belong to the same VLAN.

- Failover is enabled on both security Cisco ASA.

- Failover configuration is valid on both security Cisco ASA.

The security Cisco ASA supports a number of **debug** commands for troubleshooting purposes. Use the **debug fo** commands as shown in Example 11-37 to enable the failover debug messages.

CAUTION   The failover debug commands produce a lot of output. Do not enable these debugs without consulting a TAC engineer.

Example 11-37 *Available Failover Debugs*

```
Chicago(config)# debug fo ?
exec mode commands/options:
  cable   Failover LAN status
  fail    Failover internal exception
  fmsg    Failover message
  ifc     Network interface status trace
  open    Failover device open
  rx      Failover Message receive
  rxdmp   Failover recv message dump (serial console only)
  rxip    IP network failover packet recv
  switch  Failover Switching status
  sync    Failover config/command replication
  tx      Failover Message xmit
  txdmp   Failover xmit message dump (serial console only)
  txip    IP network failover packet xmit
  verify  Failover message verify
```

To troubleshoot issues related to failover timing, use the **debug fo rxip** and **debug fo txip** commands to determine if the packets are being exchanged according to the configured polltimes. As illustrated in Example 11-38, the FHELLO (failover hello) packets are received on all the configured interfaces.

Example 11-38 *Output of* **debug fo rxip** *and* **debug fo txip**

```
Chicago# debug fo rxip
Chicago# debug fo txip
fover_ip: fover_ip(): ifc 3 got Fover Msg 10.10.10.2 -> 10.10.10.1
fover_ip: fover_ip(): ifc 1 209.165.200.226 -> 209.165.200.225
fover_ip: fover_ip(): ifc 1 got FHELLO
fover_ip: fover_ip(): ifc 2 192.168.10.2 -> 192.168.10.1
fover_ip: fover_ip(): ifc 2 got FHELLO
```

It is recommended that you enable logging of failover messages to either an internal buffer or an external syslog server to avoid overwhelming the console or remote administrative session. In Example 11-39, the administrator sets up buffer logging for the failover (ha) logging class, represented as **fo_logging**, with a logging buffer size of 20,000 bytes.

Example 11-39 *Enable Failover Logging*

```
Chicago(config)#  logging enable
Chicago(config)#  logging list fo_logging level debugging class ha
Chicago(config)#  logging buffer-size 20000
Chicago(config)#  logging buffered fo_logging
Chicago(config)#  logging class ha buffered debugging
```

After enabling failover logging, the administrator can use the **show logging** command. In Example 11-40, the primary security Cisco ASA is changing its role from active to standby. The failover was initiated by the secondary Cisco ASA. The physical interfaces change their state from waiting to normal.

Example 11-40 *Output of* **show logging**

```
Chicago# show logging
Syslog logging: enabled
    Facility: 20
    Timestamp logging: enabled
<snip>
    Buffer logging: list test, class ha, 19073 messages logged
<snip>
Oct 1 2005 11:36:39: %ASA-1-104002: (Primary) Switching to STNDBY - Other unit
want me Standby
Oct 1 2005 11:36:40: %ASA-1-105003: (Primary) Monitoring on interface outside
waiting
Oct 1 2005 11:36:40: %ASA-1-105003: (Primary) Monitoring on interface inside waiting
Oct 1 2005 11:36:42: %ASA-6-210022: LU missed 317 updates
Oct 1 2005 11:36:52: %ASA-1-105004: (Primary) Monitoring on interface outside normal
Oct 1 2005 11:36:52: %ASA-1-105004: (Primary) Monitoring on interface inside normal
```

Summary

The failover feature in the Cisco Cisco ASA is designed to allow network administrators to achieve near 100-percent uptime for their network devices. The robust Cisco ASA operating system allows administrators to have both Cisco ASA in the active state to pass traffic. It also allows Cisco ASA to support asymmetric routing to load-balance traffic across multiple service providers. This chapter covered extensive **show** and **debug** commands to assist in troubleshooting simple and complicated failover deployments.

This chapter covers the following topics:

- Architectural overview
- Configuration of quality of service
- Deployment scenarios
- Monitoring quality of service

CHAPTER 12

Quality of Service

In a standard IP network, all packets are processed identically based on best effort. The network devices usually ignore the importance or criticality of the data that is passing through the network. This creates problems in deployments where time-sensitive traffic, such as voice and video packets, is delayed or dropped because the network devices do not prioritize it over other traffic. The feature of prioritizing some traffic over other traffic is known as *quality of service (QoS)*.

QoS is useful in the following network deployments:

- You run voice, video, and data traffic on the same network. Because voice and video streams are time sensitive and do not tolerate network delays, QoS policies must be implemented to ensure traffic prioritization.

- You run data applications such as time sensitive databases that require traffic prioritization if there is congestion on the network.

- You want to prioritize management traffic, such as Telnet or SSH, so that you do not lose access to the network devices if there is an outbreak of a new virus in the local network.

- You are a service provider and want to offer different classes of service (CoS) to your customers based on their needs.

- You have virtual private networks (VPNs) deployed and you want to prioritize or rate-limit traffic going over the VPN tunnel.

Many different types of QoS mechanisms are available in the Cisco devices, such as the following:

- Traffic policing
- Traffic prioritization
- Traffic shaping
- Traffic marking

NOTE   QoS is useful in policing and prioritizing packets only when there is congestion in the network. For end-to-end QoS, all network devices along the path should be QoS capable.

Architectural Overview

Cisco ASA supports two types of QoS:

- Traffic policing
- Traffic prioritization

Both of these methods are configured by using the robust Modular Policy Framework (MPF), discussed briefly in Chapter 8, "ASA Application Inspection."

NOTE   Cisco ASA supports QoS only in the single-mode firewall. QoS will not work if the security appliance is configured in multiple-mode security contexts, discussed in Chapter 9, "Security Contexts."

The following sections discuss the two supported types of QoS, the packet flow sequence in the security appliance, the packet-classification process, and the QoS features with respect to VPNs.

Traffic Policing

Traffic policing, also known as *traffic rate-limiting,* allows you to control the maximum rate of traffic eligible to pass through an interface. Traffic that falls within the configured parameters is allowed to pass, whereas traffic that exceeds the limit is dropped.

In Cisco ASA, if traffic is not classified as "priority," as discussed in the following "Traffic Prioritization" section, it is processed through the rate limiter. The security appliance tries to look for an existing flow and tags the packet for QoS. Thereafter, it sends the packet to the QoS engine for processing. The packet passes through the rate limiter, which determines if the packet conforms to the configured rate. If it does not, then the packet can be forwarded for additional processing or can be dropped based on the policies. If it conforms to the configured rate, the packet is flagged to take the nonpriority queue. Figure 12-1 illustrates how a packet is processed in the security appliance when it passes through the QoS engine.

When traffic leaves the QoS engine, it is forwarded to the egress interface for physical transmission. The security appliance implements another level of QoS processing at the interface to guarantee traffic with a non-priority flag gets proper handling. Packet processing at the interface depends on the depth of the low-priority queue and the conditions of the transmit ring. Transmission ring is the buffer space used by the security appliance to hold packets before transmitting them at the driver level. If the ring is congested, the packet is queued to the low-priority queue. If the transmit ring has room, the packet is sent immediately after ensuring that the high-priority queue is empty. If the high-priority queue has traffic to send, the transmit ring will service it first.

Figure 12-1 *Packet Flow Through the QoS Engine*

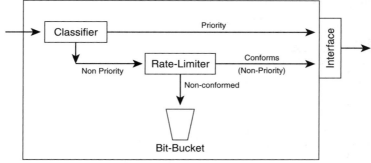

QoS Engine

With QoS rate limiting, the security appliance implements a tail drop mechanism when a packet does not conform to the configured profile. The tail drop mechanism drops the packets at the end of the queue if the queue is already full. Cisco ASA logs this event through syslog locally in the buffer or to an external server.

Traffic Prioritization

Traffic prioritization, also known as *class of service (CoS)* or *low-latency queue (LLQ)*, is used to give important network traffic precedence over normal or unimportant network traffic. It assigns different priority levels or classes (such as high, medium and low) to traffic. The lower the packet's importance, the lower its priority, and thus the greater its chances of getting dropped in case of network congestion.

In the current implementation of Cisco ASA, two classes of traffic prioritization are supported: priority QoS and nonpriority QoS. Priority QoS means that packets are prioritized over regular traffic, whereas nonpriority QoS means that packets are processed by the rate limiter, as discussed earlier.

When traffic is classified as priority, it will be express-forwarded without passing through the rate limiter. The traffic is then flagged to take the priority queue at the egress interface level.

To ensure priority forwarding of traffic at the interface, the security appliance looks at the flag for priority queue and sends the packet for immediate transmission unless the transmit ring is congested. In that case, traffic is queued to the high-priority queue. As soon as the transmit ring has room available, the security appliance services the high-priority queue and transmits the packet.

NOTE   Traffic prioritization and traffic policing are the two mutually exclusive methods for setting up QoS. You cannot prioritize some traffic and simultaneously police it in same class map configuration, discussed in the section, "Configuring Quality of Service." If you try to configure traffic policing while priority is configured, you will receive an error as follows:

```
ERROR: Must deconfigure priority in this class before issuing this command
```

Table 12-1 displays QoS compatibility on the security appliance when other features, such as a transparent firewall, are implemented.

Table 12-1   *Support of QoS with Other Features*

Feature	Support Under QoS
ToS byte preservation	Yes
Packet prioritization	Yes
Packet policing	Yes
Class-based weighted fair queuing (CBWFQ)	No
QoS for the VPN tunnels	Yes
Security contexts	No
Transparent firewall	No
Routed firewall	Yes
Packet marking	No

The next section discusses the packet flow sequence in the security appliance when QoS is applied on the interface.

Packet Flow Sequence

When a packet passes through a security appliance configured for QoS, the following sequence of events occurs, as illustrated in Figure 12-2:

1   The packet arrives at the ingress interface. If it is the first packet of the flow, the security appliance attempts to route the packet out to the proper interface and creates a flow for the subsequent packets. The flow contains the rules and actions associated with the packets.

2   Based on the QoS rules, the security appliance takes one of the following two actions:

   — If the packet matches the priority queue, it is directed to the high-priority queue for express handling. For the high-priority queue, there is no rate limiting on the packets.

   — If rate limiting is configured on the security appliance, the packet is checked to see if a flow for QoS is already established. If there is none, a flow is created based on the source and destination IP address, source and destination ports, IP protocol, and the interfaces forwarding the packets. The security appliance checks that it conforms to the configured rate-limiting parameters. If the flow exceeds the threshold, the security appliance drops the packet.

3   At this point, the QoS flow is up and the packet is forwarded to the egress interface for physical transmission.

4 The egress interface has two allocated queues for QoS. One is used for the prioritized traffic and the other is used for the rate-limited traffic. If traffic is rate-limited and there are packets to be sent in the high-priority queue, the security appliance services the high-priority queue first and then processes the rate-limited queue.

5 The security appliance transmits the packet over the physical interface.

NOTE If a packet does not match traffic priority or traffic rate limiting, it is forwarded to the nonpriority queue without applying the rate-limiting policies.

Figure 12-2 *Packet Flow Through the Security Appliance*

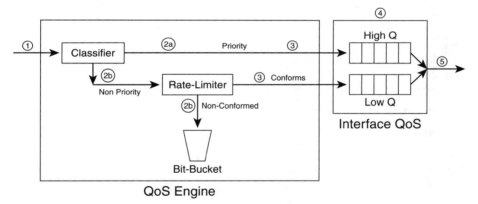

Packet Classification

Packet classification is a way to identify packets on which QoS policies need to be applied. This can range from simple functions such as IP precedence and DSCP fields to complicated methods such as complex access lists. The following subsections discuss the supported packet-classification methods.

IP Precedence Field

IP packets contain a type of service (ToS) byte, which is used to indicate the priority in which the packets should be processed. In the ToS byte, the leftmost 3 bits set the IP precedence, as shown in Figure 12-3. The network devices use the next 4 bits, known as the ToS bits, to determine how a packet should be handled by looking at delay (D), throughput (T), reliability (R), and cost (C). However, these bits are not currently used in the IP network infrastructures. The last bit in the ToS byte is typically referred as MBZ (abbreviation for "must be zero"). This bit is not used either.

Figure 12-3 *ToS Byte Displaying IP Precedence Bits*

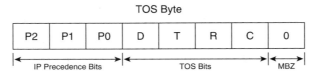

Table 12-2 lists all the IP precedence bits along with their IP precedence names as defined in RFC 791.

Table 12-2 *IP Precedence Bits and IP Precedence Names*

Precedence Value	Precedence Bit	Precedence Name
0	000	Routine
1	001	Priority
2	010	Immediate
3	011	Flash
4	100	Flash Override
5	101	Critical
6	110	Internetwork Control
7	111	Network Control

IP DSCP Field

Differentiated Services Code Point (DSCP) is intended to replace the definitions of the IP ToS byte. It uses the 6 most significant bits for packet classification. The 2 least significant bits are currently unused, as shown in Figure 12-4. By using the 6 bits in DSCP, you can classify up to 64 streams of packets.

Figure 12-4 *DSCP Field*

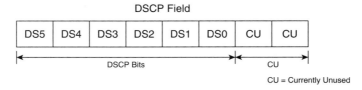

DSCP provides backward compatibility to IP precedence. Table 12-3 lists the IP precedence values with the corresponding DSCP values.

Table 12-3   *Correlation of IP Precedence Bits to DSCP Bits*

Precedence Value	Precedence Bit	DSCP Bit
0	000	000 000
1	001	001 000
2	010	010 000
3	011	011 000
4	100	100 000
5	101	101 000
6	110	110 000
7	111	111 000

While DSCP offers packet classification similarly to IP precedence, it also offers fine granularity to packet identification by using the additional 3 bits. The Internet Engineering Task Force (IETF) has divided the DSCP bits into four service concepts:

- Default DCSP, defined as 000 000, offers the best-effort packet switching through the network devices.

- Class selector provides backward-compatibility bits, shown in Table 12-3. All the DSCP bits shown in the table belong to this service.

- Expedited Forwarding (EF) per-hop behavior (PHB), with the DSCP bit of 101 110, defines the premium service for the IP packets.

- Assured Forwarding (AF) PHB, with four different classes and three different class levels, defines a total of 12 code points for packet classification.

Example 12-1 lists the well-known DSCP bits supported by Cisco ASA.

Example 12-1 *Available DSCP Options in Class Maps*

```
Chicago(config-cmap)# match dscp ?
  <0-63>   Differentiated services codepoint value
  af11     Match packets with AF11 dscp (001010)
  af12     Match packets with AF12 dscp (001100)
  af13     Match packets with AF13 dscp (001110)
  af21     Match packets with AF21 dscp (010010)
  af22     Match packets with AF22 dscp (010100)
  af23     Match packets with AF23 dscp (010110)
  af31     Match packets with AF31 dscp (011010)
  af32     Match packets with AF32 dscp (011100)
  af33     Match packets with AF33 dscp (011110)
  af41     Match packets with AF41 dscp (100010)
  af42     Match packets with AF42 dscp (100100)
  af43     Match packets with AF43 dscp (100110)
  cs1      Match packets with CS1(precedence 1) dscp (001000)
  cs2      Match packets with CS2(precedence 2) dscp (010000)
```

continues

Example 12-1 *Available DSCP Options in Class Maps (Continued)*

```
cs3       Match packets with CS3(precedence 3) dscp (011000)
cs4       Match packets with CS4(precedence 4) dscp (100000)
cs5       Match packets with CS5(precedence 5) dscp (101000)
cs6       Match packets with CS6(precedence 6) dscp (110000)
cs7       Match packets with CS7(precedence 7) dscp (111000)
default   Match packets with default dscp (000000)
ef        Match packets with EF dscp (101110)
```

NOTE   The QoS implementation in Cisco ASA observes and honors the DSCP and IP precedence bits in the packet. For the IPSec VPN tunnels, the security appliance preserves the ToS byte from the inner header to the outer header. By doing so, the security appliance and the devices along the VPN tunnel can correctly prioritize traffic.

IP Access Control List

Access control lists (ACLs) are the most commonly used form of packet classification. They can identify traffic based on many Layer 3 as well as Layer 4 headers of the packet. Please consult Chapter 5, "Network Access Control," for more information about ACL.

IP Flow

Classification based on IP flow is usually done by looking at the following five tuples:

- Destination IP address
- Source IP address
- Destination port
- Source port
- IP Protocol field

In Cisco ASA, flow-based classification is done based on the destination IP address. That means that if the traffic is destined to an IP address, an IP flow is created and the appropriate policies are applied to it.

VPN Tunnel Group

Cisco ASA can also classify packets destined to an IPSec tunnel. When a packet is received by the security appliance and matches a particular tunnel group (whether site-to-site or remote-access), the security appliance applies the configured QoS policies before transmitting the packet.

NOTE	The security appliance restricts one **match** command in the class map. However, you can have two **match** commands when setting up QoS for the VPN tunnels. Use the **match tunnel-group** *<tunnel-group-name>* command in the class map first before specifying a second qualifying **match** statement in the class map. Currently, **match flow ip destination-address** is the only supported second **match** command.

QoS and VPN Tunnels

Cisco ASA supports full QoS implementation on both the site-to-site and remote-access VPN tunnels. For the best-effort method, the site-to-site QoS implementation rate-limits traffic for the entire tunnel. This means that all hosts within the tunnel share the same bandwidth. However, for the remote-access VPN tunnels, the QoS implementation rate-limits traffic per remote-access peer. This means that each and every VPN tunnel within a remote access group gets the configured data throughput.

NOTE	Even though there is a static ACL for each site-to-site tunnel, the QoS rules will not be inserted into the database until there is an active VPN tunnel. This ensures that the security appliance does not allocate bandwidth for the IPSec security associations (SAs) that are not being used.

When both QoS and VPN engines are set up on the security appliance, the following events can occur during device configuration:

- **New QoS policy is setup for existing tunnels**—If a QoS policy is applied to an interface with an active VPN tunnel, the security appliance invokes the IPSec engine to apply the appropriate QoS parameters to the IPSec SAs.

- **Tunnel goes down for QoS-enabled group**—When a VPN tunnel goes down (whether a user deletes the connection or the administrator clears the established SA), the security appliance invokes the QoS process to delete the appropriate QoS parameters for that particular IPSec SA.

- **QoS policy is removed for the group**—When the VPN commands are removed from the QoS configuration, the security appliance invokes the QoS engine to clear up relevant parameters. The security appliance also makes sure not to call the QoS engine for the future VPN tunnels.

Configuring Quality of Service

The QoS configuration on Cisco ASA is broken down into the following four simple steps:

Step 1   Set up a class map.

> **Step 2**   Configure a policy map.
>
> **Step 3**   Apply the policy map on the interface.
>
> **Step 4**   Tune the priority queue (optional).

Step 1: Set Up a Class Map

A traffic class identifies packets on which you want to apply the QoS policies. In the security appliance, there are many ways to classify traffic, as shown in Example 12-2. Use of an ACL is the most robust method available for setting up a class map. You can specify the Layer 3 and Layer 4 information in the packets when ACLs are used. The security appliance can also match based on the DSCP and IP precedence bits in the IP header.

A traffic class is created by using the **class-map** command, followed by the name of the class. As shown in Example 12-2, a traffic class named **traffic-class** is created. Packet classification is done by using the **match** statements along with the appropriate option, described in Table 12-3.

NOTE   You cannot configure multiple **match** statements under one class map, with one exception: one additional **match** statement is allowed when you have **match tunnel-group** or **default-inspect-traffic** commands configured in a class map.

Example 12-2 *Available Options in Class Maps*

```
Chicago(config)# class-map traffic-class
Chicago(config-cmap)# match ?
  access-list                  Match an Access List
  any                          Match any packet
  default-inspection-traffic   Match default inspection traffic:
                               ctiqbe----tcp--2748     dns-------udp--53
                               ftp-------tcp--21        gtp-------udp--2123,3386
                               h323-h225-tcp--1720      h323-ras--udp--1718-1719
                               http------tcp--80        icmp------icmp
                               ils-------tcp--389       mgcp------udp--2427,2727
                               netbios---udp--137-138   rpc-------udp--111
                               rsh-------tcp--514       rtsp------tcp--554
                               sip-------tcp--5060      sip-------udp--5060
                               skinny----tcp--2000      smtp------tcp--25
                               sqlnet----tcp--1521      tftp------udp--69
                               xdmcp-----udp--177
  dscp                         Match IP DSCP (DiffServ CodePoints)
  flow                         Flow based Policy
  port                         Match TCP/UDP port(s)
  precedence                   Match IP precedence
  rtp                          Match RTP port numbers
  tunnel-group                 Match a Tunnel Group
```

Table 12-4 defines all the methods available in the **class-map** command.

Table 12-4   *Definition of* **match** *Options in the* **class-map** *Command*

Feature	Description
access-list	Packet classification is done based on an ACL. The ACL can have source and destination addresses and can optionally contain Layer 4 port information.
any	Any keyword is used to classify all packets flowing through the security appliance.
default-inspection-traffic	This option is used by the inspection engines, discussed in Chapter 8.
dscp	Packet classification is done based on the IETF-defined DSCP value in the IP header.
flow	Packets are classified using the destination IP address of the flow. This option is used along with the **tunnel-group** option.
port	Packets are classified based on the TCP or UDP destination ports for any source or destination address.
precedence	The security appliance classifies packets based on the ToS byte in the IP header.
rtp	Using RTP (real-time protocol) as the keyword, packets are matched based on the RTP stream on the even UDP port number. This even ports acts as a starting point for a range of UDP ports to identify the RTP streams.
tunnel-group	Packet classification is done based on the tunnel group. This is used for site-to-site and remote-access VPN tunnels.

In Figure 12-5, SecureMe, a fictional company, has Cisco ASA set up to classify traffic sourced from the 192.168.10.0/24 subnet and destined to the mail server, 209.165.201.1. The administrator of the security appliance also prefers to identify the Voice over IP (VoIP) traffic passing through the security appliance.

Figure 12-5   *Packet Classification in an Appliance*

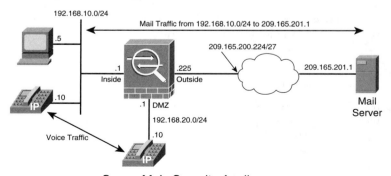

SecureMe's Security Appliance

Example 12-3 shows how to configure a class map for identifying mail and VoIP packets. An ACL named **mail-traffic** is configured to specify the source and destination IP addresses and the TCP destination port 25 (SMTP). This ACL is mapped to a class map called **mail**. Two additional class maps, **voip-sig** and **voip-rtp**, are set up to identify VoIP packets. VoIP uses DSCP values **af31** and **ef** for voice signaling and RTP streams, respectively. Class map **voip-sig** is set up to match the packets that have a DSCP value of **af31** to identify voice signaling, and class map **voip-rtp** is set up to identify the RTP streams using DSCP value of **ef**.

Example 12-3 *Class Maps to Identify Mail and VoIP Traffic*

```
Chicago(config)# access-list mail-traffic extended permit tcp 192.168.10.0
  255.255.255.0 host 209.165.201.1 eq smtp
Chicago(config)# class-map mail
Chicago(config-cmap)# match access-list mail-traffic
Chicago(config-cmap)# exit
Chicago(config)# class-map voip-sig
Chicago(config-cmap)# match dscp af31
Chicago(config-cmap)# exit
Chicago(config)# class-map voip-rtp
Chicago(config-cmap)# match dscp ef
```

NOTE   If you configure two classes with overlapping traffic and then apply policies to rate-limit traffic, the security appliance applies the most stringent traffic policy.

The security appliance can also match traffic destined to go over a tunnel. By using the **match tunnel-group** command, you can identify packets if they match against a VPN connection. In Example 12-4, the administrator has configured a class map called **tunnel-traffic** to identify traffic destined to go over a VPN group called **SecureMeGroup**. The administrator also matches traffic using destination-based IP flow.

NOTE   The use of **match flow ip destination-address** along with **tunnel-group** is mandatory if the VPN traffic needs to be rate-limited. You do not need to use **match flow ip destination-address** if the VPN traffic needs to be prioritized.

Example 12-4 *Class Maps to Identify Tunnel Traffic*

```
Chicago(config)# class-map tunnel-traffic
Chicago(config-cmap)# match flow ip destination-address
Chicago(config-cmap)# match tunnel-group SecureMeGroup
```

NOTE	If you configure two classes with overlapping traffic, and apply priority to one class and rate limiting to the other class, the security appliance matches traffic to the priority queue and does not apply the rate-limited policies.

Step 2: Configure a Policy Map

The configured class maps are bound to a policy map that defines the action to be applied on the identified traffic. You can apply the priority and the rate-limit QoS functions under the **policy-map** sub-configuration mode. Example 12-5 shows a policy map called **traffic-map** configured to apply actions to the class maps, defined in the previous step. The class map, such as **voip-sig**, **voip-rtp**, and/or **tunnel-traffic**, is linked to the policy map by using the **class** command. The security appliance also provides a way to apply actions to traffic not matched by the configured class maps. This is done by using the **class-default** command.

Example 12-5 *Configuration of Policy Maps in the Security Appliance*

```
Chicago(config)# policy-map traffic-map
Chicago(config-pmap)# class ?
  WORD             class-map name
  class-default    System default class matching otherwise unclassified packets
Chicago(config-pmap)# class voip-sig
Chicago(config-pmap-c)#
```

After mapping the class and the policy maps, Cisco ASA needs to be configured for an action that can be applied to the identified traffic. The two supported actions, as discussed earlier, are traffic prioritization and traffic policing. In Example 12-6, the security appliance is configured to prioritize VoIP traffic by using the **priority** statement.

Example 12-6 *Traffic Prioritization for the VoIP Traffic*

```
Chicago(config)# policy-map traffic-map
Chicago(config-pmap)# class voip-sig
Chicago(config-pmap-c)# priority
Chicago(config-pmap)# exit
Chicago(config-pmap)# class voip-rtp
Chicago(config-pmap-c)# priority
```

Cisco ASA uses the **police** command to define the rate-limiting actions on the identified traffic. If traffic falls in the police rate and burst size, the security appliance can transmit traffic. The police rate is the actual rate that can pass through the QoS engine. It ranges from 8000 bps (bits per second) to 2 billion bps.

The burst size is the amount of instantaneous burst that the security appliance can send at any given time without applying the exceed action. The burst size can be configured by using the following formula:

Burst size = (Policing Rate) $* 1.5 / 8$

For example, if traffic needs to be limited to a police rate of 56,000 bps, the burst size will be 10,500 bytes. The valid range for burst size is from 1000 to 512,000,000 bytes.

NOTE   The policing rate is in bits per second while the burst size is in bytes.

In Example 12-7, the security appliance is configured to rate-limit the tunnel traffic to 56 kbps, with a burst size of 10,500 bytes. If traffic falls within this range, the security appliance transmits it as it conforms to the configured policy. Otherwise, traffic that exceeds these rates will be dropped.

Example 12-7 *Rate-Limiting of Tunnel Traffic*

```
Chicago(config)# policy-map traffic-map
Chicago(config-pmap)# class tunnel-traffic
Chicago(config-pmap-c)# police 56000 10500 conform-action transmit exceed-action
  drop
```

The default conform action is to transmit traffic, while the default exceed action is to drop it.

Step 3: Apply the Policy Map on the Interface

The next step in completing the QoS configuration is the association of the policy map to an interface. This is achieved by using the **service-policy** command along with the policy name and the interface that the policy needs to be applied on. Example 12-8 demonstrates how to apply a policy map called **traffic-map** to the outside interface.

Example 12-8 *Applying QoS on the Outside Interface*

```
Chicago(config)# service-policy traffic-map interface outside
```

NOTE   Cisco ASA supports policing and prioritizing traffic only in the outbound direction. That means that if the service policy is applied to the outside interface, then all the packets leaving the security appliance on the outside interface will be inspected for QoS.

NOTE   An interface-based QoS policy overrides a global QoS policy. The global QoS policy is applied to all the interfaces.

Step 4: Tune the Priority Queue (Optional)

When the QoS engine has processed the packets, they are queued to the interface for transmission on the wire. The security appliance implements the priority queue at the interface to ensure that prioritized packets are preferred over nonprioritized packets. You can fine-tune the transmit ring and the depth of the priority queues to minimize the delay for the high-priority packets. The transmit ring, **tx-ring-limit**, specifies the number of packets allowed into the transmit queue of the interface driver.

Additionally, the security appliance allows you to set the depth of the priority queues by using the **queue-limit** command. When both queues are full, and the QoS engine forwards more traffic, the security appliance simply drops the received data. Moreover, it processes the transmit ring first before servicing the priority queues. In Example 12-9, the administrator of the security appliance has fine-tuned the priority queue parameters on the outside interface. The transmit-ring limit is changed to hold up to 100 packets in the queue, while the high- and low-priority queue depth is set up to hold 200 packets. This allows the priority queue to be processed efficiently with minimum latency caused by the transmit ring.

Example 12-9 *Configuration of Priority Queue*

```
Chicago(config)# priority-queue outside
Chicago(priority-queue)# tx-ring-limit 100
Chicago(priority-queue)# queue-limit 200
```

NOTE   The security appliance transmits the priority queue packets before servicing the nonpriority queue.

QoS Deployment Scenarios

The QoS solution is extremely useful when organizations run into network congestion, or when they want to prioritize some network traffic over other traffic. Although this important feature can be deployed in many ways, this section covers two design scenarios for the ease of understanding:

- QoS for VoIP traffic
- QoS for the remote-access VPN tunnels

NOTE   The design scenarios discussed in this section should be used solely to enforce learning. They should be used for reference purposes only.

QoS for VoIP Traffic

SecureMe's information technology (IT) group is responsible for providing network services to its internal users. The IT group hosts an e-mail server and uses Cisco IP Phones for telecommunications. SecureMe management has some specific requirements that the IT group is obliged to meet:

- Full Internet web access to the internal clients. They should get bandwidth based on best effort and should be restricted to 56 kbps.

- For VoIP calls, there should not be any network-related delays.

- Do not allow Internet e-mail users to fully utilize the bandwidth when they download their e-mail using POP3. They should be restricted to have up to 56 kbps bandwidth. Additionally, restrict users to 56 kbps when they upload their e-mail via SMTP.

- Log all the system-generated syslog messages to a server.

Figure 12-6 shows SecureMe's topology that will be used to meet the network requirements.

Figure 12-6 *SecureMe's VoIP and E-Mail QoS Policy*

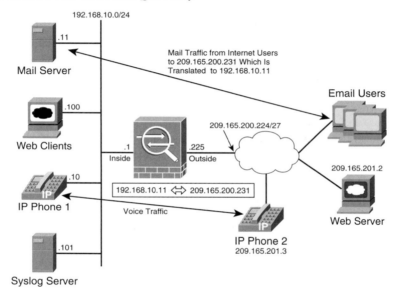

The administrator has put together the following list to meet the requirements:

- The administrator has set up five class maps to identify traffic.

- A class map called **mail-pop** is configured to classify all the packet sources from the mail server to the e-mail users when users download their emails using POP3.

- The second class map, called **mail-smtp**, identifies SMTP traffic from the e-mail users to the e-mail server when they upload their e-mails. The email server is translated to 209.165.200.231.

- The third class map, called **web**, classifies the web traffic destined to the Internet. The internal hosts are translated to the public interface's IP address.

- The last two class maps, **voip-sig** and **voip-rtp**, identify VoIP traffic.

- All class maps except for **mail-smtp** are linked to a policy map called **voip-qos-policy**, whereas the **mail-smtp** class is mapped to a policy map called **SMTP-policy**.

The **voip-qos-policy** policy map is applied to the outside interface and the **SMTP-policy** policy map is applied to the inside interface. Example 12-10 shows the relevant configuration of SecureMe's ASA to achieve the previously listed requirements.

Example 12-10 *ASA's Full Configuration Showing QoS for VoIP*

```
SecureMe# show run
ASA Version 7.0(1)
! ip address on the outside interface
interface GigabitEthernet0/0
 nameif outside
 security-level 0
 ip address 209.165.200.225 255.255.255.224
! ip address on the inside interface
interface GigabitEthernet0/1
 nameif inside
 security-level 100
 ip address 192.168.10.1 255.255.255.0
!
hostname SecureMe
!Access-list to classify Mail-traffic. SecureMe uses SMTP to upload emails
access-list Mail-ACL-in extended permit tcp any host 209.165.200.231 eq smtp
!Access-list to classify Mail-traffic. SecureMe uses POP3 to download emails
access-list Mail-ACL-out extended permit tcp host 209.165.200.231 eq pop3 any
!Access-list to classify Web-traffic to the internet.
access-list web-out extended permit tcp host 209.165.200.225 any eq www
!Syslog Server information to log the dropped packets.
logging enable
logging trap informational
logging host inside 192.168.10.101
!NAT configuration to allow inside hosts to get Internet connectivity
global (outside) 1 interface
nat (inside) 1 192.168.10.0 255.255.255.0
!Static address translation for the Mail-Server
static (inside,outside) 209.165.200.231 192.168.10.11 netmask 255.255.255.255
!
route outside 0.0.0.0 0.0.0.0 209.165.200.230 1
!Class-map to classify Mail traffic in the outbound direction
class-map mail-pop
 match access-list Mail-ACL-out
!Class-map to classify Mail traffic in the inbound direction
class-map mail-smtp
 match access-list Mail-ACL-in
!Class-map to classify Web traffic in the outbound direction
class-map web
 match access-list web-out
!Class-maps to classify VoIP traffic
class-map voip-sig
 match dscp af31
class-map voip-rtp
 match dscp ef
! Policy-map to define rules applied on traffic-class
policy-map voip-mail-qos-policy
```

continues

Example 12-10 *ASA's Full Configuration Showing QoS for VoIP (Continued)*

```
! POP mail is rate-limited to 56kbps
 class mail-pop
  police 56000 10500
! VoIP signal is prioritized
 class voip-sig
  priority
! VoIP data is prioritized
class voip-rtp
  priority
! Web-mail is rate-limited to 56kbps
class web
 police 56000 10500
! Policy-map to define rules applied on inbound mail (SMTP)
policy-map SMTP-policy
! SMTP mail is rate-limited to 56kbps
 class mail-smtp
  police 56000 10500
! Inspection Policies
policy-map global_policy
 class inspection_default
  inspect ctiqbe
  inspect http
<snip>
  inspect xdmcp
  inspect icmp
! Global Policy - applied for traffic inspection
service-policy global_policy global
! QoS policy is applied to the outside interface
service-policy voip-mail-qos-policy interface outside
! QoS policy is applied to the inside interface
service-policy SMTP-policy interface inside

! Priority Queue is setup on the outside interface for QoS efficiency
priority-queue outside
 tx-ring-limit 100
 queue-limit 200
```

QoS for the Remote-Access VPN Tunnels

Figure 12-7 shows network topology for SecureMe's London's office. It has a Cisco ASA that it uses to provide VPN services for remote users. These users use the security appliance to connect to a file server to access their home directories. SecureMe does not want its broadband VPN users to fully utilize the bandwidth for its office. Therefore, it is interested in using QoS for the VPN tunnels to restrict the users to 256 kbps. SecureMe also hosts a web server at this location. However, it does not want to restrict the Internet web clients when they connect to the web server.

Figure 12-7 *SecureMe Network Using QoS for VPN Tunnels*

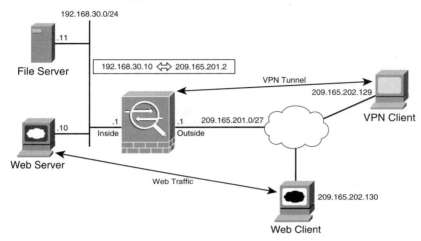

NOTE   Refer to Chapter 16, "Remote Access VPNs," for detailed VPN configuration examples.

Example 12-11 shows the running configuration of the security appliance in London. A class map called **VPN-traffic** is configured to match all the packets destined to the VPN group called **SecureMeGroup**. To provide Internet users access to the web server, another class map called **web** is set up. The traffic is matched against an ACL that is configured to identify TCP port 80 packets. Both of these classes are linked to a policy map called **VPN-Policy**, where the VPN traffic is rate-limited to 256 kbps for normal traffic with a burst rate of 48000 bytes. The security appliance is also configured to prioritize web traffic passing through it. The policy is then applied to the outside interface.

Example 12-11 *Full Configuration of the ASA in Chicago Using QoS*

```
London# show running
! ip address on the outside interface
interface GigabitEthernet0/0
 nameif outside
 security-level 0
 ip address 209.165.201.1 255.255.255.224
! ip address on the inside interface
interface GigabitEthernet0/1
 nameif inside
 security-level 100
 ip address 192.168.30.1 255.255.255.0
!
hostname London
```

continues

Example 12-11 *Full Configuration of the ASA in Chicago Using QoS (Continued)*

```
!ACL to classify Web-traffic
access-list HTTP_ACL extended permit tcp host 209.165.201.2 eq www any
!ACL to bypass address translation for the traffic destined to the VPN clients
access-list nonat extended permit ip 192.168.30.0 255.255.255.0 192.168.50.0
255.255.255.0
!NAT 0 to bypass traffic identified in ACL nonat
nat (inside) 0 access-list nonat
!Static address translation for the web server
static (inside,outside) 209.165.201.2 192.168.30.10 netmask 255.255.255.255
! Local pool of addresses to be assigned to the VPN clients
ip local pool vpnpool 192.168.50.1-192.168.50.199
! sysopt to bypass traffic filters
sysopt connection permit-ipsec
! Transform set to specify encryption and hashing algorithm
! Crypto map configuration
crypto ipsec transform-set myset esp-aes-256 esp-sha-hmac
crypto dynamic-map dynmap 10 set transform-set myset
crypto map IPSec_map 10 ipsec-isakmp dynamic dynmap
crypto map IPSec_map interface outside
! isakmp configuration
isakmp enable outside
isakmp policy 10 authentication pre-share
isakmp policy 10 encryption aes-256
isakmp policy 10 hash sha
isakmp policy 10 group 2
isakmp policy 10 lifetime 86400
! Remote Access tunnel-group configuration
tunnel-group SecureMeGroup type ipsec-ra
tunnel-group SecureMeGroup general-attributes
 address-pool vpnpool
tunnel-group SecureMeGroup ipsec-attributes
 pre-shared-key *
! Class-map to classify VPN packets
class-map VPN-traffic
 match flow ip destination-address
 match tunnel-group SecureMeGroup
!Class-map to classify Web traffic
class-map web
 match access-list HTTP_ACL
! Policy-map to define rules applied on traffic-class
policy-map VPN-Policy
 class VPN-traffic
  police 256000 48000
 class web
  priority
! Inspection Policies
policy-map global_policy
 class inspection_default
  inspect ctiqbe
  inspect http
<snip>
  inspect xdmcp
```

Example 12-11 *Full Configuration of the ASA in Chicago Using QoS (Continued)*

```
   inspect icmp
! Global Policy - applied for traffic inspection
service-policy global_policy global
! Priority Queue is setup on the outside interface for QoS efficiency
priority-queue outside
 tx-ring-limit 100
 queue-limit 200
! QoS policy is applied to the outside interface
service-policy VPN-Policy interface outside
```

Monitoring QoS

Cisco ASA includes a set of **show** commands to check the health of the security appliance and to ensure guaranteed QoS through the security appliance. These commands are also helpful in isolating any configuration-related issues. Most of the QoS-related commands start with **show service-policy**, as shown in Example 12-12.

Example 12-12 *Options Available in the* **show service policy** *Command*

```
Chicago# show service-policy ?
   flow      Show all policies that are enabled on a flow
   global    show status/statistics of the global policy
   inspect   Show status/statistics of 'inspect' policy
   interface show status/statistics of an interface policy
   ips       Show status/statistics of 'ips' policy
   police    Show status/statistics of 'police' policy
   priority  Show status/statistics of 'priority' policy
   set       Show status/statistics of 'set' policy
   <cr>
```

Cisco ASA also allows you to display the global and interface-specific policies when the **show service-policy** command is used with **global** and **interface** sub-options. Example 12-13 shows a global service policy that is usually used by the inspection engine. There are two highlighted entries: the HTTP traffic and the ICMP traffic. You can see that 8 packets were inspected by the HTTP engine and 43 were inspected by the ICMP engine. All of these packets passed the inspection engine and were allowed to travel through. The security appliance also shows any dropped packets, if the inspection engines do not permit them. Chapter 8 covers these inspections in detail.

Example 12-13 *Output of* **show service policy global** *Command*

```
Chicago# show service-policy global
Global policy:
   Service-policy: global_policy
     Class-map: inspection_default
       Inspect: ctiqbe, packet 0, drop 0, reset-drop 0
       Inspect: dns, packet 0, drop 0, reset-drop 0
       Inspect: ftp, packet 0, drop 0, reset-drop 0
       Inspect: h323 h225, packet 0, drop 0, reset-drop 0
```

continues

Example 12-13 *Output of* **show service policy global** *Command (Continued)*

```
          Inspect: h323 ras, packet 0, drop 0, reset-drop 0
          Inspect: http, packet 8, drop 0, reset-drop 0
          Inspect: ils, packet 0, drop 0, reset-drop 0
!Output omitted for brevity
          Inspect: sqlnet, packet 0, drop 0, reset-drop 0
          Inspect: tftp, packet 0, drop 0, reset-drop 0
          Inspect: xdmcp, packet 0, drop 0, reset-drop 0
          Inspect: icmp, packet 43, drop 0, reset-drop 0
Interface outside:
  Service-policy: VPN-Policy
    Class-map: VPN-traffic
      police Interface outside:
        cir 64000 bps, bc 10000 bytes
        conformed 128 packets, 137472 bytes; actions:  transmit
        exceeded 6 packets, 6444 bytes; actions:  drop
        conformed 0 bps, exceed 0 bps
    Class-map: web
      Priority:
        Interface outside: aggregate drop 0, aggregate transmit 250
```

The **show service-policy interface** command also displays the QoS interface policy name of the class map along with the configured policies within each class. In Example 12-14, two class maps are configured: **VPN-traffic** and **web**. The VPN-traffic class is configured to rate-limit the traffic to 256,000 bps with burst size of 48,000 bytes. The security appliance dropped 6 packets because they exceeded the rate-limiting policies, and transmitted 128 packets. On the other hand, the web class, being the priority class, transmitted 250 packets.

Example 12-14 *Output of* **show service-policy interface outside** *Command*

```
Chicago# show service-policy interface outside

Interface outside:
  Service-policy: VPN-Policy
    Class-map: VPN-traffic
      police Interface outside:
        cir 256000 bps, bc 48000 bytes
        conformed 128 packets, 137472 bytes; actions:  transmit
        exceeded 6 packets, 6444 bytes; actions:  drop
        conformed 0 bps, exceed 0 bps
    Class-map: web
      Priority:
        Interface outside: aggregate drop 0, aggregate transmit 250
```

The robust CLI of the security appliance allows you to monitor the depth of interface priority queues. As shown in Example 12-15, **show priority-queue statistics** displays the queue statistics of the inside and outside interfaces. There are two queue types for each interface: one for the priority traffic (LLQ) and the other for best-effort (BE) traffic. The outside interface best-effort queue transmitted 84,792 packets and dropped 1056.

The priority queue, shown as LLQ, forwarded 6589 packet and dropped none. The inside interface transmitted 442 packets on the best-effort queue.

Example 12-15 *Output of* **show priority-queue** *Command*

```
Chicago# show priority-queue statistics
Priority-Queue Statistics interface outside
Queue Type       = BE
Packets Dropped  = 1056
Packets Transmit = 84792
Packets Enqueued = 0
Current Q Length = 0
Max Q Length     = 0

Queue Type       = LLQ
Packets Dropped  = 0
Packets Transmit = 6589
Packets Enqueued = 0
Current Q Length = 0
Max Q Length     = 0

Priority-Queue Statistics interface inside
Queue Type       = BE
Packets Dropped  = 0
Packets Transmit = 44902
Packets Enqueued = 0
Current Q Length = 0
Max Q Length     = 0

Queue Type       = LLQ
Packets Dropped  = 0
Packets Transmit = 0
Packets Enqueued = 0
Current Q Length = 0
Max Q Length     = 0
Chicago#
```

Summary

QoS is a robust feature that provides network professionals a means to prioritize time-sensitive and critical data over regular traffic. The two modes, traffic prioritization and traffic policing, can be deployed in Cisco ASA to guarantee that important traffic goes through during network congestion. Cisco ASA allows you to fine-tune the QoS engine by setting the transmit ring and priority queue depths to control data delay. This chapter also assists in monitoring traffic statistics such as the number of packets matching the priority and best-effort QoS policies.

PART **III**

Intrusion Prevention System (IPS) Solution

This chapter covers the following topics:

- IPS integration
- Overview of the AIP-SSM
- Directing traffic to the AIP-SSM
- AIP-SSM management and software recovery
- Legacy IPS features

CHAPTER 13

Intrusion Prevention System Integration

Cisco ASA integrates firewall capabilities with sophisticated intrusion prevention features that provide a deep-packet inspection solution. Cisco Intrusion Prevention System (CIPS) integration provides the ability to effectively mitigate a wide range of network attacks without compromising Cisco ASA's performance.

This chapter covers Cisco ASA IPS integration at a glance and provides several deployment examples and considerations.

Adaptive Inspection Prevention Security Services Module Overview (AIP-SSM)

Cisco ASA supports the Adaptive Inspection Prevention Security Service Module (AIP-SSM) running Cisco Intrusion Prevention System (CIPS) software version 5.0 or later. One of the major features of CIPS 5.x is its ability to process and analyze traffic inline. This qualifies Cisco ASA to be classified as an IPS. The system image file is similar to the ones that run on the Cisco IPS 4200 Series sensors, Cisco IDS Services Module-2 (IDSM-2) for Cisco Catalyst 6500, and Cisco IDS Network Module for Cisco IOS routers.

Cisco ASA also provides basic IPS support if an AIP-SSM module is not present. This capability is achieved with the cuse of the IP audit feature, which is the traditional IP audit feature supported by the Cisco Secure PIX Firewall. The IP audit feature supports a basic list of signatures. It allows the appliance to perform one or more actions on traffic that matches such signatures. This feature is discussed later in the chapter, in the section "IP Audit."

Two different AIP-SSM modules exist:

- AIP-SSM-10
- AIP-SSM-20

NOTE Cisco ASA 5510 supports the AIP-SSM-10 only. Cisco ASA 5520 support both the AIP-SSM10 and AIP-SSM-20. The Cisco ASA 5540 supports the AIP-SSM-20.

The AIP-SSM is a diskless (Flash-based) module. The CIPS software runs in the Flash of the module to provide more flexibility and reliability. The module includes an Fast Ethernet port designed for out-of-band management. Figure 13-1 illustrates the front of the AIP-SSM module.

Figure 13-1 *AIP-SSM Module Front View*

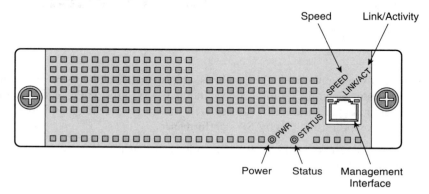

The AIP-SSM has four LED indicators that are visible to the end user. Table 13-1 describes the function of each indicator.

Table 13-1 *AIP-SSM LEDs*

LED Indicator	Color	Description
Power	Green	Indicates that the AIP-SSM card is on.
Status	Green/yellow	Green indicates that software-driven tests have passed and the card is operational. Yellow indicates that the unit is under test or indicates the proper time to remove the AIP-SSM from the ASA chassis.
Link/Activity	Green	Indicates 10/100/1000 Ethernet link and activity.
Speed	Green/orange	Green indicates that it is operating at 100 Mbps. Orange indicates that it is operating at 1000 Mbps.

AIP-SSM Management

The AIP-SSM can be managed from the management interface port, which is illustrated in Figure 13-1, by using Telnet, SSH, or Cisco Adaptive Security Device Manager (ASDM). It can also be managed from the ASA's backplane by using the **session** command:

```
session module-number
```

where *module-number* is the slot number in the Cisco ASA. Because there is only one available slot, the module number is always 1. Example 13-1 demonstrates how to open a command session to the AIP-SSM module. The AIP-SSM module prompts the user for authentication credentials.

Example 13-1 **session** *Command*

```
Chicago# session 1
Opening command session with slot 1.
Connected to slot 1. Escape character sequence is 'CTRL-^X'.
login: cisco
Password:
```

Once the user session is connected to the AIP-SSM, the configuration steps are the same as for any other system running CIPS 5.*x* or later software.

NOTE   Chapter 14, "Configuring and Troubleshooting Cisco IPS Software via CLI," covers CIPS software configuration.

To view the module statistics, use the **show module** command from the ASA CLI, as demonstrated in Example 13-2.

Example 13-2 *Output of* **show module** *Command*

```
Chicago# show module
Mod Card Type                                        Model           Serial No.
--- -------------------------------------------- ------------------- ------------
  0 ASA 5540 Adaptive Security Appliance           ASA5540          P0000000227
  1 ASA 5500 Series Security Services Module-20    ASA-SSM-20       01234567890
Mod MAC Address Range                    Hw Version   Fw Version    Sw Version
--- -------------------------------- ------------- ------------ --------------
  0 000b.fcf8.c6d2 to 000b.fcf8.c6d6  1.0             1.0(6)5       7.0(1)
  1 000b.fcf8.012c to 000b.fcf8.012c  1.0             1.0(7)2       5.0(2)S152.0
Mod Status
--- -----------------
  0 Up Sys
  1 Up
```

The first highlighted line shows the card type. In this case, the Chicago ASA 5540 is running an AIP-SSM-20 with serial number 01234567890. The second highlighted line shows the MAC address of the card and the software version it is running. The third highlighted line shows the status of the module, Up, meaning it is operational.

Inline Versus Promiscuous Mode

Cisco ASA supports both inline and promiscuous IPS modes. When configured as an inline IPS, the AIP-SSM module can drop malicious packets, generate alarms, or reset a connection, allowing the ASA to respond immediately to security threats and protect the network. Inline IPS configuration forces all traffic to be directed to the AIP-SSM. The ASA will not forward any traffic out to the network without the AIP-SSM first inspecting it.

Figure 13-2 shows the traffic flow when the Cisco ASA is configured in inline IPS mode.

Figure 13-2 *Inline IPS Traffic Flow*

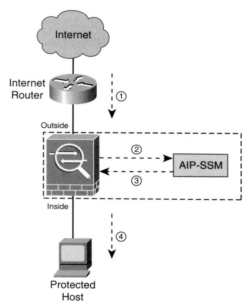

The following is the sequence of events illustrated in Figure 13-2:

1 The Cisco ASA receives an IP packet from the Internet.

2 Because the Cisco ASA is configured in inline IPS mode, it forwards the packet to the AIP-SSM for analysis.

3 The AIP-SSM analyzes the packet and, if it determines that the packet is not malicious, forwards the packet back to the Cisco ASA.

4 The Cisco ASA forwards the packet to its final destination (the protected host).

NOTE   Inline IPS mode is the most secure configuration because every packet is inspected by the AIP-SSM; however, this may affect the overall throughput. The impact depends on the type of attack, signatures enabled on the system, and amount of traffic passing through the appliance.

When the Cisco ASA is set up to use the AIP-SSM in promiscuous mode, the ASA sends a duplicate stream of traffic to the AIP-SSM. This mode has less impact on the overall throughput. Promiscuous mode is considered to be less secure than inline mode because the IPS module can only block traffic by forcing the ASA to shun the malicious traffic or sending a TCP-RST (reset) message to terminate a TCP connection.

NOTE   Promiscuous mode has less impact on performance because the AIP-SSM is not in the traffic path. A copy of the packet is sent to the AIP-SSM. If a packet is dropped, there is no effect on the ASA.

Figure 13-3 illustrates an example of how traffic flows when the AIP-SSM is configured in promiscuous mode.

Figure 13-3 *Promiscuous Mode Traffic Flow*

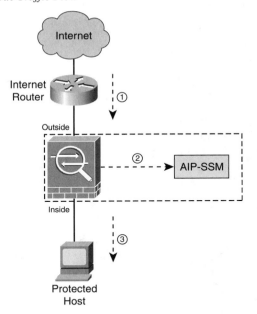

The following is the sequence of events illustrated in Figure 13-3:

1 The Cisco ASA receives an IP packet from the Internet.

2 Because the Cisco ASA is configured in promiscuous IPS mode, the AIP-SSM silently snoops the packet.

3 The ASA forwards the packet to its final destination (protected host) if the packet conforms to security policies (i.e., it does not match any of the configured signatures).

NOTE   If the ASA firewall policies deny any inbound packet at the interface, the packet will not be inspected by the AIP-SSM. This applies to both inline and promiscuous IPS modes.

In the example illustrated in Figure 13-4, SecureMe's Chicago headquarters has two redundant Cisco ASAs as Internet firewalls configured in promiscuous IPS mode. It also has an ASA configured with a site-to-site IPSec tunnel to a partner company. In this case, the ASA is configured in inline IPS mode. The traffic that this ASA inspects depends on SecureMe's security policy's site-to-site VPNs.

Figure 13-4 *SecureMe IPS Example*

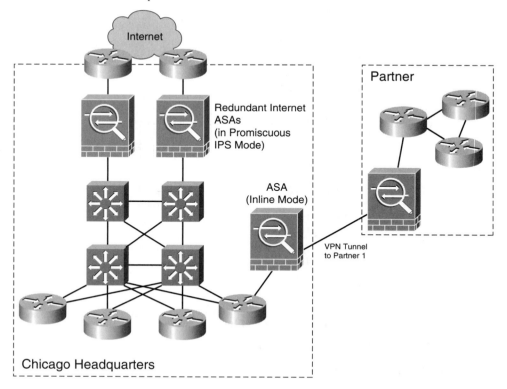

Directing Traffic to the AIP-SSM

This section covers how to configure the Cisco ASA to direct traffic to the AIP-SSM for inline and promiscuous modes. The following steps specify how traffic will be forwarded to the AIP-SSM:

Step 1   To classify how and what traffic will be forwarded to the AIP-SSM, configure a class map by using the **class-map** command. A class map named IPSclass is configured in this example to match all traffic passing through the security appliance:

```
Chicago# configure terminal
Chicago(config)# class-map IPSclass
Chicago(config-cmap)# match any
```

Step 2   Add a policy map with the **policy-map** command. A policy map named IPSpolicy is configured in this example:

```
Chicago(config)# policy-map IPSpolicy
Chicago(config-pmap)#
```

Step 3   Associate the previously configured class map to the new policy map as follows:

```
Chicago(config-pmap)# class IPSclass
```

Step 4   Use the **ips** subcommand to specify the IPS mode of operation (inline vs. promiscuous) and what the failover mechanism will be. The command syntax is as follows:

```
ips {inline | promiscuous} {fail-close | fail-open}
```

In this example, the ASA is configured with the **inline** keyword placing the AIP-SSM directly in the traffic flow.

```
Chicago(config-pmap-c)# ips inline fail-close
```

The **fail-close** keyword is used in this example. This forces the ASA to block all traffic if the AIP-SSM fails.

NOTE   The AIP-SSM is not hot-swappable. You can shut down the module by using the **hw-module module 1 shutdown** command.

Step 5   Activate the policy map globally or on one or more interfaces with the **service-policy** command. The command syntax is as follows:

```
service-policy policymap_name {global | interface interface_name}
```

The **global** keyword applies the policy to all interfaces. The **interface** keyword applies the policy to a specific interface. In this example, the policy is applied to the outside and dmz1 interfaces:

```
Chicago(config)# service-policy IPSpolicy interface outside
Chicago(config)# service-policy IPSpolicy interface dmz1
```

NOTE   Only one policy map can be applied to a specific interface.

AIP-SSM Module Software Recovery

This section covers how you can do a software recovery on the AIP-SSM through the Cisco ASA operating system. The Cisco IPS system recovery image completely refreshes the AIP-SSM to its initial state for a given software release. You can use the **hw-module module** command to recover, reload, reset, or shut down the AIP-SSM. The following is the command syntax:

```
hw-module module slot reload
hw-module module slot reset
hw-module module slot shutdown
hw-module module slot recover [boot | configure | stop]
```

The following steps are necessary to completely refresh the AIP-SSM:

Step 1   Use the **hw-module module 1 recover configure** command to configure the recovery parameters for the AIP-SSM:

```
Chicago# hw-module module 1 recover configure
Image URL [tftp://0.0.0.0/]: tftp://172.18.124.9
/IPS-SSM-K9-sys-1.1-a-5.0-2-s152.img
Port IP Address [0.0.0.0]: 172.18.124.11

VLAN ID [0]:
Gateway IP Address [0.0.0.0]: 172.18.124.1
```

After invoking the **hw-module module 1 recover configure** command, the ASA asks you for the complete URL for the TFTP server from which the AIP-SSM will pull the recovery image. This TFTP server must be accessible by the AIP-SSM management port. The port IP address is the IP address of the AIP-SSM management port. You are also asked for the VLAN ID and default gateway IP address. A VLAN ID of 0 represents that VLANs are not used. You can use the **show module** *module* **recover** command to display and verify the configured recovery parameters:

```
Chicago# show module 1 recover
Module 1 recover parameters...
```

```
Boot Recovery Image: Yes
    Image URL:            tftp:// 172.18.124.9
/IPS-SSM-K9-sys-1.1-a-5.0-2-s152.img
Port IP Address:      172.18.124.11

Gateway IP Address:   172.18.124.1
VLAN ID:              0
```

Step 2   To initiate the recovery, use the **hw-module module 1 recover boot command**. The Cisco ASA displays a warning message about erasing all configuration and data on the module. It prompts the user to confirm the recovery process:

```
Chicago# hw-module module 1 recover boot
The module in slot 1 will be recovered. This may
erase all configuration and all data on that device and
attempt to download a new image for it.
Recover module in slot 1? [confirm]
Reset issued for module in slot 1
```

You must first configure the recovery parameters before invoking the previous command. If you do not configure these parameters, the following error is displayed:

```
Chicago# hw-module module 1 recover boot
The module in slot 1 can not be recovered.
The tftp url and port address must be configured via
    hw-module module 1 recover configure
```

Previously in this chapter, you learned that you can use the **show module** command to obtain information about the modules installed on your ASA. You can also use the **show module** *module-number* **details** command to obtain more detailed information about the AIP-SSM module installed on the system. Example 13-3 includes the output of this command.

Example 13-3 *Output of* **show module details** *Command*

```
Chicago# show module 1 details
Getting details from the Service Module, please wait...
ASA 5500 Series Security Services Module-20
Model:            ASA-SSM-20
Hardware version: 1.0
Serial Number:    0
Firmware version: 1.0(7)2
Software version:  5.0(2)S152
Status:           Up
Mgmt IP addr:     172.18.124.11
Mgmt web ports:   443
Mgmt TLS enabled: true
```

Additional IPS Features

Cisco ASA provides other limited IPS features that are available without the need of the AIP-SSM module:

- IP audit
- Shunning

IP Audit

The IP audit feature is a legacy IDS feature supported in Cisco Secure PIX Firewalls. It provides basic IDS functionality to ASA systems that do not have the AIP-SSM installed. The IP audit feature enables the ASA to generate alarms based on a limited number of signatures.

To enable the IP audit feature, use the **ip audit** command. The following is the command syntax:

```
ip audit name name info [action [alarm] [drop] [reset]]
ip audit name name attack [action [alarm] [drop] [reset]]
```

name can be any arbitrary identifier for the **ip audit** policy.

There are two different categories of IP audit alarms/events:

- **info**—For informational signatures
- **attack**—For attack signatures

The **alarm** action generates an event that alerts the administrator that a packet matched a specific signature. The **drop** action enables the ASA to drop any offending packets. The **reset** action forces the ASA to drop the packet and close the connection.

NOTE   The default action is to generate an alarm.

The configured IP audit policy can be assigned to an interface with the following command:

```
ip audit interface interface_name policy_name
```

In Example 13-4, the ASA is configured to generate alarms for informational signatures and to reset connections and generate alarms for attack signatures.

Example 13-4 *IP Audit Configuration Example*

```
ip audit name secureme info action alarm
ip audit name secureme attack action alarm reset
ip audit interface outside secureme
ip audit interface dmz secureme
```

The IP audit policy shown in Example 13-4 is applied to the ASA's outside and dmz interfaces.

The Cisco ASA running basic IPS features with the IP audit feature or running advanced IP features with the AIP-SSM triggers an alarm when a given packet or sequence of packets matches the characteristics of available signatures. In both cases, it is crucial to minimize the occurrence of false positive alarms. False positives occur when the ASA triggers alarms for benign activities. A large number of false positives can be a nightmare when analyzing and correlating the events generated. You can use the **ip audit signature** command to disable or exclude a signature from being used by the IP audit feature. In Example 13-5, signature number 1005 is disabled.

Example 13-5 *Disabling Specific Signatures*

```
Chicago(config)# ip audit signature 1005 disable
```

NOTE   Chapter 14 includes detailed step-by-step information on how to tune your AIP-SSM.

Example 13-6 shows all the valid signature ranges when using IP audit.

Example 13-6 *Valid Signature Ranges when Using IP Audit*

```
Chicago(config)# ip audit signature ?
  <1000-9999>  Valid signatures are in the following range:
               { 1000, 1006 }, { 1100, 1103 }, { 2000, 2012 }, { 2150, 2151 },
               { 2154, 2154 }, { 3040, 3042 }, { 3153, 3154 }, { 4050, 4052 },
               { 6050, 6053 }, { 6100, 6103 }, { 6150, 6155 }, { 6175, 6175 },
               { 6180, 6180 }, { 6190, 6190 }
```

NOTE   These built-in signatures are not upgradeable. You can obtain detailed information on IPS signatures at the Cisco website at http://www.cisco.com/go/ips.

Shunning

The AIP-SSM can automatically shun (block) a connection when it detects malicious activity. You can also manually shun a connection if you do not have an AIP-SSM installed in your system. However, this process requires manual intervention and can be very inefficient.

NOTE   Be careful when deploying automatic shunning. An attacker may spoof its source address and, consequently, cause automatic shunning to be very ineffective and dangerous.

You can use the **show conn** command to view the existing connections on your ASA. Example 13-7 shows the output of the **show conn** command.

Example 13-7 *Displaying Connection Information with the* **show conn** *Command*

```
Chicago# show conn
1 in use, 7 most used
TCP out 10.83.145.166:3598 in 192.168.1.12:445 idle 0:00:00 bytes 6295 flags UIOB
```

TIP   The output of the **show conn** command can be lengthy and difficult to read. To display only specific information, use the **include**, **grep**, or **exclude** operands. For example,
```
show conn | include 10.83.145.166
```

You can use the **shun** command to block connections from a specific source IP address. The following is the command syntax:

```
shun src_ip [dst_ip src_port dest_port [protocol]] [vlan vlan_id]
```

Example 13-8 demonstrates how to shun port 445 connections from 10.83.145.166 to 192.168.1.12.

Example 13-8 *Shunning Specific Traffic*

```
Chicago(config)# shun 10.83.145.166 192.168.1.12 2035 445
Shun 10.83.145.166 added in context: single_vf
Shun 10.83.145.166 successful
```

NOTE   Shunning configuration and settings do not time out. A user must manually disable shunning if required.

TIP   Shunning is dynamic in nature. Consequently, ACLs modified by shunning are not saved on NVRAM. The **show shun** command displays existing shuns. The **show shun statistics** command displays the number of packets dropped because of shunning.

Summary

This chapter covered how Cisco ASA integrates and enhances the firewall, IDS, and IPS features. A detailed introduction to the AIP-SSM IPS capabilities was provided. Legacy IDS/IPS features were also discussed. Cisco ASA has the ability to integrate all of these features while blending the use of pattern matching, stateful-pattern matching, protocol decodes, and heuristic-based signatures, making the security appliance a very robust security system.

This chapter covers the following topics:

- Cisco IPS software architecture
- Introduction to the CIPS 5.x command-line interface (CLI)
- User administration
- AIP-SSM maintenance
- Advanced features and configuration

Configuring and Troubleshooting Cisco IPS Software via CLI

The integration of Cisco Intrusion Prevention Software (IPS) into Cisco ASA enables you to effectively detect and react to security threats. In this chapter, you will learn the Cisco IPS software architecture, how to configure and monitor the Adaptive Inspection and Prevention Security Services Module (AIP-SSM), and several troubleshooting techniques.

Cisco IPS Software Architecture

The Cisco IPS 5.x software was built based on its predecessor, CIDS 4.x. The architecture is similar to the 4.x software, but with several enhancements. This section provides a complete overview of the CIPS 5.x architecture while highlighting some of these differences.

One of the major differences of CIPS 5.x is that it uses the Security Device Event Exchange (SDEE) protocol instead of the Remote Data Exchange Protocol (RDEP) used in versions 4.x. SDEE is a standardized IPS communication protocol developed by Cisco for the IDS Consortium at the International Computer Security Association (ICSA). Remote applications such as Adaptive Security Device Manager (ASDM), IPS Device Manager (IDM), Intrusion Prevention System Management Console (IPSMC) and Cisco Security Monitoring, Analysis and Response System (CS-MARS) can retrieve events from the sensor through this protocol.

NOTE   ASDM/IDM IPS configuration and troubleshooting is covered in Chapter 19, "Firewall Management Using ASDM."

Cisco IDS Event Viewer (IEV) does not support 5.x events; however, it can still accept 4.x events. SDEE is not backward compatible with RDEP.

Another difference of CIPS 5.x over 4.x is its ability to run IPS operations in inline mode.

The major components of CIPS 5.x software include the following:

- MainApp
- SensorApp

- Network Access Controller (NAC)
- AuthenticationApp
- cipsWebserver
- LogApp
- EventStore
- Transactional Services for Security Device Event Exchange (SDEE)
- CLI

Figure 14-1 illustrates the main components of CIPS 5.x in correlation with the AIP-SSM.

Figure 14-1 *CIPS 5.x Architecture Overview*

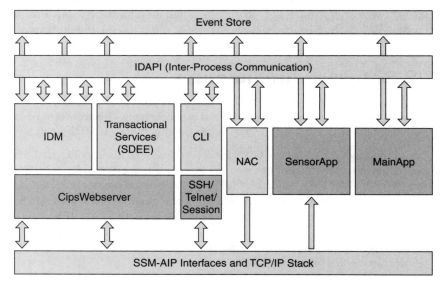

MainApp

MainApp is responsible for several critical tasks in the AIP-SSM (as well as all other platforms that support CIPS 5.x software). These tasks include:

- Initializing all CIPS components and applications
- Scheduling, downloading, and installing software updates
- Configuring communication parameters
- Managing the system clock
- Gathering system statistics and software version information
- Cleanly shutting down/restarting all CIPS services

MainApp is initialized by the CIPS operating system and starts the CIPS applications in the following sequence:

1 Reads and validates dynamic and static configurations.

2 Synchronizes dynamic configuration data to system files.

3 Creates EventStore and the Intrusion Detection Application Programming Interface (IDAPI) shared components.

4 Initializes status event subsystem.

5 Launches IPS applications as stated in the static configuration.

6 Waits until an initialization status event from each application is sent.

7 Generates an error event identifying all applications that did not start, if all status events are not received within 60 seconds.

8 Listens for control transaction requests and processes them accordingly.

MainApp controls the CIPS software installation and upgrades. It also controls network communication parameters such as:

- AIP-SSM host name
- IP addressing and default gateway configuration for the AIP-SSM command and control interface
- Network access control list

MainApp manages the system clock (whether NTP is configured or not) and collects system statistics.

SensorApp

SensorApp is the application that is responsible for the analysis of network traffic, examining it for any malicious content. The packets flow through it from the Gigabit Ethernet network interface on the AIP-SSM which is directly connected to the Cisco ASA's backplane.

If the Cisco ASA AIP-SSM configuration is set for promiscuous mode, the packets are discarded after processing by SensorApp. If configured for inline operation, the packets will either be forwarded back to the Cisco ASA or dropped according to the defined policy.

SensorApp has two modules crucial for the operation of the AIP-SSM or any other device running CIPS 5.x:

- Analysis Engine Configuration Module (Virtual Sensor)
- Alarm Channel Module (Virtual Alarm)

The Virtual Sensor is the Analysis Engine Configuration Module, which handles the AIP-SSM configuration. This module interprets the configuration and maps it into internal configuration objects. Figure 14-2 illustrates both of these modules.

Figure 14-2 *SensorApp Virtual Sensor and Virtual Alarm*

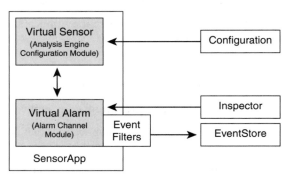

In CIPS 5.x, a new protocol is introduced called the Intrusion Detection Configuration (IDCONF) protocol. This framework provides clean, consistent, and accurate signature definitions. This replaces the old IDIOM framework in previous versions. It supports multiple layers of parameters to ensure that a signature is defined in terms that are understandable and valid for the inspection engines. The Virtual Alarm is the alarm channel module, which is responsible for processing all signature events generated by the traffic inspector engine. The primary function of the Alarm Channel Module is to generate alarms for each event as it is passed. Event or alarm filters may be configured and will be processed by the alarm channel module, as illustrated in Figure 14-2.

Network Access Controller

NAC is the application that is responsible for communicating with the Cisco ASA or any other supported device while shunning (blocking) connections if the AIP-SSM is configured in promiscuous mode.

NOTE   Do not confuse this application with the Cisco Network Admission Control industry-wide initiative sponsored by Cisco to enforce endpoint security policy compliance to mitigate damage from viruses and worms.

One of the functions of CIPS NAC is to forward shunning information to other IPS devices on the network to collectively control network access devices. IPS sensing devices that perform this operation are referred to as master blocking sensors.

AuthenticationApp

AuthenticationApp, as its name suggests, is the process that controls user authentication on the AIP-SSM or any other device running Cisco IPS 5.x software. Additionally, it administers all the user accounts, privileges, Secure Shell (SSH) keys, and digital certificates, while also controlling what authentication method is used.

AuthenticationApp controls authentication when the user connects via Telnet, SSH, a session through ASA, ASDM, IDM, or IDSMC. This is illustrated in Figure 14-3.

Figure 14-3 *AuthenticationApp Architecture*

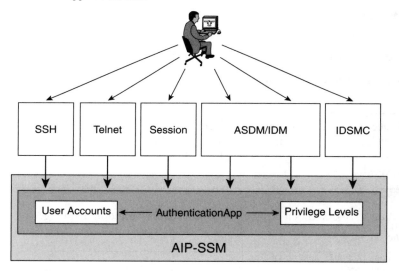

cipsWebserver

The CIPS web server (cipsWebserver) within AIP-SSM provides configuration support for IDM and provides support for SDEE transactions such as:

- Reporting security events
- Receiving IDCONF transactions
- Processing IP logs

ASDM is hosted and controlled by the Cisco ASA; however, it launches IDM, which uses SDEE to communicate with the AIP-SSM hosted by the CIPS web server. The CIPS web server supports HTTP 1.0 and 1.1 running Secure Sockets Layer (SSL)/Transport Layer Security (TLS).

LogApp

The AIP-SSM logs alert, error, status, and debug messages as well as IP logs. These messages and IP logs are accessible through the CLI and SDEE clients such as IDM, IDSMC, CiscoWorks Security Monitor, and CS-MARS. LogApp sends log messages with the following five levels of severity:

- Debug
- Timing
- Warning
- Error
- Fatal

These messages are written to the following file on AIP-SSM module:

/usr/cids/idsRoot/log/main.log.

NOTE	To access this file, you must be logged in with the service account. Instructions on how to create the service account are discussed later in this chapter, in the "User Administration" section. These messages are mostly used by Cisco TAC engineers for troubleshooting purposes.

Example 14-1 shows a sample of the information stored in main.log.

Example 14-1 *The main.log File*

```
-bash-2.05b$ more main.log
01Feb2005 20:44:49.643 0.001 cidwebserver[447] Cid/E errTransport WebSession::
    sessionTask(10) TLS connection exception: handshake incomplete.
01Feb2005 20:45:09.646 20.003 cidwebserver[4548] tls/W errWarning received
    fatal alert: certificate_unknown
```

EventStore

All IPS events are stored in the EventStore with a time stamp and a unique ascending identifier. Additionally, CIPS internal applications write log, status, and error events into the EventStore.

NOTE	IPS alerts are only written by the SensorApp application.

The EventStore is designed to store CIPS events in a circular fashion. In other words, when it reaches the configured size, the oldest events are overwritten by new events and log messages.

TransactionSource

SDEE and HTTP remote-control transactions are handled by an internal application called TransactionSource. It handles all TLS communications with external management servers and monitoring systems. TransactionSource performs basic authentication to remote management applications and monitoring systems. When an application attempts a remote-control transaction, IDAPI redirects the transaction to TransactionSource, as shown in Figure 14-4.

Figure 14-4   *TransactionSource Functionality*

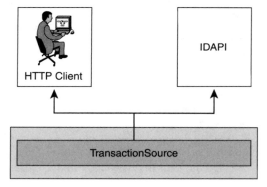

Introduction to the CIPS 5.x Command-Line Interface

The CIPS 5.x CLI provides a user interface for all direct connections to the AIP-SSM (e.g., Telnet, SSH, and session from the ASA). This section covers:

- How to log in to the AIP-SSM via the CLI
- CLI command modes
- Initial AIP-SSM configuration

Logging In to the AIP-SSM via the CLI

You can connect to the AIP-SSM CLI via the ASA backplane using the **session** command, or by initiating an SSH or Telnet connection via the external management Ethernet port.

NOTE	The Cisco ASA **session** command is covered in detail in Chapter 13, "Intrusion Prevention System Integration."

The default username is **cisco** and the default password is **cisco**. The user is forced to change his password after the first login. Example 14-2 shows the user **cisco** successfully logging in to the AIP-SSM CLI via the ASA backplane using the **session** command.

Example 14-2 *Logging In to the CLI*

```
Chicago# session 1
Opening command session with slot 1.
Connected to slot 1. Escape character sequence is 'CTRL-^X'.
login: cisco
Password: <password>
Last login: Tue Feb  1 12:53:12 from 127.0.1.1
***NOTICE***
This product contains cryptographic features and is subject to United States
and local country laws governing import, export, transfer and use. Delivery
of Cisco cryptographic products does not imply third-party authority to import,
export, distribute or use encryption. Importers, exporters, distributors and
users are responsible for compliance with U.S. and local country laws. By using
this product you agree to comply with applicable laws and regulations. If you
are unable to comply with U.S. and local laws, return this product immediately.
A summary of U.S. laws governing Cisco cryptographic products may be found at:
http://www.cisco.com/wwl/export/crypto/tool/stqrg.html
If you require further assistance please contact us by sending email to
export@cisco.com.
ChicagoSSM#
```

NOTE   There are four major user account roles that determine which operations a user is allowed to perform. They are covered later in this chapter under "User Administration."

CLI Command Modes

The CIPS 5.x CLI is similar to the Cisco ASA and IOS CLIs. It has a configuration command mode that is entered by invoking the **configure terminal** command. Example 14-3 demonstrates how to enter into global configuration mode.

Example 14-3 *Entering Configuration Mode*

```
ChicagoSSM# configure terminal
ChicagoSSM(config)#
```

The **(config)#** prompt is displayed after you invoke the **configure terminal** command.

Just like in Cisco IOS and ASA, you can display the help for a specific command by typing a question mark (**?**) after the command. You can also type a question mark to view the valid keywords that complete the command. There are certain commands that generate user interactive prompts. An example of this is the **setup** command, which is covered in the following section.

Initializing the AIP-SSM

Before the AIP-SSM can communicate with any management station and start analyzing data from the network, you must first configure basic settings using the **setup** command. The AIP-SSM will first display the current configuration and then generate user interactive prompts that will guide you to complete the initial settings.

NOTE   The default input is displayed inside brackets, [ ]. To accept the default input, press **Enter**.

Example 14-4 includes the output of the **setup** command.

Example 14-4 *Configuring Initial Settings with the* **setup** *Command*

```
ChicagoSSM# setup
     --- System Configuration Dialog ---
At any point you may enter a question mark '?' for help.
User ctrl-c to abort configuration dialog at any prompt.
Default settings are in square brackets '[]'.
Current Configuration:
service host
network-settings
host-ip 127.0.0.1
host-name sensor
telnet-option enabled
ftp-timeout 300
login-banner-text
exit
time-zone-settings
offset -420
standard-time-zone-name GMT-07:00
exit
summertime-option recurring
offset 60
summertime-zone-name PDT
start-summertime
month april
week-of-month first
day-of-week sunday
time-of-day 02:00:00
exit
end-summertime
month october
week-of-month last
day-of-week sunday
time-of-day 02:00:00
exit
exit
ntp-option disabled
exit
```

continues

Example 14-4 *Configuring Initial Settings with the* **setup** *Command (Continued)*

```
service web-server
port 443
exit
Current time: Thu Feb 23 08:05:26 2005
Setup Configuration last modified: Thu Jan 27 21:32:55 2005
Continue with configuration dialog?[yes]: yes
Enter host name[sensor]: ChicagoSSM
Enter IP interface[10.1.9.201/24,10.1.9.1]: 192.168.10.28/24,192.168.10.1
Enter telnet-server status[disabled]:enable
Enter web-server port[443]:
Modify current access list?[no]: yes
Current access list entries:
Delete:
Permit: 192.168.10.0/24
Modify system clock settings?[no]: yes
  Use NTP?[no]: yes
    NTP Key ID[]: 1
    NTP Key Value[]: cisco
    NTP Server IP Address[]:192.168.10.123    NTP Key ID[1]:
  Modify summer time settings?[no]:
  Modify system timezone?[no]:
Modify virtual sensor "vs0" configuration?[no]: yes
Current interface configuration
  Command control: GigabitEthernet0/0
  Unused:
    GigabitEthernet0/1
  Monitored:
    None
Add Monitored interfaces?[no]: yes
Interface[]:
```

Follow these steps after the AIP-SSM prompt asks you if you would like to continue with the configuration dialog:

Step 1   The configuration dialog asks you to enter the host name to be assigned to the AIP-SSM. The default host name is *sensor*. Enter the new host name (case sensitive) as follows:

```
Enter host name[sensor]: ChicagoSSM
```

Step 2   You are asked to enter the IP address and default gateway for the management interface of the AIP-SSM. The default IP address is 10.1.9.201 and the default gateway is 10.1.9.1. Enter the IP address and gateway configuration in the following format:

<ip address>/<mask-bits>,<gateway>

The IP address 192.168.10.28 with a 24-bit mask and gateway of 192.168.10.1 is entered in the following example:

```
Enter IP interface[10.1.9.201/24,10.1.9.1]: 192.168.10.28/
  24,192.168.10.1
```

Step 3   Telnet services are disabled by default. The AIP-SSM allows you to
enable Telnet services at this point:

```
Enter telnet-server status[disabled]:enable
```

Step 4   The default web server port is TCP port 443 (because it is the default for
most web servers that support SSL/TLS). The configuration dialog
allows you to change the port at this point:

```
Enter web-server port[443]:
```

The default port is selected in this example.

Step 5   The configuration dialog prompts you to modify the current access list.
Enter **yes** to add or delete hosts or networks that will be allowed to
communicate with the AIP-SSM.

```
Modify current access list?[no]: yes
Current access list entries:
Delete:
Permit: 192.168.10.0/24
```

The 192.168.10.0/24 network is added to the list in this example.

Step 6   After adding or deleting entries to your access list, the configuration
dialog prompts you to change the clock settings. In the following
example, NTP is enabled:

```
Modify system clock settings?[no]: yes
Use NTP?[no]: yes
    NTP Key ID[]: 1
    NTP Key Value[]: cisco
    NTP Server IP Address[]: 192.168.10.123
```

The NTP key ID is set to **1**, the key is **cisco**, and the NTP server address
is **192.168.10.123**.

Step 7   You can also modify daylight savings time settings. The default is
recurring, which automatically adjusts the time:

```
Modify summer time settings?[no]: yes
    Recurring, Date or Disable?[Recurring]:
    Start Month[april]:
    Start Week[first]:
    Start Day[sunday]:
    Start Time[02:00:00]:
    End Month[october]:
    End Week[last]:
    End Day[sunday]:
    End Time[02:00:00]:
    DST Zone[PDT]:
    Offset[60]:
```

Step 8   The configuration dialog asks you to specify the time zone to be
displayed when standard time is in effect:

```
Modify system timezone?[no]: yes
    Timezone[GMT-07:00]: GMT-05:00
    UTC Offset[-420]:
```

Step 9   The last step is to modify the monitored interface. In case of the AIP-
SSM, the only interface used for monitoring is the internal Gigabit
Ethernet interface:

```
Modify virtual sensor "vs0" configuration?[no]: yes
Current interface configuration
  Command control: GigabitEthernet0/0
  Unused:
    GigabitEthernet0/1
  Monitored:
    None
Add Monitored interfaces?[no]: yes
```

Step 10   The AIP-SSM displays a summary of the configuration entered:

```
The following configuration was entered.
service host
network-settings
host-ip 192.168.10.28/24,192.168.10.1
host-name ChicagoSSM
telnet-option enabled
access-list 192.168.10.0/24
ftp-timeout 300
no login-banner-text
exit
time-zone-settings
offset -420
standard-time-zone-name GMT-05:00
exit
summertime-option recurring
offset 60
summertime-zone-name PDT
start-summertime
month april
week-of-month first
day-of-week sunday
time-of-day 02:00:00
exit
end-summertime
month october
week-of-month last
```

```
day-of-week sunday
time-of-day 02:00:00
exit
exit
ntp-option enabled
exit
service web-server
port 443
exit
[0] Go to the command prompt without saving this config.
[1] Return back to the setup without saving this config.
[2] Save this configuration and exit setup.
Enter your selection[2]:
```

From the menu, you can select any of the available options:

— Go to the command prompt without saving the configuration

— Return back to the setup without saving the configuration

— Save the configuration and exit setup

Select option 2 if you are satisfied with the configuration and you want to save it in the system.

User Administration

Different types of users can be configured in the AIP-SSM with different roles associated to them. This section covers the AIP-SSM user administration.

User Account Roles and Levels

Each AIP-SSM user account has a role associated to it. There are a total of four roles that can be assigned to a specific account:

- Administrator
- Operator
- Viewer
- Service

Administrator Account

The administrator account has the highest privilege level. Users with this role are able to do the following:

- Add users
- Assign passwords

- Control all interfaces on the AIP-SSM
- Configure IP addressing
- Add and delete hosts allowed to connect to the AIP-SSM
- Tune signatures
- Perform all virtual sensor configurations
- Configure shunning

Operator Account

The operator account has the second highest privilege level. These users can view the configuration and statistics. They can also perform some administrative tasks such as modifying their own passwords, tuning signatures, and configuring shunning.

Viewer Account

Users with viewer privileges can view events and some configuration files. They can also change their own passwords.

IPS monitoring applications only require viewer access to perform their monitoring operations. However, if the application is used to perform administrative tasks, a higher privilege account is needed.

NOTE   The viewer account has the lowest of the privilege levels.

Service Account

The service account does not have direct access to the AIP-SSM CLI. It has access to a bash shell, which enables it to perform specific administrative tasks on the AIP-SSM. This account is not enabled by default.

NOTE   Only one service account can be configured in the AIP-SSM and any other device running CIPS software. The service account should be created only at the request of the Cisco Technical Assistance Center (TAC).

Adding and Deleting Users by Using the CLI

This section guides you on how to create and delete users on the AIP-SSM. It also shows you how to assign different privilege levels to the users depending on their role.

Creating Users

You can add users on the AIP-SSM by using the **username** command. The following is the command syntax:

```
username name [password password] [privilege privilege]
```

Example 14-5 demonstrates how to create the service account, called **service** with a password of **cisco12345**.

Example 14-5 *Creating the Service Account*

```
ChicagoSSM# configure terminal
ChicagoSSM(config)# username service password cisco12345 privilege service
ChicagoSSM(config)# exit
```

Example 14-6 demonstrates how two accounts are created and assigned operator and viewer roles, respectively.

Example 14-6 *Creating Other Accounts*

```
ChicagoSSM# configure terminal
ChicagoSSM(config)# username opuser password cisco12345 privilege operator
ChicagoSSM(config)# username viewuser password cisco12345 privilege viewer
```

A user called **opuser** is created and assigned operator role privileges, and a user called **viewuser** is created and assigned viewer privileges.

NOTE   Usernames must begin with an alphanumeric character and can be 1 to 64 characters in length. The minimum password length is 6 characters, and passwords can be up to 32 characters in length. All characters except spaces and ? are allowed to be used in passwords.

Deleting Users

To delete users in the AIP-SSM, use the **no username** *username* command. Example 14-7 demonstrates how the opuser is deleted from the AIP-SSM.

Example 14-7 *Deleting a User*

```
ChicagoSSM# configure terminal
ChicagoSSM(config)# no username opuser
```

Changing Passwords

You can change your own or other user passwords by using the **password** command. To change the password for another user, you must be logged in using an account with administrator privileges. Example 14-8 demonstrates how the AIP-SSM administrator changes the password for user **viewuser**.

Example 14-8 *Changing viewuser's Password*

```
ChicagoSSM# configure terminal
ChicagoSSM(config)# password viewuser
Enter New Login Password: ******
Re-enter New Login Password: ******
```

Example 14-9 demonstrates how you can change your own password by just invoking the **password** command from configuration mode.

Example 14-9 *Changing Your Own Password*

```
ChicagoSSM# configure terminal
ChicagoSSM(config)# password
Enter New Login Password: ******
Re-enter New Login Password: ******
```

AIP-SSM Maintenance

This section includes information on administrative maintenance tasks on the AIP-SSM. These tasks include the following:

- Adding trusted hosts to connect to the AIP-SSM
- Upgrading the CIPS software and signatures via the CLI
- Displaying software version and configuration information
- Backing up the AIP-SSM configuration
- Displaying and clearing events
- Displaying and clearing AIP-SSM statistics

Adding Trusted Hosts

In order for a device to be able to connect to the AIP-SSM for management and monitoring purposes, it needs to be added to the trusted host list. You can add trusted hosts that will be able to communicate with the AIP-SSM by following these steps:

Step 1 Enter configuration mode and invoke the **service host** command. You will be placed into host configuration mode.

```
ChicagoSSM# configure terminal
ChicagoSSM (config)# service host
ChicagoSSM (config-hos)#
```

Step 2 Invoke the **network-settings** command to start adding entries to the ACL for hosts or networks allowed to connect to the AIP-SSM:

```
ChicagoSSM (config-hos)# network-settings
ChicagoSSM (config-hos-net)# access-list 192.168.10.123/32
```

```
ChicagoSSM (config-hos-net)# exit
ChicagoSSM (config-hos)# exit
Apply Changes:?[yes]: yes
ChicagoSSM (config)#
```

In this example, a host with IP address 192.168.10.123 is added to the ACL.

Once you exit from both configuration modes, the AIP-SSM will prompt you to apply the changes to the configuration. Enter **yes** if the configuration parameters are correct.

SSH Known Host List

In order for any SSH client or any SSH server to communicate with the AIP-SSM, you must first add it into the SSH known host list. Use the **ssh host-key** command to add a host to the AIP-SSM SSH known host list. Example 14-10 shows how a host with IP address 192.168.10.33 is added to the Chicago SSM.

Example 14-10 *Adding an Entry to the SSH Known Host List*

```
ChicagoSSM# configure terminal
ChicagoSSM(config)# ssh host-key 192.168.10.33
Would you like to add this to the known hosts table for this
host?[yes] yes
```

The AIP-SSM asks the administrator to confirm the addition of the SSH host entry. Type **yes** or press **Enter** to confirm.

TLS Known Host List

The CIPS software allows you to restrict what systems are able to establish a TLS/SSL session to the AIP-SSM. To add a TLS trusted host to the AIP-SSM, use the **tls trusted-host** command. Example 14-11 demonstrates how to add a TLS host configured with IP address 192.168.10.34. The AIP-SSM does an SSL/TLS exchange with the specified host to obtain its SSL/TLS certificate.

Example 14-11 *Adding a TLS Known Host*

```
ChicagoSSM# configure terminal
ChicagoSSM(config)# tls trusted-host ip-address 192.168.10.34
```

Upgrading the CIPS Software and Signatures via the CLI

You can apply the CIPS software service packs and signature updates by using the CLI. The following protocols are supported:

- File Transfer Protocol (FTP)
- Hypertext Transfer Protocol (HTTP)

- Hypertext Transfer Protocol Secure (HTTPS)
- Secure Copy Protocol (SCP)

NOTE   If HTTPS/SSL is used, a trusted TLS host entry must be added for the server from which you will retrieve the service pack or signature update file.

You can perform one-time upgrades or schedule recurring automatic upgrades.

One-Time Upgrades

The **upgrade** command is used to apply service packs and signature updates to the AIP-SSM. The following is the command syntax:

```
upgrade source-url
```

The *source-url* is the location where the AIP-SSM retrieves the upgrade file.

The following is the URL syntax if FTP is used:

> **ftp:**[[//username:*password@]location]/relativeDirectory/filename*
> or
> **ftp:***[[//username@]location]//absoluteDirectory/filename*

The syntax for HTTP is

> **http:***[[//username@]location]/directory]/filename*

The syntax for HTTPS is

> **https:**[[//username@]location]/directory]/filename

The syntax for SCP is

> **scp:***[[//username@]location]/relativeDirectory]/filename*
> or
> **scp:**[[//username@]location]/absoluteDirectory]/filename

---

TIP   If you just enter the **upgrade** command followed by a protocol prefix (**ftp:**, **http:**, **https:**, or **scp:**), the CLI prompts you for all the required information.

In Example 14-12, a signature update is retrieved from the HTTP server that was previously entered into the TLS trusted list (192.168.10.34). A user called httpsuser is being used for authentication purposes. After invoking the command, the AIP-SSM prompts you to enter the password for the HTTPS server user.

Example 14-12 *Applying Signature Updates*

```
ChicagoSSM# configure terminal
ChicagoSSM(config)# upgrade https://httpsuser@192.168.10.34/upgrade/sigupdate.pkg
Enter password: *****
Re-enter password: *****
```

Scheduled Upgrades

As a best practice, you may want to configure automatic service pack upgrades or signature updates. This eases administration and provides a mechanism to make sure that your AIP-SSM is running updated signatures.

NOTE   Cisco offers a service where customers can subscribe to obtain IPS signatures shortly after security threats and vulnerabilities are announced. For more information, visit http://www.cisco.com/go/ipsalert/.

In the example illustrated in Figure 14-5, the goal is to configure the AIP-SSM module in the Chicago ASA appliance to automatically retrieve signature updates every Monday, Wednesday, and Friday at 1:00 a.m.

Figure 14-5 *Scheduled Upgrades*

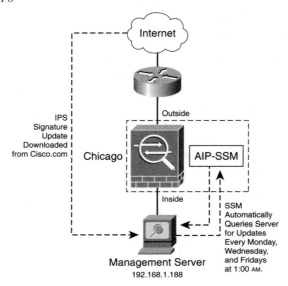

The following steps are completed on each device to achieve this goal:

Step 1 The IPS signature update from Cisco.com is downloaded and saved on the management server. To enable automatic upgrades and configure auto-upgrade settings go into service host configuration mode and enable the auto-upgrade option as follows:

```
ChicagoSSM(config)# service host
ChicagoSSM(config-hos)# auto-upgrade-option enabled
```

Step 2 Specify the IP address of the server from which the AIP-SSM will retrieve the update file. In this case, the server is 192.168.1.188:

```
ChicagoSSM(config-hos-ena)# ip-address 192.168.10.188
```

Step 3 Specify the file copy protocol used to download files from the server. SCP is used in this example:

```
ChicagoSSM(config-hos-ena)# file-copy-protocol scp
```

Step 4 Define the username for authentication on the 192.168.10.188 server. The user in this example is called scpuser:

```
ChicagoSSM(config-hos-ena)# user-name scpuser
```

Step 5 Enter the user password for authentication on the 192.168.10.188 server with the **password** command. The AIP-SSM prompts you to enter and confirm the password:

```
ChicagoSSM(config-hos-ena)# password
Enter password[]: *****
Re-enter password: *****
```

Step 6 Specify the directory where upgrade files are located on the server. A leading forward slash (/) indicates an absolute path. The directory in this example is called **updates** and the update file is called sigupdatefile.pkg:

```
ChicagoSSM(config-hos-ena)# directory/updates/sigupdatefile.pkg
```

Step 7 You can configure two types of scheduled updates:

— **Calendar based**—Specify what days and times of the week the AIP-SSM will attempt the updates.

— **Periodic**—Configure the time that the first automatic upgrade should occur, and how long the AIP-SSM will wait between automatic upgrades.

In this example, the AIP-SSM will automatically retrieve signature updates every Monday, Wednesday, and Friday at 1:00 a.m.:

```
ChicagoSSM(config-hos-ena)# schedule-option calendar-schedule
ChicagoSSM (config-hos-ena-cal)# times-of-day 01:00:00
ChicagoSSM (config-hos-ena-cal)# days-of-week Monday
ChicagoSSM (config-hos-ena-cal)# days-of-week Wednesday
```

```
ChicagoSSM (config-hos-ena-cal)# days-of-week Friday
ChicagoSSM (config-hos-ena-cal)# exit
```

Step 8   Use the **show settings** command to view and confirm all the settings entered:

```
ChicagoSSM(config-hos-ena)# show settings
   enabled
   -----------------------------------------------
      schedule-option
      -----------------------------------------------
         calendar-schedule
         -----------------------------------------------
            times-of-day (min: 1, max: 24, current: 1)
            -----------------------------------------------
               time: 01:00:00
               -----------------------------------------------
            -----------------------------------------------
            days-of-week (min: 1, max: 7, current: 3)
            -----------------------------------------------
               day: monday
               -----------------------------------------------
               day: wednesday
               -----------------------------------------------
               day: friday
               -----------------------------------------------
            -----------------------------------------------
         -----------------------------------------------
      -----------------------------------------------
      ip-address: 192.168.10.188
      directory: /updates/sigupdatefile.pkg
      user-name: scpuser
      password: <hidden>
      file-copy-protocol: scp default: scp
   -----------------------------------------------
```

Step 9   Exit configuration mode. You will be asked to apply the changes. Enter **yes** if the information is correct.

```
ChicagoSSM(config-hos-ena)# exit
ChicagoSSM(config-hos)# exit
Apply Changes:?[yes]: yes
```

Displaying Software Version and Configuration Information

You can use the **show version** command to display the version of the CIPS software, signature packages, and IPS processes running on the AIP-SSM. Example 14-13 shows the output of the **show version** command at the ChicagoSSM.

Example 14-13 *Output of AIP-SSM* **show version** *Command*

```
ChicagoSSM# show version
Application Partition:
Cisco Intrusion Prevention System, Version 5.0(1)S149.0
OS Version 2.4.26-IDS-smp-bigphys
Platform: ASA-SSM-20
Serial Number: 1234567890
Trial license, expires: 21-Feb-2005 UTC
Sensor up-time is 12 days.
Using 501858304 out of 1984704512 bytes of available memory (25% usage)
system is using 17.3M out of 29.0M bytes of available disk space (59% usage)
application-data is using 49.1M out of 166.6M bytes of available disk space (31%
usage)
boot is using 34.9M out of 68.5M bytes of available disk space (54% usage)
MainApp         2005_Jan_05_11.54   (Release)   2005-01-05T12:06:57-0600   Running
AnalysisEngine  2005_Jan_05_11.54   (Release)   2005-01-05T12:06:57-0600   Running
CLI             2005_Jan_05_11.54   (Release)   2005-01-05T12:06:57-0600
Upgrade History:
  IDS-K9-maj-5.0.1.S141.pkg    11:00:00 UTC Sat Dec 18 2004
Recovery Partition Version 1.1 - 5.0(1)S149.0
```

The first shaded line in Example 14-13 shows the CIPS software version running on the AIP-SSM. The second shaded line shows that the AIP-SSM has been up for 12 days. The third shaded line shows information about previous upgrades and updates to this AIP-SSM. Other information such as disk and memory utilization is also displayed.

You can use the **show configuration** command to display the current configuration on the AIP-SSM, as shown in Example 14-14.

Example 14-14 *Output of AIP-SSM* **show configuration** *Command*

```
ChicagoSSM# show configuration
! -----------------------------
! Version 5.0(1)
! Current configuration last modified Tue Feb 08 15:54:43 2005
! -----------------------------
service analysis-engine
exit
! -----------------------------
service authentication
exit
! -----------------------------
service event-action-rules rules0
exit
! -----------------------------
service host
network-settings
host-ip 172.23.62.92/24,172.23.62.1
host-name ChicagoSSM
telnet-option enabled
access-list 192.168.10.123/32
exit
```

Example 14-14 *Output of AIP-SSM* **show configuration** *Command (Continued)*

```
time-zone-settings
offset -420
standard-time-zone-name GMT-07:00
exit
summertime-option recurring
summertime-zone-name PDT
exit
auto-upgrade-option enabled
schedule-option calendar-schedule
times-of-day 01:00:00
days-of-week monday
days-of-week wednesday
days-of-week friday
exit
ip-address 192.168.10.188
directory /updates/sigupdatefile.pkg
user-name scpuser
password cisco
file-copy-protocol scp
exit
exit
! ----------------------------
service interface
exit
! ----------------------------
service logger
exit
! ----------------------------
service network-access
general
never-block-hosts 10.0.0.1
exit
user-profiles a
exit
exit
! ----------------------------
service notification
snmp-agent-port 165
exit
! ----------------------------
service signature-definition sig0
exit
! ----------------------------
service ssh-known-hosts
exit
! ----------------------------
service trusted-certificates
exit
! ----------------------------
service web-server
enable-tls true
port 443
exit
```

Backing Up Your Configuration

It is recommended that you back up your configuration on a regular basis. You can back up your configuration to the local Flash on the AIP-SSM or to a remote server.

Use the **copy current-config backup-config** command to make a backup of the current configuration to a file (called backup-config) locally stored on the AIP-SSM. You can merge the backup configuration file with the current configuration file or overwrite the current configuration file with the backup configuration file. In Example 14-15, the AIP-SSM merges the backup configuration into the current configuration.

Example 14-15 *Merging the Backup Configuration*

```
ChicagoSSM# copy backup-config current-config
```

In Example 14-16, the AIP-SSM overwrites the backup configuration file into the current configuration file.

Example 14-16 *Overwriting the Backup Configuration into Current AIP-SSM Configuration*

```
ChicagoSSM# copy /erase backup-config current-config
```

As a best practice, you should back up your configuration file to an external server. In the example illustrated in Figure 14-6, SecureMe's Chicago AIP-SSM copies a backup of its configuration file to FTP server 192.168.10.159.

Figure 14-6 *Configuration Backup*

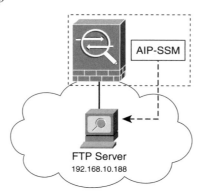

Example 14-17 shows the command entered on the AIP-SSM.

Example 14-17 *Backing Up the Configuration to an FTP Server*

```
ChicagoSSM# copy current-config ftp://192.168.10.159
User: ftpuser
File name: ChicagoSSM_Config
Password: ********
```

The configuration is successfully copied to a file named **ChicagoSSM_Config** on the FTP server **192.168.10.159**. The AIP-SSM prompts the administrator to enter the FTP user, file name, and password.

Displaying and Clearing Events

The **show events** command enables you to view the events stored in the AIP-SSM's local event log. After invoking this command, all the events are displayed as a live feed (to exit, press **Ctrl-C**). Example 14-18 lists all the available options for the **show events** command.

Example 14-18 show events *Command Options*

```
ChicagoSSM#  show events ?
<cr>
alert          Display local system alerts.
error          Display error events.
hh:mm[:ss]     Display start time.
log            Display log events.
nac            Display NAC shun events.
past           Display events starting in the past specified time.
status         Display status events.
¦              Output modifiers.
```

In Example 14-19, the AIP-SSM displays past events since 8:00 a.m.

Example 14-19 *Displaying Past Events*

```
ChicagoSSM# show events past 08:00:00
evStatus: eventId=1104988000052754141 vendor=Cisco
  originator:
    hostId: ChicagoSSM
    appName: cidwebserver
    appInstanceId: 276
  time: 2005/02/09 18:54:56 2005/02/09 11:54:56 GMT-09:00
  controlTransaction: command=getEventServerStatistics successful=true
    description: Control transaction response.
    requestor:
      user: cisco
      application:
        hostId: 127.0.1.1
        appName: -cidcli
        appInstanceId: 13200
evStatus: eventId=1104988000052754142 vendor=Cisco
  originator:
    hostId: ChicagoSSM
    appName: mainApp
    appInstanceId: 276
  time: 2005/02/09 18:55:06 2005/02/09 11:55:06 GMT-07:00
  controlTransaction: command=getEventStoreStatistics successful=true
    description: Control transaction response.
```

continues

Example 14-19 *Displaying Past Events (Continued)*

```
requestor:
  user: cisco
  application:
    hostId: 127.0.1.1
    appName: -cidcli
    appInstanceId: 13200
```

You can clear events stored locally in the AIP-SSM by using the **clear events** command, as demonstrated in Example 14-20.

Example 14-20 *Clearing Events*

```
ChicagoSSM# clear events
Warning: Executing this command will remove all events currently stored in the event
store.
Continue with clear? []: yes
```

The AIP-SSM displays a warning message asking you to confirm the removal of all the events stored on the system, because they will be lost if they have not been retrieved by a management or monitoring device.

Displaying and Clearing Statistics

The CLI enables you to collect statistics about different CIPS services, components, and applications. The **show statistics** command is used to display such information. Example 14-21 shows the **show statistics** command options.

Example 14-21 **show statistics** *Command Options*

```
ChicagoSSM# show statistics ?
analysis-engine       Display analysis engine statistics.
authentication        Display authentication statistics.
denied-attackers      Display denied attacker statistics.
event-server          Display event server statistics.
event-store           Display event store statistics.
host                  Display host statistics.
logger                Display logger statistics.
network-access        Display network access controller statistics.
notification          Display notification statistics.
sdee-server           Display SDEE server statistics.
transaction-server    Display transaction server statistics.
transaction-source    Display transaction source statistics.
virtual-sensor        Display virtual sensor statistics.
web-server            Display web werver statistics.
```

The **show statistics analysis-engine** command displays traffic statistics and health information about the AIP-SSM analysis engine. Example 14-22 includes the output of this command.

Example 14-22 show statistics analysis-engine *Command Output*

```
ChicagoSSM# show statistics analysis-engine
Analysis Engine Statistics
   Number of seconds since service started = 1665921
   Measure of the level of current resource utilization = 0
   Measure of the level of maximum resource utilization = 0
   The rate of TCP connections tracked per second = 0
   The rate of packets per second = 0
   The rate of bytes per second = 0
   Receiver Statistics
      Total number of packets processed since reset = 0
      Total number of IP packets processed since reset = 0
   Transmitter Statistics
      Total number of packets transmitted = 0
      Total number of packets denied = 0
      Total number of packets reset = 0
   Fragment Reassembly Unit Statistics
      Number of fragments currently in FRU = 0
      Number of datagrams currently in FRU = 0
   TCP Stream Reassembly Unit Statistics
      TCP streams currently in the embryonic state = 0
      TCP streams currently in the established state = 0
      TCP streams currently in the closing state = 0
      TCP streams currently in the system = 0
      TCP Packets currently queued for reassembly = 0
   The Signature Database Statistics.
      Total nodes active = 0
      TCP nodes keyed on both IP addresses and both ports = 0
      UDP nodes keyed on both IP addresses and both ports = 0
      IP nodes keyed on both IP addresses = 0
   Statistics for Signature Events
      Number of SigEvents since reset = 0
   Statistics for Actions executed on a SigEvent
      Number of Alerts written to the IdsEventStore = 0
```

You can use the **show statistics authentication** command to display statistics on failed and total authentication attempts to the AIP-SSM module. Example 14-23 shows the output of this command.

Example 14-23 show statistics authentication *Command Output*

```
ChicagoSSM# show statistics authentication
General
   totalAuthenticationAttempts = 144
   failedAuthenticationAttempts = 9
```

In Example 14-23, there were 9 failed authentication attempts out of 144 total attempts.

Example 14-24 includes the output of the **show statistics event-server** command. This command is used to only display the number of open and blocked connections o the AIP-SSM from event management stations.

Example 14-24 show statistics event-server *Command Output*

```
ChicagoSSM# show statistics event-server
General
   openSubscriptions = 10
   blockedSubscriptions = 0
Subscriptions
```

The **show statistics event-store** command gives you more useful information. It displays detailed information about the event store. Example 14-25 includes the output of this command.

Example 14-25 show statistics event-store *Command Output*

```
ChicagoSSM# show statistics event-store
Event store statistics
   General information about the event store
      The current number of open subscriptions = 10
      The number of events lost by subscriptions and queries = 0
      The number of queries issued = 0
      The number of times the event store circular buffer has wrapped = 0
   Number of events of each type currently stored
      Debug events = 0
      Status events = 59
      Log transaction events = 0
      Shun request events = 0
      Error events, warning = 1
      Error events, error = 8
      Error events, fatal = 0
      Alert events, informational = 2
      Alert events, low = 0
      Alert events, medium = 0
      Alert events, high = 0
```

Another command that is very useful for troubleshooting is the **show statistics host** command. It includes network and link statistics, health of the AIP-SSM module (i.e., CPU and memory utilization), and other administrative items such as NTP and auto-update statistics. Example 14-26 includes the output of this command.

Example 14-26 show statistics host *Command Output*

```
ChicagoSSM# show statistics host
General Statistics
   Last Change To Host Config (UTC) = 03:00:39  Tue Feb 15 2005
   Command Control Port Device = GigabitEthernet0/0
Network Statistics
   ge0_0     Link encap:Ethernet  HWaddr 00:0B:FC:F8:01:2C
             inet addr:172.23.62.92  Bcast:172.23.62.255  Mask:255.255.255.0
             UP BROADCAST RUNNING MULTICAST  MTU:1500  Metric:1
             RX packets:3758776 errors:0 dropped:0 overruns:0 frame:0
             TX packets:272436 errors:0 dropped:0 overruns:0 carrier:0
             collisions:0 txqueuelen:1000
```

Example 14-26 **show statistics host** *Command Output (Continued)*

```
                RX bytes:471408183 (449.5 MiB)   TX bytes:183240697 (174.7 MiB)
                Base address:0xbc00 Memory:f8200000-f8220000
NTP Statistics
   status = Not applicable
Memory Usage
   usedBytes = 500649984
   freeBytes = 1484054528
   totalBytes = 1984704512
Swap Usage
   Used Bytes = 0
   Free Bytes = 0
   Total Bytes = 0
Summertime Statistics
   start = 03:00:00 PDT Sun Apr 03 2005
   end = 01:00:00 GMT-08:00 Sun Oct 30 2005
CPU Statistics
   Usage over last 5 seconds = 0
   Usage over last minute = 0
   Usage over last 5 minutes = 0
Memory Statistics
   Memory usage (bytes) = 500559872
   Memory free (bytes) = 1484144640
Auto Update Statistics
   lastDirectoryReadAttempt = 01:03:09 GMT-08:00 Mon Feb 14 2005
     Read directory: scp://scpuser@192.168.10.188//updates/sigupdatefile.pkg/
   Error: Failed attempt to get directory listing from remote auto update server:
     ssh: connect to host 192.168.10.188 port 22: Connection timed out
   lastDownloadAttempt = N/A
   lastInstallAttempt = N/A
   nextAttempt = 01:00:00 GMT-08:00 Wed Feb 16 2005
```

In the shaded lines in Example 14-26, you can see that the AIP-SSM attempted to connect to the server with IP address 192.168.10.188 over SSH (TCP port 22) without success. The connection timed out because of network connectivity problems.

To display IP logger statistics, use the **show statistics logger** command. The output of this command is included in Example 14-27.

Example 14-27 **show statistics logger** *Command Output*

```
ChicagoSSM#  show statistics logger
The number of Log interprocessor FIFO overruns = 0
The number of syslog messages received = 331
The number of <evError> events written to the event store by severity
   Fatal Severity = 0
   Error Severity = 78
   Warning Severity = 358
   TOTAL = 436
```

continues

Example 14-27 **show statistics logger** *Command Output (Continued)*

```
The number of log messages written to the message log by severity
    Fatal Severity = 0
    Error Severity = 78
    Warning Severity = 27
    Timing Severity = 0
    Debug Severity = 0
    Unknown Severity = 62
    TOTAL = 167
```

IP logging is covered in detail in the following section.

Advanced Features and Configuration

This section covers advanced configuration topics and features on the AIP-SSM CIPS software. These topics include the following:

- IPS tuning
- Custom signatures
- IP logging
- Shunning

IPS Tuning

IPS devices (such as the AIP-SSM) can be configured to generate alarms when traffic matches any available and enabled signature. This can cause the number of false alarms to increase dramatically and diminish the value of the IPS device logs. To avoid these consequences, you must tune your IPS devices, including the AIP-SSM. As a result, real intrusions are quickly identified and addressed, saving you time, resources, and the high costs of recovering from a security threat.

Tuning is the process by which you configure the AIP-SSM appropriately to decrease the number of false positives and false negatives. Figure 14-7 shows the guidelines to be followed when deploying and tuning IPS devices.

NOTE   The process outlined in Figure 14-7 is based on the guidelines and recommendations of the Cisco SAFE architecture.

Figure 14-7 *IPS Deployment and Tuning Process*

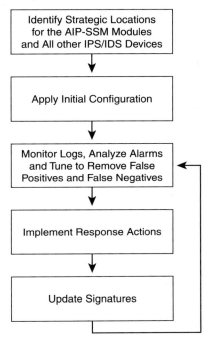

The following are the IPS deployment and tuning steps outlined in Figure 14-7:

Step 1   Identify strategic locations for all IPS devices and identify how they will be configured. For example, you should take into consideration performance, scalability, and what traffic you are trying to monitor. The Cisco SAFE blueprint recommends that you place IPS devices behind firewalls and any traffic-filtering devices. Traffic is filtered and only traffic destined for the internal devices will be processed by the IDS/IPS device. This reduces the device workload and increases performance. This can be easily accomplished with Cisco ASA and AIP-SSM module.

Step 2   Apply the initial configuration, as covered earlier in this chapter in the section "Initializing the AIP-SSM."

Step 3   Monitor and analyze the IPS logs and identify what alarms are being triggered due to malicious activity versus normal network activity. Disable alarms that are creating false positives, as discussed later in this section.

The initial monitoring period can last several days to generate sufficient logs and create a baseline of network activity.

You can also deploy a threat-analysis system to help validate the alarms' significance, impact, and appropriate response. Cisco Threat Response (CTR) and Cisco MARS provide an automated, real-time analysis of IPS alarms to eliminate false positives.

Step 4 Implement the most adequate response actions, such as TCP resets, drop, shunning, and IP logging.

Step 5 Continuously update the IPS signatures. Automatic signature updates are recommended for ease of management and scalability.

Disabling and Retiring IPS Signatures

You can change the status of a signature by using the **status** subcommand in signature definition submode. With the use of this command, you can disable or retire a specific signature.

If a signature is just disabled, it will still be processed by the signature engine and configuration list, but will not generate any logs. The following steps demonstrate how to disable a specific signature on the AIP-SSM:

Step 1 Log in to the CLI and enter into signature configuration submode:

```
ChicagoSSM# configure terminal
ChicagoSSM(config)# service signature-definition sig0
```

Step 2 Select the signature to be disabled:

```
ChicagoSSM(config-sig)# signatures 12345 0
```

Signature 12345 is selected in this example.

Step 3 Change the status of the selected signature:

```
ChicagoSSM(config-sig-sig)# status
ChicagoSSM(config-sig-sig-sta)# enabled false
```

Step 4 You can verify the settings by invoking the **show settings** command:

```
ChicagoSSM(config-sig-sig-sta)# show settings
   status
   -----------------------------------------------
      enabled: false default: false
      retired: false <defaulted>
   -----------------------------------------------
```

Step 5 Exit signature configuration submode and apply the changes to the configuration:

```
ChicagoSSM(config-sig-sig-sta)# exit
ChicagoSSM(config-sig-sig)# exit
ChicagoSSM(config-sig)# exit
Apply Changes:?[yes]:yes
```

When a signature is retired, it is removed from the engine but remains in the signature configuration list. This signature can later be activated. However, when you reactivate a retired signature, the AIP-SSM needs to rebuild the signature list for that engine, which could delay signature processing. This process could take several minutes.

The following steps demonstrate how to retire a specific signature on the AIP-SSM:

Step 1   Log in to the CLI and enter into signature definition submode:

```
ChicagoSSM# configure terminal
ChicagoSSM(config)# service signature-definition sig0
```

Step 2   Select the signature to be retired:

```
ChicagoSSM(config-sig)# signatures 23456 0
```

Signature 23456 is selected in this example.

Step 3   Change the status of the selected signature and retire the signature:

```
ChicagoSSM(config-sig-sig)# status
ChicagoSSM(config-sig-sig-sta)# retired true
```

Step 4   You can verify the settings by invoking the **show settings** command:

```
ChicagoSSM(config-sig-sig-sta)# show settings
   status
   -----------------------------------------------
      enabled: false default: false
      retired: true default: false
   -----------------------------------------------
```

Step 5   Exit signature configuration submode and apply the changes to the configuration:

```
ChicagoSSM(config-sig-sig-sta)# exit
ChicagoSSM(config-sig-sig)# exit
ChicagoSSM(config-sig)# exit
Apply Changes:?[yes]:yes
```

Custom Signatures

The capability to create custom signatures provides you with more flexibility in identifying security threats and network misconduct in a very effective fashion. To create custom signatures, you must know what exactly you want to detect in your network. This section demonstrates how to create a TCP custom signature.

Figure 14-8 illustrates our first example.

Figure 14-8 *CP Custom Signature*

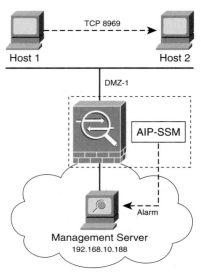

In this example, the security administrator knows that a new vulnerability exists whereby a machine can compromise other hosts and install malicious software while creating a TCP connection on port 8969. Unfortunately, this port is used by other critical applications in the network. The idea is to create a custom signature to detect this behavior, generate an alarm, and report it to a management station from hosts that are not supposed to send any traffic on TCP port 8969. In Figure 14-8, a custom signature on the AIP-SSM will trigger an alarm if Host 1 attempts to establish a connection to Host 2 over TCP port 8969. The following steps are followed to accomplish this task:

Step 1   Select the signature engine and signature identifier. Custom signature identifier values are in the range of 60000 to 65000. Log in with a user that has administrator privileges and enter into signature definition submode:

```
ChicagoSSM# configure terminal
ChicagoSSM(config)# service signature-definition sig0
ChicagoSSM(config-sig)# signatures 60088 0
```

The signature ID for the new custom signature is 60088. The subsignature ID is 0 because we will have only one signature ID for this example.

Step 2   Enter into signature description submode and define a name for the new signature:

```
ChicagoSSM(config-sig-sig)# sig-description
ChicagoSSM(config-sig-sig-sig)# sig-name TCP port 8969 Custom Signature
ChicagoSSM(config-sig-sig-sig)# exit
```

The new signature name is TCP port 8969 Custom Signature.

Step 3   Define the service port under the **string-tcp** engine configuration, as well as the direction of the connection, as follows:

```
ChicagoSSM(config-sig-sig)# engine string-tcp
ChicagoSSM(config-sig-sig-str)# service-ports 8969
ChicagoSSM(config-sig-sig-str)# direction to-service
```

The direction is configured with the **to-service option**. By selecting this option the AIP-SSM will inspect connections from all clients to the server listening on port 8969.

Step 4   Enter the regular expression (regex) string to search for in the TCP packet:

```
ChicagoSSM(config-sig-sig-str)# regex-string malwareconnect
ChicagoSSM(config-sig-sig-str)# exit
```

In this case, there is a known string that the offending host sends to its victim (malwareconnect). Once this is detected, the AIP-SSM will generate an alarm and alert the administrator.

Step 5   To verify the settings, enter the **show settings** command under the signature definition submode for the new custom signature (60088):

```
ChicagoSSM(config-sig-sig)# show settings
   sig-id: 60088
   subsig-id: 0
   -----------------------------------------------
      sig-description
      -----------------------------------------------
         sig-name: TCP port 8969 Custom Signature default: My Sig
         sig-string-info: My Sig Info <defaulted>
         sig-comment: Sig Comment <defaulted>
         alert-traits: 0 <defaulted>
         release: custom <defaulted>
      -----------------------------------------------
      sig-fidelity-rating: 75 <defaulted>
      promisc-delta: 0 <defaulted>
      alert-severity: medium <defaulted>
      status
      -----------------------------------------------
         enabled: true <defaulted>
         retired: false <defaulted>
         obsoletes (min: 0, max: 999999999, current: 0)
         -----------------------------------------------
      -----------------------------------------------
```

```
engine
- - - - - - - - - - - - - - - - - - - - - - - - - - - - - - - - - - - - - - - - - -
  string-tcp
  - - - - - - - - - - - - - - - - - - - - - - - - - - - - - - - - - - - - - - - - -
      event-action: produce-alert <defaulted>
      swap-attacker-victim: false <defaulted>
      specify-exact-match-offset
      - - - - - - - - - - - - - - - - - - - - - - - - - - - - - - - - - - - - - - -
          no
          - - - - - - - - - - - - - - - - - - - - - - - - - - - - - - - - - - - - -
              specify-min-match-offset
              - - - - - - - - - - - - - - - - - - - - - - - - - - - - - - - - - - -
                  no
                  - - - - - - - - - - - - - - - - - - - - - - - - - - - - - - - - -
              - - - - - - - - - - - - - - - - - - - - - - - - - - - - - - - - - - -
              specify-max-match-offset
              - - - - - - - - - - - - - - - - - - - - - - - - - - - - - - - - - - -
                  no
                  - - - - - - - - - - - - - - - - - - - - - - - - - - - - - - - - -
          - - - - - - - - - - - - - - - - - - - - - - - - - - - - - - - - - - - - -
      direction: to-service default: to-service
      service-ports: 8969
      regex-string: malwareconnect
      specify-min-match-length
      - - - - - - - - - - - - - - - - - - - - - - - - - - - - - - - - - - - - - - -
          no
          - - - - - - - - - - - - - - - - - - - - - - - - - - - - - - - - - - - - -
      - - - - - - - - - - - - - - - - - - - - - - - - - - - - - - - - - - - - - - -
      strip-telnet-options: false <defaulted>
      - - - - - - - - - - - - - - - - - - - - - - - - - - - - - - - - - - - - - - -
  - - - - - - - - - - - - - - - - - - - - - - - - - - - - - - - - - - - - - - - - -
event-counter
- - - - - - - - - - - - - - - - - - - - - - - - - - - - - - - - - - - - - - - - - -
    event-count: 1 <defaulted>
    event-count-key: Axxx <defaulted>
    specify-alert-interval
    - - - - - - - - - - - - - - - - - - - - - - - - - - - - - - - - - - - - - - - -
        no
        - - - - - - - - - - - - - - - - - - - - - - - - - - - - - - - - - - - - - -
    - - - - - - - - - - - - - - - - - - - - - - - - - - - - - - - - - - - - - - - -
alert-frequency
- - - - - - - - - - - - - - - - - - - - - - - - - - - - - - - - - - - - - - - - - -
    summary-mode
    - - - - - - - - - - - - - - - - - - - - - - - - - - - - - - - - - - - - - - - -
        summarize
        - - - - - - - - - - - - - - - - - - - - - - - - - - - - - - - - - - - - - -
```

```
                    summary-interval: 15 <defaulted>
                    summary-key: Axxx <defaulted>
                    specify-global-summary-threshold
           -------------------------------------------------
               no
           -------------------------------------------------
```

The shaded lines show the parameters entered for the TCP signature.

NOTE This process also applies to UDP and ICMP custom signatures. The parameters will depend on the specific protocol services and ports.

IP Logging

The IP Logging feature allows the AIP-SSM to capture IP packet data if an attack or security threat is seen. This section demonstrates how to configure IP Logging to help perform deep analysis of a security threat on the network.

CAUTION IP Logging can affect performance on the AIP-SSM. You can limit the size of log files so that performance is not degraded. As an alternative, you might want to transfer the data to a dedicated management server.

The AIP-SSM can also be configured to capture all IP traffic from a specific host on the network. You can also specify the following:

- The duration in time the IP traffic should be logged
- The amount of packets to be logged
- The maximum number of bytes to be logged

NOTE The AIP-SSM stops logging packets if any of these parameters is met.

Automatic Logging

The goal in the following example is to configure the AIP-SSM to automatically log IP packets for attacker or victim traffic if a signature is triggered. The AIP-SSM logs the packet until any of the following criteria are met:

- No more than 250 packets
- No more than 45 minutes of logging
- No more than 81920 bytes of data

To accomplish this goal, complete the following steps:

Step 1 Log in to the AIP-SSM and enter into signature IP log configuration submode:

```
ChicagoSSM# configure terminal
ChicagoSSM(config)# service signature-definition sig0
ChicagoSSM(config-sig)# ip-log
```

Step 2 Configure the AIP-SSM to only log 250 packets, using the **ip-log-packets** subcommand:

```
ChicagoSSM(config-sig-ip)# ip-log-packets 250
```

Step 3 Specify the duration you want the AIP-SSM to log packets:

```
ChicagoSSM(config-sig-ip)# ip-log-time 45
```

Step 4 Specify the number of bytes to be logged:

```
ChicagoSSM(config-sig-ip)# ip-log-bytes 81920
```

Step 5 Invoke the **show settings** command to verify the parameters entered:

```
ChicagoSSM(config-sig-ip)# show settings
   ip-log
   -----------------------------------------------
      ip-log-packets: 250 default: 0
      ip-log-time: 45 default: 30
      ip-log-bytes: 81920 default: 0
   -----------------------------------------------
ChicagoSSM(config-sig-ip)#
```

The shaded lines show the parameters entered and the default values.

Manual Logging of Specific Host Traffic

In the example illustrated in Figure 14-9, the goal is to capture all packets from a host with IP address 10.10.10.21. The security administrator was informed that other hosts in the network are seeing unusual packets from this host.

The administrator uses the **iplog** command to configure manual IP logging to log IP packets only from and to **10.10.10.21** during a 3-minute period, as demonstrated in Example 14-28.

Example 14-28 *Configuring Manual IP Logging*

```
ChicagoSSM# iplog vs0 10.10.10.21 duration 3
Logging started for virtual sensor vs0, IP address 10.10.10.21, Log ID 1
Warning: IP Logging will affect system performance.
ChicagoSSM#
```

Notice the warning the AIP-SSM gives the administrator about the performance impact of the IP Logging feature.

Figure 14-9 *Manual IP Logging*

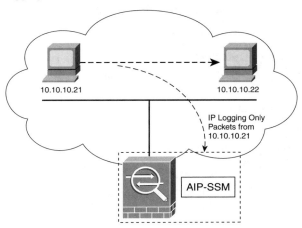

The following is the **iplog** command syntax and all the available parameters:

```
iplog name ip-address [duration minutes] [packets numPackets] [bytes numBytes]
```

You can monitor the status of the packets logged by using the **iplog-status** command, as demonstrated in Example 14-29.

Example 14-29 *IP Logging Status*

```
ChicagoSSM# iplog-status
Log ID:          1
IP Address 1:    10.10.10.21
Virtual sensor:  vs0
Status:          added
Event ID:        0
Bytes Captured:  3693
Packets Captured: 3
ChicagoSSM#
```

To stop logging packets, use the **no iplog** command. This will not delete any captured packets from the system.

After capturing the respective IP packets, you can copy the IP log files to an FTP or SCP server. This allows you to examine those files using different sniffing tools, such as tcpdump or Ethereal. Use the **copy iplog** command to copy the IP log files. The following is the command syntax:

```
copy iplog log-id destination-url
```

In Example 14-30, the IP log file that was previously captured is copied to an FTP server with IP address 192.168.10.44.

Example 14-30 *IP Logging Status*

```
ChicagoSSM# copy iplog 1 ftp://user1@192.168.10.44/iplog1
```

The IP Log ID displayed in the **iplog-status** command output is copied to the FTP server 192.168.10.44 and saved as a file named iplog1 by user1 (username on the FTP server).

Configuring Blocking (Shunning)

This section demonstrates how you can configure the AIP-SSM to interact with Cisco IOS routers, switches, PIX firewalls, and Cisco ASA appliances to block (shun) network devices. It is important that you analyze your network topology to understand which devices should be blocked by the AIP-SSM and what devices should never be blocked.

The NAC application within the CIPS software interacts with Cisco IOS routers and Catalyst 6500 Series switches by applying ACLs or VACLs to permit or deny their interfaces or VLANs. The Cisco PIX Firewall does not use ACLs or VACLs; it uses the **shun** command to perform this operation. You can view a list of all the supported devices at http://www. cisco.com/go/ips.

You can configure the AIP-SSM to be able to block itself with the **allow-sensor-block [true | false]** command in the service network-access submode. However, this action is not recommended, because it will cause all packets to be dropped to and from the blocking devices.

In the example illustrated in Figure 14-10, the AIP-SSM is configured to interact with a Cisco IOS router (10.10.12.254) that provides extranet connectivity on a dedicated link to a partner connection.

Figure 14-10 *Configuring Blocking to a Cisco IOS Router*

The following steps demonstrate how to configure the AIP-SSM:

Step 1 A user profile is configured called **myprofile**. Within this profile is stored the information that will be sent to the router for the AIP-SSM to be able to log in and manage it.

```
ChicagoSSM# configure terminal
ChicagoSSM(config)# service network-access
ChicagoSSM(config-net)# user-profiles myprofile
ChicagoSSM(config-net-use)# username admin
ChicagoSSM(config-net-use)# password
Enter password[]: ********
Re-enter password ********
ChicagoSSM(config-net-use)# enable-password
```

```
Enter enable-password[]: ********
Re-enter enable-password ********
ChicagoSSM(config-net-use)# exit
```

The username in this example is admin. You must also enter the router enable password.

Step 2   After configuring the user profile, enter into service network access submode and enter the IP address of the router:

```
ChicagoSSM(config-net)# router-devices 10.10.12.254
```

Step 3   The previously configured user profile (myprofile) is associated to the NAC configuration:

```
ChicagoSSM(config-net-rou)# profile-name myprofile
```

Step 4   Specify the protocol the AIP-SSM will use to communicate with the router:

```
ChicagoSSM(config-net-rou)# communication ssh-3des
```

SSH using the 3DES encryption algorithm is selected. You can use **telnet**, **ssh-des**, or **ssh-3des**. The default is **ssh-3des**.

Note   If you select DES or 3DES, you must add the router to the trusted SSH hosts in the AIP-SSM with the **ssh host-key** command.

Step 5   Optionally, you can specify the AIP-SSM NAT address (if the module is behind a NAT device) with the **nat-address** *nat_address* subcommand. NAT is not used in this example.

Step 6   Set the router's interface name and direction in which the ACL will be applied (inbound or outbound):

```
ChicagoSSM(config-net-rou)# block-interfaces ethernet0 in
```

The ACL will be applied inbound to the ethernet0 interface on the router.

Step 7   Optionally, you can add a preblock ACL. This is generally used for permitting the traffic that the AIP-SSM should never block. A preblock ACL named **preACL** is configured in this example:

```
ChicagoSSM(config-net-rou-blo)# pre-acl-name preACL
```

Step 8   You can also (optionally) add a post-block ACL. This is mainly used to block or permit additional traffic on the same interface or direction.

```
ChicagoSSM(config-net-rou-blo)# post-acl-name postACL
```

Step 9   Exit service network access submode and apply the changes:

```
ChicagoSSM(config-net-rou-blo)# exit
```

```
ChicagoSSM(config-net-rou)# exit
ChicagoSSM(config-net)# exit
Apply Changes:?[yes]: yes
ChicagoSSM(config)# exit
```

You can also configure the AIP-SSM to not block specific IP addresses or networks. In Example 14-31, the host with IP address 192.168.10.1 and the network 192.168.10.0/24 will never be blocked.

Example 14-31 *Avoiding Blocking Critical Devices and Networks*

```
ChicagoSSM# configure terminal
ChicagoSSM(config)# service network-access
ChicagoSSM(config-net)# general
ChicagoSSM(config-net-gen)# never-block-hosts 192.168.10.1
ChicagoSSM(config-net-gen)# never-block-networks 192.168.10.0/24
```

To allow the AIP-SSM to save the router's configuration after sending the respective commands, use the procedure demonstrated in Example 14-32.

Example 14-32 *Enabling the AIP-SSM to Write Configuration to NVRAM*

```
ChicagoSSM# configure terminal
ChicagoSSM(config)# service network-access
ChicagoSSM(config-net)# general
ChicagoSSM(config-net-gen)# enable-nvram-write true
```

The default value of the maximum number of devices or networks that can be blocked in the AIP-SSM is 250. However, you can use the **max-block-entries** command, as demonstrated in Example 14-33, to set how many blocks are maintained simultaneously. The range is from 0 to 65535.

Example 14-33 *Maximum Block Entries*

```
ChicagoSSM# configure terminal
ChicagoSSM(config)# service network-access
ChicagoSSM(config-net)# general
ChicagoSSM(config-net-gen)# block-max-entries 500
```

The maximum number of block entries is 500 in Example 14-33.

You should implement blocking/shunning very carefully, because it can disrupt legitimate services within your network caused by false positives. This is why the tuning process is so important. Attackers can launch a DoS attack if they know about your shunning configuration. These DoS attacks can be orchestrated spoofing legitimate source addresses, consequently causing disruption of legitimate hosts and services.

Summary

Cisco ASA in conjunction with the AIP-SSM modules delivers a new generation of highly accurate and intelligent inline prevention services. This provides security administrators an Adaptive Threat Defense (ATD) across their business networks and applications. This chapter provided an overview of the Cisco IPS 5.x software architecture that runs in the AIP-SSM to provide IPS services. It included an introduction to the CLI, user administration, and maintenance tasks, and explained in depth advanced configuration tasks such as custom signatures and blocking.

PART IV

Virtual Private Network (VPN) Solution

This chapter covers the following topics:

- Preconfiguration checklist
- Configuration steps
- Advanced features
- Optional commands
- Deployment scenarios
- Monitoring and troubleshooting

CHAPTER 15

Site-to-Site IPSec VPNs

Corporations continuously expand their operations by adding remote offices. These offices need network connectivity back to the corporate network for data transfer. Network administrators must evaluate the requirements and create the design to meet them. This includes selecting the network hardware platforms and the WAN technology to interconnect the branch and small offices. Some point-to-point WAN technologies include Frame Relay, Integrated Services Digital Network (ISDN), and Asynchronous Transfer Mode (ATM). Though these technologies do provide connectivity between locations, they are not very cost effective. Corporations look for ways to cut costs, for increased profitability.

Network professionals can reduce the high maintenance cost of point-to-point WAN links by using the IPSec VPN tunnel in site-to-site mode. They can use broadband connections, including digital subscriber line (DSL) or cable modem, to achieve Internet connectivity at a considerably cheaper rate, and they can deploy IPSec VPN on top of that to connect the remote locations to the central site. This allows them to accomplish both goals in a cost-effective manner:

- Internet access for clear-text traffic
- Intranet connectivity over the VPN tunnel

This chapter focuses on configuring and troubleshooting site-to-site IPSec tunnels on the Cisco Adaptive Security Appliances. It discusses a preconfiguration checklist, configuration steps, and different design scenarios. This chapter also discusses how to monitor the IPSec site-to-site tunnel to make sure that the traffic is flowing flawlessly. If the IPSec VPN is having connectivity issues, the chapter provides extensive troubleshooting help later in this chapter.

Preconfiguration Checklist

As discussed in the VPN section of Chapter 1, "Introduction to Network Security," IPSec can use Internet Key Exchange (IKE) for key management and tunnel negotiation. IKE uses a combination of different Phase 1 and Phase 2 attributes that are negotiated between the peers. If any one of the attributes is misconfigured, the IPSec tunnel will fail to establish. It is therefore highly recommended that security professionals understand the importance of a preconfiguration checklist and discuss it with other network administrators in case the far end of the VPN tunnel is managed by a different organization.

Table 15-1 lists all the possible values of Phase 1 attributes that are supported by Cisco ASA. It also includes the default values for each attribute. Highlighting the options and parameters that will be configured on the other end of the VPN tunnel is recommended.

Table 15-1   *ISAKMP Attributes*

Attribute	Possible Values	Default Value
Encryption	DES 56-bit 3DES 168-bit AES 128-bit AES 192-bit AES 256-bit	3DES 168-bit or DES 56-bit, if 3DES feature is not active
Hashing	MD5 or SHA	SHA
Authentication method	Preshared keys RSA signature DSA signature	Preshared keys
DH group	Group 1 768-bit field Group 2 1024-bit field Group 5 1536-bit field Group 7 ECC 163-bit field	Group 2 1024-bit field
Lifetime	120–2,147,483,647 seconds	86,400 seconds

NOTE   DH group 7 is used only for telecommuters who use VPN clients on PDAs.

For 3DES and AES encryption, you must have a VPN-3DES-AES feature set enabled license key.

In addition to the IKE parameters, the two IPSec devices also negotiate the mode of operation. Cisco ASA uses main mode as the default mode for the site-to-site tunnels but it can use aggressive mode if set up for it. After discussing Phase 1 attributes, it is important to highlight Phase 2 attributes for the VPN connection. The Phase 2 security associations (SAs) are used to encrypt and decrypt the actual data traffic. These SAs are also referred as the IPSec SAs. Table 15-2 lists all the possible Phase 2 attributes and their default values, offered by Cisco ASA.

Table 15-2   *IPSec Attributes*

Attribute	Possible Values	Default Values
Encryption	None DES 56-bit 3DES 168-bit AES 128-bit AES 192-bit AES 256-bit	3DES 168-bit or DES 56-bit, if 3DES feature is not active
Hashing	MD5 , SHA or None	None
Identity information	Network protocol and/or port number	No default parameter
Lifetime	120–2,147,483,647 seconds 10–2,147,483,647 KB	28800 seconds 4,608,000 KB
Mode	Tunnel or transport	Tunnel
PFS group	None Group 1 768-bit DH prime modulus Group 2 1024-bit DH prime modulus Group 5 1536-bit DH prime modulus Group 7 ECC 163-bit field	None

Once you determine which Phase 1 and Phase 2 attributes to use, the next step is to configure the site-to-site tunnel.

NOTE   Advanced Encryption Standard (AES) is a new standard developed by two Belgian cryptographers—Joan Daemen and Vincent Rijmen. AES is expected to replace the aging Data Encryption Standard (DES), which is commonly implemented by the IPSec vendors.

It is a best practice to use AES encryption over DES for enhanced security. Make sure that both IPSec devices support AES, because it is a fairly new standard.

Configuration Steps

The configuration of a site-to-site IPSec tunnel is broken down into 10 steps:

Step 1   Enable ISAKMP.

Step 2   Create ISAKMP policy.

Step 3   Set the tunnel type.

Step 4 Configure preshared keys.

Step 5 Define the IPSec policy.

Step 6 Specify interesting traffic.

Step 7 Configure the crypto map.

Step 8 Apply the crypto map to the interface.

Step 9 Configure traffic filtering.

Step 10 Bypass NAT (optional).

Figure 15-1 illustrates a network topology for SecureMe, Inc. It has two locations—one in Chicago and one in London. We will use its Chicago ASA device to demonstrate how it can be configured for a site-to-site tunnel.

Figure 15-1 *Network Topology for SecureMe, Inc.*

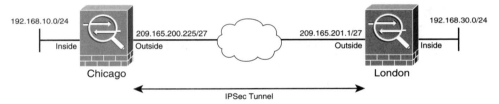

Step 1: Enable ISAKMP

IKE Phase 1 configuration starts by enabling ISAKMP on the interface that terminates the VPN tunnels. Typically, it is enabled on the Internet-facing or the outside interface. The command syntax to enable ISAKMP on an interface is

```
isakmp enable interface-name
```

Example 15-1 shows ISAKMP is enabled on the outside interface that is setup to terminate the VPN tunnels.

Example 15-1 *Enabling ISAKMP on the Outside Interface*

```
Chicago# configure terminal
Chicago(config)# isakmp enable outside
```

NOTE   IPSec VPN functionality is not available if the Cisco ASA is deployed in multiple mode. If site-to-site tunnels are required, then the Cisco ASA has to be set up in single mode. This functionality is considered for the future releases.

There are certain limitations on Cisco ASA's VPN feature, if it is deployed in transparent mode. Review Chapter 10, "Transparent Firewalls," for additional details.

Step 2: Create the ISAKMP Policy

After you enable ISAKMP on the interface, the next step is to create a Phase 1 policy that matches the other end of the VPN connection. The **isakmp policy** command accomplishes this task. Refer to the previous "Preconfiguration Checklist" section for a list of all the available options in Cisco ASA. The complete command syntax of **isakmp policy** is as follows:

```
isakmp policy priority authentication {dsa-sig | pre-share | rsa-sig}
isakmp policy priority encryption {3des | aes | aes-192 | aes-256 | des}
isakmp policy priority group {1 | 2 | 5 | 7}
isakmp policy priority hash {md5 | sha}
isakmp policy priority lifetime {120-2147483647}
```

If multiple ISAKMP policies are configured, the Cisco ASA checks the ISAKMP policy with the highest priority first. If there is no match, it checks the policy with the next higher priority, and so on until all policies have been evaluated. A priority value of 1 is the highest priority, while a priority value of 65535 is the lowest.

NOTE   If one of the ISAKMP attributes is not configured, the security Cisco ASA adds that attribute with its default value. Consult Table 15-1 for the ISAKMP attributes and the default values.

Example 15-2 illustrates how to configure an ISAKMP policy for AES-256 encryption, MD5 hashing, DH group 5, and preshared keys authentication with 28,800 seconds as the lifetime.

Example 15-2 *Creating an ISAKMP Policy*

```
Chicago# configure terminal
Chicago(config)# isakmp policy 10 authentication pre-share
Chicago(config)# isakmp policy 10 encryption aes-256
Chicago(config)# isakmp policy 10 hash md5
Chicago(config)# isakmp policy 10 group 5
Chicago(config)# isakmp policy 10 lifetime 28800
```

NOTE   If the VPN-3DES-AES feature is not enabled, the security Cisco ASA only allows DES encryption for the ISAKMP and IPSec policies.

Step 3: Set the Tunnel Type

An IPSec tunnel can be configured for two different types:

- Remote access
- Site to site

The remote-access tunnel type is used for Cisco IPSec VPN client, discussed in Chapter 16, "Remote Access VPNs." The following command sets up a tunnel type on the security Cisco ASA:

```
tunnel-group tunnel-group-name type tunnel_type
```

For a site-to-site connection, the tunnel type is set to **ipsec-l2l**, whereas the *tunnel-group-name* is the IP address of the peer. The tunnel group creates and manages a database of the static site-to-site tunnels and the remote-access groups.

Example 15-3 illustrates how to configure a site-to-site tunnel on the Cisco ASA if the peer's public IP address is 209.165.201.1.

Example 15-3 *Tunnel Group Definition*

```
Chicago(config)# tunnel-group 209.165.201.1 type ipsec-l2l
```

If a site-to-site tunnel is initiated by an IPSec device whose IP address is not defined as the tunnel group, then the security Cisco ASA tries to map the remote device to the default site-to-site group called **DefaultL2LGroup**, given that the preshared key between the two devices matches. DefaultL2LGroup does not appear in the configuration unless the default attributes within that tunnel-group are modified.

NOTE   The concept of tunnel group is taken from the VPN 3000 Series Concentrators.

Step 4: Configure ISAKMP Preshared Keys

If the ISAKMP policy is set up to use preshared keys as the authentication method, then a preshared key must be configured under the **ipsec-attributes** submenu of the **tunnel-group** command. The command syntax to map IPSec attributes to a peer is

```
tunnel-group tunnel-group-name ipsec-attributes
```

This takes you into an **ipsec-attributes** subconfiguration menu, where you can specify the key. Use the following command to set up a preshared key:

```
pre-shared-key preshared-key
```

As shown in Example 15-4, the Cisco ASA in Chicago is configured for a preshared key of **cisco123** for the peer **209.165.201.1**.

Example 15-4 *Preshared Key Configuration*

```
Chicago(config)# tunnel-group 209.165.201.1 ipsec-attributes
Chicago(config-ipsec)# pre-shared-key cisco123
```

Step 5: Define the IPSec Policy

An IPSec transform set specifies what type of encryption and hashing to use on the data packets after the tunnel is established. The IPSec transform set is negotiated during quick mode. To configure the transform set, use the following command syntax:

```
crypto ipsec transform-set transform-set-name {esp-3des | esp-aes | esp-aes-192 | esp-
aes-256 | esp-des | esp-md5-hmac | esp-null | esp-sha-hmac}
```

Table 15-3 lists the encryption and hashing algorithms that can be used in a transform set.

Table 15-3   *IPSec Transform Set*

Type	Available Options	Default Option
Encryption	**esp-3des** **esp-aes** **esp-aes-192** **esp-aes-256** **esp-des** **esp-null**	**esp-**3DES, **or esp-des** if 3DES, feature is not active
Hashing	**esp-md5-hmac** **esp-sha-hmac** **esp-none**	**esp-none**

NOTE   If the VPN-3DES-AES feature is not enabled, the security Cisco ASA allows DES encryption only for ISAKMP and IPSec policies.

If an IPSec policy is set up with a transform set to use an encryption algorithm such as **esp-aes** encryption, the security Cisco ASA adds **esp-none** as a default option for hashing. Additionally, if hashing is specified without an encryption algorithm, the Cisco ASA adds **esp-3des** as the default encryption algorithm. Example 15-5 shows that the Cisco ASA has been configured for AES-256 encryption and SHA hashing for data packets. The transform-set name is **myset**.

Example 15-5   *Transform-Set Configuration*

```
Chicago(config)# crypto ipsec transform-set myset esp-aes-256 esp-sha-hmac
```

NOTE   Cisco ASA supports only ESP as the encapsulation protocol. The support for AH currently is not planned.

Step 6: Specify Interesting Traffic

Cisco ASA uses an access control list (ACL) to define interesting traffic that it needs to encrypt. When a packet enters the security Cisco ASA, it gets routed based on the destination IP address. When it leaves the interface, which is set up for a site-to-site tunnel, the encryption engine intercepts that packet and matches it against the crypto access control entries (ACEs) to determine if it needs to be encrypted. If a match is found, the packet is encrypted and then sent out to the VPN peer.

An ACL can be as simple as permitting all IP traffic from one network to another or as complicated as permitting traffic originating from a unique source IP address on a particular port destined to a specific port on the destination address.

NOTE   Deploying complicated crypto ACLs using TCP or UDP ports is not recommended. Many IPSec devices do not support port-level crypto ACLs.

The command syntax for creating a crypto access list is as follows:

```
access-list id [line line-num] [extended] {deny | permit}{protocol | object-group
    protocol_obj_grp_id {source_addr source_mask} | object-group network_obj_grp_id |
    host src_host_addr [operator port [port] | object-group service_obj_grp_id]
    {destination_addr destination_mask} | object-group network_obj_grp_id | host
    dst_host_addr [operator port [port] | object-group service_obj_grp_id]}
```

For more details on the arguments used in an access control entry (ACE), consult Table 5-2 in Chapter 5, "Network Access Control."

Access lists also perform a security check for the inbound encrypted traffic. If a clear-text packet matches one of the crypto ACEs, the security Cisco ASA drops that packet and generates a syslog message indicating this incident.

NOTE   Each ACE creates two unidirectional IPSec SAs. If you have 100 entries in your ACL, then the ASA will create 200 IPSec SAs. Using host-based crypto ACEs is not recommended because Cisco ASA uses system resources to maintain the SAs which may affect system performance.

As shown in Example 15-6, the Chicago ASA is set up to protect all IP traffic sourced from **192.168.10.0** with a mask of **255.255.255.0** and destined to **192.168.30.0** with a mask of **255.255.255.0**. The ACL name is **encrypt-acl**.

Example 15-6 *Encryption ACL*

```
Chicago# configure terminal
Chicago(config)# access-list encrypt-acl extended permit ip 192.168.10.0
   255.255.255.0 192.168.30.0 255.255.255.0
```

The security Cisco ASA does not allow access to the inside interface if the traffic is coming over the VPN tunnel. This is true even if the inside network is included in the encryption ACL. You can enable management on the inside interface for the VPN traffic by using the **management-access** command followed by the name of the interface. Management applications such as SNMP polls, HTTPS requests, ASDM access, Telnet access, SSH access, ping, syslog polls, and NTP requests are allowed when management-access is enabled. In Example 15-7, the inside interface is being set up for management access.

Example 15-7 *Management Access on the Inside Interface*

```
Chicago(config)# management-access inside
```

NOTE   You can make only one interface as the management-access interface.

Step 7: Configure a Crypto Map

Once you have configured both Phase 1 and Phase 2 policies, the next step is to create a crypto map to use these policies. A crypto map is considered complete when it has the following parameters:

- At least one transform set
- At least one VPN peer
- A crypto ACL

The command syntax to configure a crypto map is

```
crypto map map-name seq-num set transform-set transform-set-name1
  [... transform-set-name9]
crypto map map-name seq-num set peer {ip_address | hostname} [..{ip_address10 |
  hostname10}]
crypto map map-name seq-num match address acl_name
```

Table 15-4 lists and defines the arguments used in a crypto map.

Table 15-4   *Crypto Map Argument Definitions*

Syntax	Syntax Description
map-name	Alphanumeric name of this crypto map.
seq-num	The number you assign to the crypto map entry. It can range from 1 to 65,535. The crypto map with the lowest sequence number is checked first.
set transform-set	Used to specify which transform sets can be used with the crypto map entry.
transform-set-name1	Name of the transform set. You can specify up to nine transform sets in a single crypto map instance.

continues

Table 15-4 *Crypto Map Argument Definitions (Continued)*

Syntax	Syntax Description
set peer	Used to specify an IPSec peer in a crypto map entry.
ip_address	Used to specify a peer by its IP address. You can have up to ten peers if the connection type is set as originate-only. Connection types are discussed later in this chapter.
hostname	Used to specify a peer by its host name as defined by the ASA's **name** command.
match address	Used to specify an access list for a crypto map entry.
acl_name	Alphanumeric name of the encryption ACL.

Example 15-8 shows **crypto map** configuration on the Chicago ASA. The crypto map name is **IPsec_map** and the sequence number used is 10.

Example 15-8 *Crypto Map Configuration*

```
Chicago# configure terminal
Chicago(config)# crypto map IPsec_map 10 set peer 209.165.201.1
Chicago(config)# crypto map IPsec_map 10 set transform-set myset
Chicago(config)# crypto map IPsec_map 10 match address encrypt-acl
```

The crypto map sequence number is used to define multiple IPSec tunnels destined to different peers. If the security Cisco ASA terminates an IPSec tunnel from another VPN peer, the second VPN tunnel can be defined using the existing crypto map name with a different sequence number. Each sequence number uniquely identifies a site-to-site tunnel. However, the security Cisco ASA evaluates the site-to-site tunnel with the lowest sequences number first.

NOTE   Cisco ASA does not support manual keying for IPSec tunnels. Manual keying is vulnerable to security flaws because the VPN peers always use the same encryption and authentication keys.

Step 8: Apply the Crypto Map to an Interface

After successfully configuring a crypto map, the final step is to bind it to an interface. Typically, it is applied to the Internet-facing interface that terminates the VPN connections. The command syntax is as follows:

```
crypto map  map-name interface interface-name
```

Cisco ASA limits applying more than one crypto map per interface. If there is a need to configure multiple site-to-site tunnels, use the same crypto map name with different sequence numbers. Please consult deployment scenario 2 "fully meshed topology with RRI" for an example of multiple crypto map sequence numbers.

Example 15-9 shows how a crypto map is applied to the outside interface.

Example 15-9 *Applying a Crypto Map on the Outside Interface*

```
Chicago# configure terminal
Chicago(config)# crypto map IPsec_map interface outside
```

Step 9: Configuring Traffic Filtering

Like a traditional firewall, the Cisco ASA protects the trusted network from outside traffic, unless the ACLs explicitly permit traffic to pass through it. The same concept is applied when the packets are decrypted by the IPSec engine. If there are no permits in the outside interface access list, the security Cisco ASA drops the decrypted packets as its default behavior. In Figure 15-2, Host B is only allowed to send traffic to Host A, located across the VPN tunnel, on TCP port 23. The Chicago ASA has an inbound access list called **outside_acl** applied to its outside interface, illustrated in Example 15-10.

Figure 15-2 *Filtering Traffic Across a VPN Tunnel*

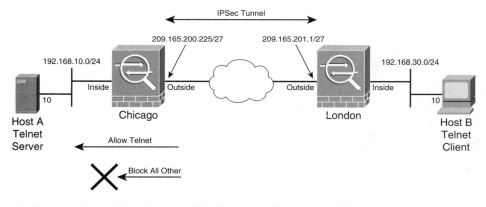

Example 15-10 *Access List to Allow Decrypted Traffic to Pass Through the ASA*

```
Chicago(config)# access-list outside_acl extended permit tcp host 192.168.30.10 host
  192.168.10.10 eq 23
Chicago(config)# access-group outside_acl in interface outside
```

In most VPN implementations, the remote private network is completely trusted, and it becomes cumbersome to create multiple entries in the outside interface ACL to allow the decrypted IPSec traffic. For the ease of configuration, Cisco ASA allows you to configure an IPSec **sysopt**, which permits all decrypted IPSec packets to go through it without inspecting them against the interface ACL. Example 15-11 illustrates that Chicago ASA is allowing all decrypted traffic by configuring the IPSec **sysopt**.

Example 15-11 *Sysopt Configuration to Bypass Traffic Filtering*

```
Chicago(config)# sysopt connection permit-ipsec
```

NOTE	The **sysopt connection permit-ipsec** command is a global command. If enabled, the security Cisco ASA bypasses the ACL check for all the IPSec tunnels.

Step 10: Bypassing NAT (Optional)

In most cases, you do not want to change the IP addresses for the traffic going over the tunnel. If NAT is configured on the security Cisco ASA to change the source or destination IP addresses, you can set up the NAT exempt rules to bypass address translation, as discussed in Chapter 5.

You need to create an ACL to specify what traffic needs to be bypassed by the NAT engine. Example 15-12 shows an access list, named **nonat**, to match the VPN traffic from **192.168.10.0/24** to **192.168.30.0/24**.

Example 15-12 *Access List to Bypass NAT*

```
Chicago(config)# access-list nonat extended permit ip 192.168.10.0 255.255.255.0
   192.168.30.0 255.255.255.0
```

Once the access list is defined, the next step is to configure the **nat 0** command. Example 15-13 demonstrates how to configure **nat 0** statement if the protected private LAN is toward the inside interface.

Example 15-13 *Configutration of nat 0 ACL*

```
Chicago(config)# nat (inside) 0 access-list nonat
```

Example 15-14 shows a complete IPSec site-to-site configuration on the Chicago ASA for peer 209.165.201.1.

Example 15-14 *Complete Site-to-Site IPSec Configuration*

```
access-list encrypt-acl extended permit ip 192.168.10.0 255.255.255.0 192.168.30.0
   255.255.255.0
access-list nonat extended permit ip 192.168.10.0 255.255.255.0 192.168.30.0
   255.255.255.0
nat (inside) 0 access-list nonat
crypto ipsec transform-set myset esp-aes-256 esp-sha-hmac
crypto map IPSec_map 10 match address encrypt-acl
crypto map IPSec_map 10 set peer 209.165.201.1
crypto map IPSec_map 10 set transform-set myset
crypto map IPSec_map interface outside
isakmp enable outside
isakmp policy 10 authentication pre-share
isakmp policy 10 encryption aes-256
isakmp policy 10 hash sha
isakmp policy 10 group 2
isakmp policy 10 lifetime 28800
tunnel-group 209.165.201.1 type ipsec-l2l
tunnel-group 209.165.201.1 ipsec-attributes
 pre-shared-key cisco123
sysopt connection permit-ipsec
```

Advanced Features

Cisco ASA provides many advanced features to suit your site-to-site VPN implementations. These features include the following:

- OSPF updates over IPSec
- Reverse route injection
- NAT Traversal (NAT-T)
- Tunnel default gateway

OSPF Updates over IPSec

As discussed in Chapter 6, "IP Routing," Open Shortest Path First (OSPF) uses multicast methodology to communicate with its neighbors. IPSec, on the other hand, does not allow encapsulation of the multicast traffic. Cisco ASA solves this problem by statically defining neighbors using the **neighbor** command, which sends unicast OSPF packets to the remote VPN peer. Refer to Chapter 6 for in-depth coverage of this feature.

Example 15-15 shows how to set up the outside interface as a nonbroadcast media and specify the remote VPN peer as the OSPF neighbor on the outside interface.

Example 15-15 *OSPF Updates over IPSec*

```
Chicago(config)# interface GigabitEthernet0/0
Chicago(config-if)# nameif outside
Chicago(config-if)# security-level 0
Chicago(config-if)# ip address 209.165.200.225 255.255.255.224
Chicago(config-if)# ospf network point-to-point non-broadcast
Chicago(config)# router ospf 1
Chicago(config-router)# network 209.165.200.225 255.255.255.255 area 0
Chicago(config-router)# neighbor 209.165.201.1 interface outside
```

NOTE   The security Cisco ASA uses the outside interface as the source of the OSPF packets and the neighbor's IP address as the destination address. Verify that the crypto ACL includes an entry to encrypt packets from 209.165.200.225 to 209.165.201.1.

Reverse Route Injection

Reverse route injection (RRI) is a way to distribute remote network information into the local network with the help of a routing protocol. With RRI, the Cisco ASA automatically adds static routes to the routing table and then announces these routes to its neighbors on the private network using OSPF. To configure RRI, you simply set the crypto map instance for reverse route:

```
crypto map  map-name seq-num set reverse-route
```

Figure 15-3 shows an IPSec topology that is using OSPF to propagate the remote private network information into the local LAN of the Chicago ASA.

Figure 15-3 *Example of RRI in the ASA*

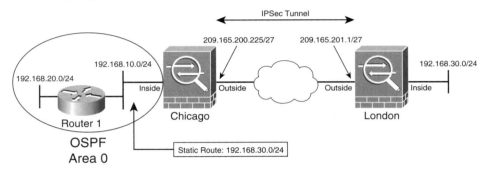

Example 15-16 illustrates how RRI can be enabled on the ASA in Chicago as depicted in Figure 15-3.

Example 15-16 *Configuration of Reverse Route Injection*

```
Chicago(config)# crypto map IPSec_map 10 match address encrypt-acl
Chicago(config)# crypto map IPSec_map 10 set peer 209.165.201.1
Chicago(config)# crypto map IPSec_map 10 set transform-set myset
Chicago(config)# crypto map IPSec_map 10 set reverse-route
```

To check if the ASA is adding the remote network information in the routing table, type **show route**, as illustrated in Example 15-17.

Example 15-17 *Routing Table on the ASA*

```
Chicago# show route
S    0.0.0.0 0.0.0.0 [1/0] via 209.165.200.226, outside
C    192.168.10.0 255.255.255.0 is directly connected, inside
C    209.165.200.224.0 255.255.255.224 is directly connected, outside
S    192.168.30.0 255.255.255.0 [1/0] via 209.165.200.226, outside
```

If you see the static route for the remote private network in the routing table, the next step is to advertise it to local OSPF peers, as shown in Example 15-18.

Example 15-18 *OSPF Configuration on the ASA*

```
Chicago(config)# router ospf 10
Chicago(config-router)# network 192.168.10.0 255.255.255.0 area 0
Chicago(config-router)# redistribute static subnets
```

The internal router (Router1) will receive this route and install it in its routing table, as demonstrated in Example 15-19.

Example 15-19 *Routing Table on a Router*

```
Router1# show ip route
C    192.168.10.0/24 is directly connected, Ethernet0
C    192.168.20.0/24 is directly connected, FastEthernet0
O E2 192.168.30.0/24 [110/20] via 192.168.10.1, 00:00:03, Ethernet0
```

NAT Traversal

Traditionally, the IPSec tunnels fail to pass traffic if there is a PAT device between the peers. Cisco ASA uses ESP which does not have any Layer 4 information. Thus a PAT device usually drops IPSec packets. To remedy this problem, Cisco drafted an IETF standard called NAT Traversal (NAT-T) to encapsulate the ESP packets into UDP port 4500 so that the PAT device knows how to translate the encrypted packets. NAT-T is dynamically negotiated if the following two conditions are met:

- Both VPN peers are NAT-T capable.
- There is a NAT or PAT device between the peers.

To enable NAT-T globally on the ASA, the command syntax is

```
isakmp nat-traversal [keepalives]
```

Keepalives range between 10 and 3600 seconds. If you don't specify the keepalive, the ASA uses 20 seconds as the default. In many cases, the NAT/PAT devices time out the UDP port 4500 entries if there is no active traffic passing through them. NAT-T keepalives are used so that the security Cisco ASA can send periodic keepalive messages to prevent the entries from timing out.

If NAT-T is globally enabled, and you do not want one of the peers to negotiate it, you can use the **crypto map nat-t-disable** command for that specific sequence number. The command syntax is

```
crypto map map-name seq-num set nat-t-disable
```

Example 15-20 illustrates how to disable NAT-T for a peer defined in sequence map 10.

Example 15-20 *Disabling NAT-T for a Peer*

```
Chicago(config)# crypto map IPSec_map 10 set nat-t-disable
```

Tunnel Default Gateway

A Layer 3 device typically has a default gateway that is used to route packets when the destination address is not found in the routing table. *Tunnel default gateway,* a concept first introduced in the VPN3000 concentrators, is used to route the packets if they reach the security Cisco ASA over an IPSec tunnel and if their destination IP address is not found in the routing table. The tunneled traffic can be either remote access or site-to-site VPN traffic. The tunnel default gateway next-hop address is generally the IP address of the inside router, Router1 (illustrated in Figure 15-3), or any Layer 3 device.

The tunnel default gateway feature is important if you do not want to define routes about your internal networks to the Cisco ASA and you rather want the tunneled traffic to be sent to the internal router for routing. To set up a tunnel default gateway, add the keyword **tunneled** to the statically configured default route. Example 15-21 shows the configuration of the Cisco ASA with the tunnel default gateway specified as 192.168.10.2, located on the inside interface.

Example 15-21 *Tunnel Default Gateway Configuration*

```
Chicago(config)# route inside 0.0.0.0 0.0.0.0 192.168.10.2 tunneled
```

Optional Commands

In addition to the advanced features discussed in the preceding section, you can optionally tweak many default parameters to optimize the site-to-site connections. This section discusses these parameters.

- Perfect forward secrecy
- Security Association Lifetimes
- Phase 1 mode
- Connection type
- Inheritence
- ISAKMP keepalives

Perfect Forward Secrecy

Perfect Forward Secrecy (PFS) is a cryptographic technique where the newly generated keys are unrelated to any previously generated key. With PFS enabled, the security Cisco ASA generates a new set of keys which is used during the IPSec Phase 2 negotiations. Without PFS, the Cisco ASA uses Phase 1 keys during the Phase 2 negotiations. The Cisco ASA uses Diffie-Hellman group 1, 2, 5, and 7 for PFS to generate the keys. Diffie-Hellman group 1 uses 768-bits modulus size to generate the keys, while group 2 uses 1024-bits and group 5 uses a 1536 bits modulus size. Group 7, where the elliptical curve field size is 163 bits, is designed for the faster computation of keys usually used by the handheld PCs. Group 5 is the most secure technique but requires more processing overhead. The syntax to configure PFS is

```
crypto map map-name seq-num set pfs {group1 | group2 | group5 | group7}
```

Example 15-22 shows you how to enable PFS group 5 for a peer with a sequence number 10.

Example 15-22 *Configuring PFS Group 5 for a Peer*

```
Chicago(config)# crypto map IPSec_map 10 set pfs group5
```

Security Association Lifetimes

If you do not specify the IPSec security association lifetimes, the Cisco ASA uses the default values of 28,800 seconds or 4,275,000 KB. The IPSec security association lifetimes can be set either globally or per crypto map instance. To configure it globally, the command syntax is

```
crypto ipsec  security-association lifetime [{seconds 120-2147483647 kilobytes 10-
   2147483647}]
```

Lifetime in seconds can vary between 120 and 2,147,483,647, and lifetime can range from 10 to 2,147,483,647 KB.

If you only want to specify unique security association lifetime values per crypto map instance, the command syntax is

```
crypto map map-name seq-num set security-association lifetime [{seconds 120-
   2147483647 kilobytes 10-2147483647}]
```

Phase 1 Mode

ISAKMP implementation in the Cisco ASA uses main mode for Phase 1 negotiations, by default. If you want to change Phase 1 mode for a specific peer, use the following command syntax:

```
crypto map map-name seq-num set phase1-mode {main | aggressive [group1 | group2 |
   group5 | group7]}
```

If the remote VPN peer initiates a site-to-site tunnel using aggressive mode, then the ASA uses that for tunnel negotiations. Aggressive mode has some security weaknesses, so it is recommended to use main mode where possible. However, if you do not want to accept connections using aggressive mode, you can disable it globally, as shown in Example 15-23.

Example 15-23 *Disabling Aggressive Mode*

```
Chicago(config)# crypto isakmp am-disable
```

Connection Type

The Cisco ASA in the site-to-site tunnel can respond and initiate a VPN connection. This bidirectional default behavior can be changed to answer-only or originate-only mode. For example, if you want to limit the security Cisco ASA to just initiate IKE tunnels, you can set the connection type to **originate-only.** This way, if the remote VPN peer tries to initiate the connection, the local Cisco ASA will not honor the request. Similarly, if you want the security Cisco ASA to accept IKE tunnels only from the peer, then you can set the connection type to **answer-only**. The command syntax to set the connection type is

```
crypto map map-name seq-num set connection-type {answer-only | bidirectional |
   originate-only}
```

NOTE	If you need to specify multiple peers in your crypto map sequence number for redundancy, then you need to set your connection type to originate-only mode.

Example 15-24 shows that Chicago ASA's connection type is set up as originate-only for the peer 209.165.201.1.

Example 15-24 *Configuring Connection Type to Originate-Only for a Peer*

```
Chicago(config)# crypto map IPSec_map 10 set connection-type originate-only
```

Inheritance

Inheritance is a way to specify how the security Cisco ASA creates the Phase 2 IPSec SAs. You can either use ACL or data rules to configure inheritance. In ACL rule inheritance, the default behavior, all the hosts in a proxy identity can use the same IPSec SA given that the crypto ACL contains an IP network. However, in data rule inheritance, the security Cisco ASA creates one tunnel for every address pair within the address ranges specified in the encryption ACL. Thus, each host uses a separate tunnel, and consequently separate keys. While this selection is more secure, it requires additional processing overhead. Thus, it is recommended to use the data rules to achieve optimum performance.

Example 15-25 shows how to change behavior to data rule inheritance.

Example 15-25 *Changing Inheritance from ACL to Data*

```
Chicago(config)# crypto map IPSec_map 1 set inheritance data
```

ISAKMP Keepalives

The ISAKMP keepalives feature is a way to determine whether the remote VPN peer is still up and whether there are lingering SAs. The Cisco ASA starts sending Dead Peer Detection (DPD) packets once it stops receiving encrypted traffic over the tunnel from the peer. By default, if it does not hear from its peer for 10 seconds, it sends out a DPD R_U_THERE packet. It keeps sending the R_U_THERE packets every 2 seconds. If it does not receive R_U_THERE_ACK for the four consecutive DPDs, the security Cisco ASA deletes the corresponding ISAKMP and IPSec SAs.

The DPD messages are sent out once the IKE and IPSec SAs are negotiated and the Cisco ASA does not receive any traffic from the other side. If you are not interested in sending DPD messages for a specific peer, it can be disabled under the tunnel-group IPSec subconfiguration menu. Example 15-26 illustrates how to disable ISAKMP keepalives for peer 209.165.201.

Example 15-26 *Disabling ISAKMP Keepalives*

```
Chicago(config)# tunnel-group 209.165.201.1 ipsec-attributes
Chicago(config-ipsec)# isakmp keepalive disable
```

You can also tweak the keepalive parameters to suit your needs. Example 15-27 shows that if the Cisco ASA does not receive encrypted traffic for 30 seconds, it will send out the first DPD packet. It is also configured to send periodic DPDs every 5 seconds if it fails to get an ACK.

Example 15-27 *Changing the Default ISAKMP Keepalive Timers*

```
Chicago(config)# tunnel-group 209.165.201.1 ipsec-attributes
Chicago(config-ipsec)# isakmp keepalive threshold 30 retry 5
```

Deployment Scenarios

The ASA VPN solution can be deployed in many different ways. In this section, we cover two design scenarios for ease of understanding:

- Single site-to-site tunnel configuration using NAT-T
- Fully meshed topology with RRI

NOTE   The design scenarios discussed in this section should be used solely to reinforce learning. They should be used for reference purposes only.

Single Site-to-Site Tunnel Configuration Using NAT-T

Figure 15-4 shows a network topology of SecureMe in which it has deployed two Cisco ASAs—one at the hub site in Chicago and the other at its London location. However, the London ASA is connected to the Internet using a broadband connection that is set up to perform PAT for the traffic passing through it. Because the PAT device does not allow passing the non-TCP and non-UDP traffic, the security Cisco ASA are set up for NAT-T. During the ISAKMP negotiations, the security Cisco ASA will detect that a PAT device exists between them, therefore forcing the traffic to be encapsulated into UDP port 4500. These security Cisco ASA are set up to send NAT-T keepalives every 20 seconds to keep the connection entries active.

Figure 15-4 *SecureMe Network Using NAT-T*

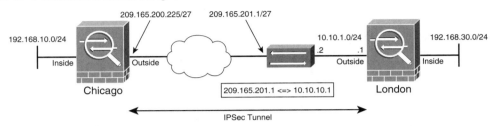

Example 15-28 shows the relevant configuration of both Cisco ASAs configured for NAT-T.

Example 15-28 *Full Configuration of the Chicago and London ASAs*

```
                              Chicago ASA:
Chicago# show run
! outside interface configuration
interface GigabitEthernet0/0
 nameif outside
 security-level 0
 ip address 209.165.200.225 255.255.255.224
! inside interface configuration
interface GigabitEthernet0/1
 nameif inside
 security-level 100
 ip address 192.168.10.1 255.255.255.0
!
hostname Chicago
! Encryption Access-list to encrypt the traffic from 192.168.10/24 to 192.168.30.0/24
access-list encrypt_acl extended permit ip 192.168.10.0 255.255.255.0 192.168.30.0
  255.255.255.0
! Access-list to bypass address translation from 192.168.10/24 to 192.168.30.0/24
access-list nonat_acl extended permit ip 192.168.10.0 255.255.255.0 192.168.30.0
  255.255.255.0
! NAT entry to bypass address translation from 192.168.10/24 to 192.168.30.0/24
nat (inside) 0 access-list nonat_acl
route outside 0.0.0.0 0.0.0.0 209.165.200.226
! sysopt to bypass traffic filters
sysopt connection permit-ipsec
! Transform set to specify encryption and hashing algorithm
crypto ipsec transform-set myset esp-3aes-256 esp-sha-hmac
! Crypto map configuration
crypto map IPSec_map 10 match address encrypt_acl
crypto map IPSec_map 10 set peer 209.165.201.1
crypto map IPSec_map 10 set transform-set myset
crypto map IPSec_map interface outside
! isakmp configuration
isakmp enable outside
isakmp policy 1 authentication pre-share
isakmp policy 1 encryption aes-256
isakmp policy 1 hash sha
isakmp policy 1 group 2
isakmp policy 1 lifetime 86400
```

Example 15-28 *Full Configuration of the Chicago and London ASAs (Continued)*

```
! NAT-T configuration
isakmp nat-traversal 20
! L2L tunnel-group configuration
tunnel-group 209.165.201.1 type ipsec-l2l
tunnel-group 209.165.201.1 ipsec-attributes
 pre-shared-key cisco123
```

London ASA:

```
London# show run
! outside interface configuration. The outside address is translated to
  209.165.201.1 by PAT
interface GigabitEthernet0/0
 nameif outside
 security-level 0
 ip address 10.10.1.1 255.255.255.0
! inside interface configuration
interface GigabitEthernet0/1
 nameif inside
 security-level 100
 ip address 192.168.30.1 255.255.255.0
!
hostname London
! Encryption Access-list to encrypt the traffic from 192.168.30/24 to 192.168.10.0/24
access-list encrypt_acl extended permit ip 192.168.30.0 255.255.255.0 192.168.10.0
  255.255.255.0
! Access-list to bypass address translation from 192.168.30/24 to 192.168.10.0/24
access-list nonat_acl extended permit ip 192.168.30.0 255.255.255.0 192.168.10.0
  255.255.255.0
! NAT entry to bypass address translation from 192.168.30/24 to 192.168.10.0/24
nat (inside) 0 access-list nonat_acl
route outside 0.0.0.0 0.0.0.0 10.10.1.2 1
! sysopt to bypass traffic filters
sysopt connection permit-ipsec
! Transform set to specify encryption and hashing algorithm
crypto ipsec transform-set myset esp-aes-256 esp-sha-hmac
! Crypto map configuration
crypto map IPSec_map 1 match address encrypt_acl
crypto map IPSec_map 1 set peer 209.165.200.225
crypto map IPSec_map 1 set transform-set myset
crypto map IPSec_map interface outside
! isakmp configuration
isakmp enable outside
isakmp policy 1 authentication pre-share
isakmp policy 1 encryption aes-256
isakmp policy 1 hash sha
isakmp policy 1 group 2
isakmp policy 1 lifetime 86400
! NAT-T configuration
isakmp nat-traversal 20
! L2L tunnel-group configuration
tunnel-group 209.165.200.225 type ipsec-l2l
tunnel-group 209.165.200.225 ipsec-attributes
 pre-shared-key cisco123
```

Fully Meshed Topology with RRI

SecureMe is planning to add a new site, Paris, into its existing network. Figure 15-5 shows the new network topology. SecureMe wants to have a fully meshed topology so that each site will have two IPSec tunnels going to the respective IPSec peers. It also wants to use RRI to distribute remote network information into the local network of Chicago using OSPF.

Figure 15-5 *SecureMe Network Using RRI in a Fully Meshed VPN*

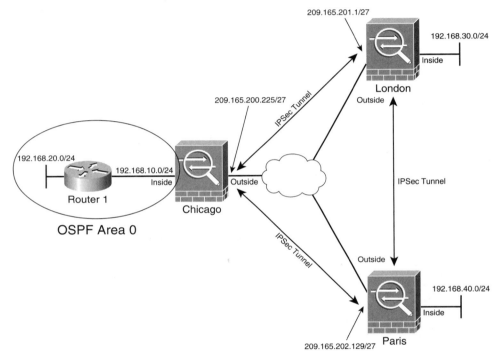

Example 15-29 shows the relevant configuration of all the Cisco ASA devices set up in a fully meshed IPSec network. There are two crypto map instances—one for each peer configured on the security Cisco ASA.

Example 15-29 *Full Configuration of the Chicago, London, and Paris ASAs*

```
                          Chicago ASA:
Chicago# show run
! outside interface configuration
interface GigabitEthernet0/0
 nameif outside
 security-level 0
 ip address 209.165.200.225 255.255.255.0
! inside interface configuration
interface GigabitEthernet0/1
 nameif inside
 security-level 100
 ip address 192.168.10.1 255.255.255.0
```

Example 15-29 *Full Configuration of the Chicago, London, and Paris ASAs (Continued)*

```
hostname Chicago
! Encryption Access-list to encrypt the traffic from Chicago to London
access-list london_acl extended permit ip 192.168.10.0 255.255.255.0 192.168.30.0
    255.255.255.0
! Encryption Access-list to encrypt the traffic from Chicago to Paris
access-list paris_acl extended permit ip 192.168.10.0 255.255.255.0 192.168.40.0
    255.255.255.0
! Access-list to bypass address translation from Chicago to other locations
access-list nonat_acl extended permit ip 192.168.10.0 255.255.255.0 192.168.30.0
    255.255.255.0
access-list nonat_acl extended permit ip 192.168.10.0 255.255.255.0 192.168.40.0
    255.255.255.0
! NAT entry to bypass address translation from Chicago to other locations
nat (inside) 0 access-list nonat_acl
! OSPF configuration for reverse-route injection
router ospf 10
 network 192.168.10.0 255.255.255.0 area 0
 log-adj-changes
 redistribute static subnets
!
route outside 0.0.0.0 0.0.0.0 209.165.200.226 1
! sysopt to bypass traffic filters
sysopt connection permit-ipsec
! Transform set to specify encryption and hashing algorithm
crypto ipsec transform-set myset esp-aes-256 esp-sha-hmac
! Crypto map configuration for London
crypto map IPSec_map 1 match address london_acl
crypto map IPSec_map 1 set peer 209.165.201.1
crypto map IPSec_map 1 set transform-set myset
! Crypto map configuration to enable RRI for London
crypto map IPSec_map 1 set reverse-route
! Crypto map configuration for Paris
crypto map IPSec_map 2 match address paris_acl
crypto map IPSec_map 2 set peer 209.165.202.129
crypto map IPSec_map 2 set transform-set myset
! Crypto map configuration to enable RRI for Paris
crypto map IPSec_map 2 set reverse-route
crypto map IPSec_map interface outside
! isakmp configuration
isakmp enable outside
isakmp policy 1 authentication pre-share
isakmp policy 1 encryption aes-256
isakmp policy 1 hash sha
isakmp policy 1 group 2
isakmp policy 1 lifetime 86400
! L2L tunnel-group configuration for London
tunnel-group 209.165.201.1 type ipsec-l2l
tunnel-group 209.165.201.1 ipsec-attributes
 pre-shared-key cisco123
! L2L tunnel-group configuration for Paris
tunnel-group 209.165.202.129 type ipsec-l2l
tunnel-group 209.165.202.129 ipsec-attributes
 pre-shared-key cisco123
```

continues

Example 15-29 *Full Configuration of the Chicago, London, and Paris ASAs (Continued)*

London ASA:

```
London# show run
! outside interface configuration
interface GigabitEthernet0/0
 nameif outside
 security-level 0
 ip address 209.165.201.1 255.255.255.0
! inside interface configuration
interface GigabitEthernet0/1
 nameif inside
 security-level 100
 ip address 192.168.30.1 255.255.0.0
!
hostname London
! Encryption Access-list to encrypt the traffic from London to Chicago
access-list chicago_acl extended permit ip 192.168.30.0 255.255.255.0 192.168.10.0
  255.255.255.0
! Encryption Access-list to encrypt the traffic from London to Paris
access-list paris_acl extended permit ip 192.168.30.0 255.255.255.0 192.168.40.0
  255.255.255.0
!
! Access-list to bypass address translation from London to other locations
access-list nonat_acl extended permit ip 192.168.30.0 255.255.255.0 192.168.10.0
  255.255.255.0
access-list nonat_acl extended permit ip 192.168.30.0 255.255.255.0 192.168.40.0
  255.255.255.0
! NAT entry to bypass address translation from London to other locations
nat (inside) 0 access-list nonat_acl
route outside 0.0.0.0 0.0.0.0 209.165.201.2
! sysopt to bypass traffic filters
sysopt connection permit-ipsec
! Transform set to specify encryption and hashing algorithm
crypto ipsec transform-set myset esp-aes-256 esp-sha-hmac
! Crypto map configuration for Chicago
crypto map IPSec_map 1 match address chicago_acl
crypto map IPSec_map 1 set peer 209.165.200.225
crypto map IPSec_map 1 set transform-set myset
! L2L tunnel-group configuration for Paris
crypto map IPSec_map 2 match address paris_acl
crypto map IPSec_map 2 set peer 209.165.202.129
crypto map IPSec_map 2 set transform-set myset
crypto map IPSec_map interface outside
! isakmp configuration
isakmp enable outside
isakmp policy 1 authentication pre-share
isakmp policy 1 encryption aes-256
isakmp policy 1 hash sha
isakmp policy 1 group 2
isakmp policy 1 lifetime 86400
! L2L tunnel-group configuration for Chicago
tunnel-group 209.165.200.225 type ipsec-l2l
tunnel-group 209.165.200.225 ipsec-attributes
 pre-shared-key cisco123
```

Example 15-29 *Full Configuration of the Chicago, London, and Paris ASAs (Continued)*

```
! L2L tunnel-group configuration for Paris
tunnel-group 209.165.202.129 type ipsec-l2l
tunnel-group 209.165.202.129 ipsec-attributes
 pre-shared-key cisco123
```

Paris ASA:

```
Paris# show run
! outside interface configuration
interface GigabitEthernet0/0
 nameif outside
 security-level 0
 ip address 209.165.202.129 255.255.255.0
 !
! inside interface configuration
interface GigabitEthernet0/1
 nameif inside
 security-level 100
ip address 192.168.40.1 255.255.255.0
hostname Paris
! Encryption Access-list to encrypt the traffic from Paris to Chicago
access-list chicago_acl extended permit ip 192.168.40.0 255.255.255.0 192.168.10.0
  255.255.255.0
! Encryption Access-list to encrypt the traffic from Paris to London
access-list london_acl extended permit ip 192.168.40.0 255.255.255.0 192.168.30.0
  255.255.255.0
! Access-list to bypass address translation from Paris to other locations
access-list nonat_acl extended permit ip 192.168.40.0 255.255.255.0 192.168.10.0
  255.255.255.0
access-list nonat_acl extended permit ip 192.168.40.0 255.255.255.0 192.168.30.0
  255.255.255.0
! NAT entry to bypass address translation from Paris to other locations
nat (inside) 0 access-list nonat_acl
route outside 0.0.0.0 0.0.0.0 209.165.202.130 1
! sysopt to bypass traffic filters
sysopt connection permit-ipsec
! Transform set to specify encryption and hashing algorithm
crypto ipsec transform-set myset esp-aes-256 esp-sha-hmac
! Crypto map configuration for Chicago
crypto map IPSec_map 1 match address chicago_acl
crypto map IPSec_map 1 set peer 209.165.200.225
crypto map IPSec_map 1 set transform-set myset
! Crypto map configuration for London
crypto map IPSec_map 2 match address london_acl
crypto map IPSec_map 2 set peer 209.165.201.1
crypto map IPSec_map 2 set transform-set myset
crypto map IPSec_map interface outside
! isakmp configuration
isakmp enable outside
isakmp policy 1 authentication pre-share
isakmp policy 1 encryption aes-256
isakmp policy 1 hash sha
isakmp policy 1 group 2
isakmp policy 1 lifetime 86400
```

continues

Example 15-29 *Full Configuration of the Chicago, London, and Paris ASAs (Continued)*

```
! L2L tunnel-group configuration for Chicago
tunnel-group 209.165.200.225 type ipsec-l2l
tunnel-group 209.165.200.225 ipsec-attributes
 pre-shared-key cisco123
! L2L tunnel-group configuration for Chicago
tunnel-group 209.165.201.1 type ipsec-l2l
tunnel-group 209.165.201.1 ipsec-attributes
 pre-shared-key cisco123
```

Monitoring and Troubleshooting Site-to-Site IPSec VPNs

Cisco ASA comes with many **show** commands to check the health and status of the IPSec tunnels. For troubleshooting purposes, Cisco ASA provides a rich set of **debug** commands to isolate the IPSec-related issues.

Monitoring Site-to-Site VPNs

If you want to check the status of the IPSec tunnels, you can start by looking at Phase 1 SA state. You can type **show crypto isakmp sa detail**, as demonstrated in Example 15-30. If the ISAKMP negotiations are successful, you should see the state as MM_ACTIVE. It also displays the type of the IPSec tunnel and the negotiated Phase 1 policy.

Example 15-30 *Output of* **show crypto isakmp sa detail**

```
Chicago# show crypto isakmp sa detail
   Active SA: 1
   Rekey SA: 0 (A tunnel will report 1 Active and 1 Rekey SA during rekey)
Total IKE SA: 1
1   IKE Peer: 209.165.201.1
    Type    : L2L          Role      : responder
    Rekey   : no           State     : MM_ACTIVE
    Encrypt : aes-256       Hash      : MD5
    Auth    : preshared     Lifetime: 86400
    Lifetime Remaining: 36536
```

You can also check the status of the IPSec SA by using the **show crypto ipsec sa** command, as shown in Example 15-31. It displays the negotiated proxy identities along with the actual number of packets encrypted and decrypted by the IPSec engine.

Example 15-31 *Output of* **show crypto ipsec sa**

```
Chicago# show crypto ipsec sa
interface: outside
    Crypto map tag: IPSec_map, local addr: 209.165.200.225

        local ident (addr/mask/prot/port): (192.168.10.0/255.255.255.0/0/0)
        remote ident (addr/mask/prot/port): (192.168.30.0/255.255.255.0/0/0)
        current_peer: 209.165.201.1
        #pkts encaps: 2023, #pkts encrypt: 2023, #pkts digest: 2023
        #pkts decaps: 2112, #pkts decrypt: 2112, #pkts verify: 2112
```

Example 15-31 *Output of* **show crypto ipsec sa** *(Continued)*

```
            #pkts compressed: 0, #pkts decompressed: 0
            #pkts not compressed: 2023, #pkts comp failed: 0, #pkts decomp failed: 0
            #send errors: 0, #recv errors: 0

            local crypto endpt.: 209.165.200.225, remote crypto endpt.: 209.165.201.1

            path mtu 1500, ipsec overhead 60, media mtu 1500
            current outbound spi: 0B77BCE7

        inbound esp sas:
          spi: 0x4FEDC46D (1340982381)
             transform: esp-aes-256 esp-sha-hmac
             in use settings ={L2L, Tunnel, }
             slot: 0, conn_id: 1, crypto-map: IPSec_map
             sa timing: remaining key lifetime (kB/sec): (9276/28646)
             IV size: 16 bytes
             replay detection support: Y
        outbound esp sas:
          spi: 0x0B77BCE7 (192396519)
             transform: esp-aes-256 esp-sha-hmac
             in use settings ={L2L, Tunnel, }
             slot: 0, conn_id: 1, crypto-map: IPSec_map
             sa timing: remaining key lifetime (kB/sec): (9276/28644)
             IV size: 16 bytes
             replay detection support: Y
```

If a hardware encryption card is installed in the security Cisco ASA and you want to look at the counter information to monitor how many packets have gone through the card, you can type the **show crypto accelerator statistics** command, as demonstrated in Example 15-32.

Example 15-32 *Output of* **show crypto accelerator statistics**

```
Chicago# show crypto accelerator statistics
Crypto Accelerator Status
- - - - - - - - - - - - - - - - - - - - - -
[Capability]
   Supports hardware crypto: True
   Supports modular hardware crypto: False
   Max accelerators: 1
   Max crypto throughput: 100 Mbps
   Max crypto connections: 750
[Global Statistics]
   Number of active accelerators: 1
   Number of non-operational accelerators: 0
   Input packets: 14606
   Input bytes: 3364752
   Output packets: 3648
   Output error packets: 0
   Output bytes: 3828341
[Accelerator 0]
   Status: OK
   Software crypto engine
```

continues

Example 15-32 *Output of* **show crypto accelerator statistics** *(Continued)*

```
    Slot: 0
    Active time: 286241 seconds
    Total crypto transforms: 7
[Accelerator 0]
  Status: OK
  Software crypto engine
  Slot: 0
  Active time: 286241 seconds
[Accelerator 1]
  Status: OK
  Encryption hardware device : Cisco ASA-55x0 on-board accelerator (revision 0x0)
                         Boot microcode   : ?CNlite-MC-Boot-Cisco-1.2
                         SSL/IKE microcode: ?CNlite-MC-IPSEC-Admin-3.03
                         IPSec microcode  : ?CNlite-MC-IPSECm-MAIN-2.03
  Slot: 1
  Active time: 286242 seconds
  Total crypto transforms: 186516
  Total dropped packets: 0
  [Input statistics]
    Input packets: 14606
    Input bytes: 3364752
    Input hashed packets: 13060
    Input hashed bytes: 1165772
    Decrypted packets: 14606
    Decrypted bytes: 2655536
  [Output statistics]
    Output packets: 3648
    Output bad packets: 0
    Output bytes: 3828341
    Output hashed packets: 455
    Output hashed bytes: 61880
    Encrypted packets: 3648
    Encrypted bytess: 3747517
```

Troubleshooting Site-to-Site VPNs

If the IPSec tunnel is not working for some reason, make sure that you have the proper debug turned on. The two most important debug commands to look at are the following:

debug crypto isakmp [*debug level 1-255*]

and

debug crypto ipsec [*debug level 1-255*]

By default, the debug level is set to 1. You can increase the debug level up to 255 to get detailed logs. However, in most cases, setting the logging level to 127 gives enough information to determine the root cause of an issue.

Refer to Figure 15-1 for a site-to-site tunnel between the ASA in Chicago and London. To enforce learning, the ISAKMP and IPSec negotiations are discussed on the security Cisco ASA in Chicago. The following debug commands are enabled on the security Cisco ASA.

debug crypto isakmp 127

and

```
debug crypto ipsec 127
```

As mentioned in Chapter 1, the tunnel negotiations begin by exchanging the ISAKMP proposals. If the proposal is acceptable, the ASA displays the **IKE SA proposal transform acceptable** message, as shown in Example 15-33.

Example 15-33 *Debugs to Show ISAKMP Proposal Is Acceptable*

```
[IKEv1 DEBUG], IP = 209.165.201.1, processing SA payload
[IKEv1 DEBUG], IP = 209.165.201.1, Oakley proposal is acceptable
.....
[IKEv1 DEBUG], IP = 209.165.201.1, IKE SA Proposal # 1, Transform # 1 acceptable
  Matches global IKE entry # 5
```

NOTE   The VPN debugs messages on the security Cisco ASA are very similar to the log messages generated on the VPN 3000 Series Concentrators.

During the ISAKMP SA negotiations, the security Cisco ASA matches the IP address of the VPN peer with the tunnel group. If it finds a match, it displays a "Connection landed on tunnel group" message, as shown in Example 15-34, and continues with the rest of the negotiations (shown as ...). The Cisco ASA displays a "Phase 1 completed" message when the ISAKMP SA is successfully negotiated.

Example 15-34 *Debugs to Show Phase 1 Negotiations Are Completed*

```
[IKEv1]: IP = 209.165.201.1, Connection landed on tunnel_group 209.165.201.1
...
[IKEv1]: Group = 209.165.201.1, IP = 209.165.201.1, PHASE 1 COMPLETED
```

After completing Phase 1 negotiations, the security Cisco ASA maps the remote VPN peer to a static crypto map sequence number and checks the IPSec Phase 2 proposal sent by the remote VPN peers. If the received proxy identities and the IPSec Phase 2 proposals match on the security Cisco ASA, it displays an "IPSec SA proposal transform acceptable" message, as demonstrated in Example 15-35.

Example 15-35 *Debugs to Show Proxy Identities and Phase 2 Proposals Are Accepted*

```
[IKEv1 DECODE]: ID_IPV4_ADDR_SUBNET ID received--192.168.30.0--255.255.255.0
[IKEv1]: Group = 209.165.201.1, IP = 209.165.201.1, Received remote IP Proxy Subnet
data in ID Payload:   Address 192.168.30.0, Mask 255.255.255.0, Protocol 0, Port 0
[IKEv1 DEBUG]: Group = 209.165.201.1, IP = 209.165.201.1, Processing ID
[IKEv1 DECODE]: ID_IPV4_ADDR_SUBNET ID received--192.168.10.0--255.255.255.0
[IKEv1]: Group = 209.165.201.1, IP = 209.165.201.1, Received local IP Proxy Subnet
data in ID Payload:   Address 192.168.10.0, Mask 255.255.255.0, Protocol 0, Port 0
...
 [IKEv1]: Group = 209.165.201.1, IP = 209.165.201.1, Static Crypto Map check,
checking map = IPSec_map, seq = 10...
[IKEv1]: Group = 209.165.201.1, IP = 209.165.201.1, Static Crypto Map check, map
IPSec_map, seq = 10 is a successful match
```

continues

Example 15-35 *Debugs to Show Proxy Identities and Phase 2 Proposals Are Accepted (Continued)*

```
[IKEv1]: Group = 209.165.201.1, IP = 209.165.201.1, IKE Remote Peer configured for
SA: IPSec_map
[IKEv1]: Group = 209.165.201.1, IP = 209.165.201.1, processing IPSEC SA
[IKEv1 DEBUG]: Group = 209.165.201.1, IP = 209.165.201.1, IPSec SA Proposal # 1,
Transform # 1 acceptable  Matches global IPSec SA entry # 10
```

After accepting the transform set, both VPN devices agree on the inbound and outbound IPSec SAs, as shown in Example 15-36. Once the IPSec SAs have been created, both VPN devices should be able to pass traffic bidirectionally across the tunnel.

Example 15-36 *Debugs Showing IPSec SAs Are Activated*

```
[IKEv1 DEBUG]: Group = 209.165.201.1, IP = 209.165.201.1, loading all IPSEC SAs
...
[IKEv1]: Group = 209.165.201.1, IP = 209.165.201.1, Security negotiation complete
  for LAN-to-LAN Group (209.165.201.1)  Responder, Inbound SPI = 0xf798f8e5,
  Outbound SPI = 0x56029210
```

The following four scenarios discuss how to troubleshoot the common issues related to IPSec tunnels. The debug messages are shown if **debug crypto isakmp 127** is enabled on the security Cisco ASA.

ISAKMP Proposal Unacceptable

In this scenario, if the ISAKMP proposals are mismatched between the two VPN devices, the Cisco ASA Cisco ASA displays an "All SA proposals found unacceptable" message after processing the first main mode packet, as shown in Example 15-37.

Example 15-37 *Debugs to Show Mismatched ISAKMP Policies*

```
[IKEv1 DEBUG]: IP = 209.165.201.1,, processing SA payload
[IKEv1]: IP = 209.165.201.1, IKE DECODE SENDING Message (msgid=0) with payloads :
  HDR + NOTIFY (11) + NONE (0) total length : 96
[IKEv1 DEBUG]: IP = 209.165.201.1, All SA proposals found unacceptable
```

Mismatched Preshared keys

If the preshared key is mismatched between the VPN devices, the Cisco ASA Cisco ASA displays a "Error, had problems decrypting packet, probably due to mismatched pre-shared key" message after processing the fourth main mode packet. This is shown in Example 15-38.

Example 15-38 *Debugs to Show Mismatched Preshared Keys*

```
[IKEv1]: Group = 209.165.201.1, IP = 209.165.201.1Received encrypted Oakley Main
  Mode packet with invalid payloads, MessID = 0
[IKEv1]: IP = 209.165.201.1, IKE DECODE SENDING Message (msgid=0) with payloads :
  HDR + NOTIFY (11) + NONE (0) total length : 104
IKEv1]: Group = 209.165.201.1, IP = 209.165.201.1, ERROR, had problems decrypting
  packet, probably due to mismatched pre-shared key.  Aborting
```

Incompatible IPSec Transform Set

The security Cisco ASA displays an "All IPSec SA proposals found unacceptable" if the IPSec transform set is mismatched between the VPN devices. In this case, the Phase 1 SA gets established and the VPN devices fail to negotiate the IPSec SA. The Cisco ASA checks the validity of the crypto map before rejecting the IPSec SA, as shown in Example 15-39.

Example 15-39 *Debugs When Incompatible IPSec Transform Set Is used*

```
[IKEv1]: Group = 209.165.201.1, IP = 209.165.201.1, Static Crypto Map check,
   checking map = IPSec_map, seq = 10...
[IKEv1]: Group = 209.165.201.1, IP = 209.165.201.1, Static Crypto Map check, map
   IPSec_map, seq = 10 is a successful match
[IKEv1]: Group = 209.165.201.1, IP = 209.165.201.1, IKE Remote Peer configured for
   SA: IPSec_map
[IKEv1]: Group = 209.165.201.1, IP = 209.165.201.1, processing IPSEC SA
[IKEv1]: Group = 209.165.201.1, IP = 209.165.201.1, All IPSec SA proposals found
   unacceptable!
```

Mismatched Proxy Identities

If the encryption ACL on the security Cisco ASA does not match the encryption ACL offered by the other end of the VPN tunnel, the Cisco ASA rejects the IPSec SA and displays a "Crypto Map Policy not found" error with the associated local and remote subnets that the remote VPN device offered. In Example 15-40, the VPN peer 209.165.201.1 wants to negotiate IPSec SAs between 192.168.20.0 and 192.168.30.0, which the security Cisco ASA rejects because the received identities do not match the configured crypto ACL.

Example 15-40 *Debugs to Show Mismatched Proxy Identities*

```
[IKEv1 DECODE]: ID_IPV4_ADDR_SUBNET ID received--192.168.30.0--255.255.255.0
[IKEv1]: Group = 209.165.201.1, IP = 209.165.201.1, Received remote IP Proxy Subnet
   data in ID Payload:   Address 192.168.30.0, Mask 255.255.255.0, Protocol 0, Port 0
[IKEv1 DEBUG]: Group = 209.165.201.1, IP = 209.165.201.1, Processing ID
[IKEv1 DECODE]: ID_IPV4_ADDR_SUBNET ID received--192.168.20.0--255.255.255.0
[IKEv1]: Group = 209.165.201.1, IP = 209.165.201.1, Received local IP Proxy Subnet
   data in ID Payload:   Address 192.168.20.0, Mask 255.255.255.0, Protocol 0, Port 0
...
[IKEv1]: Group = 209.165.201.1, IP = 209.165.201.1, Static Crypto Map check,
   checking map = IPSec_map, seq = 10...
[IKEv1]: Group = 209.165.201.1, IP = 209.165.201.1, Static Crypto Map check, map =
   IPSec_map, seq = 10, ACL does not match proxy IDs src:192.168.30.0
   dst:192.168.20.0
[IKEv1]: Group = 209.165.201.1, IP = 209.165.201.1, Tunnel rejected: Crypto Map
   Policy not found for Src:192.168.30.0, Dst: 192.168.20.0!
```

Summary

Everyday, more and more organizations are deploying IPSec site-to-site tunnels to cut costs on traditional WAN links. It is a responsibility of the security professional to design and implement an IPSec solution that will fit the needs of an organization. If the other end of the IPSec VPN tunnel is managed by a different security professional, make sure that you consult with them before configuring the ISAKMP and IPSec attributes in the ASA. This chapter discussed the configuration guide on how to implement the site-to-site tunnels and discussed the two deployment scenarios. If you implement the solution, and the IPSec tunnel is not working as expected, use the appropriate **show** commands and monitor the status of the SAs. You can also turn on the ISAKMP and IPSec debugs to help narrow down the issue.

This chapter covers the following topics:

- Cisco IPSec Remote Access VPN Solution
- Advanced Cisco Remote Access VPN features
- Deployment scenarios of Cisco Remote Access VPN
- Monitoring and troubleshooting Cisco Remote Access VPN
- Cisco WebVPN Solution
- Advanced WebVPN features
- Deployment scenarios of WebVPN Solution
- Monitoring and troubleshooting WebVPN Solution

CHAPTER 16

Remote Access VPN

Remote-access VPN services provide a way to connect home and mobile users to the corporate network. Until half a decade ago, the only way to provide this service was through dialup connections using analog modems. Corporations had to maintain a huge pool of modems and access servers to accommodate remote users. Additionally, they were billed for providing toll-free and long-distance phone services. With the rapid growth of the Internet technologies, more and more dialup mobile users are migrating to broadband DSL and cable-modem connections. As a result, corporations are in the process of moving these dialup users to remote-access VPNs for faster communication.

There are many remote-access VPN protocols available to provide secure network access. The commonly used ones include the following:

- Point-to-Point Tunneling Protocol (PPTP)
- Layer 2 Tunneling Protocol (L2TP)
- Layer 2 Forwarding (L2F) Protocol
- IPSec
- L2TP over IPSec

Cisco ASA supports native IPSec to provide VPN services in the most secure fashion. It also incorporates the new WebVPN technology, discussed later in this chapter.

Cisco IPSec Remote Access VPN Solution

With the Cisco IPSec solution, Cisco ASA allows mobile and home users to establish a VPN tunnel by using the Cisco software and Cisco hardware VPN clients.

The Cisco VPN client uses aggressive mode if preshared keys are used, and uses main mode when public key infrastructure (PKI) is used during Phase 1 of the tunnel negotiations. After bringing up the ISAKMP SA for secure communication, Cisco ASA prompts the user to specify the user credentials. In this phase, also known as X-Auth or extended authentication, the security appliance validates the user against the configured authentication database. If the user authentication is successful, Cisco ASA sends a successful authentication message back to the client. After X-Auth, the Cisco VPN client requests configuration parameters such as the assigned IP address and the DNS and WINS server IP addresses, to name a few. During this phase, known as mode-config, the security appliance sends the configured parameters back to the client. The final step for a successful VPN tunnel is the negotiation of Phase 2 parameters, as illustrated in Figure 16-1. After completing the tunnel negotiations, the client can send or receive traffic over the connection.

Figure 16-1   *Tunnel Negotiations for Cisco VPN Client*

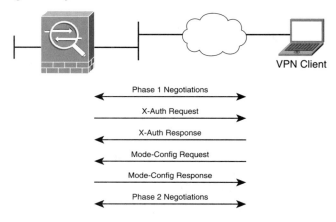

NOTE   It is recommended to use main mode for IKE authentication using RSA signatures because of the known vulnerabilities in aggressive mode.

Configuration Steps

Figure 16-2 illustrates SecureMe's Chicago hub office to be configured for the Cisco remote-access VPN solution. This topology will be used to show the following configuration steps required to establish a successful VPN tunnel. Many of these steps are identical to the steps discussed in Chapter 15, "Site-to-Site IPSec VPNs."

Step 1   Enable ISAKMP.

Step 2   Create the ISAKMP policy.

Step 3   Configure remote-access attributes.

Step 4   Define the tunnel type.

Step 5   Configure preshared keys.

Step 6   Configure user authentication.

Step 7   Assign an IP address.

Step 8   Define the IPSec policy.

Step 9   Set up a dynamic crypto map.

Step 10   Configure the crypto map.

Step 11   Apply the crypto map on the interface.

Step 12   Configure traffic filtering.

Step 13   Set up the tunnel default gateway (Optional).

Step 14   Bypass NAT (Optional).

Step 15   Set up split tunneling (Optional).

Figure 16-2   *Remote-Access Network Topology for SecureMe*

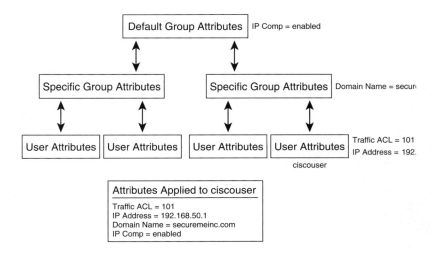

Step 1: Enable ISAKMP

By default, ISAKMP is disabled on all the interfaces. If the remote VPN device sends a tunnel initialization message, the security appliance drops it until ISAKMP is enabled on the interface terminating the VPN tunnels. Typically, it is enabled on the Internet-facing or outside interface, as demonstrated in Example 16-1.

Example 16-1   *Enabling ISAKMP on the Outside Interface*

```
Chicago# configure terminal
Chicago(config)# isakmp enable outside
```

Step 2: Create the ISAKMP Policy

The **isakmp policy** commands define ISAKMP Phase 1 attributes that are exchanged between the VPN peers. Cisco ASA supports digital signature authentication using Digital Signature Algorithm (DSA) and Rivest-Shamir-Adleman (RSA), and preshared keys as the authentication method. For encryption, Cisco ASA uses both Advanced Encryption Standard (AES) and the aging Data Encryption Standard (DES).

Additionally, Cisco ASA supports Diffie-Hellman (DH) groups 1, 2, 5, and 7. The complete command syntax of the **isakmp policy** command is as follows:

```
isakmp policy priority authentication dsa-sig I pre-share I rsa-sig
isakmp policy priority encryption 3des I aes I aes-192 I aes-256 I des
isakmp policy priority group 1 I 2 I 5 I 7
isakmp policy priority hash md5 I sha
isakmp policy priority lifetime 120-2147483647
```

If multiple ISAKMP policies are configured, the Cisco ASA checks the ISAKMP policy with the highest priority first. If there is no match, it checks the next higher priority policy, and so on until all policies have been evaluated. A priority value of 1 is the highest priority, while a priority value of 65535 is the lowest.

Example 16-2 shows an ISAKMP policy t o negotiate preshared keys for authentication, AES-256 for encryption, SHA for hashing, group 2 for DH, and 86400 seconds for lifetime.

Example 16-2 *Configuration of ISAKMP Policy*

```
Chicago# configure terminal
Chicago(config)# isakmp policy 10 authentication pre-share
Chicago(config)# isakmp policy 10 encryption aes-256
Chicago(config)# isakmp policy 10 hash sha
Chicago(config)# isakmp policy 10 group 2
Chicago(config)# isakmp policy 10 lifetime 86400
```

Step 3: Configure Remote-Access Attributes

Cisco ASA allows the configuration of most of the mode-config parameters in three different places:

- Under default group-policy
- Under user group-policy
- Under user policy

Cisco ASA implements the inheritance model, where a user inherits the mode-config attributes from the user policy, which inherits its attributes from the user group-policy, which in turn inherits its attributes from the default group-policy, as illustrated in Figure 16-3. A user, ciscouser, will receive traffic ACL and an assigned IP address from the user policy, the domain name from the user group-policy, and IP Compression along with the number of simultaneous logins from the default group-policy.

Figure 16-3 *Mode-Config Inheritance Model*

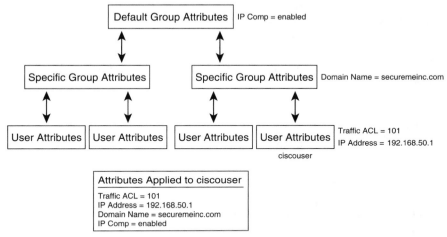

You can use the **group-policy attributes** command to specify the default and user group-policy mode-config attributes. Example 16-3 shows how to configure the default group attributes on Cisco ASA by setting **DfltGrpPolicy** as the group name in the group-policy. The administrator has limited the simultaneous logins to 3, and has enabled IP Compression for data payload.

Example 16-3 *Configuration of Default Group-Policy*

```
Chicago(config)# group-policy DfltGrpPolicy attributes
Chicago(config-group-policy)# vpn-simultaneous-logins 3
Chicago(config-group-policy)# ip-comp enable
```

NOTE   DfltGrpPolicy is a special group name, used solely for the default group-policy.

The user group-policy is set up similarly to a default group-policy, by configuring the attributes under the group-policy submenu. In Example 16-4, a group called SecureMeGrp is being set up to send the domain-name securemeinc.com attribute during mode-config exchange. One major difference between the default group-policy and the user group-policy is that you can define the latter as an internal or external group. *Internal group* means that all the policy attributes are defined locally on the security appliance, while *external group* means that all the attributes are stored on an external server such as RADIUS. In Example 16-4, SecureMeGrp is set up as an internal group, which is why the domain-name VPN attribute is defined locally.

Example 16-4 *Configuration of Group-Specific Group Policy*

```
Chicago(config)# group-policy SecureMeGrp internal
Chicago(config)# group-policy SecureMeGrp attributes
Chicago(config-group-policy)# default-domain value securemeinc.com
```

The user policy is defined by using the **username attributes** command. The user account is usually mapped to the user group-policy, discussed in the previous example. If an attribute is configured under both the user group-policy and under the user policy, then the user account attribute takes precedence over the group-policy attribute. In Example 16-5, a user account ciscouser is defined and mapped to the SecureMeGrp group. This user is configured to receive an IP address of 192.168.50.1 and a filtering ACL of 102 as the user attributes.

Example 16-5 *Configuration of User Policy*

```
Chicago(config)# username ciscouser password cisco123
Chicago(config)# username ciscouser attributes
Chicago(config-username)# vpn-group-policy SecureMeGrp
Chicago(config-username)# vpn-framed-ip-address 192.168.50.1 255.255.255.255
Chicago(config-username)# vpn-filter value 102
```

Table 16-1 lists all the mode-config attributes that you can set up under the default and user group-policies.

Table 16-1 *Configurable Mode-Config Attributes*

Attributes	Purpose
backup-servers	Set up backup servers on the client in case the primary server fails to respond
banner	Send a banner to the client after establishing a tunnel
client-access-rule	Apply rules allowing or denying access to certain VPN hosts
client-firewall	Set up the firewall parameters on the VPN client
default-domain	Send a domain name to the client
dhcp-network-scope	Specify the IP subnetwork to which users within this group will be assigned an address from the DHCP server
dns-server	Specify the IP address of a DNS server
group-lock	Specify a tunnel group to ensure that users get connected to that group
ip-comp	Enable IP Compression for the client tunnels
ip-phone-bypass	Allow Cisco IP Phones to bypass Individual User Authentication if they reside behind the hardware-based VPN clients
ipsec-udp	Use UDP encapsulation for the IPSec tunnels
ipsec-udp-port	Specify the port number that IPSec over UDP will use; default is port 10000

Table 16-1   *Configurable Mode-Config Attributes (Continued)*

Attributes	Purpose
leap-bypass	Allow Cisco wireless devices to bypass Individual User Authentication if they reside behind the hardware-based VPN clients
nem	Enable network extension mode
password-storage	Let the VPN users save their user password in the profile
pfs	Inform the VPN client to use Perfect Forward Secrecy (PFS)
re-xauth	Launch the XAUTH authentication process when IKE rekeys
secure-unit-authentication	Enable interactive authentication for the hardware-based VPN clients
split-dns	Pass down a list of domains for name resolution
split-tunnel-network-list	Pass down a list of IP networks that the VPN clients are allowed to encrypt
user-authentication	Enable individual user authentication for the hardware-based VPN clients
vpn-access-hours	Restrict VPN users based on preconfigured time range
vpn-filter	Apply a filter for the VPN traffic
vpn-idle-timeout	Specify the timeout, in minutes, if a VPN session is idle
vpn-session-timeout	Specify the timeout, in minutes, when a VPN session reaches maximum connection time
vpn-simultaneous-logins	Specify the maximum number of simultaneous logins
vpn-tunnel-protocol	Specify the permitted tunneling protocols
wins-server	Specify the IP address of a WINS server

Step 4: Define the Tunnel Type

As briefly mentioned in Chapter 15, Cisco ASA can be configured for two different tunnel types, as shown in Example 16-6.

Example 16-6 *Supported Tunnel Types*

```
Chicago(config)# tunnel-group ciscovpn type ?
  ipsec-l2l    IPSec Site to Site group
  ipsec-ra     IPSec Remote Access group
```

In this example, the **tunnel-group** tag is named ciscovpn. The tunnel type **ipsec-l2l** is used for site-to-site VPN tunnels, while the tunnel type **ipsec-ra** is used for the Cisco IPSec VPN solution. In the **ipsec-ra** type, the security appliance expects the Cisco VPN clients to initiate a tunnel and send vendor identity as Cisco client during the ISAKMP negotiations. Example 16-7 shows the Cisco ASA in Chicago configured for remote-access tunnels.

Example 16-7 *Configuration of Remote-Access Tunnels*

```
Chicago(config)# tunnel-group ciscovpn type ipsec-ra
```

NOTE   The tunnel-group name, ciscovpn in the preceding example, is the group name that needs to be configured on the Cisco VPN clients.

Step 5: Configure ISAKMP Preshared Keys

If you want to use a preshared key as the authentication method, then you must configure a shared secret which is used to validate the identity of both VPN devices. The preshared key is configured under the **ipsec-attributes** submenu of the tunnel group, as shown in Example 16-8.

Example 16-8 *Preshared Key Configuration*

```
Chicago(config)# tunnel-group ciscovpn ipsec-attributes
Chicago(config-ipsec)# pre-shared-key cisco123
```

In Example 16-8, all Cisco VPN clients configured for the ciscovpn group must use cisco123 as the preshared key. If there is a mismatch on the key, the security appliance denies group authentication for the client.

NOTE   Preshared key is also known as group password in the Cisco remote-access VPN.

NOTE   This step is not necessary if the security appliance is set up for RSA signatures. This will be discussed in Chapter 17, "Public Key Infrastructure (PKI)."

Step 6: Configure User Authentication

Cisco ASA supports a variety of authentication servers, such as RADIUS, Windows NT domain, Kerberos, SDI, and local database. For small organizations, a local database can be set up for user authentication. In Example 16-9, the Chicago ASA has two user accounts, ciscouser and adminuser, configured for IPSec authentication.

Example 16-9 *Local User Accounts*

```
Chicago# configure terminal
Chicago(config)# username ciscouser password cisco1
Chicago(config)# username adminuser password cisco2
```

The tunnel group must be configured with the corresponding authentication server, under general attributes. The **authentication-server-group** subcommand specifies the authentication server. Example 16-10 illustrates how to configure the security appliance to use the local database for the **ciscovpn** group.

Example 16-10 *Local Authentication Configuration*

```
Chicago(config)# tunnel-group ciscovpn general-attributes
Chicago((config-group-policy)# authentication-server-group LOCAL
```

For configuration of external servers, consult Chapter 7, "Authentication, Authorization, and Accounting (AAA)."

CAUTION   In the first few releases of the Cisco ASA image, if user authentication is not configured, you need the authorization server command to push the mode-config attributes.

Step 7: Assign an IP Address

During mode configuration, the Cisco VPN client requests an IP address to be assigned to the VPN adapter on the workstation. Cisco ASA supports three different methods to assign an IP address back to the client:

- Local address pool
- DHCP server
- RADIUS server

Example 16-11 shows the available address assignment methods in the **vpn-addr-assign** command. The security appliance uses the **aaa** option to use the RADIUS server for address assignment, the **dhcp** keyword to contact a DHCP server when it needs to assign an address to the VPN user, and the **local** option to use the local database.

Example 16-11 *Available Address Assignment Methods*

```
Chicago(config)# vpn-addr-assign ?
  aaa    Allow AAA servers to specify an IP address
  dhcp   Allow DHCP servers to specify an IP address
  local  Allow local pools to specify an IP address
Chicago(config)# vpn-addr-assign local
```

For small to midsize deployments, the preferred method for assigning an IP address is through the local database. When the client requests an IP address, Cisco ASA looks at the tunnel group configuration and checks the address assignment method. If local pool is the configured option, the security appliance checks the address assignment in the following order:

1 user policy configuration

2 group address pool

A static IP address can be assigned to a user under the user policy. The VPN user will receive the same IP address regardless of the number of times they connect to the Cisco

ASA. In Example 16-12, a static IP address of 192.168.50.1 is assigned to ciscouser by using the **vpn-frame-ip-address** command.

Example 16-12 *Address Assignment Under User Policy*

```
Chicago(config)# username ciscouser attributes
Chicago(config-username)# vpn-framed-ip-address 192.168.50.1
```

The second option of assigning an IP address is by configuring the address pool and then linking it to the VPN group under **tunnel-group** general attributes. Example 16-13 shows the necessary commands to configure an address pool called vpnpool, and map it for address assignment for a VPN group ciscovpn. The pool range starts from 192.168.50.2 and ends at 192.168.50.199.

Example 16-13 *Address Assignment from Local Pool*

```
Chicago(config)# ip local pool vpnpool 192.168.50.2-192.168.50.199
Chicago(config)# tunnel-group ciscovpn general-attributes
Chicago(config-general)# address-pool vpnpool
```

For ease of management, the security appliance can contact a DHCP server when allocating an IP address. After the DHCP server assigns an address, Cisco ASA forwards that IP address to the client. Example 16-14 illustrates how the security appliance in Chicago can be configured to use a DHCP server with an IP address of 192.168.10.10 for address assignment.

Example 16-14 *Address Assignment from a DHCP Server*

```
Chicago(config)# vpn-addr-assign dhcp
Chicago(config)# tunnel-group ciscovpn general-attributes
Chicago(config-general)# dhcp-server 192.168.10.10
```

Many large enterprises prefer to authenticate users on the external RADIUS servers, which can assign IP addresses to the client after successfully authenticating the users. Example 16-15 shows the configuration of the Cisco ASA if RADIUS, set up as an authenticating device, is assigning the IP address.

Example 16-15 *Address Assignment from an AAA Server*

```
Chicago(config)# aaa-server Radius protocol radius
Chicago(config-aaa-server-group)# exit
Chicago(config)# aaa-server Radius (inside) host 192.168.10.10
Chicago(config-aaa-server-host)# key cisco123
Chicago(config-aaa-server-host)# exit
Chicago(config)# vpn-addr-assign aaa
```

NOTE   If all three methods are configured for address assignment, Cisco ASA prefers RADIUS over DHCP and address pool. If Cisco ASA is not able to get an address from the RADIUS server, it contacts the DHCP server for address allocation. If that method fails as well, Cisco ASA checks the local address pool as the last resort.

Step 8: Define the IPSec Policy

An IPSec transform set specifies the encryption and hashing method to be used on the data packets once the tunnel is up. To configure the transform set, use the following command syntax:

```
crypto ipsec transform-set transform-set tag {esp-3des | esp-aes | esp-aes-192 |
    esp-aes-256 | esp-des | esp-md5-hmac | esp-null | esp-none | esp-sha-hmac}
```

Table 16-2 lists the encryption and hashing algorithms that can be used in a transform set.

Table 16-2 *IPSec Transform Set Arguments*

Type	Available Options	Default Option
Encryption	**esp-3des** **esp-aes** **esp-aes-192** **esp-aes-256** **esp-des** **esp-null**	**esp-3DES, or** **esp-des** if VPN-3DES-AES feature is not active
Hashing	**esp-md5-hmac** **esp-sha-hmac** **esp-none**	**esp-none**

NOTE   If the VPN-3DES-AES feature is not enabled, the security appliance allows DES encryption only for ISAKMP and IPSec policies.

In Example 16-16, the Chicago ASA is set up for AES-256 encryption and SHA hashing. The transform set name is myset.

Example 16-16 *Transform Set Configuration*

```
Chicago(config)# crypto ipsec transform-set myset esp-aes-256 esp-sha-hmac
```

Step 9: Set Up a Dynamic Crypto Map

VPN clients often get dynamic IP addresses from their ISPs. In a crypto map, which requires a static IP address for the VPN peer, there is no way to map those dynamic IP addresses. Cisco ASA solves this problem by allowing configuration of a dynamic crypto map. Example 16-17 demonstrates the configuration of the Cisco ASA in Chicago to use the defined transform set. The dynamic crypto map name is dynmap and it is configured with a sequence number of 10. Setting up a transform set in a dynamic crypto map is a required attribute. The dynamic crypto map becomes incomplete if there is no transform set applied to it.

Example 16-17 *Dynamic Crypto Map Configuration*

```
Chicago(config)# crypto dynamic-map dynmap 10 set transform-set myset
```

You can optionally configure many IPSec attributes in the dynamic crypto map. They include disabling NAT-T, configuring PFS and reverse-route injection (RRI), and setting security association (SA) lifetimes. Chapter 15, "Site-to-Site IPSec VPNs," covers these attributes.

Step 10: Configure the Crypto Map

The dynamic map is associated to a crypto map entry, which eventually gets applied to the interface terminating the IPSec tunnels. The crypto map can have both static and dynamic crypto map entries, discussed later in the deployment section "Load-Balancing and Site-to-Site Integration."

Example 16-18 shows crypto map configuration on the Chicago ASA. The crypto map name is IPSec_map and the sequence number is 65535.

Example 16-18 *Crypto Map Configuration*

```
Chicago(config)# crypto map IPSec_map 65535 ipsec-isakmp dynamic dynmap
```

The Cisco ASA limits one crypto map per interface. If there is a need to configure multiple VPN tunnels, use the same crypto map name with a different sequence number. However, the security appliance evaluates a VPN tunnel with the lowest sequence number first.

Step 11: Apply the Crypto Map to an Interface

The next step in setting up a remote-access tunnel is to bind the crypto map to an interface, using the following command syntax:

```
crypto map map-name interface interface-name
```

In Example 16-19, the crypto map, IPSec_map, is applied to the outside interface of the Chicago ASA.

Example 16-19 *Applying a Crypto Map to the Outside Interface*

```
Chicago# configure terminal
Chicago(config)# crypto map IPSec_map interface outside
```

Step 12: Configure Traffic Filtering

In its default firewall role, the Cisco ASA blocks decrypted traffic and protects the trusted network, unless the ACLs explicitly permit traffic to pass through it. In Figure 16-2, the VPN clients are being assigned an IP address from the 192.168.50.0 address pool. They are allowed to send traffic to a Telnet server located at 192.168.10.20 on TCP port 23 across the VPN tunnel. The Chicago ASA has an inbound access list called outside_acl applied to its outside interface which only allows the telnet traffic to pass through it, as shown in Example 16-20.

Example 16-20 *Access List to Allow Decrypted Traffic to Pass Through the Cisco ASA*

```
Chicago(config)# access-list outside_acl extended permit tcp 192.168.50.0
255.255.255.0 host 192.168.10.20 eq 23
Chicago(config)# access-group outside_acl in interface outside
```

If you trust all of your private networks, including all of your remote VPN clients, Cisco ASA can be configured to permit all decrypted IPSec packets to pass through it without inspecting them against the configured ACL. This is done with the use of the **sysopt connection permit-ipsec** command, as shown in Example 16-21.

Example 16-21 *Sysopt Configuration to Bypass Traffic Filtering*

```
Chicago(config)# sysopt connection permit-ipsec
```

Step 13: Set Up a Tunnel Default Gateway (Optional)

A Layer 3 device typically has a default gateway that is used to route packets when the destination address is not found in the routing table. *Tunnel default gateway*, a concept first introduced in the VPN 3000 Series Concentrators, is used to route the packets if they reach the security appliance over an IPSec tunnel and if their destination IP address is not found in the routing table. The tunneled traffic can be either remote-access or site-to-site VPN traffic. The tunnel default gateway next-hop address is generally the IP address of the inside router, Router1 (illustrated in Figure 16-2), or any Layer 3 device.

The tunnel default gateway feature is important if you do not want to define routes about your internal networks to the Cisco ASA and instead want the tunneled traffic to be sent to the internal router for routing. To set up a tunnel default gateway, add the keyword **tunneled** to the statically configured default route. Example 16-22 shows the configuration of the security appliance with the tunnel default gateway specified as 192.168.10.2, located on the inside interface.

Example 16-22 *Tunnel Default Gateway Configuration*

```
Chicago(config)# route inside 0.0.0.0 0.0.0.0 192.168.10.2 tunneled
```

Step 14: Bypass NAT (Optional)

If NAT is configured on the security appliance but you do not want to change the source IP address of traffic going over the VPN tunnel, you need to configure the NAT exempt rules, as discussed in Chapter 5, "Network Access Control."

You need to create an access list to specify what traffic needs to be bypassed by the NAT engine. Example 16-23 shows an access list that is permitting the VPN traffic from 192.168.10.0/24 to the pool of addresses in 192.168.50.0/24.

Example 16-23 *Access List to Bypass NAT*

```
Chicago(config)# access-list nonat extended permit ip 192.168.10.0 255.255.255.0
    192.168.50.0 255.255.255.0
```

After defining the access list, the next step is to configure the **nat 0** command. Example 16-24 demonstrates how to configure the **nat 0** statement if the private LAN that is being protected is toward the inside interface.

Example 16-24 *Configuration of* **nat 0** *access-list*

```
Chicago(config)# nat (inside) 0 access-list nonat
```

Step 15: Set Up Split Tunneling (Optional)

Once the tunnel is up, the default behavior of the Cisco VPN client is to encrypt traffic destined to all the IP addresses. This means that if a VPN user wants to browse www.cisco.com over the Internet as illustrated in Figure 16-4, the packets will get encrypted and sent to the Cisco ASA. After decrypting them, Cisco ASA will look at its routing table and forward the packet to the appropriate next-hop IP address in clear-text. These steps are reversed when traffic returns from the web server and is destined to the VPN client.

Figure 16-4 *Traffic with No Split Tunneling*

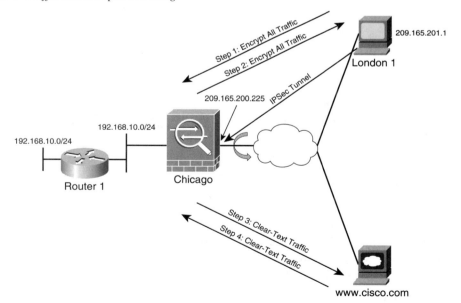

This behavior might not always be desirable, for the following two reasons:

- Traffic destined to the nonsecured networks traverses over the Internet twice — once encrypted and once in clear text.
- Cisco ASA handles extra VPN traffic destined to the nonsecured subnet.

With split tunneling, Cisco ASA can notify the VPN client for the secured subnets. The VPN client, using the secured routes, encrypts only those packets that are destined for the networks behind the security appliance.

CAUTION   With split tunneling, the VPN client is susceptible to a hacker, who can potentially take control over the computer and direct traffic over the IPSec tunnel. To mitigate this behavior, a personal firewall is highly recommended on the Cisco VPN clients.

Additionally, Cisco ASA also supports tunneling all traffic except for a list of networks that require clear-text access. This feature is useful if users require clear-text access to their local LAN and an encrypted tunnel to the corporate network.

As mentioned earlier, the security appliance provides three modes for split tunneling:

- Tunnel all traffic (no split tunneling)
- Tunnel specific networks (split tunneling)
- Tunnel all but specific networks (exclude split tunneling)

These modes can be configured under the group and user policy by using the **split-tunnel-policy** command followed by the split-tunneling mode. If split-tunneling and exclude split-tunneling modes are used, you need to configure a standard access list to specify all the destination networks to be included or excluded. Example 16-25 shows the configuration for the SecureMeGrp user group-policy to tunnel specific networks. Additionally, this configuration defines a standard ACL called Spt_tnl to include the 192.168.0.0/16 network for split tunneling. The ACL is then linked to the group-policy by using the **split-tunnel-network-list value** command followed by the name of the ACL, Spt_tnl.

Example 16-25 *Split-Tunnel Configuration*

```
Chicago(config)# access-list Spt_tnl standard permit 192.168.0.0 255.255.0.0
Chicago(config)# group-policy SecureMeGrp attributes
Chicago(config-group-policy)# split-tunnel-policy tunnelspecified
Chicago(config-group-policy)# split-tunnel-network-list value Spt_tnl
```

Cisco VPN Client Configuration

The Cisco VPN Client, also known as the Cisco Easy VPN Client, initiates the IPSec tunnel to the security appliance. If the configuration and user credentials are valid, the tunnel is established and traffic is processed over it. The Cisco VPN clients come in two different flavors, which are discussed in the sections that follow:

- Software-based VPN clients
- Hardware-based VPN clients

Software-Based VPN Clients

The software-based VPN client runs on a variety of operating systems, such as Windows, Solaris, Linux, and Mac OS/X. It can be downloaded from Cisco.com free of charge as long as the Cisco ASA is under a valid service contract.

Before you configure the Cisco VPN client, it needs to be installed on the host machine. Please refer to http://www.cisco.com/go/vpnclient for the installation instructions. Cisco ASA supports version 3.x or higher VPN clients.

NOTE   The installation of Cisco VPN Client requires administrative privileges on the workstation.

In the Windows-based operating systems, the Cisco VPN client can be launched by running the VPN client executable found under **Start > Program files > Cisco Systems VPN Client** once it is installed. The operating system runs the executable and displays the VPN Client utility, as depicted in Figure 16-5.

Figure 16-5 *Initial VPN Client Window*

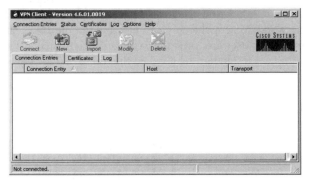

The configuration of a Windows-based VPN client requires five parameters:

- Name of the connection entry
- Public IP address of the Cisco ASA
- Group name that the VPN client will be connecting to

- Group preshared key
- Tunnel encapsulation

You can configure these parameters on the Cisco VPN client by clicking the **New** icon. The Cisco VPN client shows a different window in which you can enter the necessary information. In Figure 16-6, the user has specified the Connection Entry as Chicago ASA. You can name this entry any name you like. It only has local significance and is not forwarded to the security appliance. You can optionally enter the description for this connection entry. In this example, the connection description is Connection to Chicago ASA. The VPN client requires you to input the IP or the hostname of the security appliance. Because the public IP address of the security appliance in Chicago is 209.165.200.225, the VPN client is set up to use this address. The group name that the VPN client is configured to use is ciscovpn, and the group password is cisco123, displayed as asterisks. The group password on the client is the preshared key configured on the security appliance.

Figure 16-6 *VPN Client Configuration*

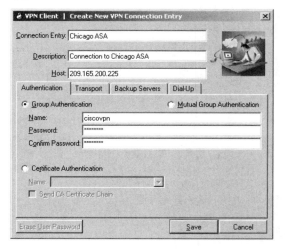

You can specify what type of data encapsulation the Cisco VPN client should be using. This is set up under the Transport tab, as shown in Figure 16-7. If IPSec over UDP or NAT-T is the encapsulation mode, then check the **Enable Transparent Tunneling** box with **IPSec over UDP (NAT/PAT)** as the selected option. If IPSec over TCP is the required encapsulation, then select **IPSec over TCP** and specify the appropriate port number. In this example, IPSec over UDP is the selected transport protocol.

NOTE	The headend side needs to be set up for transparent tunneling as well. Consult the upcoming section "Transparent Tunneling" for a detailed explanation and configuration.

Figure 16-7 *Transparent Tunneling Configuration*

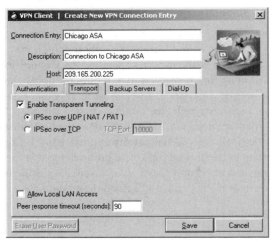

NOTE If the Enable Transparent Tunneling box is disabled, the VPN client uses only the native IPSec encapsulation mode using ESP.

After configuring the VPN client, the user can click the Connect icon to establish the connection to the security appliance. This is shown in Figure 16-8.

Figure 16-8 *VPN Connection Establishment*

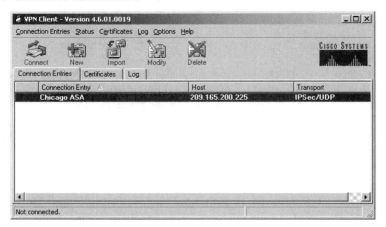

Hardware-Based VPN Clients

The Cisco hardware-based VPN clients implement the same functionality as discussed in the earlier section using the dedicated Cisco hardware devices. Easy VPN is supported on the following platforms:

- Cisco IOS router
- Cisco PIX Firewall
- Cisco VPN 3002 Hardware Client

A Cisco small office, home office (SOHO) router can act as a VPN client and initiate a VPN tunnel on behalf of the hosts residing on the private subnet, as shown in Figure 16-9. When the Cisco IOS router receives interesting traffic destined to pass over the VPN tunnel, it determines the IP address of the security appliance by checking the configuration.

Figure 16-9 *Cisco IOS based Easy VPN Client Connecting to Cisco ASA*

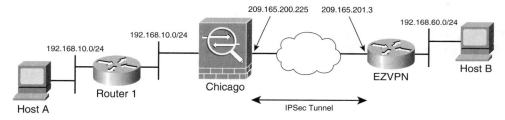

NOTE   For a list of Cisco IOS routers supported for Easy VPN deployment, refer to the following Cisco.com page:

http://www.cisco.com/go/easyvpn

Two connection modes are supported by the hardware based Easy VPN devices:

- **Client mode** — Also called Port Address Translation (PAT) mode, isolates all hosts on the private side of the hardware VPN client from those on the corporate network. The hardware based Easy VPN client translates all traffic initiated by the hosts on the private side to a single source IP address before sending it over the tunnel. This source IP address is assigned to the client by the security appliance during the mode-config exchange. The client translates the original source IP address by assigning a random source port. The client keeps and maintains a port translation table to identify where to send responses on the private network.

Using the client mode, the hosts on the private network can initiate traffic destined to the corporate network. However, the hosts on the corporate network cannot initiate traffic back to the private network of the Easy VPN client.

- **Network Extension Mode (NEM)**—Acts similarly to a site-to-site tunnel in that hosts behind the corporate network can initiate traffic destined to the network behind the Easy VPN client, and vice versa. Thus, hosts on either side know each other by their actual addresses. The major difference between the site-to-site and NEM VPN tunnels is that the IPSec connection has to be initiated by the Easy VPN client.

  Using NEM, there is no need for the security appliance to assign an IP address to the client. Therefore, the client does not participate in PAT for traffic destined over the VPN tunnel.

The Easy VPN configuration on the Cisco IOS routers requires the use of **crypto ipsec client ezvpn** followed by the name of the Easy VPN profile. The profile name has only local significance and is not used for tunnel negotiation. Under the EZVPN subconfiguration mode, you can specify the IP address of the security appliance, the group name, and the group password. In Example 16-26, an Easy VPN profile called EZVPN_Client is set up to automatically connect to the security appliance public IP address of 209.165.200.225, as soon as the Easy VPN interface configuration is done. The group name that the Cisco IOS Easy VPN client is using is ciscovpn with the group password of cisco123. The administrator has set up NEM for this connection. For X-Auth, a username of ciscouser with a password of cisco1 is being configured.

Example 16-26 *Easy VPN Client Configuration*

```
EZVPN-client(config)# crypto ipsec client ezvpn EZVPN_Client
EZVPN-client(config-crypto-ezvpn)# connect auto
EZVPN-client(config-crypto-ezvpn)# group ciscovpn key cisco123
EZVPN-client(config-crypto-ezvpn)# mode network-extension
EZVPN-client(config-crypto-ezvpn)# peer 209.165.200.225
EZVPN-client(config-crypto-ezvpn)# username ciscouser password cisco1
```

After configuring the profile, the next step is to identify the inside and outside Easy VPN interfaces. This is achieved by using the **crypto ipsec client ezvpn inside** and **crypto ipsec client ezvpn outside** commands on the correct interfaces. Example 16-27 shows how to bind the configured EZVPN_Client profile on the inside and outside interfaces.

Example 16-27 *Configuring the Inside and Outside Cisco IOS Easy VPN Interfaces*

```
EZVPN-client(config)# interface Ethernet0
EZVPN-client(config-if)# ip address 192.168.60.1 255.255.255.0
EZVPN-client(config-if)# crypto ipsec client ezvpn EZVPN_Client inside
EZVPN-client(config-if)# exit
EZVPN-client(config)# interface Ethernet1
EZVPN-client(config-if)# ip address 209.165.201.3 255.255.255.248
EZVPN-client(config-if)# crypto ipsec client ezvpn EZVPN_Client outside
```

NOTE	For Cisco PIX and VPN 3002 Hardware Client installation and configuration documents, refer to the following links.
	PIX Easy VPN Client:
	http://www.cisco.com/univercd/cc/td/doc/product/iaabu/pix/pix_sw/v_63/config/ pixclnt.htm#wp1032561
	VPN 3002 Hardware Client:
	http://www.cisco.com/univercd/cc/td/doc/product/vpn/vpn3002/4-1/referenc/tunnel.htm

Advanced Cisco IPSec VPN Features

Cisco ASA provides many advanced features to suit your remote-access VPN implementations. Some of these features are listed here:

- Transparent tunneling
- IPSec hairpinning
- VPN load-balancing
- Client auto-update
- Client firewalling
- Easy VPN features

The sections that follow cover these features in more detail.

Transparent Tunneling

In many network topologies, the VPN clients reside behind a SOHO NAT/PAT device that inspects the Layer 4 port information for address translation. Because IPSec uses ESP (IP protocol 50), which does not have Layer 4 information, the NAT device is usually incapable of translating the encrypted packets going over the VPN tunnel. To remedy this problem, Cisco ASA offers three different options:

- NAT Traversal (NAT-T)
- IPSec over UDP
- IPSec over TCP

The sections that follow cover these options in greater detail.

NAT Traversal

NAT-T, currently an IETF draft, is a feature that encapsulates the ESP packets into UDP port 4500 packets. NAT-T is dynamically negotiated if the following two conditions are met:

- Both VPN devices are NAT-T capable
- A NAT or PAT device exists between VPN peers

If both conditions are true, the VPN client tries to connect to the security appliance using UDP port 500 for IKE negotiations. As soon as the VPN peers discover that they are NAT-T capable and a NAT/PAT device resides between them, they switch over to UDP port 4500 for the rest of tunnel negotiations and data encapsulation.

The command syntax to enable NAT-T globally on Cisco ASA is as follows:

```
crypto isakmp nat-traversal [keepalives]
```

Here, the *keepalives* range is between 10 and 3600 seconds. If you don't specify the keepalives range, Cisco ASA uses 20 seconds as the default. NAT-T keepalives are used to make sure that a NAT or PAT device does not age out the VPN tunnel on UDP port 4500. The security appliance sends periodic keepalives to keep them active even if there is no data flowing over the VPN connection.

If NAT-T is globally enabled, but if you do not want to use NAT-T for the remote-access tunnel, you can use the **crypto dynamic-map set nat-t-disable** option, the command syntax for which is as follows:

```
crypto dynamic-map map-name seq-num set nat-t-disable
```

Example 16-28 illustrates how to disable NAT-T for a dynamic map, called outside_dyn_map.

Example 16-28 *Disabling NAT-T for Remote-Access Tunnels*

```
Chicago(config)# crypto dynamic-map outside_dyn_map 20 set nat-t-disable
```

IPSec over TCP

IPSec over TCP is an important feature used in scenarios where:

- UDP port 500 is blocked, resulting in incomplete IKE negotiations.
- ESP (IP protocol 50) is not allowed to pass, and as a result encrypted traffic does not traverse.
- The network administrator prefers to use a connection-oriented protocol such as TCP.

With IPSec over TCP, the security appliance negotiates the VPN tunnel using TCP as the protocol over a preconfigured port. When the tunnel is up, both VPN devices (Cisco ASA and the VPN client) pass traffic using the same connection. Example 16-29 illustrates how to configure IPSec over TCP on Cisco ASA. The administrator of the box prefers to use TCP port 10000 for tunnel setup and data transport. Cisco ASA allows up to ten TCP ports to be used for this feature.

Example 16-29 *IPSec over TCP Configuration*

```
Chicago(config)# isakmp ipsec-over-tcp port 10000
```

To verify whether the VPN clients are using IPSec over TCP, you can use the **show crypto ipsec sa | include settings** command, as demonstrated in Example 16-30. The "in use settings" option indicates that the particular VPN connection is a remote-access tunnel using TCP encapsulation.

Example 16-30 *Verifying VPN Client Use of IPSec over TCP*

```
Chicago(config)# show crypto ipsec sa ¦ include settings
         in use settings ={RA, Tunnel,  TCP-Encaps, }
         in use settings ={RA, Tunnel,  TCP-Encaps, }
```

IPSec over UDP

IPSec over UDP, similar to NAT-T, is used to encapsulate the ESP packets using a UDP wrapper. This is useful in scenarios where the VPN clients do not support NAT-T and are behind a firewall that does not allow ESP packets to pass through. In IPSec over UDP, the IKE negotiations still use UDP port 500. During the negotiations, Cisco ASA informs the VPN client to use IPSec over UDP for data transport. Additionally, Cisco ASA updates the VPN client about the UDP port it should use. Example 16-31 configures Cisco ASA to use IPSec over UDP for the remote-access group DfltGrpPolicy. Cisco ASA will push UDP port 10000 as the data encapsulation port to the VPN client.

NOTE   NAT-T is supported on Cisco VPN clients running version 3.6 or higher.

Example 16-31 *IPSec over UDP Configuration*

```
Chicago(config)# group-policy DfltGrpPolicy attributes
Chicago(config-group-policy)# ipsec-udp enable
Chicago(config-group-policy)# ipsec-udp-port 10000
```

IPSec Hairpinning

Cisco ASA does not allow a packet to leave the same interface on which it was originally received, because of security reasons. However, in case of an IPSec VPN tunnel, Cisco ASA supports receiving the IPSec traffic from one VPN tunnel and then redirecting it into the other one, if both tunnels terminate on the same interface. This feature is known as *IPSec hairpinning.* Using this feature, you can implement a true hub-and-spoke scenario, as shown in Figure 16-10. If Client1 needs to send traffic to Client2, it will send that traffic to the hub Cisco ASA. The hub Cisco ASA, after checking the routing table for the destination address, sends traffic to Client2 over the other VPN tunnel, and vice versa. However, this feature requires both remote VPN devices to be a part of the same crypto map. Additionally, the crypto map must be applied to the same interface.

Figure 16-10 *IPSec Hairpinning*

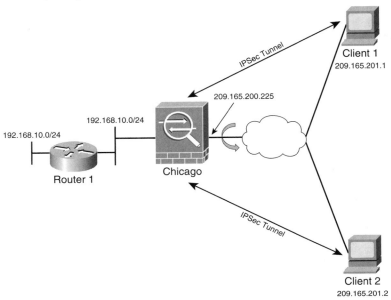

Example 16-32 shows the related IPSec configuration to implement the IPSec hairpinning feature. This configuration uses the **same-security-traffic permit intra-interface** command to permit VPN traffic to leave the same physical interface once traffic needs to go over the other VPN tunnel.

Example 16-32 *IPSec Hairpinning*

```
Chicago(config)# same-security-traffic permit intra-interface
```

Cisco ASA also supports receiving traffic over the VPN tunnel and then redirecting it back out to the Internet in clear text. This feature, also known as *Client U-turn,* is useful if you do not want the VPN traffic destined to the Internet to enter the inside network of your organization.

Cisco ASA applies firewall rules (ACL checking, packet inspection, NAT, IDS, URL filtering) before sending traffic out to the same interface for both IPSec hairpinning and Client U-turn.

VPN Load-Balancing

VPN load-balancing is a way to distribute remote-access VPN and WebVPN connections across multiple security appliances. When two or more Cisco ASA devices are deployed in load-balancing, they form a virtual cluster, with one of the security appliances acting as the cluster master. All Cisco ASA devices in the cluster are configured with a virtual IP address, and the cluster master takes ownership of that IP address, as illustrated in Figure 16-11.

Figure 16-11 *HTTP VPN Load-Balancing*

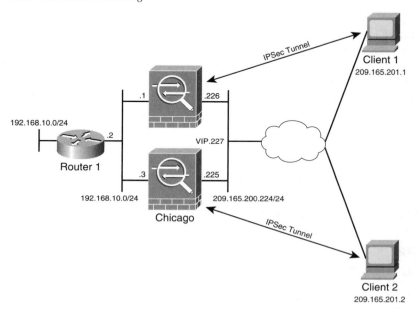

The VPN clients use this IP address to initiate the tunnel request. The master appliance, after receiving the request, looks at the load-balance database and determines which security appliance has the least load. The master appliance sends a redirect message back to the client with the IP address of the security appliance the client should connect to. The client, after receiving the IP address of the Cisco ASA, initiates a new request to the Cisco ASA and goes through the IKE negotiations.

NOTE   Cisco ASA load-balancing feature is fully compatible with the load-balancing feature on the VPN3000 concentrators.

To set up VPN load-balancing, the first thing to do is to get into the load-balancing submenu. This is achieved by issuing the **vpn load-balancing** command from configuration mode, as shown in Example 16-33. The Cisco ASA devices are configured to use a virtual IP address of 209.165.200.227, which will be used on the VPN clients as the primary host address. The last step in setting up load-balancing is to enable it by using the **participate** command.

Example 16-33 *VPN Load-Balancing Configuration*

```
Chicago(config)# vpn load-balancing
Chicago(config-load-balancing))# cluster ip address 209.165.200.227
Chicago(config-load-balancing))# participate
```

If the Cisco ASA devices are behind a firewall using NAT, then you can configure the translated IP address using the **nat** command under the load-balancing submenu, as illustrated in Example 16-34. The virtual IP address is 209.165.200.227, but the firewall is translating this address to 209.165.202.140.

Example 16-34 *VPN Load-Balancing Configuration with NAT*

```
Chicago(config)# vpn load-balancing
Chicago(config-load-balancing)# nat 209.165.202.140
Chicago(config-load-balancing)# cluster ip address 209.165.200.227
```

Additionally, you can set the appropriate priority to indicate the likelihood of a Cisco ASA device becoming the cluster master either during bootup or when the existing cluster master fails to respond. The default priority of Cisco ASA devices is determined based on the model number. Table 16-3 lists all the default priorities of the Cisco ASA devices.

Table 16-3   *Appliances and the Default Load-Balancing Priorities*

Cisco ASA Model	Default Priority
ASA 5520	5
ASA 5540	7

If two Cisco ASA devices with the same priority are powered up simultaneously, then the security appliance with the lowest IP address becomes the cluster master. Otherwise, the security appliance with the highest priority assumes the role of master cluster.

NOTE   Cisco ASA 5510 does not support VPN load-balancing.

If the cluster master fails to respond during operation, the secondary appliance with the highest priority becomes the new cluster master. The default priority of an appliance can be changed by using the **priority** command in the load-balancing menu. You can specify a priority between 1 and 10. When the original master appliance comes online, it does not preempt to regain control.

TIP   Cisco ASA uses UDP port 9023 when communicating in the load-balancing cluster. However, you can change this port by using the **cluster port** command.

Cisco ASA also allows you to set up a secured connection between the security appliances when they exchange load-balancing information. This is achieved by using the **cluster encryption** and **cluster key** commands. In Example 16-35, a key of cisco123 is used to encrypt traffic between the security appliances in the cluster. If there is a mismatch in the key, the security appliance fails to join the cluster.

Example 16-35 *VPN Load-Balancing Configuration with Encryption*

```
Chicago(config)# vpn load-balancing
Chicago(config-load-balancing)# priority 9
Chicago(config-load-balancing)# cluster key cisco123
Chicago(config-load-balancing)# cluster ip address 209.165.200.227
Chicago(config-load-balancing)# cluster encryption
Chicago(config-load-balancing)# participate
```

NOTE   VPN load-balancing requires you to enable ISAKMP on all the interfaces participating in load-balancing.

Client Auto-Update

The client auto-update feature helps you to ensure that all of the Cisco VPN clients (whether software or hardware based) are running the same version of code. When a software-based VPN client connects to Cisco ASA, it sends its software version information to the security appliance. Cisco ASA checks the received version with the configured revision of code. If the received and configured revised versions do not match, the security appliance sends a notification back to the client informing it to download the newer version. This notification is sent after the tunnel is established and it contains a link of an HTTP or HTTPS server that stores the Cisco VPN client image. Once the user clicks the link, the image is downloaded in the machine and the upgrade process can start.

NOTE   Cisco ASA supports only Windows-based software VPN clients for auto-update.

Example 16-36 shows the configuration for Cisco ASA to use the client auto-update feature for the ciscovpn tunnel group. The client auto-update feature is configured by using the **client-update** command under the **ipsec-attributes** submenu of the group to which all the Windows (including 95, 98, Me, NT, 2000, and XP) VPN clients connect. The software VPN client software image is stored on an HTTP server with an IP address of 192.168.10.10, and the image name is vpnclient-win-4.05.Rel-k9.exe. Cisco ASA checks the received revision number with the configured revision of 4.05.Rel. If the revision numbers do not match, Cisco ASA sends a notification to the VPN client, as shown in Figure 16-12. Once Cisco ASA is set up for the update URL, the final step is to enable it globally by using the **client-update enable** command.

Example 16-36 *Client Auto-Update Feature on a Tunnel Group*

```
Chicago(Config)# tunnel-group ciscovpn ipsec-attributes
Chicago(Config-ipsec)# client-update type Windows url http://192.168.10.10/
  vpnclient-win-4.05.Rel-k9.exe rev-nums 4.05.Rel
Chicago(Config-ipsec)# exit
Chicago(Config)# client-update enable
```

Figure 16-12 *Notification Message Sent to the Client*

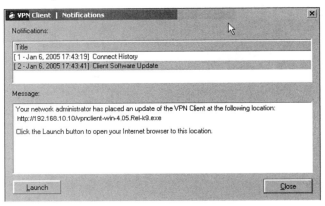

NOTE	If you want to update software only on particular Windows operating systems, you can specify the OS-specific keyword, such as Win9X for Windows 95, 98, and Me, and WinNT for Windows NT, 2000, and XP.

Additionally, if you want all Windows clients to get notified with the new image regardless of their tunnel group membership, you can configure the client auto-update in global configuration mode, as demonstrated in Example 16-37.

Example 16-37 *Client Auto-Update Feature in Global Configuration Mode*

```
Chicago(Config)# client-update type Windows url http://192.168.10.10/vpnclient-win-
  4.05.Rel-k9.exe rev-nums 4.05.Rel
Chicago(Config)# client-update enable
```

The client auto-update feature works differently for the Cisco VPN 3002 Hardware Client. When the security appliance detects that the Cisco VPN 3002 HW Client is running a different image, it sends a notification along with the URL of a TFTP server. The VPN 3002 HW Client starts the upgrade process automatically without user interruption. After downloading the image, it reboots itself to load the new code. Example 16-38 shows the configuration excerpt from the Chicago ASA, which is set up with the client auto-update feature for the Cisco VPN 3002 HW clients. The image is stored on a TFTP server with an IP address of 192.168.10.10 and an image name of vpn3002-4.7.2.Rel-k9.bin.

Example 16-38 *Client-Update Feature for Cisco VPN 3002 HW Clients*

```
Chicago(config)# client-update type vpn3002 url tftp://192.168.10.10/vpn3002-
  4.7.2.Rel-k9.bin rev-nums 4.7.2
Chicago(config)# client-update enable
```

Client Firewalling

The Cisco VPN client has an integrated personal firewall that protects a machine from the Internet by inspecting packets both inbound and outbound. By having the firewall option enabled on the VPN client, the client provides extra security if the VPN group the user is connecting to has split tunneling enabled. In this way, the firewall denies packets received from the unprotected networks, resulting in securing corporate networks from unauthorized intruders. Cisco ASA supports two different scenarios for client firewalling, discussed in the sections that follow.

NOTE   Only Windows VPN clients support the client firewalling feature.

Personal Firewall Check

The Cisco VPN client can check to see if the firewall service on the machine is running by sending periodic keepalives, also known as "Are you there" (AYT) messages, to the specified firewall. If the firewall service on the client machine is not running, the VPN client fails to establish the secured connection. Additionally, if the VPN tunnel is up and the user manually turns off the firewall service, the keepalives time out and the Cisco VPN client drops the connection. An administrator can set up Cisco ASA for three firewall check modes:

- **no firewall**—The personal firewall check is disabled. This mode is useful if non-Windows clients are connecting to a group.

- **firewall optional**—Cisco ASA checks to see if the firewall services on the VPN client are running. If they are disabled, Cisco ASA still allows the VPN connection to come up. This mode is useful if Windows and non-Windows clients connect to a group.

- **firewall required**—If the firewall service is not running, Cisco ASA will not allow the VPN tunnel to be established. This mode is recommended if Windows clients connect to a group.

All of these modes are configured under the group configuration menu using the **client-firewall** command, as shown in Example 16-39.

Example 16-39 *Modes in Client Firewall*

```
Chicago(config)# group-policy ciscovpn attributes
Chicago(config-group-policy)# client-firewall ?
  none  No firewall is required for remote users in this group
  opt   optional
  req   required
```

For optional (**opt**) and required (**req**) modes, Cisco ASA provides a list of currently supported personal firewalls, including the built-in Cisco Integrated Client Firewall, as shown in Example 16-40. This example also shows that Zone Labs' ZoneAlarm Pro is the required firewall. If the VPN clients don't have this firewall running, Cisco ASA will stop the tunnels from getting formed.

Example 16-40 *List of Supported Firewalls*

```
Chicago(config-group-policy)# client-firewall req ?

    cisco-integrated        Cisco Integrated Client Firewall
    cisco-security-agent    Cisco Security Agent
    custom                  Custom Firewall
    networkice-blackice     Network ICE BlackICE Defender
    sygate-personal         Sygate Personal Firewall
    sygate-personal-pro     Sygate Personal Firewall Pro
    sygate-security-agent   Sygate Security Agent
    zonelabs-zonealarm      Zone Labs ZoneAlarm
    zonelabs-zonealarmorpro Zone Labs ZoneAlarm or ZoneAlarm Pro
    zonelabs-zonealarmpro   Zone Labs ZoneAlarm Pro
Chicago(config-group-policy)# client-firewall req zonelabs-zonealarmpro policy AYT
```

NOTE   You can define a customized firewall if you know the vendor ID and product ID, by using the **custom** keyword.

Central Protection Policy

When split tunneling is employed, Cisco ASA can additionally send security policies to the client machine and restrict its clear-text traffic capabilities. This deployment scenario, known as *Centralized Protection Policy (CPP)* or *policy pushed,* uses ACLs that can be pushed to the client firewall. This ensures that traffic matching the permitted entries is allowed to pass through, and the unwanted traffic is filtered out.

Example 16-41 shows that Cisco ASA requires that the VPN client use the Cisco Integrated Client Firewall (CIC). Cisco ASA also restricts the client machine to send and receive traffic based on the configured inbound ACL, named Inbound_FW_ACL, and the outbound ACL, named Outbound_FW_ACL. These ACLs allow IP traffic only from 192.168.100.0/24 to 192.168.50.0/24 and vice versa.

Example 16-41 *Configuration of Central Protection Policy*

```
Chicago(config)# access-list Inbound_FW_ACL extended permit ip 192.168.100.0
  255.255.255.0 192.168.50.0 255.255.255.0
Chicago(config)# access-list Outbound_FW_ACL extended permit ip 192.168.50.0
  255.255.255.0 192.168.100.0 255.255.255.0
Chicago(config)# group-policy SecureMeGrp attributes
Chicago(config-group-policy)# client-firewall req cisco-integrated acl-in
  Inbound_FW_ACL acl-out Outbound_FW_ACL
```

Hardware based Easy VPN Client Features

Cisco ASA can provide further security for the Hardware based Easy VPN client that is connecting to it by controlling specific features, as discussed in the sections that follow.

Interactive Hardware Client Authentication

Cisco ASA can use the interactive hardware client authentication feature, also known as secure unit authentication, which ensures that the Hardware based Easy VPN client provides user credentials every time the tunnel is negotiated. That way, the security appliance does not allow user passwords to be saved on the hardware based Easy VPN client, which provides additional security. If the user password is saved on the hardware based Easy VPN client, Cisco ASA pushes down a policy during mode-config to delete the saved password from the hardware based Easy VPN client configuration. The interactive hardware client authentication is configured under group parameters using the **secure-unit-authentication** command followed by the **enable** or **disable** option. Example 16-42 shows configuration to set up Cisco ASA for interactive hardware client authentication for the SecureMeGrp group.

Example 16-42 *Configuration of Interactive Client Authentication*

```
Chicago(config)# group-policy SecureMeGrp attributes
Chicago(config-group-policy)# secure-unit-authentication enable
```

Individual User Authentication

Using the Individual User Authentication feature, Cisco ASA secures the VPN tunnel by making sure that users behind the Hardware based Easy VPN Client are authenticated before they can access corporate resources. To be able to pass traffic over the tunnel, a user behind the hardware based Easy VPN client must launch a web browser and present valid user credentials. The hardware based Easy VPN client forwards the user information to Cisco ASA, which in turn validates the user information using the configured authentication method.

TIP   The user does not have to manually point the web browser to the IP address of the Hardware based Easy VPN client. Instead, users can try to browse to any server behind the security appliance, and the hardware based Easy VPN client will redirect them for user credentials.

The Individual User Authentication is configured under group parameters using the **user-authentication** command followed by the **enable** or **disable** option. Example 16-43 shows the Cisco ASA configuration for Individual User Authentication for the SecureMeGrp group.

Example 16-43 *Configuration of Individual User Authentication*

```
Chicago(config)# group-policy SecureMeGrp attributes
Chicago(config-group-policy)# user-authentication enable
```

You can specify the idle-time period if there is no activity over a user's connection. When the idle-time period expires, Cisco ASA terminates that particular connection. The timeout period can be enabled by using the **user-authentication-idle-timeout** command followed by the timeout value in minutes. In Example 16-44, group SecureMeGrp is configured to time out inactive users after 10 minutes.

Example 16-44 *Configuration of Individual User Timeout*

```
Chicago(config)# group-policy SecureMeGrp attributes
Chicago(config-group-policy)# user-authentication-idle-timeout 10
```

NOTE The user authentication is done based on the source IP address of the clients.

Cisco IP Phone Bypass

When individual hardware client authentication is enabled, Cisco ASA tries to authenticate Cisco IP Phones if they send traffic to go over the tunnel. You can set up the security appliance to bypass authentication for Cisco IP Phones by configuring the **ip-phone-bypass** command under a group-policy, as shown in Example 16-45.

Example 16-45 *Configuration of Cisco IP Phone Bypass*

```
Chicago(config)# group-policy SecureMeGrp attributes
Chicago(config-group-policy)# ip-phone-bypass enable
```

NOTE For this feature to work, make sure that the hardware based Easy VPN client is using network extension mode.

Leap Bypass

Leap bypass is a feature in the security appliance that allows the Lightweight Extensible Authentication Protocol (LEAP) packets to go over the VPN tunnel when individual hardware client authentication is configured. LEAP bypass is configured under group parameters using the **leap-bypass** command followed by the **enable** or **disable** option. Example 16-46 shows the Cisco ASA configuration for LEAP bypass for the SecureMeGrp group.

Example 16-46 *Configuration of Cisco Aironet LEAP Bypass*

```
Chicago(config)# group-policy SecureMeGrp attributes
Chicago(config-group-policy)# leap-bypass enable
```

NOTE This feature only works with Cisco Aironet access points using LEAP for authentication.

Hardware Client Network Extension Mode

You have the option to configure a group-policy to disable network extension mode (NEM) on Cisco ASA. When you use this option, the hardware based Easy VPN clients are restricted to using client/PAT mode for VPN tunnels. If they try to use NEM, Cisco ASA blocks the tunnel from being established. NEM is configured under group parameters using the **nem** command followed by the **enable** or **disable** option. Example 16-47 shows the Cisco ASA configuration to allow NEM for the SecureMeGrp group.

Example 16-47 *Configuration to Allow NEM for Hardware based Easy VPN Clients*

```
Chicago(config)# group-policy SecureMeGrp attributes
Chicago(config-group-policy)# nem enable
```

Deployment Scenarios of Cisco IPSec VPN

The Cisco remote-access solution is useful in deployments where remote and home users need corporate access without being physically connected to the corporate LAN. The remote-access solution can be deployed in many ways; however, this section covers the following two design scenarios for ease of understanding:

- IPSec hairpinning with Easy VPN and Firewalling
- Load balancing and site-to-site integration

NOTE   The design scenarios discussed in this section should be used solely to reinforce learning. They should be used for reference purposes only.

IPSec Hairpinning with Easy VPN and Firewalling

SecureMe has recently installed a Cisco ASA in its Brussels office to provide VPN access to its mobile users. Figure 16-13 shows SecureMe's network topology in Brussels.

The security requirements for SecureMe are as follows:

- Use split tunneling and encrypt the traffic going over to the 192.168.0.0/16 network.
- Enforce Cisco Integrated Client Firewall and only allow HTTP and DNS traffic in clear text.
- Use IPSec over TCP on port 9000 as the encapsulation protocol.
- Allow one VPN client to be able to talk to the other client.
- Use local database for user authentication.
- Log all the system-generated syslog messages to a server.

Figure 16-13 *SecureMe's Remote-Access Topology in Brussels*

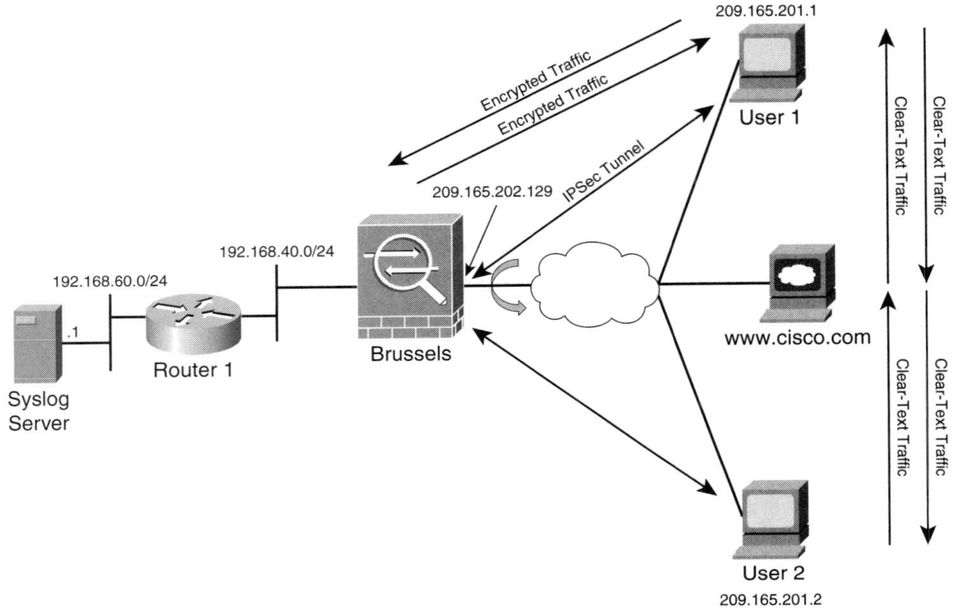

Example 16-48 shows the relevant Cisco ASA configuration in Brussels.

Example 16-48 *Cisco ASA Full Configuration Having Multiple Security Contexts*

```
Brussels# show running-config
: Saved
:
ASA Version 7.0(1)
! ip address on the outside interface
interface GigabitEthernet0/0
 nameif outside
 security-level 0
 ip address 209.165.202.129 255.255.255.0
! ip address on the inside interface
interface GigabitEthernet0/1
 nameif inside
 security-level 100
 ip address 192.168.40.1 255.255.255.0
!
hostname Brussels
domain-name securemeinc.com
! To Allow IPSec hairpinning on the same interface
same-security-traffic permit intra-interface
! ACL to define Split-tunnel policy. This will allow the Client to send encrypted
! traffic to 192.168.0.0/16
access-list ST_ACL standard permit 192.168.0.0 255.255.0.0
! ACL to define Inbound FW policy to restrict inbound clear-text traffic
```

Example 16-48 *Cisco ASA Full Configuration Having Multiple Security Contexts (Continued)*

```
access-list Inbound_FW_ACL extended permit tcp any eq www any
access-list Inbound_FW_ACL extended permit udp any eq domain any
! ACL to define Outbound FW policy to restrict outbound clear-text traffic
access-list Outbound_FW_ACL extended permit tcp any any eq www
access-list Outbound_FW_ACL extended permit udp any any eq domain
! Enable logging to send syslog messages to 192.168.60.150
logging enable
logging timestamp
logging host inside 192.168.60.150
logging trap notifications
! IP Pool used to assign IP address to the VPN client
ip local pool ippool 192.168.50.1-192.168.50.100 mask 255.255.255.0
! Default gateways.
route outside 0.0.0.0 0.0.0.0 209.165.202.130 1
route inside 192.168.60.0 255.255.255.0 192.168.40.2
route inside 0.0.0.0 0.0.0.0 192.168.40.2 tunneled
! Configuration of an internal user-group called SecureMeGrp
group-policy SecureMeGrp internal
! Configuration of user-group attributes
group-policy SecureMeGrp attributes
 split-tunnel-policy tunnelspecified
 split-tunnel-network-list value ST_ACL
 default-domain value secureminc.com
 client-firewall req cisco-integrated acl-in Inbound_FW_ACL acl-out Outbound_FW_ACL
! Configuration of LOCAL user database
username ciscouser password aE.CsXUz4UT9JfjO encrypted
username adminuser password aE.T9JfjOCsXUz4U encrypted
username poweruser password sXUzaE.C4UT9JfjO encrypted
! Configuration of ASDM for Appliance management
http server enable
http 0.0.0.0 0.0.0.0 inside
! sysopt to bypass traffic filters
sysopt connection permit-ipsec
! Transform set to specify encryption and hashing algorithm
crypto ipsec transform-set ESP-3DES-SHA esp-3des esp-sha-hmac
! Dynamic crypto-map for Remote-Access Clients
crypto dynamic-map outside_dyn_map 10 set transform-set ESP-3DES-SHA
! Dynamic crypto-map is mapped to the static crypto-map
crypto map outside_map 65535 ipsec-isakmp dynamic outside_dyn_map
! Static crypto-map is applied to the outside interface
crypto map outside_map interface outside
! isakmp configuration
isakmp enable outside
isakmp policy 10 authentication pre-share
isakmp policy 10 encryption 3des
isakmp policy 10 hash md5
isakmp policy 10 group 2
isakmp policy 10 lifetime 86400
! Tunnel Encapsulation to use IPSec over TCP over port 9000
isakmp ipsec-over-tcp port 9000
! tunnel-group configuration for VPN client. The groupname is ciscovpn
```

continues

Example 16-48 *Cisco ASA Full Configuration Having Multiple Security Contexts (Continued)*

```
tunnel-group ciscovpn type ipsec-ra
tunnel-group ciscovpn general-attributes
 address-pool ippool
 default-group-policy SecureMeGrp
tunnel-group ciscovpn ipsec-attributes
 pre-shared-key *
```

Load-Balancing and Site-to-Site Integration

SecureMe's headquarters office in Chicago wants to deploy Cisco ASA to be used for remote-access VPN tunnels that will support about 2000 users. However, SecureMe wants to make sure that users do not overburden the system and therefore wants to use two security appliances in load-balancing mode. Figure 16-14 shows SecureMe's network topology in Chicago.

Figure 16-14 *SecureMe's Remote-Access Topology in Chicago*

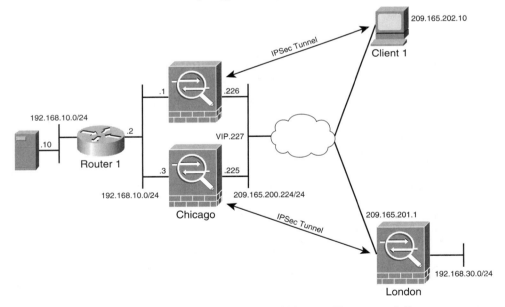

The security requirements for SecureMe's Chicago office are as follows:

- Load-balance Cisco IPSec VPN connections across two Cisco ASA devices.
- Use NAT-T if there is a NAT device between the VPN peers.
- Use a RADIUS server as the external database for user lookup.
- Configure a site-to-site VPN tunnel to the London ASA.

- Assign the DNS and WINS server addresses as 192.168.20.100 and 192.168.20.101, respectively.

- Limit the number of simultaneous sessions per users to two.

- Display a banner warning authorized users.

- Translate the clear-text traffic if it is originated from the inside network and destined to the outside network.

Example 16-49 shows the complete configuration of SecureMe's Cisco ASA in Chicago.

Example 16-49 *Cisco ASA Relevant Configuration Using Load-Balancing and Site-to-Site Integration*

```
Chicago# show running-config
: Saved
ASA Version 7.0(1)
! ip address on the outside interface
interface GigabitEthernet0/0
 nameif outside
 security-level 0
 ip address 209.165.200.225 255.255.255.0
! ip address on the inside interface
interface GigabitEthernet0/1
 nameif inside
 security-level 100
 ip address 192.168.10.1 255.255.255.0
!
hostname Chicago
domain-name securemeinc.com
! Access-list entries to bypass NAT for the traffic going from Chicago to London
access-list inside_nat0_outbound extended permit ip 192.168.10.0 255.255.255.0
  192.168.30.0 255.255.255.0
access-list inside_nat0_outbound extended permit ip 192.168.20.0 255.255.255.0
  192.168.30.0 255.255.255.0
! Access-list entries to bypass NAT for the traffic going from Chicago to RA_clients
access-list inside_nat0_outbound extended permit ip 192.168.10.0 255.255.255.0
  192.168.60.0 255.255.255.0
access-list inside_nat0_outbound extended permit ip 192.168.20.0 255.255.255.0
  192.168.60.0 255.255.255.0
! Encryption Access-list to encrypt the traffic from Chicago to London
access-list to_London extended permit ip 192.168.10.0 255.255.255.0 192.168.30.0
  255.255.255.0
access-list to_London extended permit ip 192.168.20.0 255.255.255.0 192.168.30.0
  255.255.255.0
! IP Pool used to assign IP address to the VPN client
ip local pool ippool 192.168.60.1-192.168.60.100 mask 255.255.255.0
! NAT ACL is bound to NAT 0 statement to bypass address translation
nat (inside) 0 access-list inside_nat0_outbound
! Address Translation for the inside network
nat (inside) 1 192.168.10.0 255.255.255.0
nat (inside) 1 192.168.20.0 255.255.255.0
global (outside) 1 interface
 Default gateways.
route outside 0.0.0.0 0.0.0.0 209.165.200.226 1
route inside 192.168.20.0 255.255.255.0 192.168.10.2 1
```

continues

Example 16-49 *Cisco ASA Relevant Configuration Using Load-Balancing and Site-to-Site Integration (Continued)*

```
route inside 0.0.0.0 0.0.0.0 192.168.10.2 tunneled
! Radius configuration to enable user authentication
aaa-server Radius protocol radius
aaa-server Radius (inside) host 192.168.10.10
 key cisco123
! Configuration of an internal user group-policy called SecureMeGrp
group-policy SecureMeGrp internal
! Configuration of user-group attributes
group-policy SecureMeGrp attributes
 banner value Unauthorized Users will be prosecuted
 vpn-simultaneous-logins 2
 wins-server value 192.168.20.101
 dns-server value 192.168.20.100
 default-domain value securemeinc.com
! Configuration of ASDM for Appliance management
http server enable
http 0.0.0.0 0.0.0.0 inside
! Transform set to specify encryption and hashing algorithm
crypto ipsec transform-set ESP-3DES-SHA esp-3des esp-sha-hmac
! Dynamic crypto-map for Remote-Access Clients
crypto dynamic-map outside_dyn_map 10 set transform-set ESP-3DES-SHA
! Crypto map configuration for London
crypto map outside_map 20 match address to_London
crypto map outside_map 20 set peer 209.165.201.1
crypto map outside_map 20 set transform-set ESP-3DES-SHA
! Dynamic crypto-map is mapped to the static crypto-map
crypto map outside_map 65535 ipsec-isakmp dynamic outside_dyn_map
! Static crypto-map is applied to the outside interface
crypto map outside_map interface outside
! isakmp configuration- Enabled on the outside interface
isakmp enable outside
! isakmp configuration- Enabled on the inside interface for VPN LB
isakmp enable inside
! isakmp policy configuration
isakmp policy 10 authentication pre-share
isakmp policy 10 encryption 3des
isakmp policy 10 hash md5
isakmp policy 10 group 2
isakmp policy 10 lifetime 86400
! NAT-T is enabled with a default keepalive of 20 seconds
isakmp nat-traversal 20
! tunnel-group configuration for VPN client. The group-name is ciscovpn
tunnel-group ciscovpn type ipsec-ra
tunnel-group ciscovpn general-attributes
 address-pool ippool
 authentication-server-group Radius
 authentication-server-group (inside) Radius
 default-group-policy SecureMeGrp
tunnel-group ciscovpn ipsec-attributes
 pre-shared-key *
```

Example 16-49 *Cisco ASA Relevant Configuration Using Load-Balancing and Site-to-Site Integration (Continued)*

```
! L2L tunnel-group configuration for London
tunnel-group 209.165.201.1 type ipsec-l2l
tunnel-group 209.165.201.1 ipsec-attributes
 pre-shared-key *
! VPN Load-balancing. The virtual IP address is  209.165.200.227. Encryption is
  enabled with using cisco123 as the key
vpn load-balancing
 cluster key cisco123
 cluster ip address 209.165.200.227
 cluster encryption
 participate
```

Monitoring and Troubleshooting Cisco Remote Access VPN

Cisco ASA comes with many **show** commands to check the health and status of the IPSec tunnels. For troubleshooting purposes, there is a rich set of **debug** commands to isolate the IPSec-related issues.

Monitoring Cisco Remote Access IPSec VPNs

If you want to see if the IPSec tunnels are working and passing traffic, you can start by looking at the status of Phase 1 SA. Type **show crypto isakmp sa detail**, as demonstrated in Example 16-50. If the ISAKMP negotiations are successful, you should see the state as **AM_ACTIVE**.

Example 16-50 **show crypto isakmp sa detail** *Command Output*

```
Chicago# show crypto isakmp sa detail
   Active SA: 1
    Rekey SA: 0 (A tunnel will report 1 Active and 1 Rekey SA during rekey)
Total IKE SA: 1

1   IKE Peer: 209.165.201.10
    Type    : user          Role  : responder
    Rekey   : no            State : AM_ACTIVE
    Encrypt : 3des          Hash  : MD5
    Auth    : preshared     Lifetime: 86400
    Lifetime Remaining: 86331
```

You can also check the status of the IPSec SA by using the **show crypto ipsec sa** command, as shown in Example 16-51. This command displays the negotiated proxy identities along with the actual number of packets encrypted and decrypted by the IPSec engine.

Example 16-51 *Output of* **show crypto ipsec sa** *Command*

```
Chicago# show crypto ipsec sa
interface: outside
    Crypto map tag: outside_dyn_map, local addr: 209.165.200.225
       local ident (addr/mask/prot/port): (0.0.0.0/0.0.0.0/0/0)
       remote ident (addr/mask/prot/port): (192.168.50.60/255.255.255.255/0/0)
       current_peer: 209.165.201.10
       dynamic allocated peer ip: 192.168.50.60

       #pkts encaps: 10, #pkts encrypt: 10, #pkts digest: 10
       #pkts decaps: 10, #pkts decrypt: 10, #pkts verify: 10
       #pkts compressed: 0, #pkts decompressed: 0
       #pkts not compressed: 0, #pkts comp failed: 0, #pkts decomp failed: 0
       #send errors: 0, #recv errors: 0
```

You can check the status of a hardware encryption card with the **show crypto accelerator statistics** command. In Example 16-52, the important output from this command is shown, which displays the counter information, such as the number of packets going through the encryption card.

Example 16-52 **show crypto accelerator statistics** *Command Output*

```
Chicago# show crypto accelerator statistics
Crypto Accelerator Status
------------------------
[Capacity]
   Supports hardware crypto: True
   Supports modular hardware crypto: False
   Max accelerators: 1
   Max crypto throughput: 200 Mbps
   Max crypto connections: 750
[Global Statistics]
   Number of active accelerators: 1
   Number of non-operational accelerators: 0
   Input packets: 18
   Input bytes: 5424
   Output packets: 223
   Output error packets: 0
   Output bytes: 172405
[Accelerator 0]
   Status: Active
! Output omitted for brevity.
```

Cisco ASA can display global IKE and IPSec counter information, which is helpful in isolating VPN connection problems. Information such as the number of total requests, the number of total SAs created, and the number of failed requests is useful to determine the failure rate for IKE and IPSec SAs in the security appliance. As shown in Example 16-53, you can view this information by using the **show crypto protocol statistics ikev1** and **show crypto protocol statistics ipsec** command.

Example 16-53 *Output of* **show crypto protocol statistics ikev1** *Command*

```
Chicago# show crypto protocol statistics ikev1
[IKEv1 statistics]
    Encrypt packet requests: 23
    Encapsulate packet requests: 23
    Decrypt packet requests: 23
    Decapsulate packet requests: 23
    HMAC calculation requests: 63
    SA creation requests: 3
    SA rekey requests: 0
    SA deletion requests: 1
    Next phase key allocation requests: 4
    Random number generation requests: 0
    Failed requests: 1
Chicago# show crypto protocol statistics ipsec
[IPsec statistics]
    Encrypt packet requests: 0
    Encapsulate packet requests: 0
    Decrypt packet requests: 0
    Decapsulate packet requests: 0
    HMAC calculation requests: 0
    SA creation requests: 4
    SA rekey requests: 0
    SA deletion requests: 2
    Next phase key allocation requests: 0
    Random number generation requests: 0
    Failed requests: 1
```

Troubleshooting Cisco IPSec VPN Clients

If the IPSec tunnel is not working for some reason, make sure that you have the proper debug turned on. The following are the two most important debugs to look at:

- **debug crypto isakmp** [*debug level 1-255*]
- **debug crypto ipsec** [*debug level 1-255*]

By default, the debug level is set to 1. You can increase the severity level up to 255 to get detailed logs. However, in most cases, setting this to 127 gives enough information to determine the root cause of an issue.

Refer to Figure 16-13 and look at the tunnel negotiation between the Cisco ASA and the VPN client. To enforce learning, the following debugs have been enabled:

- **debug crypto isakmp 127**
- **debug crypto ipsec 127**

As mentioned in Chapter 1, "Introduction to Network Security," the tunnel negotiations begin by exchanging the ISAKMP proposals. The security appliance shows the tunnel group, ciscovpn in this case, that the VPN client is trying to connect to. If the proposal is acceptable, the Cisco ASA displays a message indicating that the IKE SA proposal is acceptable, as shown in Example 16-54.

Example 16-54 debug *Output to Show ISAKMP Proposal Is Acceptable*

```
Chicago# debug crypto isakmp 127
Chicago# debug crypto ipsec 127
[IKEv1 DEBUG]: Group = , IP = 209.165.201.10, processing SA payload
[IKEv1 DEBUG]: Group = , IP = 209.165.201.10, processing ke payload
[IKEv1 DEBUG]: Group = , IP = 209.165.201.10,processing VID payload,
<snip>
[IKEv1]: IP = 209.165.201.10, Connection landed on tunnel_group ciscovpn
[IKEv1 DEBUG]: Group = ciscovpn, IP = 209.165.201.10, processing IKE SA
[IKEv1 DEBUG]: Group = ciscovpn, IP = 209.165.201.10, IKE SA Proposal # 1, Transform
   # 10 acceptable  Matches global IKE entry # 1,
```

If the proposal is acceptable, the VPN devices try to discover if they are NAT-T capable and if there is an address-translation device between them. If NAT-T is not negotiated or a NAT/PAT device is not detected, they display the **Remote end is NOT behind a NAT device. This end is NOT behind a NAT device** message, as shown in Example 16-55.

Example 16-55 debug *Output to Show NAT-T Discovery Process*

```
[IKEv1 DEBUG]: Group = ciscovpn, IP = 209.165.201.10, processing NAT-Discovery
payload
[IKEv1 DEBUG]: Group = ciscovpn, IP = 209.165.201.10, computing NAT Discovery hash
[IKEv1 DEBUG]: Group = ciscovpn, IP = 209.165.201.10, processing NAT-Discovery
   payload
[IKEv1]: Group = ciscovpn, IP = 209.165.201.10, Automatic NAT Detection Status:
   Remote end is NOT behind a NAT device. This end is NOT behind a NAT device
```

After NAT-T negotiations, Cisco ASA prompts the user to specify user credentials. Upon successful user authentication, the security appliance displays a message indicating that the user (ciscouser in this example) is authenticated, as shown in Example 16-56.

Example 16-56 debug *Output to Show User Is Authenticated*

```
[IKEv1]: Group = ciscovpn, Username = ciscouser, IP = 209.165.201.10, User
   (ciscouser) authenticated.,

[IKEv1 DEBUG]: Group = ciscovpn, Username = ciscouser, IP = 209.165.201.10,
   constructing blank hash
[IKEv1 DEBUG]: Group = ciscovpn, Username = ciscouser, IP = 209.165.201.10,
   constructing qm hash
```

The client requests mode-config attributes by sending a list of client-supported attributes, as shown in Example 16-57. Cisco ASA replies back with all of its supported attributes and the appropriate information.

Example 16-57 debug *Output to Show Mode-Config Requests*

```
[IKEv1 DEBUG]Processing cfg Request attributes,
[IKEv1 DEBUG]MODE_CFG: Received request for IPV4 address!,
[IKEv1 DEBUG]MODE_CFG: Received request for IPV4 net mask!,
[IKEv1 DEBUG]MODE_CFG: Received request for DNS server address!,
[IKEv1 DEBUG]MODE_CFG: Received request for WINS server address!,
```

After pushing down the attributes, Cisco ASA displays the "PHASE 1 COMPLETED" message indicating that the ISAKMP SA is successfully negotiated, as demonstrated in Example 16-58.

Example 16-58 debug *Output to Show Phase 1 Negotiations Are Completed*

```
[IKEv1]: Group = ciscovpn, Username = ciscouser, IP = 209.165.201.10PHASE 1
  COMPLETED,
<snip>
[IKEv1 DEBUG]: Group = ciscovpn, Username = ciscouser, IP = 209.165.201.10
  Processing ID,
[IKEv1 DECODE]ID_IPV4_ADDR ID received 192.168.50.60,
[IKEv1]: Group = ciscovpn, Username = ciscouser, IP = 209.165.201.10 Received remote
  Proxy Host data in ID Payload:  Address 192.168.50.60, Protocol 0, Port 0,
```

After completing Phase 1 negotiations, the VPN peers try to negotiate Phase 2 SA by exchanging the proxy identities and the IPSec Phase 2 proposal. If they are acceptable, Cisco ASA displays a message indicating that the IPSec SA proposal is acceptable, as shown in Example 16-59.

Example 16-59 debug *Output to Show Proxy Identities and Phase 2 Proposal Are Accepted*

```
[IKEv1 DEBUG]: Group = ciscovpn, Username = ciscouser, IP = 209.165.201.10, IPSec
  SA Proposal # 12, Transform # 1 acceptable  Matches global IPSec SA entry # 10,
[IKEv1 DEBUG]: Group = ciscovpn, Username = ciscouser, IP = 209.165.201.10 ,
  Transmitting Proxy Id:
  Remote host: 192.168.50.60  Protocol 0  Port 0
  Local subnet:  0.0.0.0  mask 0.0.0.0 Protocol 0  Port 0
```

After accepting the transform set values, both VPN devices agree on the inbound and outbound IPSec SAs, as shown in Example 16-60. Once the IPSec SAs have been created, both VPN devices should be able to pass traffic bidirectionally across the tunnel.

Example 16-60 debug *Output to Show IPSec SAs Are Activated*

```
IKEv1 DEBUG]: Group = ciscovpn, Username = ciscouser, IP = 209.165.201.10 , loading
  all IPSEC SAs
[IKEv1]: Group = ciscovpn, Username = ciscouser, IP = 209.165.201.10 Security
  negotiation complete for User (jazib)  Responder, Inbound SPI = 0x00c6bc19,
  Outbound SPI = 0xa472f8c1,
[IKEv1]: Group = ciscovpn, Username = ciscouser, IP = 209.165.201.10 Adding static
  route for client address: 192.168.50.60 ,
[IKEv1]: Group = ciscovpn, Username = ciscouser, IP = 209.165.201.10 , PHASE 2
  COMPLETED (msgid=8732f056)
```

Cisco WebVPN Solution

WebVPN is an evolving method to establish remote-access VPN tunnels without having to install the Cisco VPN Client. A VPN user establishes the secure connection to the Cisco ASA by using a web browser such as Internet Explorer, Netscape, or FireFox. A WebVPN tunnel can easily be created from a computer that has Secure HTTP (HTTPS) access to the public interface of a Cisco ASA. Thus, using WebVPN, the client machine establishes a Secure Sockets Layer (SSL) connection to Cisco ASA, providing easy access to a broad range of applications, including intranet web browsing, e-mail, and Windows file sharing. The list continues on by implementing the robust port-forwarding feature, which provides secure access to most of the TCP-based applications.

Figure 16-15 illustrates a WebVPN connection initiated by UserA going to the SecureMe Chicago ASA. When the SSL tunnel is authenticated, the user can access the servers on the inside network of the Cisco ASA.

Figure 16-15 *WebVPN Topology for SecureMe*

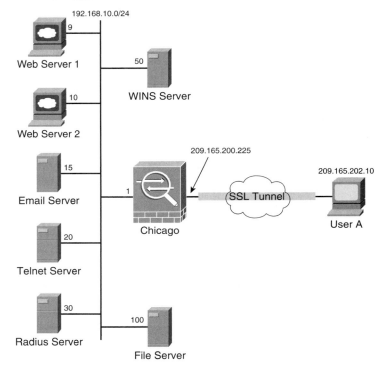

CAUTION The WebVPN functionality on Cisco ASA does not affect in any way the other VPN implementations such as site-to-site or remote-access tunnels. However, WebVPN tunnels are memory-intensive, which can indirectly affect the overall performance of the security appliance.

Table 16-4 lists the major differences between the Cisco VPN client solution and the WebVPN solution. WebVPN is an obvious choice for someone who wants to check their e-mail from a hotel or an Internet café without the need to install and configure a Cisco VPN client.

Table 16-4 *Contrasting Cisco VPN Client and WebVPN*

Feature	Cisco VPN Client	WebVPN
VPN Client	Uses Cisco VPN Client software for complete network access.	Uses a standard web browser to access limited corporate network resources. Eliminates need for separate client software.
Management	You have to go through the installation and configuration on the VPN client.	You do not need to install a VPN client. No configuration is required on the client machine.
Encryption	Uses a variety of encryption and hashing algorithms.	Uses SSL encryption native to web browsers.
Connectivity	Establishes seamless connection to network.	Supports application connectivity through browser portal.
Applications	Encapsulates all IP protocols, including TCP, UDP, and ICMP.	Supports limited TCP-based client/server applications.

In WebVPN, a web client starts an HTTPS session to the public IP address of the security appliance. After processing the request, the security appliance presents a certificate to the web client to authenticate it. Once the secure connection is established, the web client is presented with a login screen to specify the user login credentials. If authentication is successful, a cookie is presented to the user. This cookie is valid until the session is over. When the user clicks the logout icon, or the idle timeout or the maximum connect time is reached, the session cookie is deleted, thus terminating the connection.

NOTE   Stateful failover for WebVPN is currently not supported.

Configuration Steps

The configuration of WebVPN can be broken down into five steps. Figure 16-15 is used throughout this section to demonstrate how to set up Cisco ASA.

Step 1   Enable the HTTP server.

Step 2   Enable WebVPN on the interface.

Step 3   Configure WebVPN look and feel.

Step 4   Configure WebVPN group attributes.

Step 5   Configure user authentication.

Step 1: Enable the HTTP Service

The first step in configuring WebVPN is to enable the HTTP service on the security appliance. Once the HTTP service is enabled, Cisco ASA listens on TCP port 80 for HTTP traffic and on TCP port 443 for HTTPS traffic. You can access the WebVPN interface by one of the following methods:

- Make a request on TCP port 443
- Make a request on TCP port 80, which Cisco ASA will redirect to port 443 if port-redirection is enabled

Example 16-61 shows the configuration for the Chicago ASA to make it act as an HTTP server that is also configured to redirect the requests made for TCP port 80.

Example 16-61 *Enabling the HTTP Service on the Chicago ASA*

```
Chicago(config)# http server enable
Chicago(config)# http redirect outside 80
```

NOTE In the current implementation, both WebVPN and ASDM cannot be enabled on the same interface. Chapter 21, "VPN Management Using ASDM," covers ASDM for VPNs in more detail.

Step 2: Enable WebVPN on the Interface

After setting up the web services on Cisco ASA, the second step is to enable WebVPN on the interface where the WebVPN connections will be terminated. If WebVPN is not enabled on the interface, Cisco ASA will not accept any connections even if WebVPN is globally set up.

To enable WebVPN on an interface, you must use the **enable** command followed by the name of the interface in the WebVPN subconfiguration menu. The configuration in Example 16-62 shows the Chicago ASA is using the outside interface for the termination of WebVPN sessions.

Example 16-62 *Enabling the WebVPN on the Chicago ASA Outside Interface*

```
Chicago# config terminal
Chicago(config)# webvpn
Chicago(config-webvpn)# enable outside
```

Once WebVPN is enabled on an interface, the security appliance is ready to accept the connections. However, recommended practice is to follow all the steps for a complete WebVPN implementation.

Step 3: Configure WebVPN Look and Feel

Figure 16-16 shows the default WebVPN page when a connection is made from a web browser. The title of the page is "WebVPN Service" and the Cisco Systems logo is displayed in the upper-left corner of the web page. The initial page prompts the user for user authentication credentials.

Figure 16-16 *Default WebVPN Page*

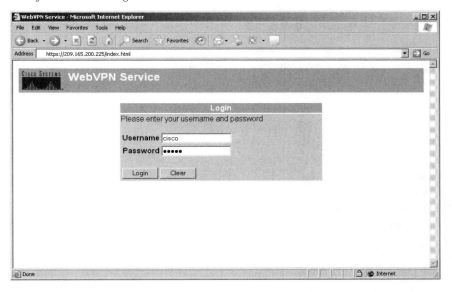

You can customize the WebVPN login page to accommodate an organization's security policy. Figure 16-17 shows the customized login page for SecureMe. The title of the login page has been changed to "Chicago ASA", and the login message has been changed to "Welcome to SecureMe's VPN". The user prompt message has been set to "Enter Username". The primary and secondary title colors are changed to 108,108,108 (dark gray) and 161,161,161 (light gray), respectively. Additionally, the primary and secondary title text colors are set to white and black, respectively. SecureMe does not want to display the Cisco Systems logo in its login page. Therefore, the logo is removed from the upper-left corner of the page. When users log out, the security appliance will display the message **You are not logged into SecureMe's Network**.

Example 16-63 shows the corresponding Cisco ASA configuration for customization. The WebVPN configuration parameters are specified in the WebVPN submenu.

Figure 16-17 *Customized WebVPN Page*

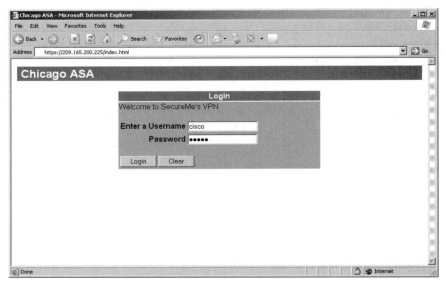

Example 16-63 *Customizing the WebVPN Login Page on Cisco ASA*

```
Chicago(config)# webvpn
Chicago(config-webvpn)# enable outside
Chicago(config-webvpn)# title Chicago ASA
Chicago(config-webvpn)# username-prompt Enter a Username
Chicago(config-webvpn)# login-message Welcome to SecureMe's VPN
Chicago(config-webvpn)# logout-message You are not logged into SecureMe's Network
Chicago(config-webvpn)# logo none
Chicago(config-webvpn)# title-color 108,108,108
Chicago(config-webvpn)# secondary-color 161,161,161
Chicago(config-webvpn)# text-color white
Chicago(config-webvpn)# secondary-text-color black
```

You can upload a customized logo file in Flash. The accepted formats are JPEG, GIF, and PNG.

Step 4: Configure WebVPN Group Attributes

Cisco ASA allows you to configure most of the WebVPN parameters in three different places:

- Under default group-policy
- Under user group-policy
- Under user policy

As mentioned earlier, Cisco ASA implements the inheritance model and applies attributes from the user policy first, then from the user group-policy, and finally from the default group-policy. The same concept is true for WebVPN implementations.

NOTE   The default and user group policies are set up to allow both Cisco IPSec VPN and WebVPN tunnels. If you want to restrict a policy to solely use WebVPN, use the **vpn-tunnel-protocol webvpn** command, as demonstrated later in Example 16-66.

The user group and default group policies are configured by using the **group-policy** command followed by the name of the group-policy. Cisco ASA uses DfltGrpPolicy as the group-policy name for the default group-policy. A group-policy name other than DfltGrpPolicy is treated as a user group-policy. In Example 16-64, SecureMeWebGrp is set up as an internal group-policy.

Example 16-64 *User Group-Policy Configuration*

```
Chicago(config)# group-policy SecureMeWebGrp internal
Chicago(config)# group-policy SecureMeWebGrp attributes
```

The WebVPN attributes are configured under the WebVPN subconfiguration mode of the group-policy menu, as shown in Example 16-65.

Example 16-65 *WebVPN User Group-Policy Configuration*

```
Chicago(config)# group-policy SecureMeWebGrp internal
Chicago(config)# group-policy SecureMeWebGrp attributes
Chicago(config-group-policy)# webvpn
Chicago(config-group-webvpn)#
```

Table 16-5 lists all the WebVPN attributes that can be mapped to user, user group, and default group policies.

Table 16-5   *Configurable WebVPN Attributes*

Attribute	Purpose
filter	Apply a WebVPN ACL for traffic filtering.
functions	Enable features such as file access, file browsing, and file entry.
homepage	Set an initial web page when users log in.
html-content-filter	Filter HTML content, such as Java and images, from the WebVPN sessions.
port-forward	Map the port-forwarding list to the group.

continues

Table 16-5 *Configurable WebVPN Attributes (Continued)*

Attribute	Purpose
port-forward-name	Configure the name to be shown on the WebVPN page for the port-forwarding applet.
url-list	Map the URL-mangling list to the group.

All of these attributes are discussed in detail in the next section, "Advanced WebVPN Features." Example 16-66 shows the Cisco ASA configuration for a user group-policy named SecureMeWebGrp that permits only WebVPN connections. The WebVPN users are allowed to browse, access, and enter file information using the **functions** command.

Example 16-66 *Configuration of User Group Attributes*

```
Chicago(config)# group-policy SecureMeWebGrp internal
Chicago(config)# group-policy SecureMeWebGrp attributes
Chicago(config-group-policy)# vpn-tunnel-protocol webvpn
Chicago(config-group-policy)# webvpn
Chicago(config-group-webvpn)# functions file-access file-entry file-browsing
```

Step 5: Configure User Authentication

Cisco ASA supports many authentication servers, such as RADIUS, NT domain, Kerberos, SDI, TACACS+, and local database. For small organizations, a local database can be set up for user authentication. In Example 16-67, the Chicago ASA has a user account, cisco, set up for authentication.

Example 16-67 *Local User Accounts*

```
Chicago# configure terminal
Chicago(config)# username cisco password cisco123
```

The WebVPN submenu must be configured with the corresponding authentication server. The **authentication-server-group** command is used to specify the authentication server. Example 16-68 illustrates the necessary commands required to use a local database.

Example 16-68 *Local Authentication Database Configuration*

```
Chicago(config)# webvpn
Chicago(config-webvpn)# authentication-server-group LOCAL
```

For configuration of external servers, consult Chapter 7.

Advanced WebVPN Features

Cisco ASA provides many advanced WebVPN features to suit the VPN implementations:

- Port forwarding
- URL mangling

- E-mail proxy
- Windows file sharing
- WebVPN access lists

The sections that follow cover these features in more detail.

Port Forwarding

Once a session is established, users can use the features offered by WebVPN. One of the important features is port forwarding, which provides client access to the servers over the known and fixed TCP ports. VPN users connect to the TCP applications offered by the server using Cisco ASA. To use this feature, the authenticated WebVPN users click the "Start Application Access" link on the main page, which launches a Java applet on the client machine showing the IP address and the port number that can be used for the session. Figure 16-18 illustrates the Java applet launched in the client machine.

Figure 16-18 *Port-Forwarding Applet*

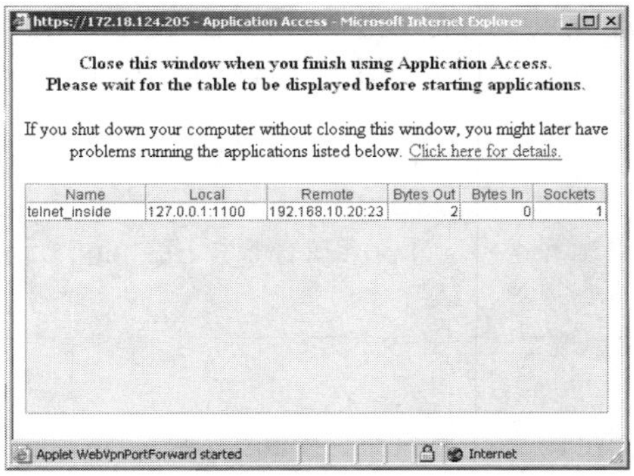

The port-forwarding feature requires you to install Sun Microsystems' Java Runtime Environment (JRE) and configure applications on the end user's PC. If users are establishing the WebVPN tunnel from public machines, such as Internet kiosks or web cafés, they might not be able to use this feature. The installation on Sun's JRE requires administrative rights on the client machine.

You can enable or disable port forwarding by configuring the **functions** command under the webvpn menu of a default, user group, or user policy. To enable port forwarding, use the **functions** command with the **port-forward** parameter, as shown in Example 16-69.

Example 16-69 *Enabling Port Forwarding*

```
Chicago(config)# group-policy SecureMeWebGrp attributes
Chicago(config-group-policy)# vpn-tunnel-protocol webvpn
Chicago(config-group-policy)# webvpn
Chicago(config-group-webvpn)# functions port-forward
```

Port forwarding is configured by using the **port-forward** command followed by the name of the list in the global configuration mode. The Cisco ASA configuration in Example 16-70 specifies a list called telnet_inside to forward information about a Telnet server located at 192.168.10.20.

Example 16-70 *Port-Forwarding List Configuration*

```
Chicago(config)# port-forward telnet_inside 1100 192.168.10.20 23
```

NOTE   When port forwarding is in use, the HOSTS file on the WebVPN client is modified to resolve the host name using one of the loopback addresses. Cisco ASA uses an available address in the range from 127.0.0.2 to 127.0.0.254.

If the HOSTS file cannot be modified, the host listens on 127.0.0.1 and the configured local port.

Once the applet is loaded on the client, the user can establish a Telnet connection to the server by using the loopback IP address of 127.0.0.1 on the local port 1100. This will redirect the connection over the WebVPN tunnel to the server at 192.168.10.20 on port 23.

NOTE   It is recommended to use a local port between 1024 and 65535 to avoid conflicts with the existing network services.

The port list can then be mapped to a default, user group, or user policy. In Example 16-71, the port list telnet_inside is mapped to a user group-policy named SecureMeWebGrp under the WebVPN submenu. Mapping of the list to a policy is done by using the **port-forward value** command followed by the name of the list.

Example 16-71 *Port-Forwarding List Mapping*

```
Chicago(config)# group-policy SecureMeWebGrp attributes
Chicago(config-group-policy)# vpn-tunnel-protocol webvpn
Chicago(config-group-webvpn)# webvpn
Chicago(config-group-webvpn)# functions port-forward
Chicago(config-group-webvpn)# port-forward value telnet_inside
```

The login page shows a default link of "Start Application Access" to launch the port-forwarding applet. This link can be renamed to accommodate the security policy of an organization. In Example 16-72, the link for the port-forwarding applet on the main login page is changed to "SecureMe Port-Forwarding".

Example 16-72 *Configuration of Port-Forwarding Applet name*

```
Chicago(config)# group-policy SecureMeWebGrp attributes
Chicago(config-group-policy)# vpn-tunnel-protocol webvpn
Chicago(config-group-policy)# webvpn
Chicago(config-group-webvpn)# functions port-forward
Chicago(config-group-webvpn)# port-forward value telnet_inside
Chicago(config-group-webvpn)# port-forward-name value SecureMe Port-Forwarding
```

Configuring URL Mangling

Using WebVPN, remote users can browse their internal websites. Cisco ASA terminates the
HTTPS connections on the public interface, and then forwards the HTTP or HTTPS
requests to the specified server. The response from the web server is then encapsulated into
HTTPS and forwarded to the client. This feature, known as URL mangling, is illustrated in
Figure 16-19. The following sequence of events takes place when UserA tries to connect to
a web server located at 192.168.10.10:

Step 1   User A initiates an HTTP request to the web server, located on the other
side of the WebVPN tunnel. The user request is encapsulated into the
SSL tunnel and is then forwarded to the security appliance.

Step 2   The security appliance de-encapsulates the traffic and initiates a
connection to the server on behalf of the web client.

Step 3   The response from the server is sent to the security appliance.

Step 4   The security appliance, in turn, encapsulates and sends it to UserA.

Figure 16-19 *HTTP Requests Using URL Mangling*

With URL mangling, the original protocol, host address, port number, and path get
manipulated to establish connectivity to the Cisco ASA. The original protocol field is
replaced with https, while the original address and port are replaced with the IP address
and port of the security appliance. The mangled path in the URL is augmented with the
protocol, port, and host elements of the original URL. Figure 16-20 shows the original and
the modified URLs.

Figure 16-20 *URL Mangling in WebVPN*

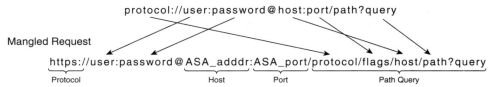

Table 16-6 lists four examples of the original and the mangled URLs. The Cisco ASA IP address is 209.165.200.225.

Table 16-6 *Original and Mangled URLs in WebVPN*

Original URL	Mangled URL
http://www.securemeinc.com	https://209.165.200.225/http/0/ www.securemeinc.com
https://internalweb.securemeinc.com/ index.html	https://209.165.200.225/https/0/ internalweb.securemeinc.com/index.html
http://freedom.securemeinc.com/~free/ protect-cgi-bin/simple_query.cgi	https://209.165.200.225/http/0/freedom. securemeinc.com/~free/protect-cgi-bin/ simple_query.cgi
http://metrics.securemeinc.com:675	https://209.165.200.225/http/675/ metrics.securemeinc.com:675

The flags parameter, shown in Figure 16-20, integrates the original port number and a set of other flag values. It is the ASCII representation in decimal, with the lower 16 bits reserved for the port and the upper 16 bits reserved for flags. Port 0 is used if the original URL either contains 80 (for HTTP) or 443 (for HTTPS). The upper 16 bits are currently not used.

NOTE   The current implementation of WebVPN cannot modify Java and ActiveX coding in a web page. Additionally, Cisco ASA does not mangle non-HTTP-based URLs such as ftp:// or telnet://.

The configuration of URL mangling involves setting up a URL list to specify the IP address of the web server(s). The command syntax to define a URL list is as follows:

```
url-list listname displayname url
```

where:

• *listname* is the name that is then used to map the **url-list** to a user or group-policy.

- *displayname* is the name that is shown to the WebVPN user after a successful user authentication.

- *url* is the actual URL to a web-server that resides toward the inside interface.

In Example 16-73, a URL list named HTTP_Link is set up with a displayname of Internal and the host URL of http://192.168.10.10.

Example 16-73 *URL Mangling List*

```
Chicago(config)# url-list HTTP_Link "Internal" http://192.168.10.10
```

The URL list is then linked to a user or group-policy by using the **url-list** command followed by the name of the URL list. In Example 16-74, the URL list HTTP_Link is applied to the SecureMeWebGrp group under the webvpn submenu.

Example 16-74 *URL List Mapping to a Group-Policy*

```
Chicago(config)# group-policy SecureMeWebGrp attributes
Chicago(config-group-policy)# webvpn
Chicago(config-group-webvpn)# url-list value HTTP_Link
```

Cisco ASA can optionally forward HTTP WebVPN sessions to either an HTTP or HTTPS server. These proxy servers act as the intermediary servers between the WebVPN users and the Internet. This greatly enhances network security by filtering unnecessary web traffic in the network. Example 16-75 shows the configuration for Cisco ASA to be set up as an HTTP server located at 192.168.10.100 and as an HTTPS server with an IP address of 192.168.10.200.

Example 16-75 *HTTP/HTTPS Proxy Configuration*

```
Chicago(config)# webvpn
Chicago(config-webvpn)# http-proxy 192.168.10.100 80
Chicago(config-webvpn)# https-proxy 192.168.10.200 443
```

As a security device, Cisco ASA has the capability to filter out Java or ActiveX applets, script tags, display images, and delete cookies from the HTML pages when they are sent over a WebVPN connection. This is done by using the **html-content-filter** command followed by the selected parameter to filter. The Cisco ASA configuration in Example 16-76 sets up the capability to filter out Java/ActiveX and display images when the HTML pages are sent to the client.

Example 16-76 *HTML Content Filtering*

```
Chicago(config)# group-policy SecureMeWebGrp attributes
Chicago(config-group-policy)# vpn-tunnel-protocol webvpn
Chicago(config-group-webvpn)# webvpn
Chicago(config-group- webvpn)# html-content-filter java images
```

E-Mail Proxy

WebVPN provides a way for the remote users to check e-mail using the secure HTTP connection. This feature, known as e-mail proxy, provides a seamless connection from an e-mail client to the server. Users have the option to either authenticate themselves to the GUI WebVPN authentication screen or set up the e-mail client for automatic user authentication.

Cisco ASA supports three types of e-mail proxies: SMTP, IMAP4, and POP3. All of these proxies use their own unique SSL/TLS ports. Cisco ASA uses the default TCP ports of 988, 993, and 995 for SMTP, IMAP4, and POP3, respectively. All of these proxies are disabled until explicitly enabled on the physical interface by configuring the **enable** command, followed by the name of the interface terminating the connections, under the e-mail proxies' subconfiguration menu. The Cisco ASA configuration in Example 16-77 enables the security appliance to accept IMAP4, POP3, and SMTP proxies on the outside interface.

Example 16-77 *Enabling E-Mail Proxy on the Outside Interface*

```
Chicago(config)# imap4s
Chicago(config-imap4s)# enable outside
Chicago(config-imap4s)# pop3s
Chicago(config-pop3s)# enable outside
Chicago(config-pop3s)# smtps
Chicago(config-smtps)# enable outside
```

Cisco ASA provides protection against denial of service (DoS) attacks against the e-mail servers when deployed as an e-mail proxy. The user has to be authenticated first by the security appliance before the session is opened for e-mail transfer, as illustrated in Figure 16-21. After a successful user authentication, Cisco ASA opens a session to the e-mail server and forwards the user credentials for validation.

Figure 16-21 *User Authentication Using E-Mail Proxy*

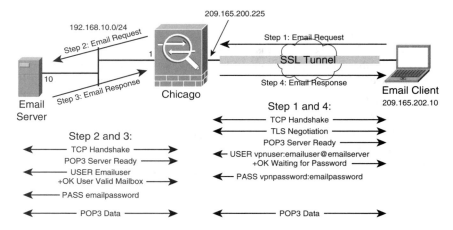

Once the WebVPN session is authenticated, the Cisco ASA's default behavior is to apply the attributes configured under the DfltGrpPolicy group-policy. However, a user group-policy can be applied to the e-mail proxies by configuring the **default-group-policy** command followed by the name of the user group-policy. In Example 16-78, the IMAP4 proxy is associating the SecureMeWebGrp user group-policy with the authenticated IMAP4 sessions.

Example 16-78 *Mapping of User Group-Policy on the IMAP4 Proxy*

```
Chicago(config)# imap4s
Chicago(config-imap4s)# enable outside
Chicago(config-imap4s)# default-group-policy SecureMeWebGrp
```

Authentication Methods for E-Mail Proxy

Cisco ASA supports three methods for e-mail proxy authentication:

- Piggyback authentication
- AAA authentication
- Certificate authentication

Piggyback Authentication

With piggyback HTTPS, a user is required to have a WebVPN session already established before connecting to the e-mail server. The user provides their e-mail username and passwords for authentication. If the VPN and e-mail usernames are different, the user is required to provide both of them, separated by a VPN delimiter (discussed later in this chapter). The VPN user credentials are used to verify only that the WebVPN session is already established. If the session is not established, the user is not allowed to connect to the e-mail server.

CAUTION   Due to an inherit flaw in SMTP, if piggyback authentication is used with SMTP, an attacker can potentially send spam e-mail messages using any name and using a legitimate user account. This typically happens when the attacker spoofs the IP address and the VPN name of the legitimate user. To remedy this problem, consider using IMAP4 or POP3 for piggyback authentication. Alternatively, you can use certificate authentication for SMTP.

Example 16-79 shows that piggyback authentication is enabled for users who use IMAP4 for e-mail messages.

Example 16-79 *Piggyback Authentication for IMAP4*

```
Chicago(config)# imap4s
Chicago(config-imap4s)# enable outside
Chicago(config-imap4s)# authentication piggyback
```

AAA Authentication

AAA authentication is a way to authenticate the VPN users using either the internal or external database. For AAA authentication, users do not need to have a pre-established WebVPN session. When a user checks e-mail, the e-mail client opens the secured connection to Cisco ASA and presents the VPN user credentials. Cisco ASA checks the configured user database and authenticates the user if credentials are valid. After a successful authentication, Cisco ASA forwards the e-mail user credentials to the e-mail server. If the VPN and e-mail usernames are different, a VPN delimiter is used to differentiate them.

Cisco ASA uses an authentication server to validate user accounts. Example 16-80 shows the AAA authentication configuration for RADIUS users who use POP3 for e-mail. The RADIUS server is defined under tag Rad and is located at 192.168.10.30. This tag is then mapped to the POP3 proxy by using the **authentication-server-group** Rad command.

Example 16-80 *AAA Authentication for POP3*

```
Chicago(config)# aaa-server Rad protocol radius
Chicago(config-aaa-server-group)# exit
Chicago(config)# aaa-server Rad host 192.168.10.30
Chicago(config-aaa-server-host)# exit
Chicago(config)# pop3s
Chicago(config-pop3s)# enable outside
Chicago(config-pop3s)# authentication aaa
Chicago(config-pop3s)# authentication-server-group Rad
```

Certificate Authentication

Certificate authentication requires the e-mail user to present the certificate to the security appliance for validation. If the certificate authentication is unsuccessful, the secured connection is terminated, and the e-mail client fails to connect to the server. This method requires two certificates to be installed on the devices:

- A certificate authority (CA) certificate on Cisco ASA and on the e-mail client
- An identity certificate on the client machine that is signed by a CA and authenticated by Cisco ASA

Example 16-81 shows that certificate authentication is enabled for users who check their e-mail using SMTPS.

Example 16-81 *Certificate Authentication for SMTPS*

```
Chicago(config)# smtps
Chicago(config-smtps)# enable outside
Chicago(config-smtps)# authentication certificate
```

NOTE	SMTP e-mail proxy allows mailhost authentication for additional security. Mailhost authentication requires the use of username, password, and server information. Cisco ASA does not allow the configuration of mailhost authentication for POP3 and IMAP4, because they always perform mailhost authentication. SMTP e-mail proxy is enabled by configuring **authentication mailhost** under the SMTP proxy.

Identifying E-Mail Servers for E-Mail Proxies

After you configure the authentication methods, the next step is to identify the e-mail servers to be used for each proxy. To specify an e-mail server, you can use the **server** command followed by the IP address or the host name of the server. In the configuration in Example 16-82, one email server, called secureme-email, is set up to serve both IMAP and POP3 users. The server is defined under both the IMAP and POP3 configuration menus.

Example 16-82 *Configuration of E-Mail Proxy Servers*

```
Chicago(config)# imap4s
Chicago(config-imap4s)# enable outside
Chicago(config-imap4s)# server secureme-email
Chicago(config-imap4s)# authentication piggyback
Chicago(config-imap4s)# pop3s
Chicago(config-pop3s)# enable outside
Chicago(config-pop3s)# server secureme-email
Chicago(config-pop3s)# authentication aaa
```

Delimiters

Cisco ASA can differentiate the WebVPN username from the e-mail username by using specific delimiters for each of the e-mail proxies. There are two types of supported delimiters:

- Username delimiter
- Server delimiter

Username Delimiter

A *username delimiter* is used to separate out the VPN username from the e-mail username in the username string when configuring the e-mail client. However, this delimiter is necessary only when both usernames are different from each other. The same username delimiter is used to differentiate the user password from the e-mail server password. The username delimiter can be specified by using the **name-separator** command followed by the actual delimiter. Cisco ASA supports the following valid username delimiters:

- hash (#)
- comma (,)

- colon (:)
- semicolon (;)
- at (@)
- pipe (|)

The Cisco ASA configuration in Example 16-83 specifies the use of # for the username delimiter for the IMAP4 and POP3 proxies. The default username delimiter on Cisco ASA is the colon (:).

Example 16-83 *Configuration of E-Mail Proxy Username Delimiter*

```
Chicago(config)# imap4s
Chicago(config-imap4s)# enable outside
Chicago(config-imap4s)# server secureme-email
Chicago(config-imap4s)# name-separator #
Chicago(config-imap4s)# authentication piggyback
Chicago(config-imap4s)# pop3s
Chicago(config-pop3s)# enable outside
Chicago(config-pop3s)# server secureme-email
Chicago(config-pop3s)# name-separator #
Chicago(config-pop3s)# authentication aaa
```

NOTE   You cannot have a username delimiter as a valid character in the user password.

Server Delimiter

A *server delimiter* is used to differentiate the username from the e-mail server name when the username string is entered in the e-mail client. A server name can be either the host name or the IP address of the e-mail server. The server delimiter can be specified by using the **server-separator** command followed by the actual delimiter. Cisco ASA supports the following valid server delimiters:

- hash (#)
- comma (,)
- colon (:)
- semicolon (;)
- at (@)
- pipe (|)

However, the server delimiter must be different from the username delimiter. Example 16-84 demonstrates the Cisco ASA configuration to use | as the server delimiter for the IMAP4 and POP3 proxies. The default server delimiter on Cisco ASA is at (@).

Example 16-84 *Configuration of E-Mail Proxy Server Delimiter*

```
Chicago(config)# imap4s
Chicago(config-imap4s)# enable outside
Chicago(config-imap4s)# server secureme-email
Chicago(config-imap4s)# name-separator #
Chicago(config-imap4s)# server-separator |
Chicago(config-imap4s)# authentication piggyback
Chicago(config-imap4s)# pop3s
Chicago(config-pop3s)# enable outside
Chicago(config-pop3s)# server secureme-email
Chicago(config-pop3s)# name-separator #
Chicago(config-pop3s)# server-separator |
Chicago(config-pop3s)# authentication aaa
```

TIP   The e-mail client must be properly configured for the e-mail proxy feature to work. Consult the following link for an e-mail client sample configuration:

http://www.cisco.com/en/US/partner/products/hw/vpndevc/ps2284/
products_configuration_guide_chapter09186a00801f1fb6.html

Windows File Sharing

Cisco ASA supports network file sharing using Common Internet File System (CIFS), a file system that uses the original IBM and Microsoft networking protocols. Using CIFS, users can access their file shares located on the file servers, as illustrated in Figure 16-22. Users can download, upload, delete, or rename the files under the shared directories, but only if the file system permissions allow them to perform those actions.

To access the shared resources, users can click the Browse Network link and select the proper domain or workgroup. They can browse to the desired shared resource and take the appropriate actions (read, write, delete, rename filename). They can even create subdirectories, assuming that they are allowed to do so. Alternatively, they can enter the NetBIOS name of the server in the Enter Network Path field to display all the shared resources available for that server, as depicted in Figure 16-23.

Figure 16-22 *CIFS Browsing on the Security Appliance*

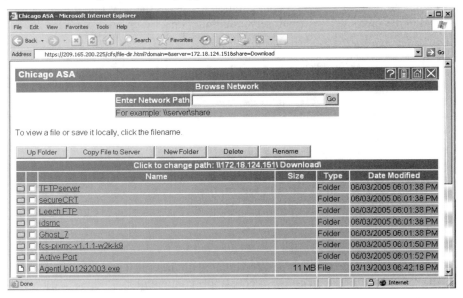

Figure 16-23 *CIFS Support on Cisco ASA*

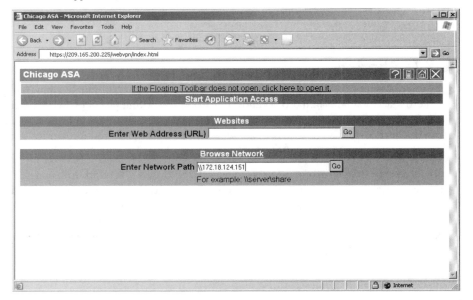

The configuration of CIFS requires the use of a NetBIOS Name Server (NBNS), also known as Windows Internet Naming Server (WINS). When a WebVPN user queries to browse the network, the Cisco ASA contacts the WINS server and acquires the list of available domains, workgroups, and workstations. The command syntax to configure an NBNS server is as follows:

```
nbns-server ipaddr [master] [timeout timeout] [retry retries]
```

The **nbns-server** command can be found under webvpn subconfiguration mode. The *ipaddr* is the IP address of the NBNS server for CIFS name resolution. The **master** keyword specifies that the configured NBNS server acts as the master browser in addition to being a WINS server. The **timeout** value instructs an appliance to wait for the configured number of seconds (default is 2 seconds) before sending another query to the next server. The **retry** option is used to specify the number of times Cisco ASA has to go through the list of the configured NBNS servers. The default retries is 2, and it ranges from 0 to 10.

NOTE   You can specify up to three WINS servers in the current version.

The configuration in Example 16-85 sets up Cisco ASA to use three NBNS servers. The first server, 192.168.10.50, acts as a master browser rather than a WINS server. The other two servers, 192.168.10.51 and 192.168.10.52, are the WINS servers. The **timeout** and **retry** values are set to their defaults.

Example 16-85 *CIFS—NBNS Server Configuration*

```
Chicago(config)# webvpn
Chicago(config-webvpn)# nbns-server 192.168.10.50 master timeout 2 retry 2
Chicago(config-webvpn)# nbns-server 192.168.10.51 timeout 2 retry 2
Chicago(config-webvpn)# nbns-server 192.168.10.52 timeout 2 retry 2
```

Cisco ASA does not enable CIFS functionality until the **functions** parameter is set up to allow file browsing, file access, and file entry. The configuration in Example 16-86 sets up Cisco ASA with a user group-policy named SecureMeWebGrp, which allows users to browse, access, and enter file information using the **functions** attribute.

Example 16-86 *Configuration of User Group Attributes*

```
Chicago(config)# group-policy SecureMeWebGrp attributes
Chicago(config-group-policy)# webvpn
Chicago(config-group-webvpn)# functions file-access file-entry file-browsing
```

WebVPN Access Lists

Cisco ASA enables network administrators to further their WebVPN security by configuring WebVPN access control lists (ACLs) to manage access to web, file, and e-mail servers. These ACLs affect only the WebVPN traffic and are processed in sequential order until there is a match. If there is an ACL defined but no match, the default behavior on Cisco ASA is to drop the packets. On the other hand, if there is no ACL defined, Cisco ASA allows all traffic to pass through it.

Moreover, this robust WebVPN feature allows these ACLs to be downloaded from a Cisco Secure Access Control Server (CS-ACS) by using the vendor specific attributes (VSAs). This allows central control and management of user access into the corporate network by offloading ACL definitions locally on the security appliance.

TIP   Using CS-ACS Server, a WebVPN ACL can be configured by specifying the **webvpn:inacl#** prefix in the downloadable ACLs, where # indicates the sequence number of an access control entry (ACE).

The command syntax to create a WebVPN ACL is as follows:

```
access-list id webtype {deny | permit} url [url_string | any] [log [[disable | default]
| level][interval secs] [time_range name]]
```

and

```
access-list id webtype {deny | permit} tcp [host ip_address | ip_address subnet_mask
| any] [oper port [port]] [log [[disable | default] | level] [interval secs]
[time_range name]]
```

A URL-based WebVPN ACL is used to filter out WebVPN packets if they contain a URL such as http://. A TCP-based WebVPN ACL is used to filter out WebVPN packets if they use TCP encapsulation based on the IP address and the Layer 4 port number.

Table 16-7 describes all the options available in the WebVPN ACL.

Table 16-7   *WebVPN ACL Parameters*

Feature	Description
any	Specifies all IP addresses or all URLs.
deny	Denies access if packets match the condition.
permit	Permits access if packets match the condition.
tcp	A keyword to specify a TCP-based ACE.
host	A keyword to specify a host IP address.
oper	The operator that is used to compare destination ports in WebVPN packets. The security appliance supports **lt** (less than), **gt** (greater than), **eq** (equal), **neq** (not equal), and **range** (inclusive range) as operators.

Table 16-7   *WebVPN ACL Parameters (Continued)*

Feature	Description
port	Specifies the TCP or UDP port in the range of 0 to 65535 used for WebVPN packets.
ip_address	The actual IP address of the host or the network address.
subnet_mask	The actual subnet mask when a network address is specified as the IP address.
url	A keyword to specify a URL-based ACE.
url-string	The actual URL used for filtering.
log	Sends a syslog message whenever there is a hit on the ACL .
disable	Does not send a syslog message if packets hit the configured ACE.
default	Uses the default behavior, which generates a syslog 106023 message whenever a packet matches a deny in the ACE.
level	Changes the syslog level when a message is generated. The default level is 6 (informational).
interval	A keyword to specify the time interval to generate the subsequent new syslog messages.
secs	The actual time interval, in seconds. The default time interval is 300 seconds, and it ranges from 1 to 600 seconds.
time_range	A keyword to specify the time-range name.
name	The predefined time-range name.

NOTE   If you want to include all URLs that are not explicitly matched in the ACL, you can include an asterisk (*) as a wildcard. The following example shows how to block POP3 e-mail access and allow all other protocols:

```
access-list blockpop3 webtype deny url pop3://*
access-list blockpop3 webtype permit url any
```

In Example 16-87, there is a WebVPN ACL configured called HTTP. The first entry in the list denies WebVPN HTTP traffic destined to an internal server located at wwwin.securemeinc.com. The logging is set to debugging (level 7) with the subsequent syslog messages generated every 60 seconds. The second entry in the list permits all other WebVPN traffic.

Example 16-87 *WebVPN ACL Configuration*

```
Chicago(config)# access-list HTTP webtype deny url http://wwwin.securemeinc.com log
  debugging interval 60
Chicago(config)# access-list HTTP webtype permit url any
```

Once the WebVPN ACL is configured, the next step is to link it to a default, user group, or user policy under the WebVPN configuration menu. Example 16-88 shows that the configured HTTP ACL is mapped to a user group called SecureMeWebGrp by using the **filter value** command.

Example 16-88 *WebVPN ACL Mapping*

```
Chicago(config)# group-policy SecureMeWebGrp attributes
Chicago(config-group-policy)# webvpn
Chicago(config-group-webvpn)# filter value HTTP
```

Cisco ASA does not apply the WebVPN ACL feature to the user until the **functions** parameter is set up to filter traffic. In Example 16-89, SecureMeWebGrp is configured for **filter** function, which turns on WebVPN traffic filtering on the security appliance.

Example 16-89 *WebVPN ACL Filtering*

```
Chicago(config)# group-policy SecureMeWebGrp attributes
Chicago(config-group-policy)# webvpn
Chicago(config-group-webvpn)# functions filter
Chicago(config-group-webvpn)# filter value HTTP
```

CAUTION   WebVPN ACLs do not block a user from accessing the resources outside the company. These ACLs ensure that WebVPN traffic denied by the ACLs will not pass through the security appliance.

Deployment Scenarios of WebVPN

The Cisco WebVPN solution is useful in deployments where remote and home users need limited application support without installing a separate VPN client. The WebVPN solution can be deployed in many ways; however, the sections that follow cover two design scenarios for ease of understanding:

- WebVPN with external authentication
- WebVPN with e-mail proxies

NOTE   The design scenarios discussed in this section should be used solely to reinforce learning. They should be used for reference purposes only.

WebVPN with External Authentication

SecureMe has recently learned about the WebVPN functionality in Cisco ASA and wants to deploy it for a group of mobile contractors in London who do not have access to Cisco VPN Client. These contractors use a web server for browsing, a terminal server, and a Windows file server to save and retrieve their documents.

Figure 16-24 shows SecureMe's network topology for WebVPN.

Figure 16-24 *SecureMe's WebVPN topology in London*

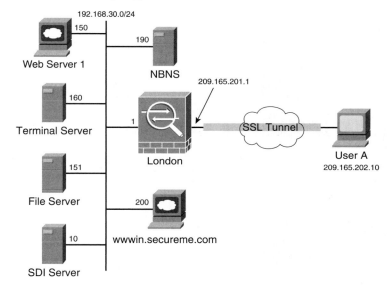

The security requirements for SecureMe's London office are as follows:

- Allow access to a web server with an IP address of 192.168.30.150
- Deny access to the internal web-server located at wwwin.securemeinc.com
- Allow access to a file server with an IP address of 192.168.30.151
- Allow access to a terminal server with an IP address of 192.168.30.160
- Use an SDI server as the external database for user lookup

Example 16-90 shows the relevant configuration of the London ASA.

Example 16-90 *Relevant WebVPN Configuration for the London ASA*

```
London# show running-config
: Saved
:
ASA Version 7.0(1)
! ip address on the outside interface
interface GigabitEthernet0/0
```

continues

Example 16-90 *Relevant WebVPN Configuration for the London ASA (Continued)*

```
 nameif outside
 security-level 0
 ip address 209.165.201.1 255.255.255.0
! ip address on the inside interface
interface GigabitEthernet0/1
 nameif inside
 security-level 100
 ip address 192.168.30.1 255.255.255.0
!
hostname London
domain-name securemeinc.com
! DNS lookup for hostname
dns domain-lookup inside
dns name-server 192.168.30.200
! WebVPN ACL to deny users to access wwwin.securemeinc.com using HTTP
access-list HTTP webtype deny url http://wwwin.securemeinc.com
access-list HTTP webtype permit url any
! Default Gateway
route outside 0.0.0.0 0.0.0.0 209.165.201.2 1
! URL Mangling. A link to an internal web-server at 192.168.30.150 is displayed
url-list HTTP_Link "Internal" http://192.168.30.150
! Port Forwarding for Terminal Services using local port 1100
port-forward TerminalServer 1100 192.168.30.160 3389
! SDI configuration for user authentication
aaa-server SDI_Server protocol sdi
aaa-server SDI_Server host 192.168.30.10
! Configuration of an internal user-group called SecureMeWebGrp configured for
  WebVPN
group-policy SecureMeWebGrp internal
group-policy SecureMeWebGrp attributes
 vpn-tunnel-protocol webvpn
 webvpn
! The allowed list of functions
   functions url-entry file-access file-entry file-browsing port-forward filter
! WebVPN ACL is applied under the group WebVPN menu
   filter value HTTP
! URL Mangling list is applied under the group WebVPN menu
   url-list value HTTP_Link
! Port Forwarding List is applied under the group WebVPN menu
   port-forward value TerminalServer
! Configuration of ASDM for Appliance management
http server enable
http 0.0.0.0 0.0.0.0 inside
! WebVPN global configuration
webvpn
 enable outside
 logo none
! WebVPN users will be authenticated against an SDI server
 authentication-server-group SDI_Server
! WebVPN user group-policy is applied
 default-group-policy SecureMeWebGrp
! Configuration of WINS server located at 192.168.30.190
 nbns-server 192.168.30.190 master timeout 2 retry 2
```

WebVPN with E-Mail Proxies

SecureMe is looking to deploy the WebVPN e-mail proxy functionality for its remote users who need to check their corporate e-mail. These users generally use either POP3 or IMAP4 depending on their email client configuration. Figure 16-25 shows SecureMe's network topology for e-mail proxy.

Figure 16-25 *SecureMe's E-Mail Proxy WebVPN Topology*

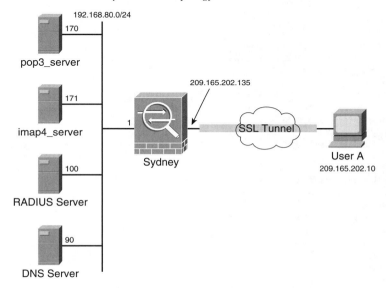

The security requirements for SecureMe's Sydney office are as follows:

* Allow POP3 and IMAP4 access to the e-mail server with a hostname of email-server.securemeinc.com. Use port 1000 for secure POP3 and 1010 for secure IMAP4. The users specify the pipe (|) as the username delimiter and the at (@) symbol as the server delimiter.

* Use a RADIUS server as the external user database.

* Use a DNS server to resolve email server name

Example 16-91 shows the complete configuration of the Sydney ASA.

Example 16-91 *Sydney ASA Configuration to Implement E-Mail Proxies*

```
Sydney# show running-config
: Saved
:
ASA Version 7.0(1)
! ip address on the outside interface
interface GigabitEthernet0/0
 nameif outside
 security-level 0
```

continues

Example 16-91 *Sydney ASA Configuration to Implement E-Mail Proxies (Continued)*

```
 ip address 209.165.202.135 255.255.255.224
! ip address on the inside interface
interface GigabitEthernet0/1
 nameif inside
 security-level 100
 ip address 192.168.80.1 255.255.255.0
 !
hostname Sydney
domain-name securemeinc.com
! DNS lookup for hostname
dns domain-lookup inside
dns name-server 192.168.80.90
! Default Gateway
route outside 0.0.0.0 0.0.0.0 209.165.202.136 1
! Radius configuration for user authentication
aaa-server Radius_Server protocol radius
aaa-server Radius_Server host 192.168.80.100
 key cisco123
! Configuration of an internal user-group called SecureMeWebGrp configured for
  WebVPN
group-policy SecureMeWebGrp internal
group-policy SecureMeWebGrp attributes
 vpn-tunnel-protocol webvpn
 webvpn
! Configuration of ASDM for Appliance management
http server enable
http 0.0.0.0 0.0.0.0 inside
! WebVPN global parameters
webvpn
 enable outside
 logo none
 authentication-server-group Radius_Server
 default-group-policy SecureMeWebGrp
! IMAP4 configuration
imap4s
 enable outside
 port 1010
 server email-server
 name-separator |
 server-separator @
 default-group-policy SecureMeWebGrp
 authentication-server-group Radius_Server
 authentication aaa
! POP3 configuration
pop3s
 enable outside
 port 1000
 server email-server
 name-separator |
 server-separator @
 default-group-policy SecureMeWebGrp
 authentication-server-group Radius_Server
 authentication aaa
```

Monitoring and Troubleshooting WebVPN

This section discusses the **show** and **debug** commands that are available to monitor and troubleshoot WebVPN-related issues on the security appliance.

Monitoring WebVPN

To monitor the WebVPN sessions, the first step is to check how many active WebVPN tunnels are established on the security appliance. You can achieve this by issuing the **show vpn-sessiondb summary** command, as shown in Example 16-92. This command displays the summary of all the active VPN tunnels including WebVPN. In this example, the security appliance allows up to 300 WebVPN connections, and there are currently 101 active sessions.

Example 16-92 *Output of* **show vpn-sessiondb summary** *Command*

```
Chicago# show vpn-sessiondb summary

Active Sessions:                        Session Information:
  LAN-to-LAN          : 1                 Peak Concurrent       : 200
  Remote Access       : 48                Concurrent Limit      : 300
  WebVPN              : 101               WebVPN Limit          : 300
  Email Proxy         : 0                 Cumulative Sessions   : 409
  Total Active Sessions : 150             Weighted Active Load  : 150
                                          Percent Session Load  : 50%
                                          VPN LB Mgmt Sessions  : 0
```

To monitor specific information about the WebVPN users, you can use the **show vpn-sessiondb webvpn** command. In Example 16-93, a WebVPN session for user ciscouser is displayed. The IP address of the WebVPN client is 209.165.201.10 and the negotiated encryption type is 3DES. The security appliance has received 33,149 bytes of traffic, while it has transmitted 34,375 bytes of data to the client. The security appliance has enforced policies from a user group called SecureMeWebGrp. The user is connected for about 10 minutes and 41 seconds.

Example 16-93 **show vpn-sessiondb webvpn** *Command Output*

```
Chicago# show vpn-sessiondb webvpn

Session Type: WebVPN

Username     : ciscouser
Index        : 1                  IP Addr      : 209.165.201.10
Protocol     : WebVPN             Encryption   : 3DES
Bytes Tx     : 34375              Bytes Rx     : 33149
Client Type  : Mozilla/4.0 (compatible; MSIE 6.0; Windows NT 5.1; SV1)
Group        : SecureMeWebGrp
Login Time   : 22:08:19 UTC Mon Oct 1 2005
Duration     : 0h:10m:41s
Filter Name  :
```

If the security appliance acts as an e-mail proxy, you can use the **show vpn-sessiondb email-proxy** command to check the statistics of e-mail proxy sessions. In Example 16-94, a user, ciscouser, is checking e-mails using POP3S. The security appliance has received 1632 bytes and transmitted 1892 bytes.

Example 16-94 show vpn-sessiondb email-proxy *Command Output*

```
Chicago# show vpn-sessiondb email-proxy
Session Type: Email-Proxy

Username     : ciscouser
Index        : 1              IP Addr      : 209.165.201.10
Protocol     : POP3S          Encryption   : 3DES
Bytes Tx     : 1892           Bytes Rx     : 1632
Group        : SecureMeWebGrp
Login Time   : 22:08:19 UTC Mon Oct 1 2005
Duration     : 0h:10m:41s
```

Troubleshooting WebVPN

Cisco ASA provides a number of troubleshooting and diagnostics command for WebVPN. This section focuses on three troubleshooting scenarios related to WebVPN.

SSL Negotiations

If you have a user who is not able to connect to the security appliance using SSL, you can enable the **debug ssl cipher** command to isolate the SSL negotiation issues. The security appliance shows the proposed SSL ciphers and, if the WebVPN client picks one cipher, the chosen cipher. As shown in Example 16-95, the WebVPN client has chosen DES-CBC3-SHA.

Example 16-95 debug menu webvpn *Command Output*

```
Chicago# debug ssl cipher 1
debug ssl cipher enabled at level 1
SSL: Choosing cipher
Proposed:
  RC4-MD5
  RC4-SHA
  DES-CBC3-SHA
  DES-CBC-SHA
  EXP1024-RC4-SHA
  EXP1024-DES-CBC-SHA
  EXP-RC4-MD5
  EXP-RC2-CBC-MD5
  EDH-DSS-DES-CBC3-SHA
  EDH-DSS-DES-CBC-SHA
  EXP1024-DHE-DSS-DES-CBC-SHA
Prefer:
  DES-CBC3-SHA
```

Example 16-95 debug menu webvpn *Command Output (Continued)*

```
      DES-CBC-SHA
      RC4-MD5
      RC4-MD5
SSL: OK  [00000021:00000121]:DES-CBC3-SHA
SSL: Chose cipher DES-CBC3-SHA (IP=209.165.201.10)
SSL, ssl3_get_client_hello: client (IP=209.165.201.10) sent 11 ciphers
     client [ 0 of 11]:RC4-MD5
     client [ 1 of 11]:RC4-SHA
     client [ 2 of 11]:DES-CBC3-SHA
```

WebVPN Data Capture

The WebVPN data capture tool is useful to troubleshoot WebVPN issues related to web browsing and browser-based applications such as Outlook Web Access (OWA). When this tool is enabled, it creates two text-based files in the local flash:

- **ORIGINAL.<nnn>**—Contains the web transactions between the security appliance (which acts as a web client) and the web server

- **MANGLED.<nnn>**—Contains communication between the security appliance (which acts a web server) and the WebVPN client

The security appliance uses a three-digit extension, represented as <nnn>, to pair up the two files. It ranges between 0 and 999.

CAUTION   When this capture tool is enabled, the security appliance creates ORIGINAL.<nnn> and MANGLED.<nnn>, which impacts the overall performance. Use a very specific URL for data capture and disable this tool when data has been captured.

Use the **debug menu webvpn 67** command to enable or disable the WebVPN data capture tool. The complete command syntax for this command is

```
debug menu webvpn {cmd} {user} {url}
```

where:

- *cmd* is a command to enable or disable this tool. If you specify 1, the security appliance enables this capture tool, and if you specify 0, the tool is disabled.

- *user* is the username for which you want to enable data capturing.

- *url* is the actual HTTP URL used to capture the data. You can enable this tool to capture all or specific HTTP transactions for a user.

In Example 16-96, the administrator enables this tool to capture data traffic destined to a web server (wwwin.securemeinc.com) from a WebVPN user, ciscouser.

Example 16-96 debug menu webvpn *Command Output*

```
Chicago# debug menu webvpn 67 1 ciscouser /http/0/wwwin.securemeinc.com
Mangle Logging: ON
Name: "ciscouser"
URL: "/http/0/wwwin.securemeinc.com"
```

NOTE   To capture HTTPS-based packets, use /https/0/<*actual url*> as the URL.

Once the files are captured, you can move them to an FTP or a TFTP server so that they can be analyzed.

NOTE   You can engage a TAC engineer to help you analyze and resolve the issue.

E-Mail Proxy Issues

If the security appliance is set up for e-mail proxy, and you have a user who is not able to connect to check his e-mail, follow these guidelines:

1   Verify that the e-mail client is set up to use an SSL connection to the ports configured on the security appliance.

2   Use the show **vpn-sessiondb email-proxy** command to display the status of the WebVPN e-mail proxy for that user. You can see that the security appliance received 1632 bytes from the client but there were no bytes transmitted.

```
Chicago# show vpn-sessiondb email-proxy
Session Type: Email-Proxy


Username     : ciscouser
Index        : 1                      IP Addr      : 209.165.201.10
Protocol     : POP3S                  Encryption   : 3DES
Bytes Tx     : 0                      Bytes Rx     : 1632
Group        : SecureMeWebGrp
Login Time   : 22:08:19 UTC Mon Oct 1 2005
Duration     : 0h:01m:01s
```

3   Enable packet capture on the inside interface to check if the packets are transmitted and received by the security appliance. In the following example, the administrator enables packet capture on the inside interface for the traffic sourced from its inside

interface, 192.168.80.1, and destined to an e-mail server located at 192.168.80.170 on TCP port 110.

```
access-list email-acl permit tcp host 192.168.80.1 host 192.168.80.170 eq
pop3
access-list email-acl permit tcp host 192.168.80.170 eq smtp host
192.168.80.1
capture email-cap access-list email-acl interface inside
```

4 You can also enable logging for e-mail proxy by creating a logging list for e-mail proxy and then linking the list to a logging type. As shown in the following example, the administrator has defined a logging list for e-mail proxy called email-pxy with the severity level set to debugging. The list is bound to buffered logging.

```
logging enable
logging timestamp
logging list email-pxy level debugging class email
logging buffered email-pxy
```

Summary

Using the remote-access methods available with Cisco ASA, security administrators can deploy Cisco ASA into almost any network topology. The Cisco IPSec VPN solution is available if users want to access the entire secured network. On the other hand, WebVPN provides application-based connectivity from the SSL-enabled browsers. To reinforce learning, many different deployment scenarios were discussed along with their configurations. This chapter covered extensive **show** and **debug** commands to assist in troubleshooting complicated Remote Access VPN and WebVPN deployments.

This chapter covers the following topics:

- Introduction to PKI
- Enrolling the Cisco ASA to a CA using SCEP
- Manual (cut-and-paste) enrollment
- Configuring CRL options
- Configuring IPSec site-to-site tunnels using certificates
- Configuring the Cisco ASA to accept remote-access VPN clients using certificates
- Troubleshooting PKI

CHAPTER 17

Public Key Infrastructure (PKI)

PKI is usually defined as a set of standards and systems whose main purpose is to verify and authenticate the validity of each party involved in a network transaction. This chapter starts with an introduction to PKI and then shows you how to configure, enroll, and troubleshoot the Cisco ASA with digital certificates.

Introduction to PKI

As previously mentioned, PKI is a security architecture that provides a higher level of confidence for exchanging information over insecure networks. PKI is based on public key cryptography, a technology that was first created to encrypt and decrypt data involving two different types of keys: a public and a private key. A user gives their public key to other users, keeping the private key. Data that is encrypted with the public key can be decrypted only with the corresponding private key, and vice versa. Figure 17-1 illustrates how this works.

Figure 17-1 *Private and Public Keys*

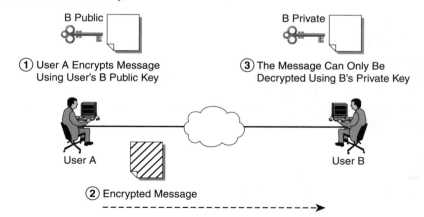

The following is the sequence in Figure 17-1:

1   User A obtains User B's public key and uses it to encrypt a message destined for User B.

2   User A sends the encrypted message over the unsecured network.

3   User B receives the encrypted message and decrypts it using his own private key.

The following are several key terms and concepts used in PKI:

- Certificates
- Certificate authority (CA)
- Certificate revocation list (CRL)
- Simple Certificate Enrollment Protocol (SCEP)

The following subsections define each of these terms and concepts in turn.

Certificates

Digital certificates are commonly used to authenticate and validate users and devices while securing information exchanged over unsecured networks. Certificates can be issued for a user or a network device. Certificates securely bind the user's or device's public key and other information that identifies them.

The certificate syntax and format are defined in the X.509 standard of the International Telecommunication Union-Telecommunication Standardization Sector (ITU-T). An X.509 certificate includes the public key and information about the user or device, information about the certificate itself, and optional issuer information. Generally, certificates contain the following information:

- The entity's public key
- The entity's identifier information, such as the name, e-mail address, organization, and locality
- The validity period (the length of time that the certificate is considered valid)
- Issuer's information
- CRL distribution point

Digital certificates can be used in many implementations, such as IPSec and Secure Sockets Layer (SSL), secure e-mail using Secure/Multipurpose Internet Mail Extensions (S/MIME), and many others. The same certificate might have different purposes. For example, a user certificate can be used for remote access VPN, accessing application servers, and for S/MIME e-mail authentication.

NOTE   Cisco ASA supports digital certificates for remote-access and site-to-site IPSec VPN session authentication, as well as for WebVPN and SSL administrative sessions.

The CA that issues the certificate determines the implementations for each certificate. The usage of the certificate is recorded to the CA (e.g., SSL, IPSec, etc.)

Certificate Authority

A CA is a device or entity that can issue a certificate to a user or network device. Before any PKI operations can begin, the CA generates its own public key pair and creates a self-signed CA certificate. A fingerprint in the certificate is used by the end entity to authenticate the received CA certificate. The fingerprint is created by calculating a hash (MD5 or SHA-1) on the whole CA certificate. This corresponds to the ultimate root certificate, in cases in which multiple level of CA exists.

CAs can be configured in a hierarchy. The CA at the top of a certification hierarchy is usually referred as the main root CA. Figure 17-2 illustrates this concept.

Figure 17-2 *Certification Hierarchy*

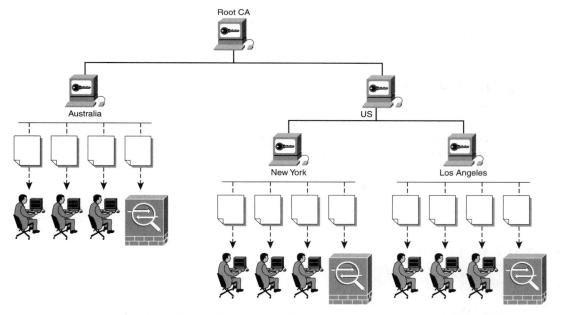

In the example in Figure 17-2, the root CA server has two subordinate CAs, US and Australia. The US CA server also has two subordinates, New York and Los Angeles. Each CA server grants or denies certificate enrollment requests from its corresponding users and network devices (Cisco ASAs in this example).

A user or network device chooses the certificate issuer as a trusted root authority by accepting the issuer CA's self-signed certificate containing the issuer's public key. The certificate information from all trusted CAs within the hierarchy is often referred to as the certificate chain of trust.

There are several CA vendors. The following are some of the CAs supported by Cisco ASA:

- Microsoft Windows 2000 and 2003 CA Server(s)
- VeriSign

- Baltimore UniCERT
- RSA Keon
- Entrust
- Cisco IOS router configured as a CA server

Several PKI implementations also include the use of registration authorities (RAs). An RA acts as an interface between the client (user or network device) and the CA server. An RA verifies and identifies all certificate requests and requests the CA to issue them. RAs can be configured within the same CA (server) or in a separate system. Microsoft CA server, RSA Keon, and Entrust are examples of PKI servers that utilize RA.

A certificate is valid only for the period of time specified by the issuing CA. Once a certificate expires, a new certificate must be requested. You also have the ability to revoke a specific user and device certificate. The inventory of serial numbers of revoked certificates is maintained on a certificate revocation list (CRL).

Certificate Revocation List

When you revoke a certificate, the CA publishes its serial number to the CRL. This CRL can be maintained on the same CA or a separate system. The CRL can be accessed by any entity trying to check the validity of any given certificate. LDAP and HTTP are the most commonly used protocols when publishing and obtaining a CRL. Storing CRLs in a separate system other than the CA server is often recommended for large environments, for better scalability and to avoid single points of failure.

Figure 17-3 illustrates how a certificate can be revoked on a CA and subsequently published to a CRL server.

Figure 17-3 *Certificate Revocation and CRL Example*

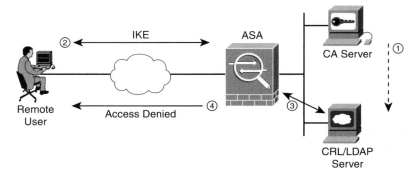

The following is the sequence of events in Figure 17-3:

1 The user certificate is revoked in the CA server. The CA server updates the CRL/ LDAP server.

2 The user attempts to establish an IPSec VPN connection to the Cisco ASA.

3 The Cisco ASA is configured to query the CRL server. It downloads the CRL and finds the certificate serial number on the list of revoked certificates.

4 The Cisco ASA denies access to the user and sends an IKE delete message.

There are several reasons why you need to use CRLs. Revoking a certificate is crucial if it might have been compromised or if the user might not have authority to use such certificate. For example, you should always revoke certificates when employees leave your organization.

Simple Certificate Enrollment Protocol

Simple Certificate Enrollment Protocol (SCEP) is a protocol developed by Cisco. SCEP provides a secure issuance of certificates to users and network devices in a scalable manner. It uses HTTP for the transport mechanism for enrollment and uses LDAP or HTTP for CRL checking. SCEP supports the following operations:

- CA and RA public key distribution
- Certificate enrollment
- Certificate revocation
- Certificate query
- CRL query

Cisco ASA supports enrollment via SCEP and manually via a cut-and-paste method.

TIP Using SCEP is recommended for better scalability. The manual cut-and-paste method is normally used when the CA server does not support SCEP or an HTTP connection is not possible.

Enrolling the Cisco ASA to a CA Using SCEP

Enrollment is the process of obtaining a certificate from a CA server. This section covers the necessary steps to configure and enroll a Cisco ASA to a CA server.

Generating the RSA Key Pair

Before starting the enrollment process, you must generate the RSA key pair with the **crypto key generate rsa** command. To generate the keys, you must first configure a host name and domain name. Example 17-1 demonstrates how to configure the Cisco ASA host name and domain name and generate the RSA key pair.

Example 17-1 *Generating the RSA Key Pair*

```
ASA(config)# hostname Chicago
Chicago(config)# domain-name securemeinc.om
Chicago(config)# crypto key generate rsa modulus 1024
INFO: The name for the keys will be: <Default-RSA-Key>
Keypair generation process begin.
```

NOTE   In Example 17-1, the name for the key pair is <Default-RSA-Key>. The <Default-RSA-Key> is replaced with a key pair label if configured.

Use the **crypto key zeroize rsa** command if an RSA key pair exists and a new pair needs to be regenerated. Example 17-2 demonstrates how to remove existing RSA key pairs.

Example 17-2 *Removing Existing RSA Key Pair*

```
Chicago(config)# crypto key zeroize rsa
WARNING: All RSA keys will be removed.
WARNING: All certs issued using these keys will also be removed.
Do you really want to remove these keys? [yes/no]: yes
```

To verify the generation of the RSA key pair, use the **show crypto key mypubkey rsa** command. Example 17-3 shows the output of this command.

Example 17-3 *Viewing RSA Key Pair Information*

```
Chicago# show crypto key mypubkey rsa
Key pair was generated at: 08:46:31 UTC Jul 10 2005
Key name: <Default-RSA-Key>
 Usage: General Purpose Key
 Modulus Size (bits): 1024
 Key Data:
  30819f30 0d06092a 864886f7 0d010101 05000381 8d003081 89028181 00f26be4
  08b00ac5 fb06adda 7c7a2ae6 26c136ce 990f5612 41d6fa09 79ef251f d229dcc0
  64bc15f8 1b3a4f1e 131f1765 866dfb3a bb8c3a59 f8605625 8e8ff0ca 90d291d0
  75c753c3 dd5f55f3 6d49d774 523b9d8b 78ad05b4 efd75793 88ac9646 7e8c8816
  017d464d 4a817041 a559dc63 2532c657 cc12373a c7b733f1 a50bdb82 61020301 0001
```

NOTE   The same RSA key pair is used for Secure Shell (SSH) connections to the security appliance.

Configuring a Trustpoint

The Cisco ASA certificate configuration commands are similar to Cisco IOS commands. The **crypto ca trustpoint** command declares the CA that your Cisco ASA should use and allows you to configure all the necessary certificate parameters. Invoking this command puts you in ca-trustpoint configuration mode, as shown in Example 17-4.

Example 17-4 *Configuring a Trustpoint*

```
Chicago# configure terminal
Chicago(config)# crypto ca trustpoint CISCO
Chicago(ca-trustpoint)#
```

Table 17-1 lists and describes all the ca-trustpoint subcommands.

Table 17-1   *Enrollment Configuration Subcommands*

Subcommand	Description
accept-subordinates	Allows the Cisco ASA to accept subordinate CA certificates
crl	CRL options (explained later in this chapter)
default	Returns all enrollment parameters to their default values
email	Used to enter the e-mail address to be used in the enrollment request
enrollment	Enrollment parameters: **retry**—Polling retry count and period **self**—Enrollment will generate a self-signed certificate **terminal**—Used for manual enrollment (cut-and-paste method) **url**—The URL of the CA server
fqdn	Includes fully qualified domain name
id-cert-issuer	Accepts ID certificates
ip-address	Includes IP address
keypair	Specifies the key pair whose public key is to be certified
password	Returns password
serial-number	Includes serial number
subject-name	Subject name
support_user_cert_validation	Validates remote user certificates using the configuration from this trustpoint, provided that this trustpoint is authenticated to the CA that issued the remote certificate

Figure 17-4 illustrates a topology that is used in the next example. A Cisco ASA is configured to enroll via SCEP to the CA server 209.165.202.130.

Figure 17-4 *Enrollment via SCEP Example*

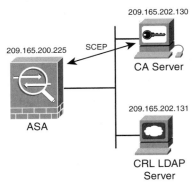

Example 17-5 includes the Cisco ASA trustpoint configuration.

Example 17-5 *Configuring the ASA to Enroll via SCEP*

```
Chicago# configure terminal
Chicago(config)# crypto ca trustpoint CISCO
Chicago(ca-trustpoint)# enrollment url http://209.165.202.130/certsrv/mscep/
  mscep.dll
Chicago(ca-trustpoint)# enrollment retry count 3
Chicago(ca-trustpoint)# enrollment retry period 5
Chicago(ca-trustpoint)# fqdn Chicago.securemeinc.com
Chicago(ca-trustpoint)# exit
Chicago(config)# exit
Chicago#
```

In Example 17-5, the Cisco ASA is configured with a trustpoint named **CISCO. The enrollment url** subcommand is used to declare the location of the CA server.

NOTE   In this example, the CA server is a Microsoft Windows CA Server with SCEP services. The complete URL is http://209.165.202.130/certsrv/mscep/mscep.dll.

The SCEP plug-in for Microsoft Windows can be downloaded from Microsoft's website at www.microsoft.com

---

The Cisco ASA is configured to retry three times in case the certificate is not successfully obtained from the CA Server. It is also configured to wait 5 minutes between each request to the CA. The fully qualified domain name (FQDN) used in the enrollment request is configured to be Chicago.securemeinc.com.

In this example, the Cisco ASA enrolls with the CA to use certificates for IPSec authentication. The Cisco ASA needs to obtain the CA certificate and request an ID certificate from the CA server. To obtain the CA certificate, use the **crypto ca authenticate** command. Example 17-6 demonstrates how to use this command to retrieve the CA certificate from the CA server.

Example 17-6 *Obtaining the CA Certificate from the CA Server*

```
Chicago# configure terminal
Chicago(config)# crypto ca authenticate CISCO
INFO: Certificate has the following attributes:
Fingerprint:    3736ffc2 243ecf05 0c40f2fa 26820675
Do you accept this certificate? [yes/no]: yes
```

In Example 17-6, **CISCO** is the name of the previously configured trustpoint. After executing this command, the Cisco ASA establishes a TCP port 80 connection to the 209.165.202.130 CA server (via SCEP). While doing this transaction, the Cisco ASA prompts you to accept the certificate.

NOTE   The Cisco ASA also retrieves RA certificates from the server if an RA is used.

After the CA certificate is obtained from the CA server, use the **crypto ca enroll** command to generate an identity certificate request to the 209.165.202.130 CA server. Example 17-7 demonstrates how to use this command to obtain the ID certificate.

NOTE   The request is a PKCS#7 certificate request.

Example 17-7 *Obtaining the ID Certificate from the CA Server*

```
Chicago(config)# crypto ca enroll CISCO
%
% Start certificate enrollment ..
% Create a challenge password. You will need to verbally provide this
    password to the CA Administrator in order to revoke your certificate.
    For security reasons your password will not be saved in the configuration.
    Please make a note of it.
Password:
Re-enter password:
% The fully-qualified domain name in the certificate will be:
Chicago.securemeinc.com
% Include the router serial number in the subject name? [yes/no]: no
Request certificate from CA? [yes/no]: yes
% Certificate request sent to Certificate Authority
Chicago(config)# The certificate has been granted by CA!
```

The word **CISCO** is the name of the previously configured trustpoint. After invoking the **crypto ca enroll** command, the Cisco ASA asks you for a password to be used for this certificate. The Cisco ASA displays the FQDN to be used in the certificate. As shown in the third shaded line, the Cisco ASA asks if you would like to include its serial number in the subject name of the certificate. This is not selected in this example. The serial number is not used by IKE but may be used by the CA server to authenticate certificates or to associate a certificate with a particular device. If you are in doubt, ask your CA administrator if you need to include the serial number in your certificate request. In the fourth shaded line, the Cisco ASA finally asks if you would like to request the certificate from the CA. If your answer is **yes** and the subsequent request is successful, the message in the fifth shaded line is shown, indicating a successful certificate enrollment.

Use the **show crypto ca certificates** command to verify and display the root/CA and ID certificate information. Example 17-8 shows the output of this command.

Example 17-8 *Output of* **show crypto ca certificates**

```
Chicago# show crypto ca certificates
Certificate
  Status: Available
  Certificate Serial Number: 1c91af4500000000000d
  Certificate Usage: General Purpose
  Issuer:
    cn=SecuremeCAServer
    ou=ENGINEERING
    o=Secureme
    l=Chicago
    st=IL
    c=US
    ea=administrator@securemeinc.com
  Subject Name
    Name: Chicago.securemeinc.com
    Serial Number:
    hostname=Chicago.securemeinc.com
  CRL Distribution Point:
    http://chicago-ca.securemeinc.com/CertEnroll/SecuremeCAServer.crl
  Validity Date:
    start date: 02:58:05 UTC Sep 2 2005
    end   date: 03:08:05 UTC Sep 2 2007
  Associated Trustpoints: CISCO
 !
CA Certificate
  Status: Available
  Certificate Serial Number: 225b38e6471fcca649427934cf289071
  Certificate Usage: Signature
  Issuer:
    cn=SecuremeCAServer
    ou= ENGINEERING
    o=Secureme
    l=Chicago
    st=IL
    c=US
    ea=administrator@securemeinc.com
```

Example 17-8 *Output of* **show crypto ca certificates** *(Continued)*

```
   Subject:
     cn=SecuremeCAServer
     ou=ENGINEERING
     o=Secureme
     l=Chicago
     st=IL
     c=US
     ea=administrator@securemeinc.com
   CRL Distribution Point:
     http://chicago-ca.securemeinc.com/CertEnroll/SecuremeCAServer.crl
   Validity Date:
     start date: 20:15:19 UTC Jun 25 2005
     end   date: 20:23:42 UTC Jun 25 2008
   Associated Trustpoints: CISCO
Chicago#
```

The certificate information is shown in Example 17-8 which includes the following:

- The status of each certificate
- The certificate usage
- The issuer distinguished name (DN) information (i.e., organization, organizational unit, locality, etc.)
- CRL distribution point (CDP)
- The validity period of each certificate
- The trustpoint associated to the certificate

This command is very useful for troubleshooting and verification purposes.

Manual (Cut-and-Paste) Enrollment

The manual, or cut-and-paste, enrollment method is mostly used in any of the following circumstances:

- The CA server does not support SCEP.
- There is no IP connectivity between the Cisco ASA and the CA server.
- TCP port 80 is blocked between the Cisco ASA and the CA server.

Configuration for Manual Enrollment

The configuration of the Cisco ASA for manual enrollment is very similar to its configuration for the SCEP enrollment process. However, the **enrollment terminal** subcommand is used instead of the **enrollment url** subcommand. Example 17-9 shows the trustpoint configuration for manual enrollment.

Example 17-9 *Configuring the Cisco ASA for Manual Enrollment*

```
Chicago# configure terminal
Chicago(config)# crypto ca trustpoint MANUAL
Chicago(ca-trustpoint)# enrollment terminal
Chicago(ca-trustpoint)# exit
Chicago(config)# exit
Chicago#
```

The name of the trustpoint in Example 17-9 is **MANUAL.** The **enrollment terminal** subcommand is used to specify manual enrollment.

Obtaining the CA Certificate

The administrator retrieves (copies and pastes) the certificate from the CA server. Use the **crypto ca authenticate** command to import the CA certificate. Example 17-10 demonstrates how to import the CA certificate to the Cisco ASA manually.

Example 17-10 *Importing the CA Certificate Manually*

```
Chicago(config)# crypto ca authenticate MANUAL
Enter the base 64 encoded CA certificate.
End with a blank line or the word "quit" on a line by itself
-----BEGIN CERTIFICATE-----
MIIC0jCCAnygAwIBAgIQIls45kcfzKZJQnk0zyiQcTANBgkqhkiG9w0BAQUFADCB
hjEeMBwGCSqGSIb3DQEJARYPamF6aWJAY2lzY28uY29tMQswCQYDVQQGEwJVUzEL
MAkGA1UECBMCTkMxDDAKBgNVBAcTA1JUUDEWMBQGA1UEChMNQ2lzY28gU3lzdGVt
czEMMAoGA1UECxMDVEFDMRYwFAYDVQQDEw1KYXppYkNBU2VydmVyMB4XDTA0MDYy
NTIwMTUxOVoXDTA3MDYyNTIwMjM0MlowgYYxHjAcBgkqhkiG9w0BCQEWD2phemli
QGNpc2NvLmNvbTELMAkGA1UEBhMCVVMxCzAJBgNVBAgTAk5DMQwwCgYDVQQHEwNS
VFAxFjAUBgNVBAoTDUNpc2NvIFN5c3RlbXMxDDAKBgNVBAsTA1RBQzEWMBQGA1UE
AxMNSmF6aWJDQVNlcnZlcjBcMA0GCSqGSIb3DQEBAQUAA0sAMEgCQQDnCRVLNn2L
wgair5gaw9bGFoWG2bS9G4LPl2/lTDffk9yD3h7/R3bBLIcSwy3nt1V5/brUtGFR
CoVV2XQ4RZEtAgMBAAGjgcMwgcAwCwYDVR0PBAQDAgHGMA8GA1UdEwEB/wQFMAMB
Af8wHQYDVR0OBBYEFKTqtaUJ6Pm9Pc/0IRc/EklKnT9TMG8GA1UdHwRoMGYwMKAu
oCyGKmh0dHA6Ly90ZWNoaWUvQ2VydEVucm9sbC9KYXppYkNBU2VydmVyLmNybDAy
oDCgLoYsZmlsZTovL1xcdGVjaGllXEN1cnRFbnJvbGxcSmF6aWJDQVNlcnZlci5j
cmwwEAYJKwYBBAGCNxUBBAMCAQAwDQYJKoZIhvcNAQEFBQADQQCw4XI7Ocff7MIc
LlAEyrhrTn3c2yqTbWZ6lO/QGaC4LdfyEDMeA0HvpkbB2GGJSj1AZocRCtB33GLi
QkiMpjnK
-----END CERTIFICATE-----
INFO: Certificate has the following attributes:
Fingerprint:     82a0095e 2584ced6 b66ed6a8 e48a5ad1
Do you accept this certificate? [yes/no]: yes
Trustpoint CA certificate accepted.
% Certificate successfully imported
```

As shown in Example 17-10, the CA certificate is manually imported to the Cisco ASA using the cut-and-paste method. Enter a blank line or the word **quit** after pasting the

Base64-encoded CA certificate to the Cisco ASA to exit the CA configuration screen. If the certificate is recognized, the Cisco ASA asks you if you would like to accept the certificate; enter **yes**. The "Certificate successfully imported" message is displayed if the CA certificate import is successful.

Generating the ID Certificate Request and Importing the ID Certificate

To generate the ID certificate request, use the **crypto ca enroll** command. Example 17-11 demonstrates how to generate the certificate request.

Example 17-11 *Generating the ID Certificate Request*

```
Chicago(config)# crypto ca enroll MANUAL
% Start certificate enrollment ..
% The fully-qualified domain name in the certificate will be:
Chicago.securemeinc.mom
% Include the router serial number in the subject name? [yes/no]: no
Display Certificate Request to terminal? [yes/no]: yes
Certificate Request follows:
MIIBpDCCAQ0CAQAwLTErMA4GA1UEBRMHNDZmZjUxODAZBgkqhkiG9w0BCQIWDE5Z
LmNpc2NvLmNvbTCBnzANBgkqhkiG9w0BAQEFAAOBjQAwgYkCgYEA1n+8nczm8ut1
X5PVngaA1470A1Us3YWRvOYcfwj/tosNRoJ/lY2tVQMnZ+aKlai2+PcZfyP2u2Ar
cadRwkwY0KfKrt5f7LAKrhmHyavNT0rRXBxEMPbtvWuacghmaNXAiRGNpNOHpQjB
QCth9fw7s+anAkXZlfd2ZzAu1Y60s6cCAwEAAaA3MDUGCSqGSIb3DQEJDjEoMCYw
CwYDVR0PBAQDAgWgMBcGA1UdEQQQMA6CDE5ZLmNpc2NvLmNvbTANBgkqhkiG9w0B
AQQFAAOBgQDGcYSC8VGy+ekUNkDayW1g+TQL4lYldLmT9xXUADAQqmGhyA8A36d0
VtZlNc2pXHaMPKkqxMEPMcJVdZ+o6JpiIFHPpYNiQGFUQZoHGcZveEbMVor93/KM
IChEgs4x98fCuJoiQ2RQr452bsWNyEmeLcDqczMSUXFucSLMm0XDNg==
---End - This line not part of the certificate request---
Redisplay enrollment request? [yes/no]: no
Chicago(config)#
```

Example 17-11 shows how the certificate request is generated. Copy and paste the certificate request to your CA server and generate the new ID certificate for the Cisco ASA.

TIP   Make sure not to copy and paste the second highlighted line in Example 17-11. The certificate request will be malformed if this is included.

NOTE   Obtain a Base64-encoded certificate from your CA server. You will not be able to copy and paste a Distinguished Encoding Rules (DER) encoded certificate.

The Cisco ASA gives you the option to redisplay the certificate request if needed (as shown in Example 17-11).

Once the ID certificate is approved by the CA server, use the **crypto ca import** command to import the Base64-encoded ID certificate. Example 17-12 demonstrates how to import the ID certificate.

Example 17-12 *Manually Importing the ID Certificate*

```
Chicago(config)# crypto ca import MANUAL certificate
% The fully-qualified domain name in the certificate will be:
Chicago.securemeinc.com
Enter the base 64 encoded certificate.
End with a blank line or the word "quit" on a line by itself
-----BEGIN CERTIFICATE-----
MIIECDCCA7KgAwIBAgIKHJGvRQAAAAAADTANBgkqhkiG9w0BAQUFADCBhjEeMBwG
CSqGSIb3DQEJARYPamF6aWJAY2lzY28uY29tMQswCQYDVQQGEwJVUzELMAkGA1UE
CBMCTkMxDDAKBgNVBAcTA1JUUDEWMBQGA1UEChMNQ2lzY28gU3lzdGVtczEMMAoG
A1UECxMDVEFDMRYwFAYDVQQDEw1KYXppYkNBU2VydmVyMB4XDTA0MDkwMjAyNTgw
NVoXDTA1MDkwMjAzMDgwNVowLzEQMA4GA1UEBRMHNDZmZjUxODEbMBkGCSqGSIb3
DQEJAhMMTlkuY2lzY28uY29tMIGfMA0GCSqGSIb3DQEBAQUAA4GNADCBiQKBgQDW
f7ydzOby63Vfk9WeBoDXjvQDVSzdhZG85hx/CP+2iw1Ggn+Vja1VAydn5oqVqLb4
9x1/I/a7YCtxp1HCTBjQp8qu3l/ssAquGYfJq81PStFcHEQw9u29a5pyCGZo1cCJ
EY2k04elCMFAK2H1/Duz5qcCRdmV93ZnMC7VjrSzpwIDAQABo4ICEjCCAg4wCwYD
VR0PBAQDAgWgMBcGA1UdEQQQMA6CDE5ZLmNpc2NvLmNvbTAdBgNVHQ4EFgQUxMvq
7pWbd8bye1PKnXTKYO3A5JQwgcIGA1UdIwSBujCBt4AUpOq1pQno+b09z/QhFz8S
SUqdP1OhgYykgYkwgYYxHjAcBgkqhkiG9w0BCQEWD2phemliQGNpc2NvLmNvbTEL
MAkGA1UEBhMCVVMxCzAJBgNVBAgTAk5DMQwwCgYDVQQHEwNSVFAxFjAUBgNVBAoT
DUNpc2NvIFN5c3RlbXMxDDAKBgNVBAsTA1RBQzEWMBQGA1UEAxMNSmF6aWJDQVNl
cnZlcoIQIIls45kcfzKZJQnk0zyiQcTBvBgNVHR8EaDBmMDCgLqAshipodHRwOi8v
dGVjaGllL0NlcnRFbnJvbGwvSmF6aWJDQVNlcnZlci5jcmwwMqAwoC6GLGZpbGU6
Ly9cXHR1Y2hpZVxDZXJ0RW5yb2xsXEphemliQ0FTZXJ2ZXIuY3JsMIGQBggrBgEF
BQcBAQSBgzCBgDA9BggrBgEFBQcwAoYxaHR0cDovL3R1Y2hpZS9DZXJ0RW5yb2xs
L3R1Y2hpZV9KYXppYkNBU2VydmVyLmNydDA/BggrBgEFBQcwAoYzZmlsZTovL1xc
dGVjaGllXENlcnRFbnJvbGxcdGVjaGllX0phemliQ0FTZXJ2ZXIuY3J0MA0GCSqG
SIb3DQEBBQUAA0EAQ1+WBtysPhOAhTKLYemj8X1TpGrqtUl3mCyNH5OXppfYjSGu
SGzFQHtnqURciJBtay9RNnMpZmZYpfOHzmeFmQ==
-----END CERTIFICATE-----
INFO: Router Certificate successfully imported
Chicago(config)#
```

The Base64-encoded ID certificate is successfully imported to the Cisco ASA.

Configuring CRL Options

This section teaches you how to configure CRL checking on the Cisco ASA. You can configure the Cisco ASA to do any of the following:

- Not require CRL checking

- Optionally accept the peer's certificate if the security appliance is not able to retrieve the CRL
- Require CRL checking

To bypass CRL checking, use the **crl nocheck** trustpoint subcommand.

TIP   Bypassing CRL checking is insecure and therefore is not recommended.

The **crl optional** subcommand allows the Cisco ASA to optionally accept its peer's certificate if the required CRL is not available.

Use the **crl required** subcommand to force the Cisco ASA to perform CRL checking. The CRL server must be reachable and available in order for a peer certificate to be validated. After this command is enabled, you must configure the CRL parameters. To configure the CRL options, use the **crl configure** trustpoint subcommand. After invoking this command, you will be placed in the ca-crl prompt, as shown in Example 17-13.

Example 17-13 *The* **crl configure** *Subcommand*

```
Chicago(config)# crypto ca trustpoint CISCO
Chicago(ca-trustpoint)# crl required
Chicago(ca-trustpoint)# crl configure
Chicago(ca-crl)#
```

Table 17-2 lists all the CRL configuration options.

Table 17-2   **crl configure** *Configuration Options*

Subcommand	Description
cache-time	Used to configure the refresh time (in minutes) for the CRL cache. The range is from 1 to 1440 minutes. The default value is 60 minutes.
default	Returns all the options to the default value.
enforcenextupdate	Used to define how to handle the NextUpdate CRL field. If this option is configured, CRLs are required to have a NextUpdate field that has not yet lapsed.
ldap-defaults	Used to define the default LDAP server and port to use if the distribution point extension of the certificate being checked is missing these values.
ldap-dn	Used to configure the Login DN and password which defines is used to access the CRL database.

continues

Table 17-2 crl configure *Configuration Options (Continued)*

Subcommand	Description
policy	Used to configure the CRL retrieval policy. The following options are available:
	both—The Cisco ASA use the CRL distribution points from the certificate being checked, or else uses static distribution points.
	cdp—The Cisco ASA uses the CRL distribution points from the certificate being checked.
	static—The Cisco ASA uses statically configured URLs.
protocol	The protocol used for CRL retrieval. The options are **http**, **ldap**, and **scep**.
url	A static URL for the site from which CRLs may be retrieved. You can specify up to five URLs. An index value is used to determine the rank of the configured URL.

Example 17-14 demonstrates how to configure CRL checking and the use of several of the previous options.

Example 17-14 *CRL Checking Example*

```
crypto ca trustpoint CISCO
 crl required
 enrollment retry count 3
 enrollment url http://209.165.202.130:80/certsrv/mscep/mscep.dll
 fqdn Chicago.securemeinc.com
 crl configure
  policy static
  url 1 ldap://chicago-crl1.securemeinc.com/CRL/CRL.crl
  url 2 ldap://chicago-crl2.securemeinc.com/CRL/CRL.crl
  url 3 ldap://chicago-crl3.securemeinc.com/CRL/CRL.crl
```

In Example 17-14, a Cisco ASA is configured to require CRL checking with the **crl required** trustpoint subcommand. The Cisco ASA has three CRL servers statically defined. LDAP is used as the transport protocol.

NOTE   Make sure to configure a domain name server on the Cisco ASA when using FQDN for CRL distribution points. Use the **dns name-server** *ip-address* command to specify the domain name server to be used.

The Cisco ASA will first try the CRL server named chicago-crl1.securemeinc.com. Subsequently, it will try chicago-crl2.securemeinc.com and chicago-crl3.securemeinc.com, in that order, as shown in Figure 17-5.

Figure 17-5 *CRL Checking Example*

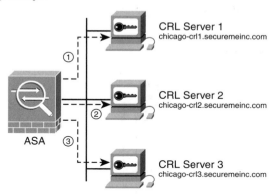

You can manually request the retrieval of the CRL by using the **crypto ca crl request**
command. Example 17-15 demonstrates how to manually retrieve the CRL.

Example 17-15 *CRL Manual Retrieval*

```
Chicago(config)# crypto ca crl request CISCO
CRL received
```

The CRL is received successfully. To view the CRL, use the **show crypto ca crls** command,
as demonstrated in Example 17-16.

Example 17-16 *Output of* **show crypto ca crls** *Command*

```
Chicago# show crypto ca crls
CRL Issuer Name:

cn=SecuremeCAServer,ou=ENGINEERING,o=Secureme,l=Chicago,st=IL,c=US,ea=administrato
  r@securemeinc.com
    LastUpdate: 14:18:11 UTC Sep 10 2004
    NextUpdate: 02:38:11 UTC Sep 18 2004
    Retrieved from CRL Distribution Point:
      http://chicago-crl1.securemeinc.com/CertEnroll/SecuremeCAServer.crl
```

The first and second shaded lines in Example 17-16 show when the last CRL update took
place and when the next one will be. The third shaded line shows the URL of the CRL
distribution point.

Configuring IPSec Site-to-Site Tunnels Using Certificates

In Chapter 15, "Site-to-Site IPSec VPNs," you learned how to configure an IPSec site-to-
site tunnel using preshared keys. This section shows you how to configure an IPSec site-
to-site tunnel between two Cisco ASAs using certificates. In this example, a branch office

in London needs to create an IPSec site-to-site tunnel to SecureMe's headquarters office in Chicago. Figure 17-6 illustrates a high-level network topology of SecureMe's implementation.

Figure 17-6 *IPSec Site-to-Site Tunnel Using Certificates*

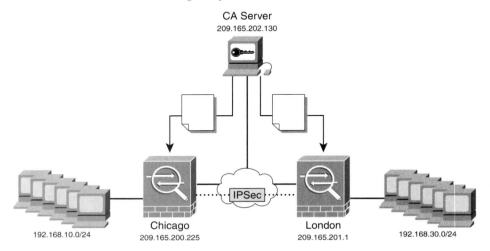

The Cisco ASAs in both locations successfully enroll with the CA server and build the IPSec site-to-site tunnel using its corresponding certificates for authentication. Example 17-17 includes Chicago's ASA trustpoint configuration.

Example 17-17 *Chicago ASA Trustpoint Configuration*

```
crypto ca trustpoint chicago
  enrollment retry period 5
  enrollment retry count 5
  enrollment url http://209.165.202.130/certsrv/mscep/mscep.dll
  fqdn Chicago.securemeinc.com
  subject-name O=secureme, OU=Chicago
```

The Cisco ASA is configured to enroll to the CA server 209.165.202.130. The certificate distinguished name information will contain **O=secureme** and **OU=Chicago** in this example. The O represents the organization name and OU represents the organizational unit. After the certificates are successfully retrieved from the CA server, you will see the certificate chain information in the configuration, as shown in Example 17-18.

Example 17-18 *Certificate Chain Information*

```
Chicago# show running-config | begin crypto ca certificate
crypto ca certificate chain chicago
  certificate 03
    30820211 308201bb a0030201 02020103 300d0609 2a864886 f70d0101 04050030
    3e311430 12060355 040b130b 454e4749 4e454552 494e4731 16301406 0355040a
```

Example 17-18 *Certificate Chain Information (Continued)*

```
     130d4369 73636f20 53797374 656d7331 0e300c06 03550403 1305696f 73636130
   quit
 certificate ca 01
     308201d0 3082017a a0030201 02020101 300d0609 2a864886 f70d0101 04050030
     3e311430 12060355 040b130b 454e4749 4e454552 494e4731 16301406 0355040a
 quit
```

NOTE   Hexadecimal certificate information has been shortened for brevity in Example 17-18.

Example 17-19 demonstrates how the ISAKMP policy is configured in Chicago's Cisco ASA. The **isakmp identity auto** command is configured in this example. Usually, the IP address identity is used for preshared key authentication. The keyword **hostname** is generally used for certificate-based connections. The **auto** keyword automatically determines the ISAKMP identity. This is recommended if you have a combination of some IPSec tunnels using preshared keys and others using certificates for authentication.

Example 17-19 *ISAKMP Policy Configuration*

```
isakmp identity auto
isakmp enable outside
isakmp policy 1 authentication rsa-sig
isakmp policy 1 encryption aes-256
isakmp policy 1 hash sha
isakmp policy 1 group 1
isakmp policy 1 lifetime 86400
```

The second shaded line in Example 17-19 shows that the Cisco ASA is configured for RSA signature authentication.

Example 17-20 includes Chicago's ASA crypto map configuration.

Example 17-20 *Crypto Map Configuration*

```
access-list 100 extended permit ip 192.168.10.0 255.255.255.0 192.168.30.0
  255.255.255.0
crypto ipsec transform-set myset esp-aes-256 esp-sha-hmac
crypto map chicago 10 match address 100
crypto map chicago 10 set peer 209.165.201.1
crypto map chicago 10 set transform-set myset
crypto map chicago 10 set trustpoint Chicago
crypto map chicago interface outside
```

The crypto map configuration is similar to the configuration examples in Chapter 15. The shaded line in Example 17-20 associates the crypto map with the trustpoint that defines the certificate used while negotiating the IPSec connection.

Example 17-21 includes the tunnel group configuration for Chicago's ASA.

Example 17-21 *Tunnel Group Configuration*

```
tunnel-group 209.165.201.1 type ipsec-l2l
tunnel-group 209.165.201.1 ipsec-attributes
  peer-id-validate cert
!used to validate the identity of the peer using the peer's certificate
  chain
! Enables sending certificate chain
  trust-point Chicago
! used to configure the name of the trustpoint that identifies the
! certificate to be used for this tunnel
```

Note the differences in the configuration in Example 17-21 in comparison to the configuration of an IPSec site-to-site tunnel using preshared keys. The **peer-id-validate cert** command is used to validate the identity of the IPSec peer using its certificate. The **chain** command enables the Cisco ASA to send the complete certificate chain to its peer. The **trust-point** command associates the trustpoint that identifies the certificate to be used for this tunnel.

Example 17-22 shows London's Cisco ASA site-to-site IPSec configuration.

Example 17-22 *London's ASA Site-to-Site IPSec Configuration*

```
access-list 100 extended permit ip 192.168.30.0 255.255.255.0 192.168.10.0
255.255.255.0
crypto ipsec transform-set myset esp-aes-256 esp-sha-hmac
! crypto transform-set and crypto map configuration matching the IPSec Policies
! from its peer
crypto map London 10 match address 100
crypto map London 10 set peer 209.165.200.225
crypto map London 10 set transform-set myset
crypto map London 10 set trustpoint London
! The trustpoint configured below is applied to the crypto map.
crypto map London interface outside
crypto ca trustpoint London
 enrollment retry period 5
 enrollment retry count 3
 enrollment url http://209.165.202.130/certsrv/mscep/mscep.dll
 fqdn London.securemeinc.com
 subject-name O=secureme, OU=London
! The certificate subject name information is defined
 crl configure
crypto ca certificate map 1
! The following is the certificate information appended to the configuration
! after enrollment
crypto ca certificate chain London
 certificate 02
    30820210 308201ba a0030201 02020102 300d0609 2a864886 f70d0101 04050030
    3e311430 12060355 040b130b 454e4749 4e454552 494e4731 16301406 0355040a
    130d4369 73636f20 53797374 656d7331 0e300c06 03550403 1305696f 73636130
    1e170d30 34303931 30313332 3230375a 170d3035 30393130 31333232 30375a30
```

Example 17-22 *London's ASA Site-to-Site IPSec Configuration (Continued)*

```
      56311030 0e060355 040b1307 41746c61 6e746131 10300e06 0355040a 13074765
      6f726769 61313030 0e060355 04051307 34343436 37303830 1e06092a 864886f7
      0d010902 16114174 6c616e74 612e6369 73636f2e 636f6d30 5c300d06 092a8648
      86f70d01 01010500 034b0030 48024100 be06c890 637c426c 5c1e431e c6247567
      c0b7c279 86f87c1f 5c01a305 cdaf699a 84dd872d 7b45b0ba 4bf7f28c 2097fe6f
      5f07926a 9bfcdc03 0a383e9f 4b32d0b3 02030100 01a3818a 30818730 39060355
      1d1f0432 3030302e a02ca02a 86286874 74703a2f 2f63726c 73657276 65722e63
      6973636f 2e636f6d 2f43524c 2f636973 636f2e63 726c301c 0603551d 11041530
      13821141 746c616e 74612e63 6973636f 2e636f6d 300b0603 551d0f04 04030205
      a0301f06 03551d23 04183016 80142ff7 332973b2 4d6ddb0d 711bd3fb b033359a
      6981300d 06092a86 4886f70d 01010405 00034100 abe66626 4d58e0d6 25fa809d
      c30bfaed 4cae7ef3 e4f6a120 206ba892 faa81224 1497ea80 f9e28bf6 4a73037f
      570c7e19 f56a05ca a6942805 508e9b37 61dac8c3
    quit
  certificate ca 01
      308201d0 3082017a a0030201 02020101 300d0609 2a864886 f70d0101 04050030
      3e311430 12060355 040b130b 454e4749 4e454552 494e4731 16301406 0355040a
      130d4369 73636f20 53797374 656d7331 0e300c06 03550403 1305696f 73636f30
      1e170d30 34303931 30313132 3035365a 170d3037 30393130 31333230 35365a30
      3e311430 12060355 040b130b 454e4749 4e454552 494e4731 16301406 0355040a
      130d4369 73636f20 53797374 656d7331 0e300c06 03550403 1305696f 73636f30
      5c300d06 092a8648 86f70d01 01010500 034b0030 48024100 dc7d0b35 1bfa7577
      99cbab8b 69c32a44 47ecd0ae 7cb13fc0 808e7520 9d5e6132 1bc4565a 1ede26a4
      fc01650e 240aa737 824e07c3 c92f9796 5dd10ac7 4e1a5b75 02030100 01a36330
      61300f06 03551d13 0101ff04 05300301 01ff300e 0603551d 0f0101ff 04040302
      0186301d 0603551d 0e041604 142ff733 2973b24d 6ddb0d71 1bd3fbb0 33359a69
      81301f06 03551d23 04183016 80142ff7 332973b2 4d6ddb0d 711bd3fb b033359a
      6981300d 06092a86 4886f70d 01010405 00034100 7982764a c82daaf0 ed3b0a6e
      25df09b2 4caa7ce8 b27098f1 982085bc 0fda9bcf 86dedda6 84c30abc 48c43fc8
      692386ad 595e2b1e aafd3388 9d711b3c 6314cb5e
    quit
  ! ISAKMP identity is set to auto
  isakmp identity auto
  isakmp enable outside
  ! ISAKMP authentication is set to rsa-sig
  isakmp policy 1 authentication rsa-sig
  isakmp policy 1 encryption aes-256
  isakmp policy 1 hash sha
  isakmp policy 1 group 1
  isakmp policy 1 lifetime 86400
  ! Tunnel group configuration for the site to site tunnel
  tunnel-group 209.165.200.225 type ipsec-l2l
  tunnel-group 209.165.200.225 ipsec-attributes
  ! The ASA will validate the identity of the peer using the peer's certificate
   peer-id-validate cert
  ! The chain subcommand enables the ASA to send the complete certificate chain
  ! the previously configured trust point is applied to the tunnel group
  trust-point London
```

The shaded lines in Example 17-22 explain the relevant configuration parameters in London's ASA.

Configuring the Cisco ASA to Accept Remote-Access VPN Clients Using Certificates

This section demonstrates how to configure the Cisco ASA to terminate Cisco VPN client IPSec connections using certificates. The configuration steps to configure remote-access VPNs using preshared keys are covered in Chapter 16, "Remote Access VPNs." Figure 17-7 illustrates the topology and components used in the following example.

Figure 17-7 *Remote-Access VPN Using Certificates*

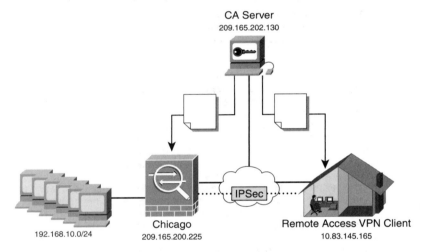

In Figure 17-7, remote-access users using the Cisco VPN Client connect to the Cisco ASA to access the corporate internal resources in Chicago. The clients and the Cisco ASA obtain certificates from the CA server 209.165.202.130. The steps necessary to enroll the Cisco ASA to the CA server are the same as those demonstrated previously in this chapter. The following subsection demonstrates how to enroll the Cisco VPN with the CA server.

Enrolling the Cisco VPN Client

The Cisco VPN client has the ability to enroll to a CA server via either SCEP or manual (file based) enrollment. Click the **Certificates** tab on the VPN Client to configure the enrollment parameters. Figure 17-8 shows the Certificates tab of the Cisco VPN Client.

NOTE   The Certificates tab toolbar is only viewable in advanced mode. Running the VPN Client in simple mode will not show these options. To change from simple mode to advanced mode, choose **Options > Advanced Mode**.

Figure 17-8 *Cisco VPN Client Certificates Tab*

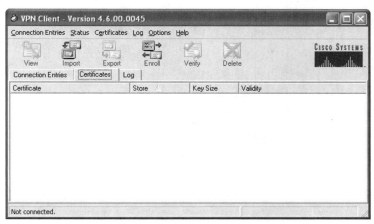

NOTE   To enroll and manage personal certificates in Cisco VPN Client version 3.x and earlier, use
          the Certificate Manager application included with the Client. This section concentrates on
          versions 4.x and later.

The Cisco VPN Client toolbar displays the tasks you can execute from the Certificates tab.
Table 17-3 lists all the toolbar options and their usage.

Table 17-3   *Cisco VPN Client Certificates Tab Toolbar Options*

Option	Description
View	Shows the details of a selected certificate. Information includes validity period, issuer information, and distinguish name information such as CN, OU, O, etc.
Import	Used to import a certificate from a file or certificate store.
Export	Used to export a selected certificate.
Enroll	Used to begin enrollment process.
Verify	Used to check if the selected certificate is valid (not expired).
Delete	Deletes the selected certificate or certificate request

SCEP provides an easy mechanism to enroll the Cisco VPN Client. The following are the
necessary steps to enroll the Cisco VPN Client via SCEP.

Step 1   Click the **Enroll** button on the toolbar. The VPN Client Certificate
             Enrollment window is displayed, as shown in Figure 17-9.

Figure 17-9 *Cisco VPN Client Certificate Enrollment Window*

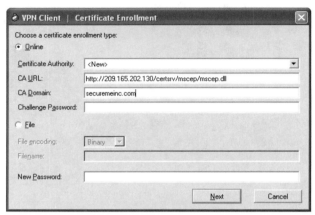

Step 2 Select **Online** as the certificate enrollment type.

Step 3 Enter the CA URL, domain, and challenge password (if applicable) and click **Next**. Various CA servers require the user to provide a password during enrollment. The Cisco VPN Client allows you to enter the password in the Challenge Password field. This password is provided by the CA administrator. The New Password option is used for the password that protects this certificate. If your connection entry requires certificate authentication, you must enter this password each time you connect.

Step 4 The VPN Client Certificate Enrollment information form is displayed, as shown in Figure 17-10.

Figure 17-10 *Cisco VPN Client Certificate Enrollment Form*

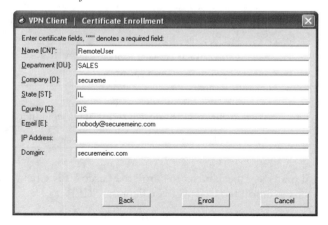

This form allows you to enter the information to be included in the certificate request. After you enter the necessary information, click **Enroll** to send the certificate enrollment request to the CA server via SCEP. The following are the parameters you can specify on the certificate request:

- **Name [CN]**—The unique common name (CN) for the user certificate. This can be the name of a user, system, or other entity. This field is required. The CN of **RemoteUser** is used in this example.

- **Department [OU]**—Usually the name of the department to which the user belongs. **SALES** is used in this example.

Note   By default, the Cisco ASA matches the OU with the VPN group name. Other DN fields can also be used for this purpose.

- **Company [O]**—The name of the company or organization to which the user belongs. **secureme** is used in this example.

- **State [ST]**—The name of the state. Illinois (**IL**) is used in this example.

- **Country [C]**—A two-letter country code. US is used in this example.

- **Email [E]**—User's e-mail address (nobody@securemeinc.com is used in this example).

- **IP Address**—The IP address of the user's system. It is recommended that you do not use this field if the system's IP address will change (for example, DHCP).

- **Domain**—The domain name to which the user's system belongs. This example uses securemeinc.com.

Step 5   The Cisco VPN Client sends the enrollment request to the CA server. After the certificate is granted, the Cisco VPN Client stores it on the Cisco certificate store, as shown in Figure 17-11.

Figure 17-11 *Cisco VPN Client Certificate Information*

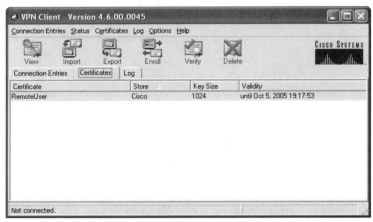

Configuring the Cisco ASA

Complete the following steps after you have enrolled the Cisco ASA to the CA server. Example 17-23 shows the ISAKMP policy configuration of the Cisco ASA.

Example 17-23 *ISAKMP Policy for Remote-Access VPN*

```
isakmp identity hostname
isakmp enable outside
isakmp policy 1 authentication rsa-sig
isakmp policy 1 encryption 3des
isakmp policy 1 hash sha
isakmp policy 1 group 2
isakmp policy 1 lifetime 86400
```

The shaded line in Example 17-23 shows how the ISAKMP authentication type is set to **rsa-sig** for certificate authentication.

Example 17-24 shows the crypto map configuration to dynamically terminate remote-access VPN client connections.

Example 17-24 *Dynamic Crypto Map Configuration for Remote-Access VPN*

```
crypto ipsec transform-set chicagotrans esp-3des esp-sha-hmac
crypto dynamic-map dynmap 10 set transform-set chicagotrans
crypto map chicagomap 65525 ipsec-isakmp dynamic dynmap
crypto map chicagomap interface outside
```

The commands in Example 17-24 are the same as those covered in Chapter 16 while using preshared keys. Example 17-25 demonstrates the VPN tunnel-group configuration parameters.

Example 17-25 *Tunnel-Group Configuration for Remote-Access VPN*

```
tunnel-group SALES type ipsec-ra
tunnel-group SALES general-attributes
 address-pool ippool
 authentication-server-group LOCAL
tunnel-group SALES ipsec-attributes
 peer-id-validate cert
 trust-point chicago
```

The first shaded line in Example 17-25 makes the Cisco ASA validate the identity of the VPN client using the peer's certificate. The second shaded line associates the group with the configured trustpoint.

The name of the VPN group in Example 17-25 is **SALES**. This matches the OU value from the client's certificate. By default, the Cisco ASA binds the client connection to a specific group using the OU value. However, you can use any DN certificate information to associate the client to a respective group. This is similar to the Cisco VPN 3000 Concentrator certificate DN matching feature.

To configure the Cisco ASA to associate a VPN client connection using the peer's certificate DN information, you can use the **tunnel-group-map** command in combination with a certificate map. Example 17-26 demonstrates how to configure the Cisco ASA to associate any VPN clients on which its certificate has an e-mail address containing **securemeinc.com** to the VPN group named **SALES**.

Example 17-26 *DN Matching Example*

```
crypto ca certificate map 10
! A certificate map is created with a sequence number of 10
 subject-name attr ea co securemeinc.com
!The Cisco ASA is configured to match the email address (ea) of the client's
!certificate. Any certificates that contains securemeinc.com in the email address
 field will be associated to the specified group.
tunnel-group-map enable rules
! A tunnel-group-map is enabled to match the previously defined rules.
tunnel-group-map 10 SALES
!The certificate map 10 is associated to the VPN group SALES.
```

The following are all the available DN attributes available:

- **c**—Country
- **cn**—Common name
- **dnq**—DN qualifier
- **ea**—E-mail address
- **genq**—Generational qualifier

- **gn**—Given name
- **i**—Initials
- **ip**—IP address
- **l**—Locality
- **n**—Name
- **o**—Organization name
- **ou**—Organizational unit
- **ser**—Serial number
- **sn**—Surname
- **sp**—State/province
- **t**—Title
- **uid**—User ID
- **uname**—Unstructured name

The following are the operands that can be used with the **subject-name** subcommand under the certificate map:

- **co**—Contains
- **eq**—Equal
- **nc**—Does not contain
- **ne**—Not equal

Troubleshooting PKI

There are several troubleshooting commands and techniques used to troubleshoot PKI on the Cisco ASA. This section covers them in detail.

Time and Date Mismatch

One of the most common problems experienced when first implementing PKI is time and date mismatch. The certificate validity period is the time period during which a certificate is valid. Incorrect time settings in the Cisco ASA, its peers, or the CA can cause the IKE negotiation to fail.

TIP	It is suggested that you configure Network Time Protocol (NTP) on the Cisco ASA and the CA server to avoid this problem.

To check the validity period of the installed certificates, use the **show crypto ca certificates** command. Example 17-27 includes an excerpt of the output of **debug crypto isakmp 127** and **debug crypto ca** while a Cisco ASA had incorrect clock settings.

Example 17-27 *Output of* **debug crypto isakmp 127** *and* **debug crypto ca** *with Incorrect Clock Settings*

```
Oct 07 11:33:16 [IKEv1 DEBUG], Group = , IP = 209.165.201.1
    processing cert payload
Oct 07 11:33:16 [IKEv1 DEBUG], Group = , IP = 209.165.201.1,
    processing cert request payload
Oct 07 11:33:16 [IKEv1 DEBUG], Group = , IP = 209.165.201.1 processing
    RSA signature,
Oct 07 11:33:16 [IKEv1 DEBUG], Group = , IP = 209.165.201.1, computing hash
Oct 07 11:33:16 [IKEv1 DECODE]0000: 8D01E129 F25F46B3 C3CA9D4E
    55571486    ...)._F....NUW..
0010: BDA26964 FA025484 03C271EB 43A7E69C    ..id..T...q.C...
0020: 2A9AD9FA 49E523B1 94AC4874 E352B13B    *...I.#...Ht.R.;
0030: 07354EA9 DB81F8E2 62276185 1A5EF2FC    .5N.....b'a..^..
0040: 7436999D A6E54E96 AB5A5023 23BD1613    t6....N..ZP##...
0050: A2CB28F6 C817A665 9140C932 21EA5AAC    ..(....e.@.2!.Z.
0060: 33D1A3C9 CC8B1B7F 792D3A63 3C220A25    3......y-:c<".%
0070: 7B3ACB97 1CC09506 879D40B7 41E28A20    {:........@.A..
Oct 07 11:33:16 [IKEv1 DEBUG], Group = , IP = 209.165.201.1,
    Processing Notify payload
Oct 07 11:33:16 [IKEv1], IP = 209.165.201.1Trying to find group
    via cert rules...,
Tunnel Group Match on map sequence # 10.
Group name is SALES
Oct 07 11:33:16 [IKEv1], IP = 209.165.201.1, Connection landed on
    tunnel_group SALES
CRYPTO_PKI: looking for cert in handle=375b290, digest=
92 3c f9 ac b2 65 e3 fe 49 5a dc b8 64 d4 cd 9e  |  .<...e..IZ..d...
CRYPTO_PKI: Cert record not found, returning E_NOT_FOUND
CRYPTO_PKI: crypto_pki_get_cert_record_by_subject()
CRYPTO_PKI: Found a subject match
CRYPTO_PKI(make trustedCerts list)Oct 07 11:33:16 [IKEv1], Group = SALES,
    IP = 209.165.201.1 Peer Certificate authentication failed,
Oct 07 11:33:16 [IKEv1 DEBUG], Group = SALES, IP = 209.165.201.1 IKE MM
    Responder FSM error history (struct &0x49cc114)
<state>, <event>:
MM_BLD_MSG6, EV_UPDATE_CERT
MM_BLD_MSG6, EV_UPDATE_CERT
MM_BLD_MSG6, EV_UPDATE_CERT
MM_BLD_MSG6, EV_UPDATE_CERT,
Oct 07 11:33:16 [IKEv1 DEBUG], Group = SALES, IP = 209.165.201.1 ,
    IKE SA MM:ce9697e1 terminating:
flags 0x0105c002, refcnt 0, tuncnt 0
Oct 07 11:33:16 [IKEv1 DEBUG], sending delete/delete with reason message
Oct 07 11:33:16 [IKEv1 DEBUG], Group = SALES, IP = 209.165.201.1 ,
    constructing blank hash
Oct 07 11:33:16 [IKEv1 DEBUG], constructing IKE delete payload
```

continues

Example 17-27 *Output of* **debug crypto isakmp 127** *and* **debug crypto ca** *with Incorrect Clock Settings*

```
Oct 07 11:33:16 [IKEv1 DEBUG], Group = SALES, IP = 209.165.201.1,
    constructing qm hash
Oct 07 11:33:16 [IKEv1],
IP:( 209.165.201.1), IKE DECODE
 SENDING Message (msgid=7bd21f5e) with payloads :
HDR + HASH (8) + DELETE (12)
total length : 80
```

Example 17-28 includes the **show crypto ca certificates** and **show clock output** showing the date mismatch.

Example 17-28 *Output of* **show crypto ca certificates** *and* **show clock**

```
Chicago# show crypto ca certificates
Certificate
  Status: Available
  Certificate Serial Number: 1c91af4500000000000d
  Certificate Usage: General Purpose
  Issuer:
    cn=SecuremeCAServer
    ou=ENGINEERING
    o=Secureme
    l=Chicago
    st=IL
    c=US
    ea=adminsitrator@securemeinc.com
  Subject Name
    Name: Chicago.securemeinc.com
    Serial Number: 46ff518
    hostname=Chicago.securemeinc.com
    serialNumber=46ff518
  CRL Distribution Point:
    http://chicago-ca.ssecuremeinc.com/CertEnroll/SecuremeCAServer.crl
  Validity Date:
    start date: 02:58:05 UTC Sep 2 2005
    end   date: 03:08:05 UTC Sep 2 2007
  Associated Trustpoints: chicago
!
CA Certificate
  Status: Available
  Certificate Serial Number: 225b38e6471fcca649427934cf289071
  Certificate Usage: Signature
  Issuer:
    cn=SecuremeCAServer
    ou= ENGINEERING
    o=Secureme
    l=Chicago
    st=IL
    c=US
    ea=administrator@securemeinc.com
```

Example 17-28 *Output of* **show crypto ca certificates** *and* **show clock** *(Continued)*

```
   Subject:
     cn=SecuremeCAServer
     ou=ENGINEERING
     o=Secureme
     l=Chicago
     st=IL
     c=US
     ea= administrator@securemeinc.com
   CRL Distribution Point:
     http://chicago-ca/CertEnroll/SecuremeCAServer.crl
   Validity Date:
     start date: 20:15:19 UTC Jun 25 2005
     end   date: 20:23:42 UTC Jun 25 2008
   Associated Trustpoints: chicago
Chicago# show clock
11:50:27.165 UTC Thu Oct 7 2010
```

The **clock set** command is used to correct the time and date settings problem.

SCEP Enrollment Problems

SCEP uses TCP port 80 for its communications. Make sure that TCP port 80 is not blocked anywhere when enrolling the Cisco ASA. The following debug commands are useful when troubleshooting certificate enrollment problems on the Cisco ASA:

- **debug crypto ca transactions**
- **debug crypto ca messages**

Example 17-29 includes the output of these **debug** commands when the Cisco ASA attempts to enroll but the CA server never responds due to communication problems.

Example 17-29 *Output of* **debug crypto ca transactions** *and* **debug crypto ca messages**

```
crypto_ca_get_ca_certificate(48b4884, 1850fa0)
crypto_pki_req(48b4884, 11, ...)
Crypto CA thread wakes up!
CRYPTO_PKI: Sending CA Certificate Request:
GET /cgi-bin/pkiclient.exe?operation=GetCACert&message=chicago HTTP/1.0
CRYPTO_PKI: status = 65535: failed to send out the pki message
CRYPTO_PKI: transaction GetCACert completed Crypto CA thread sleeps!
```

The error messages in Example 17-29 are displayed if the Cisco ASA is not able to communicate with the CA server due to any communication problems, such as routing problems, blocked ports, etc.

Time and date settings are also crucial during enrollment. Example 17-30 shows an unsuccessful enrollment request when the incorrect time and date settings were set in the Cisco ASA.

Example 17-30 *Errors Due to Incorrect Time and Date Settings During Enrollment*

```
Chicago(config)# crypto ca enroll chicago
%
% Start certificate enrollment ..
% Create a challenge password. You will need to verbally provide this
   password to the CA Administrator in order to revoke your certificate.
   For security reasons your password will not be saved in the configuration.
   Please make a note of it.
Password:
Re-enter password:
% The subject name in the certificate will be: O=secureme, OU=Chicago
% The fully-qualified domain name in the certificate will be:
Chicago.securemeinc.com
% Include the router serial number in the subject name? [yes/no]: no
Request certificate from CA? [yes/no]: yes
% Certificate request sent to Certificate Authority
Chicago(config)#
Certificate is not valid yet.
The certificate enrollment request failed!
```

The shaded lines in Example 17-30 show that the certificate enrollment request failed because the certificate received is not valid yet. The start date in the certificate validity period was later than the current date in the Cisco ASA.

CRL Retrieval Problems

During IKE Phase 1 negotiation, if CRL checking is required, the ASA verifies the revocation status of the peer certificate. CRLs exist on external servers maintained by CAs. To verify the revocation status, the Cisco ASA retrieves the CRL by using one of the available CRL distribution points and checks the peer certificate serial number against the list of serial numbers in the CRL. The Cisco ASA can use LDAP or HTTP (SCEP) for CRL checking. LDAP uses TCP port 389. Make sure that the necessary ports are not blocked by any device between the Cisco ASA and the CRL distribution point.

Use the **show crypto ca crls** command to view the CRL information on the Cisco ASA, as previously shown in Example 17-16.

If you chose a CRL retrieval policy that uses static distribution points, you must enter at least one (and not more than five) valid URL. This allows you to configure backup CRL distribution points to maximize availability.

Summary

This chapter provided an introduction to PKI and then progressed into detailed configuration and enrollment topics. To use digital certificates for authentication, you must first enroll with a CA and obtain and install a CA certificate on the Cisco ASA. Next, you must enroll and install an identity certificate from the same CA. This chapter showed how to enroll and install digital certificates on the Cisco ASA via SCEP or manually with the cut-and-paste method. It also provided detailed configuration steps for site-to-site and remote-access VPNs using digital certificates. Several troubleshooting tips and techniques were included at the end of the chapter.

Adaptive Security Device Manager

This chapter covers the following topics:

- Setting up ASDM
- Initial setup
- Functional screens
- Interface management
- System clock
- Configuration management
- Remote system management
- System maintenance
- System monitoring

CHAPTER 18

Introduction to ASDM

Cisco Adaptive Security Device Manager (ASDM) provides an easy-to-navigate and simple graphical interface to set up and manage the different features that Cisco Adaptive Security Appliance (ASA) provides. It is bundled with a variety of administrative and monitoring tools to check the health of Cisco ASA and the traffic traversing through it. This chapter introduces the ASDM GUI and helps you to complete the initial configuration parameters.

Setting Up ASDM

Before you can access the ASDM graphical console, you must install the ASDM software image on the local flash of the security Cisco ASA. The ASDM console can manage the local security Cisco ASA only; thus, if you need to manage multiple security Cisco ASA, the ASDM software must be installed on all the Cisco ASAs. However, a single workstation can launch multiple instances of ASDM clients to manage the different Cisco ASA.

A new security Cisco ASA is shipped with ASDM loaded in flash with the following default parameters:

- The GigabitEthernet0/1 interface on Cisco ASA 5520 and ASA 5540 is set up as inside with an IP address of 192.168.1.1. On Cisco ASA 5510, the Ethernet0/1 interface is set up as inside with the same address.

- The DHCP server enabled on the inside interface hands out addresses in the range of 192.168.1.2 through 192.168.1.254.

Uploading ASDM

You can use the **dir** command to determine whether or not the ASDM software is installed. In case the security Cisco ASA does not have the ASDM software, your first step is to upload the image from an external file server using the supported protocols. Refer to Chapter 4, "Initial Setup and System Maintenance," for a list of supported protocols. Cisco ASA needs to be set up for basic configuration, such as the interface names, security levels, IP addresses, and the proper routes. After setting up basic information, use the **copy** command to transfer the image file, as shown in Example 18-1, where an ASDM file, named asdm-501.bin, is being copied from a TFTP server located at 172.18.108.26. Verify the content of the local flash once the file is successfully uploaded.

Example 18-1 *Uploading the ASDM Image to the Local Flash*

```
Chicago# copy tftp flash
Address or name of remote host []? 172.18.108.26
Source filename []? asdm-501.bin
Destination filename [asdm-501.bin]? asdm-501.bin

Accessing tftp://172.18.108.26/asdm-501.bin...!!!!!!!!!!!!!!!!!!!!!!!!!!!!!!!!!!!!!
! Output omitted for brevity.
!!!!!!!!!!!!!!!!!!!!!!!!!!!!!!!!!!!!!!!!!!!!!
Writing file disk0:/asdm-501.bin...
!!!!!!!!!!!!!!!!!!!!!!!!!!!!!!!!!!!!!!!!!!!!!!!!!!!!!!!!!!!!!!!!!!!!!!!!!!!!!!!!!!!
! Output omitted for brevity.
!!!!!!!!!!!!!!!!!!!!!!!!!!!!!!!!!!!!!!!!!!!!!!!!!!!!!!!!!!!!!!!!!!!!!!!!!!!!!!!!!!
5876644 bytes copied in 161.420 secs (36500 bytes/sec)
Chicago# dir
Directory of disk0:/
1260   -rw-  5124096      16:47:34 Aug 07 2005  asa701.bin
2511   -rw-  5876644      17:38:14 Aug 07 2005  asdm-501.bin

62881792 bytes total (46723072 bytes free)
```

Setting Up Cisco ASA

When the ASDM file is accessed, the Cisco ASA loads the first ASDM image from the local Flash. If there are multiple ASDM images in the flash, use the **asdm image** command and specify the location of the ASDM image you want to load. This ensures that Cisco ASA always loads the specified image when ASDM is launched. In Example 18-2, Cisco ASA is set up to use asdm-501.bin as the ASDM image file.

Example 18-2 *Specifying the ASDM Location*

```
Chicago(config)# asdm image disk0:/asdm-501.bin
```

The security Cisco ASA uses the Secure Sockets Layer (SSL) protocol to communicate with the client. Consequently, the security Cisco ASA acts as a web server to process the requests from the clients. You can enable the web server on Cisco ASA by using the **http server enable** command.

The security Cisco ASA discards the incoming requests until the client's IP address is in the trusted network to access the HTTP engine. In Example 18-3, the administrator is enabling the HTTP engine and is setting up Cisco ASA to trust the 172.18.124.0/24 network connected toward the mgmt interface.

Example 18-3 *Enabling the HTTP Server*

```
Chicago(config)# http server enable
Chicago(config)# http 172.18.124.0 255.255.255.0 mgmt
```

NOTE	The WebVPN implementation on Cisco ASA also requires that you run the HTTP server on Cisco ASA. However, you cannot run ASDM and WebVPN on the same interface.

Accessing ASDM

The GUI of ASDM can be accessed from any workstation whose IP address is in the trusted network defined on the security Cisco ASA. Before you establish the secure connection to Cisco ASA, verify that IP connectivity exists between the workstation and the Cisco ASA.

To establish an SSL connection, launch a browser and point the URL to the IP address of Cisco ASA. In Figure 18-1, the administrator is accessing ASDM by typing in https://172.18.124.205/admin/index.html as the URL.

Figure 18-1 *Accessing the ASDM URL*

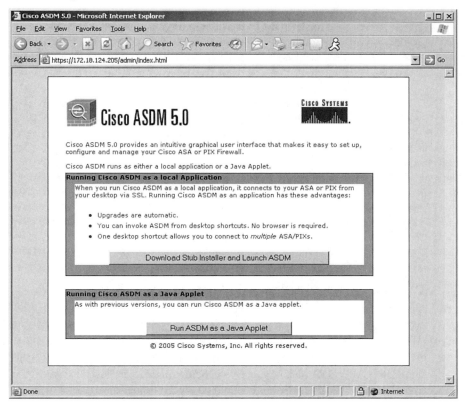

NOTE	ASDM requires Java plug-in 1.4(2) or 1.5.0 installed on the web browser.

The security Cisco ASA presents a self-signed certificate to the workstation so that a secure connection can be established. If the certificate is accepted, the security Cisco ASA prompts the user to present authentication credentials. If the ASDM authentication is not set up, there is no default username. The default password is cisco, which is actually the telnet or exec password of the security Cisco ASA.

After a successful user authentication, Cisco ASA presents two ways to launch ASDM:

- **ASDM as a Java applet**—The security Cisco ASA launches ASDM in the client's browser as a Java applet. This option is not feasible if a firewall that filters out Java applets exists between the client and the security Cisco ASA.

- **ASDM as an application**—The security Cisco ASA offers a setup utility called asdm50-install.msi, which can be saved to the local hard drive of the workstation.

  The setup utility installs the ASDM application under C:\Program Files\Cisco Systems\ASDM as the default directory which can be changed when going through the installation process. During the install process, the setup utility creates a shortcut to the application on the Desktop and on the taskbar. This option does not rely on a web browser to launch the ASDM application. Additionally, multiple instances of this application can be launched to connect to different security Cisco ASA. One of the major advantages of using ASDM as an application is the fact that whenever a newer version of an ASDM image is uploaded to the security Cisco ASA's flash, the ASDM application is automatically upgraded without user intervention.

NOTE	ASDM as an application feature is currently supported on Windows-based operating systems.

ASDM can be started either from the desktop shortcut, Quick Launch, or via **Start > Program Files > Cisco ASDM Launcher > Cisco ASDM Launcher,** depending on the user selection. After the software installation, the ASDM launcher is automatically started.

When the ASDM stub application is launched, it prompts for the IP address of the security Cisco ASA you are trying to connect and the user authentication credentials. Figure 18-2 illustrates this, where an SSL connection is being made to an Cisco ASA located at 172.18.124.205. Specify the username and password to log into ASDM.

Figure 18-2 *Launching ASDM*

NOTE   Chapters 18, 19, 20, and 21 use ASDM as an application to guide you through the configuration and monitoring features of the security Cisco ASA.

TIP   The ASDM application saves the previously connected IP addresses and username information in a file called deviceInfo.cfg. It is located under *user_home_directory\ .asdm\data*. It is highly recommended that you do not manually edit this file. It can be deleted if the IP addresses and the usernames need to be cleared.

Initial Setup

If the user authentication is successful, ASDM checks the current version of the stub application and downloads a new copy if necessary. It loads the current configuration from the security Cisco ASA and displays it in the GUI, as shown in Figure 18-3.

TIP   ASDM logs the debug and error messages into a file to troubleshoot the application-related issues. The name of the file is asdm-log-[timestamp].txt and it is located at *user_home_directory\.asdm\log*.

ASDM divides the initial screen, also known as the Home screen, into the following five sections:

* **Device Information**—Displays the hardware and software information of the security Cisco ASA, such as the current version of operating system and the device type. If the License tab is selected, ASDM shows the features that are enabled on the security Cisco ASA.

Figure 18-3 *Initial ASDM Screen*

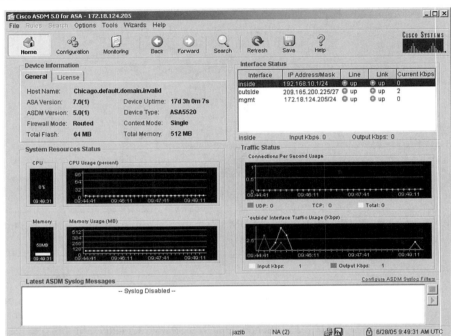

- **System Resources Status**—Provides the current status of CPU and memory usage on Cisco ASA.

- **Interface Status**—Displays the interface name and the assigned IP address. It also shows the link information of the currently configured interfaces and the rate of traffic passing through them.

- **Traffic Status**—Provides information about the number of active TCP and UDP connections and the traffic rate passing through the outside interface.

- **Latest ASDM Syslog Messages**—Shows the latest ASDM syslog messages that are generated by the security Cisco ASA. Syslogging is disabled by default and needs to be enabled for log monitoring. When enabled, the security Cisco ASA sends the messages to the ASDM client. This is discussed later in the chapter, in the section "System Logging."

The statistics on the Home screen are refreshed every 10 seconds and show the information for the last 5 minutes.

Startup Wizard

The ASDM application has seven menus on the toolbars to configure certain parameters. One of the menus is called **Wizards**, which contains two options, VPN Wizard and Startup

Wizard. To launch the Startup Wizard, choose **Wizards > Startup Wizard**, as shown in Figure 18-4.

Figure 18-4 *Launching the Startup Wizard*

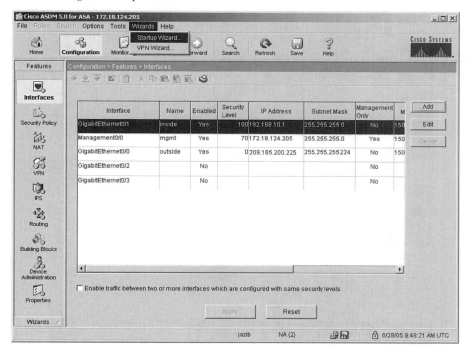

The Startup Wizard can also be launched by choosing **Configuration > Wizards > Startup**.

The next screen on the wizard prompts you to specify whether you want the wizard to continue with the existing device configuration or to reset the running configuration to its factory default values. Resetting the security Cisco ASA into default configuration is helpful if you do not want to keep the existing configuration. This option is feasible if the security Cisco ASA is deployed in a lab environment with no production traffic traversing through it. In Figure 18-5, the administrator has selected the option to modify the existing configuration.

NOTE   Chapter 4 talks about the default configuration.

The Basic Configuration screen allows you to modify the host name and domain name of the security Cisco ASA. ASDM also enables you to modify the enable password by specifying the current enable password and then entering the new enable password, as illustrated in Figure 18-6. By default, there is no enable password configured on the security Cisco ASA.

Figure 18-5 *Starting Point of the Configuration*

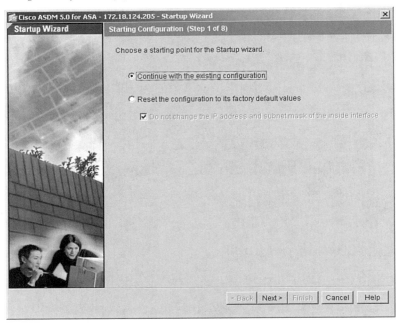

Figure 18-6 *Basic Configuration*

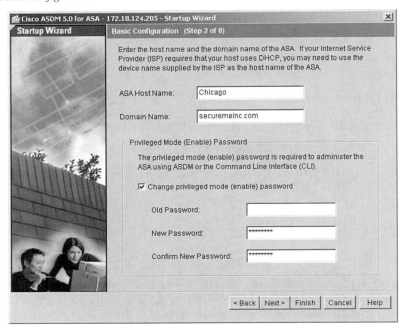

You can modify the outside interface attributes, such as the interface name and the IP address, on the next screen. If the outside interface is being assigned an IP address from the DHCP server, select the **Use DHCP** option. In Figure 18-7, the outside interface has a static IP address of 209.165.200.225/27 and a default gateway of 209.165.200.226.

Figure 18-7 *Outside Interface Configuration*

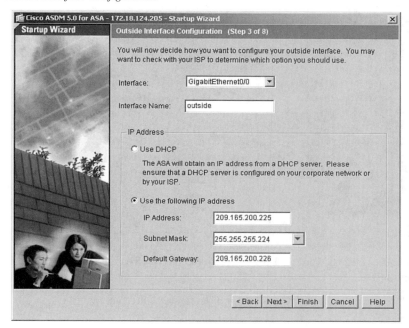

You can select the remaining interfaces and edit attributes such as the interface name, security level, and IP address/subnet mask.

NOTE   You might lose your connection to the security Cisco ASA if you modify the interface parameters that ASDM is connected to.

The wizard allows you to enable a DHCP server on the inside interface. The security Cisco ASA can assign DHCP attributes such as IP addresses from a pool, the DNS and WINS server addresses, the default gateway address, the domain name, and the lease expiration time.

As illustrated in Figure 18-8, a pool of addresses in the range of 192.168.10.10 to 192.168.10.199 is set up with DNS and WINS addresses of 192.168.10.200 and 192.168.10.201. The default domain name is securemeinc.com and the IP address lease expires in 3600 seconds. Click **Next** to proceed.

Figure 18-8 *DHCP Server*

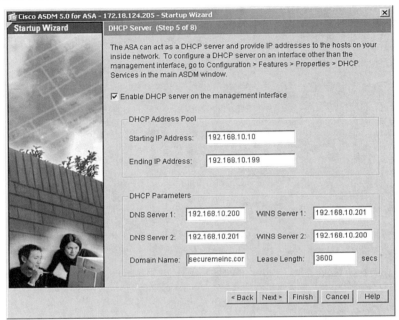

If address translation needs to be set up on Cisco ASA, the Startup Wizard presents three options:

- The first option creates a pool of addresses for dynamic NAT.
- The second option configures dynamic PAT.
- The third option bypasses address translation.

In Figure 18-9, ASDM is being set up to dynamically translate the inside hosts to the outside interface's IP address using PAT.

The last configuration step in the Startup Wizard allows you to set up administrative access to Cisco ASA. As discussed in Chapter 4, the security Cisco ASA supports Telnet and SSH as the CLI-based remote management protocols, and supports ASDM as a GUI-based application. You can specify the allowed IP addresses on each of the interfaces for each of the management protocols. In Figure 18-10, the 192.168.10.0/24 network is allowed to establish SSH connections to Cisco ASA from the inside interface, while the 172.18.124.0/24 subnet is allowed to establish SSH and HTTPS connections from the mgmt interface.

CAUTION   If the HTTP server is disabled, ASDM will stop communicating with Cisco ASA.

Figure 18-9 *Address Translation*

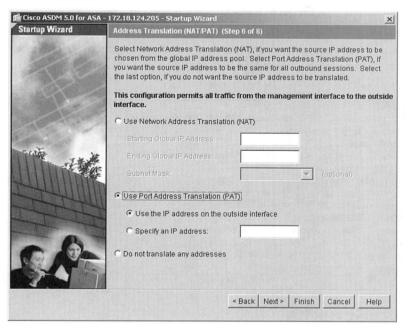

Figure 18-10 *Administrative Access*

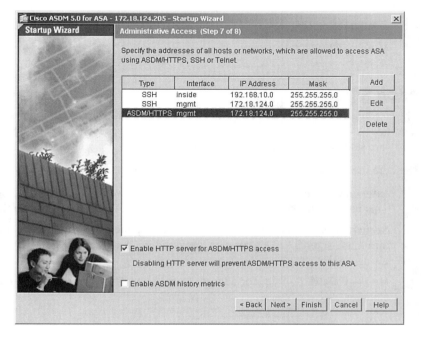

ASDM prompts you to either send the updated configuration or go back to modify the parameters. Click **Finish** to send the configuration to Cisco ASA.

If the "Preview command before sending to the device" option is enabled on ASDM under **Tools > Preferences**, the entire startup configuration is displayed before it is sent to the security Cisco ASA, as shown in Example 18-4.

Example 18-4 *Initial Configuration Generated by ASDM*

```
!DHCP server configuration
dhcpd address 192.168.10.10-192.168.10.199 inside
dhcpd enable inside
dhcpd dns 192.168.10.200 192.168.10.201
dhcpd wins 192.168.10.201 192.168.10.200
dhcpd domain securemeinc.com
!PAT configuration
global (outside) 10 interface
nat (inside) 10 0.0.0.0 0.0.0.0
!SSH configuration
ssh 172.18.124.0 255.255.255.0 mgmt
ssh 192.168.10.0 255.255.255.0 inside
!Changing the enable password
enable password cisco123
```

Functional Screens

In addition to the Home screen, the ASDM interface comes with the following two functional screens:

- Configuration screen
- Monitoring screen

Configuration Screen

The Configuration screen is useful when the new or existing configuration needs to be modified. It contains on the left side eight or nine Features icons, depending on the hardware setup of Cisco ASA, as shown in Figure 18-11.

Here are the Features icons of the Configuration screen:

- **Interfaces**—Configures interfaces and sub-interfaces on the security Cisco ASA. This panel is discussed in the section "Interface Management," later in the chapter.

- **Security Policy**—Helpful in creating security policies to filter packets traversing through Cisco ASA. This panel is discussed in Chapter 19, "Firewall Management Using ASDM."

- **NAT**—Creates policies for address translation. This panel is discussed in Chapter 19.

Figure 18-11 *Configuration Screen*

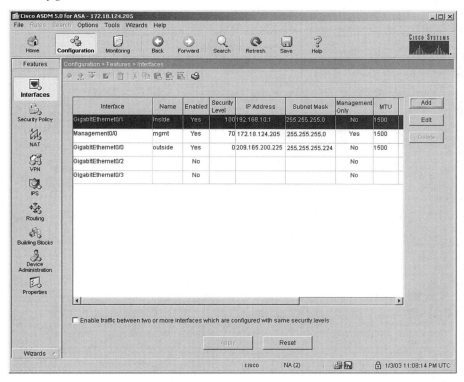

- **VPN**—Sets up the site-to-site and remote-access VPN tunnels. This panel is discussed in Chapter 21, "VPN Management Using ASDM."

- **IPS**—Sets up policies for the SSM card to monitor and drop unauthorized packets. This icon is not visible if an SSM card is not present. This panel is discussed in Chapter 20, "IDS Management Using ASDM."

- **Routing**—Helpful in setting up the static routes and dynamic routing protocols. This panel is discussed in Chapter 19.

- **Building Blocks**—Enables and modifies parameters for the inspection engines. Chapter 19 discusses this panel.

- **Device Administration**—Here, the basic device features can be set up. These features are discussed later in this chapter.

- **Properties**—Helpful in setting up the basic software features, such as system logging and failover. Some of the features are discussed in this chapter and the remaining features are introduced in Chapter 19.

Monitoring Screen

The Monitoring screen displays statistics about the hardware and software features of the security Cisco ASA. ASDM provides real-time graphs to monitor the health and status of Cisco ASA. Figure 18-12 shows the initial Monitoring screen.

Figure 18-12 *Monitoring Screen*

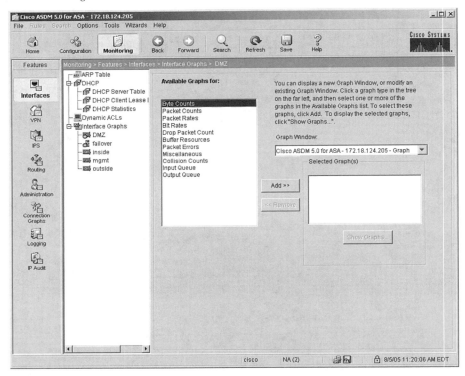

Similar to the Configuration screen, the Monitoring screen also displays seven or eight icons, depending on whether or not you have the SSM module installed.

Here are the Features icons of the Configuration screen:

- **Interfaces**—Monitors interfaces and sub-interfaces by maintaining ARP, DHCP, and dynamic ACLs tables. It also provides a graphical representation of interface utilization and packet throughput.

- **VPN**—Monitors the active VPN connections on the security Cisco ASA. This panel is discussed in Chapter 21.

- **IPS**—Provides statistical information for the packets going through the IPS engine. This panel is discussed in Chapter 20. This icon is not present if the IPS module is not installed.

- **Routing**—Displays the current routing table and OSPF LSA types.

- **Administration**—Monitors active administrative sessions such as Telnet, SSH, and ASDM. It also provides graphical information about CPU, memory, and blocks utilization.

- **Connection Graphs**—Provides graphical information about the active translations and UDP/TCP connections.

- **Logging**—Displays log messages as live events. It also shows log messages from the buffer space.

- **IP Audit**—Provides graphical information if the IP audit feature is enabled. This panel is discussed in Chapter 20.

Interface Management

Choose **Configuration > Features > Interfaces** to set up the physical interfaces and to create sub-interfaces. Select the interface you want to modify and click **Edit** to specify the interface parameters. In Figure 18-13, GigabitEthernet0/2 is being set up as a DMZ interface with a security level of 50 and an IP address of 209.165.201.1/27. If you click Configure Hardware Properties, you can set the duplex and speed manually.

Figure 18-13 *Interfaces Configuration Screen*

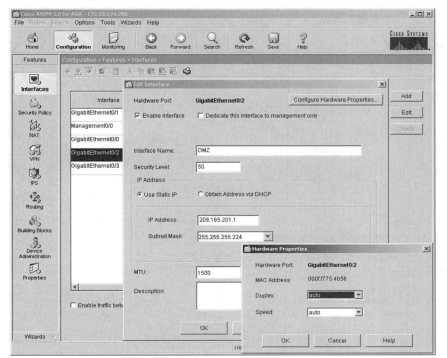

NOTE	ASDM does not support assigning IPv6 addresses to the interfaces.

To create a sub-interface, click **Add** under **Configuration > Features > Interfaces** and select the physical interface from the **Hardware Port** drop-down menu. Specify the interface name, VLAN ID, sub-interface ID, security level, and an IP address to complete the sub-interface setup, as shown in Figure 18-14. A new sub-interface is being created on the GigabitEthernet0/3 physical interface with a sub-interface and VLAN ID of 200. The interface name is Web and a security level of 20 is assigned to it. The IP address is being assigned from a DHCP server.

Figure 18-14 *Sub-interface Configuration Screen*

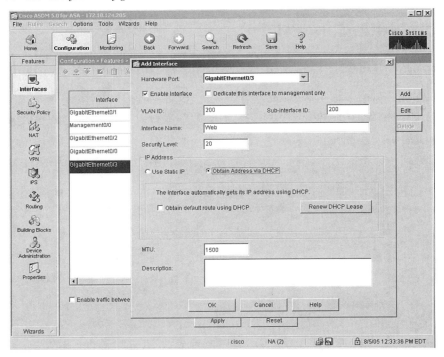

Example 18-5 shows the relevant configuration that ASDM pushes to the security Cisco ASA when a sub-interface is set up.

Example 18-5 *Configuration of a Sub-interface*

```
Interface GigabitEthernet0/3.200
  vlan 200
  no shutdown
  nameif Web
  security-level 20
  ip address  dhcp
```

System Clock

The system clock can be adjusted by choosing **Configuration > Features > Device Administration > Administration > Clock**, as shown in Figure 18-15. Select the appropriate time zone from the drop-down menu and adjust the system date by browsing through the monthly calendar. The system time can be adjusted by entering the time in the 24-hour format. In Figure 18-15, the system time is being adjusted to 5:05:05 a.m. on August 5, 2005 in the Eastern time zone. Click **Apply** to adjust the system clock.

Figure 18-15 *Adjusting the System Clock*

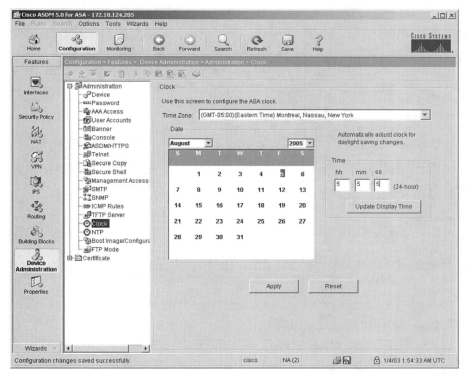

Example 18-6 displays the CLI commands to adjust the system clock that ASDM sends to the security Cisco ASA.

Example 18-6 *Adjusting the System Clock via the CLI*

```
clock timezone EST -5 0
clock summer-time EDT recurring 1 Sun Apr 2:00 last Sun Oct 2:00 60
clock set 5:5:5 AUG 5 2005
```

The system clock can be dynamically adjusted if an NTP server is specified on Cisco ASA. Set up an NTP server by choosing **Configuration > Features > Device Administration > Administration > NTP**. Click **Add** to enter a new NTP server and specify the IP address and the source interface information, as shown in Figure 18-16. If NTP authentication is being used, specify the authentication key and the key value. In this figure, a preferred NTP server located at 192.168.10.50 toward the inside interface is defined with an authentication key number of 1 and a key value of csco.

Figure 18-16 *Specifying an NTP Server*

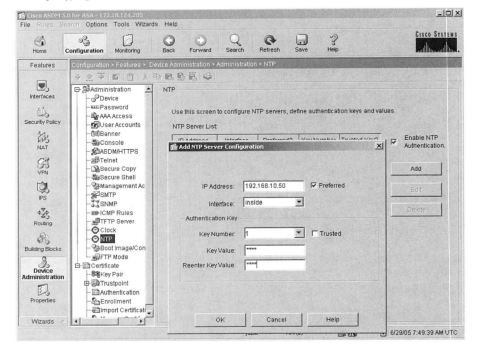

Example 18-7 shows the CLI commands that ASDM sends to the security Cisco ASA.

Example 18-7 *Specifying an NTP Server via the CLI*

```
ntp server 192.168.10.50 key 1 source inside prefer
ntp authenticate
ntp authentication-key 1 md5 csco
```

Configuration Management

As discussed in Chapter 4, the security Cisco ASA keeps two copies of the configuration:

- Active or running configuration
- Saved or startup configuration

The running configuration on the security Cisco ASA can be maintained and managed by browsing the File menu options, as shown in Figure 18-17.

Figure 18-17 *Running Configuration Management*

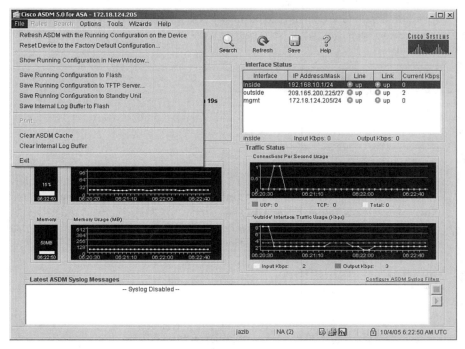

Here are the options available under the File menu:

- **Refresh ASDM with the Running Configuration on the Device**—ASDM can poll the security Cisco ASA and update its configuration using the running configuration of the Cisco ASA.

- **Reset Device to the Factory Default Configuration**—Clears the running configuration of the security Cisco ASA. This is equivalent to issuing **clear configuration all** from the CLI. This action prompts you to assign an IP address to the management interface. This way, the ASDM client can restore connectivity to the security Cisco ASA.

- **Show Running Configuration in New Window**—Opens a new window on the desktop with the current running configuration.

- **Save Running Configuration to Flash**—Saves the running configuration in the NVRAM. This is equivalent to issuing **copy running-config startup-config** from the CLI.

- **Save Running Configuration to TFTP Server**—Use this option to store a copy of the running configuration to an external TFTP server for backup purposes.

- **Save Running Configuration to Standby Unit**—If failover is set up, select this option to ensure that the backup security Cisco ASA is synchronized with the current running configuration of the active Cisco ASA.

Remote System Management

An administrator does not have to be physically connected to the console port of Cisco ASA to be able to access the CLI. The security Cisco ASA supports three remote management protocols:

- Telnet
- Secure Shell (SSH)
- SSL (ASDM)

Telnet

The security Cisco ASA comes with a Telnet server that allows users to remotely manage it. Set up a Telnet server by choosing **Configuration > Features > Device Administration > Administration > Telnet**. Click **Add** and specify the IP host, subnet, and network addresses allowed to connect from a particular interface. In Figure 18-18, the entire 192.168.10.0/24 inside network is allowed to start a Telnet connection to the security Cisco ASA.

Figure 18-18 *Setting Up the Telnet Server*

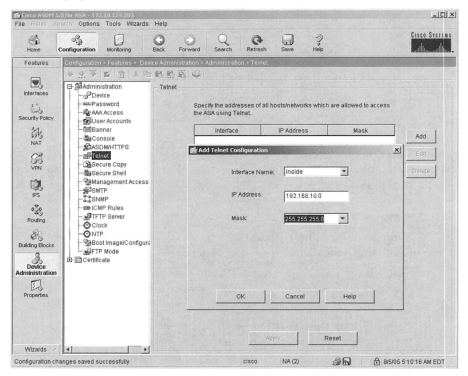

To monitor the Telnet sessions that are being established to the security Cisco ASA, choose **Monitoring > Features > Administration > Telnet Sessions**. This screen shows the session ID and the IP address of the Telnet client, as shown in Figure 18-19, where a workstation is accessing the security Cisco ASA from 192.168.10.2.

NOTE   Because the security Cisco ASA supports Telnet and SSH, using SSH for remote management is highly recommended.

Figure 18-19 *Monitoring the Telnet Sessions*

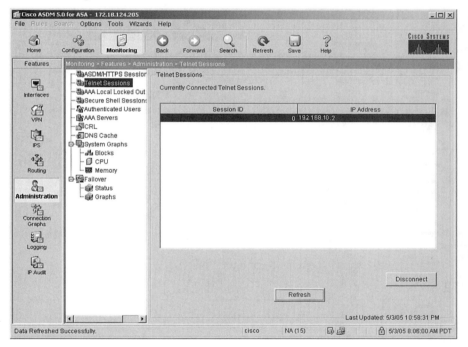

SSH

The security Cisco ASA can act as an SSH server to allow secured connections. The SSH server can be enabled by choosing **Configuration > Features > Device Administration > Administration > Secure Shell**. Click **Add** and specify the IP host, subnet, and network addresses allowed to connect from a particular interface. In Figure 18-20, the inside network of 192.168.10.0/24 and mgmt subnet of 172.18.124.0/24 are allowed to start an

SSH connection to the security Cisco ASA. Cisco ASA is allowed to accept only SSH version 2 connections.

Figure 18-20 *Setting Up the SSH Server*

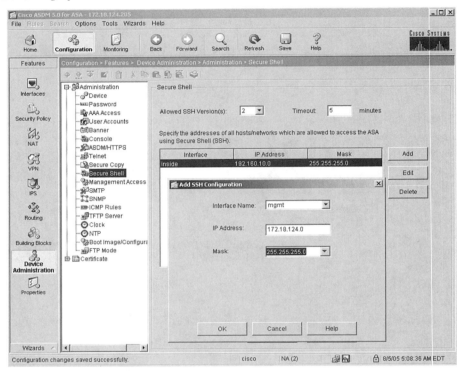

Example 18-8 shows the related configuration.

Example 18-8 *Setting Up the SSH Server via the CLI*

```
ssh version 2
ssh 192.168.10.0 255.255.255.0 inside
ssh 172.18.124.0 255.255.255.0 mgmt
```

SSL (ASDM)

The remote administration of Cisco ASA also includes managing it from ASDM. You can limit the IP addresses to manage the security Cisco ASA by setting the parameters under **Configuration > Features > Device Administration > Administration > ASDM/ HTTPS**. In Figure 18-21, the 172.18.124.0/24 subnet is allowed to establish ASDM connections from the mgmt interface.

Figure 18-21 *Managing ASDM*

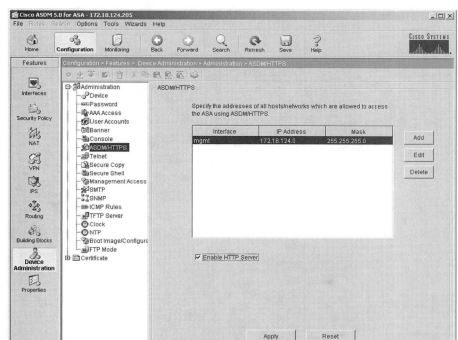

CAUTION   If the HTTP server is disabled, ASDM will stop communicating with Cisco ASA.

System Maintenance

This section explains how to manage the different system image files on the security Cisco ASA.

Software Installation

ASDM can upload either an ASA or an ASDM image to the Cisco ASA flash using the HTTPS protocol. This is done by clicking **Tools > Upload image from Local PC** on the toolbar. Select whether you want to upload an ASDM or an ASA image, and then specify the path to the image file on the local drive. For ease of use, you can also click **Browse Local** and select the file by browsing the local hard-drive file structure. Specify the destination location on the Cisco ASA flash and then click **Upload Image** to initiate the file transfer process. In Figure 18-22, an ASA image, asa701.bin, is being uploaded from the local drive C:\temp\ASA\asa701.bin to disk0:/asa701.bin on Cisco ASA.

Figure 18-22 *Image Upload*

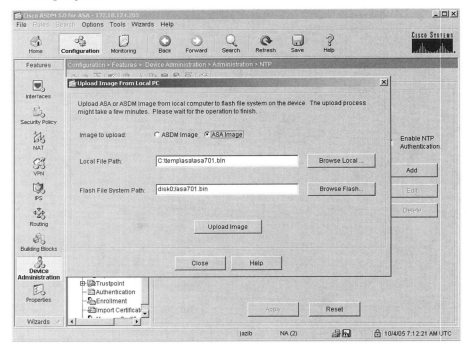

If the system Flash contains more than one system image, the security Cisco ASA boots off from the first image it finds in the flash. If the image you want to boot is not the first one on the disk, you should set the boot order to load the desired binary image file. It is set up under **Configuration > Features > Device Administration > Administration > Boot Image/ Configuration**, as shown in Figure 18-23. The system image asa701.bin is set up as the first image the security Cisco ASA will boot from.

File Management

ASDM provides an easy interface to manage the files on the security Cisco ASA. The File Management option under Tools is used to manage the system flash structure. Functions such as copy, rename and deletion of system files are supported.

Similar to the image upgrade option, the security Cisco ASA can also upload system and nonsystem files from an external server to the flash and vice versa under **Tools > File Transfer**. This is helpful in transferring syslog and other system-generated files from the security Cisco ASA.

Figure 18-23 *Setting the Boot Order*

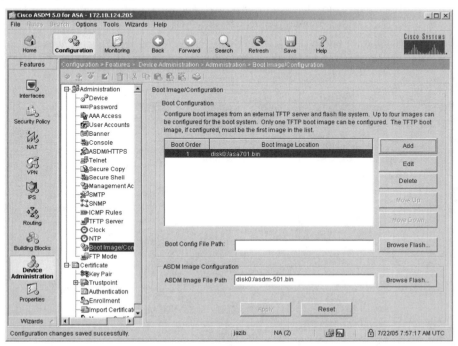

System Monitoring

The security Cisco ASA can generate system and debug messages when an event occurs. These messages can either be ignored or logged depending on the security policies of an organization.

System Logging

System logging is a process by which the Cisco security Cisco ASA generates an event for any significant occurrence that affects the system, such as network problems, error conditions, and threshold breaches. It can be enabled under **Configuration > Features > Properties > Logging > Logging Setup**. As shown in Figure 18-24, ASDM is set up to configure the security Cisco ASA for the following properties:

- Global syslogging is enabled on Cisco ASA.
- Cisco ASA will redirect the debug messages as syslogs.
- The syslog messages will be sent in the EMBLEM format.

- Cisco ASA will write the syslog messages to the local flash and to an FTP server. The FTP server is located at 172.18.124.10 and the security Cisco ASA uses a username of cisco with a password of c1sc0, shown as asterisks.

- The default buffer size is 4096 bytes. When the buffer space reaches this limit, the security Cisco ASA will save the syslog messages to the flash and the FTP server.

Figure 18-24 *Enabling Syslog*

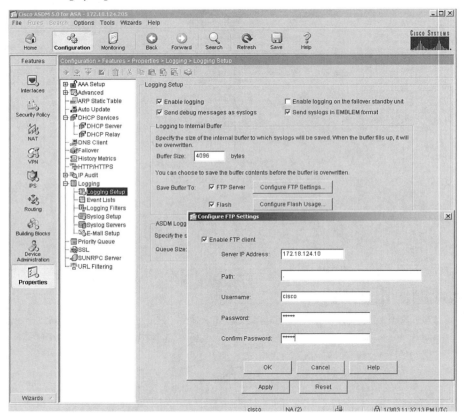

CAUTION   Logging to flash can use up most of the available space on flash and this option should be enabled only when logging either at a low level or at a selected class.

As mentioned in Chapter 4, Cisco ASA can create logging lists to filter out specific messages. In Figure 18-25, a logging list called **WebVPN** is being set up to filter webvpn class logs with the severity level set to debugging.

Figure 18-25 *Setting Up a Logging List*

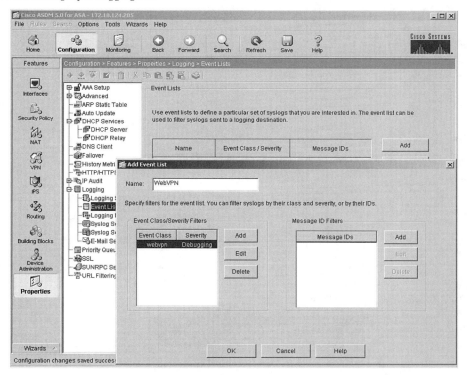

The logging list can be applied to one of the syslog types. In Figure 18-26, the ASDM interface is set up to receive the log messages identified by the WebVPN logging list. This is configured under **Configuration > Features > Properties > Logging > Logging Filters** and ASDM under Destination Logging.

Once ASDM logging is enabled, the security Cisco ASA sends the logs to the ASDM host connected to it, which ASDM displays on the Home screen, as shown in Figure 18-27.

Figure 18-26 *Applying ASDM Logging List*

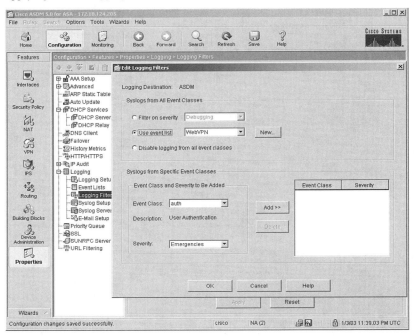

Figure 18-27 *Displaying Logs on ASDM*

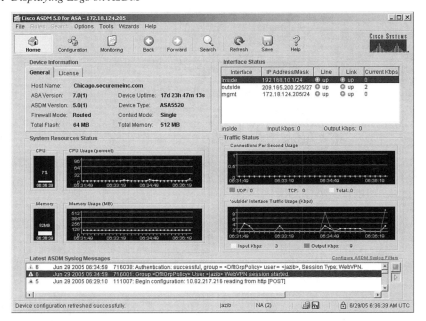

Example 18-9 shows the relevant configuration in setting up syslogging for the scenarios just discussed.

Example 18-9 *Syslog Configuration Created by ASDM*

```
logging enable
logging debug-trace
logging emblem
logging flash-bufferwrap
logging ftp-bufferwrap
logging ftp-server 172.18.124.10 . cisco c1sc0
logging list WebVPN level Debugging class webvpn
logging asdm WebVPN
```

To monitor the system logs sent to ASDM, choose **Monitoring > Features > Logging > Live Log** to view the events live as they are generated by Cisco ASA. This is useful when you are troubleshooting a problem using the security Cisco ASA. Figure 18-28 shows the live logs being displayed when the logging level is set to debugging and the buffer level is limited to 1000. These log messages can even be saved to a log file on the local workstation if needed.

Figure 18-28 *Displaying Live Logs on ASDM*

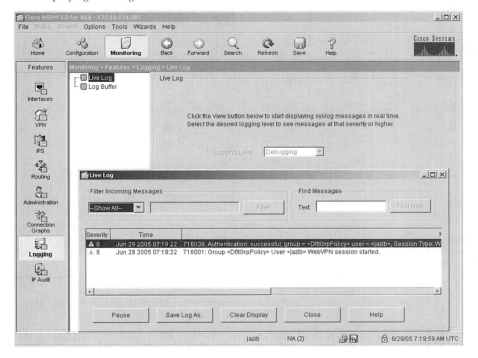

Figure 18-29 illustrates how to set up an external syslog server on ASDM. This is achieved by clicking **Add** under **Configuration > Features > Properties > Logging > Syslog Servers**. Select the interface connected to the syslog server, from the drop-down menu. Additionally, specify the IP address and the protocol/port used by the syslog server. If a UDP-based syslog server is used, you can choose to send the output in the EMBLEM format. In Figure 18-29, the syslog server is located off the mgmt interface at 172.18.124.100 using UDP port 514 and receiving the output in the EMBLEM format.

Figure 18-29 *Setting Up a Syslog Server*

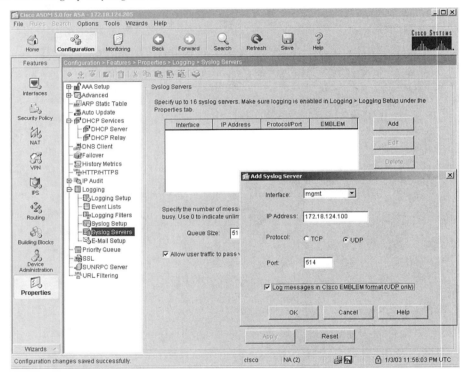

Example 18-10 demonstrates the relevant configuration that ASDM sends to the security Cisco ASA.

Example 18-10 *Specifying a Syslog Server*

```
logging host mgmt 172.18.124.100 format emblem
logging permit-hostdown
```

If a TCP-based syslog server is deployed and it is not reachable, the security Cisco ASA blocks all traffic that is passing through it to add an extra level of security. However, this default behavior can be changed if the Allow User Traffic to Pass when TCP Syslog Server Is Down option is selected.

For logging of time-sensitive events, ASDM can configure a security Cisco ASA to send logs to an e-mail address by going through an SMTP server. This is set up by clicking **Add** under **Configuration > Features > Properties > Logging > E-Mail Setup**, as shown in Figure 18-30, where the syslog messages with severity emergencies are sent to a destination e-mail address of administrator@securemeinc.com from Chicago@securemeinc.com.

Figure 18-30 *Setting Up E-Mail–Based Syslogging*

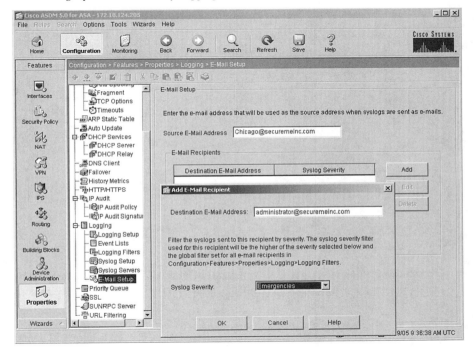

The SMTP server can be declared under **Configuration > Features > Device Administration > Administration > SMTP**. ASDM allows an administrator to enter a primary server and an optional secondary server. In Example 18-11, the configuration generated by ASDM using 192.168.10.100 as the SMTP server is shown.

Example 18-11 *Setting Up E-Mail–Based Logging*

```
logging from-address Chicago@securemeinc.com
logging recipient-address administrator@securemeinc.com level Emergencies
smtp-server 192.168.10.100
```

SNMP

Cisco ASDM can set up the security Cisco ASA for SNMP logging and traps under **Configuration > Features > Device Administration > Administration > SNMP**. Click **Configure Traps** to set up the five supported trap types, as shown in Figure 18-31. The administrator has selected all the supported SNMP traps on ASDM.

Figure 18-31 *Setting Up SNMP Traps*

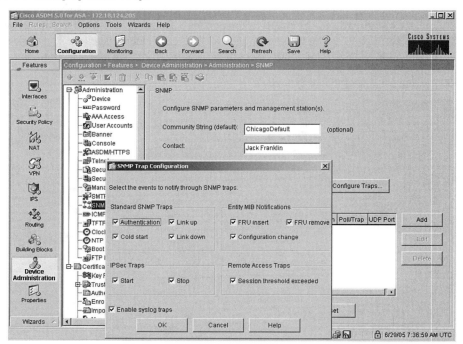

The default community string is set to **ChicagoDefault**. The contact name is Jack Franklin, while the location of Cisco ASA is Chicago. Example 18-12 shows the relevant configuration that ASDM sends to Cisco ASA.

Example 18-12 *Configuring SNMP Traps and Device Information*

```
snmp-server enable traps snmp authentication
snmp-server enable traps snmp linkup
snmp-server enable traps snmp linkdown
snmp-server enable traps snmp coldstart
snmp-server enable traps ipsec start
snmp-server enable traps ipsec stop
snmp-server enable traps entity config-change
snmp-server enable traps entity fru-insert
snmp-server enable traps entity fru-remove
snmp-server enable traps remote-access session-threshold-exceededsnmp-server
  community ChicagoDefault
snmp-server location Chicago
snmp-server contact Jack Franklin
```

After setting up the SNMP device and trap information, the last step is to configure an SNMP server to send the traps. Click **Add** under SNMP Management Station and specify the interface name, the IP address of the management server, the SNMP version, community string, and the UDP port number. You can also limit poll and trap functions for this server. As illustrated in Figure 18-32, the SNMP server is located off the mgmt interface at 172.18.124.110 and is using UDP port 162. The SNMP string is ChicagoSNMP and the server uses SNMP version 1. The SNMP host can poll and receive traps from the security Cisco ASA.

Figure 18-32 *Specifying an SNMP Server*

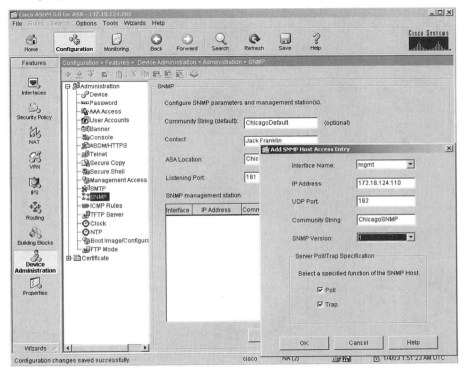

Example 18-13 shows the corresponding configuration.

Example 18-13 *Setting Up an SNMP Server*

```
snmp-server host mgmt 172.18.124.110 community ChicagoSNMP version 1
```

Summary

This chapter briefly introduced ASDM and discussed the GUI for system configuration and monitoring. The chapter also discussed how to load ASDM in Cisco ASA and launch it from a browser. Configuration examples such as the Startup Wizard and the initial parameters were also introduced.

This chapter covers the following topics:

- Access control lists
- Address translation
- Routing protocols
- AAA
- Application inspection
- Security contexts
- Transparent firewalls
- Failover
- QoS

CHAPTER 19

Firewall Management Using ASDM

This chapter focuses on the firewall features that can be configured and managed by Cisco Adaptive Security Device Manager (ASDM). The chapter also provides an overview of the different firewall features and step-by-step configuration examples using the ASDM GUI.

Access Control Lists

As discussed in Chapter 5, "Network Access Control," you can use access control lists (ACLs) to filter traffic passing through Cisco ASA. You can set up a traffic-filtering ACL under **Configuration > Features > Security Policy > Access Rules**. Click **Add** to create a new ACL. Figure 19-1 shows a new access control entry (ACE) added into ASDM to block web traffic coming in from the outside host located at 209.165.201.1 to an inside web server located at 209.165.202.131. This ACE is a part of an ACL, which is automatically created by ASDM and applied to the interface. ASDM provides a nice Rule Flow Diagram section to illustrate how the ACL policy will be applied to the traffic. The source or destination host/network addresses may be IP addresses, an interface name, or an object group. You may also enter a description at the bottom of the screen to label the purpose of this entry.

NOTE   An ACE is referred to as an access rule in the ASDM interface.

Figure 19-2 illustrates the complete ACL with two ACEs.

The first entry denies the traffic originating from the host located at 209.165.201.1. The second entry allows web traffic to pass through Cisco ASA if it is either of the following:

- Sourced from any IP address, except the one that is blocked.
- Destined for the IP address of the web server.

Figure 19-1 *Setting Up an ACE*

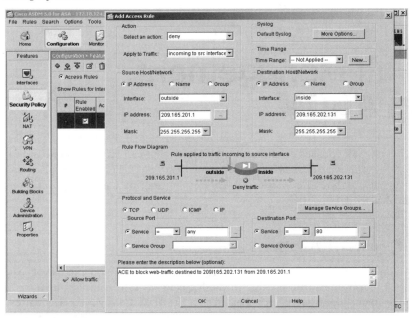

Figure 19-2 *Displaying the Entire ACL*

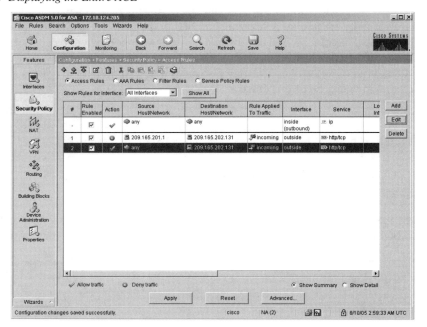

Example 19-1 shows the corresponding ACL generated by ASDM. The ACL name is **outside_access_in** and it is applied to the outside interface in the inbound direction.

Example 19-1 *ACL Generated by ASDM*

```
access-list outside_access_in remark ACE to block web-traffic destined to
   209.165.202.131 from 209.165.201.1
access-list outside_access_in extended deny tcp host 209.165.201.1 host
   209.165.202.131 eq www
access-list outside_access_in extended permit tcp any host 209.165.202.131 eq www
access-group outside_access_in in interface outside
```

The use of object groups can simplify both the CLI and GUI configuration if numerous hosts need to be filtered using similar properties. For network-based object groups, Cisco ASA needs to know where a host or a network exists. To accomplish this, navigate to **Configuration > Features > Building Blocks > Host/Networks** and then click **Add** under **Hosts/Networks Groups**. You can enter the IP addresses of the hosts either by clicking **Existing Hosts and Networks** and adding them from the list or by clicking **New Host or Network**, typing the new address, and then adding it with the **Add** button, as shown in Figure 19-3. The existing hosts are the previously added hosts in the ASDM list. The administrator has named this object group **inside_web_servers** and has grouped three inside IP addresses in the list.

Figure 19-3 *Defining an Object Group in ASDM*

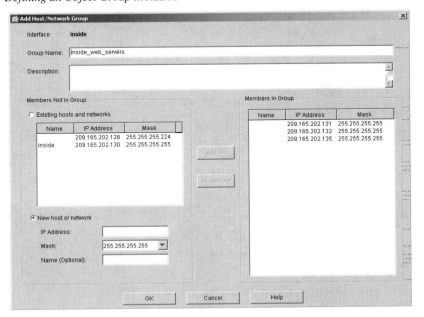

After defining the object groups, you can map an ACE, as shown in Figure 19-4. The traffic from the outside hosts defined in the outside_hosts network group is allowed to pass through Cisco ASA to the hosts on the inside network that are identified in the inside_web_servers group on TCP port 80.

Figure 19-4 *Mapping an Object Group in ASDM*

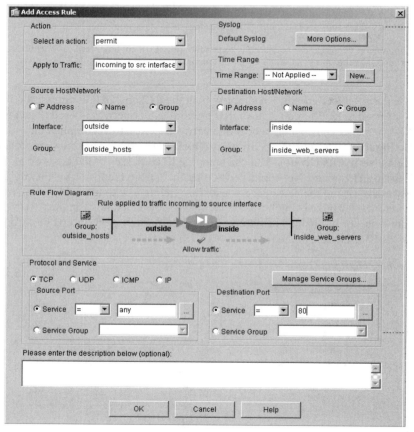

Example 19-2 shows the configuration generated by ASDM when using object groups.

Example 19-2 *ACL with Object Groups Generated by ASDM*

```
object-group network inside_web_servers
 network-object 209.165.202.131 255.255.255.255
 network-object 209.165.202.132 255.255.255.255
 network-object 209.165.202.135 255.255.255.255
object-group network outside_hosts
 network-object 209.165.201.1 255.255.255.255
 network-object 209.165.201.2 255.255.255.255
 network-object 209.165.201.10 255.255.255.255
access-list outside_access_in line 1 extended permit tcp object-group outside_hosts
object-group inside_web_servers eq 80
access-group outside_access_in in interface outside
```

Using ASDM, you can configure a security Cisco ASA to filter ActiveX and Java applets from the traffic passing through it. To set this up, choose **Configuration > Features > Security Policy > Filter Rules**, which results in the window shown in Figure 19-5. Here, Cisco ASA is being set up to filter ActiveX code from the web requests that originated from the inside network 209.165.202.128/27 and are destined for any address on the outside network.

Figure 19-5 *Content Filtering*

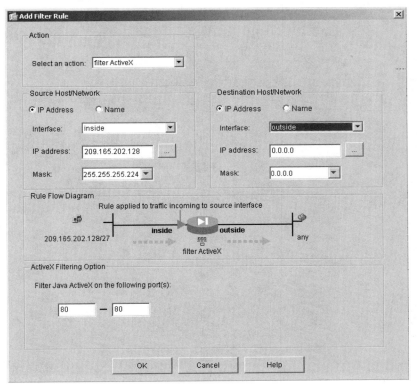

Address Translation

You can configure address translation under **Configuration > Features > NAT**. ASDM allows both dynamic and static NAT/PAT for either all or selected hosts on the inside and the outside networks. Click **Add** to define a new NAT/PAT policy in the Add Address Translation Rule window. As shown in Figure 19-6, ASDM is identifying the inside network of 192.168.10.0/24 for address translation.

In Figure 9-6, the administrator has also checked the Enable Traffic Through the Firewall Without Address Translation window. This option appears in the main window under

Configuration > Features and NAT. This option allows traffic that does not match any NAT policy to pass through the security Cisco ASA without changing the source or destination addresses. However, the packets that match the NAT/PAT policies are translated.

Figure 19-6 *Defining a NAT/PAT Policy*

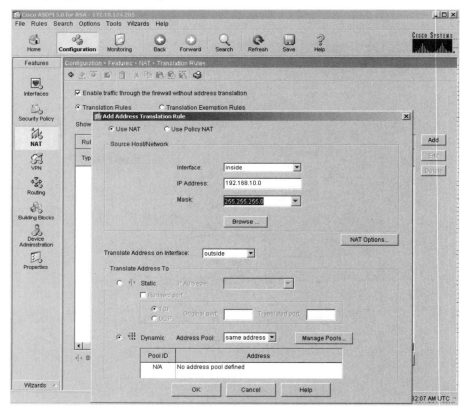

SecureMe, a fictitious company, wants to dynamically translate the inside 192.168.10.0/24 network from a pool of public addresses. Click **Manage Pools** to define a new pool of IP addresses, as shown in Figure 19-7. Because the inside hosts will be translated to the outside network, select the outside interface and click **Add** to add a range of IP addresses from **209.165.200.230** to **209.165.200.235** to be mapped to a pool ID of 10. The 209.165.200.236 address is used for PAT if all the other addresses have been assigned. Click **OK** to finish the setup.

If you need to configure static NAT, click the **Static** radio button in the Add Address Translation Rule window and specify the translated address in the **IP Address** box, as shown in Figure 19-8, in which an inside host, 192.168.10.100, is being translated to 209.165.200.240.

Figure 19-7 *Defining a Pool of Addresses*

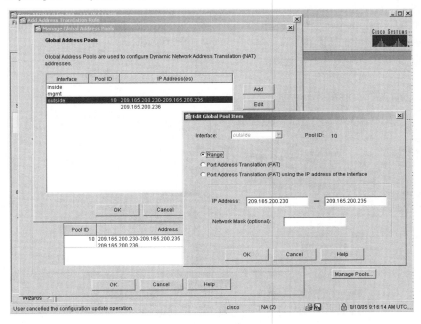

Figure 19-8 *Static Address Translation*

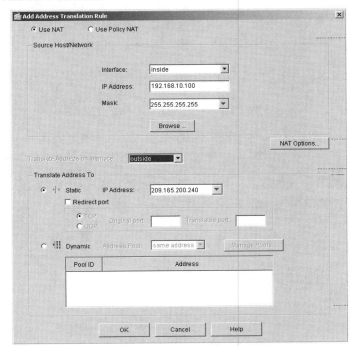

To configure DNS Doctoring and the maximum connection limits, discussed in Chapter 5, click **NAT Options** in the Add Address Translation Rule window to open the Advanced NAT Options window, shown in Figure 19-9. In this case, the administrator has restricted the maximum TCP-based connections to not exceed 500 for the static entry created in the previous step. The maximum embryonic connection limit is 200, and Cisco ASA is being set up to randomize the sequence numbers in the TCP packets.

Figure 19-9 *Setting the TCP-Based and Embryonic Connection Limits*

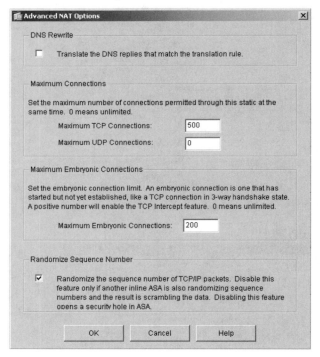

ASDM also supports NAT exemption policies to bypass address translation. You configure these policies under **Configuration > Features > NAT > Translation Exemption Rules**, as shown in Figure 19-10. This process is important if packets are traversing over a site-to-site VPN tunnel and do not need to be translated. In Figure 19-10, if packets are sourced from 192.168.10.0/24 and destined for 192.168.30.0/24, the security Cisco ASA will not translate them.

NOTE   For NAT order of operation, consult Chapter 5.

Figure 19-10 *Setting Translation Exemption Rules*

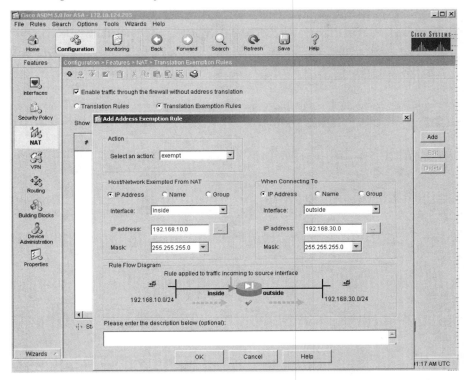

Example 19-3 shows the relevant configuration generated by ASDM for address translation.

Example 19-3 *Address Translation Configuration Generated by ASDM*

```
access-list inside_nat0_outbound line 1 extended permit ip 192.168.10.0
   255.255.255.0 192.168.30.0 255.255.255.0
nat (inside) 0 access-list inside_nat0_outbound
static (inside,outside) 209.165.200.240 192.168.10.100 netmask 255.255.255.255 tcp
   500 200 udp 0
no nat-control
nat (inside) 10 192.168.10.0 255.255.255.0   tcp 0 0 udp 0
global (outside) 10 209.165.200.230-209.165.200.235
global (outside) 10 209.165.200.236
```

Routing Protocols

As introduced in Chapter 6, "IP Routing", the security Cisco ASA supports RIP and OSPF. The following sections cover routing protocol configuration using ASDM.

RIP

To set up the RIP routing protocol, navigate to **Configuration > Features > Routing > Routing > RIP**. In Figure 19-11, SecureMe wants to configure the inside interface of Cisco ASA for RIP Version 2 with MD5 authentication. The authentication key is cisco123 and the key ID is 123. Cisco ASA will only inject a default route to the RIP-enabled devices toward the inside interface.

Figure 19-11 *Setting Up RIP as the Routing Protocol*

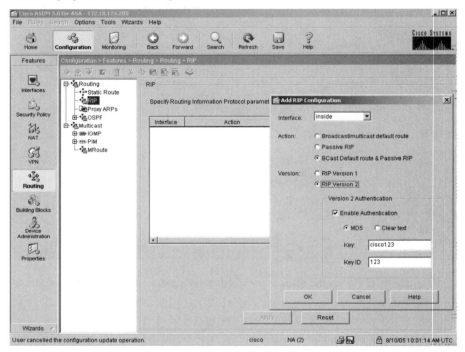

Example 19-4 shows the RIP configuration generated by ASDM.

Example 19-4 *RIP Configuration Generated by ASDM*

```
rip inside default version 2  authentication MD5 cisco123 123
rip inside passive version 2  authentication MD5 cisco123 123
```

OSPF

SecureMe is now planning to deploy OSPF in its inside network for dynamic routing. To set up OSPF, navigate to **Configuration > Features > Routing > Routing > OSPF > Setup** and click the **Process Instances** tab. You can enable OSPF globally and specify the OSPF process ID. Before you can set up OSPF, you need to disable RIP on the security

Cisco ASA, because you cannot enable both routing protocols simultaneously. After you set up the process ID, click the **Area/Networks** tab to specify the OSPF area ID, as shown in Figure 19-12, in which the OSPF Process is set to 100 and the OSPF Area ID is 0. Because SecureMe wants to run OSPF on the inside interface, which has an IP address of 209.165.202.130, SecureMe's administrator has specified the IP address with a host mask of 255.255.255.255 in Figure 19-12.

Figure 19-12 *Setting Up OSPF as the Routing Protocol*

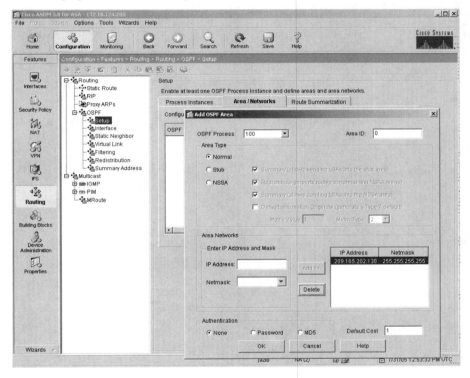

Example 19-5 shows the basic OSPF configuration that is generated by ASDM.

Example 19-5 *OSPF Configuration Generated by ASDM*

```
router ospf 100
log-adj-changes
area 0
network 209.165.202.130 255.255.255.255 area 0
```

NOTE   You can configure either RIP or OSPF as the routing protocol on Cisco ASA.

Multicast

As discussed in Chapter 6, Cisco ASA supports multicast routing and uses PIM Sparse mode for dynamic routing. You can enable multicast routing by navigating to **Configuration > Features > Routing > Multicast** and clicking **Enable Multicast Routing**, as shown in Figure 19-13.

Figure 19-13 *Enabling Multicast Routing*

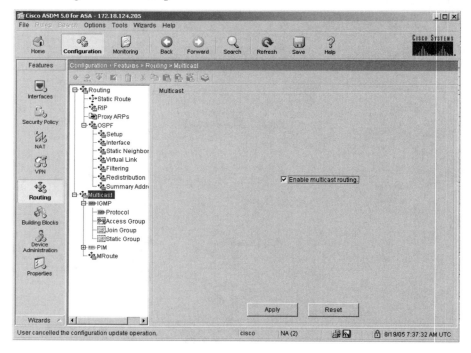

As the administrator, you can set up PIM Sparse mode by specifying a Rendezvous Point under **Configuration > Features > Routing > Multicast > PIM > Rendezvous Points**, as shown in Figure 19-14.

In Figure 19-14, SecureMe is using a Cisco IOS router at 192.168.10.2 as the Rendezvous Point and ASDM is being set up to use this address for all the multicast addresses. Example 19-6 shows the multicast configuration generated by ASDM.

Example 19-6 *Multicast Configuration Generated by ASDM*

```
multicast routing
pim old-register-checksum
pim rp-address 192.168.10.2 bidir
```

Figure 19-14 *Specifying a Rendezvous Point*

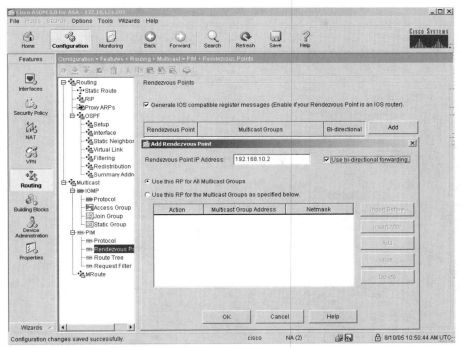

AAA

Cisco ASA can use an external authentication server such as RADIUS or TACACS to offload the authentication process. To set up an external authentication server for SecureMe, for example, follow these three simple steps:

Step 1   Select an authentication protocol.

SecureMe wants to use an external RADIUS server for the Telnet and SSH connections to the security Cisco ASA. Navigate to **Configuration > Features > Properties > AAA Setup > AAA Server Groups** and click **Add** to specify the protocol used on Cisco ASA, as shown in Figure 19-15. The server group name is **Rad** and the selected protocol is **RADIUS**.

Step 2   Define an authentication server.

To specify an authentication server, navigate to **Configuration > Features > Properties > AAA Setup > AAA Servers** and click **Add** to open the Add AAA Server window, shown in Figure 19-16. Select the server group name that is defined in the previous step. Because the AAA server resides toward the inside interface, select the **inside** interface from the drop-down menu. The IP address of the RADIUS server is 192.168.10.105 while the shared secret key between the server and the security Cisco ASA is cisco123 (which is displayed as asterisks).

Figure 19-15 *Specifying an Authentication Protocol*

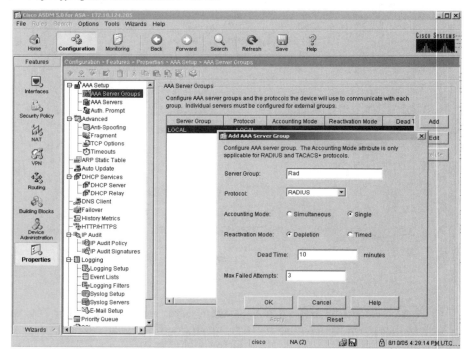

Step 3 Map the configured authentication server.

Navigate to **Configuration > Features > Device Administration > Administration > AAA Access > Authentication** to map the configured RADIUS server to the appropriate login processes. As shown in Figure 19-17, select the server group **Rad** under Enable, SSH, and Telnet connections. In case the RADIUS server is not available, the security Cisco ASA is being set up to use the local user database for authentication. Click **Apply** to send the configuration commands to the security Cisco ASA.

Figure 19-16 *Defining an Authentication Server*

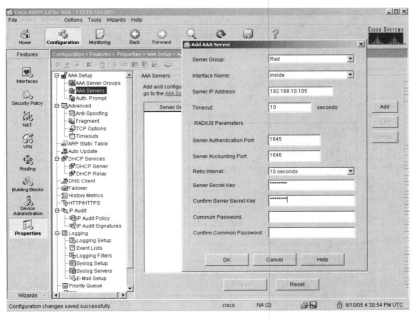

Figure 19-17 *Mapping the Authentication Server*

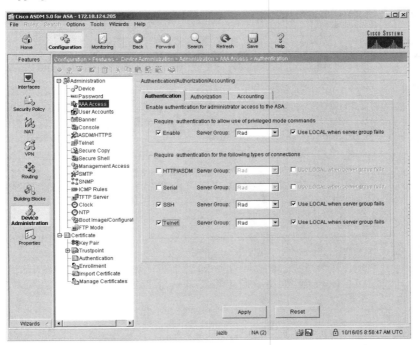

Example 19-7 shows the complete AAA configuration generated by ASDM.

Example 19-7 *AAA Configuration Generated by ASDM*

```
aaa-server Rad protocol radius
aaa-server Rad host 192.168.10.105
 key cisco123
aaa authentication enable console Rad LOCAL
aaa authentication ssh console Rad LOCAL
aaa authentication telnet console Rad LOCAL
```

Application Inspection

Application inspection can look at the application protocol content of a packet to ensure that it is allowed to pass through the security Cisco ASA. Application inspection is a three-step configuration process:

Step 1   Set up the Application Inspection Map.

You set up application inspection under **Configuration > Features > Building Blocks > Inspect Maps**.

SecureMe is looking to enable inspection for the HTTP data packets at its Chicago location. SecureMe would like to do the following:

— Drop connections if they are not RFC 2616 compliant. RFC 2616 defines the HTTP 1.1 protocol specification.

— Allow connections after verifying the content-type field.

— Reset connections if the MAX URI exceeds 250 bytes.

— Drop connections for P2P applications such as Kazaa and Gnutella.

The RFC compliance and content-type verification are checked under the General tab, as shown in Figure 19-18, in which an HTTP map called web-traffic is set up. Select **Drop Connection** as the action under RFC Compliance. Because SecureMe is interested in looking at the logs whenever a noncompliant packet tries to traverse through Cisco ASA, also check the **Generate Syslog** option. To enable content-type verification, check **Verify Content-Type Field Belongs to the Supported Internal Content-Type List** and specify **Allow Connection** as the action and check **Generate Syslog** to log this event.

Figure 19-19 shows how to specify the maximum URL length when an HTTP packet traverses through the security Cisco ASA. It is set up under the **Entity Length** tab in the Add HTTP Map window. Check **Inspect URI Length** and specify the maximum length of **250** bytes.

Figure 19-18 *RFC Compliance and Content-Type Verification*

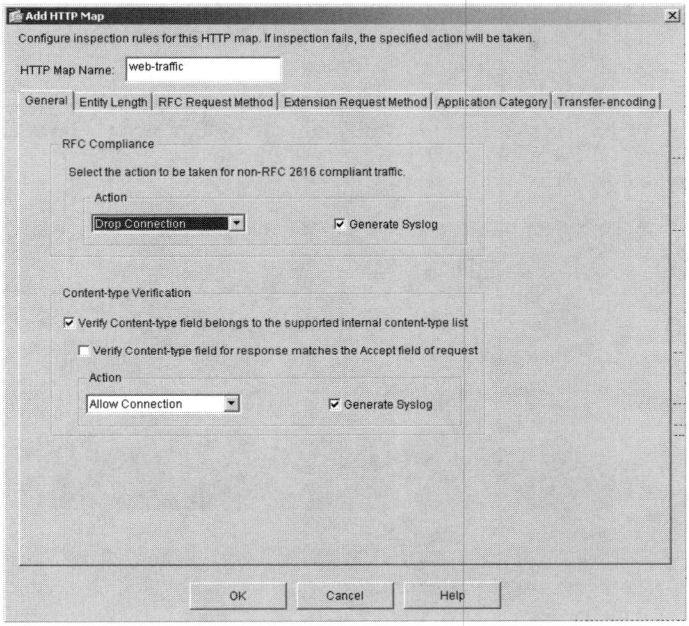

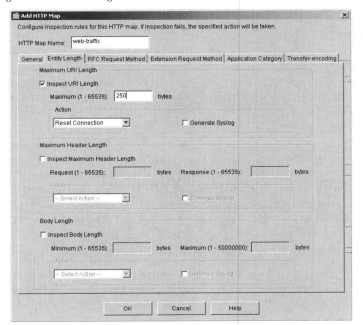

Figure 19-19 *Setting Maximum URI Length*

Click the **Application Category** tab to set up inspection for specific application types that are included in an HTTP request. Choose **P2P** under **Available Categories** and select **Drop Connection** as the applied action. Enable **Generate Syslog** to log an entry if Cisco ASA drops the P2P HTTP packets. Click **Add** to move the entry with the selected action to the specified category table. Figure 19-20 illustrates how to set it up.

Figure 19-20 *Application Inspection*

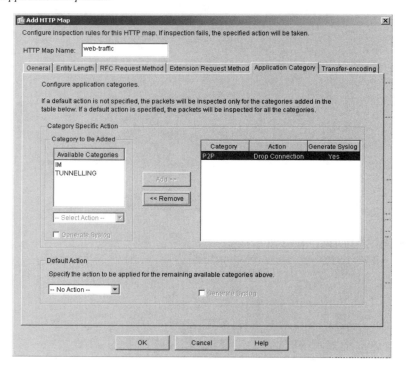

Step 2 Define a policy map.

After setting up the application map, the next step is to map it to a service policy so that Cisco ASA can start inspecting the traffic traversing through it. Create a new service policy map by navigating to **Configuration > Features > Security Policy > Service Policy Rules** and clicking **Add**. The application inspection can either be a part of the global policy or a separate interface policy. In Figure 19-21, an interface policy is being created called **inside-policy** that will be applied to the inside interface.

The next configuration window prompts you to choose how to classify the traffic when it passes through Cisco ASA. Because SecureMe is interested in inspecting the web traffic, choose as the traffic match criteria **TCP or UDP Destination Port**, as shown in Figure 19-22. The next window (not shown) prompts you to specify at which Layer 4 port number to inspect the traffic. SecureMe uses port 80 for all of its web traffic, and consequently the selected TCP destination port is 80.

Figure 19-21 *Adding a New Service Policy*

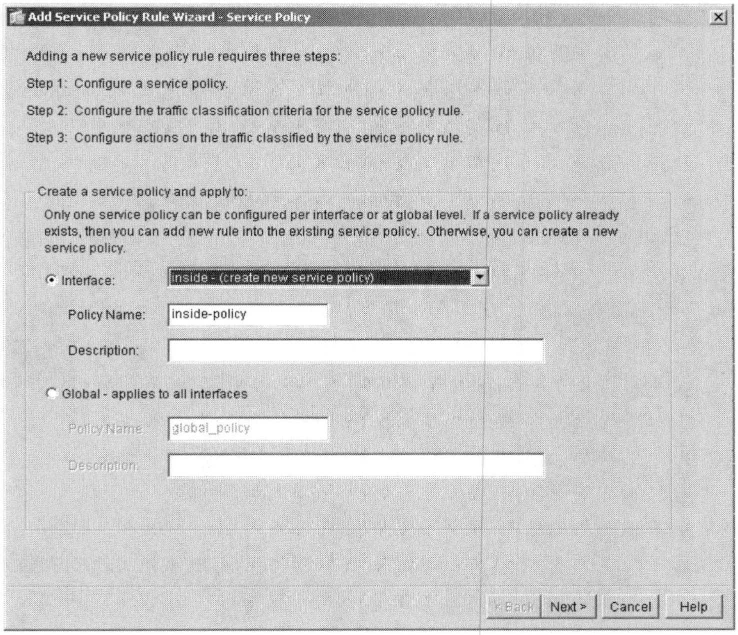

Step 3   Link the inspection map to the service policy.

Click **Configure** and select the inspection map called web-traffic from the list, as shown in Figure 19-23. Click **OK** and then **Finish** to complete the setup of the service policy.

Example 19-8 shows the complete configuration of an HTTP map and the service policy.

Example 19-8 *HTTP Map Configuration Generated by ASDM*

```
http-map web-traffic
  strict-http action drop log
  content-type-verification  action allow log
  max-uri-length 250 action reset
  port-misuse p2p action drop log
class-map inside-class
  match port tcp eq 80
policy-map inside-policy
  class inside-class
    inspect http web-traffic
service-policy inside-policy interface inside
```

Figure 19-22 *Classifying Traffic*

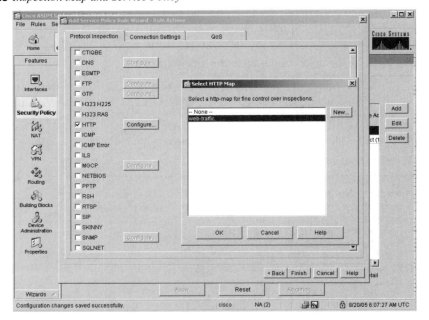

Figure 19-23 *Inspection Map and Service Policy*

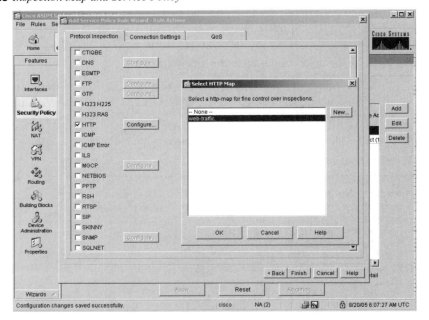

Security Contexts

ASDM allows you to manage new and existing security contexts, if the security Cisco ASA is already running in the multicontext mode. Consult Chapter 9, "Security Contexts," on how to set up an Cisco ASA for multiple security contexts.

When an Cisco ASA is converted from single to multiple mode, the security Cisco ASA saves the default configuration under the admin context. To create a new context, navigate to **Configuration > Features > Security Contexts** under the System context and click **Add**. ASDM prompts you to specify the name of the new context and the associated interfaces, as shown in Figure 19-24. The name of the security context is Cubs, and GigabitEthernet0/1 and GigabitEthernet0/2 are the two interfaces allocated to this context. The configuration of this context is saved in the local Flash (disk0:) as Cubs.

Figure 19-24 *Creating a New Security Context*

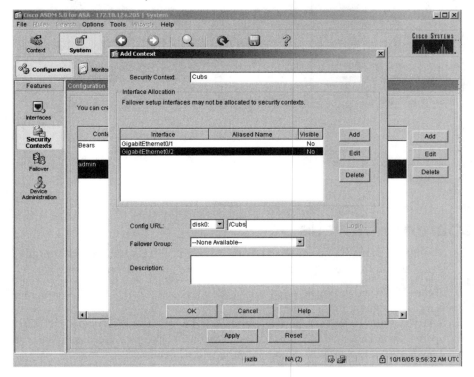

All other features in a security context are set up the same as discussed earlier in this chapter. To switch from one security context to another, select the desired security context from the Context drop-down menu, as shown in Figure 19-25.

Figure 19-25 *Selecting the Desired Security Context*

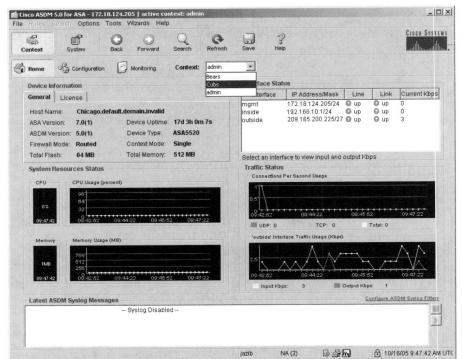

Transparent Firewalls

Similar to security contexts, Cisco ASA can be enabled for transparent firewalls from the CLI. Consult Chapter 10, "Transparent Firewalls," for configuration steps.

Figure 19-26 shows how to set up an EtherType ACL on ASDM if the security Cisco ASA is already running in transparent firewall mode. Navigate to **Configuration > Features > Security Policy > Ethertype Rules** and click **Add**. Figure 19-26 shows an ACE being set up to allow all inbound IPX traffic to enter the inside interface. Because there is an implicit deny at the end of an ACL, all other traffic will be denied.

Figure 19-26 *Setting Up an EtherType ACL*

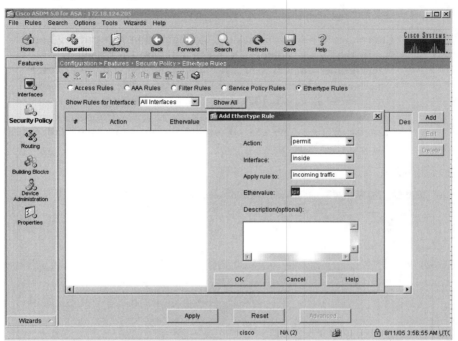

Failover

The failover feature on Cisco ASA ensures that the secondary Cisco ASA takes over the connections if the primary device fails to respond. The security Cisco ASA also supports Active/Active failover, in which both Cisco ASA are active and standby at the same time.

For this example, SecureMe is trying to set up two security Cisco ASA in failover mode. There are two security contexts configured: Cubs and Bears. The requirements for the Cisco ASA devices are as follows:

- The primary Cisco ASA will act as an active unit for the Cubs context while the secondary Cisco ASA will act as an active unit for the Bears context. These Cisco ASA will act as a backup for the other context.
- Use GigabitEthernet0/3 for both LAN failover and stateful failover updates.

To achieve the preceding listed requirements, use the following steps:

Step 1 Enable failover.

To configure failover, navigate to **Configuration > Features > Failover** under the System context, as shown in Figure 19-27. Select GigabitEthernet0/3 as the **LAN Failover** and the **Stateful Failover** interface. The interface is labeled **FOCtrlIntf**. The primary failover interface IP address is 10.10.10.1, while the standby address is 10.10.10.2. The shared key is set to cisco123 (which appears in asterisks). Once done, check **Enable Failover** to turn on the failover on the security Cisco ASA.

Figure 19-27 *Enabling Failover*

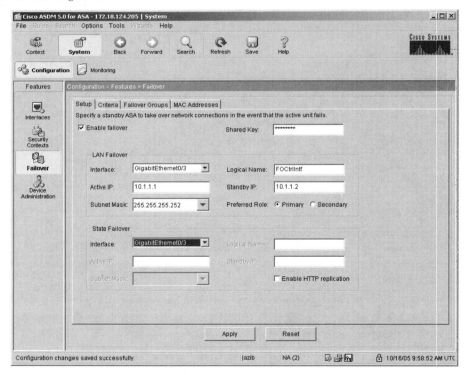

Step 2 Define failover groups.

You can define failover groups by clicking the **Failover Groups** tab and then clicking **Add**. A security Cisco ASA is being configured for Failover Group 1 in the Primary preferred role, as shown in Figure 19-28. Because stateful failover is enabled, the security Cisco ASA will replicate the stateful connections to the standby firewall. Additionally, this security Cisco ASA is set up to preempt the state if it is acting as a primary device for Failover Group 1.

Figure 19-28 *Setting Failover Groups*

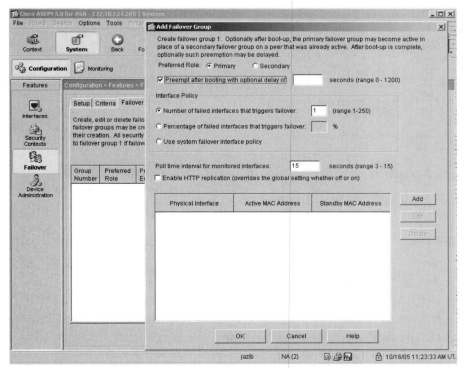

Similarly, add another failover group to be in the Secondary role with the preempt option enabled.

Step 3 Map failover groups to security contexts.

Set up the Active/Active failover to map the failover group to the appropriate security contexts. To do so, navigate to **Configuration > Features > Security Contexts** and select the security context that needs to be enabled for failover. In Figure 19-29, the Cubs context is modified to make it a member of Failover Group 1, while the Bears context is a part of Failover Group 2.

Figure 19-29 *Mapping of Failover Group to Security Context*

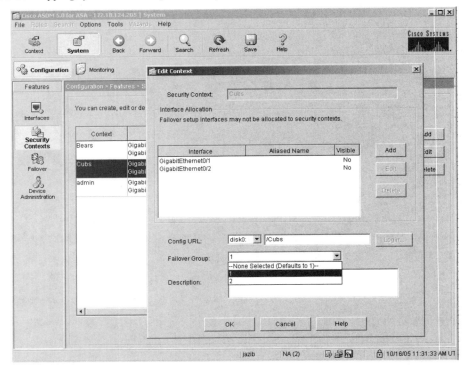

Example 19-9 shows the complete configuration of failover as generated by ASDM.

Example 19-9 *Failover Configuration Generated by ASDM*

```
failover group 1
  primary
  polltime interface 15
  interface-policy 1
failover group 2
  secondary
  polltime interface 15
  interface-policy 1
failover
context Cubs
  join-failover-group 1
context Bears
  join-failover-group 2
failover active
```

If you navigate to **Monitoring > Features > Failover > System** under the System context, ASDM displays the output of **show failover** in the GUI. You can choose to make an Cisco ASA active or standby, reset failover, and reload the standby Cisco ASA, as shown in Figure 19-30.

Figure 19-30 *Monitoring Failover*

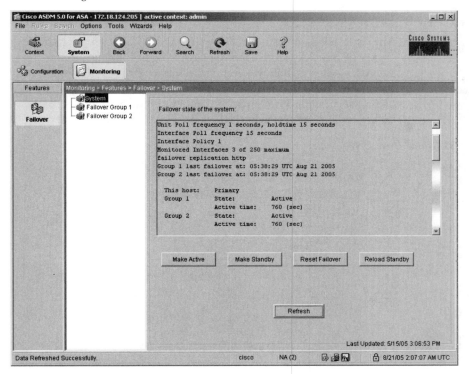

QoS

As discussed in Chapter 12, "Quality of Service," QoS is used to either prioritize or rate-limit certain traffic based on the match criteria. You can set up QoS using ASDM under **Configuration > Features > Security Policy > Service Policy Rules**.

SecureMe is interested in using the rate-limiting feature as well as the prioritization features of the security Cisco ASA by using ASDM. SecureMe's requirements to implement QoS are as follows:

- Do not allow Internet e-mail users to hog the bandwidth when they download e-mail using SMTP. They should be restricted to a maximum of 560 kbps. The e-mail server is located on the inside interface, while the Internet e-mail users are located on the outside interface.

- The VoIP calls should get prioritized over other traffic.

In ASDM, QoS is set up using the following three steps:

Step 1 Configure a service policy.

Similar to setting up an inspection policy, QoS also uses service policies. A new QoS policy can be added by navigating to **Configuration > Features > Service Policy**, selecting the **Service Policy Rules** radio button and clicking Add. The next screen allows you to specify a policy name, as shown in Figure 19-31. A service policy of **outside-policy** is being configured on the outside interface. Click **Next** to move to the next step.

Figure 19-31 *Setting Up a Service Policy*

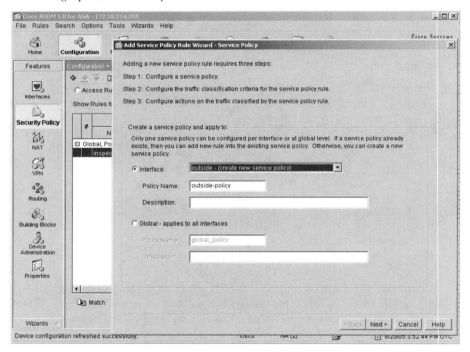

Step 2 Classify interesting traffic.

The next step guides you to identify the interesting traffic that needs to be rate-limited or prioritized. There are eight ways to classify packets, as discussed in Chapter 12. For e-mail users who access an e-mail server located at 209.16.200.231 on TCP port 25, you can configure a source and destination based ACL. When you select this option, ASDM allows you to define the source and destination IP addresses, as shown in Figure 19-32. If the traffic is sourced from 209.165.200.231 on port 25 destined to any address, then treat that traffic as interesting. Click **Next** to configure the last step.

Figure 19-32 *Classifying Mail Traffic*

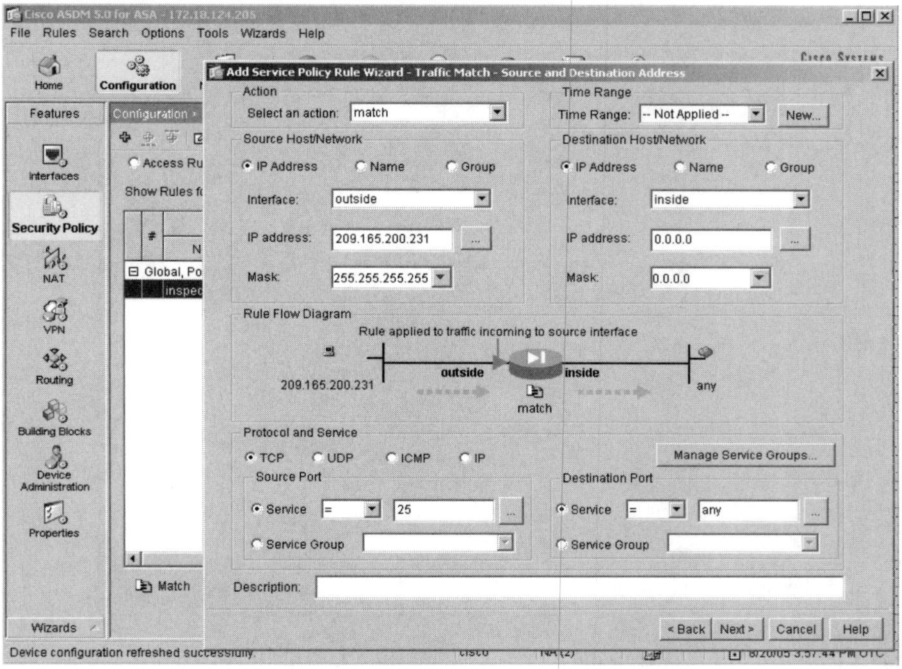

Note	ASDM does not allow setting up source and destination ACLs if the default service group is used.

Step 3   Set up QoS action.

Click the **QoS** tab on the next configuration screen to specify the traffic prioritization or rate-limiting. Because the mail traffic needs to be restricted to a committed rate of 560,000 bps with a burst size of 10,000 bytes, check the **Police Output** option and select the rates shown in Figure 19-33.

Note	The QoS policies are applied only on the egress interface.

Step 4   Set up additional policies (optional).

You can set up additional QoS policies to prioritize the voice traffic based on the DSCP values. Create a new policy by clicking **Add** under **Service Policy Rules** and using the same interface service policy. Specify a new traffic class name and check **IP DiffServ CodePoints (DSCP)**, as shown in Figure 19-34, in which a traffic class called voip is being configured.

Figure 19-33 *Applying a QoS Policy*

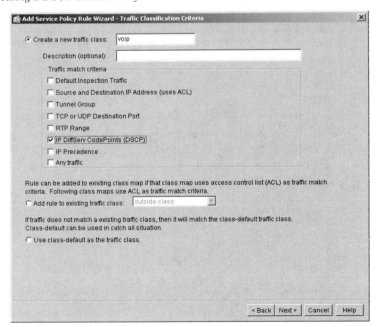

Figure 19-34 *Creating a DSCP-Based Policy*

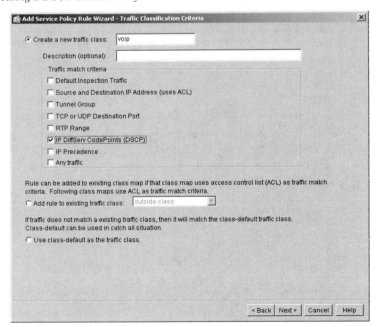

On the next configuration window, specify the DSCP values that are
going to be used for traffic classification. In Figure 19-35, DSCP values
of af31 and ef are selected because they are used by the voice traffic.
Click **Next** to set up the QoS policies.

Figure 19-35 *Selecting the DSCP Values*

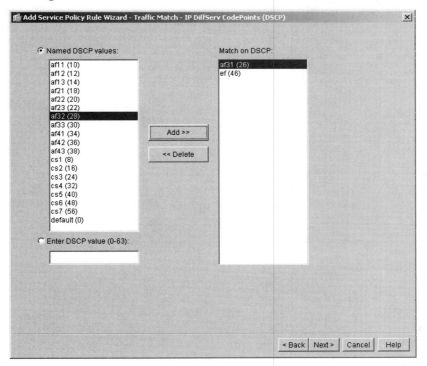

Click the **QoS** tab and check **Enable Priority for This Flow** as the
action for the voice traffic, as shown in Figure 19-36. Once you apply the
policy, the security Cisco ASA warns you that the priority queue limit
must be set up on the interface before traffic can be prioritized.

The priority queue can be set up under **Configuration > Features >
Properties > Priority Queue**. In Figure 19-37, a priority queue is being
set up on the outside interface with a queue limit of 200 packets and a
transmit ring buffer of 200 packets.

Figure 19-36 *Setting Up QoS Action as Priority*

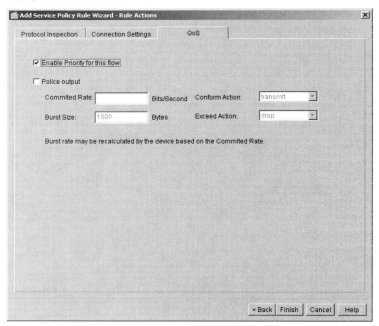

Figure 19-37 *Setting Up Interface Priority Queue*

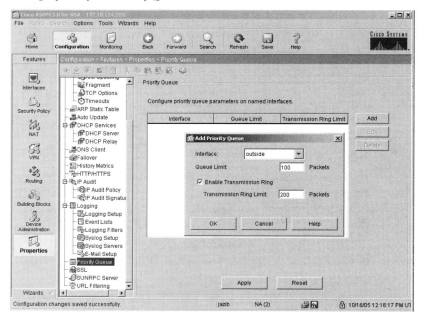

Example 19-10 shows the relevant configuration of QoS policies generated by ASDM.

Example 19-10 *QoS Configuration Generated by ASDM*

```
access-list outside_mpc_in line 1 extended permit tcp host 209.165.200.231 eq 25 any
class-map outside-class
  match access-list outside_mpc_in
class-map voip
  match dscp 26 46
policy-map outside-policy
  class outside-class
    police 560000 10000 conform-action transmit exceed-action drop
  class voip
    priority
service-policy outside-policy interface outside
priority-queue outside
  tx-ring-limit 200
  queue-limit 100
```

Summary

This chapter briefly talked about the firewall features that are offered by the Cisco ASA devices and how to configure them using the ASDM GUI. Features such as ACLs, address translation, routing protocols, authentication, security contexts, transparent firewalls, failover, and QoS were discussed with accompanying configuration examples.

This chapter covers the following topics:

- Accessing the IPS Device Management Console from ASDM
- Basic configuration
- Advanced configuration and monitoring

CHAPTER 20

IPS Management Using ASDM

This chapter covers the configuration, monitoring, and management of the Adaptive Inspection and Prevention Security Services Module (AIP-SSM) using ASDM. It provides real-life examples of how a network security administrator performs basic and advanced configuration and administration tasks.

Accessing the IPS Device Management Console from ASDM

ASDM is loaded from Cisco ASA and is used to launch the IPS Device Management Console to configure, monitor, and manage the AIP-SSM.

To access the AIP-SSM IPS Device Management Console, first launch ASDM and connect to Cisco ASA from your local workstation. When you first install the AIP-SSM into the Cisco ASA appliance, you must configure the initial settings using the **setup** command via the CLI.

NOTE	The initialization and initial setup of the AIP-SSM is covered in Chapter 14, "Configuring and Troubleshooting Cisco IPS Software via CLI."

You can use the **setup** command to configure basic settings such as the following:

- The AIP-SSM host name
- IP addressing
- AIP-SSM web server port
- Access control lists
- Time settings

After you run the **setup** command and set up these parameters, you can connect to the AIP-SSM via ASDM.

To configure the AIP-SSM, launch ASDM and click the **IPS** icon under the Configuration section, as illustrated in Figure 20-1.

Figure 20-1 *Accessing IPS Configuration Window*

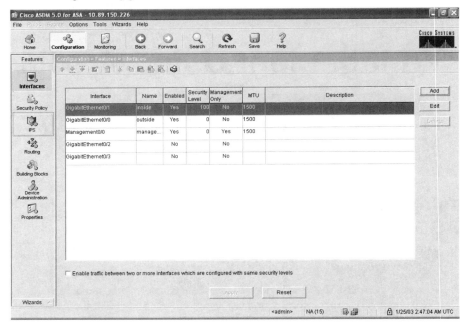

After you click the IPS icon, ASDM warns you that it will make a connection to the AIP-SSM. You can choose to connect to it via the management IP address or a different address. As shown in Figure 20-2, ASDM is making a connection to 10.89.149.226, which is the management IP address of the AIP-SSM.

Figure 20-2 *ASDM Connecting to the AIP-SSM*

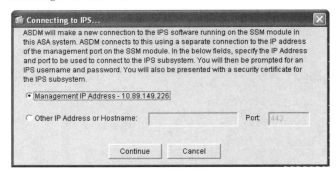

You are prompted to log in to the AIP-SSM. You can use the default user (cisco) to log in and access the configuration windows.

The following sections demonstrate how SecureMe's IPS administrator at the Los Angeles, California branch configures an AIP-SSM on a Cisco ASA 5520. Figure 20-3 shows a high-level overview of the network topology at the Los Angeles branch.

Figure 20-3 *SecureMe Los Angeles Branch*

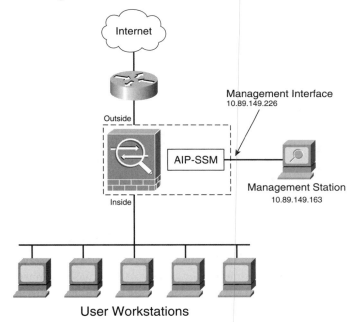

The AIP-SSM management interface is configured with the IP address 10.89.149.226. A management station (10.89.149.163) from which ASDM is launched is located in the same subnet.

Configuring Basic AIP-SSM Settings

This section demonstrates how SecureMe's IPS administrator uses ASDM to configure basic settings on the AIP-SSM.

Licensing

When SecureMe's IPS administrator first launches ASDM, he discovers that the system does not have a valid license. To correct this problem, the administrator chooses **Cisco Connection Online** to obtain the license directly from Cisco.com, as shown in Figure 20-4.

Figure 20-4 *Licensing*

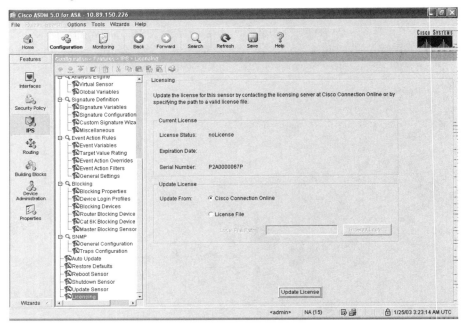

ASDM sends the serial number to Cisco over an HTTP connection to obtain the license key. The license key is displayed after it is retrieved.

Optionally, the IPS administrator can also upload the license information from a file stored on his local workstation.

Verifying Network Settings

The IPS administrator is informed that a new router is installed in the management subnet. The AIP-SSM gateway information needs to be updated with the router's IP address (10.89.149.254). Figure 20-5 shows how to add the new IP address under the ASDM network settings.

The administrator notices that Telnet access is enabled on the AIP-SSM. He proceeds and disables it, because SSH and ASDM access is only required by SecureMe's security policy. Under the network settings, you can modify any of the following options:

- Host name of the AIP-SSM.
- IP address of the management interface on the AIP-SSM (the default IP address is 10.1.9.201).
- Network mask.

- Default gateway address (the default is 10.1.9.1).

- The FTP timeout when an FTP client communicates with the AIP-SSM (default is 300 seconds).

- The AIP-SSM web server security level and port. It is strongly recommended that you enable TLS/SSL.

- Whether Telnet access is enabled or disabled. It is not enabled by default, because it is not a secure method.

Figure 20-5 *AIP-SSM Network Settings*

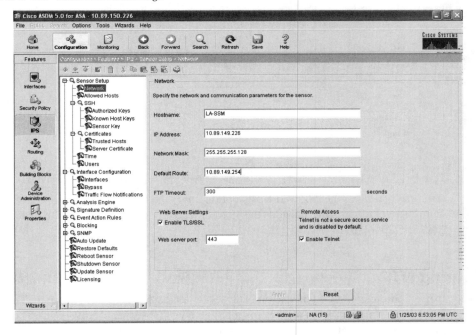

Adding Allowed Hosts

The IPS administrator wants to connect to the IPS from his home workstation when connecting using the Cisco VPN client. He connects to a cluster of Cisco ASA appliances in Chicago to gain access to the private networks. These appliances are configured to always assign his VPN client a static IP address (192.168.75.34). Consequently, he adds this IP address in the Allowed Hosts section on ASDM, as shown in Figure 20-6.

Figure 20-6 *Allowed Hosts Section*

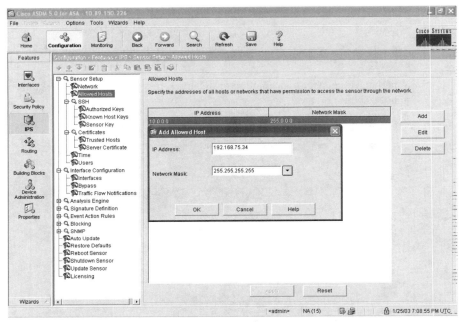

After navigating to the Allowed Hosts option under the Sensor Setup section, the IPS administrator clicks **Add** and adds the 192.168.75.34 IP address with a 32-bit subnet mask (255.255.255.255).

Configuring NTP

It is recommended that you use an NTP server as the AIP-SSM time source. The IPS administrator in Los Angeles installed a new NTP server (10.89.149.207) on the management network. He configures the NTP server parameters by choosing **Configuration > Features > IPS > Sensor Setup > Time**, as shown in Figure 20-7.

The IPS administrator adds the IP address of the NTP server (10.89.149.207). He also enters the NTP MD5 key (cisco123) and key ID (1) for NTP authentication. The NTP server uses the associated key when transferring data to the AIP-SSM.

Adding Users

Four different types of users can be configured in the AIP-SSM:

- Viewers
- Operators

- Administrators
- Service

Figure 20-7 *NTP Configuration*

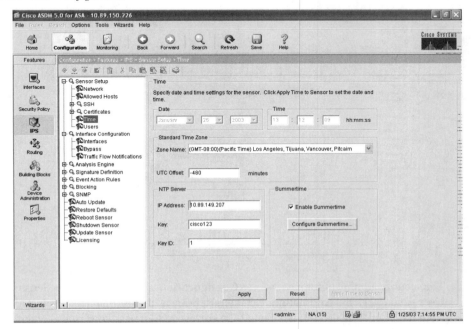

The definition of each account type is discussed in Chapter 14.

In the following scenario, the IPS administrator needs to create the service account to be able to enter into the AIP-SSM service mode.

NOTE

The service user cannot log in to ASDM. This user is only used to log in to the AIP-SSM service mode (bash shell) for administrative purposes. The service account should only be used for troubleshooting purposes with the assistance of the Cisco Technical Assistance Center (TAC).

The service account is added as illustrated in Figure 20-8.

Figure 20-8 *Adding Users*

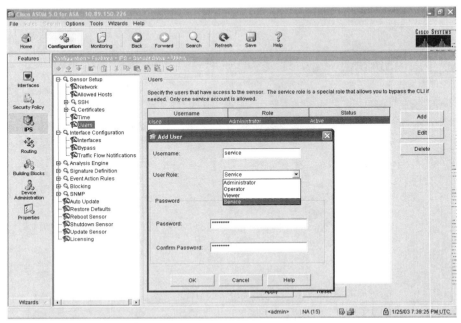

The security administrator navigates to **Configuration > Features > IPS > Sensor Setup > Users** and clicks the **Add** button. He enters **service** as the username and selects **Service** from the User Role drop-down menu. The corresponding password is also entered and confirmed, as shown in Figure 20-8.

Advanced IPS Configuration and Monitoring Using ASDM

This section provides examples on advanced IPS configuration tasks and monitoring using ASDM. The examples include the following:

- Disabling and enabling signatures (signature tuning to eliminate false positives and false negatives)
- Configuring blocking
- Creating custom signatures
- Creating event action filters
- Installing signature updates and service packs
- Configuring auto-update

Disabling and Enabling Signatures

The IPS administrator needs to view all the events generated by the AIP-SSM during the last hour. To view these events, he navigates to **Monitoring > Features > IPS > Events**, as shown in Figure 20-9.

Figure 20-9 *Monitoring IPS Events in ASDM*

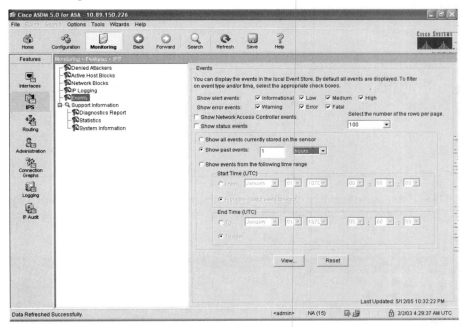

In the Events pane, the IPS administrator filters all alert and error events for the past one hour and accesses these events by clicking **View**.

NOTE   ASDM confines the number of events you can view to a maximum 500 rows per page. This is done to allow better manageability of the data when retrieving large numbers of events from the AIP-SSM.

Figure 20-10 shows the list of IPS events generated by the AIP-SSM during the last hour.

The IPS administrator is surprised by the large number of ICMP echo requests and echo reply events generated by signatures 2000 and 2004. Hundreds of these events are displayed, as shown in Figure 20-10. After more investigation, the IPS administrator notices that these events are false positives and unnecessary. He decides to disable signatures 2000 and 2004 to avoid the generation of all of these unnecessary events.

Figure 20-10 *Viewing IPS Events*

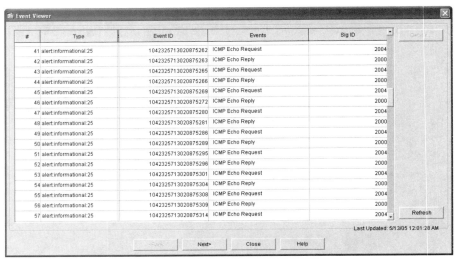

To disable the signatures, the IPS administrator navigates to **Configuration > Features > IPS > Signature Definition > Signature Configuration**, as illustrated in Figure 20-11.

Figure 20-11 *Configuring Signatures with ASDM*

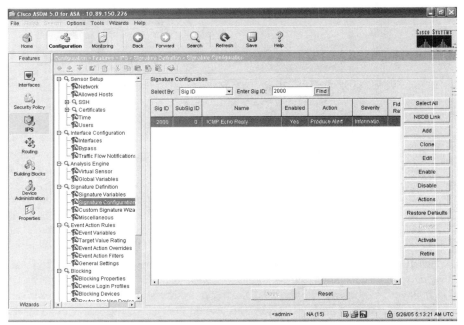

In the Signature Configuration pane, you can sort and view all signatures available on the AIP-SSM. You can sort and find signatures by any of the following fields:

- Attack type
- Protocol
- Service
- Operating system
- Action to be performed
- Engine
- Signature ID
- Signature name

In this case, the IPS administrator finds the signature by doing a search by signature ID (Sig ID). He first finds signature 2000 and clicks **Edit**. The dialog box shown in Figure 20-12 is displayed, allowing the IPS administrator to disable the signature. The administrator also follows this procedure to disable signature 2004.

Figure 20-12 *Disabling Signatures with ASDM*

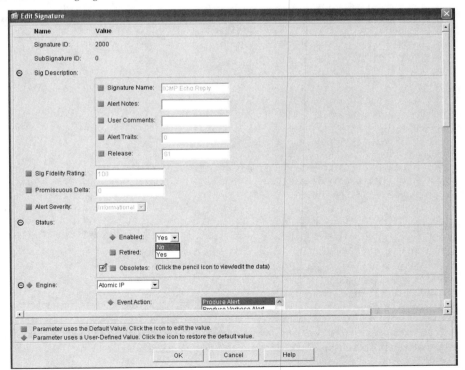

TIP	You can also enable or disable a signature by choosing **Configuration > Features > IPS > Signature Definition > Signature Configuration** and clicking the **Enable** or **Disable** button.

After disabling these signatures, the IPS administrator is able to pay more attention to events that reveal real threats, because the number of false positives is reduced. He notices that client 10.120.2.2 attempted to retrieve password files via a CGI script on server 10.120.3.34. The IPS administrator is able to see the detailed information about this event by clicking the Details button on the ASDM Event Viewer. The output shown in Example 20-1 describes an attempt to illegally access the /etc/shadow file 10.120.3.34.

Example 20-1 *Detailed Information About IPS Events*

```
evIdsAlert: eventId=1042325713020875362  vendor=Cisco  severity=high
  originator:
    hostId: LA-SSM
    appName: sensorApp
    appInstanceId: 339
  time: May 22, 2005 7:53:03 PM UTC  offset=-360  timeZone=GMT-06:00
  signature:  description=Unix Password File Access Attempt  id=3201  version=S2
    subsigId: 2
    sigDetails: /etc/shadow
  interfaceGroup:
  vlan: 0
  participants:
    attacker:
      addr: 10.120.2.2  locality=OUT
      port: 1070
    target:
      addr: 10.120.3.34  locality=OUT
      port: 80
  actions:
    ipLoggingActivated: true
    logAttackerPacketsActivated: true
  context:
    fromAttacker:
000000  67 65 74 20 2F 65 74 63  2F 73 68 61 64 6F 77 0D  get /etc/shadow.
  ipLogIds:
    ipLogId: 9
  riskRatingValue: 75
  interface: ge0_1
  protocol: tcp
```

The organization's security policy dictates that hosts that attempt to access password files on a system should be blocked (shunned), as discussed next.

Configuring Blocking

The IPS administrator decides to configure blocking (shunning) for all connections matching signature 3201, except for a server (10.33.33.31) that is critical to SecureMe's operations.

TIP   As a best practice, you must identify critical hosts and networks that should never be blocked. Sometimes, a trusted network device's normal behavior may appear to be a specific attack, and shunning such a device will cause disruption of legitimate services.

Figure 20-13 shows how the IPS administrator navigates to **Configuration > Features > IPS > Blocking > Blocking Properties** and clicks on **Add** to configure the AIP-SSM to never block the 10.33.33.31 server.

Figure 20-13 *Configuring Devices to Never Be Blocked*

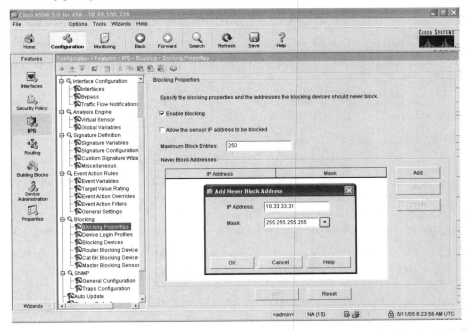

The IPS administrator also confirms that the Enable Blocking option is checked. Blocking is enabled by default. An error message is generated if blocking is disabled and other fields under **Configuration > Features > IPS > Blocking** have non-default values.

CAUTION   Always make sure that you add AIM-SSM's address under Never Block Addresses. Blocking the AIP-SSM will stop communication with the blocking device.

When using blocking, the AIP-SSM is configured to log in to Cisco ASA to deliver the respective block rules. The IPS administrator navigates to **Configuration > Features > IPS > Blocking > Device Login Profiles** and enters the Cisco ASA login profile containing the username, login password, and enable password information under a new policy named ASA, as shown in Figure 20-14.

Figure 20-14 *Device Login Profile*

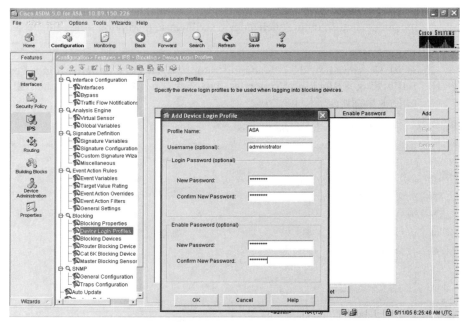

After configuring the new device login profile, the IPS administrator navigates to **Configuration > Features > IPS > Blocking > Blocking Devices** and adds the Cisco ASA information, as illustrated in Figure 20-15.

The AIP-SSM will connect to the Cisco ASA appliance using the SSH protocol (with the 3DES encryption algorithm) when delivering the block rules.

CAUTION   A single IPS device (sensor) can control blocking (shunning) in multiple devices. However, you cannot configure two IPS sensors or AIP-SSM to control blocking on the same device. It is suggested to use a master blocking sensor to avoid this problem. A master blocking sensor controls the blocking configuration in all the network devices specified (that is, Cisco routers, Cisco ASA, Cisco PIX, and Cisco switches). In this example, only the LA-SSM will control blocking on Cisco ASA. If more than one IPS device is configured to perform blocking, you must enter the master blocking sensor under **Configuration > Features > IPS > Blocking > Master Blocking Sensor**.

Figure 20-15 *Adding Cisco ASA as a Blocking Device*

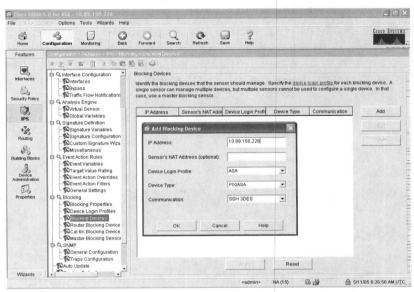

In Figure 20-16, the signature 3201 event action is configured to produce verbose alerts and to block the connection that triggered such alarm.

Figure 20-16 *Enabling Signature Event Actions*

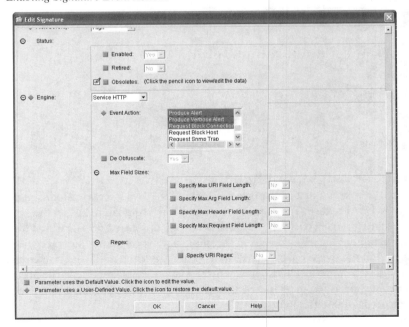

Creating Custom Signatures

ASDM enables you to create custom signatures using a step-by-step wizard. The IPS administrator uses this wizard to create a custom signature for a new security threat on a third-party web application that SecureMe users access on a daily basis. By using a long Arg (argument value) on the HTTP Uniform Resource Identifier (URI), the attacker can disrupt internal services on this third-party web application. URI Arg values should not be longer than 15 characters.

The IPS administrator navigates to **Configuration > Features > IPS > Signature Definition > Custom Signature Wizard** to access the Customer Signature Wizard, as illustrated in Figure 20-17.

Figure 20-17 *Accessing the Custom Signature Wizard*

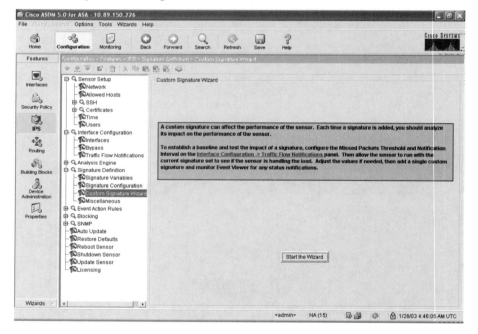

CAUTION	Note the warning that is displayed in Figure 20-17. Adding a custom signature can affect sensor performance. To monitor the effect the new signature has on the sensor, click **Configuration > Features > IPS > Interface Configuration > Traffic Flow Notifications** and configure the Missed Packet Threshold and Notification Interval options. You can configure the missed packet threshold within a specific notification interval and also configure the interface idle delay before a status event is reported. The notification interval specifies how often the AIP-SSM checks for the missed packets percentage. The values depend on your environment.

The IPS administrator launches the wizard and completes the following steps to create a signature that will trigger an alarm when URI arguments are longer than 15 characters:

Step 1   The wizard asks the administrator to select a specific signature engine from the Select Engine list. In this case, the administrator does not know what engine to select. He selects **No**, as shown in Figure 20-18, and then clicks **Next**.

Figure 20-18   *Selecting a Specific Signature Engine*

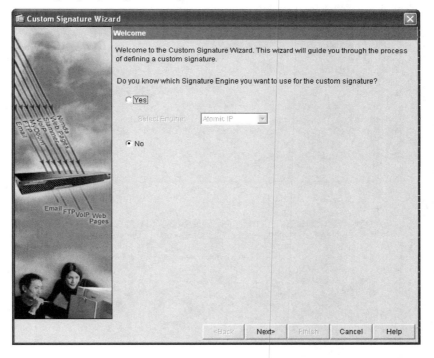

Step 2   The wizard allows the administrator to select the protocol that matches the type of traffic the signature should inspect. He selects **TCP** and then clicks **Next**, as illustrated in Figure 20-19.

Step 3   In the TCP Traffic Type window, the IPS administrator selects **Single TCP Connection**, as shown in Figure 20-20, and then clicks **Next**, because he is creating a signature to detect an attack in a single TCP connection.

Figure 20-19 *Selecting the Respective Protocol*

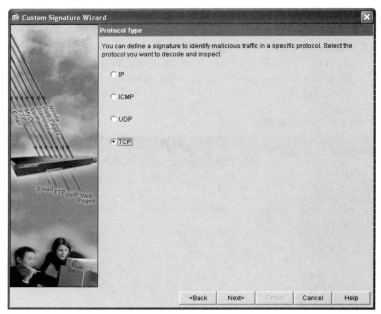

Figure 20-20 *Selecting the TCP Traffic Type*

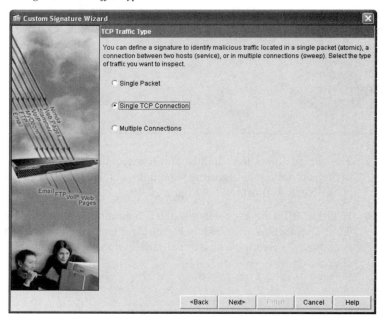

Step 4   The administrator selects **HTTP** as the service type, as shown in
Figure 20-21.

Figure 20-21 *Selecting the TCP Service Type*

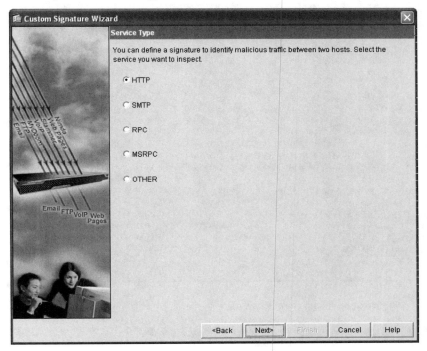

Step 5   The IPS administrator enters the required information to specify the
attributes that uniquely identify the custom signature, as shown in
Figure 20-22, and then clicks **Next**. The signature ID configured is 60099,
the subsignature ID is 0, and the signature name is My HTTP Custom
Signature. Alert notes and user comments are also entered to provide
more information.

Note	Custom signature IDs can be in the range of 60000 to 65000. Signature ID 60099 is used in this example.

Step 6   The maximum URI Arg field length field is configured to 15 in the
Engine Specific Parameters window. The event action is configured to
produce verbose alerts and block the offending connection. This is
illustrated in Figure 20-23.

Figure 20-22 *Specifying Signature ID and Attributes*

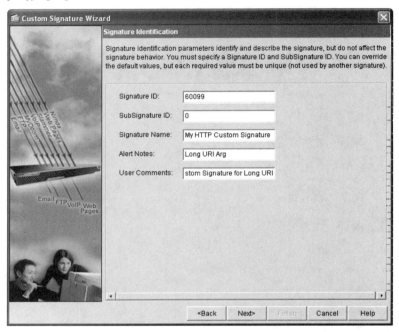

Figure 20-23 *Setting Engine Specific Parameters*

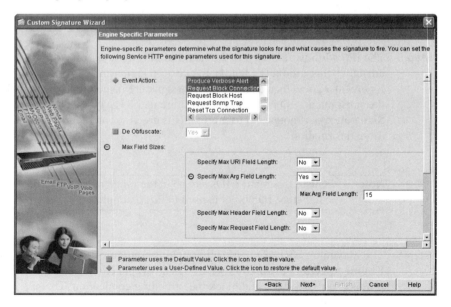

Step 7   The Signature Fidelity Rating is configured to its default value (75), as shown in Figure 20-24. This value indicates your confidence in the signature in a range from 0 to 100 (100 being the most confident). The alert severity to be reported by the AIP-SSM is configured to High for this custom signature.

Figure 20-24 *Specifying Signature Fidelity Rating and Severity*

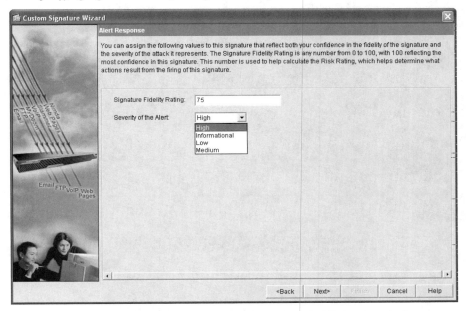

Step 8   The IPS administrator clicks **Finish** in the Alert Behavior window to save the new signature. A dialog box appears to confirm the creation of the custom signature, as illustrated in Figure 20-25.

NOTE   You can change the default alert behavior of a custom signature by clicking **Advanced** in the Alert Behavior window. For example, the administrator can control how often this signature produces an alert if it is triggered.

Creating Event Action Filters

The IPS administrator does not want to log any events for traffic sourced by any host in the 10.10.123.0/24 network. Therefore, he navigates to **Configuration > Features > IPS > Event Action Rules > Event Action Filters > Add** and adds a new filter, as illustrated in Figure 20-26.

Figure 20-25 *Confirming and Saving Custom Signature*

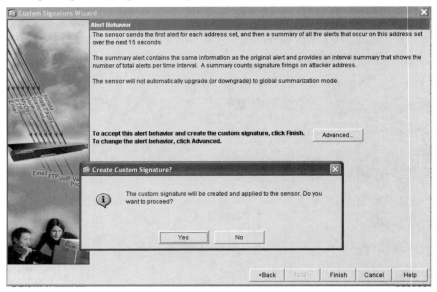

Figure 20-26 *Adding an Event Action Filter*

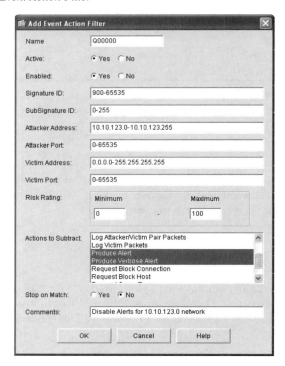

The 10.10.123.0/24 network is entered under the attacker's address, and the filter is configured to not log any events from any hosts in this network.

TIP   Event action filters are processed in the order in which they were entered. However, you can move filters up or down in the list to change the order in which they are processed.

Installing Signature Updates and Software Service Packs

This section shows how to install signature updates and IPS software service packs on the AIP-SSM using ASDM. In this scenario, the IPS administrator downloads a signature update from Cisco.com to his FTP server (10.89.149.55) and then navigates to **Configuration > Features > IPS > Update Sensor** to immediately apply the signature update to the AIP-SSM. This is illustrated in Figure 20-27.

Figure 20-27 *Installing a Signature Update Using ASDM*

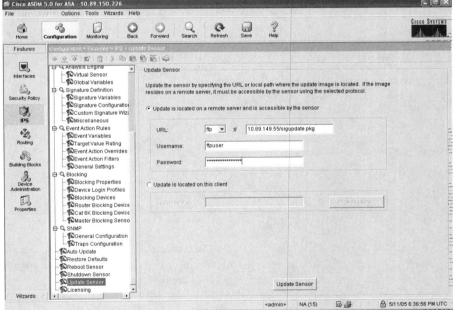

The AIP-SSM connects to the FTP server and retrieves the signature update (sigupdate.pkg) using the ftpuser user credentials.

Configuring Auto-Update

ASDM enables you to configure the AIP-SSM to automatically query an SCP or FTP server for signature updates at a given time interval. You set this up under **Configuration > Features > IPS > Auto Update**. In the example shown in Figure 20-28, the IPS administrator has configured the AIP-SSM to retrieve updates from the 10.89.149.55 FTP server every Monday, Wednesday, and Friday at 1:00 a.m.

Figure 20-28 *Configuring Auto-Update Using ASDM*

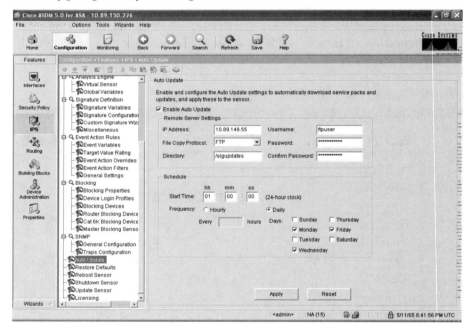

NOTE   You should always be careful when implementing automatic updates. A corrupted signature update or service pack can cause disruption of services in the AIP-SSM.

Summary

ASDM provides a user-friendly interface to configure Cisco ASA and the AIP-SSM. This chapter covered how ASDM can be used to configure, monitor, and manage the AIP-SSM IPS services. It started by introducing basic configuration tasks and advanced into more in-depth topics, providing real-life examples to assist your understanding.

This chapter covers the following topics:

- Site-to-site VPN setup using preshared keys
- Site-to-site VPN setup using PKI
- Cisco remote-access IPSec VPN setup
- WebVPN
- VPN monitoring

CHAPTER 21

VPN Management Using ASDM

This chapter guides you in setting up the different types of VPNs available in Cisco ASA. It provides an overview and step-by-step configuration examples using the ASDM GUI.

You can set up the VPN parameters by navigating to **Configuration > Features > VPN**, as shown in Figure 21-1.

Figure 21-1 *VPN Configuration Window*

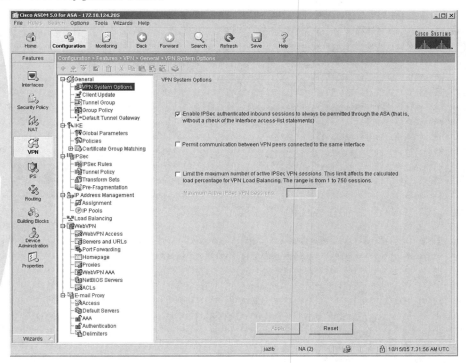

Site-to-Site VPN Setup Using Preshared Keys

To set up a site-to-site VPN tunnel, launch the VPN Wizard. The VPN Wizard guides you through an easy to follow set of configuration steps that results in a properly configured VPN tunnel.

Figure 21-2 illustrates a VPN topology between two sites, Chicago and London. The inside interface of Cisco ASA in Chicago is directly connected to the 192.168.10.0/24 subnet, while there is another inside network, 192.168.20.0/24, behind Router1. The public interface's IP address is 209.165.200.225/27, and the default route sends all traffic to the next-hop router toward the Internet. The ASDM client with an IP address of 172.18.124.100 is connected to the mgmt interface of the security Cisco ASA, which has an IP address of 172.18.124.205.

Cisco ASA in London is set up in a similar way with two inside networks, 192.168.30.0/24 and 192.168.40.0/24. The public interface's IP address is 209.165.201.1/27.

Figure 21-2 *Site-to-Site ASA Setup*

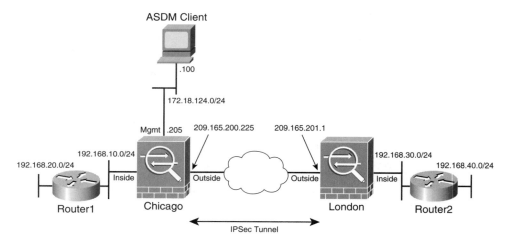

Use the following configuration steps to set up Cisco ASA in Chicago for a site-to-site tunnel using the preshared keys for IKE authentication:

Step 1   Launch the VPN Wizard by choosing **Wizards > VPN Wizard**, as shown in Figure 21-3.

You can also launch the VPN Wizard by navigating to **Configuration > Wizards > VPN**.

ASDM launches the VPN Wizard with the option to choose a tunnel type. Click the **Site-to-Site** radio button, as shown in Figure 21-4.

Figure 21-3 *Launching the VPN Wizard Through the Menu Bar*

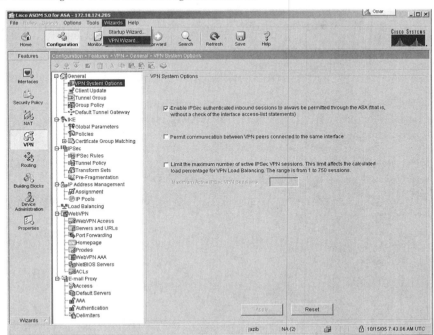

Figure 21-4 *Choosing the Site-to-Site Tunnel Type*

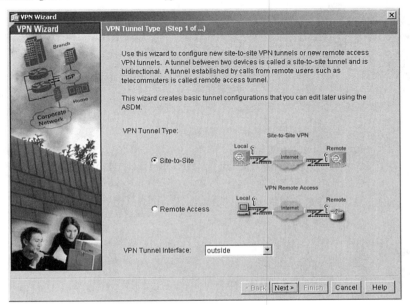

Because the remote peer of the site-to-site VPN tunnel resides toward the outside interface of Cisco ASA, the Outside interface is chosen from the drop-down menu in the VPN Tunnel Interface field. Click **Next** to move to the Remote Site Peer window.

Step 2 Specify the peer's identity.

The VPN Wizard prompts you to specify peer information, such as its public IP address and ISAKMP authentication method. In the example, the public IP address of Cisco ASA in London is 209.165.201.1, as specified in the Peer IP Address field in Figure 21-5.

Figure 21-5 *Site-to-Site ASA Setup*

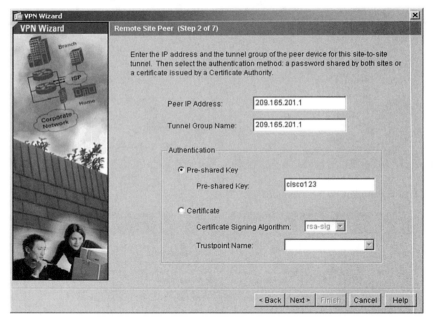

As mentioned in Chapter 15, "Site-to-Site IPSec VPNs," Cisco ASA supports two authentication methods: preshared keys and RSA signatures (PKI). In this topology, preshared keys are used to authenticate the VPN peer. The administrator has chosen to use **cisco123** as the preshared secret key for peer authentication. Click **Next** to move to the IKE Policy window.

Step 3 Select the IKE policy.

Cisco ASA allows you to choose the IKE parameters such as the encryption and authentication types and the Diffie-Hellman (DH) group. In Figure 21-6, the administrator has selected **3DES** for encryption, **SHA** for authentication, and **DH group 2** for key generation. Click **Next** to move to the IPSec Encryption and Authentication window.

Figure 21-6 *Selecting the IKE Policy*

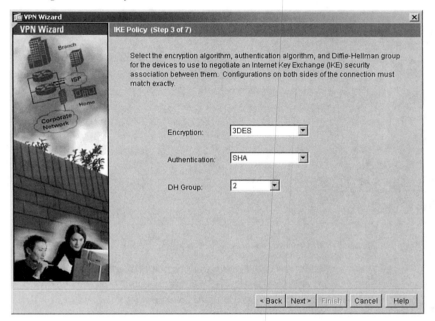

> **Note**   It is recommended to use AES-256 as an encryption algorithm. However, AES is a new standard and is not supported by all VPN devices. Check with the remote VPN device administrator to confirm whether it supports this standard.

Step 4   Set up the IPSec transform set.

Configuring the IPSec transform set is accomplished by selecting an encryption and authentication algorithm. In Figure 21-7, the administrator has chosen **3DES** for encryption and **SHA** for hash authentication. Click **Next** to move to the Local Hosts and Networks window.

Figure 21-7 *Selecting the IPSec Transform Set*

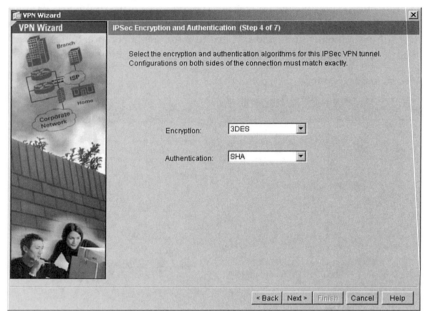

Step 5   Identify local networks.

Select the hosts/subnets or networks to be used as the local proxy during the IPSec negotiation. Cisco ASA recognizes all the local networks, if their routes are in the routing table. You can click the **. . .** button to see a list of the local networks, as shown in Figure 21-8.

Optionally, you may manually add an address in the IP Address field with the appropriate subnet mask. After you enter the IP address, click **Add** to move the address to the Selected Hosts/Networks pane, as illustrated in Figure 21-9. In this example, the administrator has added **192.168.10.0/24** and **192.168.20.0/24** as local networks.

Cisco ASA also allows you to specify the interface name or a tunnel group that identifies traffic. These options are hardly used in real-world site-to-site VPN deployments. Click **Next** to move to the next window.

Step 6   Define remote networks.

The Remote Hosts and Networks window allows you to identify the remote private network. This window looks very similar to the one in Step 5. In Figure 21-10, the administrator has identified two remote private networks: 192.168.30.0/24 and 192.168.40.0/24. Click **Next**.

Figure 21-8 *Selecting Networks from the List*

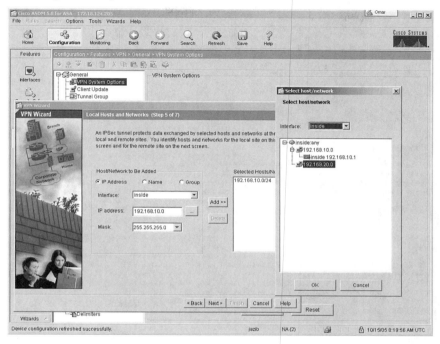

Figure 21-9 *Adding Selected Networks as the Local Proxy*

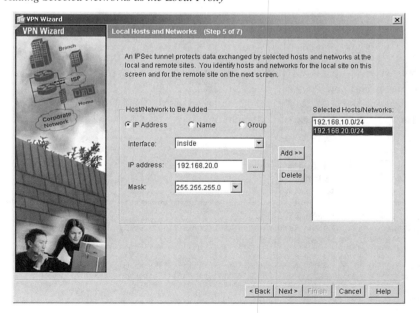

Figure 21-10 *Adding Selected Networks as the Remote Proxy*

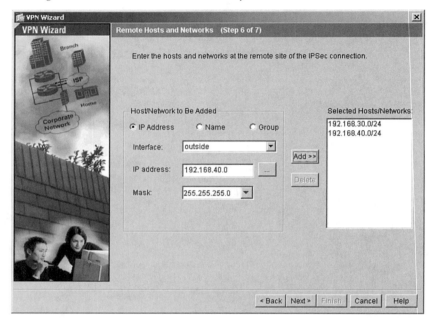

Step 7 Verify the site-to-site configuration.

The last step in setting up a site-to-site VPN tunnel is to verify that all the parameters are accurate. If they look correct, click **Finish** to complete the VPN Wizard.

If the Preview Command Before Sending to the Device option is enabled on ASDM, the entire site-to-site configuration is displayed before being sent to the security Cisco ASA. If the configuration looks accurate, click **Send** to push it to Cisco ASA. Example 21-1 shows the site-to-site configuration generated by ASDM. ASDM does not add comments, but they are added here for ease of understanding.

Example 21-1 *Complete Site-to-Site Configuration Sent by ASDM*

```
!Access-list to bypass Address Translation
access-list inside_nat0_outbound extended permit ip 192.168.10.0 255.255.255.0
  192.168.30.0 255.255.255.0
access-list inside_nat0_outbound extended permit ip 192.168.10.0 255.255.255.0
  192.168.40.0 255.255.255.0
access-list inside_nat0_outbound extended permit ip 192.168.20.0 255.255.255.0
  192.168.30.0 255.255.255.0
```

Example 21-1 *Complete Site-to-Site Configuration Sent by ASDM (Continued)*

```
access-list inside_nat0_outbound extended permit ip 192.168.20.0 255.255.255.0
   192.168.40.0 255.255.255.0
!Access-list is linked to NAT 0
nat (inside) 0 access-list inside_nat0_outbound
!IPSec transform-set for data encryption
crypto ipsec transform-set ESP-3DES-SHA esp-3des esp-sha-hmac
!Access-list to define interesting traffic for the encryption process
access-list outside_cryptomap_20 extended permit ip 192.168.10.0 255.255.255.0
   192.168.30.0 255.255.255.0
access-list outside_cryptomap_20 extended permit ip 192.168.10.0 255.255.255.0
   192.168.40.0 255.255.255.0
access-list outside_cryptomap_20 extended permit ip 192.168.20.0 255.255.255.0
   192.168.30.0 255.255.255.0
access-list outside_cryptomap_20 extended permit ip 192.168.20.0 255.255.255.0
   192.168.40.0 255.255.255.0
!Crypto map configuration
crypto map outside_map 20 match address outside_cryptomap_20
crypto map outside_map 20 set peer 209.165.201.1
crypto map outside_map 20 set transform-set ESP-3DES-SHA
!Crypto map is applied to the outside interface
crypto map outside_map interface outside
!ISAKMP Phase 1 policy
isakmp enable outside
isakmp policy 10 authentication pre-share
isakmp policy 10 encryption 3des
isakmp policy 10 hash sha
isakmp policy 10 group 2
isakmp policy 10 lifetime 86400
!Tunnel-group configuration to set 209.165.201.1 as a site-to-site peer
tunnel-group 209.165.201.1 type ipsec-l2l
tunnel-group 209.165.201.1 ipsec-attributes
 pre-shared-key *
!Sysopt to bypass packet filtration
sysopt connection permit-ipsec
```

Site-to-Site VPN Setup Using PKI

ASDM supports VPN tunnels using RSA signatures (PKI) for IKE authentication. Before a site-to-site tunnel can be set up, ASDM must have knowledge of the preinstalled certificates. If certificates are not installed on Cisco ASA, you need to follow the steps discussed in this section to retrieve both root and identity certificates from the certificate authority (CA). Figure 21-11 illustrates two Cisco ASA set up for a site-to-site tunnel using PKI. The CA server resides on the outside interfaces of Cisco ASA at **209.165.202.130**.

Figure 21-11 *Site-to-Site Tunnel Using PKI*

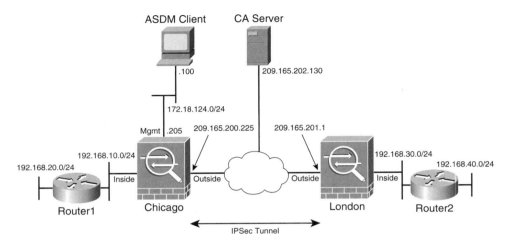

Most steps in setting up a site-to-site tunnel using PKI are identical to those discussed in the previous section. The following steps are used to retrieve the certificates from a CA server:

Step 1 Generate the RSA keys.

If Cisco ASA does not have RSA keys generated, or if you want to create new keys, choose **Configuration > Features > Device Administration > Certificate > Key Pair** and click **Add** to create a new set of keys, as shown in Figure 21-12. ASDM prompts you to specify a label for the keys or to use the default RSA key name. Additionally, you can select the modulus size and the usage of the key. A modulus size of 1024 bits is selected in this example.

Step 2 Configure the trustpoint.

The next step after generating the RSA keys is to configure the PKI trustpoint. A trustpoint declares a CA server and creates a device identity based on the certificate issued by the CA. Choose **Configuration > Features > Device Administration > Certificate > Trustpoint > Configuration** to create a trustpoint. Click **Add** to define a trustpoint, called **ChicagoPKI** in the example, and go through the enrollment process, as shown in Figure 21-13. In the Key Pair field, the administrator is using the default RSA keys that were generated in Step 1. The enrollment mode is set to automatic, in which Cisco ASA submits a PKI

request dynamically using the Simple Certificate Enrollment Protocol
(SCEP). The enrollment URL guides Cisco ASA to submit the request at
http://209.165.202.130/certsrv/mscep/mscep.dll.

Figure 21-12 *Generating the RSA Keys*

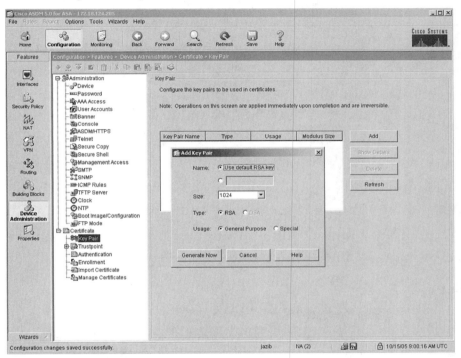

Note	Each CA server vendor uses a different enrollment URL. Please consult the CA server documentation for the correct syntax.

You can optionally set the Fully Qualified Domain Name (FQDN) and
Distinguished Name (DN) for the certificates. Click the **Certificate
Parameters** button to specify the FQDN or DN or both, as shown in
Figure 21-14, where a DN with an attribute of Common Name (CN)
Chicago is being configured.

Figure 21-13 *Setting Up an Enrollment URL*

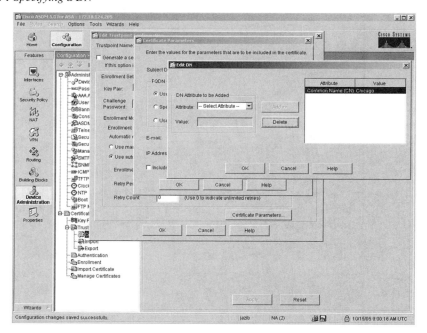

Figure 21-14 *Specifying a DN*

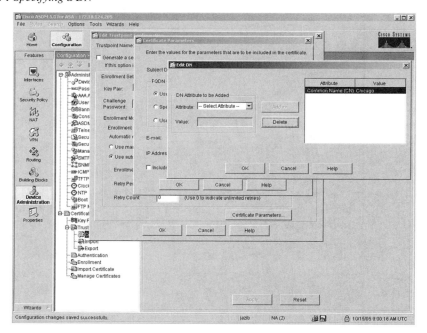

Step 3 Set up CRLs.

A certificate revocation list (CRL) is a list of all the certificates that have been revoked by the CA server's administrator. Cisco ASA can use this list to validate a certificate received from the VPN peer. If the received certificate has already been revoked, Cisco ASA denies the IKE negotiation. Cisco ASA can either use the CRL distribution point (CDP) from the certificate or use the statically configured one. In Figure 21-15, Cisco ASA is relying on the CDP embedded in the certificate.

Figure 21-15 *Specifying the CDP*

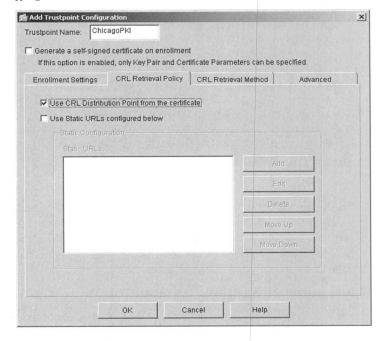

Cisco ASA supports three protocols for retrieving the CRL from the CA servers:

— LDAP

— HTTP

— SCEP

Click the **CRL Retrieval Method** tab to select at least one of the protocols. In Figure 21-16, the administrator is using HTTP and SCEP as the CRL retrieval protocols.

Figure 21-16 *Specifying the CRL Retrieval Protocols*

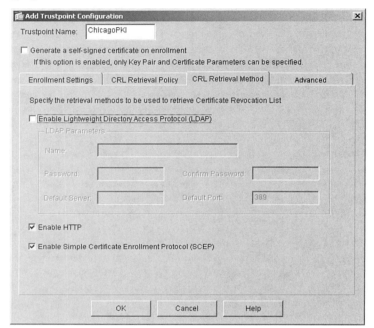

The Advanced tab enables you to specify the CRL checking and caching timers. You can choose to require CRL checking for all the received certificates, as shown in Figure 21-17. In this example, the administrator has also enabled Enforce Next CRL Update, which requires having a valid and nonexpired next update value.

Step 4 Authenticate and enroll in the CA server.

For a successful PKI implementation, Cisco ASA needs to receive both the root certificate and the identity certificate from the CA server. Choose **Configuration > Features > Device Administration > Certificate > Authentication** to request the root certificate. Click **Authenticate** after selecting the configured trustpoint to submit a request, as shown in Figure 21-18.

Figure 21-17 *Setting Advanced Trustpoint Attributes*

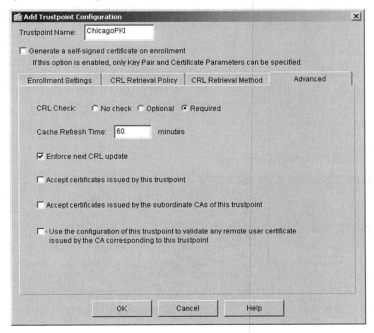

Figure 21-18 *Requesting Root Certificate*

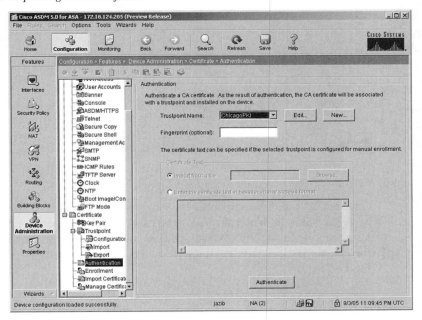

To request an identity certificate, choose **Configuration > Features > Device Administration > Certificate > Enrollment** and click **Enroll**, as shown in Figure 21-19.

Note	It is recommended to verify the fingerprint of the received CA certificate with the fingerprint on the CA server to ensure that the CA certificate has not been compromised.

Figure 21-19 *Requesting Identity Certificate*

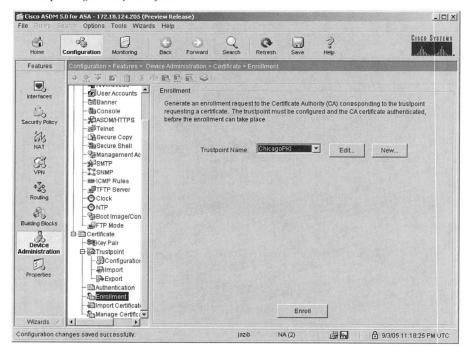

Step 5   Select a certificate for the site-to-site tunnel.

Once the CA administrator approves the requested certificate, Cisco ASA loads it in flash and allows it to be used for the VPN connections. Using the site-to-site VPN Wizard, you can select an available certificate for IKE authentication in the Remote Site Peer window, as shown in Figure 21-20.

Figure 21-20 *Selecting Certificates for VPN Tunnels*

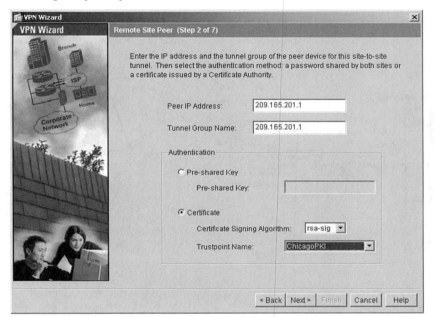

Cisco Remote-Access IPSec VPN Setup

ASDM also provides a VPN Wizard that configures remote-access IPSec VPN connections for the Cisco EasyVPN clients. This wizard guides you through the step-by-step configurations required for a successful EasyVPN client tunnel. In this section, Figure 21-21 is used as a reference topology in which a security Cisco ASA is being set up to accept VPN connections on the outside interface from multiple remote-access clients. The inside interface of Cisco ASA in Chicago is directly connected to the 192.168.10.0/24 subnet, while another inside network, 192.168.20.0/24, is behind Router1. The public interface's IP address is 209.165.200.225/27, and the default route sends all traffic to the next-hop router toward the Internet.

The goal of this example is to enable split tunneling such that the clients encrypt only traffic destined for the inside networks on Cisco ASA. All other traffic destined for the Internet, such as web traffic to www.cisco.com, should flow in clear text directly from the remote VPN clients.

Figure 21-21 *Remote-Access Topology*

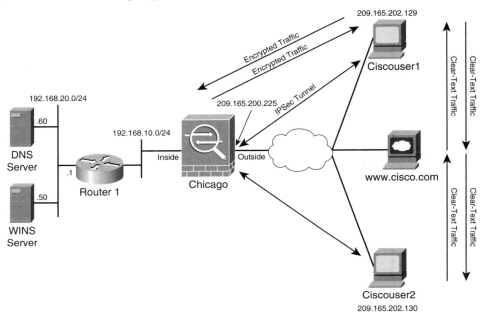

Use the following procedure for step-by-step configuration of ASDM:

Step 1   Launch the VPN Wizard.

To launch the VPN Wizard, click **Wizards > VPN Wizard**, as shown earlier in Figure 21-3.

ASDM launches the VPN Wizard, which provides an option to select the VPN tunnel type. Click the **Remote Access** radio button, as shown in Figure 21-22.

In this example, because VPN clients connect to Cisco ASA on the outside interface, the Outside interface is chosen from the drop-down menu in the VPN Tunnel Interface field. Click **Next** to move forward to the Remote Access Client window.

Step 2   Select the type of remote-access VPN tunnel.

The current version of Cisco ASA supports only Cisco IPSec remote-access VPNs, which is the default remote-access VPN tunnel type, as shown in Figure 21-23. Click **Next** to move to the VPN Client Tunnel Group Name and Authentication Method window.

Figure 21-22 *Selecting Remote-Access Tunnel*

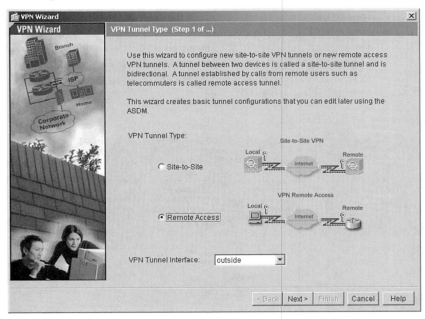

Figure 21-23 *Selecting the Type of Remote-Access VPN*

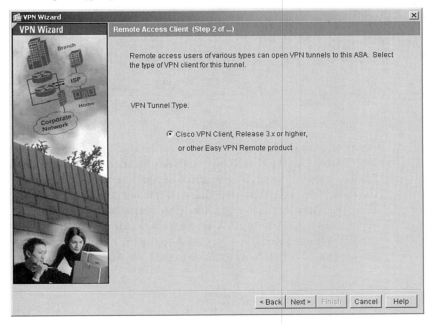

Step 3   Set up the tunnel group name.

Specify the tunnel group name and the password if preshared keys are used. If PKI is being used, select the server certificate from the drop-down menu. In Figure 21-24, the administrator is setting up Cisco ASA with a tunnel group name of **SecureMeTnlGrp** with the associated preshared key of **cisco123**. Click **Next** to move to the Client Authentication window.

Figure 21-24 *Specifying a Tunnel Group Name*

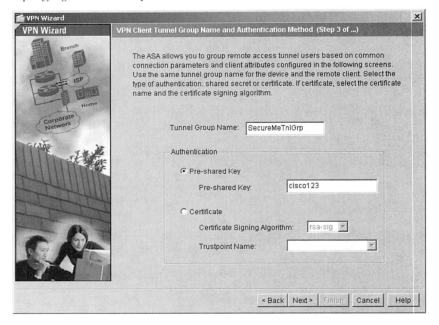

Step 4   Set the user authentication method.

As mentioned in Chapter 7, "Authentication, Authorization, and Accounting (AAA)," Cisco ASA supports local and external databases for user authentication. If an external database server is used for authentication, you must predefine it. If it is not defined earlier, you can leave the wizard and set it up under **Configuration > Features > Properties > AAA Setup > AAA Servers**. In Figure 21-25, the administrator is setting up Cisco ASA to use the local database for user authentication. Click **Next** to move to the User Accounts window.

Figure 21-25 *Selecting the Local User Database*

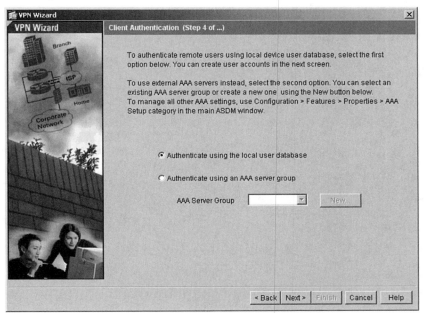

Step 5 Create the user database.

In Step 4, the administrator is using the local user database for user authentication. ASDM allows you to create additional user accounts, if necessary. In Figure 21-26, the administrator is setting up an account for ciscouser2 with a password of 123cisco (shown in asterisks). Click **Add** to instruct ASDM to create a user account. Click **Next** to move to the Address Pool window.

Step 6 Assign IP addresses.

An important step in setting up the remote-access VPN connection is to assign an IP address to the client during the tunnel negotiation. ASDM prompts you to create an address pool and specify a range of IP addresses. In Figure 21-27, the administrator has set up an IP pool called **ippool,** which starts at **192.168.50.1** and ends at **192.168.50.127**. The subnet mask for the range of addresses is **255.255.255.128**. Click **Next** to move to the Attributes Pushed to Client (Optional) window.

Figure 21-26 *Creating User Accounts*

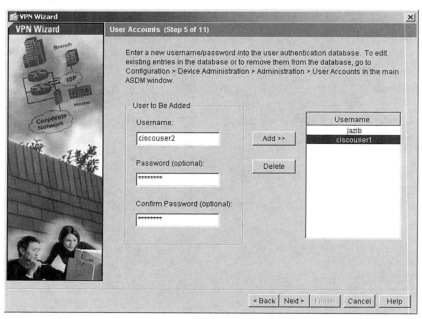

Figure 21-27 *Assigning IP Addresses*

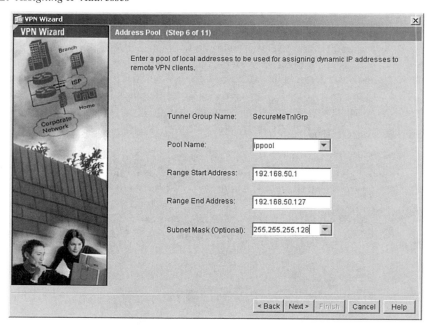

Step 7   Set up mode configuration attributes.

The VPN Wizard allows you to configure three basic mode configuration attributes, which include the DNS and WINS servers, IP addresses, and the domain name of an organization, as shown in Figure 21-28. In this example, **192.168.10.10** and **192.168.10.20** are being used as the DNS addresses, and **192.168.10.20** and **192.168.10.10** are being used as the WINS addresses. The domain name is **securemeinc.com**. Click **Next** to move to IKE Policy window.

Figure 21-28 *Assigning Mode Configuration Attributes*

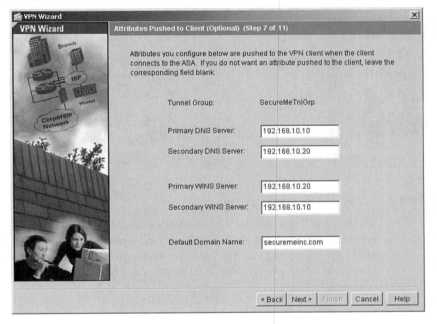

Step 8   Select the IKE policy.

Cisco ASA allows you to choose the IKE parameters such as the encryption and authentication types and the Diffie-Hellman (DH) group. In Figure 21-29, the administrator has selected 3DES for encryption, SHA for authentication, and DH group 2 for key generation. Click **Next** to move to the IPSec Encryption and Authentication window.

Note	Cisco VPN Client supports DH groups 2 and 5, by default. You have to select one of these groups to match the client settings.

Figure 21-29 *IKE Policy*

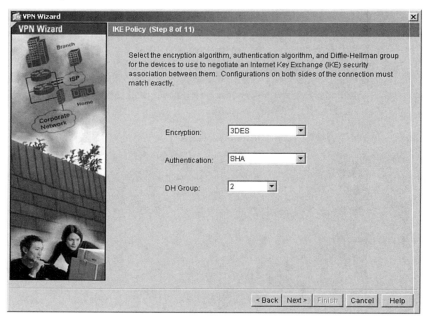

Step 9 Set up the IPSec transform set.

Set up the IPSec transform set by selecting the IPSec encryption and authentication methods. In Figure 21-30, the administrator has chosen 3DES for encryption and MD5 for hash authentication. Click **Next** to move to the Address Translation Exemption and Split Tunneling (Optional) window.

Step 10 Bypass address translation.

If NAT control is enabled on the security Cisco ASA, you can choose to bypass address translation for the traffic sourced from the inside network of Cisco ASA and destined for the VPN client's assigned addresses. ASDM creates an access list to identify traffic traveling over the tunnel, and applies NAT exemption to bypass address translation. To identify local networks, add the local hosts/subnets/networks in the Selected Hosts/Networks pane, as shown in Figure 21-31. In this example, the administrator does not want **192.168.10.0/24** and **192.168.20.0/24** addresses to be translated if they are sending traffic to the VPN pool of addresses, **192.168.50.0/25**.

Figure 21-30 *IPSec Transform Set*

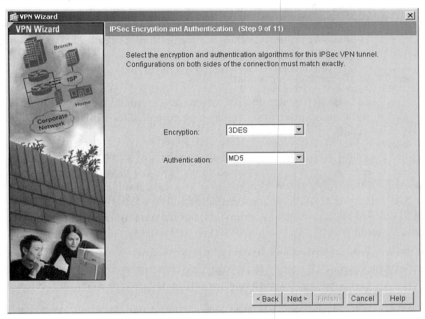

Figure 21-31 *Enabling Split Tunneling and NAT Exemption*

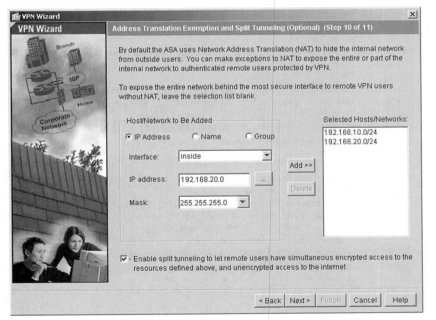

By using split tunneling, you can enforce the remote VPN users to encrypt only the traffic destined for the inside networks of Cisco ASA. All other traffic can go to the Internet in clear text. Enable split tunneling by checking off the box shown at the bottom of Figure 21-31. Click **Next** to move to the last step of the VPN Wizard.

Step 11 Verify remote-access configuration.

The last step in setting up a remote-access tunnel is to verify that all the parameters are accurate. If they look correct, click **Finish** to complete the wizard.

If the Preview Command Before Sending to the Device option is enabled in ASDM, the entire remote-access VPN configuration is displayed to you before being sent to the security Cisco ASA. If the configuration looks accurate, click **Send** to push it to Cisco ASA. Example 21-2 shows the complete remote-access VPN configuration created by ASDM. ASDM does not add comments, but they are added here for ease of understanding.

Example 21-2 *Complete Remote-Access Configuration Created by ASDM*

```
!Access-list to bypass Address Translation
access-list inside_nat0_outbound permit ip 192.168.10.0 255.255.255.0
 192.168.50.0 255.255.255.128
access-list inside_nat0_outbound permit ip 192.168.20.0 255.255.255.0
 192.168.50.0 255.255.255.128
!Access-list is linked to NAT 0
nat (inside) 0 access-list inside_nat0_outbound
!Access-list is identify traffic for Split tunneling
access-list SecureMeTnlGrp_splitTunnelAcl standard permit 192.168.10.0
 255.255.255.0
access-list SecureMeTnlGrp_splitTunnelAcl standard permit 192.168.20.0
 255.255.255.0
!User Accounts for local X-Auth
username ciscouser1 password ffIRPGpDSOJh9YLq encrypted privilege 0
username ciscouser2 password ffIRPGpDSOJh9YLq encrypted privilege 0
!Pool of addresses to be assigned to the VPN users
ip local pool ippool 192.168.50.1-192.168.50.127 mask 255.255.255.128
!Configuration of VPN group-policy
group-policy SecureMeTnlGrp internal
!group-policy to send mode-config attributes
group-policy SecureMeTnlGrp attributes
  split-tunnel-policy tunnelspecified
  split-tunnel-network-list value SecureMeTnlGrp_splitTunnelAcl
  dns-server value 192.168.10.10 192.168.10.20
  wins-server value 192.168.10.20 192.168.10.10
  default-domain value securemeinc.com
!Configuration of Remote Access VPN group called SecureMeTnlGrp
tunnel-group SecureMeTnlGrp type ipsec-ra
tunnel-group SecureMeTnlGrp general-attributes
```

Example 21-2 *Complete Remote-Access Configuration Created by ASDM (Continued)*

```
!The VPN Group is using VPN attributes from the group-policy
  default-group-policy SecureMeTnlGrp
  address-pool  ippool
!Configuration of preshared key for SecureMeTnlGrp
tunnel-group SecureMeTnlGrp ipsec-attributes
  pre-shared-key cisco123
!IPSec transform-set for data encryption
crypto ipsec transform-set ESP-3DES-MD5 esp-3des esp-md5-hmac
!ISAKMP Phase 1 policy
isakmp enable outside
isakmp policy 30 authen pre-share
isakmp policy 30 encrypt 3des
isakmp policy 30 hash sha
isakmp policy 30 group 2
isakmp policy 30 lifetime 86400
!Dynamic Crypto map configuration
crypto dynamic-map outside_dyn_map 20 set transform-set ESP-3DES-MD5
!Static crypto map configuration
crypto map outside_map 65535 ipsec-isakmp dynamic outside_dyn_map
crypto map outside_map interface outside
!Sysopt to bypass packet filtration
sysopt connection permit-ipsec
```

WebVPN

As discussed in Chapter 16, "Remote Access VPNs," Cisco ASA allows mobile and home users to create a secure WebVPN tunnel to access corporate resources. ASDM allows you to configure and customize the WebVPN service. In this section, Figure 21-32 is used as a reference topology in which a Cisco ASA is being set up to accept the WebVPN connections on the outside interface from the web clients. The inside interface of Cisco ASA in Chicago is directly connected to the 192.168.10.0/24 subnet, while another inside network, 192.168.20.0/24, is behind Router1. The public interface's IP address is 209.165.200.225/27, and the default route sends all traffic to the next-hop router toward the Internet.

By setting up WebVPN, SecureMe wants to accomplish the following:

- Customize the WebVPN page and include SecureMe's name and logo.

- Allow access to a web server behind Cisco ASA at 192.168.20.10.

- Allow access to a Telnet server located at 192.168.20.20.

- Allow access to an e-mail server running the IMAP, POP3, and SMTP services. The server is located at 192.168.20.30.

- Set up DNS and WINS servers to permit access to the inside hosts by the domain and NetBIOS names.

Figure 21-32 *WebVPN Topology*

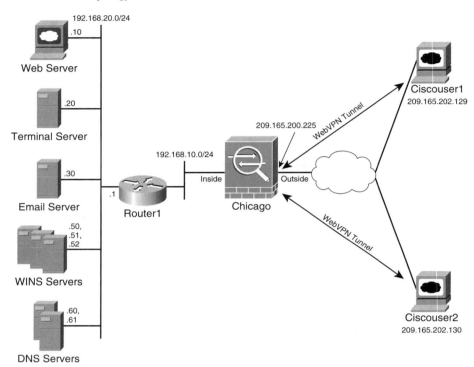

The following steps guide you through configuring the ASA to meet the preceding objectives:

Step 1 Enable WebVPN.

The first step in setting up WebVPN is to enable it on the interface that is going to terminate the connections. To configure the WebVPN parameters, choose **Configuration > Features > VPN > WebVPN.** Figure 21-33 illustrates that WebVPN is being enabled on the outside interface under the WebVPN Access parameter. After you are done, click **Apply** to commit the changes.

Note   ASDM and WebVPN are not supported on the same interface.

Step 2 Customize the look and feel.

To customize the WebVPN homepage, click the **Homepage** parameter and configure the organization-specific values. In Figure 21-34, the administrator has changed the title of the page to SecureMe WebVPN Service and has formatted the logo of the organization.

Figure 21-33 *Enabling WebVPN*

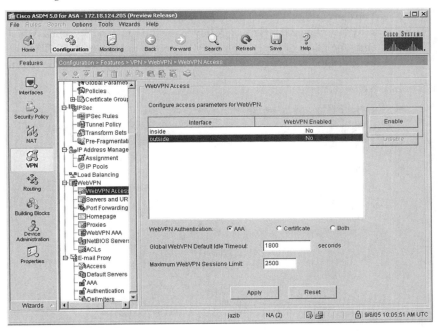

Figure 21-34 *Customizing Look and Feel*

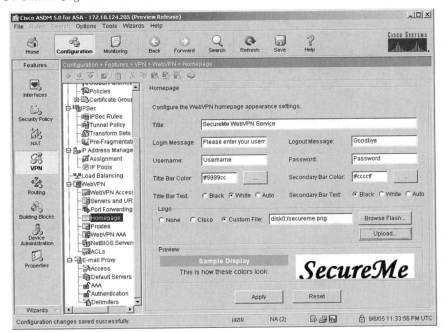

Step 3   Set up WebVPN group attributes.

You can configure group policies by choosing **Configuration > Features > VPN > General > Group Policy**. To set up a new policy, click **Add** and enter the name of the group policy, as shown in Figure 21-35. The group policy name is **SecureMeWebGrp** and it is configured as type internal.

Figure 21-35 *Creating a Group Policy*

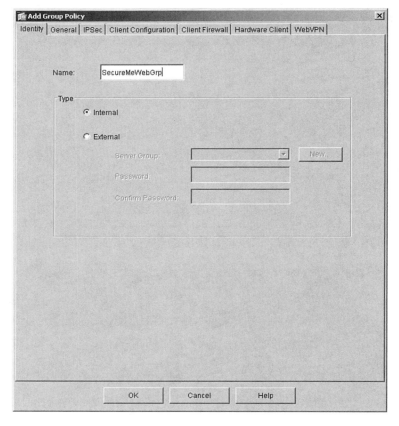

By default, a new group policy inherits all values from the default group policy, which allows both IPSec and WebVPN as the tunneling protocols. In Figure 21-36, the administrator has disabled policy inheritance for tunneling protocols and has selected WebVPN as the tunneling protocol under the General tab.

Figure 21-36 *Selecting WebVPN as the Tunneling Protocol*

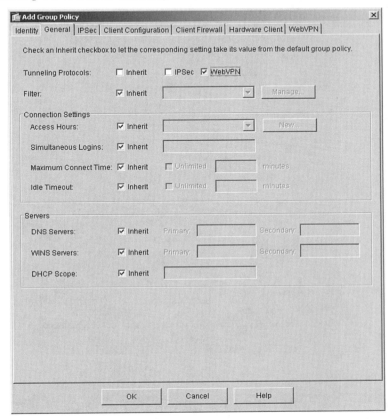

ASDM can restrict users to use certain functions such as port forwarding and Windows file browsing. These functions can be enabled under the WebVPN tab, as shown in Figure 21-37.

Step 4   Set up URL mangling.

Configure URL mangling by creating a URL list. Choose **Configuration > Features > VPN > WebVPN > Servers and URLs**. Click **Add** and specify a list name. This list name is later applied to the group policy. Figure 21-38 shows a URL list name called **HTTP_link** set up to provide URL mangling services to an internal web server at **192.168.20.10**. The display name shown on the front web page is **Internal**.

Figure 21-37 *Setting Up WebVPN Functions*

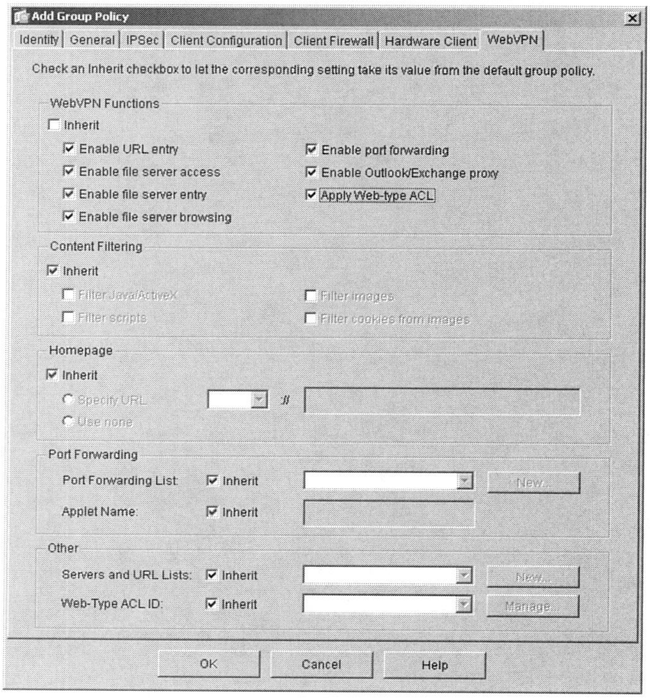

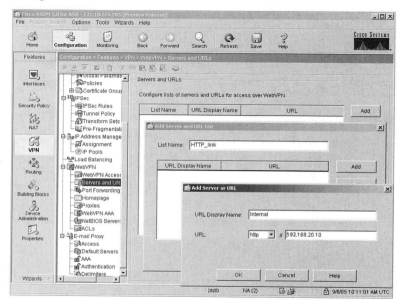

Figure 21-38 *Creating a URL List*

After you create a list, you map it to a group policy under the WebVPN tab, as shown in Figure 21-39. Click **OK** to submit these changes.

Figure 21-39 *Applying the URL List*

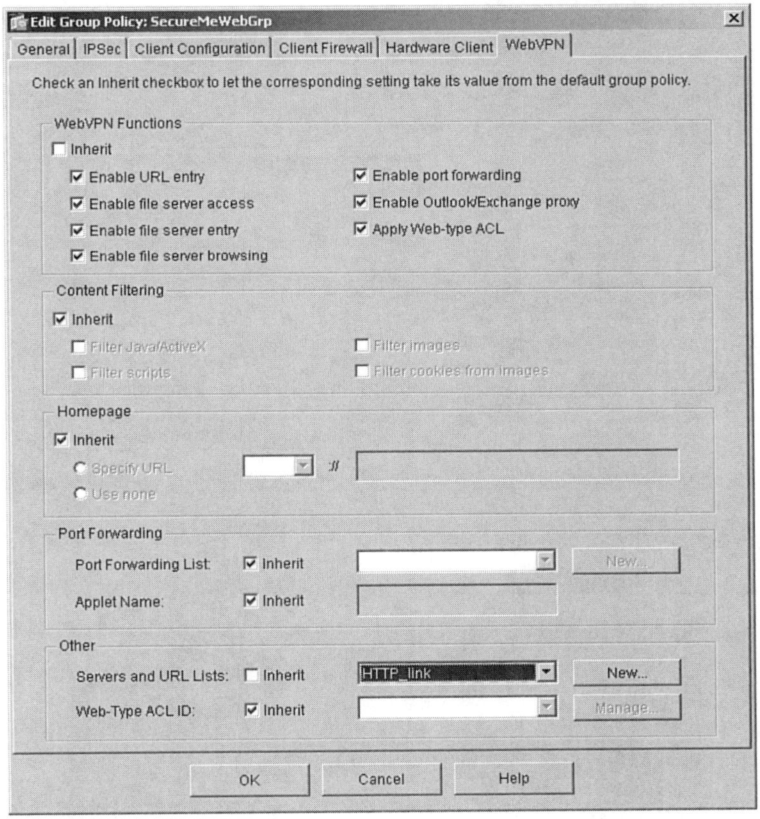

Step 5   Configure port forwarding.

As discussed in Chapter 16, the port-forwarding feature allows users to gain access to the TCP-based applications over the WebVPN connection. Configure port forwarding under **Configuration > Features > VPN > WebVPN > Port Forwarding**. To create a new port-forwarding entry, click **Add** and specify a list name, similar to URL mangling in the previous step. In Figure 21-40, the administrator has set up a list called **telnet_inside** with the local TCP port of **1100** and the remote TCP port of **23**. The server is located at **192.168.20.20** and a description of **Telnet Service** is added to the entry.

After you create a port-forwarding list, you apply it to the group policy, as shown in Figure 21-41. Click the **WebVPN** tab and select the list from the drop-down menu under Port Forwarding.

Figure 21-40 *Creating a Port-Forwarding List*

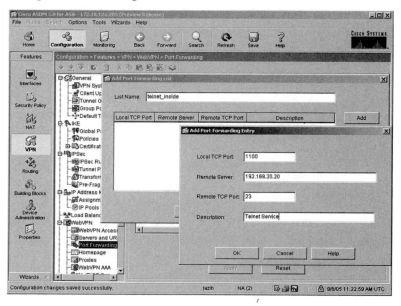

Figure 21-41 *Applying a Port-Forwarding List*

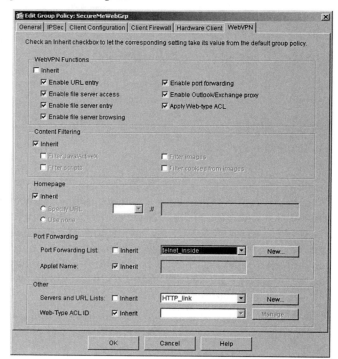

Step 6   Specify WINS and DNS servers.

A WINS server is necessary to resolve NetBIOS names. To set up these servers, choose **Configuration > Features > VPN > WebVPN > NetBIOS Servers**. As shown in Figure 21-42, ASDM is setting up three NetBIOS servers located at **192.168.20.50**, **192.168.20.51**, and **192.168.20.52**. The first server in the list also acts as a master browser in addition to being a WINS server.

Figure 21-42 *Setting Up WINS Servers*

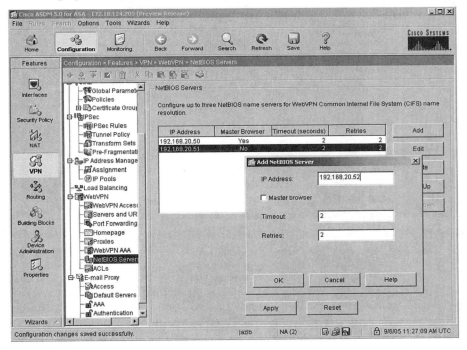

DNS servers resolve the domain names of the network devices to their configured IP addresses. To specify DNS servers, choose **Configuration > Features > Properties > DNS Client**. Cisco ASA allows up to six DNS server for name resolution. You have to instruct Cisco ASA which interface to use to send the DNS requests. Figure 21-43 illustrates that two DNS servers, located at **192.168.20.60** and **192.168.20.61**, are set up for name resolution on the inside interface. You click **Apply** to submit the changes to Cisco ASA.

Figure 21-43 *Setting Up DNS Servers*

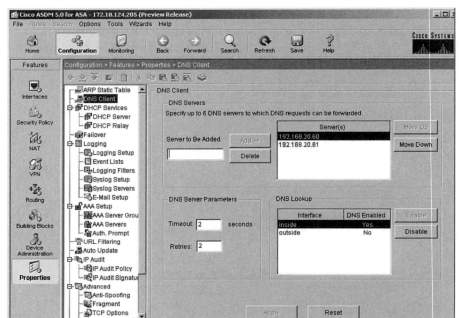

Step 7 Configure e-mail proxy functionality.

E-mail proxy functionality allows WebVPN users to access e-mail over a secured connection. Cisco ASA supports SMTPS, POP3S, and IMAPS as e-mail protocols. To enable any or all of them, choose **Configuration > Features > VPN > E-mail Proxy > Access**. You can enable one or all of these protocols per interface, as shown in Figure 21-44, where all three protocols are enabled for the outside interface.

Cisco ASA needs to know where the e-mail server(s) resides. To specify the host name or the IP addresses of the servers, choose **Configuration > Features > VPN > E-mail Proxy > Default Servers**. Figure 21-45 illustrates that Cisco ASA is being configured for **secureme-email** as the POP3S, IMAPS, and SMTPS servers using the default TCP ports of 995, 993, and 988, respectively. The DNS server resolves **secureme-email** as 192.168.20.30.

Figure 21-44 *Enabling E-Mail Proxy*

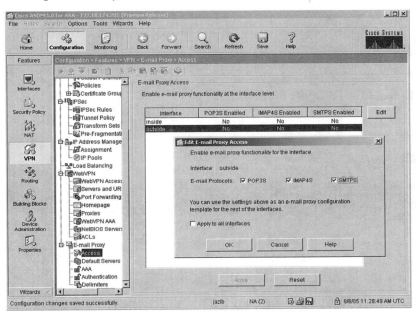

Figure 21-45 *Setting Up the E-Mail Proxy Servers*

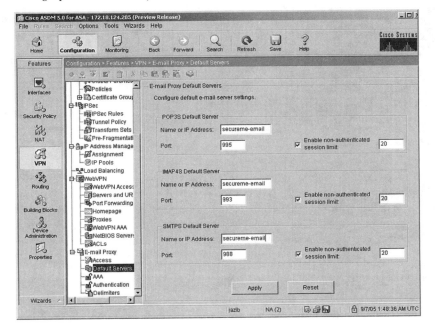

Cisco ASA allows the use of three different types of authentication:

- AAA
- Piggyback HTTPS
- Certificate

E-mail authentication methods are configured under **Configuration > Features > VPN > E-mail Proxy > Authentication.** In Figure 21-46, Cisco ASA is being configured to use AAA authentication for all three supported e-mail protocols.

Figure 21-46 *E-Mail Proxy Authentication*

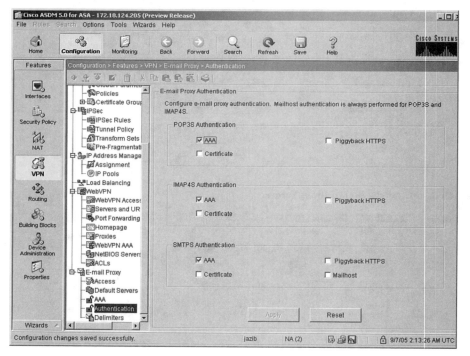

Because AAA has been selected as the authentication method, ASDM needs to map an authentication server to the e-mail protocol. In Figure 21-47, a predefined authentication group called **Rad**, which is using RADIUS authentication, is linked to the protocols. A group policy, called **SecureMeWebGrp**, is also applied to the e-mail users when they establish a connection using any one of the three e-mail protocols.

Figure 21-48 shows the username and server delimiters for the three supported e-mail protocols, which are set to their default values of colon (:) and at (@), respectively.

Figure 21-47 *E-Mail Proxy AAA Servers*

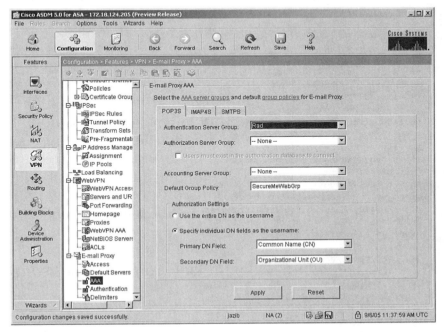

Figure 21-48 *E-Mail Proxy Delimiters*

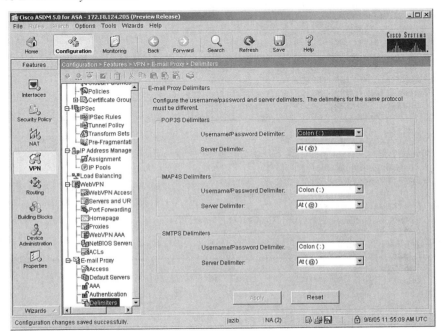

Example 21-3 shows the complete WebVPN configuration generated by ASDM.

Example 21-3 *Complete WebVPN Configuration Created by ASDM*

```
!DNS server configuration for hostname resolution
dns domain-lookup inside
dns name-server 192.168.20.60
dns name-server 192.168.20.61
!URL-List for URL-Mangling
url-list HTTP_link "Internal" http://192.168.20.10
!Port-forward List for Port Forwarding
port-forward telnet_inside 1100 192.168.20.20 telnet Telnet Service
!AAA server configuration for Email Proxy authentication
aaa-server Rad protocol radius
aaa-server Rad host 192.168.20.40
 key cisco123
!Group-policy configuration for WebVPN users
group-policy SecureMeWebGrp internal
group-policy SecureMeWebGrp attributes
!Allowed tunneling protocol is WebVPN
 vpn-tunnel-protocol webvpn
 webvpn
!Allowed functions for WebVPN
  functions url-entry file-access file-entry file-browsing mapi port-forward filter
!URL-List is applied to the group-policy
  url-list value HTTP_link
!Port-forward List is applied to the group-policy
  port-forward value telnet_inside
!WebVPN global configuration
webvpn
!WebVPN is enabled on the outside interface
 enable outside
!WebVPN homepage title and logo are modified
 title SecureMe WebVPN Service
 logo file disk0:/secureme.png
!WINS servers are setup for NetBIOS name resolution
nbns-server 192.168.20.50 master timeout 2 retry 2
nbns-server 192.168.20.51 timeout 2 retry 2
nbns-server 192.168.50.52 timeout 2 retry 2
!Email Proxy for IMAP protocol is setup on the outside interface
imap4s
 enable outside
!Declaration of IMAP Email Server
 server secureme-email
!AAA authentication for IMAP users
 authentication-server-group Rad
 authentication aaa
!Group-policy is applied to the IMAP users
 default-group-policy SecureMeWebGrp
!Email Proxy for POP3 protocol is setup on the outside interface
pop3s
 enable outside
!Declaration of POP3 Email Server
 server secureme-email
!AAA authentication for POP3 users
 authentication-server-group Rad
```

Example 21-3 *Complete WebVPN Configuration Created by ASDM (Continued)*

```
 authentication aaa
!Group-policy is applied to the POP3 users
 default-group-policy SecureMeWebGrp
!Email Proxy for SMTP protocol is setup on the outside interface
smtps
 enable outside
!Declaration of SMTP Email Server
 server secureme-email
!AAA authentication for SMTP users
 authentication-server-group Rad
 authentication aaa
!Group-policy is applied to the SMTP users
 default-group-policy SecureMeWebGrp
```

VPN Monitoring

ASDM provides a GUI to monitor the status of IPSec and WebVPN tunnels. The GUI displays information such as total number of active tunnels, the type of encryption used by the VPN connections, and so on. To view VPN statistics, choose **Monitoring > Features > VPN > VPN Statistics.** To look at the active sessions, click the **Sessions** option, as shown in Figure 21-49. There are two VPN tunnels active on this Cisco ASA:

- A site-to-site tunnel
- A remote-access VPN tunnel

Figure 21-49 *Monitoring Active Sessions*

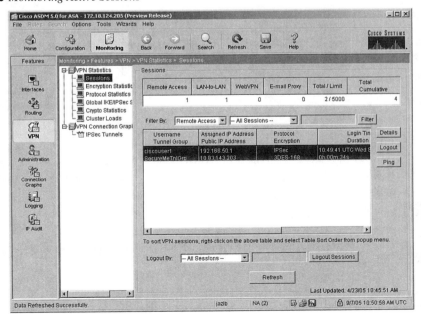

The remote username is ciscouser1, which is connected to SecureMeTnlGrp using 3DES encryption. The site-to-site tunnel attributes can be monitored by filtering on LAN-to-LAN.

Choose **Global IKE/IPSec Statistics** to monitor IKE and IPSec sessions. To look at the counters for IKE, select **IKE Protocol** in the drop-drown menu, as shown in Figure 21-50. The important information to look at is the initiator and responder fail messages, which indicate that the VPN tunnels do not establish because of mismatched parameters.

Figure 21-50 *Monitoring IKE Protocols*

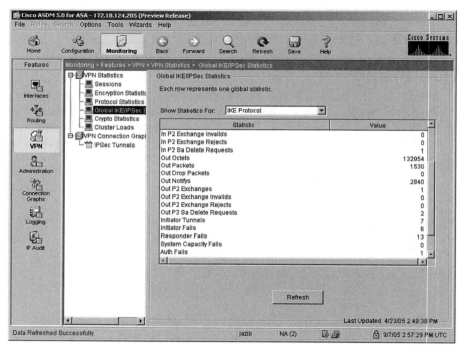

ASDM can also show the inbound and outbound information about the data packets if IPSec Protocol is selected in the drop-down menu. This includes, but is not limited to, the encrypted packets coming in and going out of Cisco ASA, the number of packets dropped, and authentication or replay failures, as shown in Figure 21-51.

Clicking **Crypto Statistics** shows the number of IKE and/or IPSec packets encrypted and decrypted by Cisco ASA, along with any failed requests. Clicking Crypto Statistics also provides information for WebVPN-based connections if **SSL Protocol** is selected in the drop-down menu, as shown in Figure 21-52.

Figure 21-51 *Monitoring IPSec Protocols*

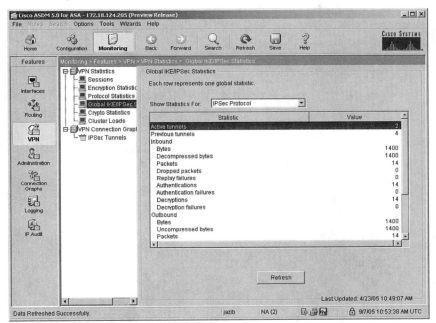

Figure 21-52 *Monitoring WebVPN Information*

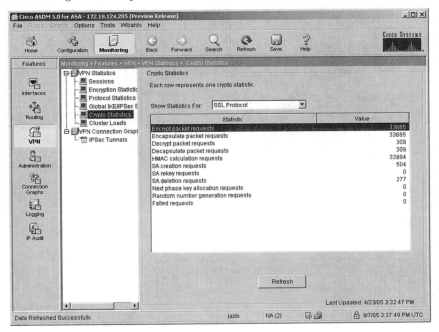

The monitoring capabilities of ASDM provide real-time graphs of active IKE and/or IPSec sessions. To set up the graphs, choose **Monitoring > Features > VPN > VPN Connection Graphs > IPSec Tunnels**. In Figure 21-53, the administrator has enabled graphs for IKE and for IPSec active sessions.

Figure 21-53 *Plotting IKE and IPSec Graphs*

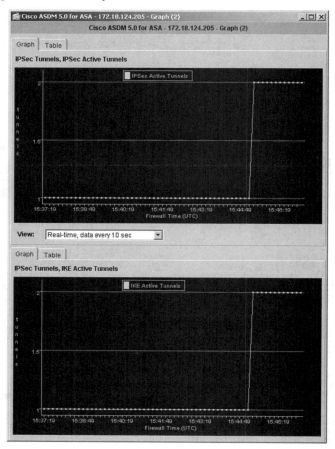

Summary

This chapter presented four VPN deployment scenarios and demonstrated how to set them up using ASDM. It also introduced the VPN monitoring capabilities of ASDM by showing the VPN statistics and graphs.

This chapter covers the following topics:

- Deploying the Cisco ASA at branch offices and small businesses
- Deploying the Cisco ASA as a large enterprise firewall, VPN, and IPS
- Deploying the Cisco ASA to provide data center security

CHAPTER 22

Case Studies

This chapter provides a series of real-life examples of how Cisco ASA appliances are deployed at small, medium, and large organizations. Several case studies, based on the organization used in previous chapters (SecureMe), demonstrate how the Cisco ASA can help secure organizations of all sizes.

The first case study demonstrates how a business partner (Partner-A) uses Cisco ASA to provide firewall protection to its network and to communicate over a secure VPN connection to SecureMe's regional site in Washington. Additionally, this case study demonstrates an example of a remote branch office implementation.

The second case study shows how SecureMe deploys Cisco ASA to provide high-availability protection from its Internet with Anti-X and Intrusion Prevention System (IPS) services. Furthermore, a cluster of Cisco ASA appliances is implemented for a remote-access VPN.

The final, third case study demonstrates how Cisco ASA is deployed to provide data center security with high availability and inline IPS services.

Case Study 1: Deploying the Cisco ASA at Branch Offices and Small Businesses

This section demonstrates how Cisco ASA appliances are deployed in SecureMe's branch offices, as well as how a business partner company uses Cisco ASA to provide firewall and site-to-site VPN connectivity to SecureMe.

Branch Offices

SecureMe has several small branch offices around the world. There are 20 to 25 users at each branch office. A Cisco ASA 5510 is deployed at each of the three branch offices (New York, Los Angeles, and Atlanta), as shown in Figure 22-1.

The Cisco ASA 5510 at each location is connected to a Cisco IOS router providing Internet connectivity. The Cisco ASAs are also connected to Cisco Catalyst switches (not shown in Figure 22-1) to provide connectivity to internal users.

Figure 22-1 *Branch Offices*

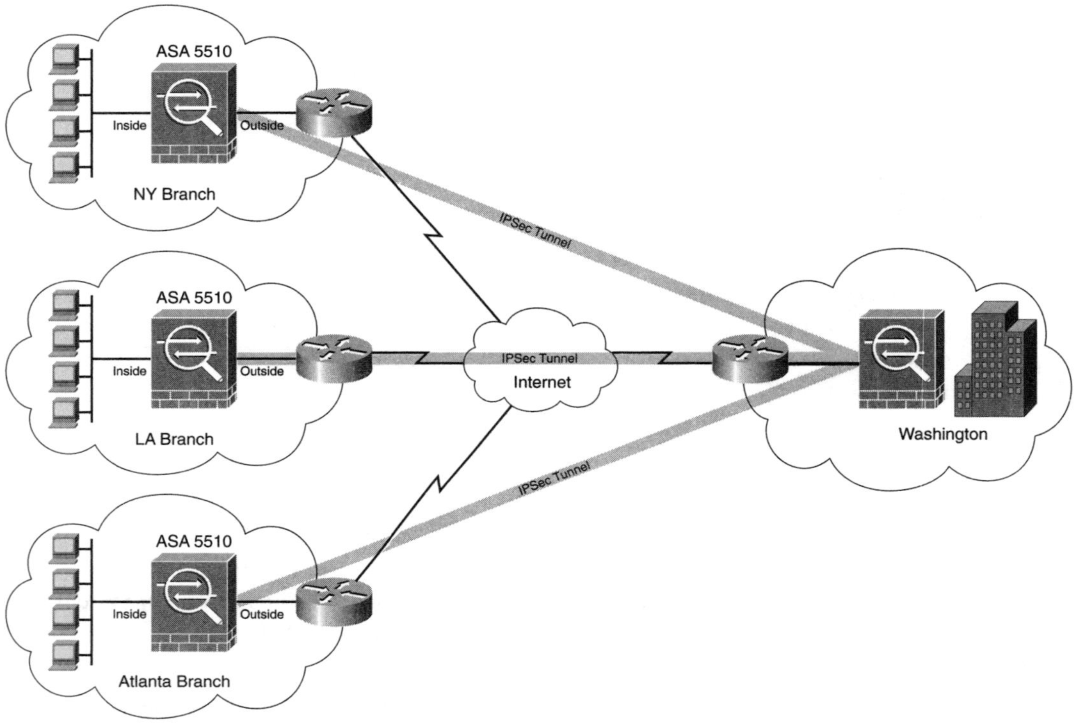

SecureMe's security policies restrict all of its branch office users from communicating to the Internet on any port other than TCP port 80 (www) and TCP port 443 (SSL). Its business model requires the following:

- The use of a third-party application that uses TCP ports 8912 and 8913. Client machines from users at remote locations will access this third-party application server over the site-to-site VPN tunnel to SecureMe's regional site in Washington.

- Users access their e-mail (Simple Mail Transfer Protocol [SMTP], Post Office Protocol [POP], and Internet Message Access Protocol [IMAP]) from an e-mail server in Washington over the VPN tunnel.

- DNS is allowed for name resolution.

The IT staff in Washington developed an application to provide the capability to remotely control user workstations at remote branch offices from the Washington regional site network. This application is also used to remotely install software (that is, operating system patches and antivirus updates) and it communicates over TCP port 7788. Figure 22-2 is a diagram of the New York branch office network with all the assigned IP addresses.

Figure 22-2 *New York Branch Office Network*

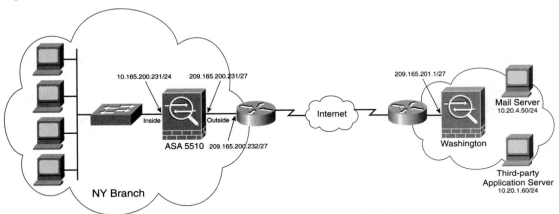

To accommodate the previously listed requirements, the configuration in Example 22-1 is deployed at the New York branch office. This same configuration is deployed on the Cisco ASA at Los Angeles and Atlanta branch offices as well, with the exception of the IP addresses corresponding to each specific location.

Example 22-1 *New York Branch Configuration*

```
! The public outside interface
interface GigabitEthernet0/0
 nameif outside
 security-level 0
 ip address 209.165.200.231 255.255.255.224
!
! The private inside interface
interface GigabitEthernet0/1
 nameif inside
 security-level 100
 ip address 10.165.200.231 255.255.255.0
!
!
hostname NewYork
!
!The following access control list entries restrict internal users to only be able to
!send HTTP, HTTPS, and DNS traffic to the Internet
access-list insideACL extended permit tcp 10.165.200.0 255.255.255.0 any eq www
access-list insideACL extended permit tcp 10.165.200.0 255.255.255.0 any eq https
access-list insideACL extended permit udp 10.165.200.0 255.255.255.0 any eq domain
!
!The following access control list entries restrict internal users to only be able to
!send TCP port 8912 and 8913 traffic to the 10.20.1.60 server in Washington, which hosts
!the previously mentioned third-party application.
access-list insideACL extended permit tcp 10.165.200.0 255.255.255.0 host 10.20.1.60
   eq 8912
```

continues

Example 22-1 *New York Branch Configuration (Continued)*

```
access-list insideACL extended permit tcp 10.165.200.0 255.255.255.0 host 10.20.1.60
  eq 8913
!
!The following access control list entries restrict internal users to only be able to
!send SMTP, POP3, and IMAP4 traffic to the 10.20.4.50 mail server in Washington.
access-list insideACL extended permit tcp 10.165.200.0 255.255.255.0 host 10.20.4.50
  eq smtp
access-list insideACL extended permit tcp 10.165.200.0 255.255.255.0 host 10.20.4.50
  eq pop3
access-list insideACL extended permit tcp 10.165.200.0 255.255.255.0 host 10.20.4.50
  eq imap4
!
!The following access control list entry allows the 10.10.220.0/24 management
  segment in
!Washington to be able to launch a remote control session to the internal user
  workstations
!in NY.
access-list outsideACL extended permit tcp 10.10.220.0 255.255.255.0 10.165.200.0
  255.255.255.0 eq 7788
!
!The following access control list entries are used to define what traffic should be
!encrypted over the IPSec site-to-site tunnel to Washington.
access-list encryptACL extended permit ip 10.165.200.0 255.255.255.0  10.20.4.0
  255.255.255.0
access-list encryptACL extended permit ip 10.165.200.0 255.255.255.0 10.20.1.0
  255.255.255.0
access-list encryptACL extended permit ip 10.165.200.0 255.255.255.0 10.10.220.0
  255.255.255.0
!
!The following access control list entries allows the ASA to bypass NAT for the IPSec
!tunnel traffic.
access-list nonat extended permit ip 10.165.200.0 255.255.255.0 10.20.4.0
  255.255.255.0
access-list nonat extended permit ip 10.165.200.0 255.255.255.0 10.20.1.0
  255.255.255.0
access-list nonat extended permit ip 10.165.200.0 255.255.255.0 10.10.220.0
  255.255.255.0
!
!The following NAT configuration allows all the internal devices within the
!10.165.200.0/24 network to be port address translated to the outside interface
  address
!except for the VPN traffic.
global (outside) 1 interface
nat (inside) 0 access-list nonat
nat (inside) 1 10.165.200.0 255.255.255.0
!
!Access-lists are applied to the corresponding access-groups
access-group insideACL in interface inside
access-group outsideACL in interface outside
!
! Default gateway pointing to the external router's IP address
route outside 0.0.0.0 0.0.0.0 209.165.200.232 1
!
```

Example 22-1 *New York Branch Configuration (Continued)*

```
!The following is the IPSec site-to-site tunnel configuration to the Washington ASA
!209.165.201.1.
crypto ipsec transform-set myset esp-aes-256 esp-sha-hmac
crypto map IPSec_map 10 set peer 209.165.201.1
crypto map IPSec_map 10 set transform-set myset
crypto map IPSec_map 10 match address encryptACL
crypto map IPSec_map interface outside
isakmp enable outside
isakmp policy 10 authentication pre-share
isakmp policy 10 encryption aes-256
isakmp policy 10 hash sha
isakmp policy 10 group 2
isakmp policy 10 lifetime 86400
tunnel-group 209.165.201.1 type ipsec-l2l
tunnel-group 209.165.201.1 ipsec-attributes
 pre-shared-key 1qaz@WSX
```

Note that the **sysopt connection permit-ipsec** command is not used in the configuration in Example 22-1. This is purposefully done to ensure that the decrypted VPN traffic passes through the interface ACL applied to the outside interface.

Small Business Partners

Partner-A is a small company that buys supplies from SecureMe on a regular basis. There is a specific ecommerce application that SecureMe and Partner-A use to do all of their business transactions. Partner-A deploys the Cisco ASA 5510 to provide site-to-site extranet VPN services and to secure its infrastructure, as shown in Figure 22-3.

Figure 22-3 *Extranet Communication*

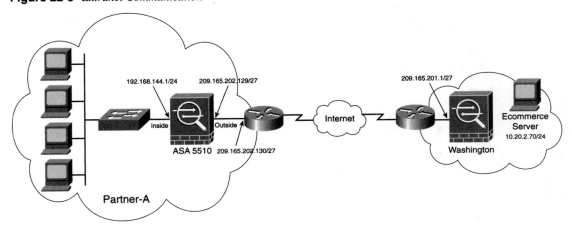

The e-commerce application used by Partner-A to buy its materials is a web-based application over Secure HTTP (HTTPS). SecureMe and Partner-A policies dictate that only TCP port 443 (HTTPS) traffic should be allowed over their site-to-site VPN connection to the e-commerce server in Washington (10.20.2.70). Traffic destined to the rest of 10.x.x.x networks in Washington is not allowed. All other traffic is allowed to leave the security appliance. Example 22-2 shows the configuration for Partner-A's Cisco ASA to achieve this goal.

Example 22-2 *Partner-A Configuration*

```
! The public outside interface
interface GigabitEthernet0/0
 nameif outside
 security-level 0
 ip address 209.165.202.129 255.255.255.224
!
! The private inside interface
interface GigabitEthernet0/1
 nameif inside
 security-level 100
 ip address 192.168.144.1 255.255.255.0
!
hostname Partner-A
! Access-list allowing only HTTPS communication to the 10.20.2.70 server and
  dropping all
! other communication to the 10.0.0.0/8 supersubnet for networks in Washington.
access-list Part_in_ACL extended permit tcp 192.168.144.0 255.255.255.0 host
  10.20.2.70 eq https
access-list Part_in_ACL extended deny ip 192.168.144.0 255.255.255.0 10.0.0.0
  255.0.0.0
access-list Part_in_ACL extended permit ip any any
!
! Access-lists to bypass NAT and classify what packets will be encrypted over the
  tunnel
access-list nonat extended permit ip 192.168.144.0 255.255.255.0 host 10.20.2.70
access-list encryptACL extended permit ip 192.168.144.0 255.255.255.0 host
  10.20.2.70
!
! NAT configuration
global (outside) 1 interface
nat (inside) 0 access-list nonat
nat (inside) 1 192.168.144.0 255.255.255.0
!
!Access-list Part_in_ACL applied to inside interface
access-group Part_in_ACL in interface inside
route outside 0.0.0.0 0.0.0.0 209.165.202.130 1
!IPSec site-to-site configuration
crypto ipsec transform-set myset esp-aes-256 esp-sha-hmac
crypto map IPSec_map 10 match address encryptACL
crypto map IPSec_map 10 set peer 209.165.201.1
crypto map IPSec_map 10 set transform-set myset
crypto map IPSec_map interface outside
isakmp enable outside
```

Example 22-2 *Partner-A Configuration (Continued)*

```
isakmp policy 10 authentication pre-share
isakmp policy 10 encryption aes-256
isakmp policy 10 hash sha
isakmp policy 10 group 2
isakmp policy 10 lifetime 86400
tunnel-group 209.165.201.1 type ipsec-l21
tunnel-group 209.165.201.1 ipsec-attributes
 pre-shared-key 3edc$RFV
```

Partner-A has a total of 75 users. Its Network Address Translation (NAT) configuration is designed to allow all of its users to have Port Address Translation (PAT) resolve the address of the ASA's public interface.

The network security administrator at Partner-A receives a call from Partner-A's Chief Information Officer (CIO) mentioning that the security policy has been changed such that ActiveX and Java should be blocked for all of Partner-A's user web traffic to the Internet. The commands shown in Example 22-3 are appended to SecureMe's Cisco ASA configuration to fulfill this requirement.

Example 22-3 *Blocking ActiveX and Java*

```
filter activex 80 0.0.0.0 0.0.0.0 0.0.0.0 0.0.0.0
filter java 80 0.0.0.0 0.0.0.0 0.0.0.0 0.0.0.0
```

ActiveX and Java are filtered for all sources, and destinations on port 80.

Case Study 2: Large Enterprise Firewall, VPN, and IPS Deployment

This section demonstrates how Cisco ASA can provide multifunction solutions for large enterprise networks. Figure 22-4 shows how different Cisco ASAs are deployed within SecureMe's headquarters offices.

The Cisco ASA appliances are deployed as follows:

1 The Cisco ASA 5540s at the Internet edge provide internal users connectivity to Internet services and provide external users access to information on public servers in a demilitarized zone (DMZ) network. These appliances are configured in failover mode. An AIP-SSM module is installed on each appliance to provide IPS services.

2 A cluster of Cisco ASA 5520s is configured to provide remote-access VPN services to telecommuters and remote users.

3 Two Cisco ASA 5520s (in failover mode) provide security services to servers at SecureMe's data center.

Figure 22-4 *Network Topology for Regional Site Offices*

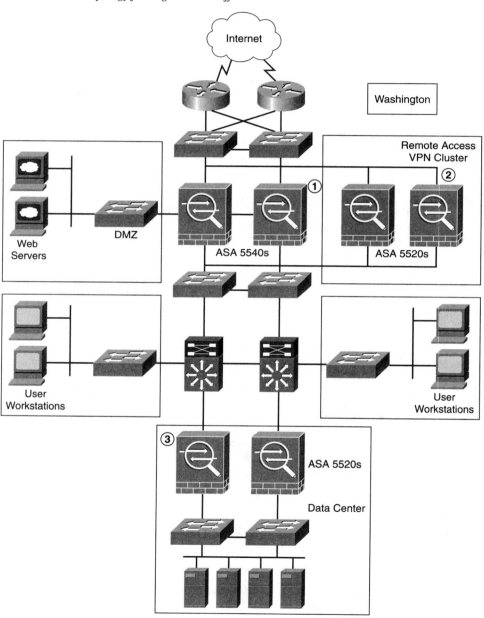

Internet Edge and DMZ

The Cisco ASA 5540s (5540-1 and 5540-2) at the Internet edge of SecureMe's main office network are configured in failover mode and are connected to two Catalyst switches on their outside (public) interface, as illustrated in Figure 22-5.

Figure 22-5   *Regional Site Offices: Cisco ASA Deployment at the Internet Edge and DMZ*

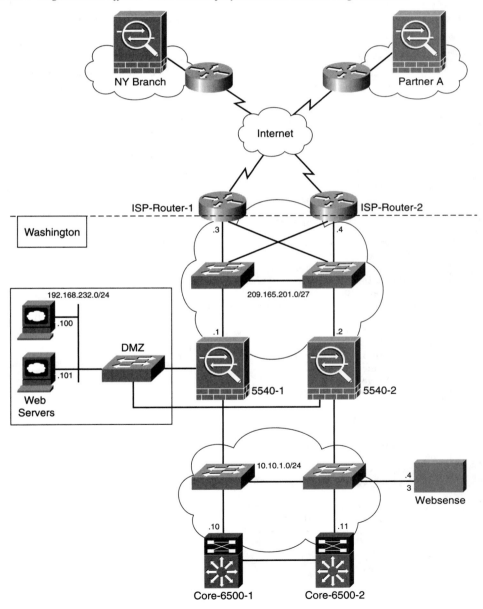

These two switches are connected to Cisco IOS routers (ISP-Router-1 and ISP-Router-2) connected to two different ISPs. These routers are configured with the Hot Standby Router Protocol (HSRP) to provide redundant links to the Internet.

The LAN switches are connected to each other via 100BASE-T trunk ports, and each LAN switch is, in turn, connected to the routers and the Cisco ASA 5540s (subnet 209.165.201.0/27). The HSRP virtual address of the routers is 209.165.201.5/27. The default gateway configuration at each of the Cisco ASA 5540s is set to the virtual address of the routers.

There are two web servers in a DMZ network (192.168.232.100 and 192.168.232.101). These servers are statically translated to two public IP addresses (209.165.201.25 and 209.165.201.26, respectively). Only HTTP and HTTPS communication is allowed to these servers from Internet users. These servers retrieve information from an internal database hosted at the 10.20.3.80 server running MySQL (an open-source database). The web servers use TCP port 3306 to communicate to the internal database. This is the only communication allowed from these servers to the internal network.

Example 22-4 includes the commands to configure Washington ASA 5540-1 to achieve these goals. The site-to-site tunnel configuration to the New York branch office and Partner-A is also included in Example 22-4. A crypto map called **Washington_map** is configured with two separate instances.

Example 22-4 *Washington ASA 5540-1 Configuration*

```
!Configuration of public interface facing the Internet routers
interface GigabitEthernet0/0
 description outside interface
 nameif outside
 security-level 0
 ip address 209.165.201.1 255.255.255.224
 !
!Configuration of the inside interface
interface GigabitEthernet0/1
 description inside interface
 nameif inside
 security-level 100
 ip address 10.10.1.1 255.255.255.0
 !
!DMZ Interface with security level 50
interface GigabitEthernet0/2
 description DMZ interface
 nameif DMZ
 security-level 50
 ip address 192.168.232.1 255.255.255.0
 !
! Interface used for failover communication
interface GigabitEthernet0/3
 description Failover Interface
 no nameif
 no security-level
 no ip address
 !
```

Example 22-4 *Washington ASA 5540-1 Configuration (Continued)*

```
!Management interface configuration ASA and AIP-SSM management interfaces are in the
!10.10.220.0/24 management network.
interface Management0/0
 nameif mgmt
 security-level 70
 ip address 10.10.220.1 255.255.255.0
 management-only
!
!
hostname Washington5540-1
!
!Access control list to bypass NAT for the IPSec communication  to the New York branch
!office and Partner-A networks.
access-list nonat extended permit ip host 10.20.2.70 192.168.144.0 255.255.255.0
access-list nonat extended permit ip 10.20.4.0 255.255.255.0 10.165.200.0 255.255.255.0
access-list nonat extended permit ip 10.20.1.0 255.255.255.0 10.165.200.0 255.255.255.0
access-list nonat extended permit ip 10.10.220.0 255.255.255.0 10.165.200.0 255.255.255.0
!
!Access control list to classify what traffic will be encrypted to the IPSec
! site-to-site tunnel to Partner-A

access-list encryptPartA extended permit ip 10.20.2.0 255.255.255.0 192.168.144.0
    255.255.255.0!
!Access control list to classify what traffic will be encrypted to the IPSec site-to-site
!tunnel to the New York branch office.
access-list encryptNY extended permit ip 10.10.1.0 255.255.255.0 10.165.200.0
    255.255.255.0
access-list encryptNY extended permit ip 10.20.2.0 255.255.255.0 10.165.200.0
    255.255.255.0
access-list encryptNY extended permit ip 10.10.220.0 255.255.255.0 10.165.200.0
    255.255.255.0
!
!Access control list applied to the DMZ interface to allow only communication from the
!web servers to the 10.20.3.80 MySQL server over TCP port 3306
access-list dmzACL extended permit tcp host 192.168.232.100 host 10.20.3.80 eq 3306
access-list dmzACL extended permit tcp host 192.168.232.101 host 10.20.3.80 eq 3306
!
!NAT configuration - a global pool of addresses (209.165.201.10 to 209.165.201.15) is
!configured. After these addresses are allocated all connections will be port
!address translated to 209.165.201.16.
global (outside) 1 209.165.201.10-209.165.201.15
global (outside) 1 209.165.201.16
nat (inside) 0 access-list nonat
nat (inside) 1 10.0.0.0 255.0.0.0
!
!Static NAT configuration for the web servers in the DMZ network.
static (DMZ,outside) 209.165.201.25 192.168.232.100 netmask 255.255.255.255
static (DMZ,outside) 209.165.201.26 192.168.232.101 netmask 255.255.255.255
!
!Access group for dmzACL
access-group dmzACL in interface DMZ
!
!IPSec site-to-site tunnel configuration - two crypto maps are configured (one for the
```

continues

Example 22-4 *Washington ASA 5540-1 Configuration (Continued)*

```
!tunnel to the branch office in New York and a second for the tunnel to Partner-A).
crypto ipsec transform-set myset esp-aes-256 esp-sha-hmac
crypto map Washington_map 10 match address encryptPartA
crypto map Washington_map 10 set peer 209.165.202.129
crypto map Washington_map 10 set transform-set myset
crypto map Washington_map 20 match address encryptNY
crypto map Washington_map 20 set peer 209.165.200.231
crypto map Washington_map 20 set transform-set myset
crypto map Washington_map interface outside
isakmp enable outside
isakmp policy 10 authentication pre-share
isakmp policy 10 encryption aes-256
isakmp policy 10 hash sha
isakmp policy 10 group 2
!
```

Filtering Websites

There is a Websense server for URL filtering (10.10.1.43) in the inside interface of the Internet edge firewalls. The security administrator configures Cisco ASA to send all the user web requests to the 10.10.1.43 filtering server, except requests to the two web servers located in SecureMe's DMZ network (192.168.232.100 and 192.168.232.101). The goal is that, after an internal user accesses a site, the Cisco ASA will cache the address (if permitted by the Websense server).

The cache size configured is 64 KB. Therefore, when the same or another user accesses the cached website, the Cisco ASA will not query the Websense server again, increasing performance. The URL memory pool size is configured with 10 KB. An additional requirement the security administrator dictates is for Cisco ASA to allow long URLs of 4 KB in size. To increase performance, 128 blocks are kept in the Cisco ASA buffer. Example 22-5 includes the command the security administrator enters in Cisco ASA 5540-1 to achieve these goals.

Example 22-5 *URL Filtering*

```
!Specifying the Websense server
url-server (inside) vendor websense host 10.10.1.43
!
!Filtering all URLs except for the two servers in the DMZ

filter url except 0.0.0.0 0.0.0.0 192.168.232.101 255.255.255.255
filter url except 0.0.0.0 0.0.0.0 192.168.232.100 255.255.255.255
filter url http 0.0.0.0 0.0.0.0 0.0.0.0 0.0.0.0
!
!URL block memory pool is configured to 10KB
url-block url-mempool 10
!
!Support for long URLs of up to 4KB in size
url-block url-size 4
!
!The following command enables 128 blocks to be buffered in the Cisco ASA.
```

Example 22-5 *URL Filtering (Continued)*

```
url-block block 128
!
!URL cache size of 64KB based on both the source address initiating the URL request,
  as !well as the URL destination address
url-cache src_dst 64
```

NOTE   For more information about Websense filtering server, go to http://www.websense.com.

Remote Access VPN Cluster

SecureMe has two Cisco ASA 5520s configured in a cluster for remote access VPN support.
Figure 22-6 illustrates the design, including corresponding IP addresses.

Figure 22-6 *Remote-Access VPN Cluster*

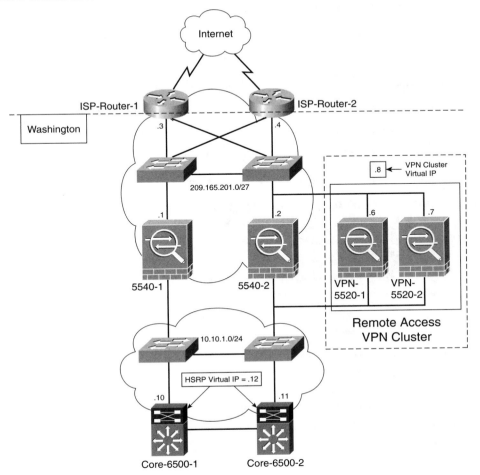

The two Cisco ASA 5520s are labeled VPN-5520-1 and VPN-5520-2. The goal is to have the VPN-5520-1 configured as the cluster master (with priority 10) and VPN-5520-2 as the cluster secondary (with priority 5). Load-balancing communication between both Cisco ASA 5520s must be encrypted. Example 22-6 shows the configuration of the cluster master (VPN-5520-1).

Example 22-6 *Remote-Access VPN Cluster Master ASA Configuration*

```
!Public/outside interface configuration
interface GigabitEthernet0/0
 nameif outside
 security-level 0
 ip address 209.165.201.6 255.255.255.224
!
!Private/inside interface configuration
interface GigabitEthernet0/1
 nameif inside
 security-level 100
 ip address 10.10.1.6 255.255.255.0
!
hostname VPN-5520-1
!
!IP Pool for remote access VPN clients
ip local pool vpnpool 10.10.253.1-10.10.253.254
!Static Routing configuration. Default gateway is pointing to the Internet router
   HSRP
!address and tunnel default gateway is pointing to the primary ASA 5540 Internet
   Firewall
!IP address.
route outside 0.0.0.0 0.0.0.0 209.165.201.5 1
route inside 10.20.0.0 255.255.0.0 10.10.1.12 1
route inside 10.10.0.0 255.255.0.0 10.10.1.12 1
route inside 0.0.0.0 0.0.0.0 10.10.1.1 tunneled
!
!RADIUS Server configuration. The RADIUS server is located in SecureMe's Data
   Center.
aaa-server Radius protocol radius
aaa-server Radius host 10.20.1.40
 key cisco123
!
!A VPN group called SecureMeGrp is configured.
group-policy SecureMeGrp internal
group-policy SecureMeGrp attributes
 banner value You have connected to VPN-5520-1. This is a restricted VPN system.
 dns-server value 10.20.4.98 10.20.4.99
 vpn-simultaneous-logins 1
 vpn-tunnel-protocol IPSec
 ipsec-udp enable
 ipsec-udp-port 10000
 split-tunnel-policy tunnelall
 default-domain value securemeinc.com
!
!IPSec transform-set configuration
```

Example 22-6 *Remote-Access VPN Cluster Master ASA Configuration (Continued)*

```
crypto ipsec transform-set ESP-3DES-SHA esp-3des esp-sha-hmac
!
!A dynamic crypto map is configured for the remote access VPN clients.
crypto dynamic-map secureme_dyn_map 10 set transform-set ESP-3DES-SHA
crypto map outside_map 100 ipsec-isakmp dynamic secureme_dyn_map
crypto map outside_map interface outside
!
! isakmp configuration - Enabled on the outside interface
isakmp enable outside
! isakmp configuration - Enabled on the inside interface for VPN LB
isakmp enable inside
!
!ISAKMP policy configuration for VPN Clients
isakmp policy 10 authentication pre-share
isakmp policy 10 encryption 3des
isakmp policy 10 hash sha
isakmp policy 10 group 2
isakmp policy 10 lifetime 86400
!
!Tunnel Group configuration for Remote Access VPN
tunnel-group securemevpn type ipsec-ra
!
!Tunnel group general attributes. The VPN Address pool vpnpool is mapped , the
  default !VPN group is SecureMeGrp, and authentication is set to RADIUS.
tunnel-group securemevpn general-attributes
 address-pool vpnpool
 authentication-server-group Radius
 authentication-server-group (inside) Radius
 default-group-policy SecureMeGrp
!
!Tunnel Group IPSec attributes
tunnel-group securemevpn ipsec-attributes
 pre-shared-key *
!
!Load-balancing configuration. Encryption for VPN load-balancing communication is
!configured. The priority 10 will force this appliance to be the master.
vpn load-balancing
 priority 10
 cluster key cisco123
 cluster ip address 209.165.201.8
 cluster encryption
 participate
```

The master Cisco ASA (VPN-5520-1) is configured to assign IP addresses to VPN clients from a pool of addresses in the range of 10.10.253.1 through 10.10.253.254. A different IP address pool must be configured in the cluster secondary appliance (VPN-5520-2). The IP address pool range is 10.10.254.1 through 10.10.254.254. Example 22-7 shows the cluster secondary Cisco ASA configuration.

Example 22-7 *Remote-Access VPN Cluster Secondary ASA Configuration*

```
!Public/outside interface configuration
interface GigabitEthernet0/0
 nameif outside
 security-level 0
 ip address 209.165.201.7 255.255.255.224
 !
!Private/inside interface configuration
interface GigabitEthernet0/1
 nameif inside
 security-level 100
 ip address 10.10.1.7 255.255.255.0
 !
hostname VPN-5520-2
 !
!IP Pool for remote access VPN clients
ip local pool vpnpool 10.10.254.1-10.10.254.254
!Static Routing configuration. Default gateway is pointing to the Internet router HSRP
!address and tunnel default gateway is pointing to the primary ASA 5540 Internet
  Firewall
!IP address.
route outside 0.0.0.0 0.0.0.0 209.165.201.5 1
route inside 10.20.0.0 255.255.0.0 10.10.1.12 1
route inside 10.10.0.0 255.255.0.0 10.10.1.12 1
route inside 0.0.0.0 0.0.0.0 10.10.1.1 tunneled
 !
! RADIUS Server configuration. The RADIUS server is located in SecureMe's Data Center.
aaa-server Radius protocol radius
aaa-server Radius host 10.20.1.40
 key cisco123
 !
!A VPN group called SecureMeGrp is configured.
group-policy SecureMeGrp internal
group-policy SecureMeGrp attributes
 banner value You have connected to VPN-5520-2. This is a restricted VPN system.
 dns-server value 10.20.4.98 10.20.4.99
 vpn-simultaneous-logins 1
 vpn-tunnel-protocol IPSec
 ipsec-udp enable
 ipsec-udp-port 10000
 split-tunnel-policy tunnelall
 default-domain value securemeinc.com
 !
!IPSec transform-set configuration
crypto ipsec transform-set ESP-3DES-SHA esp-3des esp-sha-hmac
 !
!A dynamic crypto map is configured for the remote access VPN clients.
crypto dynamic-map secureme_dyn_map 10 set transform-set ESP-3DES-SHA
crypto map outside_map 100 ipsec-isakmp dynamic secureme_dyn_map
crypto map outside_map interface outside
 !
! isakmp configuration- Enabled on the outside interface
isakmp enable outside
```

Example 22-7 *Remote-Access VPN Cluster Secondary ASA Configuration (Continued)*

```
! isakmp configuration- Enabled on the inside interface for VPN LB
isakmp enable inside
!
!ISAKMP policy configuration for VPN Clients
isakmp policy 10 authentication pre-share
isakmp policy 10 encryption 3des
isakmp policy 10 hash sha
isakmp policy 10 group 2
isakmp policy 10 lifetime 86400
!
!Tunnel Group configuration for Remote Access VPN
tunnel-group securemevpn type ipsec-ra
!
!Tunnel group general attributes. The VPN Address pool vpnpool is mapped , the
  default !VPN group is SecureMeGrp, and authentication is set to RADIUS.
tunnel-group securemevpn general-attributes
 address-pool vpnpool
 authentication-server-group Radius
 authentication-server-group (inside) Radius
 default-group-policy SecureMeGrp
!
!Tunnel Group IPSec attributes
tunnel-group securemevpn ipsec-attributes
 pre-shared-key *
!
!Load-balancing configuration. Encryption for VPN load-balancing communication is
!configured. The priority 10 will force this appliance to be the master.
vpn load-balancing
 priority 5
 cluster key cisco123
 cluster ip address 209.165.201.8
 cluster encryption
 participate
```

Notice that the configuration is almost identical to the cluster master appliance with the exception of the IP addressing, IP address pool, and VPN load-balancing priority.

Application Inspection

The Washington security administrator received calls from many users complaining that they can't access streaming video with applications using the Real-Time Streaming Protocol (RTSP) (for example, Apple QuickTime 4, RealPlayer, and Cisco IP/TV). After researching the issue, the security administrator notices that RTSP inspection is not enabled on the Internet edge Cisco ASA. The configuration commands in Example 22-8 are appended to the Internet edge appliances.

Example 22-8 *RTSP Inspection*

```
!An ACL defining the RTSP traffic over the default TCP ports (554 and 8554)
access-list rtsp_acl permit tcp any any eq 554
access-list rtsp_acl permit tcp any any eq 8554
!
!A class-map named rtsp_traffic is configured matching the previously configured ACL
class-map rtsp_traffic
 match access-list rtsp_acl
!
!A policy map called inbound_policy is configured to inspect all RTSP traffic and
   applied
!to the inside interface
policy-map inbound_policy
 class rtsp_traffic
   inspect rtsp
service-policy inbound_policy interface inside
```

IPS

The Cisco ASA 5540s at the Internet edge are running IPS services in AIP-SSM modules. Each AIP-SSM is configured in promiscuous mode. The AIP-SSM inspects all packets that enter through the outside interface and are destined for the inside and DMZ networks. The configuration in Example 22-9 is appended to each Cisco ASA 5540.

Example 22-9 *ASA IPS Redirection*

```
!A class-map is configured to capture/match all traffic
class-map IPSclass
match any
!
!A policy map is created associating the previously created class map. IPS is
   configured
!in promiscuous mode and to for the Cisco ASA to continue to pass traffic if the
   AIP-SSM fails
policy-map IPSpolicy
  class IPSclass
    ips promiscuous fail-open
!
!IPS service policy is applied globally.
service-policy IPSpolicy global
```

If the AIP-SSM fails, the Cisco ASA 5540 will continue to pass traffic normally. This is referred to as fail-open. In inline mode, if the security appliance is configured to fail-close, Cisco ASA will stop all traffic to be transmitted from and to any of its interfaces. However, in promiscuous mode the AIP-SSM will not cause the traffic passing through the Cisco ASA to stop. The fail-open or fail-close configuration only applies to inline mode.

The security administrator notices several events/alarms generated by signature 223344. After detailed analysis, the security administrator discovers that these are false positives.

The goal is to disable signature 223344. It will still be processed by the AIP-SSM without generating any logs or events. Example 22-10 shows the AIP-SSM configuration to disable signature 223344.

Example 22-10 *Disabling Signature 223344*

```
WashingtonSSM-1# configure terminal
WashingtonSSM-1(config)# service signature-definition sig0
WashingtonSSM-1(config-sig)# signatures 223344 0
WashingtonSSM-1(config-sig-sig)# status
WashingtonSSM-1(config-sig-sig-sta)# enabled false
WashingtonSSM-1(config-sig-sig-sta)# show settings
   status
   -----------------------------------------------
      enabled: false default: false
      retired: false <defaulted>
   -----------------------------------------------
WashingtonSSM-1(config-sig-sig-sta)# exit
WashingtonSSM-1(config-sig-sig)# exit
WashingtonSSM-1(config-sig)# exit
Apply Changes:?[yes]:yes
```

The tuning process is crucial for IPS management. After disabling signatures that generate false positives and making sure that the correct signatures are enabled, the security administrator can now determine threat origins and targets, and use this information to prevent attacks, protect resources, and reduce network downtime.

NOTE   The Cisco Security Monitoring, Analysis and Response System (CS-MARS) can collect IPS event information from the AIP-SSM. CS-MARS provides intelligent and sophisticated features that can help you during the IPS tuning process. You can get more information about CS-MARS at http://www.cisco.com/go/mars.

Case Study 3: Data Center Security with Cisco ASA

SecureMe builds security policies that align asset protection with business goals. To secure its data center, the security administrator defines separate security zones. These zones divide the data center into areas that are logically alienated from one another to contain security threats and anomalies at minimal impact. The individual zones in SecureMe's data center support individual application groups of servers. Each zone is protected by a virtual firewall context on the Cisco ASA 5520s at the data center (DC-5520-1 and DC-5520-2). Figure 22-7 illustrates how each zone is protected by each security context.

Figure 22-7 *Data Center Zones and Virtual Contexts*

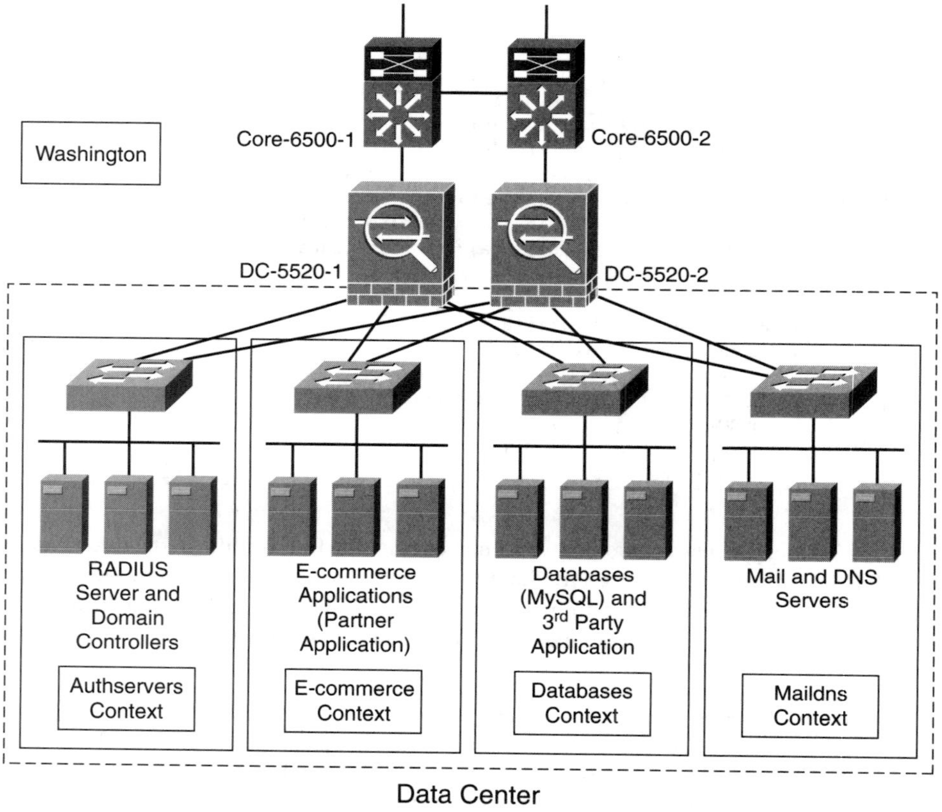

SecureMe's data center has four different zones, corresponding to individual virtual firewall contexts running in transparent mode:

- Authentication servers (authservers context)
- E-commerce applications (e-commerce context)
- MySQL database server and third-party applications (databases context)
- Mail and DNS servers (maildns context)

Communication between applications is limited to specific traffic required for application integration, data warehousing, and web services.

Interfaces cannot be shared in transparent mode, thus creating the need for different subinterfaces for the inside and outside interfaces of each virtual context. Example 22-11 shows the system context configuration and how each separate context is created.

Example 22-11 *Admin Context Configuration*

```
!Cisco ASA 5520 running in transparent multi-mode
firewall transparent
!
!Separate subinterfaces are created and associated to their respective VLANs
interface GigabitEthernet0/0
!
interface GigabitEthernet0/0.1
 vlan 200
!
interface GigabitEthernet0/0.2
 vlan 201
!
interface GigabitEthernet0/0.3
 vlan 202
!
interface GigabitEthernet0/0.4
 vlan 203
!
interface GigabitEthernet0/1
!
interface GigabitEthernet0/1.1
 vlan 100
!
interface GigabitEthernet0/1.2
 vlan 101
!
interface GigabitEthernet0/1.3
 vlan 102
!
interface GigabitEthernet0/1.4
 vlan 103
!
interface GigabitEthernet0/2
!
interface GigabitEthernet0/2.1
 vlan 501
!
interface GigabitEthernet0/2.2
 vlan 502
!
interface GigabitEthernet0/3.1
 vlan 503
!
interface GigabitEthernet0/3.2
 vlan 504
!
interface Management0/0
!
enable password 8Ry2YjIyt7RRXU24 encrypted
hostname DC-5520-1
ftp mode passive
pager lines 24
```

continues

Example 22-11 *Admin Context Configuration (Continued)*

```
no failover
no asdm history enable
arp timeout 14400
console timeout 0
!
!Admin context configuration. Management0/0 interface is allocated for the admin context
admin-context admin
context admin
  allocate-interface Management0/0
  config-url disk0:/admin.cfg
!
! Virtual context for RADIUS and Domain Controllers
context authservers
  description Virtual context for Radius and Domain Controllers
  allocate-interface GigabitEthernet0/0.1
  allocate-interface GigabitEthernet0/1.1
  config-url disk0:/authservers.cfg
!
!Virtual context for e-commerce applications
context ecommerce
  description Virtual context for e-commerce applications
  allocate-interface GigabitEthernet0/0.2
  allocate-interface GigabitEthernet0/1.2
  config-url disk0:/ecommerce.cfg
!
! Virtual context for databases and third-party application
context databases
  description Virtual context for databases and third-party app
  allocate-interface GigabitEthernet0/0.3
  allocate-interface GigabitEthernet0/1.3
  config-url disk0:/databases.cfg
!
!Virtual context for email and DNS servers
context maildns
  description Virtual context for email and DNS servers
  allocate-interface GigabitEthernet0/0.4
  allocate-interface GigabitEthernet0/1.4
config-url disk0:/maildns.cfg
!Virtual context for active/active failover
context FO_context1
  allocate-interface GigabitEthernet0/2.1
  allocate-interface GigabitEthernet0/3.1
  config-url flash:/FO_context1.cfg
  failover-group 1
!
!Virtual context for active/active failover
context FO_context2
  allocate-interface GigabitEthernet0/2.2
  allocate-interface GigabitEthernet0/3.2
  config-url flash:/FO_context2.cfg
  failover-group 2
```

The Cisco ASA 5520s at SecureMe's data center include a configuration for each context that identifies the security policy for each zone. Figure 22-8 illustrates one of the security contexts (maildns context) within the respective data center zone.

Figure 22-8 *Mail and DNS Server Data Center Zone*

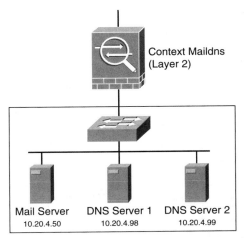

Mail Server   DNS Server 1   DNS Server 2
10.20.4.50   10.20.4.98   10.20.4.99

Example 22-12 shows the maildns virtual context configuration.

Example 22-12 maildns *Context Configuration*

```
DC-5520-1/maildns(config)# show running-config
: Saved
:
ASA Version 7.0(1) <context>
firewall transparent
names
!
interface GigabitEthernet0/1.4
 nameif inside
 security-level 100
!
interface GigabitEthernet0/0.4
 nameif outside
 security-level 0
!
enable password 8Ry2YjIyt7RRXU24 encrypted
passwd 2KFQnbNIdI.2KYOU encrypted
!
!ASA automatically configures the hostname parameters to the context name
hostname maildns
!
!ACL allowing only mail and DNS traffic to corresponding servers
access-list maildns extended permit tcp any host 10.20.4.50 eq smtp
access-list maildns extended permit tcp any host 10.20.4.50 eq pop3
```

continues

Example 22-12 maildns *Context Configuration (Continued)*

```
access-list maildns extended permit tcp any host 10.20.4.50 eq imap4
access-list maildns extended permit udp any host 10.20.4.98 eq domain
access-list maildns extended permit udp any host 10.20.4.99 eq domain
pager lines 24
mtu outside 1500
mtu inside 1500
ip address 10.10.1.55 255.255.255.0
no asdm history enable
arp timeout 14400
!
!A static NAT is configured to limit the maximum number of connections to 10000 and
!maximum embryonic connections to 500.
static (inside,outside) 10.20.4.0 10.20.4.0 netmask 255.255.255.0 tcp 10000 500
static (inside,outside) 10.20.4.0 10.20.4.0 netmask 255.255.255.0 udp 10000 500
!
!Access-group for the previously configured access-list
access-group maildns in interface outside
timeout xlate 3:00:00
timeout conn 1:00:00 half-closed 0:10:00 udp 0:02:00 icmp 0:00:02
timeout sunrpc 0:10:00 h323 0:05:00 h225 1:00:00 mgcp 0:05:00
timeout mgcp-pat 0:05:00 sip 0:30:00 sip_media 0:02:00
timeout uauth 0:05:00 absolute
no snmp-server location
no snmp-server contact
snmp-server enable traps snmp
telnet timeout 5
ssh timeout 5
!
class-map inspection_default
 match default-inspection-traffic
 !
 !
policy-map global_policy
 class inspection_default
  inspect dns maximum-length 512
  inspect ftp
  inspect h323 h225
  inspect h323 ras
  inspect netbios
  inspect rsh
  inspect rtsp
  inspect skinny
  inspect esmtp
  inspect sqlnet
  inspect sunrpc
  inspect tftp
  inspect sip
  inspect xdmcp
!
service-policy global_policy global
Cryptochecksum:00000000000000000000000000000000
: end
[OK]
DC-5520-1/maildns(config)#
```

ESMTP inspection is configured in the maildns context. All other security contexts are configured similarly to the maildns context, except for the appropriate ports and protocols allowed for each application.

Summary

This chapter covered several real-life examples of how to deploy Cisco ASA within small, medium, and large organizations. The first case study illustrated how the Cisco ASA 5510s are deployed in branch offices. The second case study detailed how a large enterprise deploys Cisco ASA at the Internet edge to protect the corporate network while running IPS services to detect and defeat today's highly complex and sophisticated security threats. Furthermore, this case study covered how to deploy a Cisco ASA cluster as a remote-access VPN solution. The final case study demonstrated how to deploy Cisco ASA to provide in-depth defense and to mitigate threats throughout the data center.

INDEX

Symbols & Numerics

? (question mark), displaying command help, 428

3-way handshakes, embryonic connections, 158

A

AAA (Authentication, Authorization, and Accounting)
Cisco ASDM connections, configuring, 227
external authentication server, configuring, 657–660
serial console connections, configuring, 227
server groups, specifying, 220–222
server reactivation policies, 221
supported protocols, 213–215
Active Directory, 219
Kerberos, 219
LDAP, 219–220
Microsoft Windows NT, 219
RADIUS, 215–217
RSA SecurID, 218–219
TACACS+, 217–218
aaa accounting command, 235
abbreviating commands, 54
ABRs (Area Border Routers), 184
absolute time restrictions, 134–135
accessing
ASDM, 613–614
LogApp, 426
accounting
configuring, 235
RADIUS, configuring, 236–237
TACACS+, configuring, 237
ACEs (access control entries), 117
arguments, 121–123
object groups, 127
defining, 131–133
ICMP-type, 130
network-based, 129
protocol-based, 128–129
service-based, 129–130

ACLs (access control lists), 6, 117, 388, 645–646
ACEs, 117
arguments, 121–123
object groups, 127–133
advanced features, 126
applying to interfaces, 124–125
configuring, 121–124
crypto ACLs, creating, 474
downloadable, 136
EtherType, 119
extended, 119
features of, comparing, 120
inbound/outbound traffic filtering, 145–147
inheritance rule, 484
IPv6, 119
arguments, 126
configuring, 125–126
monitoring, 149–152
object groups, 127
defining, 647–649
ICMP-type, 130
network-based, 129
protocol-based, 128–129
service-based, 129–130
outbound, 118
remarks, adding, 124
standard, 119
traffic filtering across site-to-site VPNs, 477–478
WebVPN ACLs, 120, 561–564
active Cisco ASA, 347
Active Directory, 219
Active/Active failover, 352–353, 667
active unit failover, specifying MAC address, 365
asymmetric routing, 353–355
configuring, 359–364
multiple security context deployment, 371–374
verifying operation, 376
Active/Standby failover, 351–352
configuring, 355–359
single mode deployment, 369–371
ActiveX content filtering, 137–138

G

gatekeepers, 263
gateways, 263
GET-NEXT messages (SNMP), 109
global configuration mode (CIPS 5.x), 428
global IPv6 addresses, configuring, 70–71
GPRS (General Packet Radio Service), 258.
  See also GTP
gratuitous ARP, 364
group attributes, 503
GTP (GPRS Tunneling Protocol), 258–259
  application inspection, 262–263
  GTPv0, 259–260
  GTPv1, 260–261

H

H.323 protocol suite, 263–265
  application inspection, 263–266
    control-signaling methods, 267–268
    enabling, 267
  FastConnect H.323 feature, 264
  FoIP, 268
hairpinning, Easy VPN and firewalling
  deployment scenario, 531–534
hardware client NEM, 531
hardware requirements for failover, 351
hardware-based VPN clients, configuring,
  517–519
header fields (IPv6), 68–69
heuristic scanning, 12
hop count, 178
host-based intrusion detection systems, 13–14
HTTP filtering, configuring, 143
HTTP inspection, 268, 287–288
  enabling, 269–275
hw-module module command, 414
HyperTerminal, establishing connection with
  console port, 50–52

I

ICMP filtering, 136–137
ICMP inspection, 276

ICMP-type object groups, 130
IDCONF (Intrusion Detection Configuration)
  protocol, 424
Identity NAT, 166
IDSM-2 (IDS Services Module-2), 33
IDSs (intrusion detection systems), 10–11
  host-based, 13–14
  network-based, 11
    anomaly-based analysis, 13
    heuristic-based analysis, 12
    pattern-matching, 11
    protocol analysis, 12
    stateful pattern-matching, 12
  NIDS, protocol analysis, 12
IGMP (Internet Group Multicast Protocol), 203
  configuration information, displaying, 208
  query timeouts, configuring, 205
IKE (Internet Key Exchange), 20
  Phase 1, 20–22
  Phase 2, 22–24
ILS (Internet Locator Service) inspection, 276
image upgrades. performing zero-downtime
  software upgrades, 367–369
images, upgrading via Cisco ASA CLI, 89–92
implementing failover, 668–670
inbound NAT, TCP intercept, 159
inbound/outbound traffic filtering, ACLs,
  145–147
Individual User Authentication feature, 529–530
inheritance, 484, 502
initial setup
  of ASDM, 615–616
  of ASA, 56
    device name, 58–59
    DHCP services, configuring, 65–67
    interface configuration, 59–62
    management interfaces, configuring, 65
    parameters, 57–58
    subinterface configuration, 63–64
initializing AIP-SSM, 429–433
Inline IPS mode, 410
inside NAT, 154
inspect dns command, 254
inspect esmtp command, 255
inspect skinny command, 283
inspection policies, provisioning, 248–249
installing ASDM system image files, 633–634
interactive hardware client authentication, 529

Cisco Systems

Cisco Press

3 STEPS TO LEARNING

STEP 1

First-Step

STEP 2

Fundamentals

STEP 3

Networking
Technology Guides

STEP 1 **First-Step**—Benefit from easy-to-grasp explanations.
No experience required!

STEP 2 **Fundamentals**—Understand the purpose, application,
and management of technology.

STEP 3 **Networking Technology Guides**—Gain the knowledge
to master the challenge of the network.

NETWORK BUSINESS SERIES

The Network Business series helps professionals tackle the
business issues surrounding the network. Whether you are a
seasoned IT professional or a business manager with minimal
technical expertise, this series will help you understand the
business case for technologies.

Justify Your Network Investment.

Look for Cisco Press titles at your favorite bookseller today.

Visit **www.ciscopress.com/series** for details on each of these book series.

DISCUSS

NETWORKING PRODUCTS AND TECHNOLOGIES WITH CISCO EXPERTS AND NETWORKING PROFESSIONALS WORLDWIDE

VISIT NETWORKING PROFESSIONALS A CISCO ONLINE COMMUNITY WWW.CISCO.COM/GO/DISCUSS

CISCO SYSTEMS

THIS IS THE POWER OF THE NETWORK. now.

Cisco Systems

 **Cisco Press**

NETWORKING TECHNOLOGY GUIDES
MASTER THE NETWORK

Turn to Networking Technology Guides whenever you need **in-depth knowledge of complex networking technologies**. Written by leading networking authorities, these guides offer theoretical and practical knowledge for **real-world networking applications and solutions**.

Look for Networking Technology Guides at your favorite bookseller

Cisco CallManager Best Practices:
A Cisco AVVID Solution
ISBN: 1-58705-139-7

Cisco IP Telephony: Planning, Design, Implementation, Operation, and Optimization
ISBN: 1-58705-157-5

Cisco PIX Firewall and ASA Handbook
ISBN: 1-58705-158-3

Cisco Wireless LAN Security
ISBN: 1-58705-154-0

End-to-End QoS Network Design:
Quality of Service in LANs, WANs, and VPNs
ISBN: 1-58705-176-1

Network Security Architectures
ISBN: 1-58705-115-X

Optimal Routing Design
ISBN: 1-58705-187-7

Top-Down Network Design, Second Edition
ISBN: 1-58705-152-4

Visit **www.ciscopress.com/series** for details about Networking Technology Guides and a complete list of titles.

 Learning is serious business.
Invest wisely.

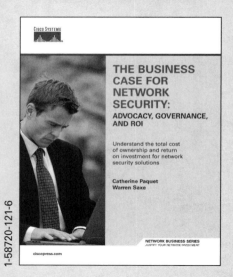

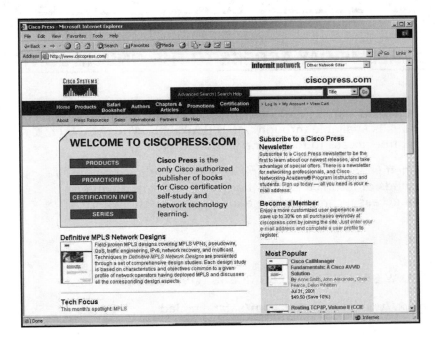
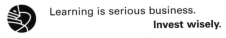

BOOKS ONLINE

ENABLED

THIS BOOK IS SAFARI ENABLED

INCLUDES FREE 45-DAY ACCESS TO THE ONLINE EDITION

The Safari® Enabled icon on the cover of your favorite technology book means the book is available through Safari Bookshelf. When you buy this book, you get free access to the online edition for 45 days.

Safari Bookshelf is an electronic reference library that lets you easily search thousands of technical books, find code samples, download chapters, and access technical information whenever and wherever you need it.

TO GAIN 45-DAY SAFARI ENABLED ACCESS TO THIS BOOK:

- Go to **http://www.ciscopress.com/safarienabled**

- Enter the ISBN of this book (shown on the back cover, above the bar code)

- Log in or Sign up (site membership is required to register your book)

- Enter the coupon code found in the front of this book before the "Contents at a Glance" page

If you have difficulty registering on Safari Bookshelf or accessing the online edition, please e-mail customer-service@safaribooksonline.com.